DOUBLEDAY
CELEBRATES
100 YEARS OF
EXCELLENCE

The American OPERA SINGER

The Lives and Adventures of America's Great Singers in Opera and Concert, from 1825 to the Present

Peter G. Davis

DOUBLEDAY
New York London Toronto Sydney Auckland

PUBLISHED BY DOUBLEDAY
a division of Bantam Doubleday Dell Publishing Group, Inc.
1540 Broadway, New York, New York 10036

DOUBLEDAY and the portrayal of an anchor with a
dolphin are trademarks of Doubleday, a division of
Bantam Doubleday Dell Publishing Group, Inc.

Book design by Richard Oriolo

Library of Congress Cataloging-in-Publication Data
Davis, Peter G.
The American opera singer : the lives and adventures of
America's great singers in opera and concert, from 1825
to the present / Peter G. Davis. — 1st ed.
p.   cm.
Includes bibliographical references and index.
1. Singers—United States—Biography.   I. Title.
ML400.D33   1997
782.1′092′273—dc21
[B]   97-9123
CIP
MN

ISBN 0-385-47495-4
Copyright © 1997 by Peter G. Davis
All Rights Reserved
Printed in the United States of America
November 1997
First Edition
1 3 5 7 9 10 8 6 4 2

For Scott

Acknowledgments

At every stage in the preparation of this book Gregor Benko, co-founder of the International Piano Archive at the University of Maryland and an unfailing resource regarding musicians past and present, directed me to a wealth of relevant material about the American singer. Biographical studies, articles, newspaper clippings, journals, collections of operatic memorabilia, pictorial material—Gregor seemed to know where everything could be located. I would never have been able to write about the American singer at all without his invaluable advice and assistance.

I also have Gregor to thank for introducing me to Dr. Girvice Archer, Jr., who so generously allowed me full access to his magnificent collection of lithographs, visiting cards, and rare photographs of opera singers. The illustrations of the following singers are from Dr. Archer's collection: Charlotte Cushman, Dolorès Nau, Adelaide Phillipps, Cora de Wilhorst, Genevieve Ward, Clara Louise Kellogg, Annie Louise Cary, Emma Abbott, Emma Albani, Emma Thursby, Minnie Hauk, Charles R. Adams, David Bispham, Lillian Nordica, Emma Eames, Olive Fremstad, Marie van Zandt, Sibyl Sanderson, Pauline L'Allemand, Mary Garden, Rosa Ponselle, Alma Gluck, Eva Gauthier, Edith Mason, Sissieretta Jones, Roland Hayes, Marian Anderson, Grace Moore, Lily Pons, Edward Johnson, Dusolina Giannini, Jennie Tourel, Helen Traubel, Risë Stevens, and Leontyne Price.

Another indispensable resource has been the Metropolitan Opera Archives, where I spent many hours being enlightened by its treasures, as well as by the informed comments of Robert Tuggle, the Archives' ever helpful director, and his assistant, John Pennino. Many other individuals have supplied aid, information, and/or patient support along the way. Among them were Walter E. Arnold; Peter Clark, General Press Representative of the Metropolitan Opera; Marc Dulman; Marylou Falcone; Johanna Fiedler; Delbert Flynn; Ernest Gilbert; Kit Gill; Alexander Holliday; Joseph Horowitz; Brian Kellow; Cory Lockhart; Jim McPherson; William Murray, Director of Press and Public Relations at the

Brooklyn Academy of Music Press Office; Jim Oleson; Elena Park, General Press Representative of the San Francisco Opera; Walter Price; James Van Sant; Ellen Schanz; Teresa Sterne; Michael Willis, Director of Public Relations at the Glimmerglass Opera; and Edgar Vincent.

Both through their writings and their conversation, numerous critics, scholars, and enthusiastic students of vocal history have helped shape my thinking on singers and singing over the years. I am especially obliged to Martin Bernheimer, Will Crutchfield, Richard Dyer, the late Dale Harris, Albert Innaurato, Conrad L. Osborne, and Michael Scott for their wisdom and knowledge, however much we may have at times wrangled and disagreed over the subject.

The suggestion that I write a book on American singers was first made by Stephen Rubin, a longtime friend, former colleague in New York's music journalism jungle, and presently chairman/CEO of the Bantam Doubleday Dell Publishing Group's international division and chairman of Transworld Publishers. Without his faith that I was the right one for the job and his gentle prodding along the way, the book would never have been written. My agent, Cynthia Robbins, also went beyond the call of duty to keep me focused and happy during the writing process, as well as tending to a host of pesky details.

I owe a debt to my editor, Jesse Cohen, whose professionalism is matched by his knowledge and enthusiasm for music—a rare combination in book publishing and a constant blessing as this lengthy project was shepherded through to press. I have also been fortunate to have had my manuscript so scrupulously copyedited by Robert D. Daniels, a former associate editor at *Opera News*. His encyclopedic knowledge of opera, singers, and America's musical past corrected many of my errors, while his delicate questioning of several overhasty pronouncements rescued me on more than one occasion.

My special thanks to Astrid Varnay for permission to quote from her autobiography, *50 Years in 5 Acts*, to be published in the spring of 1998 by Baskerville.

Finally, a deep bow to my partner, Scott Parris, for his support, patience, and help in seeing me through the rough times, ever since I first hesitantly plunged into the fascinating history of the American singer over seven years ago.

—*Peter G. Davis*
June 1997

Author's Note

Opera titles are usually given in the language sung in performance, when definitely known; otherwise, they are given in the language in which the opera was originally written. Roles generally retain their most familiar designations, for example, Marguerite in *Faust*.

Contents

Introduction		1
Prelude: The Signorina		7
One: Adventures in a New World		16
Interlude One: Lindomania		30
Two: Career Goals		38
Three: An American Prima Donna		53
Four: The Three Emmas		69
Five: "Go On, Minnie!"		87
Six: Men at Work		102
Interlude Two: Queen Adelina		118
Seven: She Did Her Damnedest		128
Eight: "Last Night There Was Skating on the Nile"		147
Nine: Anna Olivia		165
Ten: Around and About l'École Marchesi		182
Eleven: Sing Low		205
Twelve: The Divine Mary		220
Interlude Three: The Great Caruso		239
Thirteen: Gerryflappers		246
Fourteen: A Caruso in Petticoats		264

Fifteen: Going on Record   284

Sixteen: The Glory Road   303

Seventeen: Black Gold   322

Eighteen: Glamour Time   341

Interlude Four: The Yellow Brick Brewery   359

Nineteen: Johnson Babies: I   372

Twenty: If I Could Tell You   399

Twenty-one: Johnson Babies: II   416

Twenty-two: Job Hunting   448

Interlude Five: La Divina   478

Twenty-three: Homemade Goods   487

Twenty-four: At the Top   513

Twenty-five: The End of the Adventure   541

    Postlude: Life After the Three Tenors   560
    Coda   577
    Notes   583
    Bibliography   603
    Index   611

The

American

Opera Singer

Introduction

~~~~~~~~~~~~~~~~~~~~~~~~~~~~~~~~~~~~~

$\mathcal{A}$ recurrent lament in Beverly Sills's 1987 autobiography, *Beverly*, is the deplorable second-class status American singers must always endure in their uphill struggle for recognition. If only she had been born and bred in Europe, Sills seems to feel, her talents would have been immediately noted and her career swiftly launched. Instead, the road to fame was long and hard, largely because she had the misfortune to be an American. "In my own country," the soprano writes while reminiscing about her early years, "the American artist was low man, or woman, on the totem pole . . . In those days, most American singers were the Rodney Dangerfields of the opera world—we got no respect."

Nearly a century before Sills, Clara Louise Kellogg registered a similar complaint in her autobiography, *Memoirs of an American Prima Donna*. As a nineteen-year-old operatic debutante in 1861, singing Gilda in *Rigoletto* at New York's Academy of Music, Kellogg found how difficult it was for an American singer to be taken seriously: "The Italians of the chorus were always bitter against me for, up to that time, Italians had had the monopoly of music. It was not generally conceded that Americans could appreciate, much less interpret opera; and I, as the first American prima donna, was in the position of a foreigner in my own country."

Both sopranos got it wrong. Of course, competition from abroad has always been fierce, but the American singer as a scarce and perpetually underappreciated figure has long been a popular misperception. Kellogg may have been among the earliest American singers to achieve international fame, but she had several significant predecessors. Some might even have protested her claim to be the first American prima donna—Adelaide Phillipps, for example, who often shared the stage with Kellogg and by the 1860s was a prominent singer in Europe and the United States. The image of Sills as a lonely pioneer battling anti-American prejudice in mid-twentieth century is even more preposterous. At the time she was fighting for recognition, the Metropolitan Opera was crammed with Americans: Eleanor Steber, Risë Stevens, Dorothy Kirsten, Helen Traubel, Leonard Warren, Richard Tucker, Blanche Thebom, Jan Peerce, Robert Merrill, Astrid Varnay, Regina Resnik, James Melton, Margaret Harshaw, Patrice Munsel, and Nadine Conner were only the most prominent. Not only did they all sing leading roles at the Met, but most of them also had a national profile, busily performing on radio and in the new medium of television—some even made Hollywood films. Sills's main obstacle as a young singer, in fact, was fierce competition from her already securely established compatriots rather than the country's presumed overriding preference for foreigners.

By the 1950s native vocal talent was flourishing, but that hardly came as a surprise to long-time observers of the country's vocal scene. The four generations separating Kellogg and Sills had produced dozens of Americans who pursued prominent careers at home and abroad: Minnie Hauk, Emma Abbott, Lillian Nordica, Geraldine Farrar, Louise Homer, Olive Fremstad, Emma Eames, Rosa Ponselle, David Bispham, Richard Crooks, Sibyl Sanderson, Clarence Whitehill, Marian Anderson, Edith Mason, Gladys Swarthout, John Charles Thomas, Alma Gluck, Grace Moore—the list goes on and on. And of course when one looks about at the end of the twentieth century, opera and concert stages the world over are densely populated—indeed, dominated—by Americans. And yet each promising new generation of singers is invariably hailed as an unprecedented phenomenon.

What this ritual of discovery and rediscovery mostly reflects is this country's long-standing cultural inferiority complex vis-à-vis classical music—especially a glittering import like opera, which was never fully absorbed into the country's cultural fabric and remade into a living art form that America could call its own. Of course, American singers always had difficult battles to wage, especially at the beginning. The U.S. public was unprepared to deal adequately with opera when it was first imported in the early 1800s. Although the most popular airs of Rossini, Donizetti, Bellini, and, later, the young Verdi caught on immediately, often recast as ballads sung in the vernacular, it took longer for serious operatic performance to flourish. Even when it did, an American repertory never developed, and without that creative spur, the country's singers could not play the same role in the history of opera that their European counterparts did. In Europe, singing styles evolved organically over the centuries in direct response to changing styles in operatic composition, from the florid arias of the Baroque and early Romantic eras to the heavier vocal demands of Verdi, Wagner, and Puccini. By the time the North American continent was sufficiently settled for people to think about producing homegrown opera, the form's creative vitality was waning and audiences no longer clamored for new works. As a result, opera in America has always been essentially a re-creative art form, despite sporadic and, to date, unsuccessful attempts to cultivate a significant native repertory.

So it was the American singer's task to transform the great operas of all nationalities and styles from an exotic entertainment into an integral part of the country's musical culture—a formidable assignment, but one that a vigorous, ambitious, and potentially wealthy young society found to be a provocative challenge. The social and economic energies of a growing new country rather than the development of the form itself stimulated the rise of American singers. That practical reality honed their skills, and today, the American singer's high reputation for technical preparedness, stylistic flexibility, and versatility is proverbial—a facility that also has its downside in the many faceless singing personalities who now travel the globe from one opera house to another, performing a frozen repertory from the past. Since international audiences still clamor to experience these great works, expert custodians are needed to keep them alive, and with their healthy voices, smart professional skills, and vaulting ambition, American singers have rushed in to do the job. And they have succeeded spectacularly.

The country's first singers could hardly have predicted that development. As well as having to familiarize themselves with a multiplicity of foreign musical styles and languages, those pioneers faced more basic problems: finding vocal instruction, dealing with the instability of early musical institutions and the physical hardships of overland travel, not to mention an ingrained puritanical distrust of the theater—in nineteenth-century America, singing on the stage was widely perceived as an inappropriate career for a man and positively an indecent one for a young lady. Helping to change those attitudes were the periodic arrivals of exciting stars from Europe, singers whose vocal personalities and impact on the country are here treated as interludes within the main story. Maria Malibran, Jenny Lind, Adelina Patti, Enrico Caruso, and on to the Three Tenors—all captured nationwide attention, greatly heightened America's appreciation for classically trained operatic voices, and popularized operatic music wherever they went.

But there was a price to pay. If those European marvels became powerful role models as they toured the land, they also reinforced the popular prejudice that American singers were second-best. And by earning prodigious sums of money, they suggested that the life of a glittering opera star always guaranteed tremendous fame and wealth. None of that was true, of course, but whenever one of those paragons appeared on the scene, the cause of the American singer, both as artist and wage earner, suffered severe setbacks.

Who is an American singer? That question is not easily answered in a country originally created and continually renewed through immigration. Many of America's first professional singers were born in Europe, but those who spent their childhood, received their early musical education, and pursued most of their careers here must be considered native singers, along with several others who will be more controversial. The British will inevitably protest my appropriation of Mary Garden. Perhaps the Scottish-born soprano never became an American citizen (although some sources claim she did), but she arrived here as a child, grew up in rural Massachusetts, received early vocal instruction in Chicago, and spent the better part of her professional life in America—Garden knew very well where her voice and singular theatrical personality would best flourish, and it would not be in England, which heard her only briefly at the beginning of her career. Lily Pons, too, was a strictly American phenomenon. The French-born coloratura may have found it good publicity to promote herself as the essence of Parisian chic after she disarmed New Yorkers at her sensational Met debut in 1931, but her career could only have happened in America during the thirties' glamour time—even after Pons became a big New World star, her compatriots never quite got the message.

Many other foreign-born artists passed much of their lives in America and profited from it, but they were never so completely nationalized. Singers like Ezio Pinza and Lauritz Melchior were international vocal giants who would have been considered great singers no matter where they chose to live. Singers from South America have different tales to tell, but Canadians, whose musical background and experiences so closely parallel those of their colleagues to the south, fit naturally into the picture. To fill out the vocal portraits of singers from the distant past, many unjustly forgotten today, I have relied as much as possible upon their recordings and their own words, since both reveal more about the subject than even they themselves probably realized. Readers will note a more subjective tone to the narrative when it reaches the 1950s—inevitably so, since by that time I had appeared on the scene to hear and judge America's singers for myself. As this book was never intended to be a comprehensive lexicon, many worthy but minor figures from all periods have been regretfully omitted.

Most of the Americans who pursued singing careers in the nineteenth century came from the Northeast. And no wonder. Not only were the roots of European culture first firmly planted in the Boston–New York–Philadelphia area, but it took strong Yankee determination and a rugged constitution even to consider such a course. The country's earliest professional singers had to be hardy individualists simply to survive. Like many of them, Clara Louise Kellogg came from tough New England stock, and when she decided to risk everything and follow her dream, she summoned her girlhood companions and boldly announced, "Girls, I've made up my mind to go on the stage! I know just how your people feel about it, and I want to tell you now that you needn't speak to me, nor bow to me if you meet me in the street. I shall quite understand, and I shan't feel a bit badly. *Because I think the day will come when you will be proud to know me!*" The italics and exclamation point are Kellogg's, and they underscore her resolve.

Kellogg considered herself an outsider, but once she had decided on her life's course, she pursued it with determination, setting an example for her successors. American singers have had to reinvent themselves ever since, and they have been doing so with extraordinary resourcefulness and success. Faced with an ever-changing set of cultural and sociological realities and dealing mainly with music from a foreign culture, each new generation has had to seek out its own road to fame, fortune, and artistic fulfillment on the country's opera and concert stages. Colorful personalities have emerged at every stage of the journey, and this is the story of their adventures.

Prelude

The Signorina

~~~~~~~~~~~~~~~~~~~~~~~~~~~~~~~

ew York City had never seen or heard anything quite like it before: Italian opera performed in the original language and by a troupe of genuine grand-opera singers from Europe. On November 29, 1825, America's fastest-growing metropolis was to be given its first taste of a delicious imported delicacy, one that had, up till then, been available only as a crudely prepared homemade product.

The performers had been recruited in London by Dominick Lynch, a socially prominent New York wine merchant, and Stephen Price, manager of the Park Theatre, located on Park Row between Ann and Beekman streets. A passionate music-lover and amateur singer who took a vigorous interest in all aspects of the city's musical life, Lynch was determined to improve the quality of New York's music-theater offerings, which then consisted mainly of popular British ballad operas; the most famous works of Rossini, Mozart, and other well-known European composers performed in bowdlerized English versions; and a varied assortment of entertainments in which music played a subsidiary role. That was all very well, but by 1825 New York's growing monied class had begun to take an interest in European cultural refinements, and was eager to experience them firsthand.

Lynch and Price reasoned that New York was now ready to appreciate authentic grand opera, presented exactly as seen and enjoyed in Europe. Even these audacious cultural entrepreneurs knew that great risks were involved—then, as now, opera was a tremendously expensive and unpredictable proposition, the best talent would be difficult to lure across the ocean, and there was no guarantee that the city would respond. When the news got out, though, New Yorkers definitely seemed intrigued. The opening night performance of Rossini's *Il Barbiere di Siviglia* at the Park Theatre quickly became the most eagerly anticipated musical event in the city's history.

Grand opera had been the talk of the town all month long, and the local newspapers were full of excited speculations. On November 7, a day after the packet ship *New-York* docked with its precious cargo of singers on board, the daily *New-York American* breathlessly announced that one of the "highest and most costly entertainments" of the Old World would soon be revealed to the New by opera singers "so arranged with respect to their various powers, that neither London, nor Paris, nor Naples can exhibit superior performers; and in respect to some of them we use the language of a most competent judge, himself an accomplished musician, when we say that the first Soprano, the first Tenor, and the first Basse Taille of all Europe are now in New York."

That "most competent judge" was undoubtedly Lynch himself, and while he probably intentionally exaggerated his catch, he still had every reason to be proud of it. Heading the troupe was Manuel del Pópolo Vicente Rodríguez García—at fifty, no longer a tenor in his prime perhaps, but still a formidable vocal presence who had created the role of Count Almaviva in the tumultuous world premiere of *Il Barbiere* in Rome nine years earlier. He was also the patriarch of a prodigiously talented musical family, which he brought with him to perform the opera's other key roles. His wife, Joaquina Sitches García, sang the secondary soprano part of Berta. Figaro was entrusted to the couple's twenty-year-old son, Manuel Patricio Rodríguez García, eventually to become one of the century's most celebrated and influential vocal pedagogues, dying in 1906 at the age of 101. Rosina was sung by his seventeen-year-old sister, María-Felicia, who, under her married name of Malibran, would soon conquer all of Europe during a dazzling but brief career tragically cut short in 1836 by a fatal horse-riding accident. A fifth gifted García also traveled to New York, but in 1825 diva-to-be Pauline Viardot—whose voice, artistry, and musical intelligence later inspired Wagner, Verdi, Berlioz, Brahms, and Meyerbeer—was only a toddler of four. The company was rounded out by singers of solid professional standing, but hardly of the first rank. A rather seedy assortment of Italians accompanied the leading performers, mostly to sing in the chorus and to help with various duties backstage. The orchestra was a local one, staffed with twenty-five players from the Philharmonic Society and other musical organizations, all conducted from the first-violin desk by the Park Theatre's music director, Nathaniel De Luce.

When they learned of this operatic adventure, the British snickered condescendingly over what they considered little more than a rag-bag troupe, but to culture-starved New Yorkers Lynch had pulled off an amazing coup. The son of a well-to-do Irish immigrant, the socially established Lynch was ideally positioned to import opera to New York. He arrived in London prepared to use all his connections to find the finest opera singers dollars could buy, bring them to America, and astonish his fellow citizens with sights and sounds previously unimagined. One of his contacts led him to Giuditta Pasta, who would one day be Bellini's first Norma and Donizetti's first Anna Bolena. Pasta received Lynch courteously and listened with interest, but the twenty-seven-year-old soprano could not be cajoled into the project. Although not yet the glittering star she would soon become, Pasta realized that her prospects in Europe never looked better, and she had no intention of endangering the momentum of her career with an American adventure.

Pasta, though, was in a position to point Lynch in other directions. Currently the prima donna of John Ebers's opera company at London's King's Theatre, the diva had several distinguished colleagues to recommend, and the aging García with his talented brood presented themselves as the most likely candidates. Besides, the tenor would surely take along his pride and joy, young María, who shortly before Lynch's arrival in London had created a sensation substituting at the last minute for an indisposed Pasta as Rosina in *Il Barbiere* at the King's Theatre. Although María idolized Pasta, the older soprano must have felt it only prudent to have such a potentially dangerous teenage rival removed from the London scene and safely deposited in the far-off wilds of America.

Eventually the Garcías agreed to make the long journey, no doubt encouraged by the handsome sums Lynch and Price were prepared to pay for their services. The exact figures are unavailable, but when the entire troupe had finally been assembled and contracted, *Harmonicon,* an influential British music journal of the time, had some sour observations to make about its uncultured American cousins, and considered García's entourage beneath contempt, a collection of has-beens and untried youthful talent: "How an opera is to be got up by such slender means we cannot guess . . . But our transatlantic brethren have no experience in this kind of musical representation, and, therefore, will not perhaps be very discerning. The sums said to be secured to these persons are past belief, all circumstances considered. We have hitherto been the laughingstock of Europe for the preposterous manner in which we pay foreigners, but the ridicule will now be transferred to the Western continent if the statements put forth [about the singers' fees]—which we cannot credit—should actually prove true."

Although snide, *Harmonicon* was right on at least one point. America has always been willing to pay the price for the privilege of hearing the most famous foreign opera singers, from Manuel García to Luciano Pavarotti. New York's very first operatic gala may not have featured the greatest voices in the world, and perhaps it was dearly bought. But for the city's high society, that opening night performance of *Il Barbiere di Siviglia* seems to have been worth whatever princely sum it cost.

The city's fevered anticipation as it prepared for the great night of November 29 can easily be imagined from notices published in the *American* prior to the event. The paper had recently appointed its first music critic, who, under the authoritative by-line of "Musaeus," indoctrinated his readers into the mysteries of Italian opera, discussing such niceties as the differences between *aria di bravura* and *aria di mezzo carattere* as well as giving a potted history of the form. The day before the performance, the prospective audience was even lectured at length about proper dress for the occasion in an article signed by one "Cinderella."

Cinderella's sartorial recommendations and Musaeus's crash courses in opera appreciation were duly noted by fashionable New Yorkers. The *American*'s report in the November 30 edition fairly drooled over an audience that boasted the cream of society as well as such notables as Joseph Bonaparte, the ex-King of Spain; novelist James Fenimore Cooper; poet Fitz-Greene Halleck; and, one suspects, a prominent New York merchant who would soon become well known to the Garcías: François Eugène Malibran. "Never before within the walls of the Park Theatre has such an audience been assembled, and never before have they resounded to such music. By eight o'clock the pit and boxes were filled to overflowing—the lower and second circles were occupied chiefly by elegant and well-dressed females; and if our fair correspondent Cinderella was there, as doubtless she was, it must have gratified her, as it did the house at large, to perceive that no unsightly bonnets marred the view of those occupying back seats, or detracted from the array of beauteous and smiling faces, decked in native curls, or embellished with wreaths of flowers, or tasteful turbans."

A high-fashion note was firmly set right from the start, and opening night at the opera has remained the most stylish annual event in New York's social calendar ever since. Though most of the well-primed audience could not understand a word of Italian and few were able to judge the finer musical aspects of the performance, the elegant tone of the evening left no one in doubt that *something* of tremendous cultural importance had occurred.

The musical and historical significance of the occasion certainly did not escape the press, which pondered at length on the implications. On the following day an awed reporter for the *New-York Evening Post* wrote, "In what language shall we speak of an entertainment so novel in this country, but which has so long ranked as the most elegant and refined among the amusements of the higher classes of the old world? All have obtained a general idea of the opera from report. But report can give but a faint idea of it. Until it is seen, it will never be believed that a play can be conducted in recitative or singing and yet appear as natural as ordinary drama . . ."

The *New-York Literary Gazette and Phi Beta Kappa Repository* agreed, but suggested that opera's elitist nature was unlikely to appeal to the ordinary American, whose musical tastes tended toward simpler pleasures. That argument would soon be heard with increasing frequency as opera established itself as a more familiar fixture on the country's musical scene and, in its purest form, became strongly identified with moneyed high society. According to the *Gazette*, "The style of singing now introduced is, in a measure, new to this country, and the science they [the singers] display, wonderful. For ourselves (ignoramuses that we are!) we do not relish the music, because we do not understand the Italian. There are those, no doubt, who can, or pretend, to follow the composer through all his passages, even without a syllable of language: we have not so much skill, and never delight in vocal music without the words. There are some sweet English, Scotch, and Irish melodies which touch us deeply, and make us feel the poetic influence of music, and long after the strain has ceased, reverberate on the heart . . ."

Dominick Lynch and his influential wealthy friends would surely have sniffed at such a philistine attitude, but they did overestimate the city's readiness to support grand opera on a full-time basis. Despite all their efforts, Americans could hardly be transformed into knowledgeable operagoers overnight. This first exposure seems to have been greeted mainly as a seductive curiosity, only partially demystified by such self-appointed "experts" and improvers of the public mind as Musaeus and Cinderella, whose naive instruction would have struck the average Londoner as ludicrous.

After their warm initial reception, the García clan and their colleagues settled down for an extended stay in New York. The troupe's repertory consisted of nine operas: five by Rossini (*Tancredi*, *Otello*, *Il Turco in Italia*, and *La Cenerentola* in addition to *Il Barbiere*), two by García himself (*L'Amante Astuto* and *La Figlia dell'Aria*), Zingarelli's *Giulietta e Romeo*, and Mozart's *Don Giovanni*. The inclusion of Mozart's masterpiece especially gratified its famous librettist, Lorenzo da Ponte, who had lived on and off in New York since 1805 and was teaching Italian at Columbia University at the time of the Garcías' visit. Da Ponte had long dreamed of the day when Italian opera would arrive in the New World, and the aging but still colorful poet-adventurer was among the first to welcome and cheer on this extraordinary family. And yet for all the curiosity that the Garcías' arrival piqued at first, general public interest in Italian opera soon waned after the novelty wore off. Ticket sales at the Park Theatre dwindled steadily during the winter of 1825–26, especially on the evenings when María García was not singing, and eventually it became clear that New York—much less Boston, Philadelphia, or the other major East Coast cities—was hardly prepared to sustain a full-time opera company.

While opera itself may not have been established on the strongest footing, one crucial element of it was: the diva. New Yorkers may have been culturally and operatically naive, but they knew a star when they saw one, and the whole city positively lost its heart to María García. "Signorina García, of the Italian Opera," wrote the *New-York Mirror*, "charms us with sweet music, such as in days of yore caused the rocks to jump and the trees to dance." The December issue of the *New-York Review and Atheneum Magazine* warbled even more rhapsodically: "But how or in what language shall we speak of María García? How can our feeble pen portray the loveliness of this admirable creature's face and figure, or give to our distant readers any conception of the witching wonders of her almost unequalled voice? Compass, sweetness, taste, truth, tenderness, flexibility, rapidity, and force do not make up even half the sum of her vocal powers, and her voice is only one of the rare qualities with which Nature has endowed her. The audience had assembled to witness an extraordinary singer; their surprise can scarcely be imagined when she showed herself the accomplished actress as well as the enchanting vocalist."

History would soon prove that the New-York Review's critic was not entirely wallowing in naive hyperbole. Although still in her teens and just at the beginning of her brief but spectacular career, María must have been an extraordinarily potent stage presence—later, when French critics compared her to Pasta, they wrote that the older singer may have embodied the classical spirit of Sophocles and Racine, but the younger fairly seethed with the impetuous and uninhibited passions of Hugo and Shakespeare. If any singer were needed to kindle America's nascent curiosity in opera, it was María García, who even at seventeen reveled in her power to intoxicate a wide-eyed New World audience hungering for Old World culture. "Here they are already half crazy for Italian opera," she enthused in a letter to Pasta on February 18, 1826, "and I, as you can imagine, am the heroine!!! How wonderful to be in a country where they don't understand!!!" María was the first, but hardly the last, visiting operatic luminary to rejoice over, and make capital from, America's childlike delight in an exotic imported cultural phenomenon.

The raw emotions that helped make María such an exciting stage personality were surely generated in part by her tempestuous relationship with her father, both offstage and on. García was an exacting, even cruel, taskmaster who had drilled his daughter's voice unrelentingly ever since she had been a little girl in Paris. It was there one day that the composer Ferdinando Paër and a friend passed by García's house and heard agonizing screams coming from an open window. Paër's friend was horrified, but the composer smiled and said, "It's only García beating his daughter to teach her to get her trills right."

Another tale concerning María and her exigent father circulated widely through New York after the García's troupe's first performance of Rossini's Otello. Apparently the decision to add the work to the repertory was a last-minute one, and María had just six days to learn Desdemona—the title role had long been one of Manuel's specialties. To encourage his daughter to knuckle down to work, García told her, "On Saturday you are to appear, and you will excel, or, if not, in the final scene, when I am supposed to be striking you with a dagger, I will really stab you!" No doubt García spoke in jest, but on opening night María was not entirely sure. When she saw her father approach with a real knife, the terrified girl screamed, "Papá, papá, por dios no me mates!" (Papa, Papa, for God's sake don't kill me!). Since most of the audience understood Spanish no better than they did Italian, everyone assumed that it was all part of the opera, and María enjoyed her greatest triumph yet. "In the chamber scene where Otello kills his wife," the *Evening Post* breathlessly reported, "their impassioned acting, the accompaniment of the orchestra, and the concert of the elements abroad, apparently conscious of the event, combined to produce in the audience sensations of sublimity and terror beyond which no imagination can reach."

From this distance, it seems fairly clear that audiences were responding more to María's stage persona than to her musical abilities—New Yorkers would soon become more sophisticated about such things, although they never really ceased to be enchanted by anything extramusical that smacked of "sublimity and terror." "The Signorina," as she was affectionately dubbed by her fans, may have felt underappreciated for her vocal expertise, but otherwise she was clearly delighted by all the attention. At the same time, she was becoming increasingly exasperated by her father's dictatorial and abusive manner. That, more than a grand passion, threw the girl into the arms of Malibran, a wealthy New York merchant well over twice her age. García, of course, was furious, but Malibran's offer of $50,000 soon mollified him, along with a promise that María could continue to perform with the troupe at least for the duration of its New York engagement. So on March 23, 1826, María García became Maria Malibran, a name that would soon become famous the world over.

Maria continued to appear as the Park Theatre's star attraction throughout the summer. After one last *Barbiere* on September 30—in the Lesson Scene Maria enchanted "an overflowing audience" by singing English, French, and Spanish songs, some of her own composition— García and his entourage departed for Mexico on the brig *Brown*, leaving Maria behind. At first, Madame Malibran contemplated abandoning her career, and for three months she played the role of dutiful wife and socially prominent New York matron. By the end of the year, however, the country's general economic instability had undermined Malibran's business, and it was soon clear that Maria would have to go back to work—which she did, singing a repertory of ballad operas and English adaptations of popular operas at the Bowery Theatre as well as giving concerts in both New York and Philadelphia. By the fall of 1827, despite her busy schedule and large fees, Maria decided that she could earn even more money in Europe—an especially attractive proposition since her husband's debts continued to mount.

On November 1, 1827, Maria Malibran sailed to Paris, leaving her husband and a host of admirers behind. Her farewell appearance at the Bowery on October 29 was an emotional one, concluding with a song she had composed especially for the occasion. "There is no instance of so high a celebrity being gained at so early an age as that of the Signorina," wrote the *New-York Enquirer*, proud that America had played its part in establishing the reputation of a European singer obviously destined for greatness. "Nor can there be any doubt that had she remained in Europe she would have now been in the very first rank of her profession. It is gratifying to our pride to know that her fame has not diminished among us, though it is painful to our musical likings to know that it is that unlessened fame which calls her back to Europe."

Malibran never returned to the scenes of her first triumphs, but New York would not soon forget her. America had created its first operatic superstar, fell madly in love with her, and was grieved to see her go. How many young Americans who saw and heard the Signorina at the Park Theatre came away with the dream that, one day perhaps, they might become a singer able to compete with, or even surpass, her accomplishments?

One

~

Adventures

in a New

World

~~~~~~~~~~~~~~~~~~

fter the García troupe's ten-month season, activity on New York City's musical stages reverted to the popular light entertainments that had prevailed before the revelation of Italian opera in all its authentic glory. There were other faltering attempts over the years to rekindle the excitement that the García visit generated at first, but until the Academy of Music at Irving Place and Fourteenth Street firmly established itself as the city's leading venue for opera and concert in the mid-1850s, the story of operatic performance in Manhattan was turbulent and erratic as one speculative effort after another foundered in a sea of debts and backstage intrigue.

One of the most ambitious undertakings was launched in 1833 by Lorenzo da Ponte himself, still vigorous at eighty-four and undeterred in the noble ambition that more or less sustained him in old age: to see Italian opera securely established in his adopted country. Da Ponte enlisted the assistance of Dominick Lynch and Philip Hone, a former mayor of New York. Together, they succeeded in persuading a coterie of wealthy citizens to back the venture, which began grandly with the erection of a $150,000 theater especially constructed for opera. The country's first diamond horseshoe, the Italian Opera House at the corner of Church and Leonard streets, was a space any European city might have envied, a splendid auditorium where the city's well-heeled citizens could display themselves—the privilege of owning a box for the season cost $6,000. In his book *Music in America*, Frédéric Louis Ritter, European-born but a longtime resident in the country and a keen observer of the musical scene, gives a vivid description of the interior and how well it had been designed to serve the needs of high society: "The auditorium was different in arrangement than any hitherto seen in America. The second tier was composed entirely of private boxes, hung with curtains of crimson silk; and the first tier communicated with the balcony and pit, thus making the first advance toward the long-desired privilege of the ladies occupying that portion of the house. The whole interior was pronounced magnificent, and the scenery and curtains were beautiful beyond all precedent. The ground of the front-boxes was white, with emblematical medallions and octagonal panels of crimson, blue, gold. The dome was painted with representations of the Muses. The sofas and pit-seats were covered with damask, and the floors were all carpeted."

On November 18 the house was inaugurated in style when a group of Italian singers headed by Clementina Fanti, the company's prima donna and prime attraction, gave the New York premiere of Rossini's *La Gazza Ladra*. Hone, apparently not quite as avid an opera buff as his colleagues, left a frank account of the evening in his diary, once again complaining about the language problem: "The opera, they say, went off well for a first performance; but to me it was tiresome, and the audience was not excited to any degree of applause. The performance occupied four hours—much too long, according to my notion, to listen to a language which one does not understand; but the house is superb, and the decorations of the proprietors' boxes (which occupy the whole of the second tier) are in a style of magnificence which even the extravagance of Europe has not yet equaled . . . Will this splendid and refined amusement be supported in New York? I am doubtful."

Hone's doubts were soon confirmed. The company's first season ran its course as scheduled—forty performances over a six-month period, supplemented by an additional fifteen in Philadelphia and an extra twenty-eight in New York through July 1834. On a purely artistic and social level, the new Italian opera company was reckoned a success, and several other works were introduced to New York: Rossini's *Matilde di*

Shabran, Cimarosa's *Il Matrimonio Segreto*, Pacini's *Gli Arabi nelle Gallie*, Bellini's *La Straniera*, and an opera by Carlo Salvioni, the company's principal conductor: *La Casa da Vendere*. The bottom line, however, was disastrous: expenses of $81,054.98 and a resultant deficit of $29,275.09. Despite the red ink, a second season was launched, only to be canceled a few months after it had begun. Financial mismanagement, compounded by the sudden defection by Signora Fanti—the diva inexplicably packed up one day and vanished without a trace—sank the company. It also put an end to the operatic dreams of Da Ponte, who died a disappointed man on August 17, 1838, at the age of eighty-nine. A year later the grand theater he had so lovingly fathered burned to the ground.

The brief but chaotic history of Da Ponte's Italian Opera House is all too typical of the many attempts to plant opera on nineteenth-century American soil. In *Music in America*, Ritter wittily sums up the vicissitudes as he saw them from his vantage point in the 1880s:

> The faces of artists and manager have changed, but the routine of business has not altered. The opera in America vegetates sometimes luxuriantly, and sometimes poorly; but it does not grow in the sense of true growth . . . The history of Italian opera in America may, without exaggeration, be summed up in the following manner: At the beginning of a season great blowing of trumpets by the manager and his interested friends; the press generally echoes the managerial key-note, though one or the other may be found to play his own tune; a promising beginning; the manager is on the road to make a fortune in a short time; the unexpected whim of some jealous singer, a favorite with the public, threatens to spread a cloud over the manager's sanguine hopes; the orchestra and chorus strike for higher wages; or some political crisis occurs; or some novelty in a social, commercial, or other direction occupies public curiosity; the public, for one cause or another, becomes indifferent and stays away from the opera-house; the press becomes restless, and challenges the manager to reform, or fear the consequences of his shortcomings; the manager thinks it advisable to visit, with his company, other cities, in order to replenish his exchequer; he finally goes West, and experiences a grand smash-up; the company (except the one "star," who seldom suffers) in small squads succeeds in getting back to New York; general and

wholesale abuse of the manager follows; somebody gathers together the broken-up opera fragments, and manages in a short
time to run somebody else in debt; the principal singers leave in
disgust for Europe; the chorus and orchestra hold a mass-meet-
ing in some "saloon" on Third Avenue, in order to devise means
for getting their pay, and swear never to be entrapped again by
those unscrupulous managers. Sometimes the company goes to
Mexico to be robbed by banditti, or visits Havana to catch the
yellow-fever. This, until a recent period, has been the inevitable
fate of Italian opera-managers in America (of honest ones, at
least), and will probably be at least partially their fate for some
time to come.

The simple fact was that the average American of 1830 could not
really make head or tail of opera. The dramatic situations often seemed
contrived and ridiculous, and a fuller understanding of the plots was
hardly helped by hearing the works sung in an incomprehensible language. It might have been possible to appreciate the music, singing, and
magnificent scenery as abstract passing beauties, but the stylized conventions of the form and the often subtle correlations between word and
music that give opera its special lyric-dramatic character escaped most
audiences. Opera was an exotic bloom for the cultured elite and up-
wardly mobile; the general public continued to prefer more down-to-
earth musical entertainments with catchy tunes sung in the vernacular.

If audiences struggled to grasp the finer points of operatic performance, it's small wonder that, as yet, there were few native singers of
any distinction—the artists, as well as the operas, were mostly imported
for the occasion. Still, when one looks closely at the roster of the company that appeared at the Italian Opera House between 1833 and 1835,
one notes the name of Julia Wheatley, who on May 6, 1834, made her
debut, as Semira in Arne's *Artaxerxes*. "Now grown up," according to one
notice, young Julia could scarcely have been more than fifteen at the
time, since she had already appeared on a New York stage, as a dancer at
the age of six, at the old Park Theatre in September 1825—just two
months before García and his troupe arrived in town. A native-born
American and the daughter of actors—Mr. and Mrs. Frederick Wheatley
were engaged at the Park, where mother Wheatley was particularly admired for her amusing impersonations of elderly women—Julia literally
grew up in the theater. So, in fact, did her sister, Emma, and brother,

William, who also joined the family onstage as children and later became noted actors.

There is no record of Julia Wheatley's attendance at the Garcías' performances, but it is scarcely possible that, given her family's occupation, she could have stayed away. Indeed, it's not too fanciful to imagine the young girl being utterly captivated by Maria, at the Park and later at the Bowery, and finding Malibran a potent role model. As with most singers of this period, the exact nature of Wheatley's voice is difficult to pin down, and the surviving reviews of her performances give us only a spotty idea of her vocal character and technical abilities. After her first appearance in Rossini's *Edoardo e Cristina*, on November 24, 1835, the *Morning Courier & New-York Enquirer* had this to report: "The young debutante, Miss Wheatley, was received in the most flattering manner and looked the character of Edward admirably. She evidently labored under apprehension throughout the entire performance and we shall therefore suspend our opinion of her singing, until we hear her again. Her recitative and cavatina in the second act, beautifully accompanied by Mr. Taylor on the flute, gave general satisfaction."

Wheatley seemed to be something of a Rossini specialist—but then, Rossini was at the pinnacle of his European popularity and his works also dominated the young American opera scene. Since Wheatley tackled Malcolm in *La Donna del Lago*, Neocle in *L'Assedio di Corinto*, and Amaltea in *Mosè in Egitto*, one assumes that her voice lay in the mezzo-soprano range and that she must have possessed a fair coloratura technique in order to handle such florid music. Whatever the degree of her vocal expertise, she can confidently be named one of the very first American singers to take on leading operatic roles at home and more or less hold her own in the company of European-trained artists. The mild critical reaction to her singing very likely had to do with her lack of rigorous vocal training, which would scarcely have been available to her at the time. One of Wheatley's mentors was the British singer and composer Charles Edward Horn, who also appeared in *Artaxerxes*, although one wonders how much of value she learned from a singer whose own voice was judged to be a poor one and who gave up the stage entirely after a severe illness in 1835. In any case, Wheatley retired upon her marriage in 1840 and was heard from no more.

The scarcity of good teachers, questionable methods of vocal training, and unwise repertory choices surely account for the even briefer operatic career of Charlotte Cushman (1816–76), who made her debut,

as the Countess Almaviva in Mozart's *Le Nozze di Figaro*, at Boston's
Tremont Street Theatre on April 8, 1835. Although enthusiastically received, Cushman sang successfully for less than a year before her voice
completely gave out and she turned to the spoken stage, eventually
becoming one of America's most celebrated nineteenth-century actresses. As a young girl, though, she envisioned music as her lifelong
profession. Born in Boston of Puritan stock—her father, Elkanah, was a
descendant of Robert Cushman, who acted as business manager for the
Mayflower voyagers in 1620—Charlotte struggled through her early
years, helping to raise and provide for four younger brothers and sisters
after the failure of their father's West Indies merchant trade. Music seems
to have been her main diversion, and her voice attracted the attention of
John Paddon, one of Boston's most highly regarded music teachers and a
man with connections. He introduced Charlotte to Joseph and Mary
Wood, a British operatic couple then touring America. Mrs. Wood was
clearly the talent of the family—under her maiden name of Mary Ann
Paton, she had won a brilliant reputation in England, especially after
creating the role of Rezia in Carl Maria von Weber's *Oberon* at London's
Covent Garden in 1826 under the composer's baton.

The Woods were appearing at the Tremont in Boston, and they
immediately arranged for their protégée's debut as the Countess in
Figaro, a soprano role even though Cushman's voice seems always to
have been a rich contralto. Being vocally miscast at such a tender age no
doubt took its toll, and the young woman's impetuous nature probably
aggravated matters—she was famous in later years for her flamboyantly
impassioned performances, especially her signature role of the wild
Gypsy fortune-teller Meg Merrilies in a stage adaptation of Sir Walter
Scott's novel *Guy Mannering*. After Cushman's promising debut, the
Woods had no trouble in finding her an engagement with an opera tour
that had just been organized by James Maeder, music director of the
Tremont Street Theatre, and his actress wife, Clara Fisher. The 1836 trip
south was an arduous one, and eventually they reached the St. Charles
Theatre in New Orleans, described as one of the largest auditoriums in
North America. Here Cushman, apparently straining to fill the space,
came to grief, even after Maeder cautioned her to pace herself and not
to force. "But, the young lady knew more than her teacher," he said. "She
was almost insane on the subject of display and effect and altogether too
demonstrative in the way of commanding that which is only to be obtained slowly and patiently—operatic success."

Later, even Cushman admitted she tended to overdo things. "With the Maeders I went to New Orleans and sang until, owing perhaps to my youth, to change of climate, or too great a strain upon the upper register of my voice, which, as his wife's voice was a contralto, it was more to Mr. Maeder's interest to use, I found my voice suddenly failing me. In my unhappiness I went to ask counsel and advice of Mr. Caldwell, the manager of the New Orleans Theatre. He at once said to me, 'You ought to be an actress and not a singer.' " Cushman took his advice on the spot, decided to make her acting debut then and there—as Lady Macbeth, under Caldwell's aegis—and never looked back. Possessed of a young theatrical talent bursting with an aggressive urge to express itself, Cushman went on to become one of the most acclaimed and wealthiest actresses of her generation. Over thirty of her favorite parts were male roles, which caused some snide comments at the time, although, as one biographer was quick to observe, "no breath of scandal ever touched her name." When she brought her Romeo to London's Haymarket Theatre in 1845, the critics were captivated, one of them exclaiming, "I listened and gazed and held my breath, while my blood ran hot and cold."

Many years later, in her *Memoirs of an American Prima Donna*, the soprano Clara Louise Kellogg recalled an evening spent with Cushman in the 1870s, when both women were world-famous. By then the actress was living in semiretirement with her longtime companion, the noted sculptress Emma Stebbins, and suffering from the cancer that would soon kill her. It was a bittersweet occasion, and Kellogg sensed that the end was near. But the poet Sidney Lanier had brought his flute and charmed the company with his playing, and Cushman sang in what Kellogg described as her "fine baritone-contralto voice. Again I see her turning to talk to us between songs, emphasizing her points with that odd, inevitable gesture of the forefinger that was so characteristic of her, and then wheeling back to the instrument to let that deep voice of hers roll through the room in 'Will She Wake and Say Good Night?' "

Neither Wheatley nor Cushman had operatic careers in any modern sense of the term, partly because they had not been properly prepared for the job—technically, musically, artistically, or emotionally—and partly because the world of opera, volatile by nature, had just begun to be defined in America. Perhaps in a way both were fortunate, one to settle early on into contented domesticity and the other into the more manageable profession of acting. Eliza Biscaccianti (1824–96) had a less happy time of it, and in many respects what can be pieced together about her life epitomizes the dangers of pursing a career as an opera singer in early nineteenth-century America.

Biscaccianti was probably destined for some kind of a musical career. Her grandfather was James Hewitt (1770–1827), a prolific composer and a conductor—from 1792 to 1808 he was in charge of the orchestra at the old Park Theatre in New York. Hewitt mostly pursued musical activities in Boston, however, where his daughter, Sophia (1799–1845), flourished as a pianist, organist, singer, harpist, and music teacher (she is credited with what may have been the first performance in America of a Beethoven piano sonata, the composer's Op. 26). In 1822 Sophia married the Italian-born Louis Ostinelli, a violinist with whom she frequently concertized. Their daughter, Eliza, surrounded by music from birth, must have shown early vocal promise, since in 1843 her fellow Bostonians raised a subscription to support her study in Italy. There she took lessons from two of the era's most outstanding pedagogues, Nicola Vaccai and Francesco Lamperti, and, according to some accounts, was coached by Giuditta Pasta. Shortly after marrying a titled Italian cellist named Count Alessandro Biscaccianti, Eliza made her debut in May 1847 at Milan's Teatro Carcano, as Elvira in Verdi's *Ernani*. A few months later, on December 8, she sang opera in New York for the first time, appearing at the Astor Place Opera House as Amina in Bellini's *La Sonnambula.*

Enthusiastic hometown supporters traveled from Boston for the occasion, and many New Yorkers were also on hand to root for what was then an anomaly: an American prima donna. Biscaccianti's reception was mixed, to say the least, and her reputation, not to mention her talent, remained controversial for the duration of her career—by mid-century, American music criticism had taken on an aggressive, often brutally frank tone, and sometimes it is difficult to sort out personal prejudices from objective reportage. Commenting on Biscaccianti's debut in the *Courier & Enquirer*, Richard Grant White sets the scene fairly enough: "Signora Biscaccianti made her debut in this opera under more favorable circumstances than any vocalist whose first appearance we remember. Weeks before, she had become a personal favorite with many of the most influential subscribers. She had troops of friends in Boston, large numbers of whom came on here to be present at her expected triumph. She is an American born, and this justly disposed the public to exult, to feel itself flattered in any success she might achieve . . . The consequence was that at the first performance of *La Sonnambula* the house was so filled that, in spite of more than a hundred extra seats, numbers were turned from the door, and the audience was not only the most brilliant, but the best disposed that could possibly have assembled in New York.

"All went, not only expecting, but determined, to be pleased," White continues, before plunging in the knife. "What was the surprise of such an audience, so disposed, when, after a weary first act—save for the efforts of Vietti [the Elvino]—the curtain fell upon a failure so utter, so crushing, that the prospective second act seemed a self-sacrifice both to artist and audience." And yet despite these dire expectations, a total disaster managed to be averted: "Some change manifested itself in the audience in consequence of an apparent improvement in the singer; and as the act proceeded, and in the 'Ah! non giunge,' personal predilection, national pride, and perhaps good musical taste, found sufficient reason for such an outbreak of applause that one not present during the first act would have imagined the debutante successful beyond expection."

Eventually White tells us how the singer actually sounded, and his verdict is devastating: "Biscaccianti's voice is a soprano, or rather, was, for it is utterly ruined and has at present no particular character." White further opines that the singer probably started out with a promising endowment, but one that had been "destroyed, long ere she placed herself under the care of a European master . . . by an extravagant use of that vicious method of relaxing the throat and bellowing out the lower notes . . ." Complaining of attenuated pianissimos and bodiless fortes, out-of-tune singing, and bad acting, White finally throws up his hands and sententiously tells us that the whole sorry situation reflects what a distance America still must travel before reaching musical maturity: "If we wish to foster the arts among us, that our country may take in this regard the high position she holds in other matters, let us remember that it is to be done by raising America to the pure and lofty in art, and not by bringing down art to America."

For a slightly more friendly view of Biscaccianti's New York debut, readers could turn to Henry C. Watson in the *Evening Mirror*, although he, too, was determined not to be blinded by patriotic sentiment. According to Watson, Biscaccianti was hampered by her poor technical method, but he granted that "the young lady has undoubtedly remarkable talent, but her impulses run counter sometimes to good taste and correct judgment. A little thought will remedy these, and Signora Biscaccianti will become an ornament to her profession." Softening up even further, Watson gives us a charming physical description of Biscaccianti as "a petite figure, a sort of little pet, that the public will encourage and support. Her figure is good, her eyes are splendid, and her face is intellectual and passionate."

After a hundred and fifty years, it is impossible to sort out Biscaccianti's real vocal problems from the emotions she generated simply by being an American prima donna. In an attempt to offer a more objective analysis of her controversial debut, the *New-York Herald* advanced a view that placed the whole affair in a social context, a veritable skirmish of class warfare between New York's *canaille* and *haut ton:* an ecstatic public on the one hand rooting for one of their own and an elitist press on the other determined not to indulge unformed native talent. "One set have put her down as an awful failure in every particular, both in dress, in voice, in method, in everything, red stockings included. Another set consider her everything that is superb, elegant, accomplished, exquisite, unapproachable, and above all a native and a Boston girl . . . The unfortunate and lovely Biscaccianti, who has more talent and genius than she is allowed to possess, appears to be the victim of mean intrigue."

If nothing else, the heated reviews of Biscaccianti's New York performances called attention to the fact that an American opera singer had arrived on the scene. That phenomenon was bound to polarize opinions, and the controversy no doubt helped propel the soprano's career. After 1847 she traveled widely for more than a dozen years, singing up and down the Northeast Corridor as well as performing in Italy, France, and Russia, and eventually South America. Biscaccianti enjoyed an especially warm reception in Lima, Peru, in 1853. "Who, upon hearing thy song," gushed a notice signed by the obviously grateful Ladies of Lima, "would not feel his heart palpitate with enthusiasm? For thou pourest out ineffable enchantment with thy sweet tones. Favorite nightingale of the Americas! Sybil of harmony and delight, at whose voice the celestial vaults might be moved!"

In 1852, a year before receiving that extravagant apostrophe, Biscaccianti had traveled to San Francisco, the first opera singer of any renown to perform on the West Coast—even Barnum did not venture into that musical wilderness with Jenny Lind in 1851. Accompanied by her cellist husband and a piano accompanist, one George T. Evans, Biscaccianti was scheduled to make her first appearance at the Grace Church on Powell Street on March 22, but the demand for tickets was so great to see a creature who "embodied grace, domestic joys and refinements long since abandoned" that the performance was relocated in the American Theatre. Singing excerpts from operas by Verdi, Bellini, Rossini, and Adam, as well as such popular ballads as "Oh Cast That Shadow from Thy Brow" and "I Am Queen of a Fairy Band," the soprano caused such a furor that *The Alta California* exclaimed, "People went about in a daze and even the most sober minded and judicial subscribed to the decision of the press that the evening marked an era in the musical, social and fashionable progress of the city."

Biscaccianti could hardly have been that good—very likely the West Coast and the Ladies of Lima were responding to the novelty of hearing a classically trained singer, especially one so young and comely. After enjoying those pleasant adventures, the soprano headed off on an extended world tour, garnering notices that usually praised her attractive stage personality while expressing reservations about a voice that must have been seriously flawed. A thread of doubt even runs between the lines of a review of a homecoming concert, written by a loyal Boston critic and published in the February 5, 1859, number of *Dwight's Journal of Music:* "Every piece sung by our accomplished townswoman—weak as she was and nervous after a long illness—was a signal triumph. We all knew before that she was one of the most highly cultivated soprani of the day, and that she sings from a real musical passion; but the extraordinary finish and artistic refinement of her singing upon this occasion took us by surprise. Her voice, while it has naturally lost some of its power, makes up for it by the sweetness, purity, and refinement of its quality."

That concert appears to be one of the last bits of happy news to surface about Biscaccianti. Judging from her subsequent adventures, the vocal problems noted by *Dwight's* anonymous reviewer were surely due to something more serious than a temporary indisposition. That same year, 1859, the soprano returned to San Francisco with her husband and five-year-old son, Giulio. The city had changed greatly in seven years, musical and theatrical events were now plentiful, and Biscaccianti could no longer compete, especially given what must have been reduced vocal resources. Matters were hardly improved when she left her cellist husband to live with her accompanist, who apparently beat her with depressing regularity. After her singing engagements shrank to church work and appearances with a minstrel show, Biscaccianti, at the end of her rope, took to drink and was often spotted reeling in the streets and alleys of North Beach. By then she had become an entertainer at the Bella Union, a San Francisco variety hall, where, according to a contemporary report, "in a fog of tobacco fumes, in an atmosphere stale with drink and loud with the clink of glasses and the raucous talk of men who came to leer rather than listen, our prima donna, once greeted as 'a sibyl of harmony and delight, a fairy vision,' sang her old arias and popular airs, too often the worse for drink."

Calling upon what remained of her Yankee pluck, Biscaccianti eventually pulled herself together and in 1865 headed once again for South America. There she remained for the better part of a decade, enjoying something of a professional, physical, and mental rehabilitation before finding her way back to Italy. By now her career was effectively at an end, and bad times once again brought her to the brink. In 1877 she was discovered living in Rome, impoverished and ill, eking out a living as a voice teacher and trying to support her son, now twenty-three years old and serving in the Italian Army. Thirty years after her stormy New York debut, the onetime American diva reached out through the pages of *Dwight's Journal* appealing for charity from any Americans who might remember her brief years of youthful celebrity. Apparently the plate was successfully passed, or else sheer New England grit kept her going: Biscaccianti survived for another twenty years, ending her days in the Rossini Foundation Home for Musicians and Artists in Paris. The curtain fell in July 1896, but before the end came, Biscaccianti expressed a dying hope that the American press might take note of her passing. One New York paper obligingly accorded her a poignant obituary of just seventeen lines, charitably recalling that, at the time of her 1847 debut, "she was young, beautiful and possessed a sweet soprano voice that charmed her hearers, and her American tour was a continuous triumph." It wasn't, of course, but when she reached the end of a long and hard road, Eliza Biscaccianti finally did receive a bit of the unconditional approval that all divas yearn for.

Other Americans drifted in and out of the opera world before the 1850s, in Europe as well as on the more chaotic scene back home, but most of them are shadowy presences who made little impact and left few traces. The country as a whole, of course, sang with uninhibited vigor, but it was a rude song compared to European opera. America's popular hymns, ballads, bawdy limericks, political jingles, imported and self-composed folk tunes, hardly had much to do with the florid arias and sophisticated lyric dramas of Rossini, Mozart, Cimarosa, or the young Verdi, whose powerful new voice was just beginning to be heard all over the world.

Outside of New York, though—especially in Boston and Philadelphia, where opera had yet to gain an appreciable foothold—the genteel vocal traditions of Europe did flourish in another form, in the many amateur and professional performances of oratorios and other sacred works.

Here was a musical genre firmly rooted in the country's history—the first psalm of praise was heard on the shores of New England the moment the Pilgrims landed at Plymouth in 1620. Group singing in churches had always been an integral part of the service, although the idea of note-singing—that is, actually reading the written music rather than learning it by rote—was only gradually accepted as a practice that would not automatically lead to popery, let alone outright witchcraft. Eventually congregations were exhorted to become musically literate, and note-singing was formally adopted in the eighteenth century. By 1800 so-called singing schools could be found from Maine to Georgia offering instructional sessions devoted to the teaching of the rudiments of singing and note-reading, and it was only a matter of time before choral societies would be formed to give public performances of the extensive oratorio repertory. Here Boston led the way, and in 1815 the Handel and Haydn Society was founded, an organization that has functioned without interruption right up to the present day.

The repertory of the Society's early seasons was more or less restricted to brief pieces, with occasional ambitious forays into the works of its two eponymous composers, most notably Handel's *Messiah* and Haydn's *Creation*. Other composers were gradually admitted to the pantheon: Mozart, Beethoven, Spohr, Mendelssohn, Rossini, and several minor masters whose works are now forgotten. The soloists were usually drawn from local talent with, one suspects, highly variable results, although the public seemed grateful for what it could get. At a potpourri concert in 1817, according to a note in the Society's first set of annals, written in the 1870s, "The honors of the day seem to have been awarded to Oliver Shaw, the blind tenor singer, composer, and music publisher, from Providence, whose plaintive and expressive voice, as we are told, took such hold of the feelings, that, although audible applause was to have been withheld, as unsuitable to the occasion and place, the rule was disregarded. I have heard from the lips of one who listened to him, writes Mr. Samuel Jennison, that by his sweet singing, which was simple and natural, without any pretension to style or ornament, Mr. Shaw often so touched the hearts of his audience that there would be hardly a dry eye in the house."

Another solo singer whose name crops up frequently in programs of this period is a Miss Bennett, later to become Mrs. Martin, who also moved her listeners. The annals record, "If the current anecdote be true of the gentleman at Roxbury, who, on hearing this lady sing 'Angels ever bright and fair, take, oh! take me to your care,' burst into tears and audibly exclaimed, 'He will, He will!,' this lady must have sung with no little sweetness and pathos; but my duty as an historian obliges me to say that Mrs. Martin failed to recollect the incident when questioned about it in the year 1878. She had still, however, very clear ideas about the special defect in singing at these early concerts of the Society, for on being asked to name it, she replied, 'Out of tune.' "

Later on, by the 1830s, the Society would engage professional soloists whenever possible, mostly British singers on tour, but such treats were infrequent in those early years. Occasionally notables of the London concert stage—stars like tenor John Braham and soprano Anna Bishop—appeared in Boston to sing Mendelssohn's *Elijah* or Handel's *Samson,* and when they did attendance invariably soared. Even in 1850 there was a veritable stampede at the box office when the season closed with Rossini's *Stabat Mater* sung by visiting Italians. Bostonians clearly wanted to hear stellar European personalities as much as did New Yorkers, and here, too, local talent was more often than not considered second-best. That situation would soon begin to change, though. American singers had taken their first steps, however faltering, and during the latter half of the century they would begin to offer a serious challenge to their European colleagues, both at home and abroad. And an even greater vocal inspiration than Malibran was about to appear from Europe to spur them on.

Lindomania

~~~~~~~~~~~~~~~~~~~~~~~~~~~~~~~~~~~~

ℰ ven Phineas T. Barnum was flabbergasted. Thirty thousand New Yorkers turned out to greet Jenny Lind when her steamer, the *Atlantic,* docked at the foot of Canal Street on Sunday morning, September 1, 1850. They crowded onto the pier, they stared from the windows of nearby buildings, they filled the streets. They shouted, jostled, and jockeyed for position, injuring several people amid all the excitement— one man was even swept off the dock and into the water. Crowds stretched all the way back to Broadway and the singer's hotel, stopping traffic for blocks.

Lind finally managed to get off the ship and fight her way to the Irving House, where, Barnum later wrote in his autobiography, "her rooms were thronged by visitors, including the magnates of the land in both Church and State. The carriages of the wealthiest citizens could be seen in front of her hotel at nearly all hours of the day, and it was with some difficulty that I prevented the 'fashionables' from monopolizing her altogether, and thus, as I believed, sadly marring my interests by cutting her off from the warm sympathies she had awakened among the masses."

Barnum need not have worried. The impresario convinced Lind to come to America by promising her a staggering $200,000 for two hundred concerts and posting a bond of 10,000 pounds sterling with Baring Brothers in London to guarantee the tour. He then promoted it with consummate cunning, and all of his gambles were about to pay off. The country had been in a frenzy over "the Swedish Nightingale" even before she sang a note, thanks to Barnum's advance publicity. As early as November 1849, *The Message Bird*, a new semimonthly devoted to the elevation of music and literature in America, drily informed its readers, "Her fears of the water are a great hindrance to her undertaking such a journey. But if she can only be persuaded to look upon it in a purely business point of view, she will see that it is a safe operation; for if she arrives alive and in health, she will make a heap of money; and if she should happen to die on the way, her skin, properly stuffed, would be nearly as successful."

Back in England, from whence the adored songbird had flown to start her American migration, the satirical magazine *Punch* made merry. By then everyone had read Charles Dickens's withering portrait of the United States in *Martin Chuzzlewit* and the novelist's reports of his own recent travels abroad. What else could one expect from a cultural waste-land populated with crass, money-hungry philistines, only too eager to encourage a crude huckster like Barnum to exhibit their adored Jenny like one of his sideshow freaks? When her engagement with Barnum is finally over, *Punch* sarcastically predicted, "JENNY LIND does not return to Europe. On the conclusion of her engagement (which will be considerably shortened) with BARNUM, JENNY will be crowned Queen of the United States, the actual President politely retiring. JENNY accepts office under contract always to sing in so many airs, to the people of the smartest nation upon earth, what has hitherto been printed as Presidents' Speeches. Two stars and one stripe have been added to the American flag: the stars are JENNY's eyes, and the stripe a lock of JENNY's hair."

Punch's fanciful reading of the future only slightly exaggerated what would really come to pass. Having rested up sufficiently after her arduous crossing and exhausting reception, Lind was ready to sing on September 11. All New York was breathless with anticipation on the night of her first concert at Castle Garden, and the first notes the chaste northern diva sang were, appropriately, "Casta diva" from Bellini's *Norma*. The audience received that bel canto apostrophe enthusiastically, but when Lind concluded the evening with several simple but melodious folklike songs to her own guitar accompaniment, joy was unrestrained. Her last number, composed especially for the occasion, was titled "Greeting to America," with words by Bayard Taylor (who won the $200 prize Barnum offered for the best ode on the subject) and music by Sir Julius Benedict, the tour's musical director. With that, New York was at her feet.

The following months witnessed Lind's triumphant progress from one city to another, always greeted by cheering crowds at railroad stations, boat landings, and in front of her hotel. Barnum's genius for publicity was in large part responsible for all the hoopla. By mid-century the country's growing middle class was sufficiently developed and settled to demand entertainment—even entertainment presented as culture, as long as that remained unthreatening. Barnum knew precisely what was wanted, how to gratify that want, and how to beat the drum for it. He may not have exactly promoted Lind as a freak-show attraction like other famous Barnum exhibits, such as General Tom Thumb, Jumbo, and the Feejee Mermaid. But this inspired entrepreneur was the first to recognize the possibilities of advance newspaper publicity, and he lost no opportunities in taking advantage of this new art, stirring Lindomania to a frenzy in advance of her arrival in each city.

One New York paper even inaugurated a special daily column entitled "Movements of the Swedish Nightingale." The *Herald* hailed her presence "as significant an event as the appearance of Dante, Tasso, Raphael, Shakespeare, Goethe, Thorwaldsen, or Michael Angelo," and noted that she had "changed all men's ideas of music as Bacon's system revolutionized philosophy." As the Lind tour progressed, the country positively wallowed in an orgy of self-congratulation and pride that one of Europe's icons of high culture had elected to grace America with her presence. The demand for tickets to her concerts was so great that Barnum hit upon the ingenious notion of auctioning them off. The first ticket in New York brought $225, and the premium went up at each successive city. By the time Lind reached Boston, one Ossian F. Dodge made the highest bid, a lordly $625.

The soprano remained aloof from Barnum's marketing ploys ("Mr. Dodge is a fool" was her only comment about that worthy's extravagance), but she never discouraged them or other manifestations of Lindomania, which rapidly developed into a small industry. Soon sentimentalists could purchase all sorts of souvenirs to remind them of the night they heard Lind sing: Jenny Lind gloves, bonnets, riding hats, shawls, mantillas, robes, chairs, sofas, and pianos were on sale every-where—there was even a Jenny Lind teakettle, which, when filled with water and brought to the boil, was guaranteed to sing. No doubt taking a hint from Barnum's marketing tactics, more resourceful fans also found ways to cash in. A chambermaid who worked in the Providence hotel where Lind stayed was discovered selling golden hairs from her own head, claiming that she had removed them from the great singer's brush. A New Yorker, exhibiting a glove said to have once belonged to the diva, charged one dollar to kiss the outside and two to kiss the inside, where the fair hand had rested.

Cultural historians have never ceased scratching their heads over the 1850–52 Jenny Lind visit, attempting to describe, explain, and analyze the reasons for the furor. Barnum may have prepared the way, but even his magnificent publicity machine could hardly have generated so much excitement out of pure humbug. And, yes, the singer encountered the American public at exactly the time it seemed primed, if not actually yearning, to embrace a certified representative of European culture who might define and legitimize the country's growing awareness of high art. But why Lind? Even her voice, impossible to imagine today despite many contemporary attempts to describe it, cannot be the answer—most of the people who flocked to her concerts were hardly connois-seurs of vocal technique. Barnum himself later remarked that Lind "was a woman who would have been adored if she had had the voice of a crow." No, as the great impresario instinctively realized, Jenny Lind was a woman America could personalize and take to its collective heart, not so much because of her art but because of who she was.

She was never beautiful. John Addington Symonds met her ten years after her return from America—she was then forty-two—and left an unflattering portrait: "First, the face is terribly thin and worn. The eyes are small, and very glaucous grey. They soon screw up when she looks attentive. The nose is immense and broad at the base. The mouth broad, and lips thin, with the skin about it pink and irritable. Her hair is pro-fuse, and yellow. Her throat is immense, with a huge larynx. The whole face is mobile and expressive." That last observation is perhaps the key to the sense of sadness and spirituality that Lind seemed to evoke, a disappointing figure when first seen onstage but transfigured the moment she began to sing. Even everyday folk in her audiences noticed this phenomenon. "There was always a pathos about Jenny Lind," recalled Mrs. Price Newman seventy years after she had heard the singer. "Under all circumstances it remained with her." Another witness was H. R. Haweis, who wrote in 1891, "The dream-like echoes of the notes still linger in my ear; it was something unearthly—far away; like the cry of a wild bird lost in the sunset." Lind herself was aware of this, once remarking, "I become a different thing when I sing—different body, different soul."

The fact that Lind never sang opera in America probably helped rather than hindered her ability to cast that peculiar spell. She had renounced the opera stage shortly before crossing the Atlantic, and when asked why years later, she replied, "When every day it made me think less of this [laying her finger on the Bible] and nothing at all of that [pointing to the sunset], what else could I do?" Such pious statements played just as well in 1850 America as they did in Victorian England, and everywhere Lind was revered for her saintly persona, which not only deflected Barnum's often questionable promotional tactics but positively sacralized her art for most Americans. She never traveled on the Sabbath and her charities eventually became as famous as her singing. Even five months before her arrival, Nathaniel Parker Willis rhapsodized for the largely feminine readership of the *New York Home Journal:* "To a mind eminently sensitive, a heart still free from world stains, and the uninterrupted habit of a daily observance of her religious duties, may be more justly ascribed the manifestations of Jenny's humility, tender-heartedness, and sensibility." During her lengthy time in the United States, Lind could only fuel the country's uncritical acceptance of anything European, while Barnum's outrageous publicity reinforced the notion that native-born singers were second-best. Worse, the immense amount of money she made in America inspired hordes of other European singers to cross the ocean in hopes of making their fortunes. On the other hand, she removed much of the stigma that attached to any American, especially a young girl, who might wish to aim for a musical career, and many were inspired to meet the challenge.

Cynics said that Lind dissolved her relationship with Barnum after nine months—the original agreement had called for a year and a half—not because the showman tainted her reputation but because he had served his purpose and she could continue under her own management. It was an amicable parting, although later Lind was bitterly resentful over what she felt had been Barnum's exploitation of both her talent and her pious ways. She may also have resented the fact that the latter part of her American sojourn was distinctly less successful than the first had been under Barnum's aegis. The public also seemed put off when their *casta diva* took a husband in Boston during 1852. The lucky man was Otto Goldschmidt, her accompanist and a pianist of small accomplishment, who was also unromantic, unglamorous, and Jewish. Subsequent concerts by Mme. Goldschmidt somehow lacked the fantasy of those given by Jenny Lind, no longer that chaste goddess of the North, and attendance began to drop. Looking "as stingey as a hive of wasps" at one of her last concerts, the soprano set sail for Europe on May 29, 1852. Perhaps Lind herself sensed that she had outstayed her welcome and that her endless renditions of "The Last Rose of Summer," as well as her piety, had definitely begun to pall.

Had Jenny Lind come to America as an opera singer, her impact would probably have been minimal. A concert setting where she could be completely herself was more congenial for a singer whose armory of expressive effects ranged only from the lyrical to the pathetic. No doubt it was her religious nature that prevented her from giving convincing portrayals of operatic characters who betrayed baser human instincts. Even her most avid European admirers had found her Norma pallid compared to that of Grisi, let alone Pasta, still a fond memory in London when Lind sang the role there in the 1840s. Henry Chorley, Victorian England's most astute music critic, was especially appalled by her Druid priestess. He described her failure in the role as "something as entire, as aimless as it is possible for so remarkable an artist to make. The actress and the play had no agreement."

And yet Lind can scarcely be dismissed as a vocal mirage. There is too much reliable testimony about her special qualities, particularly the distinctive color of her voice. Even discriminating connoisseurs found her timbre irresistible, and the most susceptible seemed to find the sound an art unto itself. Chopin spoke of her singing as utterly magical, pervaded by the atmosphere of the North. Mendelssohn adored her: "She is as great an artist as ever lived; and the greatest I have known." Europe's music critics were also enchanted. Eduard Hanslick wrote, "An approximate imitation of the song of a bird, almost overstepping the boundaries of music, this warbling and piping becomes a thing of the most enchanting beauty in the mouth of Jenny Lind. All the fresh, natural woodland charm of the bird's joyous song reaches us here incredibly by way of the utmost technical bravura." Chorley's less poetic description, written in 1862, after most partisan passions had subsided, is perhaps the best:

It can now, however, without treason be recorded that Mdlle. Lind's voice was a soprano, two octaves in compass—from D to D—having a possible higher note or two, available on rare occasions; and that the lower half of the register and the upper one were of two distinct qualities. The former was not strong— veiled, if not husky, and apt to be out of tune. The latter was rich, brilliant, and powerful—finest in its highest portions. It can be told that the power of respiration was possessed by Mdlle. Lind in the highest perfection; that she could turn her "very long breath" to account in every gradation of tone; and thus, by subduing her upper notes, and giving other lower ones with great care, could conceal the disproportions of her organ . . .

Her execution was great; and, as is always the case with voices originally reluctant, seemed greater than it really was . . . She used her pianissimo tones so as to make them resemble an effect of ventriloquism. On every note that she sang, in every bar she delivered, a skilled and careful musician was to be detected.

No precise appreciation of her expression is possible . . . Whatsoever were the predisposing causes, and let them be allowed for ever so largely, Mdlle. Lind did without doubt satisfy the larger number of her auditors, by giving them the impression that she was the possessor of deep and true feeling. This satisfaction I only shared at intervals.

Clearly Lind was a unique vocal personality, but not—pace Chopin and Mendelssohn—a great artist. Despite all the fawning and hyperbole lavished on her in America, she could hardly be said to have raised the country's musical tastes with her endless renditions of the "Echo Song," "Home, Sweet Home," "The Herdsman's Song," and the other Victorian favorites that were the predominant works on her concert programs. Posterity has also cast doubts on her piety and regarded her celebrated acts of charity as mostly sham and hypocrisy. Liza Lehmann, the composer of *In a Persian Garden*, encountered Lind in Italy in 1871, and quotes a statement that is always cited as proof of the singer's spiritual snobbery, if not outright bigotry. As the two ladies sat at tea, an Italian boy came by to serve the muffins. "You see that boy?" Lind hissed. "I am trying to conquer myself—to bear with him—but—he is a Roman Catholic!"

The vocal historian Henry Pleasants examined this side of the Lind phenomenon and came away revolted by a creature he called "a remarkable artist and a remarkable woman—whoever she was . . . The role of the simple little Swedish girl, a Hans Christian Andersen 'Ugly Duckling,' the insignificant, snub-nosed, plain, simply dressed, hesitant, unassuming, poor-little-me, pining for the northern homeland, pure of heart and noble of thought, was the greatest of her roles." A more charitable view comes from Edward Wagenknecht, who in 1931 wrote an entire book—or psychograph, as he called it—attempting to explain who she was "without disparagement and without eulogy." For contemporary sensibilities, the woman he ends up with, sort of a cross between Mary Pickford and Queen Victoria, is not especially likable, particularly during her post-American career as Victorian England's leading oratorio singer, sentimental balladeer, and secular saint. But Wagenknecht finally has to believe that Lind, if viewed within the context of her era, really meant it when she gave up opera for the Bible and the sunset. "There is always a peculiar interest attaching to those who conquer the world and then throw it away," he concludes. "Self-indulgence and vice have generally been the most popular motives for such a relinquishment. Jenny Lind threw it away for God."

Before she did that, though, Lind threw it away for Barnum. And perhaps she found her true self and purpose in the process, as she changed the face of music in America and inspired an entire generation of young women to take the risky step toward singing as a professional career. Walt Whitman, however—an informed and astute observer of New York's musical scene in mid-century—was not buying it, and he must have spoken for a minority of other deep-feeling Americans when he wrote in the *Evening Post*, "The Swedish Swan, with all her blandishments, never touched my heart in the least. I wondered at so much vocal dexterity; and indeed they were all very pretty, those leaps and double somersets. But in the grandest religious airs, genuine masterpieces as they are, of the German composers, executed by this strangely overpraised woman in perfect scientific style, let critics say what they like, it was a failure; for there was a vacuum in the head of the performance. Beauty pervaded it no doubt, and that of a high order. It was the beauty of Adam before God breathed into his nostrils." For most Americans in 1850, this was exactly the sort of beauty they wanted.

Two

~

Career

Goals

~~~~~~

*F*ired by the Lind phenomenon, an increasing number of Americans made the dangerous commitment to pursue singing as a lifetime profession. Supported at first by parents who were either fiercely ambitious for their children or unusually enlightened, most of these daring souls found it prudent to head directly for Europe at an early age. There they could receive the finest instruction, test their talents in smaller opera companies, gain experience, establish themselves, and perhaps even become stars—a pattern most American singers would follow, with interesting variations, for more than a century. Some disappeared without a trace; others found success and never came home; still others attempted to forge careers in both the Old World and the New.

Among the first to undertake the latter was Maria-Dolorès-Bénédicta-Joséphine Nau, and her failure to pull it off may have had less to do with her intrinsic talents than with historical circumstances. As it is, one can only fantasize about the actual sound of her voice, her physical presence, and how her career might have developed had she been born a hundred years later.

In the issue dated March 4, 1854, *Dwight's Journal of Music* excitedly informed its readers that "the Grand Opéra at Paris is indebted to New York for one of the brightest stars in its galaxy of illustrious names." Gushing with florid prose, the lengthy report describes the furore stirred up by Dolorès Nau, an American-born soprano of Spanish parentage and acclaimed by the most exacting Parisian connoisseurs for her performances of such prima-donna roles as Eudoxie in Halévy's *La Juive*, Isabelle in Meyerbeer's *Robert le Diable*, Zerlina in *Don Giovanni*, and Pamyre in Rossini's *Le Siège de Corinthe*. Despite a tortured translation, one glowing French critique is clearly eager to assure *Dwight's* readers that Mlle. Nau's voice is something very special: "a high soprano, complete, of a severity full of grace, which warbles and lets fall the notes in pearls fine and delicately moulded. Its tone, usually tempered, sometimes piercing, but ever shunning the false éclat and the embroideries of the decadence, has a certain sonorous and silvery sound, and, through all its registers, is of incomparable purity and celestial sweetness."

In addition to possessing that ravishing vocal endowment, Mlle. Nau was also apparently something to see, a raven-haired beauty who, according to *Dwight's* anonymous correspondent, might have stepped from a canvas by Murillo or Ribera. The British press was equally enthusiastic. As Donizetti's Lucia di Lammermoor at the Princess's Theatre in London, Nau gave a performance that was nothing less than "a perfect triumph of Art, and at once stamped her as a prima donna assoluta." British critics even invoked the magical name of Malibran, by now a figure of misty legend, to describe a singer who, it was said, combined "expression, power of voice, taste, cultivation, musical knowledge, and immense power of execution."

The very existence of this vocal paragon from America must have been news to her compatriots, although when the above florid report appeared in *Dwight's*, Nau was no debutante. The article never divulges her age or supplies dates about her career, but in 1854 the soprano was just shy of her thirty-sixth birthday and had already been singing at the Paris Opéra for eighteen years. Nau was born on March 18, 1818, in New York, where her parents had settled after fleeing an insurrection on the island of Santo Domingo. She received early instruction in piano, harp, and voice from her mother, who sent the fourteen-year-old girl to the Paris Conservatoire in 1832. There she studied with the formidable Laure Cinti-Damoreau, who had created the leading soprano roles in Rossini's last five operas—all written for Paris—as well as Isabelle in

Robert le Diable and Elvire in Auber's *La Muette de Portici*. When Mme. Cinti-Damoreau felt the time was ripe, she introduced her star pupil to Rossini himself, who, our correspondent records, "extended a kind hand to the youthful laureate, shedding the light of his glory on the roses of her crown. Under his direction, Dolorès Nau diligently and thoroughly prepared herself for the Italian stage. And it was at his suggestion that she was induced to accept, en attendant, an engagement offered to her by the Royal Academy of Music." The soprano must have pleased the composer, since in 1846 she starred in one last Rossini premiere: as Nelly in *Robert Bruce,* a pastiche assembled from *La Donna del Lago* and various other early scores. Another of Nau's early mentors was Adolphe Nourrit, who preceded Gilbert-Louis Duprez as the Paris Opéra's leading tenor and created many important French grand-opera roles, the most celebrated being Éléazar in *La Juive.* No aspiring young singer could have been placed in more experienced or influential hands, and if her subsequent activities in Paris and the provinces did not entirely fill their highest expectations, she certainly pursued a career of consequence.

The article in *Dwight's* concludes with the exciting news of Mlle. Nau's imminent and eagerly anticipated return to her native city. Sure enough, that fall the New English Opera Company arrived in New York with Nau as the troupe's prima donna. It turned out to be less than a triumphant homecoming, judging from a review of Auber's *La Sirène* in the *Courier & Enquirer:* "Mlle. Nau, who was of course the Siren of the evening, has hardly a siren's voice; but it is agreeable in quality, and brilliant enough for all ordinary purposes, though entirely deficient in tenderness . . . She is most successful in passages of light and delicate vocalization which lie in the upper part of her high soprano voice. In these she is always satisfactory." No doubt distraught by such tepid reviews, Nau finished her short New York season and returned to Paris, where she remained until her death in 1891.

There are several possible explanations for Nau's lukewarm reception and why she left no lasting impression. For one thing, American music criticism had come a long way since 1825, when Musaeus and Cinderella, with wide-eyed wonderment, initiated their readers into the mysteries of grand opera. In mid-nineteenth-century America, reviewers could be brutally frank compared to their more accommodating, often fawning colleagues in Europe, and Nau would hardly be the last singer to arrive in New York with a fistful of rave notices, only to be brushed off with airy condescension by the local critics. By 1854 New York had already heard many of the finest singers in the world, and a high soprano of Nau's type would inevitably be compared with Lind's. Then, too, Nau's arrival could not have been more poorly timed. When the New English Opera Company reached town, all New York's attention was focused on the brand-new Academy of Music, which had been inaugurated on October 2 with *Norma* starring Grisi and Mario, indisputably two of the greatest singers of the age. Even more to the point, Nau's critical raves were probably out of date in 1854, and at the time of her New York appearances the soprano's voice was most likely in decline. Her complete retirement from the stage only two years after returning to Paris tends to support that suspicion. In the light of all this, the gushing advance attention Nau received in *Dwight's Journal* begins to read suspiciously like a publicity plant.

It may even be stretching a point to call Nau an American singer at all, considering her Spanish parentage, how young she was when she left home, and the fact that she seldom sang outside France. There were, however, several other young, unarguably American singers active in Europe during the 1850s who never lost their roots, and many of them eventually returned to make an impact at home. The most significant was surely Adelaide Phillipps, the first to have a fully rounded operatic career.

Born in Stratford-on-Avon, England, in 1833, Adelaide was seven years old when her parents emigrated to Boston, where she attended grade school. Like little Julia Wheatley in New York a decade earlier, Adelaide performed on the stage as a child, appearing at the Tremont Street Theatre at the age of eight, impersonating five characters in the comedy *Old and Young*, piping out several songs to complement her dance routines. During her precocious early days, the girl apparently had a sympathetic and sensible vocal advisor in Thomas Comer, who oversaw all the musical activities at the Boston Museum. As her voice matured, more formal instruction was clearly called for, and the girl was entrusted to the care of a local teacher, one Émilie Arnoult, who decided that her gifted pupil had a naturally placed contralto. By then Adelaide had reached the age of seventeen and it was 1850, the year when Jenny Lind visited Boston during her grand tour of America. Eager to show off their prodigy, the city's cultural elite approached the Swedish Nightingale, who graciously consented to hear Adelaide sing.

For a teenager in the 1850s to be noticed and encouraged by a media phenomenon like Lind must have been thrilling. By the time Lind reached Boston, her celebrity had spread throughout the country, and it must have taken considerable nerve for a young girl, even one as experienced as Adelaide, to be ushered before such a presence and asked to sing. Lind, apparently impressed, counseled the girl to abandon dancing and acting and concentrate exclusively on singing—abroad, of course— and as encouragement Lind presented the young woman with a check for $1,000 and a handwritten letter containing commendations to Manuel García II, now the most celebrated voice teacher in Europe (and who had come to Lind's rescue when she was experiencing vocal problems in 1841). Once again, as it had seven years earlier for Eliza Biscaccianti, the community pitched in to gather funds. The sum was raised, thanks in large part to a generous contribution from the piano manufacturer Jonas Chickering, and in 1851 Adelaide, accompanied by her father and a maiden aunt, set off for Europe.

After two years of study with García in London, Phillipps was deemed sufficiently prepared to make her Italian debut, on November 5, 1853, at the Teatro Grande in Brescia, as the warrior Arsace in Rossini's *Semiramide*. At first the young American was coolly received—evidently at the public dress rehearsal, Signorina Filippi, as she was to be known during the European phases of her career, had irritated the invited audience by unconventionally appearing in street clothes and singing in half voice. During the actual performance, however, at least by the time she had reached the cabaletta of Arsace's difficult entrance aria, the headstrong Signorina Filippi had sufficiently thawed out the cognoscenti to achieve at least a moderate success. Brescia's *La Fama* complimented the debutante, pronouncing her "young and attractive, with a genuine contralto voice, rich and strong, at the same time of true intonation, sweet and flexible."

For the next two years Phillipps, her father, and, presumably, the aunt, remained in Italy, but despite sympathetic notices in Milan, Crema, Rovereto, and a few other operatic centers, the contralto's engagements were sporadic and her fees insufficient to support three Americans used to the comfortable life in Boston. Then, too, the reality of performing opera in Italy was very likely a sobering experience for a young woman who, as a child prodigy, had been in constant demand and accustomed to uncritical adulation. Nonetheless, when Phillipps returned to Boston, she was definitely more musically finished than when she left, and no doubt wiser about the grueling life that faced an aspiring opera singer in those days. A local reviewer of her homecoming concert at the Boston Music Hall in October 1855 noted the improvement, and encouraged by such complimentary reviews, the Phillipps family felt that the time was ripe for the grown-up prodigy to try her luck on the New York opera stage.

That major event took place on March 17, 1856, at the Academy of Music, then the home of Max Maretzek's Italian Opera Company, and Phillipps sang Azucena in Verdi's *Il Trovatore*. It was treated as a genuine occasion by the press, even though her debut had not been as enthusiastically touted in advance as Biscaccianti's had been in 1847, nor did it generate such polarized reactions. As usual, though, New York's critics were guarded. Everyone seemed to agree that Phillipps had an unusually effective stage presence—after all, she had been performing since childhood and had long since learned how to handle herself in front of an audience. Years later one colleague—Henry Clay Barnabee, who performed with the Boston Ideal Opera Company in the late 1870s and 1880s—recalled how meticulously she prepared her impersonation of Rossini's Arsace: "Among a large number of distinguished characteristics of her dramatic excellence was her absolute identification with the character she assumed, and her attention to the smallest details, to attain which she availed herself of any suggestions. I remember standing in the wings and observing the military correctness and precision with which she performed the operation of sheathing her sword in the role she was performing, and learned on inquiry that she had taken lessons from an army officer."

Even Clara Louise Kellogg, America's self-proclaimed first prima donna, had to agree that Phillipps looked good onstage. Otherwise, Kellogg could find little to praise about her older compatriot. In her memoirs, Kellogg recalled her own operatic debut at the Academy of Music in February 1861, as Gilda in Verdi's *Rigoletto*, a performance she shared with Phillipps, who sang the comparatively small role of Maddalena: "One other person in the company who never gave me a kind word (although she was not an Italian) was Adelaide Phillipps, the contralto. She was a fine artist and had been singing for many years, so, perhaps, it galled her to have to 'support' a younger countrywoman. When it came to dividing the honours she was not at all pleased. As

Maddalena in *Rigoletto* she was very plain; but when she did Pierotto, the boyish, rustic lover in *Linda,* she looked well. She had the most perfectly formed pair of legs—ankles, feet and all—that I ever saw on a woman."

When reading the respectful comments about her many subsequent performances, one tends to doubt that Phillipps was ever considered a vocal phenomenon of the very first rank. Since she had the estimable benefit of García's classical training, it was quite possibly health problems that interferred with the natural development and maturation of her voice. After completing her first season with the Italian Opera Company, Phillipps traveled with the troupe to Havana, where she contracted yellow fever and apparently never fully recovered from its effects. That setback hardly impeded the progress of her career, however. During the next four years she was busy singing opera, concert, and oratorio up and down the Eastern Seaboard, and in the fall of 1861 she set off once again for Europe and more than a year of extensive touring. Her first stop was Paris—not at the celebrated Opéra, but at the Théâtre des Italiens in one of her signature roles, Verdi's Azucena. Interested as ever in the progress of its local diva, Bostonians could read a glowing report of this performance in the *Advertizer.* Significantly, the anonymous critic mainly praises her dramatic prowess, especially as compared to Paris's preferred Azucena, the adored contralto Marietta Alboni. That vocal paragon, he writes, "is so fat that she can only stand still while the music gushes from her throat like a fountain. Miss Phillipps, on the other hand, has a great deal of dramatic power, and displayed it to such purpose in her delineation of the fierce, revengeful, yet loving gypsy mother, that she would have made a hit with far less vocal excellence than she possesses . . ."

After her Paris appearances, which also included Ulrica in Verdi's new opera, *Un Ballo in Maschera,* and Arsace in *Semiramide,* Phillipps continued her European tour, singing in Madrid, Barcelona, Prague, Budapest, and Warsaw—an invitation to St. Petersburg had to be declined, since cold climates tended to aggravate the singer's health, still delicate after the yellow fever incident in Havana. The following year Phillipps was back in America, tirelessly traveling the country from coast to coast but always faithfully returning to Boston, where she sang at the Handel and Haydn Society triennial festivals as well as at the Peace Jubilee of 1869. In 1874, with her younger sister Mathilde, the indefatigable singer formed the Adelaide Phillipps Opera Company, but the venture quickly ran into financial difficulties and collapsed after just a year. From 1879 the mezzo was mainly associated with the Boston Ideal Opera Company, but recurrent illness finally forced her to abandon performing altogether, and in 1881 she retired to her brother's farm in Marshfield, Massachusetts. A year later, while taking the recuperative waters at Karlsbad, Germany, she died—a few weeks short of her forty-ninth birthday, and, one can't help thinking, totally exhausted.

Adelaide Phillipps may never have reached the heights of international stardom, but through hard work and unceasing application she was unquestionably the first American who had earned the right to be called a professional opera and concert singer in the fullest sense of the term—there was scarcely a moment in her life not devoted to honing her craft or appearing before an audience. She never married, nor are any romantic liaisons even hinted at in the surviving literature about her life. Her main extramusical concern was for her immediate family—her parents and many siblings, especially sister Mathilde (1853–1912), twenty years her junior.

In 1868 and at the height of her fame, Adelaide noticed that fifteen-year-old Mathilde showed signs of promising vocal talent. Putting her own activities on hold for the moment, Phillipps took the girl to Europe, where Mathilde was placed in the hands of Manuel García II in London, and later, in Paris, with that celebrated pedagogue's by-now famous sister, Pauline Viardot. Also a contralto, Mathilde more or less followed the same path as Adelaide had years earlier, gaining experience in Italy before venturing a New York debut at the Academy of Music. That occurred on February 18, 1876, in the title role of Rossini's *La Cenerentola*—with Adelaide onstage to lend moral support in the small part of Tisbe. Mathilde, however, apparently had a more retiring nature and less taste for travel than her elder sibling, or possibly her vocal gift was simply more limited. In any case, after the failure of the Adelaide Phillipps Opera Company, she became a permanent member of the Boston Ideal for the remainder of her singing career, concentrating mainly on Gilbert and Sullivan and other favorites in the light-opera repertory.

Boston had yet another prominent star singer to boast of during the mid-nineteenth century, and for a few years it seemed that Elise Hensler would turn out to be the most luminous of them all. Like Adelaide Phillipps, Hensler was born abroad—in 1836 in Switzerland—but brought to Boston as a tiny tot by her father, a tailor, who preferred to try his luck in the New World rather than serve in the Swiss Army.

Unlike Adelaide, however, Elise never graced the professional stage as a child, attending school in Springfield and Boston but attracting attention for the clarity and beauty of her light, high soprano. Vocal studies with local singing teachers inevitably led to the suggestion of European training, and off she went in 1853, barely sixteen years old, studying first at the Paris Conservatoire with the retired Italian tenor Giulio Bordogni, who, according to legend, once patted her on the shoulder and called her his *"petite* Sontag"—a flattering reference to Henriette Sontag (1806–54), one of the most successful and popular German sopranos of her time. After Paris, Elise moved to Milan, where she took lessons with a certain Romano, "a teacher and composer of high repute," according to a Boston newspaper report on her progress.

Elise had set her sights high and she wasted no time taking proper steps to realize her ambitions. In the spring of 1854 a group of Milanese admirers arranged a private concert in which the soprano sang, among other things, Pierre Rode's florid variations, a favorite coloratura showpiece of such celebrated divas as Catalani, Malibran, and Viardot. The select audience included representatives from La Scala management, who were apparently impressed, since they offered her a three-year contract on the spot. Elise—or more likely her father, who had given up tailoring to manage his daughter's career—decided that fifteen months would be a more prudent arrangement, especially if public acclaim was great enough to make her an instant star. He was also careful to ensure that her voice would not be overtaxed, stipulating that her roles were to be strictly *mezzo carattere:* the lighter Donizetti and Rossini heroines and nothing heavier or more strenuous by Verdi than Gilda in *Rigoletto* and Amalia in *I Masnadieri.* The contract further stated that La Scala could loan her services to other principal theaters of Italy for 1,000 lire per month and to Vienna for 1,500, all of it roughly adding up to an annual salary of $3,000—not bad for a seventeen-year-old debutante.

Before her scheduled December debut at La Scala, Hensler was heard that May in concert by a *Dwight's Journal* correspondent, who was impressed by her calm, collected, dignified manner, her clear, silvery tone, the true intonation, sweet trill, and confident but unassuming ladylike deportment. Eight months later, on December 31, Hensler made her La Scala debut, as Linda in Donizetti's *Linda di Chamounix.* Although some Milanese critics felt that her voice was a bit small for the house, most admired her precision, agility, and sentiment.

Hensler's evident success that New Year's Eve was a bittersweet one.

Several hours after the final curtain fell, her father suffered a stroke that left him paralyzed and unable to speak. Although his health gradually improved, the elder Hensler was no longer able to look after his daughter's interests, and by May 1855 it became clear that Elise would have to return to America, her promising European career cut short after less than a year before the public. So they sailed home, and on June 6 their ship docked in New York. A mere ten days later Elise made her debut at the Academy of Music, once again as Linda—an appropriate role, it was said, for a young girl born in Switzerland. Like Phillipps and Biscaccianti, Hensler did not win an unqualified rave from the stern *Times* reviewer, still determined to avoid chauvinism and indiscriminate compliments. He did praise the sweet and sympathetic nature of her voice, and pronounced her pure Italian method admirable, as far as it went, but mainly urged Hensler to keep up with her studies.

The following week Hensler was back in Boston to give a homecoming concert in the Music Hall on June 26. By now it was generally recognized that a soprano with such an ingratiating light voice would be unlikely to grow into the more dramatic roles of the earlier bel canto period, let alone the heavier new repertory represented by middle-period Verdi. Hensler continued to sing opera in Boston and at the Academy of Music in New York through the 1855–56 season, her roles including Elvire in *La Muette de Portici* and Elvira in *Don Giovanni*, as well as a leading part in the world premiere, on March 24, 1856, of *La Spia*—an opera based on James Fenimore Cooper's novel *The Spy*, by Luigi Arditi, a conductor and a composer, remembered today mainly for such lilting salon songs as "Il Bacio." On May 20, 1856, the soprano sailed for Italy, determined to pick up her European career where she had left it with her precipitate departure a year earlier. This she did, until fate brought her to the Royal Opera in Lisbon on October 29, 1857, when she caught the eye of Dom Fernando, the king emeritus of Portugal, who was sitting in the royal box that night celebrating his forty-first birthday.

The courtship was a long one, but finally Elise relented in 1869. There is scant news about her career during the interim, and by the time she became Fernando's morganatic wife, one suspects that the fresh vocal bloom of youth admired by critics in the 1850s had long since departed. The marriage took place in the chapel of Pena Castle at Cintra, fifteen miles from Lisbon, and Elise was instantly created Countess of Edla, becoming the first American to enter the *Almanach de Gotha*. Her professional life now over, Hensler lived luxuriously with her royal consort and became one of Europe's most noted hostesses. Famous guests from all over the world enjoyed the couple's hospitality, and for the international social set a visit to Pena Castle was de rigueur—General and Mrs. Ulysses S. Grant dropped by in 1878 while on their trip around the world. This blissful existence came to an abrupt halt when Dom Fernando died in 1885. Elise went into seclusion but lived on for many more years, dying at the age of ninety-three in 1929. By then even Boston had forgotten all about Hensler and her brief operatic career, one that long ago had seemed so promising.

Viewed within the larger dramatic framework of mid-nineteenth-century operatic life, Dolorès Nau, Adelaide Phillipps, and Elise Hensler played only bit parts. None had much of an impact on the development of singing, and judging from what one reads about them, even critical commentary by those inclined to be partial, they could hardly be considered major vocal presences. Still, they did find ways to train their voices, seek out professional opportunities, and get themselves noticed. Phillipps in particular was an enduring example to American singers, one who showed that, with hard work and persistence, it could be done, and her early successes in Italy encouraged a number of other Boston-born singers to follow her abroad in the mid-1850s. Baritone Edward Sumner and tenor Harrison Millard were just two colleagues who turned up on the rosters of smaller Italian theaters, where they performed briefly before returning home to sing with local organizations and teach the next generation.

A more prominent tenor was Henry Squires, who could be found singing Manrico in *Il Trovatore* in Naples early in 1854. "Sig. Squires," according to a friendly report that appeared in the *Gazetta Musicale di Napoli*, "deserves double sympathy, as being a beginner and consequently not an actor, and then as being an American and consequently a stranger to our manner and our language. Yet he has a voice fine enough to cover in many points all these disadvantages, and to enforce the liveliest applauses; his voice will be still more beautiful when a good pronunciation of the Italian language shall render it less constrained and more voluminous. For the rest, the tenor Squires has sufficient artistic feeling, and when he takes the meaning of the word, knows how to give it fit expression." Apparently the young tenor never did quite get the hang of how to fit the Italian words with the notes, since the same criticism turns up again in the Neapolitan press some two years later. Even at that, the local critics continued to be impressed by "Enrico" Squires, his sweet tenor, musical intelligence, and passionate feeling for Verdi—no small accomplishment for an American singer in Italy during the 1850s.

A number of other American singers tried their luck on the Italian stage, returned home, and were noticed briefly—Isabella Hinckley for one, a native of Albany who, after her time abroad, appeared as Donizetti's mad Lucia at New York's Academy of Music on January 3, 1861. "Trovator" of *Dwight's Journal* was there, and he praised her "excellent figure, brown hair, superb teeth, and expressive and pleasing face." She also sang, neatly and precisely according to Trovator, but "unlike Patti, she has not the art to conceal art." Once again, the New York critics were determined not to appear provincial or be taken in by advance gush from Europe. Perhaps the high point of Isabella's brief career came a month later at the Academy when, with Abraham Lincoln in attendance, she sang what must have been an especially emotional rendition of "The Star-Spangled Banner" during Rosina's Lesson Scene in *Il Barbiere di Siviglia*. A year later, the unfortunate Hinckley died after childbirth.

Cora de Wilhorst lasted a bit longer. After her Academy debut, as Lucia, on January 28, 1857, one critic proclaimed that he had witnessed a performance by an exceptional artist, ironically attributing the singer's musical excellence to the fact that she "has had the advantage of never having been to Italy." Even at that, her vocal technique struck him as half-formed (by now a familiar refrain in the reviews of American debutantes), but a few more years of hard study would surely iron out the problems, and then the young soprano should proceed directly to Paris. There, he confidently predicted, "she will be greeted by impartial judges of that capital as 'the great American vocalist.'" De Wilhorst never earned that title, either in Paris or at home. She did, however, prove that a native singer did not necessarily have to study abroad in order to present herself to the most exacting and hard-to-please musical public in the land (which, by mid-century, most certainly resided in New York City) and be taken seriously.

According to a lengthy biographical note that appeared in New York's *Evening Gazette* a few months before De Wilhorst's Academy of Music debut, the city's new diva was born Cora Withers, the daughter of Reuben Withers, a well-known New York banker. Fond of music since her earliest childhood, Cora had until then confined her singing to after-dinner entertainments for her parents' rich friends and business associates. A professional career probably never even entered her mind until she met a certain impoverished German nobleman named De Wilhorst and fell madly in love with him. If Mr. Withers was, not surprisingly, irritated at his daughter's choice of a husband, he was positively enraged when the headstrong Cora announced that she was planning to support them both by singing in public. "For a long time," continued the *Evening Gazette*, "he contended with this wish, but at length he acceded and her first appearance was announced to take place at Newport, R.I., in August last. Of course all our readers will remember what this announcement induced—an attack upon her husband by one of her brothers, who could not see that the profession of a vocalist is as good and as honorable per se as that of a banker or a merchant. Jenny Lind may be placed as an honorable contrast in juxta-position with the Fauntleroys and Schuylers, and we believe that but few of our readers are there who, should Cora de Wilhorst meet with continuous success in her new vocation, would not rank her name above that of her respectable parent (of whom we confess that we have heard nothing but good) even although he be a banker."

One has the feeling that whatever success Cora found with the public and the critics was due mainly to the romantic circumstances that brought her to the stage. But she must have had something, since more than one critic eventually did commend her for solid vocal accomplishment, although her onstage presence was generally considered to be cold and her expressive range rather narrow. She continued to sing in opera throughout the 1850s, becoming a leading member of Maurice Strakosch's American company at the Academy during the season of 1858–59. Opening night that year found De Wilhorst singing Elvira in Bellini's *I Puritani* and apparently bringing down the house with her rendition of the florid *polacca* in Act I—a brilliant upper register had evidently always been the soprano's special forte. The end of her career was near, however, for a year or two later a French paper reported the news that a certain Prussian count named Mr. de Wilhorst had succeeded in breaking the bank at Baden-Baden. The De Wilhorsts forsook the world of opera, and as far as anyone can determine, the lucky couple lived happily ever after in wealthy obscurity.

Another New York soprano from a privileged background, Genevieve Ward, was born on March 27, 1833, the daughter of Colonel Samuel Ward and the granddaughter of Gideon Lee, who at one time had been mayor of New York City. Unlike Cora de Wilhorst, the young girl was encouraged to develop her voice with professional goals in mind, and at the age of fifteen she left for study in Europe and, it is said, lessons with Rossini. Like Cora, however, Genevieve fell in love early on, but with less happy results. On a visit to Nice, the aspiring sixteen-year-old soprano encountered a Russian nobleman, Constantine de Guerbel, and married him on the spot. Unfortunately, De Guerbel already had a wife, and the marriage was immediately annulled. The disappointed Genevieve returned to her studies, and after three years of diligent application she successfully emerged on the Italian stage in 1856 as Genevra Guerrabella. If nothing else, the soprano's unhappy romance yielded a catchy stage name.

After six years on European stages, La Guerrabella came home, appearing with Jacob Grau's company at the New York Academy of Music on November 10, 1862, as Violetta in Verdi's *La Traviata*. Reviewing the event, the *Evening Post* remarked that she covered "the defects of a thin, cold voice by the most artistic management and consummate acting," and mainly admired her energy and intensity. That mixed notice prophetically pointed to the singer's future. After a few years of performances as Verdi's Amelia and Leonora, Bellini's Norma, and other heavy roles, La Guerrabella found that her voice was rapidly shredding. A practical woman, she became Genevieve Ward once again, and, like Charlotte Cushman a generation earlier, turned to the spoken stage. In fact, Ward achieved far more fame as an actress than she ever did as an opera singer, and that early phase of her career was only a dim memory by the time she died in London in 1922 at the age of eighty-nine.

By the 1860s the number of American singers appearing before the public had reached a sizable number. Alternating with Signorina Guerrabella in Grau's company at the Academy was a Signora Lorini, born Virginia Whiting. Lorini seems to have been more generously endowed than her colleague in more ways than one. Reviewing her Norma, *The Musical World and Musical Review* of November 22, 1862, commented on her "magnificent soprano voice of pure, bell-like and voluminous quality," but also went on to observe that "perhaps the considerable embonpoint of the lady interferes somewhat with an easy and fluent delivery, as well as with her acting, for only thus can we account for her failing to cause any special interest in her delineation of character." Also appearing with Grau's company was Kate Duckworth, known variously as Mme.

Morensi and Mlle. Montmorency, who was a pupil of Adelaide Phillipps and, like her teacher, much admired for the dramatic fire of her Azucena in *Il Trovatore*.

When *The Musical World and Musical Review* reviewed Genevra Guerrabella in November 1862, the journal confidently stated that although her voice might not have been especially remarkable, her overall accomplishment was sufficient to place her "foremost in the very respectable list of American prime donne, who now successfully rival the European celebrities of all nations." That may have been an overstatement, but by the time of the Civil War, American singers had definitely made their presence felt at home and abroad. If the country had not yet produced a Malibran, Lind, Pasta, Grisi, or Sontag, many observers of the American vocal scene felt that the appearance of such a phenomenon was surely not far off. By 1870 many would have nominated Clara Louise Kellogg, and that prima donna would have been the first to second it. Although she lacked the sheer star quality that might have propelled her into the pantheon of immortals, Kellogg was a formidable presence on the American opera and concert stages, from the moment of her New York debut in 1861 to her retirement in 1887.

Three

~

An American

Prima

Donna

~~~~~~~~~~~~~~~~~~~~~

Clara Louise Kellogg was only a toddler when her mother lifted her up to the keyboard of the family's parlor piano, just to see what would happen. "I played not only with my right hand," the soprano proudly recalled in her memoirs, "but also with my left hand; and I made harmonies. Probably they were not in any way elaborate chords, but they were chords, and they harmonised. I have known some grown-up musicians whose chords didn't! I was three then, and a persistent baby, already detesting failure."

Determination, perseverance, inborn musicality, awesome self-confidence—any young woman deciding to pursue an operatic career in mid-nineteenth-century America would have to possess these qualities, and Louise (the name her family and friends preferred throughout her life) was abundantly blessed with all four. The future diva arrived on July 9, 1842, in Sumterville (now Sumter), South Carolina, a descendant of old Connecticut stock. Shrewdness, practicality, and ingenuity—all the attributes one associates with Connecticut Yankees—ran deeply in both families, and Louise was particularly proud of her maternal grandmother's practical and musical accomplishments. Widowed at twenty-three and left with three small children, Lydia Atwood not only went into business for herself, setting up cotton gins in Connecticut and Massachusetts, but also gave lessons in music.

When Louise was still small, her parents moved back north to Birmingham (Derby), Connecticut, where George Kellogg opened his own shop, manufacturing new forms of hooks and eyes, surgical instruments, chain-making machinery, and other devices that could be useful to a growing industrial society. Music was not neglected around the house—George played the flute and his wife, Jane, the organ, and musical events were attended whenever the opportunity arose. A trip to New York City in 1850 to hear Jenny Lind provided the eight-year-old Louise with her first musical milestone, although her memories of it seemed more focused on the diva than the music: "I remember it clearly, and just the way in which she tripped on to the stage that night with her hair, as she always wore it, drawn down close over her ears—a custom that gave rise to the popular report that she had no ears." Unfortunately, George Kellogg's business failed in 1855, and the family was off again, this time to New York for good—a lucky move for Louise, whose musical inclinations could now be correctly encouraged and trained.

Like so many young girls, Louise at first took up singing simply to acquire a maidenly accomplishment, with no thought of going on the stage—or so she said. This ambitious teenager surely had something more in mind than singing for the local church choir or social group. While attending the Ashland Seminary and Musical Institute in the Catskills, she studied voice with one teacher after another, obviously working with more diligence and intensity than her schoolmates. The list of her mentors, all European-born musicians who had recently settled in the New York area, included Émile Millet (a graduate of the Paris Conservatoire), Achille Errani (a Vaccai student), and, perhaps most significantly, Emanuele Muzio (1821–90), a protégé of Verdi's and the great composer's musical assistant at the time of the first performances of his *Macbeth* and *I Masnadieri*. Maddeningly, Kellogg neglected to leave a detailed account of her studies with Muzio, who, although he never achieved fame as a conductor or composer, was esteemed by Verdi for his sensitivity and musicianship. He must have passed on much valuable advice to his young pupil, especially with regard to style, tradition, and an idiomatic approach to Italian opera. Such sophisticated instruction would have been otherwise unavailable to American girls like Louise, who was never given the opportunity to study voice in Europe.

Early in 1860 Muzio decided to ease his seventeen-year-old charge into the career she clearly yearned for, arranging a four-week concert tour that went as far west as Detroit. If Louise ever thought that the life of an internationally renowned opera diva was going to be one of non-stop glamour, this jolting experience quickly brought her down to earth. "That was a hard tour," wrote Kellogg. "Indeed, all tours were hard in those days. Travelling accommodations were limited and uncomfortable, and most of the hotels were very bad. Trains were slow and connections uncertain, and of course there was no such thing as a Pullman or, much less, a dining car. Sometimes we had to sit up all night and were not able to get anything to eat, not infrequently arriving too late for the meal hour of the hotel where we were to stop. The journeys were so long and so difficult that they used to say Pauline Lucca [an Austrian soprano and indefatigable barnstormer] always travelled in her nightgown and a black velvet wrapper."

After that brief trial by fire, Kellogg was ready to make her formal operatic debut, as Gilda in *Rigoletto*, on February 27, 1861, at New York's Academy of Music. The soprano had been diligently studying the role for nine months, and Muzio's coaching must have been a major factor in helping to make the evening at least a tolerable success. Kellogg may have known the role inside out by then, but she still had much to contend with. As we have already seen, her compatriot Adelaide Phillipps, as Maddalena, was apparently not especially welcoming, and her other colleagues do not seem to have been particularly helpful either. The Rigoletto, an Italian baritone named Ferri, was blind in one eye, and Kellogg found she had to resort to deft impromptu maneuvers in order to remain on his seeing side. Love scenes with the Duke required an extra amount of imagination and self-control, since Giorgio Stigelli (actually Georg Stiegele, a German tenor) reeked of beer and cheese. Despite these impediments, the New York reviewers, if not exactly ecstatic, were at least complimentary, particularly about the debutante's realistic acting.

Throughout her career Kellogg always considered dramatic presentation just as important as vocal accomplishment, a credo she shared with Phillipps and numerous other American singers of the period— perhaps, one can't help thinking, to compensate for voices and techniques that were never as finished or reliable as those of the greatest European divas of the day. A week after her Academy of Music debut, Kellogg was in Boston singing in *Linda di Chamounix*, again striving her utmost "to give a truthful and appealing impersonation of her. But the handicaps of those days of crude and primitive theatre conditions were really almost insurmountable." The lighting system was not only inadequate but dangerous, consisting mainly of an unprotected row of glaring footlights and a single calcium-generated beam for special effects. The Academy had just three all-purpose "productions" to accommodate its singers and dazzle its patrons, and all three were frequently combined and altered as required.

Kellogg struggled with the limitations of contemporary theater facilities all her life, and her ingenious methods of finding ways to surmount them registered early on. After she had sung her first Linda in Boston and was scheduled to perform the same role in New York, she was horrified to learn from the company's costumier that the gown she wore in the first act would have to make do in the last. "But I can't," she gasped. "That fresh new gown, after months are supposed to have gone by!—when Linda has walked and slept in it during the whole journey." Kellogg may have been only nineteen at the time, but her prima-donna instincts were aroused and fully prepared to deal with the crisis:

> I sent for an old shawl from the chorus and ripped my costume into rags. By this time the orchestra was almost at the opening bars of the third act and there was not a moment to lose. Suddenly I looked at my shoes and nearly collapsed with despair. One always provided one's own foot-gear and the shoes I had on were absolutely the only pair of the sort required that I possessed; neat little slippers, painfully new and clean . . . Well—there was a moment's struggle before I attacked my pretty shoes—but my passion for realism triumphed. I sent a man out into Fourteenth Street at the stage door of the Academy and had him rub those immaculate slippers in the gutter until they were thoroughly dirty, so that when I wore them onto the stage three minutes later they looked as if I had really walked to Paris and back in them. The next day the newspapers said that the part of Linda had never before been sung with so much pathos. "Aha!" said I, "that's my old clothes! That's my dirt!"

A few months after Kellogg launched her career, the Civil War erupted. If opera did not exactly vanish from the boards, performances were less frequent and audience interest waned for the duration—"Yankee Doodle" and "The Girl I Left Behind Me" seemed, for the moment at least, far more inspiring than the arias of Rossini and Verdi. Kellogg did enjoy at least one hit during the war years when she toured with Donizetti's *The Daughter of the Regiment*. Audiences were said to have responded with a frenzy of patriotic enthusiasm after seeing Kellogg beat her snare drum (a feat she had mastered especially for the occasion) and hearing her sing Donizetti's infectious tunes as well as numerous interpolated national airs. Some lads in the audience, Kellogg claimed, were so swept up by the performances that they promptly enlisted.

After two years as a successful young prima donna, Kellogg had sung leading roles in a dozen operas: *Rigoletto, Linda di Chamounix, I Puritani, La Sonnambula, Un Ballo in Maschera, The Daughter of the Regiment,* Massé's *Les Noces de Jeannette, Lucia di Lammermoor, Don Giovanni* (Zerlina), Donizetti's *Poliuto,* Flotow's *Martha,* and *La Traviata.* If she had not exactly overwhelmed the cognoscenti, her genuine talent was recognized and appreciated. "Miss Kellogg's impersonation of Martha," wrote one critic two months after her Academy debut in 1861, "confirmed our agreeable impression of her as a singer and an actress. The fresh bloom of her voice, its maiden-like, clear, penetrating quality, somewhat Patti-like, her truth of intonation and expression, and her already remarkable execution are full of promise, which is sustained by the unaffected, graceful animation, as well as a certain intellectual quality, an air of native refinement, that pervades her performance. It certainly seems unnecessary to go abroad for mere vocal study, when such singers can spring up and unfold so fair at home."

What Kellogg needed now was a vehicle to define her own special operatic persona, and she soon found one: Marguerite in Gounod's *Faust,* which she sang in the opera's New York premiere on November 25, 1863. Now generally looked upon as a quaint Victorian period piece, *Faust* was considered positively avant-garde when new—even Verdi had not yet departed so radically from the familiar formal conventions of Rossini and Donizetti. "Gounod's bold harmonies, sweeping airs, and curious orchestration were upsetting to the public ears," Kellogg reminisced, admitting that such "new music" puzzled her as well. "Also, I found it very difficult to sing. I, who had been accustomed to Linda and Gilda and Martha, felt utterly at sea when I tried to sing what at that time seemed to me the remarkable intervals of this strange, new, operatic heroine, Marguerite." Stimulated by the challenge, Kellogg applied herself with customary diligence and thoroughness in developing her interpretation, characteristically putting much thought into how to act the part. Many of her decisions were typically shrewd and perceptive, even though it was clear that she had little sympathy for Marguerite or her dilemma:

> Stupidity is really the keynote of Marguerite's character. She was not quite a peasant—she and her brother owned their own house, showing that they belonged to the stolid, sound, sheltered burgher class. On the other hand, she explicitly states to Faust that she is "not a lady and needs no escort." In short, she was the ideal victim and was selected as such by Mephistopheles who, whatever else he may have been, was a judge of character. Marguerite was an easy dupe. She was entirely without resisting power. She was dull, and sweet, and open to flattery. She liked pretty things, with no more discrimination or taste than other girls. She was a well-brought-up but uneducated young person of an ignorant age and of a stupid class, and innocent to the verge of idiocy . . .
>
> I had never been allowed to read Goethe's poem until I began to study Marguerite. But even my careful mother was obliged to admit that I would have to familiarise myself with the character before I interpreted it. It is doubtful, even then, if I entered fully into the emotional and psychological grasp of the rôle. All that part of it was with me entirely mental. I could seize the complete mental possibilities of a character and work them out intelligently long before I had any emotional comprehension of them. As a case in point, when I sang Gilda I gave a perfectly logical presentation of the character, but I am very sure that I had not the least notion of what the latter part of *Rigoletto* meant. Fear, grief, love, courage—those were emotions that I could accept and with which I could work; but I was still too immature to have much conception of the great sex complications that underlay the opera that I sang so peacefully. And I dare say that one reason why I played Marguerite so well was because I was so ridiculously innocent myself.

At first the critics found *Faust* positively incoherent, but the public flocked to see it—twenty-seven performances had to be given that season to accommodate the demand—and Kellogg, despite her scorn for what she perceived to be Marguerite's bovine density, was clearly one potent reason for its success. The critics loved her performance, and Kellogg herself most prized the comment of Henry Wadsworth Longfellow, who the day after the premiere wrote to James T. Fields of Boston, "The Margaret was beautiful. She reminded me of Dryden's lines—'So pois'd, so gently she descends from high, It seems a soft dismission from the sky.' "

Kellogg's protestations of her own maidenly innocence, even at age twenty, were undoubtedly true—the self-made prima donna had that much in common with Marguerite. As far as one can tell, Jane Kellogg consented to her daughter's career ambitions so long as she could act as vigilant chaperone. Stage kisses were permitted on the forehead only, and once, when a tussle with a villainous baritone became too realistic for Mrs. Kellogg's taste, the good woman quickly stepped in and cried, "Don't you dare touch my daughter so roughly!" Louise submitted to her mother's eagle-eyed supervision without apparent signs of rebellion, although she registered mild resentment later on: "It is all very well to be carefully guarded and to be made the archetype of American virtue on the stage, but there is a great deal of innocuous amusement that I might have had and did not have, which I should have been better off for having. My mother could hardly let me hold a friendly conversation with a man—much less a flirtation."

With the end of the war in 1865 and her career securely established in America, Kellogg inevitably began to think about a European debut that might increase her prestige and earning power at home. Although they had made no contracts abroad, nor even saw any definite prospects ahead, Kellogg and her mother set sail for London in the fall of 1867. The singer's reputation had preceded her, however, and she was met at the dock by a representative from the fabled British impresario Colonel James Henry Mapleson, at that time director of the company appearing at Her Majesty's Theatre. Arrangements were immediately concluded, and Kellogg made her London debut, as Marguerite, on November 2—a nervy decision, as it turned out. At Her Majesty's the role was then considered the private property of Christine Nilsson, and in the rival company at Covent Garden the part belonged to Adelina Patti; and both sopranos were two of the most celebrated international divas of the day. Another formidable presence at Her Majesty's was Therese Tietjens, who also had Marguerite in her repertory. At her New York debut six years earlier, Kellogg was resented by the Italians, who dominated the Academy of Music; now she had to prove herself before a chilly British audience, which was equally skeptical at the prospect of encountering an American prima donna.

Wretchedly nervous on the first night, Kellogg heard just one kind word from a colleague before going on stage: "Courage, little one, courage," whispered her Valentin, Charles Santley, the English baritone for whom Gounod had written the aria "Avant de quitter ces lieux." Buoyed by Santley's thoughtfulness, Kellogg went on with a brave heart, gave her all, won over a doubting public, and earned an encomium in *The Athenaeum* from Henry Chorley. His remarks put an interesting perspective on Kellogg's voice, temperament, and operatic priorities, which were clearly in the process of departing from the old bel canto school and indicating the later direction her career would take as she gradually added the more weighty roles of Verdi and Wagner to her repertory.

> Miss Kellogg has a voice, indeed, that leaves little to wish for, and proves by her use of it that her studies have been both assiduous and in the right path. She is, in fact, though so young, a thoroughly accomplished singer—in the school, at any rate, toward which the music of M. Gounod consistently leans, and which essentially differs from the florid school of Rossini and the Italians before Verdi. One of the great charms of her singing is her perfect enunciation of the words she has to utter. She never sacrifices sense to sound; but fits the verbal text to the music, as if she attached equal importance to each. Of the Italian language she seems to be a thorough mistress, and we may well believe that she speaks it both fluently and correctly. These manifest advantages, added to a graceful figure, a countenance full of intelligence, and undoubted dramatic ability, make up a sum of attractions to be envied, and easily explain the interest excited by Miss Kellogg at the outset and maintained by her to the end.

Additional performances of *Faust* quickly followed, and soon Kellogg was further challenging the preeminence of Patti and Nilsson by poaching on such other favorite roles as Violetta, Martha, and Linda. Kellogg claimed that the public "tacitly" preferred her to Patti in the latter role, especially after Luigi Arditi, the chief conductor at Her Majesty's, composed "The Kellogg Waltz" for the new American star to sing at the close of Donizetti's opera. The rivalry might have become even more heated had Her Majesty's not burned to the ground on December 6, a month after Kellogg's debut. Arditi had been rehearsing the orchestra when the flames broke out, and the last piece of music to be played in the old theater was, yes, "The Kellogg Waltz."

Kellogg and her mother took advantage of the sudden interruption of her London season to visit the Continent—the first time the singer had taken time off from working and studying, she admitted, since she was thirteen. The time was spent mostly in Paris, on the Riviera, and in Rome, where she was presented to Pope Pius IX—"a most lovely and genial personality with a delightful atmosphere about him." By March, however, Colonel Mapleson had regrouped his forces and had transferred them to the Drury Lane Theatre. The spring season was ready to begin, and Kellogg had been invited to rejoin the company. Mapleson was planning to stun London operagoers with a series of productions featuring all-star casts, a comparative rarity in those days, when one or, at the most, two important artists were considered sufficient. Not surprisingly, the public flocked to a *Nozze di Figaro* starring Kellogg as Susanna, Tietjens as the Countess, Nilsson as Cherubino, and Santley as the Count. "These were casts unequalled in all Europe," Kellogg informs us—"almost, I believe, in all time!"

Mapleson would probably have been happy to keep Kellogg for a while longer in London, but the soprano and her mother felt that the time had come to plan a triumphant homecoming, especially now that her English successes had enriched her reputation. When an offer came from the Strakosch management for an extended tour of North America, it was accepted, and for the next three years Kellogg more or less abandoned the opera stage and went on the road as a concert singer. Exchanging the comparatively pampered life of, by now, an internationally acclaimed opera singer for the hardships and uncertainties of touring was a bold step, but only a logical one for an ambitious American who intended to make her art and name known throughout the land. "Oh, those first tours!" wrote Kellogg about her three-year coast-to-coast marathon. "Not only was it exceedingly uncomfortable to travel in the South and West at that time, but it was decidedly risky as well. Highway robberies were numerous and, although I myself never happened to suffer at the hands of any desperadoes, I have often heard first-hand accounts from persons who have been robbed of everything they were carrying. While I was touring in Missouri, Jesse James and his men were operating in the same region and the celebrated highway man himself was once in the train with me."

For all their discomforts and real dangers, the tours did bring Kellogg to the attention of many who would otherwise have never been aware of her. By the mid-1870s few civilized citizens of the country had not at least heard of Clara Louise Kellogg, and when the three years were up, the singer was gratified to be acclaimed the leading prima donna of America by the Peace Jubilee Association, which invited her to sing at their celebration in Boston in the spring of 1871. She had to decline the honor, however, since England beckoned once again, and Mapleson made her an offer too tempting to refuse. Warmly welcomed back as Linda, Kellogg enjoyed her second stay in London even more than her first, especially after the rigors of touring. Clearly the frequent invitations to sing at Buckingham Palace and opportunities to hobnob with royalty appealed to her more than chance encounters with Jesse James. "I am an imperialist by nature," she confessed. "I love pomp and ceremony and circumstance and titles. The few times that I have ever been dissatisfied with my experiences in the lands of crowned heads, it was merely because there wasn't quite enough grandeur to suit my taste!"

It was during Kellogg's return season in London that two of the day's leading impresarios, Max Maretzek and Max Strakosch, decided to go into opera management together in America, forming a troupe with Kellogg and Pauline Lucca as the two stars. As with Callas and Tebaldi in the next century, the rivalry between two potent prima donnas was fueled more by their fans than by the ladies themselves, who seemed to get along tolerably well. Of course, there were the inevitable professional frictions during their yearlong tour. Lucca (1841–1908) was Viennese by birth, and she shared many of Kellogg's roles, such as Marguerite, Violetta, and Maria in *La Figlia del Reggimento*. The only true sore point was Lucca's secret contractual monopoly on *Faust*, and Kellogg was at first hurt and angry at being prevented from singing a signature role that she felt was hers by right of conquest. She consoled herself with the observation that the impulsive Lucca, who seems to have been a more spontaneous and less reflective singer than Kellogg, may have been "striking, effective, and piquant but not touched by much distinction. The difference between our presentations was said to be that I 'convinced by a refined perfection of detail' and Lucca by more vivid qualities. Indeed, our voices and methods were so dissimilar that we never felt any personal rivalry . . ."

Ever the pragmatist, Kellogg now began to think about the possibility of reaching an even wider American public by performing opera in English. At the time, Italian was the operatic lingua franca, even for *Faust* and Thomas's *Mignon*—Kellogg, curiously enough, refers to Thomas's perennial as an Italian opera in her memoirs. But with the Kellogg-Lucca tour behind her, she felt that the time was ripe to experiment with opera in the vernacular. After considering all the familiar objections—clumsy translations, distortions of a composer's careful word setting, the occasional necessity to alter the melodic line by adding extra syllables, etc.—she came to the not unreasonable conclusion that her audience's immediate understanding of the plot and the characters' emotions far outweighed all the liabilities.

So in 1873 the soprano organized her own English Opera Company and hired a roster of young American singers—William Castle, Joseph Maas, George Conly, Annie Montague, and Jennie van Zandt—many of whom went on to prominent careers. Kellogg, of course, was the major attraction, and the indefatigable diva gave of herself generously—during the 1874–75 season she sang no fewer than 125 performances. The repertory consisted of the established favorites, which Kellogg supplied with her own new singing translations, as well as British operas originally written in English such as Balfe's *The Talisman* and *The Bohemian Girl* and Benedict's *The Lily of Killarney*. Several novelties were also included, the most significant being Wagner's *The Flying Dutchman*, and Kellogg attacked the "music of the future" with her customary vigor, enthusiasm, and enterprise.

Kellogg was neither the first nor the last to be puzzled, if not bored, by Wagner's penchant for seeming onstage stasis, but the opera challenged her and she was determined to find some way to make sense of the long scene where Senta and the Dutchman finally meet face to face, but stand looking at each other raptly for what seems like a stage eternity. Finally she looked up Wagner's own treatise on the staging of his operas and discovered that the singers need only stand absolutely still; if they did so, that and the potency of the music would hold the public double the length of time.

We tried to stand "absolutely still." It was an exceedingly difficult thing to do. In rôles that have tense moments the whole
body has to hold the tension rigidly until the proper psychological instant for emotional and physical relaxation. The public is
very keen to feel this, without knowing how or why. A drooping
shoulder or a relaxed hand will "let up" an entire situation. The
first time I sang Senta it seemed impossible to hold the pause
until those eighteen bars were over. "I have got to hold it! I have
got to hold it!" I kept saying to myself, tightening every muscle
as if I were actually pulling on a wire stretched between myself
and the audience. I almost auto-hypnotised myself; which probably helped me to understand the Norwegian girl's own condition of auto-hypnotism! An inspiration led me to grasp the back
of a tall Dutch chair on the stage. That chair helped me greatly
and, as affairs turned out, I held the audience quite a firmly as I
held the chair!

One would be curious to know what else Kellogg thought about
Wagner, whose operas were just beginning to be heard in America.
Typically, however, her memoirs focus mainly on such mundane matters
as her costuming, the production's scenic shortcomings, and even her
wall-eyed understudy. In any case, the English Opera Company enjoyed
only a moderate success, and disbanded after touring for three years.
Although the audiences materialized in respectable numbers, financing
became increasingly difficult. The superrich, who were expected to support opera in the 1870s—and, indeed, have continued to pay the piper
right up to the present day—never saw any reason why opera should be
presented to the masses in the vernacular. For the aristocratic moneyed
classes, the form continued to be a socially structured, foreign-domi-
nated entertainment; the idea of English translations must have struck
them as totally irrelevant, especially since so many of the most desirable
stars were imported from Europe.

After dissolving her company in 1876, Kellogg agreed to appear in a
triple-star tour of America organized by Max Strakosch and Henry
Mapleson, son of the famous British impresario. Her two colleagues were
to be Marie Roze and Annie Louise Cary—"the three graces," as they
were billed, "three pure and irreproachable women appearing together
upon the operatic stage." Actually, the three divas could barely tolerate
each other, and Kellogg describes the tour as one of the most unpleasant

experiences of her professional career. Mlle. Roze—a French soprano—
was Mapleson's lover, an arrangement that scandalized the prudish Mrs.
Kellogg. Her daughter, though, saw the real problem as Mapleson, who
"always disliked me and, over and over again, he put Marie in a position
of seeming antagonism to me; but I never bore malice for she was innocent enough." There was more open hostility with Cary, even though
she was a contralto and not a direct competitor. Kellogg discreetly re-
frains from giving any details, but relations between them were constantly strained, and the press made the most of it.

One suspects that Kellogg had little respect for her rival. Ever jealous of her status as the first lady of American opera, the soprano may
have begrudged Cary's numerous distinctions, which included creating
the role of Amneris when Verdi's *Aida* received its American premiere in
1873; Kellogg was not asked to sing the title role (that coveted assignment went to an Italian soprano named Ottavia Torriani), even though
the performance was conducted by her old teacher Emanuele Muzio. To
make matters worse, Cary was a great friend of Kellogg's old nemesis,
Adelaide Phillipps. Although Phillipps never had a kind word for Kellogg, she once grandly introduced Cary to a breakfast gathering in a
New York hotel as "the greatest living contralto."

Kellogg eventually took on two important new roles during her
"three graces" tour—both, like Wagner's Senta, indicative of the fact that
either her voice was darkening or the agility and sparkling upper register
needed for florid bel canto roles perhaps no longer came quite so easily
to her. The first was Bizet's Carmen, which, like Mignon, was too juicy a
role to pass up just because it was written for a lower voice. As usual,
Kellogg was concerned about projecting a vivid dramatic presence, especially since Roze, her rival in the part, was, in her opinion, "the gentlest
mannered gypsy that was ever stabbed by a jealous lover—a handsome
Carmen but too sweet and good for anything."

It's worth remembering that when Kellogg first sang in *Carmen*, in
1878, the opera was barely three years old and still recovering from its
disastrous premiere at the Paris Opéra-Comique. Soon it would be one
of the most popular works in the repertory, but at the moment *Carmen*
was only beginning to catch on with the public, which seemed primarily
attracted to its shock value. Determined to get as deeply inside the
character as contemporary stage conventions would allow, Kellogg
hunted down the original Prosper Mérimée novel and set about to do
her homework. In spite of the pains she took over her impersonation,

Kellogg never made much of an impression as Carmen, which apparently suited her personality no better than it did Marie Roze's. "Fancy Kellogg," wrote one critic after a performance in Chicago, "the sedate, the self-conscious, the queenly, the dignified, the much-arrayed Clara Louise Kellogg, frisking about à la bouffe!"

The second new role, and one suspects a more congenial one, was Aida, which she later sang on a return visit to London on June 19, 1879. Even at that, a British critic in *The Musical World*, after noting that the soprano had managed to keep her vocal technique and dramatic intelligence largely intact since the city had last heard her eleven years previously, paid Kellogg the sort of backhanded compliment that all singers dread to read as their voices age: "If the voice—which can hardly be denied—had lost somewhat of its force and timbre, it is still under the absolute control of its possessor, retaining, when not forced, all its pleasing quality."

Although Kellogg was only thirty-seven, it was very likely that her voice had lost much of its freshness and security—certainly the coloratura roles of her earliest years were not being tossed off as easily and with the same éclat as they once had. She may have been a potentially dangerous rival for Adelina Patti during her first London season, but by 1880 Patti was at her vocal peak, her career at its zenith, and her reputation as the leading diva of the day unassailable. Kellogg did not remain in London long. She probably reasoned that if she was ever to make her mark on the Continent, it was now or never. Engagements in Paris and Vienna were arranged, followed by appearances in St. Petersburg, where, the soprano felt, "it was a criterion of artistic excellence and position" to have sung. She was right on that point, since her colleagues in the Russian capital during the winter of 1880–81 included Marcella Sembrich, Lillian Nordica, Sofia Scalchi, Angelo Masini, and Antonio Cotogni.

Not a great deal came from it all—Kellogg was, as usual, respectfully received, but the superstar mystique that continues to hover around the names of the greatest singers of her generation eluded her. She returned to America in 1881, where she found that her options had become almost entirely limited to concert tours, which once again carried her from one end of the country to another. On April 18, 1881, she appeared at the Brooklyn Academy of Music in *Il Trovatore*, announced as a "farewell." The next day the *Brooklyn Eagle* made it clear to all that the time had come: "Her best friends . . . could but regret her appearance

. . . It were far better had the memory of the noble voice, the charming stage presence and the lyrical attainments of the favorite American prima donna been permitted to linger as a fragrant recollection than that the idol which the imagination held enshrined should be rudely shattered by unwelcome actualities. Last night's performance was not a pleasant one to listen to, and its contemplation is the reverse of agreeable. The house was thin in numbers and cold . . . the truth remains, unpleasant as is its statement, that Miss Kellogg's sun as an operatic singer has set."

After six years of pursuing an exhausting nonstop itinerary, even Kellogg must have noted that her career seemed to be petering out, and that her future course was plain. She made one last concert appearance, and on November 9, 1887, at forty-five, was married in Elkart, Indiana, to Carl Strakosch, the nephew of her former manager, Max Strakosch. How this romance developed, came to be consummated, and what part, if any, Jane Kellogg had in seeing her precious daughter safely domesticated at last, is unknown. In any case, the happy couple settled in New Hartford, Connecticut, on a grand estate called Elpstone, named by Mrs. Strakosch herself after a huge elephant-shaped rock near the entrance. The only singing the former prima donna indulged in after her marriage was during occasional at-home musicales, accompanying herself at the piano and proudly listening to her husband play his own compositions. It was at Elpstone, on May 13, 1916, a few years after the couple had celebrated their silver wedding anniversary, that Clara Louise Kellogg Strakosch died of cancer at the age of seventy-three. By then, as Isabel Moore writes in her foreword to the diva's memoirs, her name was "known to the immediate generation chiefly as an echo of the past."

Kellogg was most certainly a formidable presence on the American music scene between 1861 and 1887. Her accomplishments and national renown were very real, her industry was unflagging, and her successes were hard-earned. No other American singer before her had ever achieved quite so much, and her example was a potent one—by the time she left the stage, the operatic scene was crowded with younger singers who had surely been inspired by her. Even at that, it's difficult to avoid the conclusion that she lacked the special star quality that might have turned her into a genuine international celebrity.

Kellogg would probably have blamed it all on anti-American prejudice, but reading between the lines of her memoirs and the critical notices of the day, even the most complimentary reviews, one senses a career created more from grit and determination than from an incandescent vocal, musical, or dramatic talent. The evidence is fairly clear that her voice began to deteriorate by her late thirties, which may have been the result, as with so many early American singers, of inadequate training and attempting too much too soon. For all the care she lavished on preparing her roles, the personality that emerges from her book lacks spontaneity, warmth, and emotional depth. What she finally leaves us with is the picture of an intelligent, industrious, yet vain woman, as much concerned with social advancement as artistic achievement.

And yet Kellogg proved conclusively that the American singer had finally arrived, even if she—and he—still had some distance to travel. One late-nineteenth-century journalist, Andrew C. Wheeler, whose column for the *New York Sun* appeared under the name of Nym Crinkle, got at least that part right when he commented on Kellogg's career: "For a woman who has sung everywhere, she retains a very wholesome opinion of her own country. She always seems to me to be trying to win two imperishable chaplets, one of which is for her country. So you see we have got to take our little flags and wave them whether it is the correct thing or not. And, so far as I am concerned, I think it is the correct thing . . . She has this tremendous advantage that, when she declares in print that America can produce its own singers, she is quite capable of going afterwards upon the stage and proving it!"

In many respects, Kellogg was a pioneer, and although we can never know how her voice sounded or the exact nature of her vocal personality, she did set the tone for American opera singers to come. By aspiring to sing the great soprano roles of the day and make them uniquely hers, as well as by realizing the necessity of having a European reputation before her fellow Americans would fully accept her, Kellogg pursued a career that in retrospect seems entirely modern—even conventional—in its dogged pursuit of glamour and prestige. It wasn't long, however, before other singers appeared on the scene and showed that there were different paths to take. Three of Kellogg's most famous contemporaries pointed the way: Emma Abbott to the potential of operatic success way out West, Emma Albani to a career centered in Europe, and Emma Thursby to what could be accomplished by renouncing opera altogether and making a fortune on the concert stage.

Four

~

The

Three

Emmas

~~~~~~~~~~~~~~~~~~~~~~~~

The year was 1867 and the touring Kellogg English Opera Company had just arrived in Toledo, Ohio, some hours in advance of its prima donna. Petrelli, a baritone with the troupe, met Kellogg at the train station and informed her that "a strange-looking girl" was at the hotel hoping to sing for the diva. "Oh dear," sighed Kellogg, by now accustomed to such entreaties from stagestruck hopefuls. "Another one to tell that she hasn't any ability."

Resigned, the soprano graciously granted an audience to the sixteen-year-old girl, whom she later recalled in her memoirs as "very unattractive, exceedingly plain and colorless, and with a large turned-up nose . . . She was poorly clad. She owned no warm coat, no rubbers, no proper clothing of any sort. I questioned her and she told me a pathetic tale of privation and struggle. She lived by traveling about from one hotel to the next, singing in the public parlour when the manager would permit it, accompanying herself upon her guitar, and passing around a plate or a hat afterwards to collect such small change as she could . . . Of course I, who had been so protected, was horrified by all this. I could not understand how a girl could succeed in doing that kind of thing. She told me, furthermore, that she took care of her mother, brothers, and sisters."

That bedraggled teenager was Emma Abbott, whose fortunes were destined for a dramatic improvement: at the height of her career, some twenty years later, she was reputed to be the wealthiest opera singer in America. Impressed by Abbott's vocal potential as well as her predicament, Kellogg decided then and there that she had found "the one girl in ten thousand who was really worth helping," and she urged Abbott to study in New York City with Achille Errani, one of Kellogg's former teachers. The two prima donnas left conflicting accounts of what happened next. Kellogg claimed that she not only helped raise a subscription to finance Abbott's trip East but also outfitted the girl with a proper wardrobe and introduced her to all the right people. For her part, Abbott acknowledged only the dresses, adding that tales of her extreme poverty as a young girl were greatly exaggerated.

Perhaps they were. Abbott's roots were in rural New Hampshire, where her father, Seth, after trying his hand at several trades, became an itinerant musician. He married Almira Palmer in 1842 and after several years of travel settled in Chicago, where Emma was born in 1850. An outbreak of cholera three years later sent the Abbotts to Peoria, and it was there that the little girl, along with her five brothers and sisters, attended school. Money was not plentiful, but apparently Seth Abbott always had sufficient cash in hand to keep his family decently clothed and fed—the nine-year-old Emma did indeed sing for a crowd of appreciative miners at a local schoolhouse in Peoria and went home with a sackful of coins, but the popular legend that she performed barefoot and in rags is surely an embroidery.

Thoughts of a career were already spinning in Emma's head. Even as a youngster she had heard all about such glamorous figures as Patti, Kellogg, and Nilsson, the crowds they attracted, and the immense fees they commanded, and she was determined to discover the secrets of their success. The first prima donna she accosted was the Scottish diva Parepa-Rosa, who heard "the Peoria Prodigy" (young Emma was already a local celebrity) while on an American tour in 1865 and prophesied a great career for the girl, "if her life is spared. Of course it will not be under her own name." The grandly yclept Euphrosyne Parepa-Rosa (her real name) got that last part wrong, but her words of encouragement were all Abbott needed to hear. She was soon studying in Chicago with a vocal instructor who rejoiced in the truly improbable name of Mozart, and singing whenever an occasion arose, including a brief stint with a local opera troupe. When that company failed, she was given a pass to Detroit by a "kind-hearted railroad man," and from there, despite hunger and many hardships, Abbott managed to find her way to New York.

Once in the big city, she arranged to sing for several voice teachers, but none were sufficiently impressed to take on a pupil unable to pay for her lessons. Down to her last fifteen dollars and completely discouraged, Abbott turned back home, stopping off in Toledo for her fateful meeting with Kellogg. Although Kellogg always refused in later years to acknowledge Abbott as her special protégée, she was definitely instrumental in changing the course of the girl's life. If nothing else, the older prima donna must have felt kinship with someone whose ambitions, survival instincts, stamina, and fierce determination to succeed matched her own.

Back in New York, and with Kellogg's name behind her, Abbott fared infinitely better than on her first visit. Her studies with Errani proceeded apace, and she gained valuable experience singing in Henry Ward Beecher's Plymouth Church in Brooklyn and Edwin H. Chapin's Church of the Divine Paternity—important venues in those days, since they offered a young singer not only exposure but also access to families of social and financial prominence. And one has the feeling that Abbott knew how to take full advantage of every opportunity. Eventually she made her professional debut at a benefit concert on December 12, 1871, but the notices were not complimentary: "young and attractive," admitted the Brooklyn Eagle, and "evidently ambitious," but with "a weakness of style . . . and a premature development of voice."

Clearly Abbott needed European finishing, so in 1872 Dr. Chapin's congregation chipped in to raise the necessary $10,000 to send their singer to the Continent, where she continued her studies in Milan and Paris. Despite her modest but secure financial base, Abbott was lonely and impatient for her career to start in earnest; but as always, she was more than capable of looking after herself. Early in 1873, while staying in Menton, near Nice, she sent a letter to Emma Thursby, a fellow American also studying in Milan and herself on the threshold of a big career, and its tone reveals the spunky spirit, sense of humor, and down-to-earth practicality that would later serve Abbott so well. "I have wept such gallons of tears," wrote one Emma to the other, "and have been swimming in seas of woe for such an age—that I am the most heart broken—washed out—wrung out looking 'critter' you ever did see. Me thinks I see the sympathetic moisture dimming those beauteous eyes, as you read this heart rending account of my sorrows. Nuf sed on that hed! Dry those eyes fair maid, and lets talk business! Enclosed find 5 fr. 50c in Milanese money. Will you try to get this changed into Italian paper (which will pass outside of Milan—) or better still, can you send me a 5 fr. gold piece in your letter? The 50 centimes will pay for the exchange from paper to gold I think." In later years, when Abbott was rich and ran her own opera company, many disparaged her art, but no one ever doubted her business acumen.

Two years later, while in Paris, Emma once again noticed that a great diva had arrived in town. Wasting no time, she seized the moment, summoned up what was apparently an unlimited supply of gall, approached the great Adelina Patti, and requested an opportunity to sing. After being repeatedly repulsed, Abbott finally gained entrance to Patti's hotel apartments through the help of a sympathetic doorkeeper, waited for the diva's arrival, and asked her to autograph a pocket fan. Patti did so impatiently, and brusquely handed it back to the girl. "Emma received it with a courtesy," recorded Abbott's adulatory 1891 biographer, Sadie E. Martin, "and kissed the autograph passionately; then said, 'I can sing a little and am studying very hard. May I sing just a few notes for you?' Patti nodded assent, and her visitor began. First, four lines of a simple ballad, then snatches from Italian songs, and Patti's heart was won."

According to Martin, Patti was so overwhelmed that she removed her diamond earrings, pressed them into Abbott's hands, and immediately wrote a letter to Colonel Mapleson in London, urging the impresario to find a place for this wonderful talent. The Colonel obliged after Abbott made her successful debut at Covent Garden in 1876, as Maria in *La Figlia del Reggimento*. Although Martin reports that Abbott's "singing and drumming set Londoners wild," the soprano also confided to her biographer, "When the curtain was rung down, the house became dark and quiet; and no sound reached my ears save the call of one of the chorus to another, 'Are you ready to go?' The reaction came to me. I asked myself, 'Emma, is this really you? Are you singing in London? Is it a dream or are your fond hopes fulfilled?' Oh dear! how homesick I was for a few minutes! I cried because I was so far from home, because none who loved me were near to see that I had tried to fulfill their anticipations. I would have given more just then to see pa and ma, and take my sister in my arms, than for the praise of London." One wonders about that, but at least Abbott must have figured she could afford the luxury of shedding a genuinely sentimental tear at last.

Abbott's subsequent engagement with Mapleson's company at Drury Lane had hardly begun before it was over, her contract summarily canceled. Disagreements with the impresario included his insistence that she interpolate popular ballads into performances, something Abbott claims she declined to do, and her adamant refusal to sing in La Traviata on the grounds that the opera was immoral. In retrospect, both objections seem rather odd. After the part had been "cleansed" of its more risqué allusions, Violetta later became one of Abbott's most frequently performed roles, and her habit of interpolating sentimental ditties into virtually every opera she sang was one reason why East Coast operagoers would never take her seriously as an artist after her return to America. In fact, one has to speculate on whether Abbott ever truly had the vocal goods to compete successfully in either London or New York. Although adulatory reviews were plentiful in the provinces, metropolitan critics always pointed out the limitations of her range, technique, and interpretive insights.

The other big event in Abbott's time abroad was her marriage to Eugene Wetherell, a New York druggist who had met the singer while he was on a grand tour of Europe. The union seems to have been a genuine love match between two kindred spirits, who later proved to be just as compatible as business partners as man and wife. After severing relations with Mapleson, Abbott, with her new husband, returned to New York and on February 23, 1877, made her debut at the Academy of Music, as Amina in La Sonnambula. Again, the reception was distinctly mild.

Since it seemed unlikely that New York would ever fall at her feet, Abbott looked about for other options. In 1878 she formed the Emma Abbott English Grand Opera Company, which, with Wetherell as business manager, toured the country during the 1880s, bringing opera to cities and towns that would otherwise never have experienced it. Suddenly the soprano found her element and she reveled in a populist environment, her voice and presence charming a large, unsophisticated audience that adored her. Welcomed everywhere west of the Hudson River as "the people's prima donna," Abbott was called upon to inaugurate thirty-five new opera houses between 1878 and 1890, from Waterloo, Iowa, to Ogden, Utah. Heading a company of up to sixty members, Abbott reigned as the sole star and artistic supervisor who oversaw everything from the choice of sets and costumes—in most cases based on Paris designs and unusually sumptuous for a touring group—to the careful editing of the scores to suit the tastes and expectations of her regional audiences.

Abbott also knew how to put on a good show, precisely the sort of diverting entertainment hardworking Americans who lived outside the big cities wanted—on a good week, the net profit at the box office was sometimes as much as $10,000. "The Last Rose of Summer" was the hit song of the day, and scarcely a performance of any opera passed without it, even if only as an encore. One eagerly anticipated piece of business occurred when the beauteous prima donna was actually kissed onstage by the tenor—the famous "Abbott Kiss," first introduced into Massé's *Paul et Virginie* and later incorporated into Gounod's *Roméo et Juliette*, Gilbert and Sullivan's *The Mikado*, and virtually every other opera in the repertory. That was about as naughty as the staging ever became—while not exactly a prude, Abbott prided herself on her morals and insisted that her company members toe the line. She even preferred that they marry each other than remain single while touring because, as she said, "I know what a safe-guard a husband is to a woman in my profession, when that husband is one's constant companion."

In whatever part of the country she happened to find herself on Sundays, Abbott never failed to attend church, and woe betide anyone who questioned her faith or profession—a combination of middle-class morality and showbiz savvy that has always played well in America's small towns, a fact that Abbott seemed to sense instinctively. New York sophisticates sneered at all this, of course, but what galled them especially was what they perceived as Abbott's crude popularization of an art form that, to them, represented European culture at its highest and most pure. Kellogg staked her claim on that high ground, and she spoke for America's social elite when she wrote, "Emma Abbott did appalling things with her art, of which one of the mildest was the introduction into *Faust* of the hymn 'Nearer My God to Thee'! . . . And yet she was always trying to 'purify' the stage and librettos! I have always felt about Emma Abbott that she had *too* much force of character." Abbott's response, typically practical, could be read in the *Minneapolis Sunday Tribune* at the time of her death: "The critics have said, 'Emma Abbott was not a great singer, as there are roles she cannot interpret, and heights to which she might not hope to attain.' But she was a singer of the people . . . and it was to the hearts and tastes of the people that she appealed, for, she said: 'The people pay their admission fee and thus make my future; the critics dead-head their entrance, and try to rob me of what the people give.'" Nothing could more succinctly sum up the paradoxical role opera played in America during the 1880s: a high-brow entertainment that, with some adjustments, could be made equally attractive for ordinary folk. Emma Abbott made her choice, and proudly offered her voice to the masses.

There's no telling what Abbott might have accomplished as a popularizer of opera had not she and her husband died so young. Wetherell succumbed to pneumonia during a business trip to Denver in 1889, but Abbott bravely kept the company going for another year and a half. Then, on December 29, 1890, the troupe arrived in Utah to open the new opera house in Ogden with Balfe's *The Rose of Castille.* "The house was just completed," recorded Martin, "and the walls were not thoroughly dry, but the star's dressing room was made comfortable by sufficient heat, and blanketing walls and windows. By accident, however, a window became lowered while Miss Abbott disrobed, and she was at once thrown into a terrible chill, from which it seemed impossible to recall her. She had been indisposed for several days, and had taken immense doses of quinine as a bracer, to carry her through a series of colds, each one of which seemed to settle more deeply upon her."

Despite the obvious seriousness of her condition, Abbott continued with the killing nonstop routine touring divas followed in those days: *The Bohemian Girl* on the thirtieth, *Martha* on the following afternoon, and a repeat performance of *The Rose of Castille* that evening. By then Abbott was barely able to stagger through. When she was heard muttering, "I must sing if I die for it," the company pleaded with her to ring down the curtain, but Abbott, bolstered by occasional teaspoons of champagne, wouldn't hear of it. "When the theater closed that evening," Martin wrote, "although all were well aware of her illness, not one dreamed that their favorite songstress had sung her last note on earth." Five days later, barely a month after her fortieth birthday, the people's prima donna expired in a Salt Lake City hotel room. A pro to the end, Abbott's last words to her attending physician were "Doctor, I think I am booked."

"Booked! For where Miss Abbott?"

"For Paradise, Doctor."

Although Emma Abbott and Emma Thursby met and became friendly for a brief time when both were girls studying in Europe, they seldom saw each other afterward, a fact due more to their busy schedules than to any differences in temperament, even if those were considerable. Indefatigable travelers at the height of their careers, the two sopranos did cross paths again at least once: in January 1880, when Thursby journeyed to St. Louis for three concerts and found Abbott appearing in the same city. Thursby attended a performance of *The Bohemian Girl* with Abbott as Arline, renewed old acquaintance, and, as her biographer Richard McCandless Gipson opines, doubtlessly "took silent note of the success that could easily be hers, in that other field, the opera." Although often urged and frequently tempted, Thursby never once set foot on an operatic stage. She remained a concert singer all her life, the first of any importance that America had produced and, to judge from what one reads about her successes at home and in Europe, among the very best.

When Emma Cecilia Thursby was born in Williamsburg in 1845, that sheltered corner of Brooklyn was still a quiet town of 11,000, far removed from the hustle and bustle of downtown Manhattan. Emma was the second of five children born to John Barnes Thursby, a rope manufacturer who proudly traced his roots to King Canute in the eleventh century. Emma's pretty voice was noted when she was only four, and thereafter the idea of becoming a singer seemed a foregone conclusion. Further encouragement came when the five-year-old learned about Jenny Lind, whose ship *Atlantic* docked in New York on September 1, 1850. Emma was at the pier to welcome home her grandfather, who had actually met the great lady during the crossing. That and Lind's subsequent American triumphs spurred the Thursby family to take a special interest in tending to their talented daughter's musical education.

Emma and her older sister, Alice, attended Miss E. N. Duryee's School in Flatbush, one of the best primary schools in Brooklyn for those who could afford private instruction, and both girls participated in the music programs that flourished in educational institutions in those palmy days. Having outgrown Miss Duryee's by 1857, the girls were transferred to the Moravian Seminary in Bethlehem, Pennsylvania, but in 1859 their father's failing health and growing financial difficulties brought them back to Brooklyn. By the end of the year John Thursby had died, his cordage business was in ruins, and Emma left school to put her voice to work. For the modest yearly stipend of $150, she became the soprano soloist at the Bedford Avenue Reformed Dutch Church, later stepping up to a more prominent post at Henry Ward Beecher's famous Plymouth Church in Brooklyn.

Emma's local fame grew over the next dozen years, as did the demands for her services and her annual salary—by 1876 the Broadway Tabernacle in Manhattan had lured her away from Edwin Chapin's Church of the Divine Paternity with the promise of $3,000 a year, the highest salary a church soloist could expect in those days. Meanwhile, the soprano continued studying voice, with Achille Errani in 1871, and briefly in Milan with Francesco Lamperti the following year. In addition to her Sunday singing, the soprano also arranged her own secular concerts at the church, engaging the musicians, making up the programs, and even selling the tickets. "In fact," she once said, "I was my own manager—and I fancy a rather good one, for I think I was always successful. Each time I would get more prominent artists, and always made it pay." One of her most prestigious catches was the celebrated Norwegian violinist Ole Bull, with whom Thursby maintained a close musical relationship until his death in 1880.

By 1870 Thursby's reputation had extended beyond the neighborhood churches of Brooklyn and Manhattan. More and more people were flocking to hear what vocal connoisseurs described as a fresh light soprano voice of remarkable clarity, delicacy, and flexibility, evenly developed throughout its wide-ranging compass and used with grace and expression. Speculation began to rise about her inevitable entry into opera, especially since she included many favorite florid arias on her concert programs and apparently sang them as exquisitely as any prima donna at the Academy of Music. Thursby never made the step, and not out of any particular moral objection; apparently the very notion of appearing onstage in costume and acting roles alien to her nature was always just too forbidding.

In any case, her concerts were becoming increasingly remunerative, and one that the soprano arranged herself at the Bedford Avenue Reformed Church on May 28, 1874, definitely pointed a path to the future. Determined to make the occasion truly a grand one, Thursby took a daring step by engaging Patrick Gilmore's 22nd Regiment Band, one of the most popular musical entourages in the country and guaranteed to pack the house. An appreciative audience did indeed overflow the church, the receipts rolled in, and Emma Thursby was on her way. A return concert with Gilmore's Band was held at the Brooklyn Academy of Music that November, and early the following year she accompanied the noted bandleader on a tour to Boston, Washington, Chicago, St. Louis, Louisville, and other cities. For the next two years concert work in secular venues in New York and elsewhere around the country became increasingly frequent, and in 1877 Thursby finally gave up church singing altogether.

Vigorous encouragement to make the plunge into an international career came from Erminia Mansfield-Rudersdorff, a potent personality with whom Thursby had been studying since 1875, and who soon became a major influence in the soprano's life. Rudersdorff was a German soprano whose English husband had died in 1860, leaving her with four children to raise (one of them was to become the noted actor Richard Mansfield). Gilmore brought her to America to star in his Boston Peace Jubilee of 1872, after which she retired to rural Massachusetts, where she tended, with equal enthusiasm, to her cows, chickens, and a few choice voice students. According to Gipson, "a month of instruction under Mme. Rudersdorff rewarded Emma Thursby with an improved musicianship, an enlarged repertory, an especial appreciation of the great oratorios, and an increased self-assurance."

A letter addressed to Thursby and dated March 14, 1876, indicates exactly where Rudersdorff stood: "I wish once more most earnestly to impress upon you the duty you owe to yourself and the great and exceptional gifts God has bestowed upon you. Do not be really foolish and almost wicked, my child, but grasp the fortune, which is thrown in your way. Let the churches go! If you will reflect well, you will find that owing to the fact of having to return to NY every week, you lose so many engagements, that it amounts to nearly, if not quite as much as what the church pays you. Europe for the next few years must be your field, if you have your wits about you . . . Do not be so undecided and wavering. There are turning points in every one's life, where fortune may be gained at last. You stand at one now—be firm and wise!"

Rudersdorff was right, but Thursby was never one to make hasty decisions. Finally, on March 6, 1877, she signed a contract with the impresario Maurice Strakosch, one too tempting to refuse. The terms included 120 concerts in the United States, Canada, and Europe during the year beginning on April 1. She would receive $200 for each concert plus all traveling and hotel expenses for herself and a companion (throughout her career Emma was invariably accompanied by Alice and, after her death, the youngest Thursby sister, Ina). A further condition was Strakosch's option to engage her for the following year for $250 a concert and the year after that for $350. After making the proper arithmetical calculations, the press breathlessly passed on the news of the

"$100,000 Thursby Contract," the largest concert fee that had ever been offered to an American soprano.

Just before the fall season began, though, Strakosch wrote Thursby that he would be unable to guarantee her European engagements after all—the impresario had discovered that Adelina Patti had suddenly shed her husband and was available, and no sensible manager would let a previously signed contract stand in the way of handling Europe's most popular diva. Sure enough, during the winter of 1877–78, Patti and her new love, the tenor Ernest Nicolini, were engaged by Strakosch for a highly successful season in Italy, and Thursby had to make her own arrangements for a European debut. That great moment eventually did occur a year later, in London on May 22, 1878, at a Philharmonic Society concert in St. James's Hall. A sheaf of British reviews reprinted in the June 22 issue of *Dwight's Journal* all remarked on the quality of Thursby's high soprano and unaffected style, especially admired in Mozart's florid concert aria "Mia speranza adorata," which by now had become the soprano's signature piece. Six additional concert appearances in London during June solidified the initial first impression, and Rudersdorff could write her star pupil on June 28 with congratulations and more tough advice, proving just how thoroughly this practical woman understood the realities of life facing American singers in those days:

> Now, childie, I want you to make the *very uttermost* of this most desirable success and secure for yourself a *firm standing* in America, so, that you may make a pot of money here, as Clara L. Kellogg has done. A thorough *money* success is feasible in America alone, when it is based upon a European reputation. That is why Kellogg went to London and sang for Mapleson first for nothing and then next to nothing, and why she wishes to sing in Europe again now, before commencing her next campaign.
>
> Get hold of the right Agent: *Jarrett* and *Ullman[n]* preferable to *any*, and let them "exploiter" you. Let the money point be the minor consideration, but let them undertake to make a *"star"* of you. Bring you back to London for the season of '79 and make a big show of you. Upon *that* basis, America will then in a short time give you a fortune.

Thursby obediently followed Rudersdorff's counsel and soon saw the wisdom behind it. After spending the winter in England, she turned her sights to Paris in the spring, first singing at the Concerts Colonne and later at the even more prestigious Pasdeloup concerts. Her Pasdeloup debut was reported upon at length and with delicious hyperbole in the *Chicago Times*. After registering delight with her rendition of an aria from Mozart's *Die Entführung aus dem Serail*, the reviewer rhapsodized:

> My purpose is merely to tell you what happened, to make you understand the voice. I should have to transport you to some deep shady dell in some primeval forest, where birds make it a business to sing for gladness, and when there to ask you to imagine a gentle stream plashing on the chords of an Aeolian harp, with the sustained note of the nightingale keeping up the chain of the melody . . . To imagine the effect at all you must recall all that is of sweetest and softest sound in the jangling of silver bells, the fall of padded keys on crystal strings, or any other melody-producing thing whatsoever. In the very parox-ysm of this enchanting outbreak of sensuous, delicious sound, the sun, which had been obscured all day, broke from cover and flooded the great arena with indescribable light, falling through many a colored pane in the vast circle of windows. The great masses of light in the chandeliers were completely eclipsed. The dazzling effect was so strong that the whole lower part of the arena disappeared, and only the voice of the singer could be heard floating upward from a golden mirage of trembling light . . . Miss Thursby's fortune, I presume, is made. No singer ever received such fealty from a French audience.

After that visionary revelation, no wonder French opera-lovers be-gan to speculate: "Quelle Ophélie! Quelle Marguerite! Quelle Valentine!" Ambroise Thomas inquired if Miss Thursby would be available to create the title role in his new opera-in-progress, *Françoise de Rimini*. Gounod called in person to express the hope that one day soon she would sing Marguerite in *Faust*. The soprano said she would think about it, but not even the constant urgings of Rudersdorff could persuade her. Most of 1879 was spent concertizing in England and France, and upon returning home in November, she seemed to settle the operatic issue once and for all when she told the *New York Herald*: "My ambition is satisfied when I can look in the faces of a sympathetic audience, and, whether singing the classical music of an oratorio or a simple ballad, realize that I have fulfilled the original plan and purpose of my life. The truth is, and I will frankly confess it, I do not feel equal to the task of representing a character, the instincts of which I do not feel. I am not an actress." Another oft-asked question arose once again after the soprano's European triumphs and new celebrity back home: Miss Thursby's matrimonial intentions. There had been reports of an engagement to a fellow passenger on board the ship that carried the singer back to New York— Henry F. Gillig, proprietor of the American Exchange in London—but that tidbit of gossip was emphatically denied. "Miss Thursby will remain wedded to her art," the *Herald* reported. And so she did, despite the occasional rumor of romance.

In any event, Emma Thursby, as Rudersdorff had predicted, was now more bookable than ever, and the astute Strakosch reentered the picture to become her exclusive manager. "The American Nightingale," as she was now billed, promptly set off for a whirlwind tour of the Midwest, but in the fall of 1881 she was called back to the Continent, traveling for two years through Germany, Austria, Switzerland, Holland, France, Spain, Denmark, Sweden, and Norway, where Edvard Grieg served as her accompanist. Unusually for those days, Thursby was frequently identified as a Mozart singer, which made the rave reviews she gathered in Vienna particularly gratifying. The most flattering comments came from Hanslick. "Miss Thursby possesses," he wrote, "if not a powerful, a very pleasing soprano of extensive compass, its flute-like character in the upper notes reminding one of Jenny Lind. It has been admirably trained, in portamento, in the gradations of tone, in scales, runs and command of distant intervals. We have heard very few take the highest notes more easily and correctly, execute a staccato more unerringly, or trills more close and equal than this American lady." High praise indeed from a critic who worshipped Adelina Patti above all singers.

For the next eight years Thursby toured ceaselessly and tirelessly in America—in 1883 alone she sang ninety-seven concerts from coast to coast. By the next decade, though, her appearances gradually declined. The deaths of her mother, oldest sister, Ole Bull, Mme. Rudersdorff, and Strakosch were heavy blows, removing most of the props that made a career possible for a woman whose nature was gentle, retiring, and even a trifle stolid. Indeed, one journalist probably got it right when he described the singer as "a sensible American girl of a type as esteemed as it is usual." Reading between the lines of her reviews—even Hanslick's— one senses that Thursby's art, for all its genuine vocal finish, was perhaps more decorative than emotionally compelling, and very likely by the 1890s the voice's youthful bloom and agility had begun to depart. For whatever reason, her yearly appearances soon dwindled to no more than a dozen, and in December 1895 she sang for the last time before a large audience, in Chicago.

By then Thursby was fifty and had earned a great deal of money, which she managed wisely. Other interests also began to occupy her after she attended the 1894 Greenacre Congress in Maine, a project devoted to comparative studies in religion, philosophy, ethics, and sociology. There Thursby met many kindred spirits and became particularly attracted to the Vedanta philosophy of the young Hindu monk and disciple of Ramakrishna, Swami Vivekananda, who convinced her that her mission was now to teach. Thursby promptly gave up singing professionally, settled in an elegantly appointed apartment overlooking New York's Grammercy Park; here her "Thursby Fridays" of music and talk were to become one of the city's social fixtures as she proceeded to instruct the next generation. Most of her pupils never had major careers—one of them, Blanche Yurka, did become a noted actress—but by the time she died, at the age of eighty-six in 1931, Thursby could at least congratulate herself on having nurtured a soprano who developed into one of the most scintillating opera stars America ever produced: Geraldine Farrar.

Marie Louise Cécile Emma Lajeunesse was born in Chambly, near Montreal, on November 1, 1847. Later, as Emma Albani, the singer knocked five years off her age, making her subsequent reputation as a Mozartian child genius among prima donnas something of a myth. Her father, Joseph Lajeunesse—a musician proficient on the organ, violin, harp, and piano—did indeed take his eldest daughter in hand early on and teach her the basics of music, but hardly when Emma was still in the cradle. Nor does her first public performance at a concert in Montreal in 1860 now seem quite like the miracle it once did, although the experience surely encouraged her to think about a career as a singer.

In 1866 the Lajeunesses moved south to Albany, New York, where Emma was appointed first soprano soloist at the Catholic Church of St. Joseph. By 1868 it was clear that Emma was ready for bigger things, and her father took her abroad to study with Francesco Lamperti in Milan. Lamperti always called Emma his favorite pupil—"She is like a bottle of soda-water," the great teacher once exclaimed; "I have only to draw the cork, and out it all comes"—and his essay on how to trill is dedicated to her. In two years Lamperti decreed his protégée ready for the stage, and as Emma Albani the soprano made her operatic debut in *La Sonnambula* in Messina, Sicily. Most assumed that the new surname was taken from the soprano's adopted American hometown; actually, her Italian elocution master, a Signor Delorenzi, suggested Albani, the name of an old Italian family whose members, with the exception of an aged cardinal, were all dead.

A success in Messina, Albani quickly acquired engagements in other Italian opera houses, and soon the news of a promising new diva came to the ears of Mapleson, who summoned Albani to London for an audition. In her memoirs Albani says that upon her arrival the Colonel mysteriously refused to see her, but in *his* memoirs Mapleson tells a different story. The cab that carried Albani from Victoria Station to Her Majesty's Theatre, he writes, was misdirected around the corner and stopped in front of Covent Garden. Before the mistake could be discovered, Covent Garden's director, Frederick Gye, had heard Albani sing, convinced her that his troupe was infinitely superior to Mapleson's, and promptly signed the soprano to a five-year contract. With *La Sonnambula* once again her debut vehicle, Albani enchanted her audience, and London suddenly had a new operatic pet. The tone of the adulatory reviews was set by the *Illustrated London News*, which complimented "the Canadian Songstress" for possessing a "voice of exquisite quality, the pure melodious charm of which is allied to sufficient power for the effective execution of the most brilliant and florid bravura passages."

Albani's excellent impression was soon confirmed by guest appearances in Paris and St. Petersburg, a command performance for Queen Victoria, and an 1874 American tour under the auspices of Max Strakosch. After singing her good-luck Bellini opera at her New York Academy of Music debut, Albani claimed the distinction of being one of the few North American–born singers who managed to disarm the city's music critics at first hearing—perhaps her French-Canadian background helped, adding the exotic foreign touch that New Yorkers seemed to require in their opera divas. "Her singing is perfect . . . a revelation," declared the *Times*. "Rarely has the Academy of Music witnessed a triumph so genuine," concurred the *Herald*. Before heading to Boston, Philadelphia, Baltimore, Washington, and Chicago, where she won similar praise, Albani stopped off in Albany to receive a heroine's welcome home.

Although she returned to Canada and the United States in 1883 and made several extended tours of the North American continent between 1889 and 1892, Albani was always perceived as an international figure who based her career in Europe. She traveled everywhere—not only to all the important operatic centers but also to India, Mexico, Australia, and South Africa. Like Adelina Patti, she always considered London her home, even if she never succeeded in displacing that diva as number one in the British public's affections. In 1878 she married Frederick Gye's son, Ernest, which at least guaranteed her preferential treatment at Covent Garden. Beyond that, the soprano enjoyed extra status as a particular favorite of Queen Victoria, who could never forgive Patti for eloping with the tenor Nicolini, both at the time married to others.

It was very likely the impossibility of competing with Patti in the lyric-coloratura repertory that persuaded Albani to look for other worlds to conquer, musical territory her rival would be unlikely to claim. In one area she succeeded. After the death of Therese Tietjens in 1877, Albani inherited the title of England's leading oratorio singer, taking on all of Tietjens's parts. She also appeared in numerous new works written with her voice in mind, oratorios that once enjoyed a tremendous vogue in England: Gounod's *Mors et Vita*, Sullivan's *The Martyr of Antioch*, and Dvořák's *The Spectre's Bride*. In 1893, despite audible signs of vocal decline, she sang the soprano solo of Brahms's *Ein Deutsches Requiem* for the composer, who, Albani records, "was so affected that he shed tears."

Another area that Patti had not staked out—and sensibly so, considering the nature of her light soprano—was the dramatic Wagner-Verdi repertory. Although she never wholly phased them out, Albani began to trade her lyric parts—Amina, Gilda, Martha, Lucia, Elvira, and Linda—for Wagner's Elisabeth, Elsa, Senta, Eva, and finally even Isolde. In the end, though, she seems to have overextended herself. One indefatigable observer of prima donnas during this era, Herman Klein, notes that when he first heard Albani, as Lucia in 1874, her voice was clear and resonant if somewhat thin in timbre and without much power in the lower reaches. According to Klein, she had sacrificed the chest register in order to add more resonance to those pure, long-held head tones that had become an Albani specialty. Singing the strenuous modern repertory with a technique designed for bel canto operas of an earlier generation was bound to take a toll, and it soon did.

When Albani joined the new Metropolitan Opera for its ninth season in 1891–92, she was most certainly no longer the same singer who had been so unanimously acclaimed by New York in 1874. Although she demonstrated her versatility by singing Gilda, Marguerite, Desdemona, Donna Elvira, Valentine, Elsa, Eva, and Senta, Albani was surely outshone in a company that also included Emma Eames, Lilli Lehmann, Lillian Nordica, and Adelina Patti. All mention of her brief Met career is discreetly omitted from the diva's memoirs. Perhaps even Albani felt that the time had come, since her last performance in opera occurred at Covent Garden four years later. Concert work occupied her until 1911, when she retired and hoped that her memoirs would bring in a bit of income—by then she had lost her considerable fortune through unwise stock market investments. Financially desperate by the 1920s, the seventy-eight-year-old Albani attempted to make a comeback in London's music halls, where she cut a pathetic figure trading on her name and whatever fond memories older audiences might still harbor. Near retirement herself, Nellie Melba came to the rescue by arranging a benefit concert and setting up a charity fund. That, along with a damehood in 1925, helped sustain Albani in quiet dignity until her death in 1930.

Unlike her contemporaries Kellogg, Abbott, and Thursby, Albani remained active long enough to leave a memento of her voice when, between 1904 and 1906, she recorded a few favorite arias. If connoisseurs noted that Albani was sounding a bit passé as early as 1886, one can imagine the state of the soprano's instrument twenty years later as she approached the age of sixty. Chancy intonation, awkward scooping, and shortness of breath are painfully audible, although the voice's remarkably preserved tonal purity and the neatly executed trills in "Angels ever bright and fair" from Handel's *Theodora*, an Albani specialty for forty years, are a tribute to Lamperti's classical training and show the remnants of what must once have been a polished technique. Elsewhere there is an occasional delicate phrase to savor and the long-sustained head notes, although overdone, are often ravishing—it was said that when Albani launched one onstage, Covent Garden's trombone player could amble out for a pint at the corner pub and return to his post with time to spare. Even at that, Patti, four years Albani's senior, once again trumped her rival when she consented to make recordings in 1905. Both singers may have been only shadows of their former selves, but Patti's irresistible charm and star quality still register. "Now I understand why I am Patti," the diva is said to have delightedly exclaimed when she first heard a playback of her voice and blew kisses at the acoustical horn. It's doubtful that Albani could have had a similar reaction to her meager recorded legacy, one that scarcely does her justice.

Five

—

"Go On, Minnie!"

~~~~~~~~~~~~~~~~~~~~~~~

Shortly before Minnie Hauk made her Paris debut, as Amina in *La Sonnambula* in the spring of 1869—she was only seventeen and said to be the first American-born singer since Dolorès Nau to appear in a French opera house—wondrous tales about her circulated in the press. The young singing sensation from the New World was described as a kind of half-civilized Pocahontas, who, back in the wilds of her homeland, was accustomed to riding a mustang bareback and being worshipped by the continent's aborigines as a "dusky daughter of the sun." *Le Figaro* reported how a New York millionaire, traveling one day on the vast American plains, was attacked by Indians who subjected him to the most hideous tortures. Suddenly a beautiful maiden dressed in wampum and buckskin appeared out of nowhere singing "Batti, batti" from Mozart's *Don Giovanni,* her dulcet voice instantly soothing the savage breasts. The grateful millionaire immediately whisked his mysterious savior off to New York City, where he built her a marble opera house and poured his fortune at her feet. *La Mode Illustrée* further recounted how this same Minnie Hauk, the "American miracle," had recently arrived in

Paris and sung for Auber. At the first note, the aged composer presumably threw up his hands and exclaimed "Mon Dieu! It is a crystal bell struck with a velvet hammer!" before falling insensible.

American singers, needless to say, were still considered exotic creatures by European operagoers in the 1860s, and Maurice Strakosch—Hauk's teacher and manager at the time of her first European engagements—clearly knew how to make capital of the fact by inventing a lot of fiction. "I had done everything I possibly could for the theatre was completely filled with the elite of Paris," he wrote in his memoirs. "The Imperial couple [Louis-Napoléon and Eugénie], whom I had specially invited, were present, and the little American girl really sang herself into the hearts of the French. In the last act an unforseen incident amused the audience hugely, and contributed more to her popularity than the beauty of her voice and her art in using it. When crossing the bridge, she, in her childish way, hesitated and finally stopped—frightened. Suddenly the words 'Go on, Minnie' were heard by the whole audience coming from behind the scenes. At the tittering that followed Minnie continued her walk faintheartedly, and when the curtain went down she had won the game." Of course, some critics objected to Strakosch's florid publicity and stubbornly refused to be impressed. As one wickedly observed, "All the songstresses not on duty were at the Italian Opera last night, to hear Minnie Hauk. They observed her. They studied her. All of them slept well." If so, their sleep was soon to be rudely disturbed. Perhaps a new Patti had not appeared on the scene, but less than ten years later, Hauk was an international superstar, the first American singer who could legitimately make the claim.

Actually, Strakosch's puffery was not a total fantasy: Hauk had had the sort of colorful childhood that, in those days, could only have happened in America, and it must have helped toughen her up for the hard times ahead. Amalia Mignon Hauck (the c was later dropped, but the nickname Minnie stuck) was born in New York City on November 16, 1851, the only child of James Hauck, a carpenter who fled his native Germany during the 1848 revolution, and his American wife. Soon after Minnie was born, the couple moved to Providence, Rhode Island, where at the age of five the girl attended her first theatrical performance, seated on her mother's lap. "When we returned home," she later reminisced, "I did not even look at my dolls, sitting in a row near my bed. I had seen at the theatre much larger, much finer ones." Like so many stagestruck girls of her generation, Minnie soon knew all about Jenny Lind, and the

Swedish Nightingale became an obsession: "All my dolls were named 'Jenny Lind,' and so were all those of my dogs and cats which I wished specially to honor. I possessed all the pictures of her I could find, and had read her biography at least once a week for as long as I could remember."

By then, in the late 1850s, the Haucks had moved west to the town of Sumner, just north of Kansas City on the right bank of the Missouri River. With her father now working for a boat-building firm and her mother running a boarding house, Minnie had little glamour in her tomboy life aside from her Jenny Lind fantasies. At that time, Sumner must have seemed like the farthermost edge of civilization to settlers from the East Coast. Vast plains stretched west of the Missouri, and Minnie often watched prairie schooners rumbling past her house on their way to the Colorado gold mines, the words "Pike's Peak or Bust" scrawled on the canvas.

Left to her own devices, Minnie was fond of taking strolls across the prairies, sometimes even wandering into the Indian camp. "The Indians would call me their 'Prairie flower'; they would give me fruit, carry me in their arms, and take me for a ride on their little ponies. Their children would show me how to string a bow and shoot an arrow, would dance or have a sham battle or a pony race for my amusement, and, towards evening, they would accompany me a good distance on my homeward way. I never realized for a moment how great was the danger of my being kidnapped." When Minnie's busy parents discovered how their unattended daughter was spending her days, they were horrified, and immediately packed her off to a girl's seminary in nearby Leavenworth.

Soon Minnie was expelled as an incorrigible scamp. She returned home to even worse problems when the rains came, the river rose, and a flood virtually swept Sumner away, forcing the Haucks to think about moving once again. After taking stock of the situation, James Hauck decided to build his own boat, load it up with his family and all their possessions, and head down the river to make a new life in New Orleans. Yet another disaster awaited them just south of St. Louis, however, when a river steamer rammed into the Haucks' houseboat and completely demolished it. Clutching to pieces of floating driftwood, Minnie and her parents watched everything they owned sink to the bottom of the Mississippi. At least the steamer's captain was considerate enough to fish out the bedraggled trio and take them free of charge to New Orleans, but the Haucks now had to begin from scratch. To make matters worse, the

Civil War was then at its height, New Orleans was blockaded, and business was at a standstill.

Once modestly settled, however, Minnie's education—her musical studies in particular—could finally begin in earnest. By then about nine years old, she started singing lessons, even venturing "Casta diva" from *Norma* and florid arias from Auber's *Les Diamants de la Couroune* and Rossini's *La Gazza Ladra* at a charity concert for wounded soldiers in the city's grand opera house. By then it must have been obvious to Minnie's long-suffering parents that their daughter had her heart set on a stage career, and perhaps even had the vocal talent to succeed. With her training in mind, the Haucks returned to New York City. Since the war was still raging, they sailed from New Orleans to New York via the Florida Keys, arriving safely late in 1862.

Minnie's precocious vocal prowess and her eagerness to show it off helped open the doors of New York society to the Haucks, who soon became regular visitors at the homes of Commodore Ritchie of the United States Navy, financier August Belmont, and racetrack entrepreneur Leonard Jerome (Jerome's own daughter, Jennie, would one day become Lady Randolph Churchill and the mother of Winston). While seeing her first opera—Auber's *Fra Diavolo* at the Academy of Music with Clara Louise Kellogg—Minnie made a firm resolve. "I fell on Mother's neck, and told her that I was now determined to become an opera singer. We were in the box named after Adelina Patti, and pointing to the famous name, painted on the back of the door, Mother said: 'Very well, my dear, I fully believe you have the ability, and I will help you with all my heart.' "

The very next day, Minnie arranged to see the Academy's director, Max Maretzek, certain that he would be happy to have her sing Norma with the company. An audition was actually arranged, but the fifteen-year-old soprano never got past the recitative to "Casta diva." Maretzek closed the score abruptly and said, "My child, you have done wonders and I need hear no more. But you must begin at the bottom of the ladder and not at the top." With that, Maretzek packed her off to Achille Errani, the teacher of so many successful American sopranos, although Hauk proudly maintained that Errani always called her his "first child in Art and only second in heart." After just a few months of diligent work with Errani, she seemed to make amazing progress, improving her technique as well as committing nine operas to memory. She even performed one of them—*Linda di Chamounix*—at the private theater in Leonard Jerome's mansion on West Twenty-sixth Street. That experiment was pronounced so successful that the time seemed ripe for a public debut, which occurred on October 13, 1866, in *La Sonnambula* at the Brooklyn Academy of Music. The press was generally favorable, complimenting Hauk on her pure, clear, ringing soprano as well as her spirited presence and pretty face.

A month later Hauk made her bow in Manhattan with Maretzek's company at the Winter Garden, the Academy of Music on Fourteenth Street having been destroyed by fire. This time her role was Prascovia in Meyerbeer's *L'Étoile du Nord* opposite the Catherine of Kellogg, and the *Times* was uncharacteristically ecstatic: "Her first note convinced the audience that Maretzek's judgment was, as usual, correct, and that in this lady he has found an artist who in time will rank among the foremost. Her power is quite equal to her brilliancy, and experience will beyond a doubt develop in her an artist quite equal, if not superior to any we have yet heard."

Unsurprisingly, Kellogg was not so pleased by her young colleague's success. She admitted that Hauk's voice, although very light, was pleasing and well trained, and that they had blended effectively in their long and elaborate duet. But during the ovation that followed, when flowers rained on the two singers, a classic prima-donna altercation occurred, the first but hardly the last in Hauk's stormy career. According to Kellogg, whenever she sang Catherine, she could be sure of receiving a bouquet from one shy young man who always tossed her the same kind of flowers—no card was needed to know whence they came or for whom they were intended. This time, though, Hauk had the nerve to sweep up all the flowers from the stage and "include in her general haul my own special, unmistakable bouquet! I recognised it, saw her take it, but, as there was no card, had the greatest difficulty in getting it away from her. I did, though, in the end."

Right from that first evening, Kellogg always thought she had Hauk's number, and she spiced her assessment with a typical mixture of shrewd observation, spite, and begrudging admiration, revealing as much about herself and her own limitations as those of her rival: "Minnie Hauk was very pushing and took advantage of everything to forward and help herself. She never had the least apprehension about the outcome of anything in which she was engaged and, in this, she was extremely fortunate, for most persons cursed with the artistic temperament are too sensitive to feel confident. She was clever, too. This is another exception, for very few big singers are clever. I think it is Mme. Maeterlinck who has made use of the expression 'too clever to sing well.' I am convinced that there is quite a truth in it as well as a sarcasm. Wonderful voices usually are given to people who are, intrinsically, more or less nonentities. One cannot have everything in this world, and people with brains are not obliged to sing! But Minnie Hauk was a singer and she was also clever."

There was no stopping Minnie Hauk now, and she quickly added Lucia, the two Zerlinas (Fra Diavolo and Don Giovanni), Annetta (the Riccis' Crispino e la Comare), and Marguerite to her repertory. The following season Maretzek planned to present the American premiere of Gounod's new opera, Roméo et Juliette, with a Mme. Peralta, who, Hauk tells us, "was of ponderous stature, and physically unfit to represent any such youthful character on the stage. Moreover, she was very slow in learning; weeks and months had passed, and as yet she had not mastered the part of Juliet." Just as Maretzek was on the verge of postponing the production, Hauk presented herself—she had already memorized the role months earlier—sang the famous waltz aria for the impresario, and was assigned the role on the spot. At the very least, she must have looked the part. Few subsequent Juliets in America, or in Europe for that matter, could have been closer to the real age of Shakespeare's heroine—Hauk had just turned sixteen—although the illusion was somewhat compromised by her Romeo, a diminutive tenore robusto of nearly fifty. During rehearsals Hauk playfully addressed him as "Papa Romeo."

Now a full-fledged prima donna, Hauk was ready for the inevitable European trip to secure technical finishing and, with luck, the prospect of a Continental success, as ever a necessity if an American singer hoped to enhance her image and increase her earning power. The wherewithal for the trip was supplied by the music publisher Gustave Schirmer, a loan Minnie says she repaid with interest soon after her first engagements. The soprano traveled with her mother—her best friend, constant companion, and closest advisor throughout her career—and their first stop was London. There Hauk attended the opera, made some important musical connections, and closely studied the competition, mainly Patti and Nilsson.

Nothing materialized in London, but a few months later in Paris she encountered Maurice Strakosch, who, as we have seen, wasted no time in putting her on the stage and with the happiest results. While in Paris Hauk did meet Auber, who, related Strakosch, sent her a note after her

debut in *La Sonnambula*: "Bravo, *ma chère enfant!* May 'Go on Minnie' become the device of your life! I am enchanted, and am looking forward to
the pleasure of seeing you go on as Zerlina in my *Fra Diavolo*." Hauk also
met Gounod, who is said to have kissed her hand after hearing her sing
an aria from *Faust* and solemnly proclaimed, "You will be a great singer."
Other celebrities who crossed her path included Flotow, the younger
Dumas, Bizet, writer Alphonse Daudet, diplomat Ferdinand de Lesseps,
philosopher Joseph Renan, and the celebrated voice teacher Mathilde
Marchesi. Ironically, considering her later identification with Carmen,
Hauk had no recollection of Bizet. She had to be reminded that he once
played the piano for her at a concert program during a soirée given by
Théophile Gautier.

With her career abroad successfully launched, Hauk began her
rounds of Europe's major opera houses, beginning in London with
Mapleson's company, followed by performances at The Hague and, in
the winter of 1869–70, in Moscow. It was in Russia where Hauk's reputation for backstage skirmishes really began. As the youngest and only
American singer in the company, she felt herself to be the victim of
intrigues, most of them instigated by the leading soprano, Désirée Artôt.
It all came to a head during a performance of *Don Giovanni* when Madame Artôt's husband—Mariano Padilla, who sang the title role—gave
Hauk's hand a sudden jerk at the end of their duet in Act I. Hauk,
convinced that the baritone was intentionally trying to cause her to
break a long-held high note, turned quickly and slapped him resound-
ingly on the face. The audience was enchanted, giving both singers such
an ovation that the duet had to be repeated, presumably without the
physical ornamentation.

By now men were beginning to pay attention to Hauk, who, although not conventionally beautiful, clearly radiated feminine charm.
"As to suitors," she confesses early in her memoirs, "they were to be
found in every city, but nowhere as numerous as in Moscow. Suitors of
every kind, old and young, of all classes, down to bashful students, who
admired me from a distance, parading under my windows on the iciest
days, watching at the stage door, throwing flowers into my carriage or
sending them with enthusiastic verses to my rooms . . . I remember a
handsome young fellow, who succeeded in getting at poor Mamma. He
proposed to marry me, and when Mamma indignantly told him to leave,
he made advances to her! I rarely got even as much as a glimpse of all
these unwelcome beaux, for they were invariably waylaid by Mamma

and quickly dispatched." Like Clara Louise Kellogg's Mamma, Mrs. Hauk would not even permit stage kisses, and soon one of Minnie's backstage sobriquets was "the American Icicle."

After leaving Moscow, Hauk centered her activities in Austria and Berlin for the next eight years, first appearing at the Vienna Hofoper in May 1870. Although she soon became a proficient linguist, German was still new to her and in those days all operas were sung in the language of the country. Hauk's debut role in Vienna was Marguerite in *Faust*, and, as in Paris, a charming extramusical touch, this time a slip of the tongue, seemed to win all hearts. After the new American Marguerite told Faust that she would make her way home *unbekleidet* (undressed) instead of *unbegleitet* (unaccompanied), she had the Viennese eating out of her hand.

Although she always seemed to make them work to her advantage, Hauk never made mistakes like that again—a quick study, in Budapest she once sang Mária in Ferenc Erkel's *Hunyadi László* in the original Hungarian after learning the words, as she said, like a parrot. Meanwhile, she was adding one opera after another to a repertory that would eventually extend to over one hundred roles, many of which she was prepared to sing in four languages. More than that, she instinctively sensed that the bel canto repertory was becoming passé—perhaps a blessing for a singer who was probably always more of a stage personality than a vocal miracle—and she eagerly took on any part that offered opportunities for dramatic display. It was in Budapest that she met Wagner after a performance of *Der Fliegende Holländer* and bonded with the composer. "I told him that I always tried to act in accordance with the symphonic indications of the orchestra, and that also as Senta I tried to interpret what his music so wonderfully implied." According to Hauk, Wagner gratefully replied, "That is right, that is right. Thank goodness! Here is an artist who knows how to act and sing according to my intentions."

Despite that encomium, Wagner never invited the soprano to sing at Bayreuth—for all her stage savvy and musical intelligence, Hauk probably never had the vocal heft or heroic manner to excel in Wagnerian opera—although the soprano did attend the first complete Bayreuth *Ring* cycle in 1876 and left some vivid impressions of the occasion. By then she was settled at the Court Opera in Berlin, where she admitted to being pampered and receiving "a salary much higher than that ever received before by any opera singer. Artistically as well as socially, I had everything that I could possibly desire. The *Intendant-General* gave me the welcome opportunity of creating new rôles, and the public spoiled me with its appreciation."

As usual, though, Hauk complained about her colleagues: "Never a kind word was vouchsafed . . . to the American singer who came to them; on the other hand, every obstacle was put in her way." The sharpest thorn in her side was the formidable Lilli Lehmann, who was given the honor of creating several roles at Bayreuth. Lehmann also wrote down a few perceptive comments about the nature of Hauk's voice and how she used it—specifically in Delibes's Le Roi l'a Dit, which was mounted especially for the soprano toward the end of her Berlin engagement. Apparently the production was not a success, and Lehmann, a martinet who had no patience with backstage temperament, laid the blame directly on Hauk as Gervaise. After expressing disdain for a singer she considered little more than an upstart, Lehmann went on to say:

> But one must be just. As little as Minnie Hauk had been able to give me up till now of anything special in singing or acting, so much the better did she please me on this evening. What left the audience cold that night was artistically, though unequally, more finely worked out than formerly. The guttural sound of the low tones was not given disagreeable prominence as it hitherto had been, and her singing and acting were more simple and distinguished. Then I realized that it is not in the least necessary to bellow; that one can sing well with a small voice, if it but sound nobly; that it is silly to be led astray by large rooms and the strong voices of others—merely for the sake of competition in power—into overstraining the physical forces, and that "the beautiful" remains "beautiful" under all circumstances, even though it may be recognized only by the single individual. Never again did I forget the warning. So Minnie Hauk, also, at the close of her engagement, sounded a string that was to my advantage.

Although still only twenty-six at the time Lehmann cast a critical eye on her, Hauk was clearly at a turning point and looking for juicy acting parts rather than those calling for vocal display. Chief among them was the title role in Bizet's Carmen, still a controversial work in 1877 and one that Berlin was not ready to risk. Hauk, however, had her heart set on the role, and when an offer to perform it came from the Théâtre

Royal de la Monnaie in Brussels, she immediately put Berlin behind her and set to work. She studied French, never having sung that language before. She read the Mérimée novella. She took dancing lessons from the Monnaie's ballet master. She also insisted on using the sung recitatives, which, although added by Ernest Guiraud after Bizet's death, Hauk always claimed were by the composer himself (even then *Carmen* was beset with textual confusion; Kellogg confidently tells us that Benjamin Godard wrote the bogus recitatives).

The first performance in May 1878 was a huge hit, sufficient to persuade Mapleson to stage the work a month later in London with Hauk—in Italian, of course, still the operatic lingua franca of the British. The Colonel had even given Hauk carte blanche in her choice of artists: Italo Campanini as Don José, Giuseppe del Puente as Escamillo, and, as Micaela, her compatriot Alwina Valleria (who later had the distinction of being the only American to sing during the Metropolitan Opera's 1883–84 inaugural season). It took even more persuasion to convince these singers to participate. According to Mapleson, Campanini returned the role of José (soon to become one of his most celebrated parts), "stating he would do anything to oblige, but could not think of undertaking a part in an opera of that description where he had no romance and no love duet except with the *seconda donna*. Shortly afterwards Del Puente, the baritone, entered, informing me that the part of Escamillo, which I had sent him, must have been intended for one of the chorus, and that he begged to decline it." Valleria also protested that Micaela was little more than a comprimario role. When everyone was eventually convinced that the opera might in fact be worthy of their talents, the performance finally took place on June 22, 1878, a date, said Hauk grandly, that marked "the beginning of a new era of operatic art. There was scarcely one newspaper that did not, sooner or later, acknowledge this fact. *Carmen* became the greatest attraction, not only of this but of many succeeding London seasons. We also produced it in the provinces and all over America . . ."

Many years later, while browsing through Herman Klein's *Thirty Years of Musical Life in London*, Hauk learned that none other than Manuel García II had accompanied Klein to *Carmen*'s London premiere, and that the great singing teacher, now almost as legendary as his sisters Malibran and Viardot, "was simply delighted with the artistic finish, the vivacity and charm, of [Minnie Hauk's] performance." So were American operagoers later that year when they had their first opportunity to see their own Minnie since her departure for Europe nine years earlier. In the fall of 1878 Colonel Mapleson brought his company to the rebuilt Academy of Music in New York, and *Carmen* was to be the chief novelty. The American premiere, in Italian with the same cast as London, took place on October 23, and the performance, said Hauk, "opened the eyes of New Yorkers as to the merits of good acting combined with good singing."

By the 1880s Hauk was a potent name and a drawing card in virtually every important operatic city in the world. Her career was now at its zenith. She traveled constantly (mostly under the managerial aegis of Mapleson), and Carmen remained her signature role until she retired some fifteen years later. From the perspective of more than a century and hundreds of Carmens later, one can only imagine how Hauk looked and sounded in the part. Klein speaks of her "strong sensual suggestion and defiant resolution," but it seems safe to assume that her gypsy girl never overstepped the bounds of Victorian propriety. When writing her obituary for the *New York Sun* in 1929, W. J. Henderson recalled that Hauk made Carmen "an undulating seductive creature of impulse," and that she sang the music with "a highly serviceable voice, a mezzo-soprano, rich and powerful," although, as he freely admitted, many years had elapsed since he had heard Hauk and at the time he was "very, very young and inexperienced." Also, to judge from Henderson's description of her voice, Hauk was probably in vocal decline—certainly past the stage of doing justice to Amina and the other florid bel canto roles that she sang as a teenager.

When she was not making headlines as Carmen, Hauk played her most famous scenes offstage, and frequent contretemps between the diva, dubbed "the Singing Hawk" by the press, and her fellow artists were a constant source of headaches for Mapleson. One of the most celebrated quarrels came to be known as "the Great Dressing-Room Disturbance," which occurred after the Mapleson company had completed its New York engagement and took to the road. When the singers arrived at the Chicago opera house, they found that it contained two dressing rooms, alike in every respect, situated on the right- and left-hand sides of the proscenium. The one on the right, however, was immediately designated "the prima donna's dressing room" and jealously coveted, since it was the favorite of Etelka Gerster, a Hungarian soprano who was the new sensation of Mapleson's troupe after her highly acclaimed American debut in *La Sonnambula* a month after the *Carmen* premiere.

Since Gerster was not in the cast of the first *Nozze di Figaro* performance, both Hauk, the Cherubino, and Marie Roze, the Susanna, demanded the precious space (Mapleson doesn't mention who sang the Countess, surely the most legitimate claimant). Taking no chances, Hauk and her maid arrived at the theater at three o'clock with her trunk and dresses and laid down stakes. An hour later Roze's maid appeared, found the room occupied, and informed her mistress's husband, Mapleson's son, Henry (we have already seen how Clara Louise Kellogg dealt with him and Roze), who immediately ordered the stagehands to remove Hauk's belongings and install his wife's. At five-thirty Hauk's agent arrived to check that all was in order, found Roze's boxes and costumes, tossed them out, returned Hauk's, and placed a padlock on the door. At six Roze herself came to the theater, called in a locksmith, broke into the room, and personally saw to it that Hauk's effects were transferred to the room on the left. When Hauk turned up at six-thirty and found her rival physically in possession of the premises, she left in a rage, returned to her hotel, and announced that the performance could proceed without her.

All of Mapleson's attempts to pry Hauk out of her hotel room and cajole her back to the opera house were useless. "I therefore had to commence the opera minus Cherubino," he wrote; "and it was not until the middle of the second act, after considerable persuasion by my lawyers, that Minnie Hauk appeared on the stage. This incident was taken up throughout the whole of America, and correspondence about it extended over several weeks. Pictures were published, also diagrams, setting forth fully the position of the trunks and the dressing-rooms."

Weaker mortals would probably have thrown up their hands and dispensed with Hauk's services after that, but Mapleson was a tough impresario and an old hand at dealing with prima-donna disputes. Besides, Hauk sold tickets, and both she and Mapleson knew it. Chicago was the scene of another fracas ten years later when the Mapleson company arrived for a performance of *Carmen* on February 8, 1885. According to the Colonel, the Don José, Luigi Ravelli, was about to introduce the high note that he always interpolated in the middle of Act III, since it invariably brought down the house. Just as he was about to let fly, Hauk rushed forward and locked him in a close embrace and he lost the note. Enraged, Ravelli began to scream "Laissez-moi! Laissez-moi!" and threatened to hurl Hauk into the orchestra—Mapleson says that things got so violent that the buttons on Ravelli's red waistcoat began to pop off, one by one, and he rushed to the front of the stage exclaiming, "Regardez, elle a déchiré mon gilet!" (Look, she has torn my waistcoat!). The audience, thinking it all part of the show, responded with thunderous applause.

The next day Mapleson received letters from Hauk's husband, the Baron von Hesse-Wartegg—a wealthy Austrian journalist and globetrotter she had wed in 1881—and her lawyer charging Ravelli with the use of vile language, insults, and threats against her life. They demanded a $2,000 bond to guarantee the future good conduct of the tenor and proper protection for Hauk, and Mapleson had no choice but to agree. Future performances of *Carmen* must surely have been odd affairs as Don José and Carmen maintained a discreet distance from each other, Ravelli to avoid the famous Hauk slap in the face and Hauk fearful that the tenor actually might substitute a real knife for a stage prop. Just to be safe, it was arranged to have Carmen stabbed offstage, staggering in to die just before the final curtain. "What could the public think," the bemused Mapleson asked, "of an opera company in which the tenor was always threatening to murder the prima donna, while the prima donna's husband found himself forced to take up a position at one of the wings bearing a revolver with which he proposed to shoot the tenor the moment he showed the slightest intention of approaching the personage for whom he is supposed to entertain an ungovernable passion?"

Although she was a truly international figure by the 1880s, Hauk spent much of that decade in her homeland. Her 1883–84 tour began in Washington, D.C., where she was invited to the White House by President Chester A. Arthur and his wife. Hauk seized the opportunity to interest Arthur in the idea of establishing an American National Opera, which, in conjunction with a conservatory of music, would set the same high standards for opera performance that existed in France, Germany, and Austria. Since opera was hardly one of Arthur's major priorities, the President replied diplomatically, "Your idea has my full approbation, but you see we are still too young a nation for such an enterprise. We must first make our way." Hauk drily answered that the United States had not wasted much time in accumulating the greatest wealth of any nation on earth, and perhaps the time had come to create a national institution, not just for opera, but for music in general. Surely Congress would take the matter up favorably if the project were laid before it. Arthur (who, ironically, became one of the few American Presidents to appear as a character in an opera, Douglas Moore's *The Ballad of Baby Doe*) smiled and changed the subject.

Like most singers of her generation, Hauk was also more than willing to sing all her roles in English whenever she performed in America and England, the only countries where opera was not presented in the vernacular. The Prince of Wales disabused her of that notion, telling her, "You are quite right. But the trouble is, that our so-called 'fashionable people' will not go to English opera, and consequently the thing won't pay." The Prince was correct, of course, but once again Hauk spoke back, suggesting that if His Royal Highness graciously took the lead, there would be English opera at Covent Garden and Her Majesty's in no time. Just to show that she meant what she said, Hauk temporarily abandoned her lucrative tours with Mapleson in 1880 and joined Carl Rosa's far less prestigious English company in order to sing in Hermann Goetz's *The Taming of the Shrew*, an opera she had once sung to great effect in Berlin. The soprano even went to the trouble of making a new translation that used as much of Shakespeare's language as possible. The reviews were laudatory, but the experiment did little to change high society's reluctance to hear opera in English.

Fearing that her success as Carmen was beginning to stamp her as a one-role artist in the public's eyes, Hauk was continually on the lookout for novelties. She added Wagner's Elsa to her repertory, fell in love with Berlioz's *La Damnation de Faust* and sang it with the Pasdeloup Orchestra in Paris, and fought tirelessly with Mapleson to put on Meyerbeer's *L'Africaine*. "*Carmen* fills the house," the Colonel replied. "You ought to be satisfied with your triumph in it." He finally relented, and *L'Africaine* became one of Hauk's most popular vehicles in the latter part of her career—along with Carmen, Sélika was the only other role she sang at the Metropolitan in the 1890–91 season. She also introduced Massenet's *Manon* to the United States, on December 23, 1885, at the Academy of Music in New York.

By the time of Hauk's single Metropolitan season, her career was beginning to wind down—one last performance of Carmen, she tells us, on April 2, 1891, was her final New York appearance. Later that year as a sort of last hurrah, she formed the Minnie Hauk Grand Opera Company for a tour that opened in Chicago on September 28 with the inevitable *Carmen*. Two days later Hauk appeared in what she incorrectly billed as the first performance in the United States of Mascagni's sensational new opera, *Cavalleria Rusticana*. The American premiere actually took place in Philadelphia three weeks earlier, but there's no doubt that Santuzza was ideally suited to Hauk's performance personality as well as proof of her infallible instinct in searching out the latest operatic vehicles. She never sang in Puccini's *Manon Lescaut*—far more suitable to her, one would think, than Massenet's more fragile musicalization of the Prévost novel—but in 1893 she did try out one more verismo heroine—Cristina in Umberto Giordano's *Mala Vita*—back at her old stamping grounds in Berlin.

Appearances were spotty after that, and when her mother died in 1896, Hauk and her husband retired to their elegant villa in Lucerne— Triebschen, the very same house that Wagner had occupied in the 1860s when he worked on *Die Meistersinger von Nürnberg* and completed the *Ring*. It was an idyllic existence until World War I swept away their fortune, a catastrophe that was soon followed by the Baron's death. By the time she dictated her memoirs in 1924, Hauk was enfeebled, blind, and poor. By then, another famous Carmen, Geraldine Farrar, had come to her rescue by establishing a charity fund, enabling Hauk to live comfortably in Lucerne until her death on February 6, 1929.

The three great European divas who inspired American singers in the nineteenth century—Malibran, Lind, and Patti—were primarily vocal phenomenons who possessed a natural endowment and technical virtuosity that even Minnie Hauk might have admitted were never hers to command. Even so, Hauk had the voice, temperament, stage talent, and strength of character to do the job. She started out in the most primitive surroundings, dreamed the American dream, applied it to an operatic career, and became one of the most prominent opera stars of the late nineteenth century. She sang everywhere, knew everyone, and retired loaded with honors—if they were all pinned on her at once, she claimed, her royal decorations would weigh enough to pull her dress down to the floor. Who knows? Perhaps if she had found the right teachers earlier on and had studied harder, she would have been more of a vocal sensation. As it turned out, she left her mark primarily as a singing actress whose example was not lost on her successors. As to her voice, Herman Klein may have been right when he remarked of her Carmen that "somehow its rather thin, penetrating timbre sounded just right in a character whose music called for the expression of heartless sensuality, caprice, cruelty, and fatalistic defiance."

Six

~

Men at

Work

~~~~~~~~~~~~~~~~~~~~~~~~~~~

*B*y the time Minnie Hauk was at the peak of her career, it was estimated that more than two hundred Americans were studying voice in Europe, a phenomenon taken as an encouraging sign that America would soon no longer need to import its opera stars. The January 10, 1874, issue of *Dwight's Journal* proudly announced a few of the young hopefuls active in Milan, doubtless about to embark on glorious careers: "Miss Katie Smith, a daughter of Mark Smith, the actor, who is said to have an elegant light soprano voice; Miss Wolvrin of Cincinnati, who will shortly make her debut at the Milanese carnival; Mrs. Seidenhoff of Charleston, Mass., a heavy dramatic soprano; Mr. Sprague of Boston, a very heavy basso . . ." and so on, more than a dozen names in all.

The fact that none of the budding talents listed in the article ever amounted to much is hardly surprising—the road to international success on the opera stage was no smoother in 1874 than it is today, for Europeans as well as Americans. Perhaps some of them did at least manage to get a start, and there may have been more singers from the

New World launching careers abroad than history records. Perusing the rosters of Italian companies in mid-century, one reads such suspicious names as Georgio Atry, Amalia Jachson, and Giuseppina Jones and wonders who they really were and where they came from.

A more significant point about *Dwight's* list of American operatic aspirants is that only one male name appears on it. Up to that time, the country had produced few professional tenors, baritones, or basses, and certainly none who had achieved the fame of a Kellogg, Abbott, Hauk, Albani, or Thursby. But then, for a young man in nineteenth-century America, the idea of studying to become an opera singer must have seemed utterly ridiculous. Informal community sing-alongs or, if he happened to have an especially pleasant voice, solo work in church choral groups and choirs was perfectly acceptable. Singing for a living, however, would probably have struck him as unmanly, if not downright pointless, considering the innumerable opportunities for making fortunes in speculative businesses, engaging in conventional professions, and, in general, exploiting a rich young country's seemingly endless natural resources. Women, on the other hand, played virtually no public role in this rapid economic expansion, and only the most driven and ambitious young lady would even consider the possibility of a life outside that of a homemaker and wifely helpmate. Since singing in the parlor was encouraged as a maidenly accomplishment, some girls inevitably displayed a natural musical talent; a few even had an aggressive, spirited temperament to go along with their vocal endowment, and the combination might at least give rise to the idea of becoming an opera singer. Men had no such social incentive toward a musical career.

The first American-born male to make an international name for himself as a professional singer was David Bispham, and he was sensitive to the fact. In the preface to his memoir, *A Quaker Singer's Recollections*, he touches on the division between the sexes in typical Quakerly prose, but he also notices that times were changing:

> Though more women than men turn to music for their livelihood, marriage and family cares divert many from further thought of it as a profession. Boys' voices, touchingly pellucid as they often are, seldom retain their former charm after the time of change; with manhood and its cares come thoughts, desires and urges in other directions, until most youths consider singing, after all, not to be a man's work. So we see that the number

of contestants in the field is rapidly being reduced by the operations of that same Power that gave the gift and still offers the prize to all such as are strong enough to persevere in the contest. Yet there are multitudes of all sorts and conditions of men and women pressing in, lured by the prospect of what they consider to be easy gain, but these require further weeding out if even a tolerably good standard is to be maintained in the profession.

One youth who preceded Bispham and risked everything to devote his life entirely to opera and concert work was Charles R. Adams, a tenor born in Charleston, Massachusetts, on February 9, 1834. For an American singer of his generation, male or female, Adams pursued a considerable career that took him to many of Europe's premier opera houses, where he seems to have been a welcome presence. Even the sketchy details that survive about his life and musical activities, not to mention the exact nature of his vocal endowment, make one wonder what he might have achieved had he been born a century later.

Soon after his voice changed, Adams began taking lessons with Edwin Bruce, organist of Boston's Bowdoin Street Church, where he was a choir member and a soloist at local church concerts. By the age of eighteen he was studying with Émilie Arnoult, the same French pedagogue who a few years earlier had taught Adelaide Phillipps, and his progress must have been rapid. The day after his twenty-second birthday Adams could be heard singing the tenor solos in a performance of Haydn's *Creation* on February 10, 1856, with the Handel and Haydn Society. By the early 1860s he was in demand for concerts beyond Boston, traveling as far as San Juan, Puerto Rico. There he made his debut in opera, as Alfredo in *La Traviata*, with a troupe headed by Inez Mulder-Fabbri (1831–1909), an Austrian-born soprano who was currently enjoying a brief flurry of international attention after her sensational "publicity" war with Patti, launched by Mulder-Fabbri's appearances at New York's Winter Garden in 1860. During his stint in the West Indies, Adams also appeared in *Norma, Il Trovatore,* Donizetti's *Lucia* and *Lucrezia Borgia,* and *Il Barbiere di Siviglia,* performances that apparently had their comical moments. Since no women were available for the chorus, soldiers had to be recruited from local garrisons, dressed in appropriate gowns, and daubed with white-face makeup, which tended to ooze away in the tropical heat.

After this practical introduction to operatic barnstorming, Adams remained with Mulder-Fabbri's troupe on its 1864 tour to Amsterdam, where he was noticed by several European impresarios. For the next thirteen years the tenor remained in Europe, singing in Berlin, at Covent Garden and La Scala, in Russia and Hungary, and eventually at the Vienna Hofoper, where he performed as a principal tenor from 1867 to 1876. His Viennese career was inaugurated with Arnold in Rossini's *Wilhelm Tell*. The *Wiener Zeitung* complimented Adams on his good German—like Hauk, Adams was something of a linguist, and by the time of his Vienna engagement he was prepared to sing much of his repertory in Italian, French, German, English, or Spanish—and went on to praise his "truly beautiful and well nursed vocal means, adequate to lyrical parts, although his organ appears a little weakened from much travelling about."

As it turned out, Adams was destined to be more of a useful company man in Vienna than a glittering star. Like many singers of his generation, he began to replace his lyrical Italian parts with roles from the increasingly popular Wagnerian repertory, and soon he became the company workhorse, probably singing music that was out of his reach. During his nine years with the Hofoper, Adams sang nearly forty roles, usually appearing three times a week—once he sang ten operas in the space of twelve days. No wonder critics had a few complaints about a voice that was already beginning to sound rather raw and husky.

In 1877 Adams decided the time had come to return home to Boston, where he remained active as a singer and teacher until his death in 1900 on the Fourth of July. More than a decade of wear and tear in heroic roles told in his singing, but his fellow townsmen welcomed him back warmly all the same and with understandable pride. For the next few years Adams busied himself in opera with various troupes as they came and went, most notably in 1878 with the Pappenheim Opera Company, which appeared under Max Maretzek's direction at New York's Academy of Music. On March 4 of that year Adams sang the title role in Wagner's *Rienzi*, the American premiere of the composer's early grand opera. By 1879 the tenor had settled permanently in Boston as a teacher, giving in 1881, by his own count, 4,492 lessons in the space of forty-eight weeks, as well as singing fifty-seven concerts, directing three choral societies, and singing a Sunday church service each week. In 1885, when the Damrosch Grand Opera Company came to Boston and suddenly found itself without a Tannhäuser, Adams came out of retirement to sing the role one last time, opposite two formidable prima donnas: Amalie Materna as Elisabeth and Marianne Brandt as Venus.

Another American tenor who earned a name for himself in the Wagnerian repertory was William Candidus, a son of German immigrants and born in Philadelphia on July 25, 1840. His father combined the careers of letter carrier and piano keyboard manufacturer, so young William's boyhood home was not entirely bereft of music. As a schoolboy, in fact, he played cornet in a military band and made occasional appearances in operetta at the Concordia Theatre in Philadelphia. Soon after finishing his schooling, Candidus went off to fight in the Civil War, enlisting in the 17th Pennsylvania Volunteers for two years' service with the Army of the Potomac. After his honorable discharge in 1864, and perhaps remembering his father's second profession, he went to work in New York at the Steinway piano factory. Two years later he married the boss's daughter, Wilhelmine Steinway, and began to wonder if the compliments he was getting as tenor soloist of the Liederkranz and Arion societies indicated a possible future in singing.

In 1872 the budding tenor headed for Germany, settling and studying in Berlin. His operatic debut came two years later in Weimar, followed by engagements in Hanover, Munich, and Berlin. The death of his wife in 1876 brought Candidus back to Philadelphia, but a year later he returned to Europe and became one of the leading tenors at the Opera at Frankfurt am Main. For the next five years Candidus shuttled back and forth between America and Germany. In his book *Grand Opera in America* (1902), Henry C. Lahee described the tenor as "a man of imposing stature, standing six feet, and weighing over two hundred pounds. His voice was a *tenore di forza* of phenomenal power and compass, and of sweet sympathetic quality." On his brief visits back home, Candidus was heard mostly in Wagner roles, especially with Theodore Thomas's American Opera Company, and like many American singers in those days he was fully prepared (and eager) to sing such roles as Lohengrin in English. One of his last appearances was in the first American performance, also in English, of Anton Rubinstein's *Nero*. In 1887 the tenor returned to Frankfurt for good, dying there in April 1910.

Virtually nothing is known about the personalities of Adams and Candidus, and even less has come down to us about their minor male contemporaries. We have already briefly met William Castle (1836–1909), who, as one of the first American Fausts and Roméos, was the frequent recipient of the famous "Abbott Kiss" when he toured with that redoubtable soprano-impresaria in the 1880s. Another tenor who traveled even more widely was Charles Hedmont (1857–1940). Although he was born in Portland, Maine, Hedmont was raised in Canada and spent most of his life in England and on the Continent, even making it to Bayreuth, where he sang Walther in *Die Meistersinger*. Another singer whose long career was virtually confined to London was a bass known as Signor Foli—actually Allan James Foley (1835–99), born in Tipperary, Ireland, but brought up in Hartford, Connecticut. He Italianized his surname while studying voice in Naples and continued to call himself Foli even after settling in London, where he was a mainstay at Covent Garden for twenty years.

Turning Anglo-Saxon names into more mellifluous-sounding Italian aliases was a common practice that continued well into the twentieth century, and for obvious reasons. When a singer was appearing in Italy, it facilitated pronunciation for the natives, and back home it gave a singer the necessary aura of Continental glamour, even if everyone knew that Signor Giovanni Chiari di Broccolini was really John Clarke. Such a basso actually did flourish in the 1880s, the name Broccolini being derived not from a certain delicious green vegetable but from Clarke's hometown of Brooklyn, where he was brought as a child from Cork, Ireland.

Broccolini sang for a while with Mapleson's company, and the Colonel recalls with much amusement how the singer, apparently a slow learner, used to cram as much of his part as he could onto a sword, stick, or whatever property he happened to be carrying. Once, Broccolini played the Commendatore in *Don Giovanni* and carefully wrote down all his words on the stone statue's staff. He then took up his majestic position in the cemetery on horseback, Mapleson relates, "with the *bâton* grasped in his right hand, and reposing on his right hip, and was expecting a rush of moonlight from the left, when the position of the orb of night was suddenly changed, and he was unable to read one syllable of the words on which he depended. Having to choose between two difficulties, he at once selected the least, and, to the astonishment of the audience, transferred the Commander's *bâton* from the right hand to the left." Broccolini could not have been a complete fool, however—he had a sufficient musical background to compose songs, a cantata, and several operettas. Perhaps his greatest claim to fame, though, was his appearance as the Pirate King in Gilbert and Sullivan's *The Pirates of Penzance* in New York on December 31, 1879. After participating in that historic event (the day after the operetta's world premiere, in England), Broc-colini became something of a G&S specialist, and for the next decade he appeared in one operetta after another, in New York and on tour, as Savoyard fever swept the country.

Other "Italian-Americans" included Carlo Bassetti, otherwise Charles Bassett of Toledo, who once sang the high tenor role of Idreno in *Semiramide* at New York's Academy of Music in the fast company of Adelina Patti and Sofia Scalchi. A bit more information can be gathered about a certain Chevalier Arturo Scovelli—Arthur Scovel from De-troit—mainly because he could claim the distinction of singing his first Alfredo in Brescia in 1879 opposite Lillian Nordica's first Violetta. Scovelli was forced to advance the management at Brescia a thousand lire ($200) to insure them against any loss risked by putting two Ameri-can debutants on the stage, but since the tenor's wife was Cornelia Roosevelt, a cousin of Theodore Roosevelt, the young man hardly suf-fered from money problems—Nordica even wore Cornelia's jewels in Act I. Scovelli enjoyed a mild success, but Nordica went on, as we shall soon see, to be a star. Some time later the tenor turned up briefly in Germany, as a protégé of Ludwig II, singing bits from Wagner's *Lohengrin* for the mad king's private amusement in one of his elaborate fantasy castles in lower Bavaria.

When he went off to Italy for vocal studies in 1866, Julius Edson Perkins inevitably decided to call himself Giulio, but retained his last name minus the final *s*—possibly he thought that singing under the name of Giulio Perchinsini was really going too far. Born in Stockbridge, Vermont, in 1845, the young bass was admired in Boston for his large, deep voice, but since his range was short at the top and he had trouble singing in tune, Perkins was discouraged from pursuing a career. He disregarded the advice, and by the time Mapleson engaged him in 1873, most of the vocal problems that bothered his fellow Bostonians seem to have been ironed out. Appearing in London as Mozart's Sarastro, he was judged to possess a voice that "is really superb, magnificently round and full, and his lower notes incomparably fine." As Baldassare in Donizetti's *La Favorita*, Perkins was complimented for his dignified acting, while his Méphistophélès in *Faust* combined "the demon's sardonic humor and grotesque bitterness with great skill." When Perkins married the beaute-ous French soprano Marie Roze in 1874, it looked for a time that the opera world might have a glamorous new couple to celebrate. Unfortunately, it was not to be. Perkins died less than a year later, apparently of pneumonia, not yet thirty years old.

When David Bispham was mulling over the possibilities of a singing career, one of his idols was another New England bass, Myron W. Whitney, who, he recalled, was "an ideal oratorio singer and, better than any one I ever heard, except Santley, who could negotiate the runs required of the Handelian singer, as well as the dramatic rendering of its recitative, in which so few are acceptable." Whitney was born in Ashby, Massachusetts, on September 5, 1836, and moved to Boston as a teenager. Like the few young men who eventually became professional singers in those days, he did not even begin to contemplate serious vocal study until well after his voice changed, and began to work with E. H. Frost at the age of twenty. By 1858 he was deemed sufficiently advanced to be offered principal bass parts by the Handel and Haydn Society, as well as numerous other local choral groups.

Ten years passed, and although Whitney enjoyed moderate success, he felt the need of strengthening his technique with European training, first with Luigi Vannuccini in Florence and later with Alberto Randegger in London. It was presumably the latter who gave Whitney his grounding in oratorio, and while in England he toured the country singing the major concert works in most of the major choral festivals under the batons of Sir Arthur Sullivan and Sir Julius Benedict. In 1876 the bass returned to America, a thorough professional and with all the vocal and musical attributes Bispham had so admired firmly in place. Whitney never crossed the seas again, and he remained one of the country's busiest opera and concert singers until his retirement in 1890.

In that very same year, on February 23, David Scull Bispham officially launched his career with his first appearance in London, a concert in the rooms of the Grosvenor Gallery. He was thirty-three, an age when most American sopranos and mezzos of his generation not only had been singing professionally for fifteen years but in many cases were already showing signs of vocal decline. Bispham's delay in getting started may in part be attributed to problems in finding proper vocal instruction, but more likely he was uncertain whether the life of a singer was really proper for a young American man—especially one whose strict Quaker upbringing frowned upon music-making of any kind. "My mother," Bispham once wrote, "I am sure, thought all music a wile of the Evil One, the stage a snare for every foot, old or young, and the combination, as in opera, something too appalling to contemplate."

Bispham was born in Philadelphia on January 5, 1857. As a child, he regularly attended Sunday Meeting with his parents, passing the cemetery where Benjamin Franklin was buried, the old shop where Betsy Ross made the first Stars and Stripes, the house where Thomas Jefferson wrote the Declaration of Independence, and the State House tower containing the cracked Liberty Bell. His father, a lawyer, had a more tolerant attitude toward music than his mother, although after the family moved outside Moorestown, New Jersey, Jane Bispham did eventually allow a small cabinet organ into the household, much to her son's delight. Young David never did become very proficient on that or any other instrument, although he did manage to make some headway on the zither, a gift from his uncle, John Bispham.

Uncle John also took his nephew to the opera for the first time— Clara Louise Kellogg's company in Philadelphia, where *The Bohemian Girl, Mignon, Faust,* "and kindred works, were done in our good English language." He was also fascinated by Zelda Seguin's Carmen and Charles Santley in Hérold's *Zampa,* little dreaming that both singers would one day become colleagues. Bispham's father occasionally took him to the Walnut Street Theater in Philadelphia, where the impressionable boy was much taken with Charlotte Cushman and Edwin Booth in *Hamlet.* After that, reading plays and the biographies of David Garrick, Edmund Kean, and the Kembles virtually became an obsession: "This was to me a magic country indeed, and from it came a clear call in a voice akin to that of music. These two voices joining in a fascinating duo, as it were, summoned me to join the circle haunted by the shades of those long gone . . ." His mother may have disapproved, but "even as a boy," Bispham decided, "I could not believe there was essential wrong in either music or the drama; the only wrong lay in their debasement, their unworthy presentation or immoderate or inconsiderate use."

During his years at Haverford College, Bispham joined in the usual extracurricular musical and theatrical activities, but if he had any ambition to pursue them after graduation in 1876, he kept that to himself. His first thought was to become a doctor, but he dropped the idea after being carried out of an operating room in a dead faint. Instead, he opted to join the firm of another uncle, David Scull, who was in the wool trade. For the next seven years, at $4 a week, Bispham was "occupied with the intricacies of my business, both in the office and in the warehouse among the workmen and the bales and fleeces of wool."

Music was not forgotten, however, and Bispham kept busy singing and acting as an amateur on the local stages; and in between tending to the woolly matters at his uncle's firm, he also took lunch-hour vocal lessons from Edward Giles, a bass in one of the city church choirs. At about this time, the New York critic Gustav Kobbé visited Philadelphia and, as he told Bispham many years later, encountered an elderly Quaker. "Does thee see the young man going along there singing?" the worthy Friend told Kobbé. "Well, he is the grandson of an old friend of mine, but I tell thee he isn't going to come to any good, for he is always fooling around after music." After mulling over that observation, Bispham countered by commenting "how essential it is for a person, in order to make a success of anything, to be always thinking of it and doing it, as far as lies in his power, and not to fool around after it."

By the time he had reached his late twenties, still undecided about his future, Bispham journeyed to Boston with a letter of introduction to Sir George Henschel, equally gifted as a singer, pianist, composer, conductor, and music director of the newly founded Boston Symphony Orchestra. Although he thought Bispham had a good natural voice, Henschel found the young man's musical background so deficient that he saw no possibility of a future career—a discouraging judgment that only seemed to light a fire under Bispham. Now determined to succeed, he temporarily abandoned the wool business in 1885 and went to Europe—a risky decision hardly calculated to please his mother, although he was encouraged by his bride, Caroline Russell, whom he had married in April of that year.

The trip was in the nature of a summerlong honeymoon, but Bispham heard a lot of opera in London, Paris, Milan, and Rome. In London he even bribed an attendant to allow him to join the bass chorus for a giant-sized performance of *Messiah* at the Handel Festival at the Crystal Palace. Upon returning to Philadelphia that autumn, he took a job as a railway clerk, receiving $12 a week "for doing nothing that I liked, and doing that badly." By spring Bispham decided that he had had enough and went back to Europe, determined to rise or fall as a singer. More vocal study was clearly first on the agenda, and for the next several years he placed himself under the tutelage of the tenor William Shakespeare, who, although he claimed no relation to the Bard, certainly had a name that was bound to strike Bispham as a good omen for the future. Shakespeare also sent him off to Milan for a thorough grounding in the classical Italian singing methods with Vannuccini and Lamperti. Italy in the 1880s was crammed with expatriate artists of all nationalities, and the aspiring bass-baritone encountered many of them, leaving especially amusing recollections of Robert Browning, John Singer Sargent, and Ouida.

Back in London, Bispham felt he had made sufficient progress to risk a modest concert debut in 1890, but his eye was really on the stage. He tested the waters with appearances in two long-forgotten operettas—*The Ferry Girl* by Lady Arthur Hill and *Joan, or, The Brigands of Bluegoria* by Robert Martin—and caught the attention of Sir Arthur Sullivan and Richard D'Oyly Carte, who needed an understudy for Cedric in Sullivan's grand opera, *Ivanhoe.* Bispham learned the part, and even though he was never asked to sing it, two excerpts from the opera later became standard items on his recital programs. He did win another part with D'Oyly Carte's short-lived English Opera Company, the Duc de Longueville in Messager's *La Basoche.* As Herman Klein recalls that debut performance, "There was about it an element of fantastic *bizarrerie* that was singularly attractive, and which at once drew attention to the unique personality of the artist. From that time forward, in whatever branch of his art he has elected to labor, David Bispham has consistently earned distinction and applause." Bispham, at the age of thirty-four, was finally on his way.

Like so many American singers of both sexes, Bispham must have been more impressive as a stage personality than as a singer—or so he was during the initial phase of his career. The conductor Henry Wood, one of England's most astute observers of the vocal scene, heard him around the time of *La Basoche* and commented, "His voice was of a real ugly, harsh quality. I told him not to attempt anything requiring beauty of tone for he simply had not got any. I suggested character singing." Bispham did plenty of that in the following ten years, but he also listened closely to his colleagues at Covent Garden and later at the Metropolitan—Jean de Reszke, Pol Plançon, and Jean Lassalle—and apparently benefited from their example. Wood heard Bispham again in 1904 and was amazed at the improvement: " 'What have you been doing with your voice?' I asked him. 'Nothing, except listening,' Bispham replied."

Whatever the true quality of his voice, Bispham clearly did not command the mellifluousness of a Plançon, a smooth basso cantante excelling in the Italian and French repertories. Bispham made his name principally in Wagner, encouraged in that direction not only by Wood but by the amazing Planchette, an automatic-writing machine he consulted in 1892. When asked by a psychic, the obliging contraption promptly wrote out all the roles it thought would be suitable for Bispham, who duly began to study them. Sure enough, Sir Augustus Harris, then the impresario of Drury Lane and Covent Garden, almost immediately began offering his new bass-baritone precisely the roles the Planchette had stipulated—Kurvenal, Beckmesser, Wolfram, the Dutchman, Telramund, Wotan, Alberich—and Bispham was ready to sing them. Of course, at first he had to perform Wagner in Italian, still the only operatic language Londoners would tolerate, although that would change before the new century dawned.

The singer did not go unnoticed by the large corps of British critics, and young George Bernard Shaw was especially complimentary. Once, after enduring a certain Herr Grengg as Hagen in Wagner's *Götterdämmerung*, Shaw remarked, "They are possibly proud of him [Grengg] at Bayreuth; but I am prepared to back Mr. Bispham to drain a tankard of laudanum and then play Hagen twice as smartly and ten times more artistically." By 1895 Bispham was one of the busiest singers in London, not only in opera but in oratorio, concert, and recital. After consulting his engagement book that New Year's Eve, he discovered "that I made more than 130 appearances in that twelve-month, and that during this period my repertory of songs numbered about 120 pieces, including duets and quartettes, over 30 selections sung with orchestra, about 15 oratorios given, 10 appearances in 5 operas in concert form, and 25 performances of 9 operas actually sung upon the operatic stage."

Bispham's first Metropolitan Opera season came the following year, his debut role being Beckmesser on November 18, 1896, with a distinguished cast: the De Reszke brothers as Walther and Sachs, Emma Eames as Eva, and Plançon as Pogner. Like their London counterparts, American operagoers still preferred to hear all opera in Italian, and so *Die Meistersinger von Nürnberg* became *I Maestri Cantori di Norimberga*. (Two days later, to accommodate the international cast, *Tannhäuser* was sung partly in French and partly in Italian.) Other roles for Bispham that season at the Met were Telramund, Masetto, and Kurvenal. He also sang Alberich in the famous *Siegfried* performance on December 30 when Nellie Melba, despite all attempts to dissuade her from attempting a part so ill-suited to her lyric soprano, made her disastrous first and last attempt to sing Brünnhilde (the diva even sent a letter of apology to the press).

During his extended period back home in America, Bispham hardly confined himself to the Met, singing concerts in some seventeen other cities in various parts of the country. He was already beginning to explore his other great love, the song literature, and on his tour he included such elevated fare as Brahms's rarely heard *Die Schöne Magelone* cycle and the composer's latest work, the *Vier Ernste Gesänge*. He gave an extempore performance of the latter one morning in Chicago at the request of the actress Ellen Terry, who was touring with Henry Irving and staying at Bispham's hotel. "As I finished," the singer wrote, "the tears that coursed down Miss Terry's cheeks were the most graceful tribute I had ever received, and yet the tribute was not for me, for I was merely the mouthpiece, the interpreter, of noble music wedded to words of power."

Even though his career was confined to England and America, by 1895 Bispham was regarded as one of the English-speaking world's leading singers. Although Wagner remained a specialty, his operatic repertory was diverse and included the late-Verdi baritone roles of Amonasro, Iago, and Falstaff, as well as Escamillo, Pizarro, Alfio, and parts in such forgotten operas as Paderewski's *Manru*, Floridia's *Paoletta*, and Dame Ethel Smyth's *Der Wald*. In 1898 he briefly left the opera stage to play Beethoven during a short Broadway run of Hugo Miller's play *Adelaide.* Concerts occupied him as much as opera, and his recitals often featured the now vanished genre of melodrama in which spoken verses were musically underscored by an elaborate piano accompaniment (Richard Strauss's *Enoch Arden,* composed for the Tennyson poem, was a Bispham specialty). "His gift of versatility is extraordinary," wrote Klein. "Alike in serious and comic characters, in Wagnerian music-drama and light French opera, in oratorio and Lieder, in declamation both spoken and sung, he has proved himself a thoroughly intellectual, accomplished and original artist."

Bispham's recital programs were always ambitious, making few concessions to popular taste. His vast lieder repertory went well beyond the familiar Schubert-Schumann chestnuts and delved into the rarely sung songs of Cornelius, Loewe, and Wolf—his annual New York recital in 1904 concluded with ten songs by this last composer, recently deceased and still thought to be dangerously avant-garde. Bispham also considered singing the music of contemporary American and English composers a happy duty, one that he owed to himself, his audiences, and his cultural heritage. The critic Richard Aldrich, who had attended many of Bispham's recitals over the years, was particularly impressed by the singer's intent "to emphasize every characteristic touch and significant point in music or verse and make it tell to the utmost." Beyond that, Aldrich admired "the clearness of his diction, that makes his texts for the most part easily intelligible—one of Bispham's most admirable traits, though sometimes it is exploited at the expense of the musical quality of the phrase and melodic line, his fondness for lingering on the nasal and liquid consonants, and the individual timbre of his voice has much about it that is fine."

Bispham first made records in 1902—fourteen titles for the Gramophone and Typewriter Company (G&T)—and, after 1906, many more sides for American Columbia. Although they only begin to suggest the breadth of his repertory—opera is particularly scarce, since after 1903 the singer had begun to devote himself primarily to oratorio and concert—the discs demonstrate both the versatility that Klein admired as well as the acquired vocal polish that had so impressed Wood. The best example we have of his many Wagner parts is an excerpt from Wotan's Farewell; it was recorded live, high up on the Met catwalk in 1902 by the Met's librarian, Lionel Mapleson, before his fabulous cylinder apparatus fell from its perch, nearly killed Johanna Gadski, and was banned from the house. The snippet is maddeningly brief, but the nobility of Bispham's declamatory power registers impressively, despite the dim reproduction. On another early disc from 1903 he sings Schubert's "Hark! Hark! the Lark" using the English of Shakespeare—no snob, Bispham always thought that Americans should be addressed in their own language, and he made no apologies when he sang German lieder in English. It is an extraordinarily elegant piece of singing, tripping lightly off the tongue and full of characterful vocal touches that are always musical, innately expressive, and completely devoid of artifice.

Bispham's narrative skills held audiences spellbound, and the reasons why are heard on his rendition of Walter Damrosch's "Danny Deever." This grisly-grim, proto-Mahlerian military ballad based on Rudyard Kipling's poem was wildly popular in its day, and soon became the singer's signature piece. Bispham once performed the song at a White House musicale, even rousing the enthusiasm of Theodore Roosevelt, another self-confessed tone-deaf American President. Apparently bowled over, Roosevelt exclaimed, "By Jove, Mr. Bispham, that was bully! With such a song as that you could lead a nation into battle!" It's also worth hearing Bispham relish the rollicking "Yo-ho-ho and a bottle of rum" refrain to Henry Gilbert's "Pirate Song"—a shameless potboiler perhaps, but as sung here a tour de force of vocal virtuosity. Even more impressive are the unaspirated runs and absolutely even register alignment heard in "Why Do the Nations" from *Messiah,* recorded in 1911, when Bispham was fifty-four, and audible testimony to the singer's strict Lamperti training. We are also most likely hearing many of the very same qualities that Bispham had so admired in Myron Whitney's Handel singing.

The latter phases of Bispham's career were mostly confined to frequent coast-to-coast concert tours, some of which extended to the Hawaiian Islands and Australia. In 1916 he could not resist participating in one last major operatic venture, when Albert Reiss, an old Metropolitan colleague who was famous for his interpretations of Wagner's character tenor parts, formed the Society of American Singers, yet another plan to promote opera in English. It is astonishing how many American singers bred in the late nineteenth century, when opera was sung in the vernacular in every European country except England, were still convinced that the day was near at hand when their compatriots would also demand to hear operas sung in their own language—a dream that, a hundred years later, is clearly never to come true. The company began modestly with what were then two Mozart rarities, *The Impresario* and *Bastien and Bastienne,* later exploring such offbeat fare as Donizetti's *Il Campanello,* Gounod's *Le Médicin Malgré Lui,* and Pergolesi's *La Serva Padrona.* Although Reiss and Bispham managed to attract such major artists to the cause as Florence Easton, Mabel Garrison, Herbert Witherspoon, Maggie Teyte, Riccardo Martin, Orville Harrold, and Artur Bodanzky (soon to become the Metropolitan Opera's leading Wagner conductor), the project was no more long-lasting than the many others that had preceded it.

Bispham never retired but sang right up to his death, which arrived unexpectedly on October 2, 1921, at the age of sixty-four—he had even given a voice lesson the day before. His last years could not have been entirely happy. In 1908 he was separated from his wife, and his only son, David Bispham, Jr., was killed early during World War I while on duty with the Royal Flying Corps. None of these troubles and tragedies intrude upon the singer's earnest, single-mindedly focused memoirs, which contain not one word about his personal life or even mention the existence of his wife, son, and two daughters.

Although his ego was as large and healthy as any singer's, Bispham took his calling as an artist very seriously, no less so than men of his age engaged in more conventional professions. His example of talent, hard work, and accomplishment did not go unnoticed by other American singers of both sexes, and he tried to give back as much as he received. Like Minnie Hauk, he even hoped to get a President interested in the idea of making music, vocal music in particular, an integral part of the country's educational life. After a concert in Washington, the bass-baritone called on Woodrow Wilson "in order to lay before him, as head of the nation, my wish to have vocal music taught in every school, college, or university in the land to every American from early youth to manhood." Although a man of greater culture than most U.S. Presidents—Bispham assures us that he even possessed a tenor of considerable power and sweetness—Wilson, like Chester A. Arthur, apparently had more pressing matters to attend to. In the end, Bispham must have realized, and taken solace from the fact, that his own career could stand as an eloquent model for future American singers, both male and female.

—

Queen Adelina

When Adelina Patti reigned as the world's undisputed queen of song during the latter half of the nineteenth century, many countries claimed her as their own. She was born in 1843 in Madrid, the youngest child in a large family of Italian opera singers; her girlhood was spent in New York City, where she launched her operatic career at the age of sixteen; her three husbands included a marquis and a tenor from France and a baron from Sweden; when not on tour after 1878, she made her home at Craig-y-Nos, a secluded castle in Wales, dying there in 1919. By then, although she became a British subject in 1898, Patti was truly a citizen of the world.

Patti's first American career began as early as 1851, when the eight-year-old girl sang Eckert's "Swiss Echo Song" and "I Am a Bayadère" during a concert conducted by Max Maretzek at New York's Tripler Hall—"a Jenny Lind in miniature" who "entirely astonished her audience," reported the *Tribune* two days later. By the time Patti sailed for England in 1861, her tours and operatic appearances had made her famous throughout North America, a prodigy surely destined for a brilliant career. America had proudly nurtured and made a star of Maria Malibran when she came to New York as a teenager in 1825, and the country wasted no time in congratulating itself upon discovering another fabulous vocal talent. After her debut at the Academy of Music on November 24, 1859, as Donizetti's Lucia, Patti was acclaimed a sensation by the Herald's reviewer, whose breast swelled with national pride as he boasted that Americans now no longer needed to "look to Europe for . . . singers, any more than for . . . painters, or . . . sculptors." When the soprano returned to America in 1881 after two triumphant decades on Europe's opera stages, there was no singer in the world more celebrated or highly regarded, both by vocal connoisseurs and the general public, and Patti was welcomed "home" in style.

To call America Patti's home was only a pleasant fiction, of course, one that the diva herself found convenient to endorse in the name of good public relations. America's cultured elite may have considered Patti one of their own, but by no stretch of the imagination could she be called an American, even an assimilated one, despite her formative years in New York City. Like Malibran and Lind before her, Patti viewed the New World as a good place to visit, a land with a potentially large audience eager to be entertained—an audience still musically naive beyond the major cities perhaps, but more than willing to pay top dollar for the privilege of hearing the best voices Europe could offer. As an adult, the idea of settling permanently in America surely never even occurred to Patti. Her impact when she did come, however—and she was never away for long between 1881 and 1894—was enormous. If Lind toured the country sacralizing musical culture, radiating the notion that a voice raised in song was a veritable moral force, Patti projected a completely secular image, and her arrival was eagerly awaited by whatever city she chose to include on her itinerary.

Patti traveled like a queen in her custom-designed railroad carriage, a sumptuously appointed salon followed by a long caravan to accommodate her entourage, dozens of trunks, a small menagerie of dogs and birds, her glittering costumes, and every creature comfort necessary for a diva on tour. When Patti sang Violetta in New York in February 1882 with a company formed especially for her, her fabulous diamonds dazzled audiences quite as much as her voice: "a diamond butterfly fluttered and flamed from her shoulder; nine different necklaces rainbowed around her neck and the front of her corsage; rings flashed from her fingers; and on her arms blazed bracelet after bracelet, culminating in one band of selected stones, each of which scintillated like a star." Her extravagant fees, $5,000 for each concert or opera appearance, were the highest the country had ever paid to hear a singer, and most audiences felt she was worth it. By the end of her career Patti had amassed a fortune, one probably unequaled by any other singer before or since. When a journalist once remarked to her that it was outrageous that she should earn more in a night than a United States President did in a whole year, Patti shot back, "Well, let him sing!"

Even her parents, Salvatore Patti and Caterina Barili-Patti, could hardly have foreseen all this when they brought three-year-old Adelina to New York in 1846. Both elder Pattis were attracted to the New World in hopes of extending their fading performing careers and eventually transforming Palmo's Opera House on Chambers Street into the city's premier showcase for Italian opera. By then father Patti was definitely nearing the end, pushing fifty and dealing with a weight problem that earned him the unflattering nickname "Patti de foie gras." Soon Salvatore was reduced to appearing in supporting roles, but the family had plenty of other vocal talent to draw on—Caterina's four children by a previous marriage, as well as another four sired by Salvatore, all eventually became singers. It was soon obvious that little Adelina would follow in her elder siblings' footsteps and possibly turn out to be the greatest of them all. She was certainly eager to get started. Barely out of diapers, the toddler was thrust onstage by her parents to play one of Norma's children. Since Caterina was singing the title role, Adelina saw no reason not to join in, and when Norma's duets with Adalgisa turned into a trio, the annoyed Caterina had to march her daughter into the wings and administer a spanking.

Until her early teen years Adelina lived with her parents at 170 East Tenth Street, a section of town that was not altogether hospitable to Italian immigrants, particularly a family of opera singers. The little girl was considered an exotic by her playmates, although she found she could deflect their teasing with tales of her family's colorful backstage life and her own impromptu backyard performances of such songs as "Yankee Doodle" complete with trills and embellishments. Surrounded by professional singers from birth, Patti, it seemed, learned to sing by example, just as she had learned to walk and talk as a baby. According to Herman Klein, one of her early biographers, her vocal training was nearly complete by the time she was seven—"correct breathing, scales, trills, ornaments, fioriture of every kind, all came naturally to her and required only the finishing touches." As a youngster, Patti worked diligently on her technique, mostly with her stepbrother Ettore Barili, but her facility was not the result of dogged practice, as she later admitted. No wonder her parents were soon eager to exhibit their wondrous daughter in public, and a debut was quickly arranged. Her exact contemporary, Henry James, witnessed that happy event, and he later recalled seeing "the image of the infant phenomenon Adelina Patti . . . in a fan-like little white frock and 'pantalettes' and a hussar-like red jacket, mounted on an armchair, its back supporting her, wheeled to the front of the stage and warbling like a tiny thrush even in the nest."

The success of Adelina's first local concert appearances inspired Salvatore to arrange a tour for his youngest, and to feature her precocious talents he put together an attractive package that included Maurice Strakosch at the piano, Adelina's contralto sister Amalia (now Strakosch's wife), and the Norwegian violinist Ole Bull. A few years later Louis Moreau Gottschalk replaced Bull as the principal instrumental attraction, and the public was even more entranced by that colorful piano personality. Patti was still the principal draw, and she was already well aware of her vocal gifts and her ability to manipulate an audience. One of her early fans visited her backstage and years later, when Patti was the toast of Europe, he reminisced:

She was playing with a doll, in company with a little girl of her own age, and was sitting in the artist's anteroom during the progress of a concert at which she had to sing. Our friend was fascinated by her charming and unaffected *naïveté,* and told her he should certainly go round to the front as soon as her time arrived to sing. "Oh, that *is* kind!" said the child; adding, "If you like, I'll make the people cry. Would you like to see me make the people cry? Well, when I'm encored (they are sure to encore me!), see if I don't make them cry!" As she had predicted, her first song, which was a brilliant "air and variations," was encored. On her return to the platform, she gave a glance at her new acquaintance, and sang an old English ballad, with such intensely pathetic expression, that he, as well as "the people," found it impossible to refrain from tears. On his return to the anteroom, he found the little singer, who so lately before had appeared to be overpowered with emotion, already re-possessed of her doll, and romping with her playmate; ceasing her play, for a moment only, to give him a merrily triumphant glance, as she said, "Well, the people *did* cry, *didn't* they? I told you so! And you cried, too! I saw you!"

By the time the Pattis felt that sixteen-year-old Adelina was ready for her operatic debut, she was already a household name among the country's music-loving audiences, having toured west to Chicago, north to Montreal, and south to New Orleans, in addition to a trip to the Caribbean islands with Gottschalk in 1857–58. When Patti made her bow at the Academy of Music, as Lucia, New York went mad. Her success was so sensational that other cities immediately clamored to see her, and she was more than prepared to accommodate them. During her two seasons on the American opera stage—in New York, Boston, Philadelphia, Baltimore, Washington, and New Orleans—Patti learned and sang fourteen principal roles, mostly bel canto operas that would remain central to her repertory for the next forty years.

After the soprano sailed for England in 1861, America could only read about her triumphs during the next two decades. Perhaps the best evidence we have that her successes were based on a truly amazing vocal endowment and not press hype comes from the comments of many composers whose music she sang. At first Rossini was irritated by her excessive embellishments—"By whom is this aria that you have just let us hear?" he remarked after Patti sang an especially florid rendition of Rosina's aria from *Il Barbiere* at one of the composer's musical soirées in Paris. Later, however, Rossini capitulated and often accompanied her at the piano, pronouncing her onstage performances of Rosina as "adorable." When Patti and Alboni sang the duet from the composer's *Stabat Mater* at his funeral, Gounod proclaimed that listening to them was the "most heavenly and touching musical moment of his whole existence."

Even Verdi was impressed by her Gilda in *Rigoletto*, in particular the "sublime effect" of her expressive declamation. When Tchaikovsky heard Patti in Russia, he enthused, "Aside from the artistic purity of her coloratura and the accuracy of her intonation, all the registers of her voice are of like strength and beauty; she sings with exceeding taste, and she possesses sufficient warmth and native, genuine animation in her performance." One of Patti's warmest admirers was Hanslick. He exhorted all younger singers to study her method, especially her "tone formation, portamento, scales, and interpretive art right down to the smallest mordent. There is no more perfect model." The ultimate accolade probably came from Jenny Lind herself, who once told Sir Arthur Sullivan, "There is only one Niagara; and there is only one Patti."

Despite her European fame, Patti had to reconquer America when she arrived in New York on November 3, 1881. The ticket sales for her first return concerts were disappointing, partly because of the astronomical prices ($10 for an orchestra seat) and partly because New York society, like that of London, was appalled that Patti had left her husband, the Marquis de Caux, for the tenor Ernest Nicolini and was living in sin. In 1877 the *New York Times* threw up its hands in horror, stating that Patti's "running away with a common tenor, after being for so many years a titled and respected lady, held up as a model to all young ladies upon the stage, was almost beyond conception." In London she was already socially ostracized, and New York followed suit. The soprano's voice, the spell of her musical personality, and rave reviews soon made audiences forget about Patti's morals, and her progress from New York to Brooklyn, Philadelphia, Cincinnati, Louisville, St. Louis, New Orleans, Indianapolis, and Boston was triumphant. Just before sailing back to England, the impresario managing her tour, Henry E. Abbey, presented Patti in complete operas at New York's Germania Theater, and the American public was completely hers once again. Indeed, the focus of her career during the coming years would be America. And why not? Her financial demands and the later contracts she personally drew up with Colonel Mapleson meant that Patti was now the highest paid and most pampered singer in the world, and America's wealth and the fact that the whole country was mad to hear her made it all possible.

However gloriously Patti may have sung, an aura of crass commercialism clung to her American tours. Mapleson certainly did his part to Barnumize the events, although there never was any doubt who called the shots—the impresario was even instructed to stand by the box office, take in the money, and bring her fee personally to the diva, who would never consent to appear until it was in hand. She had even trained her favorite pet parrot, Ben Butler, to shriek "Cash! Cash!" every time the hapless Mapleson entered her luxurious train carriage. The Colonel also tells us that the press had calculated precisely how much a Patti performance was worth by dividing the number of notes she sang by her fee. For *Lucia*, it was reckoned, she earned around 42 cents per note and for *Semiramide* 30 cents—about 7 cents per note more than Rossini had earned for composing the whole score.

When Patti finally reached San Francisco in March 1884, the scene at the box office was bedlam. "Long before daylight," reported Mapleson, "the would-be purchasers of Patti tickets had collected and formed into a line, reaching the length of some three or four streets; and from this time until the close of the engagement, some four weeks afterwards, that line was never broken at any period of the day or night . . . Later on it was announced that a limited number of gallery tickets would be sold, when a rush was made, carrying away the whole of the windows, glass, statuary, plants, etc. Ticket speculators were now offering seats at from £4 to £10 each, places in the fifth row of the dress circle fetching as much as £4, being 400 per cent above the box-office price." Finally 4,000 spectators crammed into an auditorium meant for 2,200. Like Lind before her, Patti never personally involved herself in the extramusical furor. She simply sang, smiled sweetly for the press, collected her fee, and returned home to Europe.

The San Francisco reviews were ecstatic, although writing in the *Argonaut*, a critic named Betsy B. found all the hoopla a bit much. "What is there to say of Patti's voice that people have not been saying for twenty-five years?" observed Miss B. "And how many went to hear her voice? She has become a spectacle, like Jumbo or any other freak, and the world goes to see her rather than to hear." Betsy B. was right, of course—in that respect it was Jenny Lind all over again, a cultural curiosity, imported from Europe, that everyone wanted to inspect. No one could compete with Patti, a star attraction who came, sang, conquered, and made a fortune while an entire generation of American singers bravely soldiered on.

Patti enjoyed one advantage over her potent European predecessors and successors: the demand for opera throughout America was at an all-time high. Patti played directly to this rage for opera, and the concert programs she sang on her regal progress across the country were not exactly the most sophisticated. All her popular arias were trotted out along with a generous selection of trivia, and audiences refused to leave until they had heard the diva's signature tune, "Home, Sweet Home." Patti's ability to stir emotions had hardly diminished with age, and the tears flowed every time she sang that Victorian chestnut. One wonders if it ever occurred to her weeping fans that the diva's own home, "be it ever so humble," was a lavish French château in Wales. Probably not. Patti played the role of immeasurably wealthy and glamorous opera diva to the hilt, and it was part of her mystique. That, coupled with her fabulous vocal endowment, made her quite literally incomparable. During the same decade Emma Abbott was at the height of her popularity, touring the land with her own road-show company, and Clara Louise Kellogg was reaching the end of her busy career, but neither American soprano could really compete. Kellogg always liked to consider herself a contender, although she was sensible enough to acknowledge, at least tacitly, a superior talent—"quite the most remarkable singer that I ever heard," she admits in her memoirs, adding with her customary waspishness, "A great deal is heard about the wonderful preservation of Patti's voice. It *was* wonderfully preserved thirteen years ago. [Kellogg's memoirs were published in 1913.] How could it have been otherwise, considering the care she has always taken of herself? Such a life! Everything divided off carefully according to *régime:* so much to eat, so far to walk, so long to sleep, just such and such things to do and no others! And, above all, she has allowed herself few emotions. Every singer knows that emotions are what exhaust and injure the voice. She never acted; and she never, never felt. As Violetta she did express some slight emotion, to be sure. Her *Gran Dio* in the last act was sung with something like passion, at least with more passion than she ever sang anything else. Yes: in *La Traviata,* after she had run away with Nicolini, she did succeed in putting an unusual amount of passion into the *rôle* of Violetta."

After that first "homecoming" tour, each subsequent return was rumored to be Patti's last, and soon her "farewell" tours of America became a joke. In 1890 the *Boston Gazette* suggested that they should be ranked as "farewell engagement. Last farewell engagement. Positively farewell engagement. Positively last farewell engagement—and so on, until she has sung the last note she has left to the public, and drawn from it the last note it is willing to pay for hearing her." After an absence of nine years Patti returned in 1903 for what was indeed to be her last visit to North America—she mainly agreed to make the return trip in order to show the country to her third husband, Baron Rolf Cederström, a man twenty-six years her junior. The soprano's new manager, Robert Grau (Maurice's younger brother), was prepared to make it worth her while. "Not only will I pay you $5,000 a night," he proposed, "but I will give you 25 per cent of the gross receipts at each concert in excess of $7,500; also I will pay transportation for your entire party to and from America and will give you a private palace car in America throughout the tour!"

When the papers got wind of the news, the Patti publicity mill began to grind and her three New York concerts—on November 2, 4, and 7—immediately sold out. The critics, however, were not inclined to be generous. Patti, after all, was sixty, her voice no longer the brilliant instrument it once had been, and times had changed. Since the soprano's heyday New York had embraced Wagnerian music drama as a virtual cult, and the city's tastemakers considered Patti's art utterly trivial and hopelessly out of date. W. J. Henderson was positively devastating: "Her audiences are curious collections of persons who never or very rarely go to hear music of a high order. She occupies much the same position in the world of art as Sousa's band . . . All of which is a pity, for Patti was in her time the greatest singer that ever lived. She . . . deliberately pandered to low tastes and cultivated cheap sensationalism. Her singing of parlor ballads, which genuine artists avoid, is a piece of cheap clap-trap which puts her outside the pale of serious criticism . . . Let it be added in conclusion of these remarks that the lady's demeanor on the concert stage was extremely undignified. To see a woman of sixty in a blonde wig trying to ogle an audience and play kittenish tricks is far from edifying."

Despite such critical thundering, enough curiosity-seekers still wanted one last look at Patti to make the tour worthwhile—at least at first—and the diva could write back to her brother-in-law, Gustaf Cederström: "You will be pleased to hear that grand success is following me everywhere we go—and that the Americans are *exceedingly* enthusiastic—Money is flowing in rapidly and if all goes well until the end, I shall have had a most brilliant season. I sang here last night to a nine thousand dollar house, which is considered enormous in St. Louis."

Patti was too optimistic. Attendance fell off as the tour progressed, and in spite of the luxurious accommodations supplied by Grau, the aging diva found cross-country travel more grueling than she had anticipated. Some concerts never took place due to insufficient receipts at the box office, and on March 8, after a concert at Hot Springs, Arkansas, Patti abruptly decided she had had enough. All remaining dates were canceled, and on March 12, 1904, Patti embarked on the *Lucania* from New York for Europe. The day before she left, she told the journalist William Armstrong, a longtime friend, that she was relieved to be going home. "She was," Armstrong later ruefully wrote, "as a queen who had returned to her own country, where once all had worshiped her, only to find pitifully few subjects loyal."

Perhaps so, but the reign of Patti had been a long and glorious one, in "her own country" as well as throughout Europe. Nowhere had she been more honored and rewarded than in America, even if she degenerated into little more than a Barnumesque sideshow at the end. During the height of her career she was paid a fealty that the country's native singers never did and could never hope to receive.

Seven

She

Did Her

Damnedest

~~~~~~~~~~~~~~~~~~~~~~~~~~~~~~~~~

*E*xactly when the true golden age of singing occurred—indeed, if one ever did—will always be a matter of debate. Most vocal connoisseurs, though, would probably agree that New York in the 1890s was a good place to see and hear opera. The assemblage of stars at the Metropolitan during that decade was truly staggering. Mario Ancona, Emma Calvé, Fernando de Lucia, Jean and Édouard de Reszke, Emma Eames, Lilli Lehmann, Félia Litvinne, Victor Maurel, Nellie Melba, Adelina Patti, Pol Plançon, Antonio Scotti, Ernestine Schumann-Heink, Francesco Tamagno, Milka Ternina, Ernest van Dyck—these were just a few of the luminaries active in New York during the Gay Nineties, and the Met mixed and matched their talents to produce casts of unparalleled magnificence. As the first generation of singers to leave substantial recorded evidence of their work, these artists are still able to offer audible proof that their reputations were neither inflated nor created by the fantasies of nostalgic opera buffs.

Among them was Lillian Nordica, born Lillian Norton on December 12, 1857, in Farmington, Maine. No American singer of her generation traveled so widely, enjoyed more glamorous triumphs, performed such a diverse repertory, or competed more comfortably with her European peers. Nordica sang it all, from the coloratura fireworks of Mozart's Queen of the Night, through the lyrical refinement of Verdi's Gilda and Gounod's Marguerite, to the vocal drama of Meyerbeer's Sélika and Wagner's Kundry. And, unlike some sopranos, she kept virtually all of these roles in her active repertory throughout her career, once singing Violetta forty-eight hours after Brünnhilde in *Götterdämmerung*. She willingly performed all three Brünnhildes on consecutive nights, and, at fifty-three, she relearned Isolde in French for a single production in Paris. "Plenty have voices equal to mine," the soprano once observed with characteristic modesty and epigrammatic flair, "plenty have talents equal to mine; but I have worked."

Perhaps the greatest night of her life, as well as the crowning achievement of her career, took place on November 27, 1895, when, at the Met, she sang her first Isolde opposite Jean de Reszke's first Tristan, with Anton Seidl in the pit. Wagner fever was then at its height in New York, and the excitement of experiencing these two popular artists singing in *Tristan und Isolde*, in German at last, was electric. And no one seems to have been disappointed. "I have heard *Tristan* in Vienna, in Munich, in Dresden, and those splendid representations here which enlisted the services of Lehmann, Niemann, Brandt, and Fischer," wrote the ecstatic critic of the *New York Herald*. "All these however pale into insignificance when compared with that of last evening. So splendidly was it sung, so passionately enacted, that one could not but regret that the composer was in his grave. For surely such things as the finale of the first act, the love duet in the second and the long Tristan scene he never heard, not even in his mind's ear . . ."

In the *Tribune*, even the chronically hard-to-please Henry E. Krehbiel was awed, especially by Nordica. "It is wonderful how Mme. Nordica rose to the opportunity which Wagner's drama opened to her. The greater the demand the larger her capacity. In the climaxes of the first act, in which Isolde rages like a tempest, her voice rang out with thrilling clearness, power and brilliancy . . ." The *Herald* concluded, "Let no one speak of Mme. Nordica as merely a beautiful singer hereafter. Her Isolde stamps her as one of the greatest lyric artists of the day. Note ye American prima donnas, what high ideals and incessant application will lead to. There are greater things to be done than Marguerite and Traviata . . ."

High ideals and incessant application were two concepts that Nordica learned from Amanda Norton, yet another tireless, strong-willed, omnipresent backstage mother who encouraged her daughter's ambitions and devoted much of her life to making sure they came true. "Give me a spoon," Amanda was fond of saying, "and I won't hesitate to dig a tunnel through a mountain." Young Lillian also must have had a keen sense of competition from birth. Not only the youngest of six girls, she was also a "repeater," having been called Lillian after an older sister with the same name who had died in infancy—a common family custom at the time in rural New England, and repeaters were expected to live for two.

The seven-year-old girl's bucolic existence in Farmington ended when her father, Edwin Norton, gave up trying to turn a profit from his farm and in 1864 moved the family to Boston. But Nordica never forgot Maine, which she always considered her home, returning whenever possible. Indeed, even as an international figure who moved commandingly across the world's opera stages and mingled easily with European royalty, she never seemed alienated from her Down East roots. They began to call her "the Yankee Diva" early on, and the nickname stuck.

Life in Boston was not much easier than it had been in Farmington, but eventually Edwin settled down as a photographer, Amanda worked at Jordan Marsh's department store, and the older girls found employment wherever they could. One of them, Wilhelmina, showed signs of vocal promise, and Amanda immediately enrolled her in the New England Conservatory of Music, which in 1867 had just opened its doors. Lillian used to copy her older sister as she drilled her voice with vocalises and scales, but no one took much notice of the little repeater. Her big treat during those meager years was being taken to the Parepa-Rosa Grand English Opera Company; the memory of *Il Trovatore* with Parepa-Rosa as Leonora, Amalia Patti (Adelina's contralto sister) as Azucena, and Pasquale Brignoli as Manrico remained a potent one that she never forgot.

By the time Willie reached sixteen, she had already had several singing engagements in the Boston area, but just as she seemed ready to embark on a professional career, tragedy struck. In the fall of 1869 Willie fell ill with typhoid fever and died. Amanda was crushed by the loss not only of her daughter but also of her own prospects. Help was on the way, however. After two years of grieving, Amanda suddenly noticed Lillian singing as she went about her household chores, and the fourteen-year-old girl was whisked off to be evaluated by John O'Neill, her sister's former teacher at the New England Conservatory. Professor O'Neill was astonished after taking Lillian up the scale and hearing her hit a secure, ringing high C. Suddenly called upon to fill the shoes of yet another dead sister, Lillian began serious work on her voice then and there, the eager pupil of an exacting teacher. After two years of intense study, she was allowed to sing a bit of Handel, some Verdi, and German lieder in school recitals, and in 1875 she was awarded the part of Lady Harriet in *Martha*, performed by the students of Charles R. Adams at the tenor's house on Tremont Street. Since a future career in opera looked like a very real possibility when Lillian graduated the following year, Amanda packed her bags and set off with her daughter to New York for lessons with Appolonia Bertucca, the wife of the conductor-impresario Max Maretzek.

Once settled in New York, Lillian took three lessons a week until it became obvious that the budding soprano would have to put her voice to work and earn a living. The obliging Mme. Maretzek took her to Patrick Gilmore, whose famous band was playing the 1876 centennial season in Gilmore's Gardens, and the bandmaster hired her on the spot. That fall she sang arias from popular Bellini and Verdi operas with such success that Gilmore took her with him on short tours of the East Coast and, the following year, proposed that Lillian accompany his entourage to Europe at $100 a week plus expenses for two (Amanda, of course, would come along).

After a year with Gilmore in England and on the Continent, Amanda felt that Lillian's favorable reception warranted taking the big chance on what both mother and daughter had hoped for all along: a career in opera. In the summer of 1878 they severed connections with the band and remained in Paris, where Lillian studied dramatic action with François Delsarte and coached repertory with Emilio Belari, a Span-ish tenor who had sung leading roles at Les Italiens. Thanks to O'Neill's thorough and effective training, European critics had already found her vocal method to be remarkably finished.

Indeed, when the Nortons moved to Milan that November and pre-sented themselves to Antonio Sangiovanni, the great teacher proclaimed that there was little room for improvement. He immediately recognized a voice that would one day mature into a dramatic instrument fit for the heaviest assignments, but forbade her to touch even Aida until she had completely mastered the bel canto masterpieces. That Lillian set out to do, although by January 1879 the money earned from Gilmore and the meager supplementary funds sent by the Nortons back home in Boston were fast running out. Thanks to Sangiovanni's influence and confidence in his new pupil, an operatic debut was arranged on the spot—as Elvira in a production of Don Giovanni to be given that March at the Teatro Manzoni in Milan. At the same time, an offer arrived to sing Violetta a month later in the same Brescia production that featured the Alfredo of her compatriot from Detroit, Arthur Scovel (alias Arturo Scovelli). Since the name "Lillian Norton" would never do in Italy, Sangiovanni suggested the more euphonious-sounding Giglio Nordica, and it was as "the Lily of the North" that Lillian made her professional debut in opera.

The Brescia Traviata must have been an occasion of sweet success for Lillian and Amanda—not only did the theater ring with bravas, but the next morning a string band appeared under their hotel window to play the opera's prelude accompanied by cries of "L'Americana Nordica! Bellissima Violetta!" When the excitement died down, Lillian wrote to her father back in Boston with girlish glee tempered by a typical Yankee no-nonsense attitude that never seemed to desert her: "Mother has written, I suppose at some length, on my grand success in opera. Well, she cannot say too much. I have had a grand success and no mistake. Such yelling and shouting you never heard. The theatre is packed. I put right into the acting, and you would not know me. It makes me laugh to see men and women cry and wipe their noses in the last act."

Even that triumph did not guarantee nonstop engagements and high fees. Opera stars were not made overnight in the Italy of the 1880s unless they had the financial wherewithal to back up their talent and aspirations. Christine Nilsson could spend $50,000 on her musical education and debuts and instantly take her place at the top, but Nordica had to make her way with hard work and sheer determination. When they returned to Milan and their lodgings on Via Palesto, mother and daughter continued to live hand-to-mouth in rooms that drained them of 45 cents a day plus an extra 7 cents for maid service. Daily meals for two cost $1.80, and domestic conveniences were practically nonexistent. Always a slow learner, Nordica laboriously worked on the new roles she had been engaged to sing after the Brescia Traviata (Marguerite in Genoa, Alice in Roberto il Diavolo in Novarra, and Gilda in Aquila), and turned down offers from London to sing opera in English. "She did not come to Italy to sing in English Opera," wrote Amanda scornfully, adding the sarcastic postscript: "It will be time enough to sing in E. O. when Miss Kellogg gets through with it."

In the summer of 1880 an emissary from the Imperial Opera of St. Petersburg arrived in Milan to engage a soprano for the coming winter season. Lillian auditioned successfully, and although the roles to be filled were not necessarily starring ones, the Nortons accepted the offer from the prestigious house. None of the parts were in the repertory Sangiovanni had asked her to learn, so the rest of the summer was spent working on her upcoming Russian assignments: Philine (*Mignon*) and three Meyerbeer roles: Marguerite (*Les Huguenots*), Inès (*L'Africaine*), and Berthe (*Le Prophète*). No doubt stimulated by singing in the company of such stars as Marcella Sembrich, Sofia Scalchi, Angelo Masini, and Antonio Cotogni, Nordica outdid herself and the public clamored for more. Soon she was being cast in prima-donna roles: Amelia (*Un Ballo in Maschera*), Sulamith (Goldmark's *Die Königin von Saba*), Cherubino (*Le Nozze di Figaro*), Simone (Delibes's *Jean de Nivelle*), Eudoxie (*La Juive*), and Isabelle (*Robert le Diable*).

Coincidentally, this was the same lyric-coloratura repertory that had once been the property of Clara Louise Kellogg, who arrived at the Imperial Opera during the same season as Nordica. Though it was late in the day for Kellogg, whose performances failed to excite audiences in St. Petersburg, she left a revealing sketch of the young Nordica in her memoirs:

We have always been good friends. At the time of the Gilmore tour she was quite a girl, but she dressed her hair in a fashion that made her look much older than she really was and that threw into prominence her admirably determined chin. Before becoming an opera singer she had done everything else. She had been a bookkeeper, had worked at the sewing machine, and sung in obscure choirs. The chin enabled her to survive such drudgery. A young person with a chin so expressive of determination and perseverance could not be downed.

She told me at that early period that she always kept her eyes fixed on some goal so high and difficult that it seemed impossible, and worked toward it steadily, unceasingly, putting aside everything that stood in the path which led to it. In later years she spoke again of this, evidently having kept the idea throughout her career. "When I sang Elsa," she said, "I thought of Brünnhilde—then Isolde."

My admiration for Mme. Nordica is deep and abounding. Her breathing and tone production are about as nearly perfect as anyone's can be, and, if I wanted any young student to learn by imitation, I could say to her, "Go and hear Nordica and do as nearly like her as you can!" There are not many singers, nor have there ever been many, of whom one could say that. And one of the finest things about this splendid vocalism is that she had had nearly as much to do with it as had God Almighty in the first place.

When I first knew her she had no dramatic quality above G sharp. She could reach the upper notes, but tentatively and without power. She had, in fact, a beautiful mezzo voice; but she could not hope for leading rôles in grand opera until she had perfect control of the upper notes needed to complete her vocal equipment . . . But it was not until after the Russian engagement that she went to [Giovanni] Sbriglia in Paris and worked with him until she could sing a high C that thrilled the soul. That C of hers in the "Inflammatus" in Rossini's *Stabat Mater* was something superb. Not many singers can do it as successfully as Nordica, although they can all accomplish a certain amount in "manufactured" notes. Fursch-Madi, also a mezzo, had to acquire upper notes as a business proposition in order to enlarge her repertoire. She secured the notes and requisite rôles; yet her voice lost greatly in quality. Nordica's never did. She gained all and lost nothing. Her voice, while increasing in register, never suffered the least detriment in tone nor timbre.

Kellogg's uncharacteristically generous assessment of Nordica has the ring of truth about it. Hard worker that she was and sorely in need of making a living as well as hungering for the big career, Lillian had perhaps pressed forward faster than her voice could carry her. In any case, the two summers spent in Paris with Sbriglia must have paid off. Not only was her voice sounding stronger and more flexible, but the director of the Opéra, Auguste Emmanuel Vaucorbeil, also offered her a contract to sing Marguerite in *Faust* on July 22, 1882. After a friendly if not sensational reception—by then, Gounod's opera had become practically a national monument in Paris, and the newcomer was competing with the memories of at least twenty previous Marguerites since the work had had its premiere in 1859—Nordica seemed to be on her way to international stardom. On November 26, 1883, under the auspices of Colonel Mapleson, she returned to New York to make her American operatic debut in the same role at the Academy of Music, now in competition with the Metropolitan, which had just opened its doors a month earlier with *Faust* starring Christine Nilsson. It was not as "Nordica" that she first sang in New York, but as Lillian Norton Gower. Earlier that year while still in Paris, she had married Frederick Allen Gower, her second cousin, an associate of Alexander Graham Bell's, and a handsome young man whose business acumen was presumed to border on genius—only thirty, he was already a millionaire.

At first the match seemed made in heaven. It soon became apparent, though, that Gower regarded Lillian's operatic career as simply a job she had taken to support herself and her mother, an occupation she need no longer pursue. After all her sacrifices, hardship, and years of separation from her family, Amanda was not about to entertain any such notion, and soon relations with her new son-in-law became frigid. Worse, the reviews of Lillian's Marguerite in New York and even in Boston were distinctly tepid. Krehbiel, who was to wax so lyrical over Nordica a decade later, acknowledged her training, intelligence, and taste, but felt that her performance cost her "a manifest effort to do what she well knew how to do, for she is not a phenomenal vocalist." The soprano continued with Mapleson's troupe as far as Chicago, but then returned to New York and set sail for London, where, for the moment, Gower's business interests lay.

Whether she did so willingly or not, Nordica temporarily retired into a marriage that was doomed from the start. Gower's resentment of her singing and hatred of music in general bordered on the psychotic. He even burned her scores—the copies of *Faust* and *Hamlet* that had been presented to her and inscribed by Gounod and Thomas—and her costumes as well. Occasionally asked to sing for her husband's business guests at social gatherings, Lillian would bravely get through the Jewel Song, only to be told later by Gower, "If you knew what a monkey it makes you look, you would never sing." One scene followed another until neither Lillian nor Amanda could bear another moment. In the summer of 1884 they returned to Boston, where Lillian sued for divorce and took the better part of a year to recuperate from what the papers described as a "chronic malady"—most likely an old-fashioned nervous breakdown. Gower fought back, but fate eventually settled the matter when his latest passion—aeronautics—proved his undoing. He made a balloon ascension from Cherbourg one July day in 1885, floated out over the English Channel, and was never seen again.

After recovering from that disaster, Nordica was soon ready to pick up her career where she had left it, and in January 1886 she rejoined Mapleson's troupe on its journey to America. This was the tour that witnessed Minnie Hauk's celebrated fracas with Ravelli during *Carmen* in Chicago, only one incident in an action-packed cross-country marathon that took the company from Boston to Chicago, St. Louis, Kansas City, St. Joseph, Denver, Cheyenne, Salt Lake City, San Francisco, and back. It was an exhausting reentry into professional life, but by now Nordica was more determined than ever to succeed and decided to make London her home base.

Still appearing under the rather tattered aegis of Mapleson, she made her London opera debut on March 12, 1887, at Covent Garden, which at the time was playing a distinct second fiddle to Augustus Harris's all-star entourage at Drury Lane. Nordica had little choice in the matter, since her marriage had undercut her international progress, and there were pressing bills to pay. Amanda was in Italy, her health having collapsed during the rigors of the North American tour, and Lillian had to take a cheap room by herself at the Charing Cross Hotel. Not having the money for a cab on the night of her London debut, she trudged on foot to Covent Garden to sing in *La Traviata* opposite an "Alfredo whom I had never seen before. And such a tenor! Of course my ensemble numbers were ruined, but I had a chance in my arias, and how hard I tried in them! The next day I was known in London." The press minced no words over the second-rate quality of Mapleson's present company, but Nordica's contribution was gratefully acknowledged by at least one critic: G. B. Shaw. In an unsigned notice in the *Pall Mall Gazette*, he wrote, "She is competence itself, with a brisk attack, bright style, good method, and admirable control over the middle of her voice, which is unforced and sound all over except for a trace of tremolo in the lowest register. She takes her high notes easily and in tune; her execution is accurate and brilliant in florid passages; and her cantabile singing is pure and pleasant. She is not an artist of the very first class; for her manner lacks exceptional distinction and grace; and her acting is the conventional opera house gesticulation which for some reason we tolerate at

Covent Garden . . . But she is far better than any experienced opera-goer had dared to expect . . ."

On the strength of that modest but real success, Nordica presented herself to Augustus Harris and requested a spot in his company. "We don't want you," she was bluntly told. "We have all these people"—and Harris reeled off one starry name after another—"and you have been singing at cheap prices for Mapleson." So had several others on Harris's roster, Nordica pointed out, and finally the impresario said he would consider her as an alternate if her services were ever needed. "I was distinctly made to feel like a fifth wheel to a coach," she said. The wheel soon sped into motion, though, when a certain Mme. Kupfer-Berger imported from the Continent arrived at rehearsals with "a vibrato of the most pronounced kind." Nordica was summoned to replace her, first as Violetta with Fernando de Lucia and Giuseppe del Puente, and later *Faust* with the De Reszke brothers and Victor Maurel. Further casting crises led to Aida and Valentine in *Les Huguenots* (sung in Italian), both roles new to Nordica's repertory. Appearing in England for the first time as a tenor, Jean de Reszke sang Raoul in Meyerbeer's opera, and their great duet that closes Act IV apparently brought down the house.

Now an established presence in London, Nordica also began to make her mark in the all-important world of oratorio by singing Elsie in Sullivan's *The Golden Legend*, winning both the composer's approval and his invaluable assistance in gaining entree to royal circles. Meeting all the right people was important, but, as she told Klein, "I feel I must work harder than ever now. I would like to settle in London and go on studying as many new roles as I can master. I know my voice is not yet under entire control. A singer should never be satisfied, but go on working, working all the time."

Nordica now had her eye on Wagner—her visit to the Bayreuth Festival in the summer of 1888, she said, was a sublime experience. "Mother," she whispered to Amanda during one performance, "I am going to sing here one day." Taking a first step in that direction, Nordica requested Harris to give her the part of Elsa in *Lohengrin*, which she sang as her major new role for the 1889 season. The reviews for her performance were mixed. Shaw admired her singing, but grumbled about her presence: "Miss Nordica turned Elsa of Brabant into Elsa of Bond-street, by appearing in a corset. She produces her voice so skillfully that its want of color, and her inability to fill up with expressive action the long periods left by Wagner for that purpose, were the more to be regretted." Nordica always took valid criticism seriously, and she went back to work.

Later that year the soprano returned to America, this time touring in a glamorous company assembled by Henry E. Abbey and Maurice Grau. Adelina Patti was the prima-donna headliner, singing Lakmé, a new role for her, and the troupe also included Emma Albani and Francesco Tamagno, Verdi's first Otello. Nordica's featured roles were Aida, Sélika, and Leonora in *Il Trovatore*. It was this last opera that brought her to the stage of the Metropolitan Opera House on March 27, 1890, when the troupe visited New York and gave the city a welcome taste of real Italian opera. For some years the Met's resident company had devoted itself to "Grand German Opera," performing even *Norma* and *Carmen* (with Minnie Hauk) in that language, a policy soon to be changed. At the beginning of the 1891–92 season Abbey and Grau had themselves taken over the Met management, and the team brought together a company of glittering stars, but, for some unexplained reason, not Nordica. The resourceful Lillian promptly arranged to make a four-month concert tour of America to coincide with the Met season, letting everyone know exactly where she would be, just in case. Sure enough, when the Nordica Concert Company was appearing in Cleveland, the call came: Albani had fallen ill and Nordica was needed to sing Valentine on December 18, once again with Jean de Reszke as Raoul. It was a bittersweet triumph, for one important ingredient was missing: Amanda Norton had died in London only a few weeks earlier.

At least Amanda died secure in the knowledge that her youngest daughter had reached the top. And yet Nordica still had much to accomplish. She was aware of her shortcomings, and continued to work hard to overcome them, but some were beyond even her power to change. She never commanded the sort of demonic presence that her younger contemporary Olive Fremstad brought to the Wagner heroines. Shaw's criticisms of her London performances almost always centered on a disconcerting expressive monotony and lack of dramatic flair, characteristics that were an integral part of a basically restrained, even plain performing persona. In most respects Nordica was the quintessential Yankee craftsman, whose art was born mainly out of stubborn enterprise and shrewd decisions. Her performances probably suffered from a lack of creative spontaneity, and apparently they could leave a chilly impression. Philip Hale, the captious critic of the *Boston Journal*, complained that Nordica—"that woman from Maine," as he often called her in his reviews—seldom touched the heart. But even Hale admitted the supremacy of her voice, which was surely then at its glorious maturity. And by the time she sang that famous *Tristan* at the Met with De Reszke in 1895, Nordica was at her height.

That historic performance was preceded by an event equally important and even more prestigious. In the summer of 1894 Nordica got her wish when, on the recommendation of conductor Hans Richter, Cosima Wagner summoned her to Bayreuth to sing Elsa in the festival's first production of *Lohengrin*. Naturally rumors began to fly. Some said that Nordica had offered to sing the part for nothing. The Germans complained that importing an American singer to sing Elsa amounted to a national affront, although there were no complaints about the Belgian Lohengrin (Ernest van Dyck), Romanian Telramund (Demeter Popovici), and English Ortrud (Marie Brema). And then there was talk about Zoltán Döme, a Hungarian baritone-turned-tenor who had been engaged as the alternate Parsifal despite a vocal endowment that was apparently of only minimal quality. Nordica had met Döme three years earlier in London when they both participated in a charity concert arranged by Nellie Melba at Marlborough House. He was young, handsome, something of a flirt, and, by the time of their summer together in Bayreuth, Nordica's lover.

Nordica had little time for romance, however. Cosima was taking no chances on her American Elsa, and Wagner's exacting widow decided to coach the debutante herself. In the month before formal rehearsals began, Nordica arrived at Wahnfried punctually at nine every morning to be drilled until each word of the text tripped flawlessly off her tongue and had been precisely matched to each note in the score. When the month was up, Cosima was satisfied, and her son, Siegfried, wrote enthusiastically to Otto Floersheim, editor of *The Musical Courier:* "About Madame Nordica I can tell you the most pleasing things. She will be a most extraordinary German Elsa. The language already causes her no more trouble. With an artist of her talent and of her reputation it is really touching to watch with what indefatigable zeal she dedicates herself to the perfection of her role. We are all highly enchanted to have found for the part, which vocally is one of the most exacting, an artist of the most eminent ability."

The big day arrived and Nordica wrote her Aunt Lina how she "felt that the eye of the musical world was upon me and that the stars and stripes were in my keeping and must be brought forth in victory . . ." Not surprisingly, the German critics were divided. Floersheim was pleased and astonished. Max Steinitzer, however, complained that the casting of Nordica as Elsa amounted to little more than a bizarre "national-psychological experiment"—a truly German soprano would surely have made a more authentic Bayreuth Elsa. Shaw was also on hand, and his critique, if full of typical Shavian feminist prejudices and tinged with an anti-American bias, is at least informed and flavorful:

> Those who have seen Nordica as Elsa in London, and who have perhaps been struck with the characteristically American shallowness and limpidity in her of the sort of sentiment of which German women possess such turbid oceanic depths, and with a certain want of color and variety of tone in the voice which she produces so skilfully, will hardly realize the effect she made here, especially at her first entrance and in the balcony scene in the second act. The unspeakable delight, after all that crude shouting and screaming in *Parsifal*, of hearing a perfectly formed voice, responding to the lightest touch, and able to caress a phrase in turning it, was as manna in the desert to starving men. That was the whole secret of it.
>
> For the rest, Nordica is built in the American way, not in the Germanic Elsa way. She was graceful, skilful, clever, at times excitable; but she was not sentimental, not naïve; and she was charming with the active charm of a capable, intelligent woman rather than with the passive appeal of the freshness and helplessness of youth. Her stage business was too well done for the age of the part: and from the latter half of the second act onward she frankly made Elsa a highly civilized modern woman of not less than twenty-seven, marrying a comparatively green Lohengrin.

However she may have divided the critics, Nordica once again captured the attention of the international opera world. One offstage incident has become legendary, a putdown that circled the globe almost immediately after it occurred. One afternoon, after a reception at Wahnfried, Nordica approached the formidable Lilli Lehmann. "May I come to see you, Madame Lehmann," Nordica asked humbly. "I am not taking any pupils this season," came the frosty reply. An arrogant woman but clearly no fool, Lehmann must have recognized a worthy rival and kindred spirit when she saw one—Nordica was unquestionably her equal in versatility, vocal grit, and sheer industry. Perhaps her retort, always cited as a classic example of prima-donna bitchery, was actually meant as a compliment.

Nordica hardly required Lehmann's approval after her Elsa at Bayreuth and Isolde at the Met. She had also become a bride once again, having finally married Döme in Chicago at the end of the 1895–96 season. The life of a diva seldom runs smoothly, however, and in November there were headlines in the New York papers: OPERA WITHOUT NORDICA! Just a week before the Met was to open, the soprano announced that she would not appear with the company as scheduled, having learned that Brünnhilde in the upcoming production of Wagner's *Siegfried*, long promised to her, would be sung by Nellie Melba. As she told the *New York Sun*, "I learned to my amazement that Mme. Melba got the role through the interference of Mr. Jean de Reszke. I was much wounded at heart when I heard the news as though I had been struck a blow in the face. But Mme. Melba was very proud of the fact, and told it everywhere. Mr. de Reszke wrote her a letter last summer after leaving London, advising her to study the part, and used his influence with Mr. Grau to see that it was assigned to her. He is a powerful man, and his support means a great deal. I was thunderstruck. I had supposed that Mr. de Reszke was my friend. I thought that we had gone hand in hand here through the success of *Tristan und Isolde*, and to learn that he had been instrumental in preventing my having the leading Wagnerian roles was more of a shock than I can tell you."

Nordica never came right out and said what many thought—that the idea of the light-voiced Melba singing Brünnhilde was truly ludicrous—but she did feel that after her Isolde and Bayreuth season she did have a legitimate claim on any future Wagner repertory at the Met. Furthermore, she was not even making an issue of an inequitable fee scale that gave her $1,000 a performance when Melba received $1,200, Emma Calvé got $1,400, and De Reszke, who was guaranteed a percentage of the house, could pocket at least $5,000 every time he sang. Nordica created a sensation by airing all this dirty operatic laundry in public, and everyone had a theory to explain what had happened. Some said it was all a mistake—De Reszke must have actually urged Melba to sing the Forest Bird. Others felt that the tenor had intentionally tricked Melba into thinking she could sing Brünnhilde, who appears only at the end of the opera, fresh and rested after Siegfried has been singing all evening. Nordica, they said, would have been sure to show him up, while Melba was bound to fail—which she did, spectacularly ("I was a fool," Melba said in her dressing room after her disastrous performance; "I will never do it again"). Of course, everyone denied everything, and Nordica went off on a cross-country concert tour. Naturally the big number on her program was the final scene from *Siegfried*, which she sang with great success in cities from New York to San Francisco.

Eventually the rift with De Reszke was breached, thanks mainly to the conductor Anton Seidl, who could not bear to see his Tristan and Isolde separated. Nordica never bore ill will toward Melba—the two had been friends for years, and would remain so. Meanwhile, Nordica continued to add Wagner to her repertory, singing her first *Götterdämmerung* Brünnhilde with the Damrosch company in Philadelphia on January 11, 1898, followed by *Die Walküre* less than four weeks later at the Met, when Damrosch brought his troupe to the house, which had no resident company in the 1897–98 season. When the Met reopened under Maurice Grau's aegis in November 1898, Nordica appeared in *Siegfried*, at last, on December 16. Between January 12 and 24, the Met performed its first uncut *Ring* cycle, although the three Brünnhildes were shared by Nordica, Lehmann, and Brema, apparently without any complaints.

By now Nordica was more than an opera star—she was a celebrity who looked and acted like one. On tour she had her own private railroad car. She had closets full of magnificent gowns designed by Worth, sable and velvet capes, and diamond tiaras that, along with her aigrettes, had virtually become a trademark. The one thorn in all this—and many had predicted it from the start—was Zoltán Döme, who had more or less given up singing to live off his rich wife. What he had not given up was philandering, and eventually his infidelities, not to mention his constant need for cash, precipitated a showdown. Nordica summoned Döme to her lawyer's office, where, according to one newspaper report, "at the sight of the soprano, whose income is so great, the agitated husband fainted." That was followed by a suicide attempt and eventually threats to shoot the soprano if she ever again appeared on a New York stage. "It is difficult," mused Walter Damrosch before conducting a Wagner concert with Nordica in Carnegie Hall, "to sing looking down the barrel of a gun." The matter dragged on until the courts finally granted the unhappy couple a divorce in February 1904.

In November of that year Nordica added Kundry and, four days later, Gioconda to her repertory—the last new roles she was to learn.

For the next ten years she toured ceaselessly, fought with the Metropolitan's new general manager, Giulio Gatti-Casazza—she left the company in 1909, never to sing opera in New York again—dreamed of establishing an American Bayreuth at Harmon, on the Hudson River, took up the cause of women's suffrage, and married for a third time: George Washington Young, a wealthy New Jersey banker and corporation director. None of these extramusical activities turned out well, especially the marriage. Nordica soon discovered that Young had been losing millions in the stock market, and much of it was her money. She also discovered that Young had been gradually replacing the precious stones in her diamond tiaras with paste. Writing to her sister, Nordica admitted that she had once again been "duped, betrayed, deceived, and abused" by a man. She was, she said philosophically, "just a poor picker of husbands." Nordica was hardly the first or last singer to find true happiness and success only when giving a performance onstage.

Saddest of all for posterity, the recordings that Nordica made for the Columbia Phonograph Company in New York between 1906 and 1911 turned out badly and do her scant justice. More than forty titles were known to have been recorded, but the results proved to be so inadequate that only twenty-two were published. Part of the problem was Columbia's technical know-how, far inferior in those days to G&T's in England and Victor's in New York. Then, too, some voices tended to be flattered by the acoustical process, while others could never be comfortably accommodated by the horn. Here again Nordica proved to be unlucky. "Her voice was huge," wrote critic Henry T. Finck; "the biggest orchestra could not submerge it in its tidal waves of sound," although Finck went on to say that Nordica's soprano was also "as beautiful, as smooth, mellow, velvety and luscious as the voice of any prima donna I have ever heard." Very little of this can be perceived on her commercial records. Even Herman Klein, who had been hired by Columbia as a "musical advisor" and persuaded Nordica to make her records, admitted defeat after listening to the playbacks. "The voice sounded thin and 'pinched' and even muffled in tone," he wrote; "in fact, so little like the original organ that one could scarcely recognize the timbre, much less the breadth and sonority, of one of the finest Elsas I have ever heard."

Although at times requiring even more "creative" listening, the surviving examples of Nordica on the famous Mapleson cylinders are a far more impressive representation of her voice. Not much, unfortunately, can be gleaned from the *Huguenots* duet performed on March 11, 1901, with Jean de Reszke (even at that there is still enough sound left in the grooves to produce a few shivers as the tenor makes his heady ascent to the high C-flat). The rest of Nordica's Mapleson legacy is all Wagner: Brünnhilde's battle cry (two versions, January 16 and February 21, 1903) and fragments from Act III of *Die Walküre* (February 21, 1903), excerpts from the *Tristan* love duet with Georg Anthes and Ernestine Schumann-Heink (February 9, 1903), a savoring of Isolde's Liebestod from two performances (January 7 and February 9, 1903), and bits from two Immolation Scenes (January 23 and February 28, 1903).

If anyone needs proof of Nordica's power, spot-on intonation, and gleaming tone, Brünnhilde's "Ho-yo-to-ho" will provide it—a truly staggering display of vocal self-assurance. Her Liebestod is phrased with an extraordinary plasticity that few Isoldes have ever matched, a noble interpretation that corresponds exactly to critic W. J. Henderson's memories of Nordica's Isolde, a recollection he wrote in 1937: "Nordica was not tempestuously temperamental and she had not a grand tragic voice. Her vocal tone was one of the most limpid, floating kind, exquisitely poised and possessing a singular bird-like quality, yet always giving the impression of largeness. But the woman was all brains. She sang Isolde so intelligently, so opulently in respect of gradation, subtlety of tone and significant treatment of text, that she left the hearer convinced that this was the real Irish princess of the drama; not a rampant passion in woman's garb, but a sensitive, responsive, and rational being, quite capable of giving herself for love, though hardly likely to suffer any agonies as a punishment for sin. Her singing was like Mme. Flagstad's, beautiful in tonal quality, sustained and exquisitely molded phrasing, and nobility of style."

The commercial records may not communicate quite the frisson of the Mapleson cylinders, but they are still precious. And it is extraordinary to hear this Isolde, in 1911 and at the age of fifty-three, sing Philine's coloratura showpiece from *Mignon* with such flair and so confidently decorate Leonora's "Tacea la notte" from *Il Trovatore* with the elaborate ornaments that her great predecessor Therese Tietjens had used back in the 1860s. The Wagner selections are admittedly disappointing after hearing the live versions from the Met, and her rhythmic freedom occasionally results in some weird dislocations—scarcely one measure of Strauss's song "Ständchen" is in the same tempo. Perhaps Nordica's most famous record is a selection from an opera she never sang—Elisabeth's aria from Erkel's *Hunyadi László*, possibly a leftover sou-

venir from her marriage to the Hungarian Zoltán Döme. It's an extravagant coloratura-dramatic tour de force in which Nordica, fearlessly and
exuberantly, attacks a series of runs and staccatos, eventually ascending
to a high B before tossing off a stunning climactic trill.

By the time she came to make her records, Nordica was nearing the
end. Her fights with opera managers in New York, Boston, and Chicago
were partly the inevitable conflict between a prima donna who had seen
better days and impresarios who did not have the nerve to tell her
outright that perhaps the time had come to retire. She couldn't stop,
though, despite fading vocal resources and the increasing discomforts of
rheumatism. David Bispham traveled with her in 1911 and he tells a sad
tale:

> Madame Nordica was determined and brave, living up to her
> undertakings in spite of everything, and on her last tour of the
> United States was so ill, during several concerts we gave jointly,
> that she could hardly reach the concert room. An extemporized
> and comfortable retreat was arranged for her behind the scenes,
> for dressing rooms are proverbially dirty in most theatres. The
> poor lady could scarcely struggle to her feet, but once up she
> went on unflinchingly behind the disguise of rouge, beautiful
> gowns, and jewels to sing to audiences that adored her, doing
> her best in selections suited to her waning vocal powers. Com-
> ing off she sank into her easy chair, almost crying with pain, but
> when the audience thundered in delight she said to me, "My
> favorite tree has always been tre-mendous applause. Listen to
> that! I must go and sing to them again; that is worth any suffer-
> ing!" Once she added, "Do you think now I am getting old I
> should be doing this if I didn't have to?"

Clearly Nordica always had to, but at least she was spared the pain
of making a fool of herself by parlaying the shreds of a once glorious
instrument or, like Fremstad, spending her old age in idle, unhappy
retirement. In June 1913 she set sail for her first tour of Australia and the
South Seas. Plagued by fatigue and neuritis, the soprano forged ahead
with a punishing schedule until she gave her last concert in Melbourne
on November 25. After that, the plan was to voyage from Sydney to
Java, then north to East Asia and westward via the Trans-Siberian railroad to Russia, London, and home. One wonders if Nordica had plunged

into this grueling itinerary with the actual intention of making a real-life Wagnerian immolation. Perhaps, but the gods had a longer, crueler death in mind. While sailing to Java, Nordica's ship encountered a hurricane and struck a coral reef in the Torres Strait on December 27, and during rescue operations that eventually brought the passengers to Thursday Island, Nordica came down with pneumonia. She lingered for weeks in a local hospital before being removed to Batavia (now Jakarta), where she died on May 10.

It was an ironic tropical death for a Yankee diva from Maine. But then, very little ever worked out well for her during a hard-lived life—except, of course, that glorious voice. Even her ashes were inappropriately placed in Young's family plot in the New York Bay Cemetery, Jersey City, New Jersey. As she lay dying, Nordica had some last requests for her memorial service: an orchestra to play Siegfried's funeral music, a baritone to sing Wotan's Farewell, and a guest speaker to say, "She did her damnedest." None of this happened either, "probably because," as one of her most fervent admirers once observed, "Lillian Nordica could no longer do her damnedest to see that it was done."

After losing her voice in 1836, Charlotte Cushman became a noted actress, famous for such male roles as Shakespeare's Romeo. (CHARLES D. FREDRICKS)

Born in New York in 1818 and for many years a favorite of Parisian operagoers, Dolorès Nau failed to impress her compatriots when she came home to sing in 1854. (MEADE BROTHERS)

When Boston soprano Eliza Biscaccianti arrived in San Francisco in 1852, she was an anomaly—an American prima donna—and the townsfolk greeted her as "a sibyl of harmony and delight."

A child star in her hometown of Boston, contralto Adelaide Phillipps grew up to be the first American singer to pursue a fully rounded operatic career. (JOHN S. NOTMAN)

Daughter of a New York banker, Cora de Wilhorst defied her father, married an impoverished German nobleman, and went on the opera stage in 1857. (SILLSBEE, CASE & CO.)

Taxing soprano roles like Violetta soon took a toll on the voice of Genevieve Ward (aka Genevra Guerrabella) in the 1860s; like Cushman, she turned to acting. (CHARLES D. FREDRICKS)

America's self-proclaimed first prima donna, Clara Louise Kellogg set aside the bel canto repertory to sing modern heroines like Verdi's Aida and soon paid the price. (WARREN'S PORTRAITS)

Annie Louise Cary, who often sang Amneris opposite Kellogg's Aida, was extravagantly admired by critics for her range of over three octaves. (MORA)

An indefatigable barn-stormer in the 1880s, Emma Abbott is about to exchange the famous, but chaste, "Abbott kiss" with tenor William Castle in Massé's *Paul et Virginie*. (GILBERT & BACON)

Emma Albani, "the Canadian Songstress," became a favorite of Queen Victoria's after the fabled Adelina Patti left her husband and eloped with a married man. (H. ROCHER)

Soprano Emma Thursby never sang in opera, but as the country's first concert singer she earned a fortune from her world tours, often sharing a program with the Norwegian violinist Ole Bull. (WEBER)

America's first international operatic superstar, Minnie Hauk sang everywhere, knew everybody, and took her impersonation of Carmen around the world. (MORA)

Charles R. Adams, as Tannhäuser, was a principal tenor at the Vienna Hofoper before he returned home in 1877 to teach dozens of young American singers.
(H. ROCHER)

The baritone David Bispham, who styled himself as a "Quaker Singer," commanded narrative skills in both opera and concert that held audiences in America and England spellbound.

The "Yankee Diva" Lillian Nordica created a sensation when she sang her first Isolde, opposite Jean de Reszke, at the Metropolitan Opera in 1895.
(DUPONT)

The beauteous, if notoriously chilly, Emma Eames achieved instant fame at age twenty-three in 1889 as Gounod's choice to sing Juliette for her Paris Opéra debut.

An incandescently charismatic singer, Olive Fremstad sang one scandalous Salome at the Met in 1907 and the opera was immediately removed from the stage.

After she created Delibes's Lakmé in 1883, Marie van Zandt from Brooklyn became the toast of Paris and "the spoiled child of the Opéra-Comique." (CHARLES BERGAMASCO)

The ill-fated Sibyl Sanderson inspired Massenet to write the role of Esclarmonde for her, an impersonation that was second only to the Eiffel Tower as the major attraction of Paris's 1889 Universal Exhibition. (BENQUE & CO.)

Delibes also coached Pauline L'Allemand in *Lakmé,* but the pressures of her unhappy life eventually unhinged the soprano and brought her to an insane asylum in Wisconsin. (FALK)

Louise Homer, the Met's leading contralto in the early 1900s, was a warm, inviting presence, even as the jealous Amneris in *Aida*.
(PHOTO BY DUPONT/METROPOLITAN OPERA ARCHIVES)

Debussy felt that "the Divine" Mary Garden had been sent to him "from the mists of the north" to create his otherworldly Mélisande.
(PAUL BERGER)

Geraldine Farrar chose
Leoncavallo's glamorous
music-hall singer, Zazà, to
be the role of her deliriously
acclaimed Met farewell in
1922. (METROPOLITAN OPERA
ARCHIVES)

In 1918 at age twenty-one,
Rosa Ponselle made one of the
Met's great Cinderella debuts
when she sang Leonora in *La
Forza del Destino* opposite
Caruso. (MISHKIN)

America's most beloved concert singer during and after World War I, Alma Gluck earned a fortune from her bestselling Victor Red Seal recordings. (UNDERWOOD & UNDERWOOD)

One of her generation's great originals and a Greenwich Village legend by the 1930s, Eva Gauthier introduced New Yorkers to the new music of Bartók, Falla, Schoenberg, and Poulenc. (ELLIOTT & FRY)

After her local debut in 1921, soprano Edith Mason continually enchanted Chicagoans while the rest of the world envied the city's luck in having the services of such an enchanting singer.

Known as "the Black Patti" and the singing star of her own troupe of "troubadours," Sissieretta Jones was a national celebrity by the turn of the century.

Even Nellie Melba wept when she heard the "divine" tenor of Roland Hayes, America's first internationally acclaimed black concert singer.

The young Marian Anderson, soon to prove that a voice such as hers, as Toscanini declared, was heard only once in a hundred years. (D'ARLENE)

The proverbial star of stage, screen, and radio, Grace Moore singlehandedly ushered in "glamour time" at the Metropolitan Opera after her much-publicized debut in 1928. (MISHKIN)

Ziegfeld star Mary Lewis brought more Broadway glamour than vocal distinction to the Met during her brief operatic career in the Roaring Twenties. (PHOTO BY MISHKIN/METROPOLITAN OPERA ARCHIVES)

The epitome of Parisian chic, Lily Pons invariably enchanted her new compatriots with Lakmé's tintinnabulations and "withering mood of ecstasy." (STUDIO LORELLE)

Mezzo-soprano Gladys Swarthout, pictured here in the film *Rose of the Rancho*, may have hated working in Hollywood, but her movies made both her voice and her face famous nationwide. (METROPOLITAN OPERA ARCHIVES)

As famous for his Hollywood films as his Met performances, baritone Lawrence Tibbett greets the audience as Tonio in *Pagliacci*. (PHOTO BY LUMIÈRE/METROPOLITAN OPERA ARCHIVES)

Eight

—

"Last Night There

Was Skating

on the Nile"

~~~~~~~~~~~~~~~~~~~

*A*lthough American singers were beginning to establish a very real presence on the international scene by the 1880s, it was still a struggle—to find proper vocal training, to comprehend the idiomatic performance styles of many foreign cultures, to keep pace with changing musical fashions, and, above all, to gain acceptance at home and abroad in a competitive field dominated by Europeans. But many more battles were being won. If Emma Eames did not exactly sail serenely to stardom, she could at least set out on a path that had been well trodden by her predecessors.

After completing her studies in Paris with Mathilde Marchesi, Eames began at the top, at the Paris Opéra in 1889 as Gounod's Juliette opposite Jean de Reszke's Roméo, and remained there until she left the Metropolitan in 1909 at the age of forty-three. At the height of her fame she had only one real rival—Nellie Melba. Even if Eames was never able to match the Australian diva's technical polish or vocal éclat, she offered formidable competition in the favorite lyric-coloratura roles of the day, while her more dramatically weighted instrument was far better suited to deal with the heavier demands of late Verdi, early Wagner, and Puccini's sensational new heroine, Tosca. Had she possessed Nordica's glowing health and stamina and had not retired so young, Eames might eventually have followed her older colleague's example by adding Brünnhilde, Isolde, and Kundry to her repertory.

Yet despite her vocal talent, physical beauty, and cleverness in managing her career, Emma Eames lacked a certain something, the one ingredient that might have made her a beloved artist rather than just a respected one. Some would have called it personal warmth. It was critic James G. Huneker, who, after being chilled by a Met *Aida* with Eames in the title role, made the famous remark "Last night there was skating on the Nile." Indeed, Eames's reputation as a cold performer runs like a leitmotiv throughout her professional life. Shaw noted her unruffled self-possession as early as 1894 when he saw the soprano as Charlotte in Massenet's *Werther*, and his comments are as devastating as they are priceless:

Whoever has not seen Miss Eames as Charlotte has not realized the full force of Thackeray's picture of the young lady who, when she saw the remains of her lover "Borne before her on a shutter / Like a well-conducted person, / Went on cutting bread and butter."

I never saw such a well-conducted person as Miss Eames. She casts her propriety like a Sunday frock over the whole stage, and gives Mr. Stedman's choirboys, as she cuts the bread and butter for them, a soapy nosed, plastery haired, respectable-aged-mothered appearance which they totally lack in *Carmen* under the influence of Calvé. Like Goldsmith's hero in *She Stoops to Conquer*, I am ill at ease in the company of ladylike women; and during the first act of *Werther* at Covent Garden I grew shyer and more awkward in my stall, until, upon Charlotte informing Werther that she was another's, I felt ready to sink into the earth with confusion. In the third act, when Werther, breaking down under the strain of a whole year's unintermitted well-behavedness, desperately resolved to have a kiss, and to that end offered the young lady violence, the whole audience shared the chills with which he was visibly struggling. Never, since Miss Mary Anderson [an American actress of great beauty and haughty mien but limited talent] shed a cold radiance on the rebuked stage, have virtue and comeliness seemed more awful than they do at Covent Garden on *Werther* nights. How I envy Miss Eames her self-possession, her quiet consciousness of being founded on a rock, her good looks (oh those calmly regular eyebrows!), and, above all, that splendid middle to her voice, enabling her to fill the huge theatre without an effort!

Shaw was clearly so struck by Eames's singular stage persona that he neglected to say much about her singing, save for that backhanded complimentary coda. But then, Charlotte is hardly a showy role. Perhaps the best description we have of how Eames's voice sounded and how it worked is the soprano's own, which she gladly offered during a broadcast of her recordings in 1939, the fiftieth anniversary of her operatic debut. In her prime, Eames said frankly, her voice was a thing of exquisite purity, lovely in quality, and "very flexible, with a natural trill and chromatic scale and a big working range from A below the line to C-sharp above and an even scale throughout. Nevertheless, I worked hard at my techniques and strove to eliminate every muscular effort unnecessary to the free production of tone, and thus the pronunciation was unfettered and the diction clear. In short, my technique had to be so sure that I was left free to think only of the feeling of the thoughts to be projected."

Those records do, in fact, reveal a far more expressive and intense vocal personality than contemporary criticism suggests. No doubt Eames was a cool presence whose impersonal grandeur must have contrasted markedly with the more natural and realistic manner of the younger generation, such smoldering singing actresses as Mary Garden and Geraldine Farrar. But she was also one of the last singers taught to uphold the classical ideals and disciplined training of Marchesi, who herself was a pupil of Manuel García II. When Eames moved from the lyrical ingénue heroines of Gounod to flamboyant roles like Tosca, she was bound to present a restrained portrait that seemed tame next to the incendiary emotionalism generated by the new Italian school. And yet Puccini himself saw her Tosca in Paris in 1904 and was fascinated. Eames, he said, was unique—rather haughty and aloof perhaps, but still a moving figure of self-contained dignity and pathos, the only Tosca in his experience who suggested and actually struck a note of Greek tragedy. Also a connoisseur of women, Puccini surely appreciated one point upon which no one disagreed: Eames was one of opera's great beauties.

At the age of sixty and long since retired, the soprano wrote her memoirs. Inevitably self-serving and all too eager to settle old scores, they are still more shrewdly observant and elegantly written than most examples of the genre and reveal much of her true character—sometimes perhaps more of it than even Eames realized. The first five years of her life were spent in Shanghai, where she was born on August 13, 1865, the daughter of Ithamar Eames, a Boston lawyer practicing in China, and his wife, Emma Hayden Eames from Bath, Maine. The Eames family lived in a typical Chinese bungalow on Bubbling Well Road, leading to the Rain God's temple—a fairy-tale setting where Emma and her older brother, Hayden, led a secluded, fantasy childhood. Although she never returned to China as an adult, Emma treasured special memories. One was of a Chinese butler who once saved her life by applying mouth-to-mouth resuscitation when she had been given up for dead after a bout of pneumonia. "I have always felt," she later wrote, "that I owed my passionate love of beauty and grace to the fact that he may have breathed into me a small part of a Chinese soul to keep me sweet in an atmosphere in which I had to live later, of rigid, loveless, cruel Puritanism."

Another childhood incident that Eames claimed provided a key to her personality occurred when her Chinese nurse attempted to put some pretty openwork silk socks on her kicking feet. Emma howled, but "being at the inarticulate age I could not explain that it was because the openwork part hurt my feet. It is a catastrophe to be so sensitive. I was always so, in mind and heart as well as body. Mentally and spiritually I have always been like a person who walked through a crowd on tender feet and dreaded their being bruised; a fact that explains, perhaps, why so many called me cold, aloof, proud. My dread of being hurt had thrown up a wall of great reserve about me without my being conscious of it."

That tender little soul left China when her mother fell ill and the family returned to the Eames estate in Portland, Maine. There Emma lived quietly until the age of eleven and an unfortunate turn in her father's financial affairs made it necessary to "give up one child," as the soprano later put it with unconcealed bitterness. Mrs. Eames packed her youngest off to her maternal grandparents in nearby Bath, where Emma was placed under the eagle-eyed care of her grandmother Hayden, "a woman of great force of character, with a sense of humor, but a warped emotional nature . . . She was a woman of fine mind, deeply founded principles and Puritanical standards, but withal human and passionate. And passionate, alas! to the point of having actual brain storms, during which all her ideals of conduct would be thrown to the winds. I learned how unlovely such exhibitions were and determined that the same wild impulses within myself should be curbed and directed. Even at this day I prefer not to remember the moments that inspired that resolution."

The future diva did admit that her severe upbringing had some rewards. She later came to appreciate the difference between real and self pride after being instilled with a strong sense of honor and self-respect, "even though it implanted in my breast an unattainable ideal of conduct that in later years caused me much unnecessary self-condemnation." Meanwhile, Emma channeled her animal spirits into tomboy activities, mostly "playing theater" and getting into trouble at school, and singing. Soon Emma's mother noticed that her daughter might have a voice worth cultivating. At the age of seventeen she was sent off to Boston for serious musical study, including piano instruction from an impetuous young man, "the blackest of black Germans," who taught Emma a great deal about Beethoven when he was not urging the teenager to marry him.

When she heard about those unwelcome attentions, and perhaps feeling guilty at neglecting her daughter as a child, Mrs. Eames moved to Boston to chaperone Emma and oversee her higher education. Already an independent spirit, this self-assured girl hardly seemed in need of supervision, and in any case, romance was not on her agenda. The days were filled mainly with voice lessons from Clara Munger; singing engagements in the local churches; an occasional bit of informal operatic experience—Eames, too, got her start in the busy classroom of tenor Charles R. Adams, performing Marguerite in the Garden Scene from *Faust;* and providing vocal illustrations for the lectures of John Knowles Paine, Harvard's first professor of music. She also attended concerts by the new Boston Symphony under George Henschel and Wilhelm Gericke, and saw her first operatic performances: *Lohengrin,* in Italian, with Nilsson and Campanini, and *Martha* and *Semiramide* with Patti. The fabled Adelina, decided Emma, already a severe judge, "had perfection of vocal art, of rhythm, of finish, of proportion, of charm, but she had the soul of a soubrette and in temperament was suited only to such rôles as Martha, Zerlina, and Rosina . . ."

In addition to her vocal studies with Munger, Emma had also begun to study the Delsarte "system of gesture and devitalization" with Miss Annie Payson Call, who taught the budding opera singer how to make each muscle of her body independent in order to achieve maximum effect through a minimum of effort. "This way lay grace," Emma later declared, and perhaps unconsciously explained why some thought her manner excessively chilly. "The hand of a child is always perfectly graceful, because there is no nervous tension. Therefore, to learn to have an entirely graceful hand, one must remove all conscious muscular effort from the hand and have the entire gesture proceed from the solar plexus, the seat of feeling. When one has this control and one's gestures are placed, one has only to feel the gesture for it to come of itself . . . I studied to such good effect that when I made my debut at the Paris Opéra, I had such possession of my body and such ease of movement and freedom of gesture that it was difficult to convince Gounod that I had never acted before."

By the time of her debut Emma also had two solid years of Marchesi training to draw upon, although she later claimed that her famous teacher's methods had actually done little to help her. In 1886, when she arrived in Paris, the celebrated école de chant on the Rue Jouffroy was already turning out many famous singers, a list that included such étoiles as Nellie Melba, Emma Calvé, Selma Kurz, Sibyl Sanderson, and Gabrielle Krauss. Born in Frankfurt in 1821, Mathilde Graumann had a brief career as a concert singer until 1852, when she married Salvatore Marchesi, an Italian baritone and singing teacher. The couple eventually settled in Paris, where Mathilde set up shop in 1881 to teach what she and her husband had learned from García. Her method differed from her mentor's in its preoccupation with placement, that is, placing the voice as high as possible on the breath in order to project the upper octave with as much brilliance as possible. Like so many specialized vocal techniques, Marchesi's worked better for some singers than for others. Melba, her most celebrated pupil, took to it naturally, but sopranos with a less responsive mechanism and weaker upper registers soon developed problems with the top voice.

Some historians feel that Eames belonged to the latter group, and that the loss of her upper notes precipitated her early retirement as much, if not more, than what she always said was her long-held decision to leave the stage at forty. In any case, there was little love lost between Eames and Marchesi after Emma's career took off, and in the soprano's memoirs her teacher is recalled as the ideal Prussian drillmaster, a woman of much character and one to gain a great ascendancy over her pupils . . . She herself was at her piano by nine in the morning every week day, was always perfectly and rather richly dressed and with never a hair out of place . . . She had intelligence and the real German efficiency, but no intuition. She had a head for business which, with her excellent musicianship gave her the position she occupied for so many years—that of owner, manager and teacher of the greatest school of her day.

That was fair enough, but Eames went on to say, incorrectly, that Marchesi

trained the voice to have three distinct registers, instead of one perfectly even in scale, in which the tones of each register melt into the next, as do the colors in a prism, which is the only logical way to sing. She believed, too, that a woman should not pronounce words above F in the medium, while I always felt that if a man could pronounce words on the highest notes in his voice, why not a woman? Owing to this conviction of hers, the voices of her pupils, such as Gerster's, gave the impression of ventriloquism, and sounded as though their owners had been taught to sing with a dropped larynx, which was indeed what we were told to do. Madame Marchesi fortunately did not attempt to change my natural singing method, and as my voice was a healthy one, she did it no harm, but neither did she give me that absolute vocal security which I was to gain for myself later.

At this point in time, it is difficult to separate Eames's resentment of Marchesi and her utter detestation of Melba, the "Prussian drillmaster's" favorite pupil. The crack about "ventriloquism" was obviously aimed in Melba's direction, since some never did care for the detached, vibrato-less resonance of her brilliant upper register. When Eames published her memoirs in 1927, it had been less than a year since Melba made her farewell, and feelings between the two sopranos still ran high. Eames writes that she was prepared to make her debut at the Monnaie in Brussels during the winter of 1887–88 until Melba, who already had a two-year contract at the theater, plotted successfully to keep her off the stage. Throughout her book, Eames never once refers to Melba by name, only to "that singer who had prevented my debut in Brussels," a hated rival destined to dog her life like some sort of evil genius. It all began in Paris, when Melba whispered poisonous gossip in Marchesi's ear, bad-mouthed her to Gounod, and even visited Eames after her tremendously successful debut as Juliette to criticize her singing.

Much of what Eames writes was probably true—Melba never cared for singers who encroached on what she considered her prerogatives—but after that first Juliette, nothing could stop this career. According to the Paris critics, Eames had sung rather well, and perhaps she had more to thank Marchesi for than she was willing to admit. Mathilde's daughter, Blanche—a Marchesi pupil herself, if hardly one of her mother's major triumphs—saw the soprano's debut and had a few things to say about what Eames owed her teacher:

> When Eames entered in the first act she looked so radiant, so graceful, so indescribably beautiful that it seemed as if Spring had taken human form and come down to earth. Her success was assured before she had opened her mouth, but when she sang her waltz the whole house rose; a scene of enthusiasm was witnessed unparalleled since the day of the great Krauss. Deeply moved, my mother asked my husband to accompany her behind the wings, so that she might congratulate her pupil. When they entered the dressing-room, my mother's emotion was so great that she nearly fell into Emma Eames's arms, thinking to find in her the same whirlwind of sentiments. To her amazement, Emma Eames was completely self-possessed, as cool as ice-cream, chaffing my mother about her emotion, and instead of covering her hands with kisses, as Krauss and all the pupils of the older generation would have done, she calmly said: "Oh, but, my dear madame, do not get so nervous. I am perfectly happy, and you have no idea how much I have learned here in these last few weeks." Thus all these years of work and toil were forgotten in an instant . . . My mother felt the shock these words gave to her loving heart for long years, and in fact she never recovered from it.

Eames, of course, blamed Melba for stirring up bad blood between her and Marchesi, and only many years later, after an *Aida* in London, did she fall into her old teacher's arms and bury the hatchet. After her wildly acclaimed debut, though, Eames had more pressing matters to consider. Her Juliette was so popular at the Opéra that she sang ten performances in one month, later adding Marguerite to her repertory. The following season, she created two roles—Colombe in Saint-Saëns's new opera, *Ascanio,* and the title part in *Zaïre* by Paul Véronge de la Nux—but she already felt unhappy about her work. She turned down Ophélie in Thomas's *Hamlet* as unsuited to her voice, and to show just how magnanimous she could be, Eames suggested that "the singer who had prevented my debut in Brussels" would be a perfect choice for the part. Melba accepted and had a grand success, but her continued intriguing, real or imagined, helped make Eames's second year in Paris "more or less of a nightmare." By now Eames was also romantically involved with Julian Story, a young American artist with a distinguished lineage, the grandson of the jurist Joseph Story and son of the poet and sculptor William Story. Since Mrs. Eames strenuously objected to the match, Emma's personal life had become as tense as her career.

Sensing that a change of environment and public would be just the thing to reinvigorate her, Eames decided to move on. Since impresarios were already knocking on her door, giving her the option to pick and choose, she accepted an engagement at London's Covent Garden during the spring of 1891 to sing Marguerite, along with such flattering roles as Elsa, Desdemona, and Gounod's Mireille. Eames also decided that the time was ripe for a triumphant return home, especially since she had an offer from the Metropolitan in New York, which was planning its first gala season that fall under the aegis of Grau, Abbey, and Schoeffel. Meanwhile, the day after her first performance in London of Verdi's *Otello,* Eames and Story were married with the blessings of the Prince of Wales, who had become a devoted fan and friend. Emma's mother was only apprised of the ceremony after it was over—it took her nine months to recover, but by then Mrs. Eames had long become resigned to her daughter's willful ways.

After her London season, Eames spent the summer resting up for her American debut with Grau's Metropolitan troupe, which opened in Chicago for a short preseason tour. Eames's first appearance in opera on her native soil was as Elsa in *Lohengrin* on November 9, 1891, and she must have been distressed by criticism that brushed her off as "charming, but not a great artist." Since the evening also marked the eagerly anticipated American debuts of Jean and Édouard de Reszke, Eames inevitably had to take second place, but a few nights afterward she offered her famous

Juliette and the Chicago critics recanted immediately: yes, she was charming, but as Gounod's teenage heroine she was also deemed gorgeous and a magnificent artist. A month later, on December 14, Eames and the De Reszke brothers opened the Met season in the same opera. Again *le beau Jean* claimed most of the press's attention, although Henderson in the *Times* paid Eames some polite compliments. In the *Tribune*, Krehbiel was more guarded. "Miss Eames," the latter grudgingly wrote, "is not a great artist, nor yet a ripe artist, but a singer of good intuitions and fine gifts."

Like so many singers past and present, Eames claimed that she never read notices of her singing, so perhaps the rather lukewarm critical reception hardly ruffled her celebrated composure. For her part, the soprano heard the applause, noted the ticket receipts, and serenely claimed that "in Grau's 'star company,' to the astonishment of every one, and to my own more than anybody's, I, who was comparatively a beginner, proved to be the greatest drawing card of the season." And perhaps she really was. At any rate, Eames was glad to be home, enchanted by the life, gaiety, and energy of New York society: the Patriarch's Balls, horse shows, grand suppers at Delmonico's, and the many private dinner parties given in her honor as a new Met star and new bride. The soprano draws a discreet veil over her relationship with Story. Whatever passion there may originally have been in their marriage probably evaporated early on—until divorced in 1907, the two were often on different continents for months at a time—but in 1891 Story's wealth and social connections must have seemed enough.

Now Eames's career had begun in earnest, and for the next sixteen years she divided her time between New York and London, with occasional restful periods at her elegantly appointed homes in Paris and Italy. There were interruptions. A fire destroyed the Met auditorium and canceled the 1892–93 season; more "machinations" by "that soprano" threatened her cordial relationship with Grau and kept her away from New York in 1895–96; "absurd" proposals to sing lesser roles finally led to a rupture with Covent Garden in 1901; and often Eames found herself laid up for months, suffering from what her physicians termed nervous exhaustion. Her initial confrontation with Tosca threatened to be her last. After her first appearance in the role at the Met on December 12, 1902, Henderson granted that it was better than he had expected but harped on a familiar motif: "There is no blood in her performance. It was impeccable in design, icy in execution . . . lyric sweetness . . . perfect poise . . . the lovely but immobile face . . . were elements in a portrait of surpassing beauty but not of tortured womanhood." The effort it cost to sing and act Tosca must have drained Eames, since she managed only three more performances before succumbing to a mysterious ailment—Henderson diagnosed it as "Toscalitis"—one that kept her away from the Met for another season.

In her memoirs Eames goes to some lengths to defend her impersonations and refute the notion that she was an icy performer. Elsa, for example, she conceived as "a medieval princess, sheltered, mentally undeveloped . . . gentle, dreamy, impressionable, poetic, overwhelmed with grief at the loss of her brother and an easy prey for the bullying militant Ortrud." How could such a creature, Eames protests, be portrayed as passionate and explosive? And what about Marguerite, chaste, innocent, and unsuspecting? "That is why I made her fearlessly and directly look at Faust when he accosted her, aware of no evil, but wrapped in poetic dreams. The school of realism destroys all the meaning of such operas; and often the realistic actress is not a reflecting or intelligent artist, but one who prefers to portray her own unbridled self and blow off steam, rather than sink her personality in that of the character she is portraying."

Despite the sense in what Eames says, the soprano's reputation as a cool performer was so widespread that any display of onstage temperament was news. During a performance of *Lohengrin* at the Cincinnati Music Hall in 1906, the Ortrud, Katherine Senger-Bettaque, did something that apparently offended Eames during Act II, and this "gentle" Elsa promptly responded by giving the "militant bullying" Ortrud a resounding slap in the face. Questioned by a reporter after the performance, Senger-Bettaque replied magnanimously, "Oh, I did not resent it. I was really surprised and delighted to see any evidence of emotion in Madame Eames."

Eames's popularity at the turn-of-the-century Met was surely due in large part to the sheer sound of what was unquestionably a quality voice. New York operagoers, then as now, responded primarily to sensual vocal beauty rather than subtle interpretive nuances, in large part because much of the audience could not understand the text. Grau certainly grasped that fact of life, and Eames was vital to him as he assembled one "ideal" cast after another. Appearing with Eames in *Otello* were the two singers chosen by Verdi to create their roles, Francesco Tamagno and Victor Maurel. In the American premiere of the same composer's *Falstaff*

Eames sang Alice Ford with Maurel, Giuseppe Campanari, Sofia Scalchi, and Zélie de Lussan. In 1908 Gustav Mahler conducted a *Don Giovanni* with an exceptionally dazzling cast of eight important singers: Eames (Anna), Johanna Gadski (Elvira), Marcella Sembrich (Zerlina), Antonio Scotti (Giovanni), Alessandro Bonci (Ottavio), Feodor Chaliapin (Leporello), Eugène Dufriche (Masetto), and Robert Blass (Commendatore).

The Metropolitan toured frequently in those days, and with a full complement of stars. The company was visiting San Francisco when the city was rudely awakened one morning by the great earthquake of 1906. Of course, everyone panicked. Enrico Caruso, dreaming that he was back home in Naples, reportedly leapt from his bed, ran to the window, screamed "Monte Vesuvio!" and promptly fled the city. Others reacted less melodramatically. Several hours after the first shock, Olive Fremstad was spotted sitting in a park across the street from her hotel. Apparently in trauma, she held the long-stemmed roses she had received after a performance of *Carmen* the night before, and amid the chaos she quietly pressed them to her breast. Marcella Sembrich, on the other hand, ran weeping from her hotel suite, still in her nightgown, convinced that the world had come to an end.

Eames, unsurprisingly, remained cool and collected. She was staying in the private home of a friend on Nob Hill and had retired early that night, since she was to sing the Countess in *Le Nozze di Figaro* the following afternoon. At 5 A.M. the soprano was startled by a tremendous roaring and rocking. "The pitching developed into more and more abrupt jerks," she recalled, "until the great bed, a heavy mahogany four-poster in which I was lying, was gradually shaken from the wall out into the center of the room." Eames devoted the next thirty pages of her memoirs to a vivid account of how she and her colleagues managed to survive the subsequent devastation and fires, eventually finding a way to leave the stricken city. Luckily, all the musicians managed to escape without serious injury, although the Met suffered a huge financial loss in sets, costumes, properties, and musical instruments. After throwing a few valuables into some bags, a small party consisting of Eames, Sembrich, Pol Plançon, and several other Met musicians set off by foot through the rubble and over hot cobblestones toward North Beach, where they spent the night on blankets by the side of the road. Plançon, that most elegant of French bassos, was still terrified. After being nuzzled awake by a friendly cow ("Emma, quelle est cette horrible bête?"), he marveled anew at Eames's eternal rocklike composure. Finally they found their way across the bay to Oakland, where Eames commandeered an automobile and a driver to transport the bedraggled survivors to what remained of her friend's country home outside San Jose, which had also been badly damaged by the earthquake. There they camped out for several days until communications were restored and the trip back East could be arranged.

By 1907 Eames sensed that her career was winding down and she cast about for one last vehicle, finally settling on Mascagni's *Iris*. Her choice was canny in one respect, since that opera was far better suited to her temperament than Puccini's more theatrical and infinitely more popular operatic excursion to Japan, *Madama Butterfly*. Mascagni's work is practically an abstraction, a delicate allegory about the fragility of art as personified by a pure, tragically ill-used little Japanese girl. "As it entailed a minimum of action," Eames reasoned, "it would be an excellent medium for a demonstration of my theory that thought, clearly directed, has a greater power of moving an audience than any theatricality of gesture." Determined to make her interpretation as authentic as possible, Eames went to Paris to study oriental gestures, costumes, and attitudes with the Japanese actress Sada Yacco. Despite the presence of Enrico Caruso and Antonio Scotti in the cast, however, Eames had to resign herself to a succès d'estime with *Iris*, which, like most of Mascagni's post-*Cavalleria* operas, was tepidly received at its Met premiere, on December 6, 1907.

After her *Iris* experiment, Eames was already two years past forty and her own self-imposed deadline for retirement, an age too old to continue singing the youthful, romantic roles that she had always felt were best fitted to her particular gifts. Then, too, life at the Metropolitan was not the same. Up to 1908 Eames had been one of the company's most pampered and highly paid artists—she always insisted that her fee be paid in gold—and the prospects presented by the new management did not please her. The estimable Grau had retired in 1903, and his obliging successor, Heinrich Conried, an interim figure whose health was failing, resigned after the 1907–08 season. The next leading candidate for the job was La Scala's Giulio Gatti-Casazza, a thoroughly modern professional who would in fact be the Met's first salaried general manager. Gatti also promised to bring with him Arturo Toscanini, already a legend in Italy but as yet virtually unknown in America.

This was all bad news to Eames and many singers of her generation, who felt that one of their own—specifically the more malleable Austrian-born tenor Andreas Dippel, a Met stalwart since 1890—would be a safer choice. "In spite of the record these two Italians had made at La Scala," Eames wrote, "I felt that with their different ideas and psychology they would destroy everything that Grau and Conried had labored so hard to build up, and that whatever practical or commercial good might come of their regime would be offset by the change in operatic ideals." The "two Italians" clearly posed a real artistic and professional threat to Eames, who claimed that her negative attitude was born of neither idle whim nor personal animosity but of "a perfect understanding of Italian operatic ideals." In Italy, she said, singers were treated as if they belonged to a lower order of beings—"the Italians do not feel that intellect or education, even musical education, is necessary to the singer." Obviously to an artist of Eames's sensibilities and background, such a philosophy was intolerable.

Besides, Toscanini thought very little of *Iris* and he promptly canceled the three performances Eames had been scheduled to sing in the 1908–09 season. Worse than that, the Italian conductor, in Eames's view,

left much to be desired by comparison with such great ones as Seidl and Mancinelli. He was charming and amiable, and rehearsed at the piano with me, taking all my shades and intentions. Once before the public, however, the opera was his and his alone. He had such a marvelous and exact memory that he could reproduce always what he had heard one do at any one particular rehearsal, and only that. He detached himself from us thereafter and interpreted his opera, even singing with us so loudly that one heard him on the stage.

Even to such as ourselves, who had an absolute respect for the music as it was written, he allowed no margin for the emotion of the moment, and his conducting was not an accompaniment but a stone wall of resistance to any personality but his own. This is all very well in a symphony conductor, but does not make for the ease and freedom necessary for the interpretation of those who have anything really to give and the authority to communicate it. Caruso and I discussed this and he was absolutely in accord with me in regard to these reasons for the difficulty of singing with Toscanini.

If Caruso really did agree with Eames, he changed his mind soon enough. The great tenor sang frequently with Toscanini in the years to come, and got pretty much whatever he wanted during his Met career. Eames, however, made up her mind to leave quietly, which she did after one last *Tosca* on February 15, 1909, a performance that passed without ceremony, no doubt due to her acrimonious relations with the new regime. Eames was not quite through with opera, though, and she decided to make her last appearances with the Boston Opera Company. "The days of resurrection continue," sighed H. T. Parker, the stern music critic of the *Boston Evening Transcript*, who often signed his glowering notices with the initials H.T.P.—"Hell To Pay" Parker, as Bostonians called him. It was a sentimental occasion for Eames, who felt it only proper to bid the operatic stage adieu in the city where she had pursued her musical education so long ago, and she ventured one more Tosca in 1911, on December 18, and a last Desdemona on December 22. Although the critics noticed that she was now looking a bit matronly, her beautiful face seemed as unchanged as her placid temperament. Distinguished by calmness, serenity, poise, and self-control, said Hale in the *Herald*, Eames was the last singer anyone would think of to portray Tosca. Parker, though, could still rejoice in the sound of this singular voice, "its individual, unique, crystal clearness, the fine bell-like chime of some higher notes, silvery in cool lusters, curiously like chastity in sound."

Now divorced from Story, Eames was married in 1911 to the baritone Emilio de Gogorza, a liaison that, one suspects, was arranged mainly for companionship. Because of his extreme shortsightedness, De Gogorza eschewed the opera stage, preferring to sing only in concert and on records—and with his suave voice and ability to master musical styles of all kinds, he made hundreds of them, under his own name and various pseudonyms, of light music as well as art songs in a variety of languages. Although his parents were Spanish—his father ran a shipping line that plied the seas between Cádiz and Brooklyn, where the baritone was born in 1874—De Gogorza lived most of his life in America. Nine years before he and Eames settled down to enjoy married life, De Gogorza had been named artistic director of the Victor Record Company, overseeing the recording activities of the great opera singers then under contract to the label: Calvé, Caruso, Homer, Farrar, Melba, Sembrich, Scotti, Journet, Gilibert, Campanari—and, finally, Eames, who made a series of recordings for Victor between 1905 and 1911.

Listening to Eames's discs in sequence is instructive, since the results improved as the years passed. The twelve titles made in February and March 1905 find the soprano sounding ill at ease, probably due to unfamiliarity with the recording process. During her little radio talk in 1939, she recalled how awkward she felt before the horn, even in later years when there was an orchestra to accompany her: "To a sensitive person the conditions were unnerving. We had to sing carefully into the very center of a horn to the accompaniment of an orchestra which invariably sounded out of tune, owing to the fact that metal horns were substituted for the wooden sounding-boxes of the violins. In the case of a brilliant and vibrant voice like mine, as one approached the climax, or high note, the climax was turned into an anti-climax for fear of a blast, so-called; one was gently drawn back from the horn, so that instead of a ringing high note one sounded as though one had suddenly retired into the next room. The process so enervated me, that I felt that with even the most satisfactory results, my voice would be diminished and deformed, and the softer vibrations eliminated completely."

Eames was quite right to be worried, for the brilliant vibrancy of her upper register does indeed often sound glaring, although the acoustical recordings of virtually all Marchesi pupils share this trait to some degree—no doubt the "softer vibrations" that would be audible only in an opera house helped take some of the ferocious edge off the tone. It is also clear from the last measures of Tosca's "Vissi d'arte" and the Gounod showpieces from *Faust* and *Roméo* that what Shaw complained about as early as 1891—a lack of free play at the top of the voice—must have always been a problem for Eames, albeit one that she had shrewdly found ways to minimize.

Despite having been coached in the roles by the composer himself, Eames no longer sounds very convincing as Gounod's heroines, and it's hard to accept her recordings, made some twenty-five years after her lessons with Le Maître, as authentic historical documents. Nowadays, as she tells us (i.e., in 1939), this music is seldom sung the way it should be, "absolutely in time and without meaningless holds and ritards"—a statement that hardly jibes with what we hear on her discs, interpretations that are in fact full of meaningless holds and ritards. Perhaps Eames's most persuasive operatic recordings are the two versions of Santuzza's anguished aria from *Cavalleria Rusticana*, especially the first, made on May 14, 1906. Here the tragic nobility of her declamation, as well as the shapely phrasing, gives the music both dignity and a searing pathos that is anything but cold or inexpressive. Even more imposing are the bits from *Tosca* recorded by Mapleson at the Met on January 3, 1903: excerpts from the Act II torture scene with Emilio de Marchi and Antonio Scotti, most of "Vissi d'arte," and the opera's final moments. This was Eames's fourth and last performance that season of the role before she succumbed to "Toscalitis," but there is little to suggest that she is under strain or overparted. One hears very precisely the classicism that Puccini was to admire in the soprano's interpretation as she charges the vocal line with extraordinary dramatic intensity. Luckily, these excerpts are among the clearest and most sonically vivid of the surviving Mapleson cylinders.

The sheer grandeur of Eames's vocal personality can sometimes sound a bit overbearing (in her pairing of "The Star Spangled Banner" and "Dixie" almost comically so), but many of her records are enchanting and full of feeling. The brief letter duet with Marcella Sembrich from Mozart's *Le Nozze di Figaro* is not only deliciously sung by both sopranos but remains a touching memento of what was apparently a genuinely close friendship between the two prima donnas. Eames also recorded a number of items with De Gogorza; the best is a captivating love duet from Messager's *Véronique* made in 1911, the year of their marriage, a performance of caressing charm and intimacy. Another irresistible song is the "Chanson de Baisers" by Herman Bemberg. Eames tosses off this lacy salon trifle (ironically written for and dedicated to Melba) with exquisite grace, her voice sounding at its freshest. Her last disc is perhaps the most impressive of all, a hauntingly eloquent rendering of Schubert's "Gretchen am Spinnrade" all the more striking for the magisterial portamento effects that would never be risked or even tolerated in lieder singing by a later generation.

Eames made concert tours after retiring from opera, making one last public appearance in 1916 at a charity recital in Boston. After that, she and De Gogorza divided their time among homes in Maine, Paris, New York, and London until they came to a friendly parting of the ways in 1936. Max de Schauensee, who studied voice with De Gogorza and pursued a brief singing career before becoming a music critic in Philadelphia, met Eames in 1927 when she was living in Paris. He won her confidence, and one day he even found enough courage to bring up the unmentionable subject: Melba. "We were driving in the Bois de Boulogne," he later recalled, "talking at random about singers, when I suddenly found myself asking: 'Madame Eames, what did you really think about Melba?' There was a silence and I wondered whether I might be requested to get out of her motor. Then, unexpectedly I heard her low voice saying: 'My dear, I would be a fool if I did not say that her voice was perfectly beautiful; she was an utterly ravishing singer,' the words gathered momentum: 'But, in *Faust*, had someone not told her, she would have hung the jewels on her nose.' "

"Emma is impossible," maintained De Gogorza, who always minimized the Melba-Eames feud, saying that much of it was in his wife's mind. "Melba didn't care," he once told De Schauensee; "she would pass Emma backstage and sing out 'Hello, Aymes!' and Emma would give no hint of being aware of her." But, De Gogorza continued resignedly, Emma seemed to make a fine art out of rudeness, a martinet who had few kind words for any singers, past or present. While attending the Paris debut of Lotte Lehmann, Eames turned to De Schauensee after the first group of songs and commented, "What is so remarkable? In my day, she would have been in the chorus!"

After her separation from De Gogorza, who died in 1949, Eames spent her final years in a New York apartment on Sutton Place. The last ten years of her life were quiet ones, spent mainly with her East Side neighbors—Gertrude Lawrence, Clifford Odets, Deems Taylor, and Helen Jepson were frequent visitors—and indulging in a newfound passion for attending such hit Broadway musicals as *South Pacific*, *Kiss Me, Kate*, and *Carmen Jones*. Death came on June 13, 1952, two years after a crippling chronic disease had confined her to a wheelchair. Apparently her prickly disposition actually mellowed toward the end, when, it was said, she lived entirely in the past and had nothing but praise for all her former colleagues—even Nellie Melba.

Nine

Anna Olivia

$\mathcal{B}$y the turn of the century the American musical scene was ready at last to produce what it had so far lacked: a home-grown singer of true incandescence. She (and it could only have been a woman) did not necessarily need to possess a glorious natural voice or be a paragon of dazzling technical virtuosity; but she would have to be a vocal and physical presence of such charismatic witchery as to drive audiences wild. Sure enough, that singer soon materialized in the person of Olive Fremstad, whose performances at the Metropolitan Opera between 1903 and 1914 were rapturously hailed by her admirers as incomparable for their emotional intensity, expressive detail, and ferocious commitment to what was then considered the operatic ultimate: the Wagnerian ideal of *Gesamtkunstwerk*—the total artwork.

Among the many discerning operagoers who worshipped Fremstad was the writer Willa Cather, who recast the soprano as Thea Kronberg, the opera singer heroine of her novel *The Song of the Lark*. Cather met Fremstad in 1913 while writing an article about three American prima donnas for *McClure's Magazine*—the other two were Geraldine Farrar and

Louise Homer—and it was clear which one had fascinated her most. Here was a woman who seemed perfectly ordinary during the day, but by evening could transform herself into a radiant operatic personality. What impressed Cather even more, and it became the central theme of her novel, was the fact that a girl born of humble Scandinavian parents and raised in rural Minnesota could even conceptualize, let alone achieve, success in such a specialized, difficult, and competitive profession—a major feminist triumph in turn-of-the-century America and made possible only through the hard work, perseverance, and extraordinary creative energy of one remarkable woman. Most of all, though, Cather marveled at the potent effect of Fremstad's interpretations of Brünnhilde, Isolde, and Kundry: "A great tragic actress . . . [Mme. Fremstad] is able to give these Wagnerian heroines color and passion and personality and immediateness. An actress with such power to create life and personality might well forget the great ideas which lie behind these women in releasing their humanity. But with Mme. Fremstad one feels that the idea is always more living than the emotion. Perhaps it would be nearer the truth to say that the idea is so intensely experienced that it becomes emotion . . . Here is a great and highly individual talent, unlike any that have gone before it. From the time [of her debut] on we have watched the rise of this great artist, the rapid crystallization of ideas as definite, as significant, as profound as Wagner's own."

On a less exalted level, the columnist Algernon St. John Brenon, never a completely uncritical fan, once mused on the Fremstad magic. "She was always an epic sort of creature," he wrote, "moving most comfortably somewhere between heaven and earth. Her personal radiation overcomes everything . . . she is a kind of dramatic potency in herself. If she were to come on the scene wearing an old dressing-gown and reading the Ladies' Home Journal, you would still rise in your seat and exclaim 'Ha, now something important is going to happen!' "

Fremstad was well aware of the effect she made on audiences, and her potent stage presence was the result of much thought, study, and preparation. She was the Met's first Salome, in 1907, and her graphic portrayal of the biblical teenager's sensual lust scandalized more than one Met patron. The uproar was so tumultuous, in fact, that the opera had to be withdrawn after a single performance. A fanatic for realistic detail, Fremstad must surely have been the first and last interpreter of Salome who took the trouble to visit a morgue and rehearse with the real thing. Only by lifting an actual human head, Fremstad reasoned, could anyone tell exactly how much it weighed—twelve pounds, she noted—and how much exertion a singer must show when triumphantly holding the grisly object aloft.

Nothing could have been in greater contrast to Nordica's chic, Paris-costumed Kundry than Fremstad's demonic creature. The soprano spent hours preparing herself for Kundry's first entrance, staining her skin brown before donning a tattered dress and a tangled black wig. Kundry is directed to enter breathlessly in Act I after her long journey in search of balsam for the suffering Amfortas. Fremstad expected the audience to know that she had indeed ridden the whirlwind from far-off Arabia to Montsalvat. To achieve the proper effect, she measured the distance from her dressing room to the wings and, at a signal from the regisseur, began her mad dash, arriving onstage exactly on the beat and looking as Wagner must have imagined his Kundry: eager, disheveled, and totally spent.

Another of Fremstad's celebrated roles was Venus in *Tannhäuser*, and after reading contemporary accounts of her impersonation, one wonders if any soprano has ever made more of a part that conventional wisdom considers short and not especially grateful. In those far-off days, the goddess of love invariably appeared on a luxuriously upholstered couch, with Tannhäuser chastely kneeling beside her. That hardly impeded the seductive image conjured up by Fremstad, who always said that the classical but strangely erotic pose she adopted had been faithfully copied from a statue she had once seen in the Vatican. Even on the few occasions when she sang Elisabeth in the same opera, the emotional temperature of that saintly creature rose several degrees, perhaps too high for most Met operagoers, who continued to prefer her as Venus. Fremstad once asked Giulio Gatti-Casazza to let her sing both roles in the same performance, a common enough tour de force nowadays. Even the canniest Met impresario can sometimes be obtuse, and Gatti, figuring that Fremstad might also demand two fees, refused. For her part, the soprano relished the challenge more than the money, but her wish was never granted, even though she offered to throw in the shepherd boy for free.

Just how thoroughly Fremstad prepared her roles and how minutely she calculated her effects is made clear by the detailed notations in her scores. Each bit of action is written down, steps are counted out, and virtually every part of the anatomy receives its own special set of instructions. As Act II of *Tristan* opens, she reminds herself to gaze "longingly into the forest where all her thoughts now are . . . whole body expecting the loved one . . . here she thinks of torch," and finally, "just sing beautifully, gestures not necessary." Occasionally her advice to herself is purely practical, such as during the Liebestod, where one reads a scrawled note to "take great breaths like a horse." None of that can really explain the mysterious alchemy that Fremstad used to hold her audiences spellbound. Cather said that even the opera glass could never penetrate her secrets. "The real machinery," the novelist wrote, "is all behind her eyebrows. When she sings Isolde, no one can say by what means she communicates the conception . . . her portrayal of character is always austere, marked by a very parsimony of elaboration and gesture." Fremstad herself told Cather, "My work is for serious people. If you ever really find anything in art, it is so subtle and so beautiful that— well, you need never be afraid any one will take it away from you, for the chances are nobody will ever know you've got it."

It is impossible, of course, to recapture the potency of Fremstad's stage presence, but we might have had a better representation of her voice. Like Nordica, she was uncomfortable in the recording studio and the handful of discs she made for Columbia are disappointing, technically and artistically. But then, again like Nordica's, this problematic voice never took kindly to the acoustical horn.

Fremstad began her career in Cologne as a contralto, making her debut there in 1895 as Azucena. Not until she reached the Met eight years later did she bill herself as a soprano, and even then many had doubts. The will-she-or-won't-she nature of a voice under audible strain has always added to the frisson of troubled but exciting singers from Pasta to Callas, and Fremstad definitely belongs in their company. Even at that, such an exacting critic as Richard Aldrich acclaimed Fremstad's Isolde in 1908 under Mahler's direction, the first uncut performances of Wagner's opera ever given at the Met. If there were any problems with the singer's upper extension, Aldrich could not have cared less: "Mme. Fremstad's voice is of indescribable beauty in this music, in its richness and power, its infinite modulation in all the shades and extremes of dramatic significance. It never sounded finer in quality and never seemed more perfectly under control. And her singing was a revelation, in the fact that the music was in very few places higher than she could easily compass with her voice. The voice seems, in truth, to have reached a higher altitude and to move in it without restraint and without effort."

Not surprisingly, Fremstad was a prickly personality offstage—"sensitive to the point of being quixotic," Gatti-Casazza recalled in his memoirs, "rather nervous and difficult to keep happy." Gatti was right, of course, but by the time he wrote those words he may have had cause to regret the insensitive treatment that led to Fremstad's premature retirement. Colleagues who functioned on a comparable level of tension, though, those who shared her exalted commitment to art, adored her— Toscanini, for example. Emma Eames may intuitively have sized up the great conductor as a natural enemy determined to usurp her prima-donna prerogatives, but Fremstad and Toscanini instantly recognized each other as kindred spirits. According to Mary Watkins Cushing, Fremstad's companion-secretary-buffer and long-suffering maid-of-all-work during the last years of her Met career, the two invariably went through the same ritual before each performance that Toscanini conducted: "Fremstad advanced, received him as if he were the Messiah, and pushed me into the hall . . . Immediately on his departure, which seemed to be accomplished in the vortex of a small, fussy whirlwind, there would follow from the closed room a golden flood of full-voiced scales, arpeggios, and snatches of First Act phrases. Three minutes of this—and then the Great Silence. No one breathed! What went on behind that scratched and shabby door was never known. Was it necromancy, prayer, or trance? Prayer, I think."

Toscanini may not have completely capitulated to Fremstad at first, but after conducting her in the title role of Gluck's *Armide*, they became lifelong soul mates. The opera achieved only a succès d'estime at the Met in 1910 despite a cast that included Enrico Caruso, Pasquale Amato, Louise Homer, Alma Gluck (no relation to the composer), and Dinh Gilly—although Pitts Sanborn, critic of the *New York Globe*, said he went to every performance just to hear Fremstad's wild exclamation in Act I: "Ciel, c'est Renaud!" Toscanini was apparently even more impressed. Many years later, on Fremstad's eightieth birthday, he sent her a memento inscribed "To my unforgettable Armida."

Fremstad treasured the gift, which was seldom out of her sight for the one month of life that was left her. She died on April 21, 1951, but in effect she had left this world long before that, at the moment the curtain fell on her final operatic performance more than thirty years earlier. At the height of her career she confided to a reporter, "I spring into life when the curtain rises, and when it falls I might as well die. The world I exist in between performances is the strange one, alien, dark, confused." And so it was in her long, lonely, useless years of retirement. When the end finally did come, her final instructions were typically theatrical: a long needle was to be thrust into her stilled heart and her body carried west, to be interred in a little cemetery in Grantsburg, Wisconsin, near the Minnesota border where she had spent her girlhood. Marked simply ANNA OLIVIA, the grave stands today in a field of windblown prairie grass next to her sisters Marie and Esther, three of the six children born to an immigrant Norwegian physician and preacher, Ole Fremstad, and his Swedish wife, Anna.

Much of Fremstad's early life is still shrouded in mystery, partly because the soprano preferred to keep it that way. Some biographical sources reverse the nationalities of her parents and others even insist that she was illegitimate. In later years Fremstad was fond of telling people that she was a "love child," but there seems little doubt that she was in fact Ole and Anna's first offspring, born in Stockholm on March 14, 1871, and that she was baptized Anna Olivia after her parents' own first names. Her American schoolmates dubbed her Olive soon after the Fremstads emigrated to Minnesota in the early 1880s, but her family and closest friends always called her Livan, a diminutive of Olivia as well as the Norwegian word for "life."

Once settled in St. Peter, Minnesota, Ole Fremstad continued his combined calling of medicine and religion—he had, in fact, been expressly called upon to join his countrymen in their journey to the New World as a minister of both professions. By then Olive had turned twelve and was already a proficient pianist, even though she still had to wear the blocks of wood that her father tied to her copper-toed shoes so that her feet could reach the pedals. Evidently a man of stern determination, Dr. Fremstad felt that if his daughter had her heart set on a musical career, the only way to achieve it was through unrelenting work, and Livan spent all her vacations and time after school practicing.

She was even enlisted as her father's musical assistant in his capacity as a preacher, and the two often traveled up and down the state in a wagon with a portable organ to conduct prairie revival meetings. Not only did Livan play the organ, but she sang. Cather hunted down several old Scandinavian settlers who had attended these services and asked them what they remembered. Some recalled the vivid effect of Fremstad's voice when she raised it to start the hymns of penitence and entreaties for pardon. It was uncanny, they said, hearing and watching this child who seldom failed to rouse the proper revivalist sense of remorse and longing. At times, when the congregation was slow to kindle, the little girl at the organ seemed overcome by emotion, with the invariable result that repentant sinners rose from every corner of the house. Surely Fremstad was thinking of this when she once commented, "I consider the whole opera *Parsifal* to be just a big elaborate revival meeting." She worked so hard at her musical duties, in fact, that neighbors eventually complained to the local chapter of the Society for Prevention of Cruelty to Children, but to no avail. Little Livan liked to work hard, and applying that ethic was to remain her life's greatest pleasure. She even began to take on piano pupils, most of them older than she was, and her father approved. The money may not have been much, but he felt that the spur it would give his daughter to even greater achievements was more than ample compensation.

Singing soon began to take precedence over the keyboard, and by sixteen Livan was a prominent soloist in churches and at local concerts in Minneapolis, where the family had recently moved. Toward the end of 1890, Fremstad got a leave of absence from her choir and came to New York, arriving on Christmas Eve. It must have been a cheerless and lonely holiday, even for this determined spirit, but on December 26 she found a teacher—Frederick E. Bristol—who tested her voice and agreed that there was indeed potential. Fremstad immediately cabled back home that she was staying on to study, and in exchange for her lessons with Bristol she labored at the piano in his studio as an accompanist for his other pupils. That meager income was soon to be augmented, mainly by a prestigious position as soloist at St. Patrick's Cathedral.

Despite the glittering casts at the Metropolitan during the Gay Nineties, the Met's future Isolde said she never once attended the opera—every cent she earned was set aside to finance her future career. Instead, she lined her pockets and enhanced her reputation by appearing occasionally with orchestras whenever she was asked, including a brief tour with Anton Seidl in 1891. By 1893 she had saved enough money for that essential trip to study in Europe, which for Fremstad, considering her background and artistic priorities, automatically meant Germany. She headed straight for Berlin and Lilli Lehmann, with whom she studied for two years.

The details of what was surely a tempestuous relationship between these two volatile women are unavailable, but there must have been many colorful moments—rumors even circulated of an affair between Fremstad and Lehmann's husband, the tenor Paul Kalisch, but little hard proof exists. The household was definitely under strain, however. David Bispham claimed that Lehmann's temper once became so frayed during a lesson that she took a book of songs from the piano and flung it at her pupil's head. Running from the room in tears, Fremstad passed Kalisch, who asked what was wrong. "I will never come here again," the girl wailed; "she has thrown a book at my head." "Never mind, my dear," said Kalisch, "she does the same to me." Neither singer mentioned the other much in later years—references to Fremstad are conspicuously absent from Lehmann's memoirs—but there must have been a healthy mutual respect between two women whose dedication to the highest artistic principles was fierce. When one innocent fan insisted that her Isolde even surpassed the great Lilli's, Fremstad brusquely replied, "Nonsense! We were all worms compared to her!"

It was Lehmann who first suspected that Fremstad might actually be a soprano, and worked with her to extend her upper register. And yet, when the younger singer's funds were beginning to run low and a position for leading contralto opened at the Cologne Opera, Lehmann, practical as ever, urged her to apply. "Don't worry," she told her protesting student, "you can sing the contralto range, can't you? This is a matter of expediency, *mein Kind*. You need the money, so take what you can get and be thankful!" Fremstad auditioned, was accepted, and made her operatic debut as Azucena in 1895. Several years later Lehmann also gave Fremstad a lesson in the sort of self-control every performer must learn, and it was one she never forgot. The two were appearing in *Tristan* in Vienna one evening—Lehmann as Isolde and Fremstad as Brangäne—when the older singer, after an especially heated and intense performance of Act I, turned to her young colleague before going onstage for her bow and said, "I wish you to put your hand down my back under my wig and cloak." The baffled Fremstad obeyed. "Observe," Frau Lilli said with pride, "not even my undershirt is damp!"

Until the Metropolitan signed her for the 1903–04 season, Fremstad was based mainly in Munich, although she sang small roles in the *Ring* at Bayreuth in 1896, Venus in London, and made guest appearances in Amsterdam and Antwerp as well as Vienna. Her Munich roles covered the basic mezzo-soprano repertory—some sixty to seventy parts, large and small—but the public, oddly enough, considering her later distinction as a Wagnerian, preferred her Carmen above all. Apparently in those days Fremstad showed a lighter side to her performing personality, which rarely surfaced at the Met. One tale has it that during carnival season she appeared at the opera house in blackface singing American ragtime with members of the male chorus, which she had trained herself.

If that giddy antic seems uncharacteristic, her request to sing Rosina in *Il Barbiere di Siviglia* (apparently ungranted) seems even more improbable.

Fremstad's Metropolitan debut came at last, as Sieglinde on November 25, 1903, and she captivated New York—especially the *Times* critic Richard Aldrich, who was to remain one of her staunchest champions. Aldrich pronounced her Sieglinde "a delight with small alloy. Her accomplishment as both a singer and an actress, the power and depth of her art, were such as to fill the lovers of the German works in which she is to appear with present satisfaction and jubilant expectation." For most New York operagoers the promise was more than fullfilled during the following decade.

Although briefly sidetracked by Carmen and Santuzza, neither of which made much of an impression, Fremstad consolidated her reputation with her first Met Kundry on December 1, 1904. Cather, who saw the soprano in the part later on, was overcome, especially by the mystery of her performance of the repentant Kundry in Act III:

Mme. Fremstad's Kundry is no exalted penitent, who has visions and ecstasies. Renunciation is not fraught with deep joys for her; it is merely—necessary, and better than some things she has known; above all better than struggle. Who can say what memories of Klingsor's garden are left in the renunciatory hands that wash Parsifal's feet?

After her ministrations to the knight, she goes to the rear of the stage and stands with her back to the audience, but there is no doubt as to what she is doing. She is not praying or looking into herself; she is looking off at the mountains and the springtime. From the audience one seems to see the ranges of the Pyrenees, to feel suddenly and sharply the beauty of the physical world. She moves toward the door with her bent step of "service." Before she disappears she turns again and looks at Parsifal. There are many degrees of resignation, it seems; the human spirit can be broken many times before it becomes insensate. Then only does she in truth renounce.

In the last scene renunciation is complete and the will to live entirely gone. This scene Mme. Fremstad continually improves. One used to feel her entrance too much, there was too much of the fixed religious idea in it. Now she effaces herself among the crowd of knights. Her personality was conflict. The struggle over, she is without personality; there is nothing of her but a desire for release. When the Grail is extended to her, she sinks slowly, and against the altar stair lie her dead hands, which have at last renounced—everything.

Cather, of course, talks mainly of what she sees—in Act III, after all, Kundry has only two words to sing. The music critics were also impressed, but they harped on a familiar refrain. "She is a trained Wagnerian performer and her voice is well suited to the low tones of the first act," wrote Henderson in the *Sun*. "Questionings arose when the high B of the second act and other top notes were recalled and the fate of other contraltos and mezzo-sopranos with soprano aspirations was remembered." Once when asked what she thought about such critical reservations, Fremstad replied flatly, "I do not claim this or that for my voice. I do not sing contralto or soprano. I sing Isolde. What voice is necessary for the part I undertake, I will produce."

Surely the greatest sensation of Fremstad's Met career was her single Salome on January 22, 1907. Technically she sang two performances, since the open dress rehearsal was also heavily attended. Heinrich Conried, the Met's general manager, perversely scheduled that unofficial performance on Sunday morning, when most of the invited audience would be coming straight from church. The faithful must have been truly chilled by what Krehbiel later said in the *Tribune*, "left the listeners staring at each other with starting eyeballs and wrecked nerves," an opera that left him with a "conscience stung into righteous fury by the moral stench with which *Salome* fills the nostrils of humanity." As for Fremstad, the *Times* reported that when she began to sing to the head before her, the horror of it all impelled men and women in the front rows and the boxes to stumble precipitately toward the exits and into the lobby to call their carriages. "But in the galleries," the *Times* continued, obviously relishing the gruesome scene, "men and women left their seats so that they might look down upon the prima donna as she kissed the dead lips of the head of John, the Baptist. Then they sank back in their chairs and shuddered." It was all too much for J. P. Morgan, who summoned an emergency meeting of the Met board, and the remaining nine performances were canceled.

Fremstad had only one other opportunity to sing the role that she had so painstakingly prepared—the Paris premiere of the Strauss work at the Théâtre du Châtelet less than five months later, a performance that won her a decoration from the French government. A poignant and telling postscript to Fremstad's Salome came many years later, in 1949, as she listened to a Met broadcast with Ljuba Welitsch, who had just created a sensation in the role. "Suddenly," records Mary Watkins Cushing, who was sitting with her, "in the midst of the noisiest climax, the aged prima donna reached out her crippled hand and switched the whole thing off. 'My God, Tinka!' she exclaimed, regarding me with deep dismay, 'for that I once shed my heart's blood!'"

Cushing's memoirs paint a vivid picture of Fremstad at the height of her Met career, a woman who lived life at a constant peak of intensity. Cushing was still a starstruck teenager at the time, a simple country girl and an unabashed fan from Vermont who had innocently presented herself one day to Fremstad backstage and was engaged to serve the soprano on the spot. What followed was a hectic, often infuriating existence, but seldom a dull one, and Tinka, as Fremstad nicknamed her young buffer, had to be ready to cope with her prima donna twenty-four hours a day. Cushing recalls sleeping with her toe attached to a string that led out the door of her bedroom and terminated in a ring hooked to Madame's bedpost, to be tweaked in time of need at any hour of the night. Outbursts were frequent and unpredictable. Once, Tinka selected some potted ivy to present her mistress as a homecoming gift. When the gift was proffered,

she erupted from her mound of pillows, blankets, and furs, and with a stride and gesture worthy of the outraged Isolde, Act I, snatched the offering brusquely from my hand. Another great step took her to the window and, with what seemed like one continuous motion, she swept aside the curtains and flung up the sash. Then, without a moment's hesitation, and no concern at all for whoever might happen to be strolling in the street nine stories beneath, she tossed the plant and pot straight into the outer air. She closed the windows, dusted off her hands and flopped back among her pillows, all without a sound. But the atmosphere around her crackled, and Mimi [Fremstad's pet dog] ran under the bed. Madame just sat there breathing hard and glaring at me, but presently she found her voice and it was impressive. "Ivy!" she cried, "she brings me ivy—right at the beginning of my season! Don't you know that ivy means death? Thank you, Tinka, thank you very much!" It took me some time to digest this incident, and even more to convince her of my innocence, but eventually I was shriven and blessed . . .

Such angry tantrums were actually rare, but they give some indication why Fremstad never had a satisfactory private life or was even able to cultivate a supportive circle of friends. She married twice, and each time anyone who knew her well must have wondered what she was thinking. Husband number one was Edson W. Sutphen, a speculator rumored to own all the gold mines in Tierra del Fuego. After a whirlwind romance, Fremstad married Sutphen in Salt Lake City in 1906 while the Met was on its ill-fated transcontinental tour that culminated in the San Francisco earthquake. The union lasted less than five years, during which time Fremstad continued to preach the gospel that marriage is not for serious artists. When it was tactfully pointed out that she herself was married, the diva retorted, "Oh, with me it is only a side show!" The next such show began in 1916, when Fremstad married an ineffectual composer and accompanist named Harry Lewis Brainard, an even more inexplicable liaison, although Tinka found him "gay and amusing and as comfortable to chat with as another woman." Perhaps Fremstad needed some kind of harmless pick-me-up, since by then it was clear that her career was effectively over. In any case, the vapid Brainard soon disappeared from her life and the marriage was officially dissolved in 1925. The most long-lasting and meaningful relationship Fremstad ever had was with her faithful Tinka, although when Cushing realized that her diva had retired for good, even she decided it was time to marry and live her own life.

Not surprisingly, Fremstad's relations with her colleagues were often rocky. Johanna Gadski, with whom she shared much of the Wagner repertory, was an especially hated rival. Gatti-Casazza soon found he could no longer cast them together in Die Walküre—particularly after the night when Gadski, who was singing Brünnhilde, dragged Fremstad's arm across her breastplate and inflicted a long wound (Fremstad had her revenge during curtain calls by ostentatiously dripping as much blood as she could on Gadski's costume). The soprano Frances Alda, at that time the all-powerful Signora Gatti-Casazza and an especially dangerous foe, was even more devilish. One night, while watching from the wings as Fremstad sang the seductive courtesan Giulietta in a performance of Offenbach's Les Contes d'Hoffmann, Alda snatched the diva's ubiquitous little dog Mimi from Tinka's arms, set the animal on the floor, gave her a shove, and said, "Go on, go find your mistress." Mimi needed no further coaxing as she delightedly scampered across the stage and bounded into the lap of an astonished and, needless to say, monumentally outraged Fremstad.

Mary Garden, reports Cushing, perhaps understood Livan best of all and "approached the Fremstad presence as might an acolyte the priestess at the altar"—two authentic "theater rats," as the Germans say, with similar theatrical instincts and, luckily, few roles in common. Fremstad admired Garden's enterprise enormously, and she once visited a movie studio in New Jersey where "the Divine Mary" was making a silent film of *Thaïs*, thinking that perhaps she should investigate this new art. Fremstad, though, was horrified when she saw Garden, blue and shivering after hours of retakes in an ice-cold studio. "My God, Mary, you must be quite mad!" exclaimed Fremstad. "Why do you let yourself in for anything like this?" The exhausted Garden answered by tracing a dollar sign in the air with one icy finger. "Only that and nothing else!" she replied. "But even so, it's not worth it . . . so DON'T!" To our eternal loss, Fremstad didn't.

In 1911 and 1912 Fremstad made fifteen records for Columbia. She apparently decided that the experience of singing before the horn wasn't worth it either, since she was displeased with the results and never bothered to try again. Nor did she ever quite get the hang of what the process was all about, let alone how to make the most of the situation. During one take, which had been proceeding with unusual smoothness, Fremstad noticed a tardy tuba player creeping through the studio doorway and she stopped at once in mid-phrase. "Ye gods," she shouted, "if I can get here on time, why can't you?" Fremstad's verdict of her recordings, according to Cushing, was of dismissal. "All that work and nothing gained!" she said. "When people play those things in years to come they will say: 'Oh ho, so that's the great Fremstad! Well, I guess she wasn't so much after all!' . . . Never again, Tinka, never again!"

Only a fool would say that, even if Fremstad's fifteen records only fitfully suggest the true nature of her vocal character. The voice itself is surprisingly sweet, warm, and rounded compared with Nordica's more brilliant instrument, and in that respect Fremstad is better suited to the primitive apparatus. The evidence of shortness up top becomes audible in Isolde's Liebestod and Brünnhilde's Battle Cry—the highest notes are certainly available to her, but as with most short voices they tend to be pitched sharp. The most impressive moments arrive mainly during introspective passages: "Vissi d'arte" is especially affecting for its inwardness and intensity, although Tosca was never a role that brought Fremstad great acclaim. Even better, oddly enough, is her delicate account of Mignon's "Connais-tu le pays?"; she makes the little waif's yearning vision of Italy unbearably poignant.

Only two items really hint at the grandeur, energy, and theatrical magic that intoxicated Fremstad's following. Elisabeth's greeting to the Hall of Song in *Tannhäuser* tumbles out impetuously and the voice opens out grandly at the climax, although here, too, the quiet intensity of the ecstatic middle section is what impresses most. Eboli's "O don fatale" is intolerably rushed in order to cram it all onto one side, but in every phrase the nobility and vibrancy of Fremstad's declamation grip the imagination. Five songs of small consequence round out this recorded legacy, a pitifully small one for a singer of such importance and stature.

At least when she made her records, Fremstad was only forty and at the peak of her career. Even she probably never dreamed that her days of glory at the Met were numbered, but eventually it became clear to all that Gatti-Casazza was determined to oust her from the company. She may not have been the easiest woman to deal with, of course, but considering her popularity with audiences and high standing with the critics, Gatti's attitude seemed positively perverse. Besides, he was an old hand at manipulating "difficult" artists to serve his advantage—even Fremstad, considering how deftly he handled what later became known as the famous "Giulietta incident." After singing a few performances of that ungrateful role in *Les Contes d'Hoffmann*, the soprano came to detest the part—one wonders why she even agreed to learn it in the first place. One night the substitute Giulietta, Maria Duchène, was scheduled to appear, but she became trapped in a hotel elevator and Fremstad was Gatti's only hope to save the performance. Deciding to use reverse psychology, the impresario phoned up the diva, apologized profusely for interrupting her evening, scarcely daring to broach the great favor he was about to beg.

"Well, why not ask it, at any rate?" came the reply.

"Never! I would not dare. I know that you are . . . well, temperamental. Sometimes . . . well, perhaps a bit difficult to deal with. For that reason I would not . . ."

"What! I, temperamental? I, difficult? Nonsense! Surely, you know me better than that. Ask what you like."

"And you promise not to be angry with me?"

"I promise. If only as a test of character!"

Gatti then recounted the sad tale of the trapped Duchène. "And what I wished to ask you," he concluded, "was to assume that role tonight. But, of course, if you are comfortably resting, I cannot ask it."

"You don't need to," said Fremstad. "I'll be down in ten minutes."

And so she was. Fremstad sang the loathed role, and even refused to be payed—her "character," she said, was worth more than a check, and in the future Gatti would kindly remember that at least one of his stars was not "difficult."

Apparently that was not the lesson Gatti took from the incident. Less than two years later Fremstad was distressed to discover that for the 1913–14 season her greatest roles had been distributed to others and her assignments consisted mostly of Sieglindes and Elsas. And when she also noticed herself slated for one Fricka in Wagner's *Das Rheingold*, Fremstad could hardly ignore the strong humiliating message: demotion. March arrived and no contract for the next season was forthcoming, and the press began to sense trouble. By then it was common knowledge that Gadski had already been reengaged for an even larger number of performances than usual, and that the Met had also discovered a new Wagner singer in Germany, Melanie Kurt. Gatti's practical reasons for easing Fremstad out had to do with her unreasonable demands, such as refusing to rehearse the day before or the day after a performance (even Toscanini resented her for that). And if Fremstad was definitely a "difficult" artist, she was also an expensive one. Perusing the Met's payment books, one notes that she received $1,000 a performance, but Kurt was available for $500—and presumably she would not make trouble over rehearsal schedules.

As Cushing reconstructs the showdown between Fremstad and Gatti, the final disagreement was over repertory, and the Met manager's velvet-gloved iron fist came down hard: "We need not go into particulars, *carina*," said Gatti coolly. "The facts are that we find ourselves dissatisfied with the limitations of your repertoire: you have repeatedly told us that you are unhappy here under conditions which we cannot ameliorate. We wish no longer to distress you and are therefore taking you at your word. We view your departure from the company with regret, of course, but will make no further effort to detain you."

Defeated, Fremstad could only request that the last *Tristan* of the season be reserved for her farewell. Gatti denied her even that small favor (the performance was sung by Gadski), and Fremstad's final Met performance took place two days earlier, on April 23, 1914, as Elsa, a part that had never been particularly identified with her and one that did not lie in the most comfortable part of her voice. Her fans, though, gave the soprano one of the longest and heartiest demonstrations the Old Met has ever witnessed, and New York's critics agreed that she was leaving at the height of her powers. Fremstad was only forty-three— Flagstad at that age had only just begun her Wagnerian career.

After leaving the Met, Fremstad sang with companies in Boston and Chicago, and there were numerous concert tours, but nothing seemed quite the same. Gatti probably realized eventually that he had made a serious tactical error—the mediocre Kurt never amounted to much, Gadski's career soon petered out, and no one of Fremstad's stature to sing the Wagner repertory was even on the horizon. There was talk of inviting the soprano back to the Met for the 1917–18 season, but during those World War I years German opera had been banished from the Met stage. At first a compromise seemed possible if Fremstad would agree to relearn her roles in English. "No!" she said emphatically. "If opera is to be given successfully in English, then the composer must have worked from a book in that language." When hostilities ceased two years later and anti-German feeling still ran high, she relented, but by then it was too late. In 1920 Fremstad, clearly desperate to sing opera once again, wrote Gatti a truly pathetic letter: "There was a time during the War when it seemed almost impossible to convert Wagner into English without a tremendous artistic loss. However, I am now convinced that it is the only way at present of giving Wagner to English-speaking audiences. Therefore, I am learning the operas in English—*Tristan*, *Parsifal*, *Lohengrin*, and *Tannhäuser*—I am also adding *Forza del Destino* to my repertoire, making in all for the present, with Tosca and Santuzza, seven roles.

"I expect to do better work than I have ever done before, and, naturally, in the event of your having a place for me, I should like to do that work at the Metropolitan, on the stage which has seen so many of my life's successes. Could you make this possible?"

Gatti's reply does not survive, but it was obviously negative: Fremstad never sang in public again. The long, unhappy years of retirement began, and Cushing poignantly describes them:

They were empty years chiefly because she did not know how to fill them, and her pride would not let her seek advice. She might have had, in spite of declining health, a happy retirement, for there were still many old admirers and many young students who would gladly have sat at her feet. Her magnetism and her charm of intellect never deserted her; and she had, moreover, thriftily laid by the means to cushion her old age in luxury. But such was not her way. She felt, instead, a grim compulsion to hasten toward that hell to which she was convinced that she was destined, by denying herself any alleviation of her misery. This self-imposed chastisement seemed to provide her with a sort of inverse consolation, although it drove to despair all who cared about her.

On one of my last visits to her sickroom (from which, at her express command, the gay spring sunshine had been rigorously excluded by shades and screens) she told me, in the half-hope that I might understand: "It is not against the pain and infirmity that I rebel, Tinka. I suppose that we poor humans must expect that sort of thing. No, it is because I cannot work that I fret and grieve. Work and hardship were my constant companions along my upward way: hardship at least I can still hold onto."

Fremstad read Willa Cather's article about her in *McClure's* shortly after it appeared in 1913, and she complimented the author on such an uncanny and penetrating insight into her artistic intentions. Later, though, early in her retirement years, Fremstad read *The Song of the Lark*, but the novel did not impress her. She had lived her own life by then, and it had been stronger than fantasy. As she told Cather—and perhaps she was speaking to an admiring posterity as well—"My poor Willa, it wasn't really much like that. But after all, what can you know about me? Nothing!"

Ten

~

Around and
About l'École
Marchesi

~~~~~~

𝓝o other American singer pursuing an international career at the turn of the century attained the eminence of Nordica, Eames, and Fremstad, but many tried. Some even managed to reach the Metropolitan—by 1900 already America's premier opera house, although its position was soon to be challenged by Oscar Hammerstein's Manhattan Opera. Opportunities to sing elsewhere in the country were limited, but it was still possible for the more modestly gifted or those with less vaulting ambition to perform with the many touring troupes that continued to crisscross the land. Other native singers eventually rose to local prominence in Boston and Chicago, where important companies would soon be established. Still other hopefuls made their way to Europe, won a certain amount of fame, and seldom, if ever, returned to sing for their compatriots.

In the latter category were two American sopranos who settled in Paris during the 1880s and won brief celebrity: Marie van Zandt (1858–1919) and Sibyl Sanderson (1865–1903). Both singers also managed to capture the attention of major French composers who wrote roles designed to exploit both their voices and physical charms. Van Zandt was Léo Delibes's first Lakmé in 1883, and the beauteous Sanderson, it was said, did much more for Jules Massenet than provide him with the inspiration for *Esclarmonde* (1889) and *Thaïs* (1894).

Van Zandt was herself the daughter of an American opera singer—Jennie van Zandt, who sang for a short time during the 1860s at La Scala under the name Vanzini. The family clearly had the theater in its blood—Jennie's father had been a Philadelphia institution in mid-century when, appearing as the magician Signor Antonio Blitz, he literally used to pull rabbits out of hats to the delight of one and all. It is almost certain that Marie was born in Brooklyn, although most biographical sketches written during her lifetime place her birth in Texas. There, the story goes, she was reared on her father's ranch, rode bareback and played with Indians as a girl, and "not only gained a lot of practical common sense, but a fine constitution." All that now seems to be fanciful invention—Marie's father, James van Zandt, was actually a Brooklyn clerk of Dutch extraction. Perhaps the publicists of the day remembered Minnie Hauk and how well that diva's Wild West childhood had played in Paris in 1869. In any case, Marie was taken to England at the age of eight and placed in a convent while Jennie fulfilled engagements on the Continent.

Marie's lessons at the convent included voice instruction, and word of her progress eventually reached Adelina Patti's ear. The diva came to visit, liked what she heard, offered encouragement, and in due time Van Zandt was sent off to Milan for lessons with Francesco Lamperti. Her operatic debut took place early in 1879—as Zerlina in *Don Giovanni* in Turin—and that May she appeared with Mapleson's London company in the same part and as Amina in *La Sonnambula*. A year later she reached the Opéra-Comique in Paris as Mignon, and audiences were enchanted. One writer in *Événement* thought her mouth "a little too Londonienne," whatever that meant, but he complimented her for possessing the "coquetry of the woman and the look of the demon, which is one and the same thing." That success led to a happy period in Paris where, according to Herman Klein, she became the "spoiled child of the Opéra-Comique," well liked by her fellow artists, appreciated by her impresario, doted on by high society, and admired by composers. Thomas declared her to be the very embodiment of Mignon, which she repeated more than sixty times to crowded houses. That was enough commendation for Delibes, who asked her to create the title role in *Lakmé* in 1883, a great triumph, as it turned out, for both him and Van Zandt.

Exactly what went wrong after that is hard to say—Henry C. Lahee reported that during an 1884 revival of Rossini's *Il Barbiere di Siviglia* Van Zandt suddenly lost her voice, "and was, in consequence, treated most shamefully by the press and public of fickle Paris." Others spoke darkly of cabals and growing chauvinistic resentment toward an American prima donna being given such preferential treatment over native French singers. Less sympathetic commentators suggested that she was drunk, and the self-righteous Gounod hardly helped matters by personally leading Cécile Mézéray onstage in mid-performance to replace the unfortunate American. Hoping that a leave of absence might cool the situation, Van Zandt took a few months off, but when she returned to Paris the next year, it was to scenes of even greater hostility. It all came to a climax at one performance when the soprano appeared with hands clasped and head dropped "as if in mute and helpless appeal" in hopes of inspiring sympathy, but to no avail. A barrage of whistles and catcalls finally led to an all-out riot, which had to be broken up by the police.

The Van Zandt ruckus of 1885 turned into one of the great operatic scandals of the season, and news of it circled the globe. One report, in Boston's *Musical Record*, included a brave quote from the soprano herself: "I believe the ringleaders had been bribed to whistle and hiss, and I made up my mind to remember that I was an American girl and to show American pluck!" Perhaps she was right about the ringleaders. When Van Zandt finally rejoined the Opéra-Comique years later in 1896, a newspaper article explained that the Paris prefect of police had actually engineered the entire incident to divert attention from a planned demonstration against an unpopular political official. By then, though, the soprano probably could have cared less. Two years later she married Mikhail Petrovitch de Tscherinoff, a Russian state councillor and a professor at the Imperial Academy of Moscow, and left the stage for good, spending the twenty comfortable years that remained to her at home in Paris and Cannes.

After leaving Paris in 1885, Van Zandt continued her career successfully in St. Petersburg, and at Covent Garden and other major European houses, eventually arriving at the Metropolitan to take her place among the many notable singers who inaugurated the starry Abbey-Grau-Schoeffel regime in 1891. During her one Met season the soprano appeared as Amina, Meyerbeer's Dinorah, Lady Harriet (*Martha*), Mignon, Zerlina, Lakmé, and Ophélie, ingenue roles requiring considerable agility and, of course, the provocative stage presence that had so charmed Parisians a decade earlier. Descriptions of her singing are scanty, but theater historian George C. D. Odell was probably correct when he wrote of her Met appearances: "She was a small, graceful woman, too small, in fact, for that large stage, and she had a pretty, light voice and she sang nicely."

If most young American singers of this period were lured to the glittering world of opera by the promise of fame, riches, and social betterment, the same material goals hardly drove Sibyl Sanderson. Born into wealth and privilege in Sacramento, California, Sibyl and her three younger sisters could have chosen any kind of life they wished. Their father, Silas Woodruff Sanderson, was one of California's most prominent citizens, serving as state legislator, justice of the California supreme court, and chief counsel of the Central and Southern Pacific railroads.

Sibyl's vocal promise was noted early, and her mother took her to Paris as a fifteen-year-old in 1881 to study music and languages. She returned to San Francisco two years later, but in 1886 she was back at the Paris Conservatoire, taking voice lessons from Giovanni Sbriglia and later with Mathilde Marchesi. Blanche Marchesi had happier memories of Sibyl than of that icy ingrate Emma Eames. "She was a kind-hearted, most beautiful and distinguished girl," Blanche recalled, "without an atom of pride or jealousy—a rara avis in her way. Her voice had not a mellow, but a brilliant quality, and she could reach easily the G or A-flat in Alt without any special effort, these notes being even especially strong, not like the usual tiny little miserable squeaks." It was exactly the sort of brilliant, high-placed voice that Marchesi loved to work on, although as matters turned out Sibyl never quite lived up to expectations.

An even greater influence soon entered Sibyl's life: Jules Massenet. During the summer of 1887 the composer was invited by a rich American family to attend an elegant salon expressly organized to show off Sibyl's vocal charms. Massenet went reluctantly, but he perked up after catching sight of the young soprano, who approached him humbly and said, "Dear Master, I have been asked to come to this friendly house this evening to have the honor of seeing you and to let you hear my voice. I am the daughter of a supreme court judge in America and I have lost my father. He left my mother, my sisters, and me a fortune, but I want to go on the stage. If they blame me for it, after I have succeeded I shall reply that success excuses everything."

Massenet immediately sat down at the piano to accompany her himself, and when Sibyl launched into the Queen of the Night's stratospheric second aria from *Die Zauberflöte*, the composer was dumbfounded. "What a fascinating voice!" he later wrote in his memoirs. "It ranged from low G to the upper G—three octaves—in full strength and pianissimo. I was astounded, stupefied, subjugated!" Sibyl may indeed have been genuinely impressive, young as she was and singing in a small room, but one suspects that the composer was responding to more than a pretty voice. The next morning Massenet excitedly told his publisher, Georges Hartmann, about his new discovery, who he felt would be the ideal choice to create the heroine of his new opera, *Esclarmonde*, planned as the major musical event at the upcoming Universal Exhibition in May 1889. Meanwhile, a stage debut was arranged for Sanderson, who made her bow at The Hague in January 1888 as Manon, singing under the name Ada Palmer. She was not exactly a sensation, but Massenet pronounced her performance as "ideal"—by now his interest in the singer definitely seemed more than merely professional.

That summer Sanderson holidayed in Switzerland with her mother, and the composer joined them at the Grand Hotel de Vevey, pointedly leaving Mme. Massenet and their daughter at home. For five weeks the composer and his muse worked on the score of *Esclarmonde* together, Sibyl wondering if she could possibly sing a role that was becoming more and more elaborate as Massenet became more and more infatuated. Only the presence of Mrs. Sanderson, suffering from an eye infection, seems to have prevented him from taking the ultimate step. Comments scribbled on his manuscripts reveal Massenet's troubled state of mind during these touchy days: "A painful evening last night . . . Sad end to the S evening . . . Sleepless night, a sad future . . ." When the opera was finished at last, Massenet insisted that Sanderson add her own signature on the last page of the manuscript—the opera was hers, he felt, as much as his, and the first audiences seemed to agree. When the soprano made her entrance in the prologue and unveiled her face, "there was," according to Mary Garden, "a gasp of adoration from one end of the house to the other." If nothing else, Sanderson's Esclarmonde became one of the season's most admired physical objects, second only to the Eiffel Tower, the 1889 Exhibition's other major attraction. All Paris, in fact, was talking about the diva's cadenzas and high G—the "sol d'Eiffel," as her fans dubbed it.

Sanderson's career was spectacularly launched, but her beauty and private life apparently interested European society more than her voice. In Brussels it was said that a young Belgian prince committed suicide for love of her, and later in St. Petersburg she was wooed by Crown Prince Nicholas, who attended all her performances and showered her with jewels. Massenet's next opera for his protégée, *Le Mage* (1891), was a dismal failure, and Saint-Saëns's *Phryné* (1893) generated only a succès de scandale with its famous disrobing scene, but something more interesting was on the horizon: Massenet's seductive Egyptian courtesan, Thaïs, which Sanderson created in 1894. Once again all Paris went wild when, at one point during the first performance, Thaïs's dress became unhooked, presumably by accident. The audience was stunned and delighted "to see Mademoiselle *Sein*derson naked to the waist," as the critic Willy reported, making a wicked pun on the soprano's name (*sein* is French for "breast").

By now America was wondering why this operatic Galatea had never sung on home ground, so in 1895 Maurice Grau took the hint and brought her to the Metropolitan to sing Manon. New York was unimpressed. In the *Tribune* Henry Krehbiel wrote, "Of Miss Sanderson's performance it is possible to speak with kindly recognition, if not with enthusiasm. Her voice is not one of the kind to be associated with serious opera. It is pure and true in intonation . . . but it is lacking in volume and in penetrative quality. It is pleasant in timbre and fairly equable throughout its natural register when not forced, but it becomes attenuate as it goes up and its high tones are mere trickles of sound. It is afflicted, moreover, with an almost distressing unsteadiness and is deficient in warmth." So much for the opinions of Marchesi, Massenet, and the *haute monde* of Paris.

Sanderson had not quite reached thirty, but her best days were already behind her and tragedy lay ahead. In 1897 she married Antonio Terry, a millionaire from Cuba, but whatever happiness that relationship might have brought her was short-lived. The soprano suffered a paralytic stroke, her newborn daughter survived only a few months, and Terry's own death soon followed—all during the unhappy years of 1898–99. Sanderson recovered sufficiently to pick up the threads of her career, which took her to Berlin, Vienna, Budapest, St. Petersburg, and Moscow—even back to the Met in 1901, although New Yorkers found her voice to be smaller and her acting colder than ever. When she was unable to finish a performance in Memphis, her western tour was cut short and she returned to Paris. Now desperate and ill, Sanderson wrote Massenet. Would the Maître please come to hear her sing and bring with him the conductor Édouard Colonne. If her voice still pleased them, perhaps a return engagement at one of the prestigious Concerts Colonne could be arranged. It was a pathetic reunion, as Blanche Marchesi recounts, and it hardly speaks well for Massenet's notoriously weak-willed character:

> Massenet was breathing heavily when the door opened and the once beautiful Sibyl came in. She was still beautiful, but there was something unspeakably sad about her, and when she stretched out both her hands to Massenet and said: "Maître, sauvez-moi de moi-même, rendez-moi à l'art et à la vie," his eyes closed, and he turned white, biting his lips, unable to utter a single word. "Come let us sing," exclaimed Colonne, cutting short the painful scene, and in saying so he opened the piano, striking some chords from *Manon*, thinking that she would feel more at home in her favorite part than in anything else. Oh, but it was not so. She could not remember a single note; not a word would come back to her memory. Some passages of agility still came out brilliantly, like sudden flashes peering through dark clouds, and she would throw them into the air to show these men that the voice was still there, but of Manon there was no more trace in her memory. When Massenet realized it, he remained motionless, leaning against the piano, the tears flowing over his cheeks. Seeing this, she was suddenly taken by an hysterical fit, and began to laugh at the top of her voice:
>
> "Et voilà l'histoire de Manon Lescaut!" she screamed—the very words with which the opera ends.
>
> After this she began to cry desperately. Massenet, seized with terror, took his hat, shouting, "Partons, Colonne, partons, je deviens fou," took him by the arm, and they fled from her who had once been the ideal Manon.

Even at this time of crisis and unhappiness, a second marriage was imminent—to Count Paul Tolstoy, a cousin of the Russian novelist—but in April 1903 Sanderson came down with a grippe that developed into pneumonia. Mary Garden visited her friend shortly before her death and was horrified at the sight of a woman whose beauty once had all Paris agape. The poor woman had baskets over her because she couldn't stand a sheet touching her body, which was all swollen and discolored. In the corner sat a man with a cigar. "Don't you think you should smoke somewhere else?" Garden politely suggested, but Sanderson motioned her friend to her side. "No, Mary," she whispered, "let him smoke; he's my fiancé."

Sanderson died two days later. Garden was summoned, but refused to view the corpse—"I'm glad," reported Sanderson's maid, "because she's frightening to look at." Badly shaken, Garden attended the funeral and afterward wrote, "I thought I never would get out of the church for pain and sorrow. I could feel something tearing and tearing within me . . . After Sibyl was cremated, they put her ashes in a box, and they put the box into the wall of the Paris crematory. Then they gave her a number, and there we leave my beautiful friend in her thirty-seventh year."

Considering her family background and musical preferences, Zélie de Lussan (1861–1949) might have joined Van Zandt and Sanderson in winning a name for herself in France, but if she ever sang there, the evidence has been well hidden. Born in Brooklyn of French parents, De Lussan was second only to Emma Calvé as the most famous Carmen of her generation, and by the time of her retirement in 1915 she claimed to have sung the role more than a thousand times opposite fifty-seven Don Josés. Her only teacher was her mother—Eugénie de Lussan, herself a singer—and little Zélie was singing in public by the age of nine, offering Mignon's "Connais-tu le pays?" at a New York church concert. Her stage debut took place with the Boston Ideal Opera Company in 1884 in New Haven, Connecticut, as Arline in a performance of The Bohemian Girl. When the Boston Ideal visited New York, De Lussan sang Marie in La Fille du Régiment and the press laughed—the company could afford a regiment consisting of only a corporal's guard, risibly costumed, and the tenor exhibited a voice "about an inch long and as thin as a hair."

De Lussan, however, was a hit, at least with the critic of the Spirit of the Times, whose review is an uncanny pre-echo of New York's favorite Marie of the 1940s, Lily Pons: "A slim, graceful, sprightly little lady, with crisp, curly black hair, large, dark eyes and plenty of what the French used to call chic and the English 'go,' Mlle. Lussan is a born actress, with quaint, pretty cunning ways that win the heart of an audience. As a singer, her voice is fresh, pure and true and she uses it artistically, but with the zeal of youth . . . If she were not a beginner she would refuse to appear with such a company as that which hampers, instead of helping, her in her New York debut. But she has the good luck of the young; for she shines amid the unrealized Ideals like a diamond in a heap of cobblestones."

Capitalizing on her success, De Lussan headed straight to London, where she made her Covent Garden debut, as Carmen, on July 8, 1888. Most critics commented on her resemblance to Patti in the role—not necessarily a compliment considering that Patti's Carmen, according to W. J. Henderson, was more of a kitten than a cat. G. B. Shaw, writing in *The Star,* was welcoming if hardly overwhelmed. De Lussan, he wrote, "looked the part well and sang it not at all badly, though the comparative weakness of the middle of her voice prevented her from doing the music the fullest justice. As an actress she shewed intelligence and self-possession; but she has hardly sufficient distinction of style to take a leading position in grand opera." The soprano's Carmen eventually became a London fixture, and even Shaw thought he detected that her voice had gathered color and individuality. Soon, though, he lost patience with "the hackneyed and trivial Carmen of Miss de Lussan, who learns nothing and forgets nothing." Nor did he care much for her Zerlina, remarking that the soprano "does not grow more interesting as her voice loses freshness and sustaining power and her manner becomes perter and trickier . . ."

Shaw was probably De Lussan's severest critic, although his prediction that she would not become one of opera's great luminaries proved to be correct. Even at that, she made her Metropolitan Opera debut, as Carmen, on November 26, 1894, with an all-star cast: Jean de Reszke as Don José, his brother Édouard as Escamillo, and Melba as Micaela. Krehbiel noted that "she has gained much from her experience and study abroad—her voice in richness, fullness and expressiveness, her acting in unconventionality, variety and forcefulness," and then, rather backhandedly, proclaimed her Carmen "an extremely interesting impersonation, worthy of separate consideration and admiration, and, if the force of circumstances did not force a comparison upon everyone who has heard and seen Mme. Calvé, it would be looked upon as a striking performance." Met audiences did indeed prefer Calvé's more fiery portrayal, and De Lussan soon relinquished the role to her rival.

De Lussan's reputation never rose higher during the next twenty years, but she was nonetheless kept busy, mainly in second-class companies. In America she sang with such touring groups as the Damrosch-Ellis Grand Opera Company and Henry W. Savage's Metropolitan English Grand Opera Company, but most of her activity was based in England, where she was always popular and referred to as "the Queen's own"—she was summoned three times to perform at Balmoral and Windsor Castle in 1899–1900 by the aging Queen Victoria. Married to the pianist Angelo Fronani in 1907 and widowed eleven years later, De Lussan then settled down to what appears to have been a long and happy retirement in London, dying there on December 18, 1949, three days shy of her eighty-eighth birthday. The soprano's few records were made in two lots: five sides for Victor recorded in New York on May 17, 1903, and four sides in 1906 for a minor label, Beka Grand, in London. The early discs reveal a pleasant vocal personality, with a pretty voice compromised by frequent dips into the chest register, doubtlessly to put a dramatic edge on a light soprano that really had no business tackling a role as heavy as Carmen. Her 1903 Habanera more or less confirms Shaw's reservations, leaving one to wonder how a soubrette, even one as accomplished as De Lussan, could possibly survive a thousand-plus Carmens. The answer, of course, was that she could not, and by 1906 the voice sounds positively raddled in an aria from Gounod's *Le Tribut de Zamora*.

One of the most admired cylinders in Mapleson's collection of live Metropolitan Opera performances contains a stunning rendition of Queen Marguerite's florid aria from *Les Huguenots*. The cylinder has no identification, and for many years it was automatically assumed that the singer had to be Nellie Melba—who else could have tossed off this tour de force with such dazzling attack and spectacular coloratura ease? Recent detective work, however, has uncovered the fact that the soprano was actually Suzanne Adams (1872–1953) in a performance now dated March 1, 1902. Not coincidentally, Adams was also a Marchesi pupil, and her singing here once again attests to that teacher's success in training perfectly placed high sopranos and developing brilliant upper registers.

A descendant of John Quincy Adams born in Cambridge, Massachusetts, Suzanne was fifteen when she was taken to Paris, first to study with Jacques Brouhy and then Marchesi. Like Eames, Adams "grieved my mother deeply," as Marchesi's daughter, Blanche, recalled, "and I hope she never realized how profoundly hurt her loving teacher was, who had even quite acted as a mother towards her, as she had no mother." The problem, as Blanche diagnosed it, arose when "mother" Marchesi told Suzanne that the girl's "delicate health" required a long rest in the south of France and another five years of study before she could accept a position at the Opéra. "Although my mother spoke with a most loving and careful wording," continued Blanche, "breaking it as gently as possible, Miss Adams took this wise advice as an insult, turned entirely against her, left her in the most cold-blooded manner and really kindled a strike in my mother's opera class."

Adams went ahead with her debut on January 9, 1895, as Juliette, and according to Blanche, her mother foresaw correctly: Adams could not fill the vast spaces of the Opéra effectively. "It was only after the five years predicted by my mother, when her physical strength returned, that she started her very fine career in America; but she never rose to be a star of the first magnitude, as she would have become had she continued under my mother's care and direction." It was, in fact, nearly five years to the day—January 4, 1899—that Adams first sang with the Metropolitan in New York, once more as Juliette, and apparently she was at her peak. Krehbiel greeted her arrival as "one of the latest illustrations of America's capacity for producing lovely voices."

Adams never did pose a serious threat to Melba or Eames, and the two Marchesis must have felt vindicated when the soprano's star flashed brightly, only to pale rapidly. After her Met debut, she divided her time between New York and London, where she created the role of Hero in Charles Villiers Stanford's *Much Ado About Nothing* with fellow Americans David Bispham (Benedick), Robert Blass (Dogberry), and Putnam Griswold (Leonato). By 1905, though, critics began to notice that a once beautiful and liquid voice had begun to wane, and two years later she was reduced to appearances in vaudeville singing the popular salon songs of her husband, Leo Stern, who had died in 1904. When even that option was no longer available, Adams reportedly opened a laundry in London, where she died on February 5, 1953.

Emma Nevada (1859–1940) was perhaps the first American soprano to search out Mathilde Marchesi, studying with the famous teacher in Vienna between 1877 and 1880, just before the Marchesis moved their school to Paris. Born Emma Wixom in Alpha, California, the future soprano spent her childhood in Austin, Nevada, where her father, William Wallace Wixom, practiced medicine and raised purebred horses. Although Emma took full advantage of her outdoor surroundings, she also loved to sing—at five, it is said, she entertained the miners in Virginia City and was showered with gold pieces. Later she arranged her own make-believe command performances by singing before cigar-box portraits of Queen Victoria and Prince Albert.

In 1873 Mr. Wixom returned to California and Emma entered Mills Seminary (later Mills College), studying voice with Alfred Kelleher and graduating in 1876. That summer she joined a group of girls on a European study tour, ending up with Marchesi in Vienna. Her career began in London on May 17, 1880, as Amina in *La Sonnambula* with Mapleson's company, when she sang for the first time under the name of Emma Nevada. A quarrel with Mapleson sent the singer off to the Continent, where she found success in Italy and France. In Paris she also encountered Marie van Zandt at the height of her popularity, and a feud, real or manufactured, sprang up between the two Americans. Both were light coloraturas, both claimed an exotic Wild West upbringing (here at least Nevada had truth on her side), and both shared the same repertory—Nevada even eventually got her hands on Lakmé. The rivalry became so heated that once, when Van Zandt fainted dead away in the middle of a performance, it was darkly rumored that Nevada had drugged her.

Paris became a quieter place when Nevada rejoined Mapleson's company for an American tour in 1884. For a time it looked as if she might give Adelina Patti some competition. Mapleson recounts an amusing incident that took place in Chicago during the 1885 tour shortly after the company arrived. The Colonel noticed Patti's husband, the tenor Ernest Nicolini, on a ladder measuring the letters of Patti's name on a playbill—the diva's contract stipulated that in all printed announcements her name would be one-third larger than the letters of anyone else's. Sure enough, Nicolini had discovered that his wife's name was a shade smaller than agreed upon. "In order to conciliate the offended prima donna and her irritated spouse," Mapleson wrote in his memoirs, "I caused the printed name of that most charming vocalist, Mdlle. Nevada, to be operated upon in this way: a thin slice was taken out of it transversely, so that the middle stroke of the letter E disappeared altogether. When I pointed out my revised version of the name to Signor Nicolini in order to demonstrate to him that he was geometrically wrong, he replied to me with a puzzled look as he pointed to the letters composing the name of Nevada: 'Yes; but there is something very strange about that E.' "

Nevada's career continued until 1910, mostly in Europe. Long before then she began to cut a rather old-fashioned figure, since her flutelike soprano never allowed her to proceed past the bel canto repertory and branch out into more modern works. The soprano had a daughter named Mignon, in honor of Thomas's opera, and she, too, became a singer. Nevada spent the rest of her life teaching in England, but her pupils had scant success, Mignon included—probably because, as Sir Thomas Beecham observed, she was imbued with "the pious belief that every soprano . . . should be a model of herself."

Marchesi's only other American pupil of note was Ellen Beach Yaw (1869–1947), who became famous for her freak upper extension and ability to trill in thirds and fifths. Those questionable feats were perhaps more remarkable than pleasing, or at least so they sound on her records—possibly Blanche Marchesi was obliquely referring to Yaw when she commended Sanderson's top notes as "not like the usual tiny miserable squeaks" (significantly, "Lark Ellen," as Yaw was later affectionately called, does not even rate a mention in Blanche's chatty memoirs). Born in upstate New York, Yaw grew up in Minnesota. After moving to Minneapolis and later Boston, she finally reached New York, where her teacher, Theodore Bjorksten, discovered her phenomenal ability to skyrocket more than an octave above high C. In order to raise funds for the trip to Europe, Yaw made a series of American tours under the aegis of Victor Thrane, who advertised her as having the highest vocal range in history. Curious audiences came to her concerts armed with pitch pipes and tuning forks to find out for themselves.

By the time she went to Marchesi in 1900, Yaw had already been touring Europe for five years, her most significant moment arriving in 1899, when she created the role Sir Arthur Sullivan had written for her in his last completed operetta, *The Rose of Persia*. After that, the soprano made only sporadic appearances in stage productions. In hopes of combatting Luisa Tetrazzini's popularity at the Manhattan Opera, Heinrich Conried engaged her as Lucia at the Metropolitan in 1908, but she sang just one performance. According to Antonio Altamirano, the soprano's record manager, she created a sensation and received twenty-nine curtain calls but turned down Conried's offer of a three-year contract as a piece of bad business. "Opera is very hard work," she later told Altamirano, "and I make more money in one concert than any opera company can pay me." That was certainly a fact of life, as singers with popular followings have discovered ever since, but if other impresarios around the world were clamoring for Lark Ellen's chirping, they were very quiet about it. The extant recordings reveal her freakish upper extension, but otherwise very little of real vocal or musical interest.

Altamirano claimed that Yaw had an operatic repertory of more than fifteen roles ranging from Ophélie in *Hamlet* to Adriana Lecouvreur, and apparently she sang most of them during a brief time on the Italian stages of Rome, Naples, and Catania in 1905. Good as her word, Yaw soon put opera aside and spent most of her career touring America with her own road show, busily giving variety concerts until 1931. By then a very rich woman, she retired to her mansion, "Lark's Nest," in Covina, California, to devote her remaining years to managing her favorite charity, the Lark Ellen Home for Newsboys.

Like Clara Louise Kellogg and Emma Abbott before her, Emma Antonia Joanna Juch (1863–1939) was an indefatigable barnstormer, touring the country as a champion of opera in English. Although born in Vienna, Juch was the daughter of naturalized American citizens who had temporarily returned home to settle litigation over the estate of the future soprano's great-grandfather, General von Juch. Along with many other American singers of her generation, Emma got her start with Mapleson at Her Majesty's Theatre in London, making her debut there as Philine in *Mignon* in June 1881. After three years with the Colonel, Juch was chosen by conductor Theodore Thomas to participate in a company that was preparing to take Wagner's operas on a coast-to-coast tour of the American continent, and she alternated with Christine Nilsson as Elsa in *Lohengrin*. When Jeannette Thurber's American Opera Company was organized in 1885, again under the musical direction of Thomas, Juch signed on as the principal soprano, singing Gluck's Eurydice, Mozart's Pamina, Marguerite, Senta, Elsa, and Chrysa in Anton Rubinstein's *Nero*.

After the collapse of Mrs. Thurber's noble project, Juch took up the gauntlet herself and became the impresaria of her own Grand Opera Company, which she established in 1889 and guided for three stormy years as it traveled throughout the United States, Canada, and Mexico. Taking Kellogg and Abbott as her role models, Juch acted as the troupe's major attraction, although she wisely did not overwork herself—her only four roles were Marguerite, Mignon, Carmen, and Weber's Agathe. Apart from the prima donna, the overall level of vocal quality apparently left much to be desired; even in the provinces—by now more musically sophisticated than in Abbott's day—critics noticed that Juch's associates lacked the "gifts and training commensurate with even the moderate requirements of her repertory." When the company played New York, lips positively curled. Oscar Hammerstein engaged Juch and her entourage for a season at the Harlem Opera House in 1889, which turned out to be both a financial and an artistic disaster. The nadir arrived on the evening when one Laura Bellini appeared as Arline in *The Bohemian Girl*. Her unfortunate attempt to sing the famous air "I dreamt I dwelt in marble halls" prompted one critic to observe sourly that Bellini clearly "resided in halls half a tone lower than those occupied by the orchestra."

Juch's company disbanded in 1891, and for the next three years the soprano devoted herself to concerts and recitals. Her last engagement was with the Toronto Music Festival in June 1894. If the reviews can be believed, Juch, at the age of thirty-three, was at the peak of her powers. Her rendition of the soprano solos in *Messiah*, said the *Toronto Globe*, revealed "an earnest, honest, soulful, conscientious singer" with a "brilliant and highly flexible voice." Two weeks later, though, on June 25, she married New York City's district attorney, Francis Lewis Wellman, who demanded that she give up her career. Juch obeyed, but the marriage did not last—Emma was the third of Wellman's five wives, and the unhappy marriage was dissolved in 1911. After that, Juch lived quietly in New York, and when she died on March 6, 1939, an article in *Musical America* claimed that she remained "a cheerful, merry person whose charm was undimmed by age and whose personality was in no way embittered by the unecessary and perhaps tragic sacrifice of one of the great American operatic careers."

Just how great that career might have been is suggested by Juch's three surviving records, made on May 7, 1904. Although ten years into her retirement, the soprano still sounds fresh-voiced, secure, and eager to communicate in three items that had always been closely identified with her: "Come unto Him" from *Messiah*, Tosti's "Serenata," and Elsa's Dream from *Lohengrin*. They are among the most enchanting records of the period. Numerous American singers had preserved samples of their voice and art by 1910, but none left a more impressive testimony—or more poignant evidence of unfulfilled promise—than Emma Juch.

Many other American sopranos passed across the scene at the turn of the century, leaving faint but far from negligible traces of their vocal talent. Frances Saville (1862–1935) was yet another product of the *école* Marchesi. Born Fanny Martina Simonsen to musicians in San Francisco, she spent her childhood roaming the globe with her peripatetic parents, settling in Australia in 1874 (one of her six brothers moved to New Zealand and fathered an even more famous operatic Frances of the next generation, Frances Alda). As a young concert singer in Australia, she impressed the British baritone Charles Santley, who urged her to seek out Marchesi. By the time she reached Paris, Fanny Simonsen had already turned into Frances Saville—she had eloped with her father's secretary, John Saville-Smith, several years earlier. By 1892 Marchesi proclaimed the soprano ready for her debut, as Juliette at the Monnaie in Brussels, and for the next decade Saville was a busy singer on the Continent and for two seasons (1895–96 and 1898–99) at the Metropolitan.

It was a brief career, which ended in 1903 in Vienna, where the soprano made her short list of nine recordings. They display an attractive light voice, although whatever florid technique she learned from Marchesi seems to have eroded, judging from her discomfort with the rapid divisions in Olympia's Doll Song from Offenbach's *Les Contes d'Hoffmann*. But then, like so many singers of her generation who were basically soubrettes, Saville could not resist tackling the increasingly popular Wagner repertory, in which she must have badly overextended herself. At the Met she ran the gamut from Juliette, Marguerite, Zerlina, Manon, Micaela, and Violetta to such unsuitable heavies as Wagner's Elsa, Elisabeth, and Gutrune.

Although she never rivaled Nordica or Fremstad, Susan Strong (1870–1946) concentrated on a weightier repertory right from the beginning, probably because she never studied with teachers like Marchesi, whose vocal precepts were grounded in the old bel canto school. Strong was born in Brooklyn, where her father had been mayor prior to its incorporation into the city of New York, and her principal musical training took place at London's Royal College of Music. Her operatic debut came in 1895, as Sieglinde at Covent Garden in a company organized by the American tenor Charles Hedmont. The American portion of her career included three Met seasons, between 1897 and 1901, in which she sang the lighter Wagnerian heroines, usually when Eames and Nordica were not available, as well as Donna Anna and Aida. Like Suzanne Adams, Strong retired to become a London laundress, opening a "Nettoyage de Linge de Luxe" on Baker Street. Her recordings, mostly of songs, display a charming manner and a sweet voice that was probably never meant for Wagner. Still, it was as Brünnhilde that Strong was affectionately known to her customers when they dropped by to pick up their fresh linens.

Even if we can no longer see her, on her recordings Alice Nielsen (1868–1943) conveys much energy, charm, and winning presence, qualities that made her such a popular stage figure in the early 1900s. She was "as pretty and dainty as a Dresden doll with the voice of a lark," wrote one appreciative critic back in Missouri, where Nielsen spent her youth as a stagestruck girl, often singing on the sidewalks of Kansas City for pennies. That, plus her subsequent adventures touring the country with various light-opera groups, recalls Emma Abbott's career, while her transformation from musical-comedy performer to opera star anticipates Grace Moore's rise to fame. Nielsen's own star began its ascent in 1897, when she was spotted by Victor Herbert, who gave her the leading ingenue role in his new operetta, *The Serenade*. That hit led to an even greater Herbert smash the following year—*The Fortune Teller*, written especially for Nielsen—and the show enoyed successful runs in both New York and London.

While performing in England, Nielsen caught the eye and ear of the impresario Henry Russell, Jr., who felt that the soprano had operatic potential and shipped her off for study in Italy. After two years of vocal finishing, and with Russell's continued support, Nielsen was ready for the important part of her career: a Covent Garden debut in 1904 and a return to America the next year at the head of her own touring company organized by Russell and two of his savvy showbiz associates, the legendary Sam and Lee Shubert. When Russell founded the Boston Opera Company in 1909, Nielsen was one of its leading attractions, and remained so until 1914. During those years she also appeared at the Metropolitan, where she made less of an impression. Her roles for both companies included Gilda, Puccini's Mimì, Nedda, Lady Harriet, Donizetti's Norina, and Rosina—all ideally suited to show off her pure, brightly focused soprano and perky stage personality. "A mobile face," as Quaintance Eaton describes Nielsen in her history of the Boston Opera Company, "with its wide, laughing eyes, sweet mouth, and the beauty spot on the left cheek that completed her piquant femininity; brown hair parted in the middle and wound behind the ears in becoming little knots; petite, yet softly rounded in figure, graceful, quicksilver in movement and glance. Cobina Wright, the socialite singer, granted Alice the most beautiful legs in the world—always excepting her own."

Nielsen's records communicate much of the sparkle of that portrait—an attractively colored, bright-textured, well-focused lyric soprano and a musical spirit eager to please. If New Yorkers never warmed to her charms as readily as Bostonians, that was undoubtedly because Nielsen's Met competition at the time included Frances Alda, Lucrezia Bori, Geraldine Farrar, and Frieda Hempel. Even if she failed to impress the New York public, two of her most appealing discs—love duets from Gounod's *Faust* and *Roméo et Juliette*, partnered by Giovanni Zenatello and Florencio Constantino, respectively—give a sampling of how charming she sounded in two of her most congenial roles, ones that Met audiences never saw her perform.

The names and reputations of Marie Engel, Sophie Traubmann, Marie Litta, Marie Louise Dotti, Lelia Lauri, Jessie Bartlett Davis, Amanda Fabris, Kate Rolla, Louise Margaret Nicholson (who billed herself as "Nikita"), and Laura Harris Zagury have faded from sight. These and numerous other American singers barely created a ripple in the waters, but let us pause briefly to shed a tear for Pauline L'Allemand, née Ellhasser, who was born in 1862 in Syracuse, New York.

The details of L'Allemand's career are sketchy, but we do know that she sang leading roles in Germany at the age of seventeen, married a handsome young actor named Henri L'Allemand, gave birth to a son named Edgar, left her husband, and settled in Paris. There she gained the patronage of both Anna de la Grange and Pauline Viardot (a feat in itself—the two ex-divas were mortal enemies), and was coached in the role of Lakmé by Delibes, who apparently had a soft spot for pretty young American sopranos. Returning to America in 1886, L'Allemand was hired by conductor Theodore Thomas for the first season of the newly formed English-language American Opera Company. On March 1 of that year the soprano sang Lakmé six years before Marie van Zandt brought her original interpretation to the Metropolitan. The critics praised L'Allemand's bell-like coloratura, and one report marveled over her realistic death scene, in which she evidently threw herself down a flight of stairs (if she did, the production was a century ahead of its time—the last act of *Lakmé* is set in a forest clearing). L'Allemand remained with the American Opera Company during its reorganization as the National Opera Company and its eventual collapse in 1888. After that, the soprano seems to have returned to Europe—a photograph from that period survives, showing her as a pretty, plump, bare-shouldered, sad-eyed creature in a cameo encircled by a poignant inscription: "To things immortal time can do no wrong. And that which never is to die forever must be young. Berlin '98."

When we next hear of L'Allemand, she is back in America with a grown-up Edgar, planning to tour the country in a German operetta of her own composition called *Die Kappe de Confucius*. After that project failed, Pauline and Edgar found themselves down on their luck in Milwaukee in 1911. With what money there was left, mother and son bought a humble cottage in nearby Black River Falls and opened what they hopefully called a "salon," where L'Allemand offered to teach voice and sing her old repertory of arias to anyone who cared to stop by and listen as Edgar accompanied her on his violin. Soon this odd duo came to be viewed by the rural community as more suspicious than eccentric, and eventually Edgar was accused of stealing four bags of cement from a local lumberyard. Pauline defended him, and she must have been a sight when she arrived in court wearing one of her old operatic costumes—a long violet gown with a row of buttons from throat to feet and a pair of broken high-heeled pumps held together by twine and rubber bands— and proceeded to ramble on incoherently about how she and her son had always been victims of an anti-Catholic conspiracy, hounded up and down Europe by secret agents. After witnessing that performance, the judge assumed that the woman was quite mad, and both Edgar and Pauline, by then unable to support themselves, were committed to the Mendota State Hospital for the Insane at Madison. Two years later, in 1922, they were released, and Edgar went on the road to play and promote his latest invention, an aluminum violin. The last news of L'Allemand surfaced in 1929, when she was living in Chicago, earning a pittance as a voice teacher, and still a bit daft. She once sought an injunction against a neighboring ventriloquist for "harassing her with annoying imitations of odd voices" through the walls. Was it inevitable? Pauline L'Allemand's unhappy life eventually became the subject of an opera: *Black River*, written in 1975 by Conrad Susa.

While sopranos of this period flourished, male singers continued to be scarce. Those who did rise to a certain prominence were mostly baritones and basses, and nearly all specialized in the Wagner repertory, which dominated at the Metropolitan Opera during the early years of the century. Among the earliest native-born singers to reach the Met were the Devriès brothers, Maurice (1854–1919) and Herman (1858–1949). Both must have been destined for singing careers from birth. Their mother was Rosa de Vries–van Os (1828–1889), a Dutch soprano who sang in New Orleans and New York during the 1850s, when her children were born—two older sisters, Jeanne (1850–1924) and Fidès (1851–1941), also pursued significant operatic careers in Europe. The most famous member of the family was David Devriès (1881–1934), Rosa's grandson and the nephew of Maurice and Herman, a French tenor whose attractive voice and stylish interpretations graced the Opéra-Comique in Paris between 1904 and 1930.

Both brothers received their training in France and sang extensively in Europe before returning to the city of their birth. Maurice arrived at the Met in 1895 and spent three seasons singing mainly supporting roles—Zuniga, Kothner, De Brétigny in *Manon*, the *Lohengrin* Herald, Silvio, and Mercutio. Herman followed in 1898 and remained for two seasons, sharing Zuniga with his brother and also tending to such bass roles as Don Basilio, the King in *Aida*, Sparafucile, and Capulet. In 1900 they both settled in Chicago to teach singing, although Herman, who survived Maurice by thirty years, branched out to become a noted composer, as well as a music critic for the *Chicago American Herald*.

The sturdy voice of Robert Blass (1867–1930) may be dimly heard on several Mapleson cylinders and a few rare Victor and Edison discs made in the 1900s. Born in New York of German parents, Blass originally went to Leipzig in 1887 to study the violin, but after a few voice lessons with the celebrated baritone Julius Stockhausen, one of García's most distinguished pupils, he soon discovered that he possessed a bass-baritone of unusual strength and substance. After a period on German stages and at Covent Garden, Blass joined the Met in 1900 and remained for ten years as a mainstay of the Wagner wing, chalking up sixty-three performances of King Henry in *Lohengrin*, fifty-two Gurnemanzes, fifty-one Hundings, forty-four Pogners, and forty-seven King Markes. He returned to Germany in 1913, but the Met called him back in 1920—at the age of fifty-three Blass was willing to relearn his entire repertory in English, the language that the Met insisted upon for Wagner in that touchy postwar era.

Born in Marengo, Iowa, Clarence Whitehill (1871–1932) was studying voice and working as an express clerk in Chicago when Nellie Melba heard him sing and encouraged his vocal ambitions. With the financial assistance of a local music patron, Whitehill headed to Paris for lessons with Giovanni Sbriglia, teacher of Plançon and the De Reszkes, and made his debut at the Monnaie in Brussels in 1898 under the name M. Clarence. He returned to New York to join Zélie de Lussan as part of Henry W. Savage's English Grand Opera Company for a series of performances at the Metropolitan, but wishing to study the Wagner repertory at the source, the baritone left once more for Europe in 1902 to study with Stockhausen. Whitehill subsequently sang Wolfram, Amfortas, and Gunther at Bayreuth, winning Cosima's seal of approval. In 1909 he joined the Met, where he remained until retiring in 1932, the year of his death.

Wagner was Whitehill's primary concern at the Met, but he was a versatile singer who drew on his early French training to excel as Golaud in Debussy's Pelléas et Mélisande, Athanaël in Messenet's Thaïs, the Father in Charpentier's Louise; he also appeared in such rarities as Goetz's Der Widerspenstigen Zähmung, Strauss's Die Ägyptische Helena, and Converse's The Pipe of Desire. Critics occasionally noted that his voice was not always under perfect control. After Whitehill's death, W. J. Henderson revealed that the baritone had had to overcome a long-standing difficulty "owing to the super sensitiveness of one vocal cord. When this was slightly congested the singer's tone acquired a little roughness . . . when the congestion was pronounced he became unmistakeably hoarse." This disability did not seem to impede his career, nor is it apparent on his records, which reveal a noble voice and a dignified if rather impersonal interpretive presence. When Whitehill was told that he bore an uncanny resemblance to George Washington, the recently retired baritone was persuaded to undertake one last new role in 1932: impersonating the first President in the Washington Bicentennial, which he carried off successfully just weeks before he died.

The most impressive American bass voice of the day was said to belong to Putnam Griswold (1875–1914). If so, he would surely have attained even greater eminence had he not died prematurely, after an appendicitis operation, at the age of thirty-eight. Griswold grew up in Minneapolis and trained his voice under Alberto Randegger at London's Royal College of Music, in Paris with Jacques Bouhy, and in Frankfurt with Stockhausen. With those impeccable credentials, he soon became a leading singer in Germany, most prominently at the Court Opera in

Berlin, where he first sang in 1904, regularly from 1906 to 1911, and was twice decorated by the Kaiser. The bass's short career ended at the Met, where he made his debut on November 23, 1911, as Hagen. He later sang Pogner, Wotan, King Marke, the Landgraf in *Tannhäuser,* and King Henry in *Lohengrin,* and participated in the world premieres of two American operas, Walter Damrosch's *Cyrano de Bergerac* and Horatio Parker's *Mona.*

Leon Rains (1870–1954) was born in New York and died in Los Angeles, but his career was almost entirely confined to Dresden, where he was principal baritone from 1899 to 1917. The United States's entry into World War I obliged him to return home; he then concentrated primarily on concert singing and, after retiring to California in 1924, teaching voice. Rains appeared at the Met during the 1908–09 season, but for two performances only, as Hagen and Méphistophélès. He also sang Wagner at Bayreuth and Covent Garden, where he was received with respect but little enthusiasm.

A Jew who grew up as a streetwise New Yorker, Rains began performing at the age of twelve in theatricals at the Old Star Theatre and later on Broadway with the Old San Francisco Minstrels, as well as singing in any church or synagogue that needed his services. It's tempting to conclude that Rains's decent if unspectacularly provincial career may have had something to do with his being Jewish. After all, a not-so-tacit anti-Semitism was prevalent at the Metropolitan during these years, far more so than in European musical circles, Vienna excepted. Siegfried Wagner's famous 1921 dictum that the Bayreuth Festival welcomed all singers—they could be Chinese, Negro, American, Indian, or Jewish, he said, as long as they delivered the goods—may have been overstated, but Bayreuth was already accommodating many *nicht-deutsch* singers when Rains sang there in 1904 and failed to create much of an impression. Around that time in Germany, he also made a number of discs, which display a warm, soft-grained voice and a pleasant outgoing manner, a singer Dresden was probably happy to have. But to audiences in New York and Bayreuth, used to the standards set by Pol Plançon in Gounod or Anton von Rooy in Wagner, Rains must have seemed like little more than a decent stopgap, no matter where he came from or what his ethnicity.

Completing the Met's extensive roster of lower-voiced American Wagnerians were Allen Hinckley (1877–1954) and Herbert Witherspoon (1873–1935), who joined the company in 1908, and William

Hinshaw (1867–1947) and Basil Ruysdael (1888–1960), who arrived in 1910. Considering the formidable competition, it's not surprising that they made only fleeting impressions, although surely all four were found to be both useful and necessary in those Wagner-mad days. Witherspoon saw the writing on the wall early on and gave up his singing career in 1916, when he went into music administration. He subsequently founded the American Academy of Teachers of Singing, served as director of the Chicago Civic Opera and the Cincinnati Conservatory of Music, and eventually joined the voice faculty of the Juilliard School in New York. By then his administrative talents had become so respected that on March 6, 1935, he was appointed to succeed Giulio Gatti-Casazza as the Met's general manager, the first native American to hold the post. Witherspoon tore into his new job enthusiastically, perhaps with too much gusto. On May 10, his head full of plans to infuse the company with young American blood after more than fifty years of European dominance, he dropped dead in his office of a heart attack.

Eleven

~

Sing Low

~~~~~~~~~~~~~~~~~~~~~~~~~~~~

Domesticity is not a role with Mme. Homer," wrote Willa Cather in her 1913 tribute to three American leading ladies of opera in *McClure's Magazine*, "it is her real self." Was Cather sneering slightly? Probably, considering the far more extensive and impassioned portrait she drew of that most undomesticated of singers, her idol Olive Fremstad. Cather was right in any case. Louise Homer was the first native-born opera and concert singer of consequence whose temperament and priorities allowed her to combine a major career with the life of a homemaker. She married the composer Sidney Homer in 1895, enjoyed fifty-two years of wedded contentment, and raised six children. Without neglecting her family between 1900 and 1929, she also sang forty-one roles at the Metropolitan, chalking up 501 performances at that house as well as many concert and opera appearances in other parts of the country, eventually retiring with the reputation as the most preeminent contralto America had yet produced.

Many factors contributed to help make Homer's remarkable double life possible. One was simply her satisfaction with the low vocal placement that nature had given her. Generally called upon to play mothers, old women, cheated rivals, servants, evil creatures, or best friends, mezzo-sopranos and contraltos have relatively few opportunities to play the dominant role usually accorded to the prima-donna soprano. (The distinction between "mezzo-soprano" and "contralto" was always vague, more subjective than scientific, but "contralto" was the preferred designation until the mid-twentieth century.) Not surprisingly, mezzos and contraltos have often coveted the higher repertory with its more glamorous—not to mention more financially remunerative—options, and many have ventured into soprano territory. Some have even permanently made the switch, often shortening their careers or even ruining their voices in the process. Fremstad was an exception, most likely a born mezzo-soprano who, through hard work and sheer will power, successfully made the adjustment upward. One of Homer's few potential rivals during her Met career, the American Edyth Walker (1867–1950), was less fortunate. After three seasons with the company sharing Amneris, Ortrud, and other major dramatic contralto/mezzo parts with Homer, Walker left for Europe in 1906. There she began to sing Isolde, Brünnhilde, and Strauss's Elektra, soon paying the price for her ambitions.

Homer, almost invariably labeled a contralto throughout her career, was never even tempted to follow suit. Azucena, Amneris, Ortrud, and Fidès in Le Prophète were her most strenuous roles, and she paced herself sensibly in them. Then, too, Homer had very little competition throughout her long Met career—only Ernestine Schumann-Heink and Margarete Matzenauer threatened her primacy, and those two formidable singers were often busy singing elsewhere. Because of Homer's need to be with her family, she was also prepared to devote herself entirely to the Met and remain in New York the whole season rather than make extensive (and more lucrative) concert tours or spend long periods of time in Europe. She was even willing to take lower fees if necessary, and the canny Gatti-Casazza knew he had a bargain. Besides, she was also easy to get along with and never made unreasonable demands. The public, the critics, her colleagues—everyone adored her. Her quiet dignity and warm, womanly charm radiate from all her photographs, even those that portray her as the evil Ortrud and the maniacal Azucena.

Since she seldom canceled, enjoyed robust health, and could always be relied upon to deliver the goods, Homer was rewarded with many plums, and she took part in some of the most memorable Met performances of the era, occasions that contributed to her prestige and post-humous legendary reputation. She sang Maddalena in *Rigoletto* on the night of Enrico Caruso's debut in 1903. Humperdinck himself coached her as his two witches, in the 1905 Met premiere of *Hänsel und Gretel* and five years later in the world premiere of *Königskinder*. She took the leading roles in the Met's initial forays into American opera—Converse's *The Pipe of Desire* and Parker's *Mona*—and in 1907 she sang Suzuki opposite Geraldine Farrar in the company's first *Madama Butterfly*, again with the composer on hand to direct her. Both Mahler and Toscanini made their Met debuts in 1908 and Homer sang in those performances too, as Brangäne for Mahler and Amneris for Toscanini. A quick study, the contralto once deputized for an ailing Olive Fremstad as Fricka in *Das Rheingold*, learning and memorizing the part in less than a day. Perhaps her greatest triumph came in 1909, when she starred in Toscanini's presentation of Gluck's *Orfeo ed Euridice*, the ideal vehicle for her voice and poised stage presence. Aldrich pronounced her impersonation as "one of nobility, dignity and plastic grace for the eye, and of full-throated and beautiful song for the ear . . . one of the finest and most artistic as well as one of the most original impersonations that Mme. Homer has given here." Homer, it seemed, had everything.

Most important of all, she had Sidney Homer. No singer could have asked for a more understanding, giving, loving helpmate, and they were deeply and genuinely in love with each other all their lives. Although his songs were popular with many American singers of his generation, Sidney made only a modest mark as a composer, and there was never any question who the breadwinner was in this large family, which always led a comfortable middle-class life. A sensitive man, Homer surely recognized that Louise, with her vocal talent and her industry, was making it all possible, and he may have resented the fact, if only unconsciously. During the busiest years of his wife's career, Sidney was often afflicted with inexplicable nervous disorders that sent him to health resorts in upstate New York for long periods. Yet if there was any marital discord, precious little evidence survives. In 1910, after fifteen years of marriage, Louise, on one of her infrequent trips out of town without Sidney, wrote home, "Darling, I'm so crazy to see you and be with you. I can't see how I can last another week. I'm not usually homesick, only I love you so, and we did have such dear times together this summer." Sidney replied, "I sort of realize that I was just about going to sleep for the rest of my life in the fall of '93 [the year the two first met], when a spark of life jumped in and set things afire. I don't care about being without that spark of life a minute."

Aside from domestic harmony, Homer also benefited from singing a stable repertory. Although she made her operatic debut in 1898 in Vichy singing Léonor in Donizetti's *La Favorite*, the contralto never really had to master the florid techniques necessary to perform the old bel canto operas. Nor, one suspects, would her ample, richly textured voice, which took so naturally to the Verdi-Wagner works that were her principal province, have been suited to the task. Here again Homer was lucky, more so than the singers of the preceding generation, who had to straddle two vocal worlds. Before taking a closer look at Homer and her achievements, it would be useful to pause and see how her most significant predecessor coped with that challenge: Annie Louise Cary (1841–1921), a contralto active in the 1870s and '80s who spent her retirement years in New York and no doubt frequently saw Homer perform at the Met.

We have already met Cary, the singer who so irritated Clara Louise Kellogg when those two pioneering Americans, along with the French soprano Marie Roze, joined forces for the Strakosch-Mapleson "three graces" tour in 1876. That cross-country marathon came at the height of Cary's professional life, which lasted little more than fifteen years. To begin one's career with such florid bel canto roles as Rossini's Arsace and Donizetti's Orsini and end it with heavy dramatic assignments like Verdi's Amneris and Wagner's Ortrud would tax any voice, and Cary's, originally admired for its extraordinary range of over three octaves, rich quality, and effortless production, had apparently begun to unravel even before she reached the age of forty. But then, so had Kellogg's voice after the soprano decided to look beyond Linda, Gilda, and Violetta and began experimenting with Aida, Senta, and Carmen.

A pure-bred Yankee from Kennebec County, Maine, Cary was encouraged to sing as a child by both her parents, who often appeared locally as amateur singers. After graduating from Maine's Gorham Seminary in 1860, the nineteen-year-old girl headed for Boston and the opportunity for serious vocal study, taking on all the concert work in local churches that she could handle and making frequent appearances with the Handel and Haydn Society. No doubt her larger career would have been launched sooner had not the Civil War intervened, but Cary was ready to take the big step by 1866, when she sailed for Europe to study with Giovanni Corsi in Milan. Like Emma Thursby, Cary was at first determined to make her name in concert and recital. The opera stage, she felt, was simply not a proper place for a well-bred girl from Maine, but fate soon made her change her mind. After a year with Corsi, she discovered that her debts had mounted to $6,000, so when an offer came from the opera in Copenhagen, she had no choice but to accept. Her debut, as Azucena, took place in 1867 (some sources cite Ulrica in *Un Ballo in Maschera* the following year), and after a successful tour of Scandinavia, Cary was quickly swept up into a busy operatic life that took her to Hamburg, Baden-Baden, and London, as well as to Paris for further studies, with Viardot and Bottesini.

In 1870 she was noticed by the Strakosch brothers, Max and Maurice, who had just formed a concert company to showcase Christine Nilsson in her first American appearances. The two impresarios also signed up Cary, who made her New York debut along with Nilsson at Steinway Hall on September 19, 1870. Naturally the local press was far more interested in the celebrated Swedish soprano than in the unknown contralto from Maine, but the *Herald* critic thought he had heard something special and singled out Cary as "a contralto of great purity, and an artist of more than ordinary merit." Also in the audience was the mighty Russian pianist and composer Anton Rubinstein, who reportedly stated, "It was the most beautiful voice I have ever heard in the whole world!" A year later, still with the Nilsson company, Cary sang her first operatic role in New York when she appeared as Nancy in *Martha* at the Academy of Music.

For the next ten years Cary was one of America's busiest singers, dividing her time among the great choral festivals in Boston, Cincinnati, and Worcester and various opera companies in the principal East Coast cities. Despite the distinction of being the first American to sing Amneris (1873) and Ortrud (1877), Cary never seemed quite comfortable singing opera, and she probably felt more at home in oratorio. On the concert stage Cary must have been something to hear, and critics of the day praised her lavishly. She also had the distinction of participating in the first American performances, according to *Dwight's Journal of Music*, of the Verdi *Requiem* (New York, November 17, 1874) as well as such major Bach scores as the *Christmas Oratorio* (Boston, May 17, 1877) and *Magnificat* (Cincinnati, May 13, 1875). Her approach to Bach would probably strike contemporary ears as woefully inauthentic, but to the exacting John Sullivan Dwight, Cary was "one of the noblest contralto singers in the world," whose treatment of Bach "more than any realized the spirit and transcendental art of this unsurpassable religious music."

Around 1880 Cary began experiencing vocal problems. Luckily, by then she had met Charles Monson Raymond, a wealthy banker and opera-hater who some years earlier had been dragged by a friend to see *Faust*. When the curtain fell, he announced to his surprised companion that one day he would marry the pretty girl who sang the trouser role of Siebel—which he eventually did, after a long courtship, on June 29, 1882. His bride retired then and there to devote the rest of her life to charitable causes and such good works as the New York Diet Kitchen, where she was often to be seen distributing food and clothing to the poor. During World War I, the first American Ortrud and Amneris took up knitting with a vengeance, setting a war-relief record by making 150 pairs of socks for the boys overseas. No doubt Louise Homer was among the first to congratulate her.

Homer had a few other immediate predecessors, and she was likely aware of them, even though Hélène Hastreiter (1858–1922) and Antoinette Sterling (1850–1904) both conducted their careers mainly in Europe. Hastreiter was the most famous American exponent of Gluck's Orfeo until Homer's Met triumph in 1909. After 1889, though, she had virtually disappeared from the local scene, having recently married Dr. C. L. Burgonzi, a noted Genoese nerve specialist. The remainder of Hastreiter's career was confined to Italy and France.

During her two Covent Garden seasons in 1899–1900, Homer must surely have encountered and taken note of Antoinette Sterling, who by then was practically a British institution. Another Yankee blueblood, she managed to avoid opera altogether, reserving her imposing contralto "of great sweetness and volume" exclusively for the concert platform. She began voice lessons in 1867 with a Signor Abella in New York, but in the following year traveled to Europe for an extensive period of study with Mathilde Marchesi in Cologne, Pauline Viardot in Baden-Baden, and Manuel García II in London. Although she returned to New York in 1871 and became a soloist at Henry Ward Beecher's prestigious church in Brooklyn, Sterling eventually settled permanently in England, where she married John MacKinlay in 1875 and became a ubiquitous presence on the London music scene as a singer of ballads and oratorios. One bit of indirect testimony regarding the size and richness of Sterling's voice is contained in Sir Arthur Sullivan's most famous song, "The Lost Chord," which was expressly written to display this singer's special qualities. Sterling lavished her booming contralto on that Victorian perennial for the first but hardly last time when she introduced it at a Boosey Ballad concert in London on January 31, 1877. Even Shaw was impressed by her singing, though he felt it had limitations when the contralto addressed the great works of opera and oratorio.

Opera, ballads, Bach, the oratorios of Handel—Louise Homer sang them all for many years, exhibiting precisely the sort of "delicate artificial refinements of correct phrasing and fluent execution" that Shaw found lacking in Sterling's limited vocal armory. Although she sang as a soloist in church choirs throughout her girlhood days, Homer never seems to have been driven to pursue a singing career, which she definitely decided upon only at the age of twenty-two. The fourth of eight children fathered by William Trimble Beatty, a Presbyterian minister, Louise Dilworth Beatty was born on April 30, 1871, in Shadyside, a rural suburb of Pittsburgh. By the time Louise reached school age, the Reverend Beatty had already begun to suffer from tuberculosis, and hoping to improve his health, he moved the family to St. Paul, Minnesota. There he died in 1882, leaving Sarah Beatty and her brood to manage as best they could. Soon the family moved back to Pennsylvania to be near relatives, and it was in West Chester, at the age of fourteen, that Louise first sang in public while simultaneously demonstrating an apparent inborn ability to take charge in any emergency. She sang not only the title role in a cantata called *Ruth, the Moabitess* but also the part of Boaz when the scheduled bass, who had gone to Harrisburg for the day on business, missed the last train home.

After graduating from high school, Louise worked first as a secretary at the William Penn Charter School in Philadelphia and later as a court stenographer, all the while continuing vocal instruction and her church work. Soon it became clear that singing meant more to her than shorthand, and time was passing. At an age when most important singers of her generation had already completed their basic training and made professional debuts, Louise decided to devote herself entirely to serious musical studies. She opted to pursue them in Boston, where, in that city of classical tradition, home of the famous St. Cecilia Chorus, Handel and Haydn Society, and Boston Symphony Orchestra, she felt could find the most promising opportunities.

Since Louise's sister Bess lived in Arlington, a brief ride from downtown Boston, the budding contralto moved in. She paid for room and board, as well as for voice lessons with William Whitney (son of the New England bass Myron Whitney), from her salary as a member of the choir at the First Universalist Church, directed by the influential Boston composer George Chadwick. Louise wanted to improve her basic musical knowledge as well as her voice, so Bess recommended a friend of the family, one Sidney Homer, a young man of twenty-nine who taught theory and harmony in a studio at the corner of Boylston and Tremont streets. Sidney needed all the pupils he could get, but since Louise couldn't afford his rate of three dollars an hour, he offered to teach her at the reduced price of two dollars for forty minutes. Not only did the lessons soon became longer, but Sidney started turning up with increasing frequency at Mrs. Barrows's boarding house in Boston, where Louise had moved in order to lead a more independent life.

Rigorously organized, Louise had an account book where she listed her expenses and engagements, and the entry for January 1894 contains revealing information: "Wednesday. Harmony lesson at 11; Apollo concert with Mr. Homer in evening. Thursday, Cecilia rehearsal with Mr. Homer. Friday, singing lesson at 11; symphony class (Mr. Homer) at 12; symphony at 2:30 (Mr. Homer). Saturday, Harmony lesson at 11; sang But the Lord at Conservatory (Mr. Homer there); choir at 4:30; lesson at six. Sunday, Church with Mr. Homer in evening . . . Am I seeing too much of Mr. Homer?"

Apparently not. Soon they were truly inseparable, and both began to discover opera and the stars who made it glitter—Melba as Juliette, De Reszke as Lohengrin, Eames as Marguerite, Calvé as Mignon—and Louise became increasingly fascinated with the idea of performing on the stage herself. That spring, on Louise's twenty-third birthday, Sidney declared himself, and four days later they were engaged. All of this news was a bit difficult for Sarah Beatty back in Pennsylvania to swallow. Not only was Sidney a nonbeliever, but the idea of her daughter going on the stage severely tested her Presbyterian morals. Love conquered all eventually, however, and the happy couple were married on January 9, 1895. For the time being, their life in Boston remained unchanged, as Louise continued her studies and Sidney taught an ever-growing number of pupils. In November the first child arrived, little Louise, but even that blessed event did not deter the new mother from her operatic ambitions. Unfortunately, though, her voice was not improving.

Naturally there was only one course: the essential trip to Europe to find the proper voice teacher who could correct such defects as heaviness and uneven placement. Then, with luck, the career would follow. So Sidney made his first sacrifice. He gave up his increasingly lucrative teaching practice, and raised the necessary $2,500 to take himself, his wife, and little daughter to Paris. The first year must have left them both discouraged. Louise's first teacher was Jacques Bouhy, whose pupils were singing opera everywhere, but after several months she was alarmed to hear her voice becoming smaller and more covered. Next she turned to an Italian, one Signor Juliani, whose methods only seemed to make matters worse—her greatest asset, those deep, low tones, suddenly began to disappear. Desperate, Louise finally put herself into the hands of Fidèle Koenig, who was not a voice teacher but a coach. Whether due to his instinctive understanding of this unique voice or the sheer chemistry that sometimes develops between teacher and pupil, Koenig's approach worked wonders. Soon, to her astonishment, Louise had not only regained what she had lost under Bouhy and Juliani but had advanced to the point where she could effortlessly sail through Fidès's demanding scene from Act V of Le Prophète, an aria of enormous range and brilliance requiring a voice of unusual power and flexibility.

In December 1897 Maurice Grau of the Metropolitan Opera was in Paris—the resident company in New York did not perform that season— and Koenig arranged for him to hear Louise. Grau was complimentary and filed the name for future reference, since the Met did not hire debutantes. No sooner had Grau urged her to get experience, then the offer came from Vichy—which did not take debutantes either, but the company desperately needed a leading contralto for the coming summer season, and Louise had impressed its impresario sufficiently for him to take a chance. And it was a formidable gamble for both. In the space of a few months Louise would have to learn Léonor in La Favorite, the Queen in Hamlet, Dalila, Ortrud, Venus, Margared in Lalo's Le Roi d'Ys, and Albine in Thaïs. The day of her debut arrived and all the hard work paid off. Her very opening duet with the Fernand, Émile Scaramberg, one of the finest tenors of the Paris Opéra, had to be encored, and her big aria, "Ô mon Fernand," brought down the house. An engagement followed immediately at Angers, and in 1899 she was appearing at Covent Garden and the Monnaie in Brussels. That was good enough for Grau, and in the spring of 1900 he deemed her ready for the Metropolitan.

Homer's debut with the company, as Amneris, took place in San

Francisco during a preseason tour, and she repeated the role for her official bow in New York on December 22. Not many operagoers took notice. The great French bass Marcel Journet also made his house debut that evening, as Ramfis, and Antonio Scotti must have been an impressive Amonasro, but the rest of the cast was mediocre and the audience was small. Minnie Tracy, an American soprano of little note, made her one and only Met appearance that night as Aida, and the poorly received Georges Imbart de la Tour, who sang Radamès, left town the next day. When Johanna Gadski and Jean de Reszke took over these roles two weeks later, Homer was heard to better advantage, obviously a singer who could hold her own in the best company. Even so, Grau proceeded cautiously with his new contralto, whose other roles that season and next—Siebel (Faust), Schwertleite (Die Walküre), Maddalena (Rigoletto), Urbain (Les Huguenots), Marta and Pantalis (Boito's Mefistofele), and Lola (Cavalleria Rusticana)—were virtually comprimario assignments.

Perhaps Grau was remembering the chance he had taken a year earlier with an even younger American contralto, Eleanor Broadfoot (1878–1934), a protégée of Jean de Reszke's. At twenty-one—and a debutante (De Reszke's influence obviously counted for much)— Broadfoot sang one Amneris along with several minor roles during her one season, and then disappeared from the Met for good. A year later, however, Broadfoot married a Cuban count named Francesco de Cisneros, headed to Paris for finishing, and emerged as Eleonora de Cisneros. Under that name she enjoyed success at Covent Garden and La Scala, and by the time Oscar Hammerstein engaged her in 1906 for his new Manhattan Opera, Cisneros was an international celebrity. And so she remained for the next two decades, singing the heavy contralto/mezzo-soprano repertory in Chicago and with many other companies all over the globe, appearing as Strauss's Herodias as late as the 1924–25 season in Milan. Why she never reappeared at the Met is perhaps a matter of opera politics. Her surviving records reveal an airy, attractive, evenly produced voice—a trifle light, considering her heavy repertory, but it was definitely a major endowment and one that may have well given Homer considerable competition.

Meanwhile, Homer was beginning to prove just how valuable she would be as a member of the Met family. Grau soon rewarded her with more prominent roles, including her first Azucena. Then, in the fall of 1902, the Met manager asked her to prepare Carmen for the first week of the season. Still recovering from the birth of her second child, Sidney junior, Homer felt unable to accept, and after Calvé returned to reclaim her most famous part, the opportunity to sing Bizet's Gypsy never presented itself again—or perhaps Homer had second thoughts and wisely decided that Carmen was simply not for her. In any case, her position was secure, her contract was renewed, and her future career and, more important, her family could now settle into a comfortable groove. Homer may have been momentarily threatened when Heinrich Conried succeeded Grau in 1903 and brought with him Edyth Walker, who, it was said, had been promised "absolute control" of the leading contralto roles. Instead of throwing a prima-donna fit, Homer, together with Sidney, paid Walker a call after her debut as Amneris, complimented her voice and effective performance, and wanted to hear all about her life at the Vienna State Opera. Soon the three were chatting about musical matters like old friends, and later Walker confessed that she was absolutely astonished: instead of plotting, intriguing, and passing sarcastic remarks, her rival always treated her with warmth and affection.

In any case, Walker soon left the company, and by 1905 Homer was solidly established with the critics and public, not only as the Met's leading contralto, but also as a much-loved presence. She opened that season as Laura in Ponchielli's *La Gioconda* with Nordica, Caruso, Scotti, and Plançon, and on the morning of the performance she welcomed a reporter from the *Mail and Express* into her West Eighty-ninth Street home, which in those days overlooked a livery stable. The scene of rural domesticity was completed by little Sidney, who, during the interview, watched the horses being fed and watered from his nursery window. "Calmest of the principals in tonight's cast," the article began, "was Louise Homer, who in private life is the wife of the composer and mother of two children. Today she was quietly going about her household duties, singing a few scales now and then, but keeping the balance between the work of a famous contralto and the routine of a happy home life, in a comfortable house west of Central Park. Tonight she will drive down to the Metropolitan and be transformed into the faithless Laura who is helped to a successful elopement with Enzo Caruso by her erstwhile rival, Nordica Gioconda."

Like many Met stars, Homer was in San Francisco that spring when the earthquake struck, and for years it was thought that she was the only singer in the company to sustain serious injury. "As soon as she was found, near the St. Francis Hotel," ran one account, "slightly harmed, she was hurried to Chicago for treatment." Another newspaper breathlessly reported that "succumbing to the nervous strain of the last few days, Louise Homer reached Chicago yesterday only to be taken to the Wesley Hospital on the verge of a nervous breakdown." Actually, Louise was three months pregnant and the earthquake had induced a miscarriage. The scars of that tragedy were slow to heal, but other healthy children were on the way: Katharine and Anne in 1907 (the "famous Homer twins," as they came to be known), Hester Makepeace in 1911, and the last daughter, Helen Joy, in 1914.

When Giulio Gatti-Casazza took over the Met in 1908, many old-timers feared for themselves and the future of the company—Eames and several others took early retirement—but by then Homer was an invaluable fixture and Gatti knew it. Besides, there was no other contralto in sight so dependable, versatile, and popular with the public. She opened Gatti's first season in *Aida* with Caruso, Destinn, Scotti, and Didur, with Toscanini making his debut, and that performance launched the greatest decade of her career. Her voice was at its zenith, and she was never busier. It was also during this time that the sensitive but ever faithful Sidney—described by his daughter Anne as needing "a refuge, a reasonable retreat from pressures that could loom, too large for one who was too easily engulfed"—was often at Kerhonkson, a health resort in the Adirondacks, where he was "still trying to allay those mysterious demons of tension and anxiety."

The pressures must also have been extreme for Louise as she prepared for the busy 1912–13 season without Sidney. There were endless rehearsals, worries about her husband, her ailing mother in West Chester, and five children coming down with one stomach ailment after another. "Hester has it now," she wrote Sidney at Kerhonkson. "It is my fault, I started giving her whole milk too soon. She woke last night and cried pathetically for hours, but by two o'clock she was asleep in my arms. Then this afternoon by five Morgenstern [a Metropolitan coach and conductor] came to put me through some stunts on Gotter and Meister. But I'm tired of all these rehearsals. Meister tomorrow at 8 P.M., Gotter Friday evening, Gioconda Saturday, Gotter with orchestra Sunday A.M. and I forget what Sunday evening. If the latter can be changed I'll go to West Chester Sunday afternoon to see Mama, and come back Monday . . ."

But she never seemed too busy to withhold attention from anyone who might need it. Mary Watkins, Olive Fremstad's young "buffer," recalled how Homer would even mother her when she spotted the girl standing backstage, wearily waiting in the wings for her mistress. "'Come on in and sit down,' she would say hospitably while adjusting her makeup. 'Let me tell you about my twins.' If the tale remained unfinished when she was called to the stage, she would follow the regisseur reluctantly, calling back over her shoulder to me, 'I'll tell you the rest when I get back!' And she always did. Dear Madame Homer! I remember her with so much affection, for she helped me over many rough places. But the fact that she had no nerves, in the Fremstad sense, made that temperamental singer frequently remark that she envied her, in tones that unmistakably implied something quite the contrary."

By 1918, after she finally added Fidès to her stage repertory and completed the cycle that had begun more than twenty years earlier in Paris, Homer decided that she would not renew her Met contract. After singing with the company for nineteen years and performing so many of her roles over and over, she needed a change. Besides, the children were growing up, and it was now possible to arrange concert tours, so much more remunerative than opera, and they could be worked around school schedules. Even better, the family could now take part. Young Louise had been studying voice, and after she displayed a promising soprano, the girl began to sing duets with her mother. Soon Katharine was accompanying them both at the piano, and of course Sidney's songs were always prominently featured on the program. Eventually Homer extended her repertory to include songs written by her precocious teenage nephew, Samuel Barber, the son of her youngest sister, Daisy.

In this way Homer passed the twenties, meshing her family and career more closely than ever. She even sang opera occasionally, mainly with the Chicago Grand Opera Company between 1922 and 1925, and in 1927 she returned to the Met for a few triumphant guest performances, singing one final Azucena on Thanksgiving Day, 1929. As usual, it was a family occasion, as the *Times* noted: "A memorable event took place at the opera house on Thursday when Louise Homer, famous American contralto, returned to the scene of her triumphs of bygone years, while three generations of her family sat in one of the boxes, among them her granddaughter and namesake, little Louise Homer . . . seldom, if ever, has an artist at the Metropolitan sung before three generations of her family, with her singing and acting as artistic and effective as ever."

With reviews like that, Homer might have considered continuing with her career. But when Sidney's poor health made life in New York

City during the winter virtually impossible, Louise effectively retired except for the occasional concert and radio appearance. Now at last she could indulge herself, her husband, her children, and her grandchildren all year round, at their Homeland estate at Lake George during the summers and, when the weather turned too cold for Sidney, in Florida's Winter Park. It was there that the couple celebrated their golden wedding anniversary in 1945, and mourned the death of their youngest daughter, Joy, in the fall of 1946. Several months later, on May 6, 1947, Louise herself succumbed, to coronary thrombosis. Sidney survived her by six years, dying in 1953 at the age of eighty-eight.

Homer's art was captured on discs, and few artists of her generation are more generously represented. Homer was one of the first Met singers the Victor company approached. Although reluctant at first—Sidney thought it somehow disreputable for a serious artist to sing into a horn like a common music-hall entertainer—Homer agreed, embarking on a recording career that lasted right up to her retirement from opera in 1929. By then she had made nearly two hundred titles (more than fifty were never released), and the royalties eventually brought her a great deal of money. Homer's discs were among the era's bestsellers, they remained in the catalogue for years, and the wide range of repertory gives a very complete picture of her musical activities: excerpts from operatic roles as well as art songs, popular ballads, and duets with such luminaries as Caruso, Farrar, Eames, Gluck, and Martinelli.

Some voices took to the acoustic process better than others, and here again Homer was lucky. The sound is huge, but the tone is wonderfully focused on the note, each attack has superb definition, and the voice's warm, natural overtones provide a cushioned sound that prevents any hint of blasting. Exposed in such an extensive recorded repertory, Homer could hardly disguise her limitations. The high notes are available to her, but just barely—she is clearly a contralto whose upper extension had to be cultivated, and sometimes the results sound white, hooty, and mostly a matter of will power. Nor does Homer always convince while executing florid work that would have come naturally to singers of an earlier generation. For some inexplicable reason she recorded Delibes's showpiece "Les Filles de Cadiz" a number of times, but this sparkling, graceful music, with its saucy embellishments and pert turns of phrase, hardly seems suited to her rather stolid, unsmiling manner. With items recorded more than once, her earliest versions are preferable, before that magisterial tone began to thicken and lose its responsiveness.

But when Homer addresses her great roles, she gives ample evidence why she was so beloved by the public and considered so valuable by three Met general managers. After admiring the columnar strength, security, and declamatory majesty of her Amneris and Azucena, her Ortrud and Dalila, her Orfeo and Fidès, contemporary listeners can turn to her affectionate, warmly intimate accounts of the songs that made up her concert repertory. Not surprisingly, she lavishes all of her vocal resources on Sidney's songs, even if this devoted wife and all her art are unable to transform such quaint period pieces into great music.

Twelve

~

The Divine

Mary

~~~~~~~~~~~~~~~~~~~~

The others 'acted' a role; I was the role. She who was Mary Garden died that it might live. That was my genius . . . and my sacrifice."

Yes, Mary Garden was unique, although whatever she may have had to sacrifice to "create" a role, her genius was not a tragic one. Garden knew precisely what she wanted, what she had to do to get it, and what she was worth, and few who saw her failed to get her message. When the petite Scottish-born soprano from Chicago met Debussy in 1902, the composer told her, "You have come from the mists of the north to create my music," and insisted that only she would sing Mélisande in the premiere of his new opera. Frances Alda, never one to offer other sopranos idle compliments, wrote that Garden's interpretation of Mélisande "remains immortal. She was so still. Just that one little phrase: 'Il fait froid ici,' as it came from her lips, and you shivered under the chill winds that blow between the worlds of the real and the unreal. Contrasted with it, [Lucrezia] Bori's rendering of the line sounded like a schoolgirl who steps out of bed without her slippers." Another admirer, Vincent

Sheean, emphasized the ethereal impression her Mélisande made: "She hardly moved her hands and arms for long stretches of the action: her head was usually bowed in submission, but when it moved it had the pallor of the tomb at times; it was difficult to understand how such misty rose-gray and blue-gray notes could spin from a human throat."

Interestingly, both Sheean and Alda—as well as dozens of others who fell under her spell—speak of Garden principally as a theatrical phenomenon. When her voice is discussed, it is usually praised for its remarkable command of coloration rather than its ability to spin musical abstractions or indulge in pyrotechnical display. More than any other singer of her era, Garden pointed up the changes that were afoot in the opera world at the turn of the century. Composers no longer wrote operas to show off a singer's bel canto training or spectacular vocal technique. Under the influence of Wagner and late Verdi, they now wrote "music dramas" with juicy acting parts like Tosca, Thaïs, and Salome—personality roles that required a new kind of singer. Old-fashioned divas like Patti, with their bag of coloratura tricks and self-conscious prima-donna attitudinizing, could never hope to perform these parts convincingly. Glamorous singing actresses were now needed to entrance audiences, and no one seduced them more potently than Garden.

The yawning chasm created by this generation gap is immediately apparent in Garden's brief encounter with Mathilde Marchesi, soon after the young soprano arrived in Paris in 1895 to look for a singing teacher. By then the formidable Marchesi was in her seventies and Garden found her totally impossible, a relic of a bygone age, "an old, curt, haughty woman who came forward like an empress and just deigned to bow to you—almost didn't bow." Marchesi was naturally determined to take her latest charge and drill her until she became, or could at least approximate, the only type of singer the old lady knew: a brilliant technician like Melba or Eames. Garden quickly realized that she was being pulled in the wrong direction, and after three weeks of lessons she wrote Marchesi that she could not continue, since she had no intention of becoming a coloratura. A few days later the reply came. "Mary Garden," it read. "A rolling stone gathers no moss. Don't cry till you come out of the woods."

Garden was not in the habit of weeping, whether in or out of the woods, and she wrote off Marchesi as an old fogey who was hopelessly out of touch. Besides, young Mary had just found a more sympathetic teacher by the name of Antonio Trabadello (or Trabadelo), who encouraged her to use her voice in a normal, natural way, as if she were singing by herself at home. This, she later said, was music to her ears. "Look out for teachers with freak methods!" Garden later advised young singers. "The chances are they are making you one of their experiments. No voice teacher has ever found anything superior to giving simple scales and exercises sung upon the syllables 'lah,' 'leh,' and 'lee.' With a good teacher to keep watch over the breathing and quality of the voice, one can feel perfectly safe. It was that way with Trabadello." Singers before and after would argue about that, but it wasn't long before Garden had acquired all the vocal technique she felt she would ever need to do the job—not just to sing a role, but to "create" it.

"I began my career at the top, I stayed at the top, and I left at the top" became one of Garden's favorite observations in her later years. Befriended in 1899 by the unfortunate Sibyl Sanderson, Garden was immediately taken by her new protectress to Albert Carré, director of the Opéra-Comique, who calmly looked her over and, impressed by her supreme self-assurance, remarked, "You know, that's a very special kind of girl. I have a feeling she will make an interesting Louise." Carré hadn't even heard her sing, but when he did he invited her to a rehearsal of Charpentier's new opera, a celebration of working-class Paris and free love. Garden was captivated. "Oh, M. Carré," she exclaimed, "what a wonderful opera! What gorgeous music and drama! How I'd like to study it!" "Very well," replied Carré, "I'll get you a score." For the next two months Garden studied the opera day and night, and she soon knew it inside out.

Louise was a sensation at its premiere on February 2, 1900, and two months later Garden got her big break. On Tuesday, April 10 (later Mary preferred to date it as Friday the thirteenth), Carré summoned her to the theater. Marthe Rioton, who had created the role, was feeling ill, and Garden was told to sit out front that evening, just in case. Sure enough, the call came after the curtain fell on Act II. Rioton had fled the theater in distress and the conductor, André Messager, insisted that they cancel the performance and refund the audience's money. Carré, however, was determined to send his protégée into the breach. As Garden recalled the scene:

We had to work fast now, since intermission time between the second and third acts was drawing to a close. They took me upstairs to the dressing room, and there they dressed me in a beautiful long blue silk gown that had nothing whatever to do with *Louise*. I then weighed ninety-eight pounds. I was so small they could find nothing else to fit me. So they pinned me into this dress and brought me downstairs again. They put me in the front part of the stage behind the chair where my lover Julien was supposed to be sitting, waiting for me. Then everybody on the stage went into the wings, hundreds of them, all waiting to see this unknown person rise—or fall. I wasn't a bit nervous. I have never been nervous in all my life and I have no patience with people who are. If you know what you're going to do, you have no reason to be nervous. And I knew what I was going to do . . .

Without so much as a rehearsal—indeed, without professional stage experience of any kind—Garden watched the curtain rise and promptly launched into Louise's aria, "Depuis le jour," confident that she would be a star the next morning. And she was right—all Paris was talking about Carré's bold *coup de théâtre* and the miraculous little soprano *écossaise*. The following Wednesday she sang the complete role, and Carré gave her a five-year contract on the spot. "Mlle. Rioton never sang Louise again at the Opéra-Comique," wrote Garden, who was to give more than a hundred performances of the part during the next eight years. "The role became exclusively mine, and I never found out if they had an understudy for me. All I know is that I never missed a performance." And then, with a touch of pretty poison, she added, "Later they gave the role of Hansel to Mlle. Rioton, and she was perfectly enchanting in it."

By 1900 there was definitely a *jeune fille américaine* tradition in Parisian opera circles. Some would dispute Garden's position in this sequence—like Maria Callas fifty years later, she resists being assigned any definitive nationality. Born in Aberdeen, Scotland, in 1874 (like most singers, she docked three years off her age while she lived), Mary was six years old when she and her two sisters were brought to America by their father, Robert Davidson Garden, an engineer. He later became a citizen—and a fourth daughter, Helen, was born in America—but Mary retained a British passport all her life, although some sources claim that she indeed acquired U.S. citizenship in 1924. Soon after her singing career was over, in 1935, Garden returned to Aberdeen, where she died in 1967 at the age of ninety-two, only days after singing one last verse of "Annie

Laurie" to a captive audience in her nursing home. But despite her British heritage, Garden was always more closely tied to America. After a brief stay in Brooklyn, the family moved to Chicopee, Massachusetts, where Mary spent her girlhood before settling as a teenager in Chicago to begin serious musical and vocal studies. The American connection became even stronger later on, for it was in New York and, even more prominently, in Chicago that Garden mainly conducted her career after leaving Paris in 1907. After her few Covent Garden appearances in 1902 and 1903, England rarely saw her perform again.

The fact that Garden's nationality seemed so elusive only added to her mystery, one more reason why Debussy instinctively felt that he had found the ideal Mélisande, an ethereal waif from nowhere. "I have nothing, absolutely nothing, to tell her" was the composer's only comment after having observed Garden in four months of rehearsal. In her score Debussy wrote, "In the future others may sing Mélisande, but you alone will remain the woman and the artist I had hardly dared hope for." Further enhancing this ideal image was the fascinating aura of unattainability that clung to Garden. She never married, but readily confessed to numerous love affairs. By the time of the *Pelléas* premiere in 1902, Messager, who conducted, was not only an ardent fan but a discarded lover. Later, Garden claimed, even Debussy made a pass but she quickly brushed him off. "I never really loved anybody," she confessed. "I had a fondness for men, yes, but very little passion and no need." She brought that enigmatic quality to Mélisande as well as her other great roles, and it fueled her legend.

In fact, the three heroines most closely associated with Mary Garden handily sum up her magnetic appeal: the free-loving Louise, the seductive courtesan Thaïs, and the otherworldly Mélisande. Garden always insisted that she never studied her roles in any analytical way, and she was surely referring to Olive Fremstad when discussing how she approached Salome at the Manhattan Opera, two years after the older soprano's single scandalous performance at the Metropolitan. "I knew everything about Salome. I didn't go to books and I didn't go to museums, as many people say they do, and I didn't go to see what death was like. Why don't these singers have the imagination to see it themselves? I just had it in me, all of it. I was Thaïs, I was Mélisande, I was Salome. That was all there was to it. I put on the clothes and the wigs and I became Salome."

Garden spent eight busy years at the Comique, learning one new role after another. Most were either world premiere creations or newer works that momentarily captured the public's imagination. By the time she retired in 1934, the soprano had sung thirty-four parts (sixteen written especially for her), but only a handful—Gounod's Marguerite and Juliette, Thomas's Ophélie, and Verdi's Violetta—came from an earlier period, and she seldom sang those in later years. Indeed, her London debut was a disastrous Juliette, although Garden blamed her inability to sing any note above A on rheumatism of the vocal cords, caught while unwisely standing in front of an open window and admiring the boats sailing down the Thames. She later redeemed herself and the *Pall Mall Gazette* proclaimed her Marguerite a lovely thing, "slender, agile, unsophisticated, and thoughtless—it was in her thoughtlessness that her originality lay—she . . . made the part far more rational than is usual, proving, indeed, that the fall of Marguerite was surely the most natural thing in the world . . . Her singing was sweet and pleasant, though not overdistinguished by strength . . ." Garden never sang Violetta in America, because, as she said, "the American brand of Violetta was a pure coloratura, a healthy, robust nightingale with a high E flat finishing the first-act aria. If she ever missed that E flat, heaven help her! Now, as far as I was concerned, that had nothing whatsoever to do with the lady of the camellias. So I left my lady in Paris." Perhaps she should have reconsidered. The American critic James Huneker saw her Violetta in Paris and thought she sang it superlatively, adding, "It was, however, the conception and acting that intrigued. Originality stamped both. The death scene was of unusual poignancy; evidently the young American had been spying upon Bernhardt and Duse."

Garden much preferred the modern repertory, not only because the operas of Massenet, Debussy, and their lesser contemporaries were better suited to her voice, but because their works left her free to create her own traditions. Most of the new operas she sang never approached the quality of *Louise* or *Thaïs*, let alone *Pelléas*, but the spirit that propelled them thrilled her. All artists inspired by the creative energy of their own time would understand precisely what Garden meant when she flatly said, "There [was] no reason in the world why modern grand opera should not come nearer expressing the essentials and realities of life than [had] been the case heretofore." True, the vast majority of the works she created were ephemera and unlikely to be revived, period pieces like Saint-Saëns's *Hélène*, Leroux's *La Reine Fiammette*, Pierné's *La Fille de Tabarin*, Bruneau's *L'Ouragan*, and Bunning's *La Princesse Osra*. But at least Garden was passionately involved with the operatic art of her time and she was perfectly capable of telling gems from paste.

The heroines she performed, even those in the trashiest vehicles, were usually dominating personalities who offered a charismatic singing actress every opportunity to summon up her feminine allure and stun audiences with her theatrical genius. Garden could hardly resist donning the clinging Grecian dresses of Chrysis in Erlanger's feeble *Aphrodite* and reveling in the opera's sensational features, which included a nude scene, overt lesbianism, the crucifixion of a black slave, and a multiracial orgy. The premiere took place in 1906 and the opera vanished soon after Garden left the cast, but as long as she appeared as Chrysis, the house sold out. The exacting Parisians even forgave Garden's pronounced English accent, which only seemed to add to her exotic appeal. Everyone waited for that priceless moment in *La Marseillaise*—an opera by one Lucien Lambert about the life of Rouget de Lisle, the author of France's national anthem—when Garden would leap up in a state of patriotic frenzy and announce with a distinct Celtic burr, "Je suis française!"

One day in 1907 Garden returned home from the Opéra-Comique to find a stranger in her drawing room. Without waiting to be introduced, he looked her over and said, "Turn around, Mary, and let me see your figure." It was Oscar Hammerstein, and Garden claims that she was enchanted and took to him instantly—"so unlike all the other impresarios I have ever known, with their usual questions about what operas you've sung, and how much money you want, and with whom you studied." Apparently Hammerstein liked what he saw, and he knew that Garden, with her flamboyant theatricality and ability to create publicity, would be a valuable asset to his newly established Manhattan Opera in its to-the-death struggle with the Metropolitan. Besides, the impresario had just bought the American rights to two of Garden's most celebrated vehicles—*Thaïs* and *Louise*—and he knew that their success would depend to a great extent on her presence. But he was uncertain whether the opera that he charmingly called *Pelzees and Maylisander* by a certain Deboozy might not be too esoteric for New Yorkers. Garden urged him to see it and make up his own mind—by then she had come to trust his breezy, straightforward manner. "I had a feeling," she said, "I was standing before a man of instinctive good taste and judgment in music."

Hammerstein saw one act of his *Pelzees and Maylisander*, immediately marched into Garden's dressing room, and said "Sold!" But before Garden would sign anything that involved transporting her beloved *Pelléas* to

America, she made Hammerstein agree to surround her with an all-French cast. The impresario went her one better by engaging three of the principals who had sung in the world premiere—Jean Périer (Pelléas), Hector Dufranne (Golaud), and Jeanne Gerville-Réache (Geneviève)—and had the original scenery reconstructed in Paris and shipped to New York. "That's what I liked about Oscar Hammerstein—" Garden enthused, "the finest, or nothing at all. Money never meant a damn to him."

To celebrate, Hammerstein suggested that they hire a car, motor out to the palace at Fontainebleau, and sign the contract there. Garden thought that a splendid idea, and suggested the very desk that Napoleon had used to sign his abdication. On the way, though, a wheel flew off their chauffeur-driven limousine, and the entire party was thrown into a poppy field at the side of the road. Both delighted by that twist of fate, Garden and Hammerstein decided that they had found an even more appropriate spot to sign their four-year contract, which they proceeded to do, flat on the ground amid the poppies. A few months later, with cries of "Ne partez pas!" from her Paris fans ringing in her ears, Mary Garden went back home to America as one of the international opera world's most provocative and controversial stars.

A ruthlessly self-aware singer who never doubted her abilities, Garden still arrived in New York with misgivings. The modern French repertory was practically unknown there—the Met concentrated mainly on Italian and German operas—and she feared that New York might not understand the works she loved or her interpretive methods, even though Hammerstein generously provided her with colleagues versed in the French tradition. As it turned out, her suspicions proved correct. She made her debut on November 25, 1907, in *Thaïs*, one of the eight new operas that Hammerstein would introduce to America that season. The opera was not generally liked—the *Herald* considered it "colorless and saccharine," although the *Sun* could at least recognize "a highly finished piece of stagecraft." Garden was also received with reservations, but most granted that she was unquestionably a fascinating personality. The *Press* critic gave the most vivid description of her performance: "Every motion of her sinuous body is visible through the thin, rose-colored drapery, which clung to limbs and torso with studied persistency. When she took breath the action of her diaphragm swayed her yielding form in wave-like undulations. At moments it seemed as if this creature of supple frame, slender as a sapling, pliant as a willow, wore only the garb of Eve as she moved along the boards with the stride of a tigress and the tortuousness of a serpent."

Many years later, in 1951, Garden wrote that the critics "didn't understand what we were doing . . . the papers just pulled me to pieces." In an interview five days after her debut, however, she remarked sweetly and with savvy diplomacy that she had been given "lovely" treatment by the press—but what a shame they had not understood what *Thaïs* was really all about. Although the reaction to her singular voice was mixed, the most influential critics—Henderson, Aldrich, Krehbiel—made a serious attempt to evaluate her unusual vocal personality, which they clearly found new and disturbing. If they occasionally seemed puzzled, that was only understandable. All three critics had heard most of the major voices of the past twenty years or more, singers rigorously trained in the classical García and Marchesi methods, and their expectations of what constituted great singing were those of an earlier generation functioning in an entirely different repertory. Garden was fully aware of this, and in her post-performance interview, she tried to make it easier for them by observing, "I know full well that I have not a great voice, and I do not make any claim to such heights. I am not a Melba or a Calvé and do not expect to be compared with such singers."

Garden's honesty does her credit, but in retrospect she seems much too modest. Her reputation as the original no-voice soprano grew during her years in New York, a legend that has been widely accepted ever since, but one that hardly bears close scrutiny. She left a handful of recordings and two silent films, ironically separating sound and sight in a performer who relied on the combination of both more than most, and perhaps the discs do her scant justice. Garden herself hated them, but still they contain enough information to prove that she would be considered a major singer in any age. The first set was made in 1902, and despite Debussy accompanying at the piano—two brief excerpts from *Pelléas* and some of his songs—these faded mementos are little more than curiosities. In 1911–12 she recorded a sampling of her more conventional operatic repertory, with Violetta's Act I scene from *La Traviata* perhaps the most revealing (Garden sings the aria in French, the language she preferred throughout her career, even for *Salome* and *Tosca*). As she warned, a listener will hear no top E-flat or virtuoso display, but her intonation is flawless and absolutely secure, the passagework smoothly managed, and the floating lyrical tone in the first part of the scene could hardly be more attractive.

The French arias recorded during this period, from *Louise* and three Massenet operas—*Le Jongleur de Notre-Dame, Hérodiade,* and *Thaïs*—are even more enjoyable. Not only do they share the same inviting vocal traits as the Verdi aria, but they also show us Garden's intuitive understanding of the style and her passionate belief in material that later generations seemed to lose. While pleasant enough, the songs she recorded are less valuable and mostly reflect the soprano's Scottish ancestry; at least they give us an even clearer idea of her singular timbre, brushed with a fast vibrato that gives the tone its individual pungency and, at times, a positively iridescent shimmer. Garden rerecorded much of this material as well as other titles between 1926 and 1929, naturally sounding less vocally seductive but with even more intensity of feeling. A contemporary listener to her recordings will likely wonder why an earlier generation had such problems with her. Perhaps Carl Van Vechten put his finger on it when he wrote *The Merry-Go-Round* in 1918: "When Mary Garden came to New York only a few of us were ready to receive her at anywhere near her true worth. In a field where mediocrity and brainlessness, lack of theatrical instinct and vocal insipidity are fairly the rule, her dominant personality, her unerring search for novelty of expression, the very completeness of her dramatic and vocal pictures, annoyed the philistines, the professors, and the academicians."

An attack of bronchitis postponed Garden's second New York appearance, but *Louise* finally arrived on January 3, 1908. This time the opera scored a tremendous public and critical hit, but again Garden divided opinion. One critic puzzled the soprano by writing that her high notes "were like the snakes of Ireland." When she asked her father what that could possibly mean, Robert Garden snorted and replied, "Mary, there aren't any snakes in Ireland." Other cynics said that Garden didn't need high notes anyway. Her stage presence was so hypnotic that when a top C came along all she had to do was open her mouth and jangle a bracelet to convince the audience that she had actually sung the note.

Garden's third New York outing was in the long-awaited American premiere of *Pelléas et Mélisande.* No one knew what to expect. Those who had some knowledge of the piece predicted that audiences would be either bored or puzzled. Hammerstein himself probably felt that he was mounting the opera only to gain prestige, and in an interview with the *Times* shortly before the premiere Garden warned unwary operagoers that even in Paris it took four years to establish the work in the Comique's repertory. After the first performance, on February 19, *Pelléas* itself may have left many people perplexed, but Garden impressed virtually everyone as poetry incarnate. Even Maurice Maeterlinck wrote a fan letter—and this from the man who claimed that Debussy had desecrated his play by setting it to music and who swore that he would never see the opera (Maeterlinck's anger in 1902 had less to with art than the fact that Debussy had refused to permit the playwright's mistress, Georgette Leblanc, to sing Mélisande).

During the next season Garden added two new roles to her repertory, further pointing up her extraordinary versatility along with her lifelong ability to capture headlines. The first was Jean in Massenet's "mystery play," *Le Jongleur de Notre-Dame*—a part written for a tenor, but one recommended to Garden by the French baritone Maurice Renaud, who had created the role of Boniface at the opera's world premiere in 1902. Garden adored the idea, and the innocent, asexual little juggler who dies in a state of grace while performing his tricks before a statue of the Virgin became a personal favorite for the rest of her career. Massenet was less than enchanted, confessing that he was "somewhat bewildered at seeing the monk discard his frock after the performance and resume an elegant costume from the Rue de la Paix" (so the composer wrote in his memoirs; his English translator, H. Villiers Barnett, adds a footnote telling us that when Massenet heard about this innovation, he was "simply furious").

As for Garden, she wrote that "it should always be a woman who sings the Jongleur. The part is so spiritual and so simple, and when a man sings it, it becomes too *terre à terre* . . . And I had just the body for it. I was built like a boy . . ." Garden also surely remembered how audiences had acclaimed her as a teenage boy in another Massenet opera, one she had created with great success in Monte Carlo in 1905: the title role in *Chérubin*, a *comédie chantée* tracing the further adventures of Mozart's Cherubino. In any case, Garden never changed a note in Massenet's score, and she was not about to take the composer's objections seriously. "He was always gushing," she once wrote. "He could say the most marvelous things to someone, pay the greatest compliments in the world. And the moment the door closed behind that someone he would turn to the others in the room and say something quite the contrary . . . He hadn't the character I liked in a man, and he hadn't the genius of Debussy, not by a long shot." But the fact that he wrote three or four of her most effective parts somewhat helped her to forgive those "endless letters" he used to write, "dripping with the most sickening kind of sentiment."

Garden's second coup that season was her first *Salome*, which she sang in Oscar Wilde's original French and, after taking lessons from the *première danseuse* of the Paris Opéra, danced herself. "It was an enchanting dance," Garden reminisced, "lovely, and classical in feeling. It wasn't a hoochi-koochi dance at all . . . Everything was glorious and nude and suggestive, but not coarse." Perhaps not, but Hammerstein was still taking a big gamble putting on *Salome* after the ruckus the opera had stirred up at the Metropolitan two years previously. This time, though, New York steeled itself to this operatic sewer, which shamelessly invites the unsuspecting "to bend over its reeking filth to inhale its mephitic vapors," and concentrated mainly on Garden's performance. Even Krehbiel, who loathed the work, was impressed: "Miss Garden has realized a conception of incarnate bestiality which has so much power that it is a dreadful thing to contemplate. She has developed the stages from a willful maiden to a human hyena, with wonderful skill and variety of phrase, and she has mastered all the agencies of expression. There is a terrible intensity in her acting, especially in the awful climax of the play, an intensity which, coupled with the music of the orchestra, is absolutely nerve racking to persons susceptible to music. Her dance is remarkable for its grace and voluptuous charm . . . Through it all she is a vision of loveliness, and if the opera has a place in the repertory it will be due wholly to this feature."

Even though some agreed with Henderson that Garden, for all her dramatic fascination, was swamped by Strauss's music, New York decided that the soprano had finally enjoyed an unequivocal triumph. *Salome* was given twelve more performances before capacity houses, and three in Philadelphia. There would have been more in the City of Brotherly Love—two thousand disappointed people had to be turned away at the box office before the first performance—but the outcry from religious leaders was so deafening that Hammerstein had to withdraw the piece. "Although I might have continued to have large houses with *Salome* in Philadelphia," he commented, "I preferred not to take the risk of being the man that taught Philadelphia anything it thinks it ought not to know."

Garden and the Manhattan Opera enjoyed one more season in New York. It was a veritable Mary Garden festival, during which the soprano added Massenet's *Sapho* and *Grisélidis* to her repertory as well as singing in

Le Jongleur, Faust, Thaïs, Pelléas, Salome, and *Louise.* But that was the end of it. Although Hammerstein had the press and the public on his side, the Metropolitan had the backing of the Vanderbilts, the Astors, the Morgans, and a mighty crew of Wall Street financiers. During 1910 Hammerstein was forced into bankruptcy, and in April he signed an agreement with the Met that gave him a cash settlement of $1,200,000 provided he did not enter the American opera scene for a period of ten years. In addition, the Met fell heir to the Manhattan's costumes, scenery, and scores, along with the rights to operas over which Hammerstein had had exclusive control. The Met insisted on the hands-off-opera clause because Hammerstein had already been in Chicago earlier that year, as usual surrounded by newspaper reporters, and looking over building sites—the Met considered this indefatigable impresario a threat even on the banks of Lake Michigan. The Chicago Grand Opera Company was indeed formed in 1910, but without Hammerstein the Met saw no danger of competition, even though the new venture included many members from the old Manhattan Opera.

Several Manhattan Opera artists also joined the Met roster, but Garden was not one of them—indeed, she never sang as a member of that company. The reason, she said, was because she had never been asked, and one can only speculate why. Possibly her strong identification with Hammerstein put off the Met, which has always preferred to create its own stars, and traditionally those singers have been vocal prodigies rather than theatrical personalities. Or perhaps Giulio Gatti-Casazza's failure to lure Garden to La Scala back in 1902, when he had managed that house, still rankled. That year the soprano had quarreled with Albert Carré (yes, even the Opéra-Comique director had proposed marriage and been turned down), and agreed to sing *Louise* in Milan. When Carré realized that he risked losing Garden, he made her a new contractual offer she could not refuse, and the world's most famous Louise left Gatti in the lurch—a slight he would not soon forget. Or it could be that the rich and powerful forces that ruled the Met objected to an opera singer who never knew her place and once had the nerve to sass the fabled New York lawyer and politician Chauncey Depew at an elegant social function. "I'm wondering, Miss Garden," Depew asked, "what keeps that gown up." Garden smiled sweetly and replied, "Two things, Mr. Depew—your age and my discretion." In any case, Garden needed a new center of operations, and she unhesitatingly chose her old hometown, Chicago. There she made her headquarters for the next twenty years, completely dominating the city's operatic life.

When Garden arrived on October 29, 1910, she was thirty-four years old, her artistic persona fully formed, and her repertory more or less fixed. So was her daily regimen, which began in the morning with two cups of café au lait and ended at bedtime with a large glass of hot milk with ten drops of iodine in it. The only meal of the day came at one in the afternoon, and that was very plain: a bit of meat or fish, two vegetables, and ice cream. Of course, no one believed anyone so newsworthy could possibly have such a Spartan lifestyle, and Garden saw no reason to disillusion them. On the day she returned to Chicago, a horde of reporters met her train and out she came, accompanied by a French maid and a valet, speaking in a foreign accent, and sporting a monocle as well as a diamond ring from a Turkish pasha rumored to be her fiancé. Interviews were freely granted, but two subjects were taboo: Oscar Hammerstein and wrinkles. "Chicago's just going to love *Salome*," she said. "I know what the girl was." As for the pasha, she denied the rumors, but promised to walk up Michigan Avenue wearing a pair of Turkish trousers.

The next day at her suite at the Blackstone Hotel, "our Mary," as Chicagoans were already calling her, summoned the press again. "The door of her bedroom jerked back as though there had been sudden application of the hind end of a strong mule," reported the *Chicago Inter-Ocean*, "and through the opening whizzed a tornado of choking perfume, shimmering silk, and carrot-red hair." She described the gown she planned to wear as Salome, and announced that Carmen would be her next role. The pasha's name came up again, since word had gotten out that he was en route to Chicago, accompanied by his seventy-eight other wives, who would plead with Mary not to marry. Whatever the subject, Garden had a quotable comment to make, and the press gleefully printed them all. Perhaps that explains an incident that occurred at the Chicago Stock Exchange. Garden had arrived to oversee an auction for a charity fund-raising drive when suddenly a man with long gray hair and shabby clothes threatened to attack her. As the police dragged him off, the would-be assassin had only one comment: "She talks too much."

With a sure sense of theatrical career-building that never seemed to desert her, Garden cleverly introduced herself to Chicago with her by now classic Mélisande on November 5, following that with Louise on the ninth and finally Salome on the twenty-fifth. Predictably, Strauss's opera, and Garden's vivid impersonation of its teenage heroine, set the town talking. Warned that something truly horrendous was about to take place, the city's Law and Order League sent Chicago's police chief, Leroy T. Steward, to assess the damage. "It was disgusting," he reported. "Miss Garden wallowed around like a cat in a bed of catnip." Garden felt that philistine critique beneath contempt, haughtily replying, "I always bow down to the ignorant and try to make them understand, but I ignore the illiterate."

Attempts to prevent a second performance failed, inspiring the League's president, Arthur Farwell (who never actually saw the opera), to fume, "Performances like that of *Salome* should be classed as vicious and suppressed along with houses in the red light district. I wish Miss Garden would come to see me; I should like to reform her. I am a normal man, but I would not trust myself to see a performance of *Salome*." To that suggestive invitation, Garden fired back with one of her own: "Anyone whose morals could have been corrupted by seeing *Salome* must already have degenerated . . . I should like to meet Mr. Farwell to see what he is like, but I do not think he could do me any good."

There was some talk of toning down Garden's ecstatic lust when presented with John the Baptist's head, but finally the Chicago Opera's board of directors stepped in and canceled the third performance. All this greatly amused Hammerstein, who, when he got wind of the controversy, said, "I don't know just what could be done to 'tone down' *Salome*, especially the head scene, unless, maybe they'd give the head a shave and a haircut . . . If they'd put some flannel petticoats and things on Miss Garden that might help tone things, too. Mary really ought to be petticoated, I think, considering Chicago's climate. You know, when she worked for me, she had a deadly fear when singing Salome of getting cold feet."

Over the next ten years Garden added Tosca and Carmen to her repertory, as well as treating Chicago to her famous Jongleur and Thaïs. As usual, this restless singer continued to search for spicy novelties, but virtually everything she came up with—Massenet's *Cléopâtre*, Février's *Monna Vanna* and *Ghismonda*, Victor Herbert's *Natoma*—seemed worth performing only as long as she was onstage. The city's favorite diva even trotted out Erlanger's *Aphrodite*, one of her mustier Opéra-Comique vehicles, but Chicago audiences were bored by it and the critics dismissed the piece as "tedious, stupid, and more or less meaningless." Even at that,

Garden still enjoyed a personal success, once again triumphantly rising above the tawdry material. "Mary Garden!" exclaimed the *Tribune* about her Chrysis. "A long, slow lift of that white arm and she has portrayed an ecstasy."

On January 6, 1921, the Chicago Opera's director and principal conductor, Gino Marinuzzi, resigned in despair. Attendance was down, internal squabbles were rife, and the five-year patronage of Harold F. McCormick, the head of International Harvester, was due to expire at the end of the following season. By then it had been hoped that the company would be operating in the black, but now the Chicago Opera needed a miracle even to stage a grand finale. McCormick decided on a gamble: Mary Garden would be the new impresario. "We want to go out in a blaze of glory," he told her, "and we need your name." The challenge appealed to Garden, who agreed to become "directa," as she wished to be called, as long as no one knew it would be for just that one year and she would be able to perform as usual. Volumes of verbiage hit the press after the announcement was made, and Garden promised the city a spectacular opera season it would never forget. "It's going to be an American opera company, too," she said. "Young American singers used to knock at the doors of American opera companies, only to have them opened by foreigners, who would say: 'Not at home.' Now they will be welcomed by an American, and that is as it should be." As the season eventually unfolded, however, that noble statement began to look more like Garden hype than any firm statement of artistic policy.

By fall, Mme. Directa had her roster and repertory all planned—twice as many singers as the company actually needed, and a list of hard-sell works that even Oscar Hammerstein might have blanched at. Garden's greatest coup was the world premiere of Prokofiev's *Love for Three Oranges*, mounted at the extravagant cost of $100,000. Otherwise, the season seemed mainly a showcase for her own unique talents. Garden sang two or three times a week, alternating in eight of her favorite parts, while other contracted stars such as Gadski, Schipa, Raisa, Galli-Curci, D'Alvarez, Muratore, Ivogün, Dux, Schwarz, and Lipkowska (not one of them an American) appeared only sporadically. On the few occasions when they did sing, the results were apparently glorious, but mostly these expensive artists sat in Chicago collecting fees for doing nothing. Vincent Sheean summed it up years later: "It was a remarkable opera season. I went as often as I could and reveled in the originality of the arrangements. An opera might be given once only—two performances was rather a long run—and a singer might make a debut which was simultaneously a farewell. These singularities are most often the prerogatives of failure . . . [but] Garden conducted her whole season through a tootling of success like the triumphal scene in *Aida*." At the end of it, McCormick reached deeply into his wallet and paid the bill—$1,100,000—and the Chicago Opera Association was dissolved. "If it cost a million dollars," Garden commented after her single year as an impresario, "I'm sure it was worth it."

The next season the company was reorganized as the Chicago Civic Opera Company, and Garden stayed on as its star member. For the next ten years she continued to enchant the public, which still flocked to see her as Thaïs, the Jongleur, and Fiora in Montemezzi's *L'Amore dei Tre Re* (the only Italian opera she ever consented to sing in its original language). The years were beginning to catch up, however. In 1924, at the age of fifty, Garden brought her Salome to Dallas. The opera was still controversial and the singer's reputation preceded her, but as one old-time Garden watcher described her performance, "Even to eyes susceptible to her usual magic she became a middle-aged woman awkwardly waving a few pieces of tulle."

There was one last "creation": Katiusha in Alfano's *Risurrezione* (or *Résurrection*), an opera based on Tolstoy's novel. Once again, the music was hardly deathless, but the opportunities it presented were precisely those that Garden relished. "Oh, how I adored that opera!" she reminisced. "That poor girl's innocence, her disillusionment with men, her crime and imprisonment, and the final resurrection of her soul. Each act was different, each about a different woman, really, yet about the different woman that is potentially in all women, and to each act I gave a different voice. Perhaps that fascinated me most of all, how I managed to be so many women and so many voices in one opera."

In 1934, after a final Katiusha at the Opéra-Comique thirty-four years after her spectacular debut, Garden had reached sixty and decided to call it quits. Although she soon moved back with her mother and sister Aggie to Aberdeen, Garden spent the rest of her life on the lecture circuit, mostly talking about herself and keeping the legend alive. At first she sang as well as spoke, and Paul Horgan describes one of these last lecture-recitals at her old stomping grounds in Chicago:

> She wore a close-fitting hat of black silk with a mesh of veil that came down just past her eyes—her eyes gleamed with a tigerish

light in a little blue cave of shadow that put the years at a
distance, and yet conveyed the vivid present. Her hair was a
tawny gold. A floor-length fall of pale yellow satin, her gown
was so tight over her straight hips that you wondered how she
could step. A short-sleeved torero jacket in black sparkling stuff
met long white gloves that reached above the elbows. A neck-
lace of big pearls was looped once about her throat, with the
rest of it swaying almost to her knees. How tall was she? A few
inches over five feet, it was recorded somewhere; but she was a
figure so commanding that illusion created height. By her valiant
posture she seemed to tell us not to be nervous—all would be
well, indeed brilliant.

And it was.

In the Hotel Plaza Grand Ballroom she was up to her old
tricks—casting a spell, as she had done in countless opera performances. With peremptory grace she turned and gave M.
Dansereau the signal to begin. Now they would give us songs by
Debussy, a dozen of them, including the air of Lia from L'Enfant
prodigue, the third of the Ariettes, "Je tremble en voyant ton image," "Green," "La Chevelure," and "Mandoline."

How to be exact in describing a performance made of
sound, that medium as fugitive as time? Her voice was without
luster—she was past the age of brilliant tone. Perfect in pitch, it
had at moments almost a parlando quality, in a timbre reminiscent of dried leaves stirred by air. But what expression, now
smoky with passion, again rueful for life's shadows! What musicality; and what sense of meaning—the texts of Guignand, Bour-
get, Pierre Louÿs, Verlaine, Baudelaire, came forth in all the
beauty and power of Debussy's description: "the spell of her
voice . . . so softly persuasive." We were persuaded. Did any
artist more fully know who, and what, she was? Was this the first
attribute of the interpretive genius?

In this case, the only answer could be a resounding yes. It would be
much too simple to reject Mary Garden as a self-made operatic personality created by smoke and mirrors, although many did. She always knew
precisely who and what she was, throughout her career and after it was
over, and she was never less than devastatingly honest about herself.
Apparently that recital, which took place on January 29, 1935, was her

very last, and for the next thirty years or so she filled only speaking engagements. Even those must have been exciting experiences because she was still Mary Garden, an artist who cut through the communication codes of her day, trusted her inner impulses, and "created" her roles from the very center of her being. Her theatrical persona, offstage and on, was so potent, in fact, that it led some critics to underestimate her vocal resources, which not only served her purposes more than adequately but were also capable of spinning out a fascinating variety of expressive gestures and coloristic nuances. She wasted far too much of her talent on trash, but it was almost invariably well-made trash that suited her style—in that respect she prefigured many of Hollywood's celebrated actresses of the 1930s and '40s.

Garden may have retired to Scotland, but significantly she seldom sang in England again after that unhappy 1902–03 season in London early in her career. She seemed to sense that America was the country where her singular gifts could ripen and be best appreciated. On her last visit to New York, she was in her late eighties. Coming down the ramp after deplaning, the Divine Mary noticed a few photographers who had been sent to greet her (newspapers still did such things for musical celebrities in those days), and she seized the moment. "Well, boys," she asked, boldly raising her skirt and displaying the famous Garden legs, "have I still got it?"

The Great

Caruso

~~~~~~~~~~~~~~~~~~~~~~~~~~~~~~~~

*B*efore Luciano Pavarotti and the Three Tenors phenomenon exploded during the 1990s, most Americans would have probably replied "Caruso" if asked to free-associate and respond to the words "opera singer." Not even Lind and Patti had succeeded in penetrating the national public consciousness quite so thoroughly as Enrico Caruso, certainly none born in the country that the Neapolitan tenor regarded as his home and the center of his career from 1903 to 1920.

During the height of his fame, around the years of World War I, Caruso reigned as the uncrowned king of the Metropolitan Opera, by far its most popular star and a ubiquitous presence who sang with the company on an average of twice a week throughout the opera year. And he was well rewarded for his services. Although Caruso received a relatively modest $2,500 for each Met performance, the company's top fee at the time, the tenor more than made up the difference during these years when other cities paid extravagantly for the privilege of hearing him sing. By 1920 Havana would offer him $10,000 each time he set foot on the stage of the Teatro Nacional.

The 1916–17 season was a typically busy one for Caruso, even though he could no longer sing in Europe because of the war. In addition to numerous concerts and an extensive summer tour of South America, he appeared in forty-nine performances of eleven roles at the Met in New York and on company visits to Philadelphia, Brooklyn, and Atlanta. He opened the Met season in November as Nadir in Bizet's *Les Pêcheurs de perles*, and the following twelve weeks found him singing an amazing variety of demanding roles from both the lyric and dramatic repertories: Puccini's Des Grieux, Saint-Saëns's Samson, Cavaradossi, Canio, Lionel in *Martha*, Nemorino in Donizetti's *L'Elisir d'Amore*, the Duke, Radamès, Rodolfo, and Don José. Audiences adored him in all of them—but so did the New York critics, who by then found themselves unusually unanimous on the subject of Caruso. At a dinner given in his honor at the Friars Club on November 26, shortly after the Met's opening night that season, a glittering show-business gathering including Victor Herbert, Irving Berlin, and George M. Cohan serenaded the great man to the tune of "Pretty Baby": "Everybody loves a tenor, that's why I'm in love with you! Oh, Caruso! Oh, Caruso!"

That refrain perfectly expressed Caruso's crossover appeal for ordinary Americans—very different from the mystique of Malibran, Lind, and Patti, but no less potent and, thanks to his many Victor recordings, one that had an even wider circulation. Every home with a windup Victrola contained Caruso discs, and the tenor's records brought his voice to thousands of people who never had the chance to hear him in the flesh. For them Caruso was a tonic, a singer who exuded forthrightness, masculinity, and all-embracing ardor, together with a popular touch that the genteel operatic tenors who preceded him never possessed. Nothing demonstrates that more dramatically than a comparison with his Met predecessor, Jean de Reszke. That beau ideal of aristocratic grace and vocal refinement was an eloquent interpreter of the courtly romantic gentlemen of French opera (Roméo, Raoul, Rodrigue in Massenet's *Le Cid*) and, later, Wagner's epic heroes. Indeed, De Reszke was the perfect symbol of opera as an elegant and elitist entertainment in New York during the 1890s. Caruso, on the other hand, specialized in the earthy, melodramatic verismo repertory that had lately come into vogue, and audiences particularly warmed to his anguished portrayal of Canio, the crazed wife-killer in Leoncavallo's *Pagliacci*, and Puccini's stressed-out lovers. Beyond that, his extensive recorded repertory embraced dozens of popular ballads that De Reszke would never have dreamed of singing, including a rousing rendition (in English and French) of Cohan's World War I morale booster, "Over There!"

Caruso arrived at the Met in 1903, precisely when he was needed, three seasons after De Reszke left the company. He made his debut as the Duke in *Rigoletto*, and his presence was gratefully noted, although at first without any special enthusiasm. But W. J. Henderson presciently noted in the *Sun*, "Caruso, the new tenor, made a thoroughly favorable impression, and will probably grow into the firm favor of the public. He has a pure tenor voice and is without the typical Italian bleat. Caruso has a natural and free delivery and his voice carries well without forcing. He phrased his music tastefully and showed considerable refinement of style. His clear and pealing high notes set the bravos wild with delight, but connoisseurs of singing saw more promise for the season in his mezza voce and his manliness. He is a good-looking man and acts with dignity, if with no great distinction."

It's to Henderson's credit that he sensed this much quality and promise in Caruso—like the other New York critics of his generation, Henderson was brought up to appreciate a rather different type of singer than the one that Caruso eventually came to personify. The young Italian, in fact, surely struck most longtime operagoers, still basking in memories of De Reszke, as a bit crude, if not vulgar. Henry T. Finck wrote scathingly later that season about Caruso's first Cavaradossi in *Tosca*, which, he complained, "lacked aristocratic flavor." Even Henderson termed his performance "bourgeois" in its portrayal of a "painter of hack portraits at job prices."

Eventually all the critics began to understand that Caruso was something new, a singer whose rules were not those of his predecessors and one whose influence was likely to prove enormous. As a leading member of the last generation of singers that sang mainly contemporary music, Caruso addressed a core repertory that would be shared by every lyric-dramatic tenor who came after him, and his method became the model for all of them. Sidney Homer heard precisely what was happening. "Before Caruso came," he wrote in his autobiography, "I never heard a voice that even remotely resembled his. Since he came I have heard voice after voice, big and small, high and low, that suggested his, reminded me of it at times even forcibly." Many other tenors from all over Europe came to sing Caruso's roles during his Met reign, and many of considerable distinction, but as long as King Enrico ruled, none could compete. As Michael Scott observes in his study of the tenor:

His is the performing style still extant today, and by the end of his life the hegemony of his style was complete. It not only succeeded the "bleating" vibrato-ridden tenor of the previous generation, which had never been popular outside the Italian operatic empire, but very soon the traditional French and Russian styles were also in retreat. No singers today are even faintly reminiscent of Alessandro Bonci, Edmond Clément, and Dmitri Smirnov. Their elegant and refined manners could not survive when they came to New York, and they failed to make any headway with a public in love with Caruso's opulent voice.

More than half a century has elapsed since his death and every modern tenor right up to Luciano Pavarotti and Plácido Domingo is a direct descendant, as his records make plain.

As the 1903–04 season wore on, New Yorkers became increasingly enamored of their new Italian star as they heard him in one role after another: Radamès, Cavaradossi, Rodolfo, Canio, Alfredo, Edgardo, and Nemorino. Significantly, audiences capitulated long before the more cautious critics. Toward the end of his first Met season the sold-out sign began to appear whenever he sang, and the fans were already crazy for him—after one performance, while Caruso was taking his curtain call, a young woman somehow managed to rush up onto the stage and tear a button from his costume before bursting into tears. Even his colleagues were overwhelmed. Geraldine Farrar recalled how staggered she was during her first Bohème with Caruso, after he had finished "Che gelida manina" and waited for her to begin "Sì, mi chiamano Mimì": "My emotions got all tangled up in the golden tones of Caruso's voice. I forgot all about the theatre, the action, everything. I sat there sobbing like a child. When my cue came, I didn't hear it. The orchestra hesitated. My mother in the wings waved dramatically at me. Then the prompter rose from his seat and started whispering: 'Well, Miss Farrar, are you going to sing or not?' "

With this phenomenon on hand, it's not surprising that the few American tenors who appeared with the Met during the Caruso years were virtually obliterated. The best of them was very likely Hugh Whitefield (1879–1952), although even changing his name to Riccardo Martin did not bring him the fame and fortune he might otherwise have earned had he not constantly sung in Caruso's shadow. Still, the company kept him busy, and during nine seasons beginning in 1907 he chalked up 281 performances of twenty roles, including such Caruso standards as Radamès, Rodolfo, Don José, Turridu, Faust (Gounod's and Boito's), Enzo, Pinkerton, Canio, Cavaradossi, and Manrico. He also came in handy when Giulio Gatti-Casazza began introducing American opera; Martin sang the leading tenor roles in the premieres of Converse's *The Pipe of Desire* (1910), Parker's *Mona* (1912), and Damrosch's *Cyrano de Bergerac* (1913)—no doubt his composition studies with Edward Mac-Dowell at Columbia University proved helpful in learning this unfamiliar repertory. Martin cut an unusually handsome figure onstage, and his voice, if not especially individual on his surviving discs, had an ingratiatingly sweet timbre as well as sufficient weight for the dramatic roles that were his principal province. Perhaps tired of being incessantly compared to Caruso, Martin left the Met in 1917 and finished up his career in Chicago.

Orville Harrold (1878–1933), Charles Hackett (1889–1942), Paul Althouse (1899–1954), and Mario Chamlee (1892–1966) continued to sing at the Met after Caruso's death in 1921, but their reputations did not noticeably rise with removal of the competition. Harrold, in fact, made his debut playing second fiddle to Caruso—as Léopold in *La Juive* on November 22, 1919—the culmination of a rough-and-ready singing career that began with close-harmony groups in midwestern saloons (he grew up in Muncie, Indiana) and continued in New York vaudeville before peaking in 1910, when he created the tenor lead in Victor Herbert's *Naughty Marietta*. After five Met seasons as a respectable pinch hitter in repertory standards that ranged from Donizetti's *Lucia* to Wagner's *Parsifal*, as well as appearing in such short-lived novelties as Leoni's *L'Oracolo* (1919), Hadley's *Cleopatra's Night* (1920), and Rimsky-Korsakov's *Snegurochka* (1922), Harrold retreated to finish his career where it began, in vaudeville and light opera.

The other three American tenors more or less tried to circumvent comparison with Caruso by addressing a different repertory. Like Martin, Althouse was recruited to participate in Gatti's American opera experiments: Herbert's *Madeleine* (1914), De Koven's *The Canterbury Pilgrims* (1917), Cadman's *Shanewis* (1918), and Breil's *The Legend* (1919). During the late 1920s he retrained as a heldentenor, but by the time he felt ready for the big Wagnerian roles, Lauritz Melchior had arrived and Althouse found himself once again outclassed. After retiring in 1941, Althouse became a successful voice teacher, including among his students Eleanor Steber, Richard Tucker, Léopold Simoneau, and Irene

Dalis. Both Chamlee and Hackett wisely stuck to a lyric repertory and enjoyed extended if comparatively modest careers, not only at the Met but in Europe and—in a medium where their light tenors perhaps bloomed best—as radio singers. Most American operagoers, however, looked elsewhere for Caruso's successor. If they mostly searched in vain, at least they felt more consoled listening to such Italian tenors as Beniamino Gigli, Giovanni Martinelli, and Giacomo Lauri-Volpi than to any of their compatriots.

Caruso, of course, was irreplaceable, and he continues to occupy a special place in the history of singing in America, as a man and artist as much as for his extraordinary vocal gift. In that respect, his impact on the country's musical life went deeper and lasted longer than that of Malibran, Lind, and Patti. Like those legendary sopranos, Caruso made a fortune here and enjoyed his share of publicity and réclame. But the tenor's career lacked the freakish sideshow aura that gave those divas' immensely profitable visits to America such a bad odor. When Caruso went back to Italy to die in 1921, he was genuinely mourned and admired by the man in the street as well as by cognoscenti, a beloved figure who left with his dignity, humanity, and artistic values intact. One feels he truly meant it when he once humbly remarked, "I feel a role too much . . . I always try to give of my best in interpreting a part. I know that I am a singer and an actor but I give an impression of being neither, but a real man conceived by the composer."

The warmth of his personality and the depth of his artistic integrity can be heard in all his recordings. Even more interestingly, these documents tell us that Caruso's vocal development was organic, dynamic and always changing, from the sunny-voiced generosity of the young tenor in 1902 to the baritonal richness and technical confidence he commanded eighteen years later. At each step along the way there were musical rewards as Caruso adapted his art to the physical changes in his maturing instrument as well as to the stylistic demands of the different kinds of music he sang.

Michael Scott cites one example when he calls attention to how carefully and thoughtfully the tenor altered his technical and stylistic approaches to the highest notes of his arias—all during one remarkable session on February 11, 1906. The top B in "Che gelida manina" from La Bohème (Caruso always sang the aria transposed down) is taken "fortissimo and in full verismo style. This is appropriate in La Bohème, where the note should be attacked in full voice. But not in 'Salut, demeure' from

Faust, which he sings next in the original key, for he manages the high C, taking the note in the head register and then increasing the resonance as he sustains the note. Lastly, in 'Spirto gentil' from *La Favorita* there is another top C, which again he executes after the correct style—lyrically and in a *voce mista* throughout."

One could go on analyzing Caruso's singing indefinitely. And critics never tired of doing precisely that back in the days when newspapers gave unlimited space to musical journalism—no wonder budding singers read the long glowing reports, listened to the recordings, and despaired of ever attaining the ideal that Caruso himself once articulated and seemed to reach so effortlessly. "I strain myself to keep my voice from sounding strained," Caruso said. "It is only after the hardest training that a man can regulate his voice so that it always sounds easy and natural. The audience should not think I am straining my voice but they should realize that I am straining every nerve to make my notes smooth and natural."

It speaks well for Caruso and his art that he never betrayed that vocal credo. He may have been off-form on occasion, but no one ever complained that he gave a sloppy, uncaring, or unmusical performance, and he clothed the most trivial song with the same vocal gold and generosity of spirit he brought to an aria by Verdi or Puccini. It probably never occurred to him that there was even a need to alter his approach. The tenor died just before the electrical process and the microphone not only revolutionized recording but put a wedge between classical and lighter music and the singing styles that came to define them. Before the microphone became standard equipment for a pop singer, audiences expected to hear ballads of the day sung in exactly the same manner as an operatic aria, by a trained, healthy voice projected unassisted and with ease into the spaces of an opera house or concert hall. Electronic amplification and a coarsening of musical taste would change all that, and soon a pop style developed, one that relied less on a singer's muscular control, breath support, and sheer tonal amplitude than on vocal color, rhythmic flexibility, and the sort of subtle manipulation of expressive dynamics made possible only by a microphone. Unlike his successors, Caruso never had to compete with crooners, and he intended everything he sang to be a song for all the people. Virtually all America heard him, and the country adored every note.

Thirteen

Gerryflappers

 huge crowd, mostly teenage girls, gathered at the Metropolitan Opera's stage door after the matinee performance of Leoncavallo's *Zazà* on April 22, 1922. Inside, a noisy demonstration was still in progress as Geraldine Farrar bade farewell to all her "Gerryflapper" fans who had been lucky enough to get tickets. It was a mad scene. During the performance banners were unfurled from the boxes, balloons thrown into the air, Farrar pennants waved frantically, and, as part of the onstage ceremony after Act II, some ardent buffs rushed up to present their idol with a homemade crown and scepter. When it was all over and the cheering had subsided, the soprano finally spoke. "Has George Cohan stopped crying?" she asked. "I don't want a tear in this house. I'm leaving this institution because I want to go." Farrar then began distributing her costumes and props to the faithful, donned her crown, swept out the stage door, and stepped into her limousine, which the throng proceeded to drag up Broadway into Times Square.

The Met has seen many emotional farewells and will no doubt witness many more, but for colorful invention and sheer theatricality Farrar's departure remains unequaled. It all began three months earlier when Farrar, shortly before a performance of *Faust* on January 20, unexpectedly announced her retirement. When the curtain fell that evening, the soprano was repeatedly called forward by an audience dabbing its eyes with handkerchiefs. "Children," was her consoling response, "this is no occasion for a funeral." The following weeks saw a procession of familiar Farrar heroines—Carmen, Manon, Louise, Butterfly, Zazà, one more Marguerite, Tosca—and the demonstrations became increasingly heated. After her last Butterfly, Farrar asked the fans which opera they would like to see her perform as her swan song, and the crowd shouted *"Tosca!"* Giulio Gatti-Casazza, an old hand at putting prima donnas in their places, would not hear of it. The scheduled opera would be *Zazà*. Gatti doubtlessly felt it more politically prudent to cater to Maria Jeritza, the Met's exciting new Tosca, rather than accommodate the departing favorite. No matter. Leoncavallo's potboiler may not be high art, but it was still an opera that Farrar had by then made very much her own and it suited her glamorous Hollywood image. In Act I Zazà performs a striptease, prefaced by a delicious moment when the music hall star lifts her skirts to spray perfume on a pair of lace panties (a naughty touch suggested by David Belasco). The Gerryflappers went wild.

"What is a Gerryflapper?" wearily asked W. J. Henderson, the *Sun's* music critic, who had coined the term. "Simply a girl about the flapper age who has created in her own half baked mind a goddess which she names Geraldine Farrar." The Gerryflappers were not the only ones to cheer this beauteous creature, who had reigned at the Met since 1906 and whose box office appeal was second only to Caruso's. Still gorgeous at forty, Farrar had long ago captured the imagination of the American public—and, like Mary Garden, with much more than her voice.

Farrar learned early in the game how to present herself as a total publicity package. Although the Met was always her principal base of operations, she seized every opportunity to branch out and capitalize on the new electronic communication tools just then in their infancy. Farrar made her first records in Berlin between 1904 and 1906, the years preceding her American debut, and she continued to record up to and even after her retirement—no other native singer prior to Farrar had been so completely documented in sound during every stage of her career. Her records graced virtually every home that boasted a crank-up Victrola, and those unable to get to the opera or afford the discs could see her in the dozen or so silent movies she made between 1915 and 1920, films with such tantalizing titles as *The Woman God Forgot* and *The Hell-Cat*.

Records and films were hardly the only items that contributed to Farrar's national celebrity. By 1920 her extravagantly photogenic face and figure graced all the magazines, and gossip columnists still speculated on her recent messy divorce from Hollywood actor Lou Tellegen. When that subject ran dry, one could always revive the juicy rumors of her prewar affair in Berlin with the Kaiser's opera-loving son—hadn't one childless couple even offered to adopt all the illegitimate offspring supposedly sired by the beauteous young diva and the dashing Crown Prince Frederick William? Some whispered that the reason behind Arturo Toscanini's abrupt departure from the Met in 1915 had been the direct result of an ultimatum from Farrar: Choose—either me or your wife. Since the Maestro, it was said, could not bear the prospect of working under the same roof with his ex-mistress, he simply packed up and left the country. Whatever she did, Farrar made news, and everyone wanted to know all about it.

Even at the height of her career, Farrar's colorful personality and theatrical glamour overshadowed her purely vocal accomplishments, and on that score many critics rated her even lower than Garden. Again, the recordings tell a different story, although Farrar was quick to point out that she never aspired to be a spectacular canary bird à la Adelina Patti. Besides, times had changed, as she emphasized in an article she contributed to a book on the "art of the prima donna" shortly before her farewell:

The scores of the older repertory are more purely vocal in general, their heroines more dramatically quiescent. There is not the same call for passionate acting, for energetic synchronization of music and physical action. The discreeter orchestrations allow full sway to the singer to develop her tones without stress. But modern opera is different. Now ninety men do their best, collectively, to make the singer shriek her head off. One has all sorts of almost impossible stage actions to contend with; running up and down stairs—which is not the best preparation for a burst of song—and all manner of violent actions up to turning somersaults is expected of the singing actress. Formerly, all she had to do was to step out on the stage and pay attention to nothing but her song. In fact, so different are the two types of opera, that to ask any great exponent of the modern dramatic score to sing a Bellini aria, would be like asking Dempsey to pick up a pin.

Farrar makes valid points, but sopranos of the post-Callas generation might legitimately claim that Bellini's Norma calls for no less dramatic vocal intensity than Puccini's Tosca, albeit of a different sort. During the first two decades of the century, though, singers were still busily performing new operas rather than singing a fixed repertory from the past, and Farrar's priorities were up to date. Critics of the time waxed hot and cold about her voice—apparently her sixteen years at the Met did witness some extreme fluctuations in vocal health—but astute observers understood precisely the historical necessities that created the Farrar phenomenon.

In many other respects, however, Farrar's background mirrored that of her most significant predecessors: Kellogg, Eames, and Nordica. Like them, young Geraldine was a strong-willed New England girl, she was guided by a determined mother, and after the proper European finishing she returned home a star. Born in Melrose, Massachusetts, on February 28, 1882, Farrar was the daughter of Sidney Farrar, a shopkeeper who played professional baseball during the summer, first base for Philadelphia in the National League. Geraldine passed most of her childhood in the care of her mother, who was only eighteen when her daughter was born. Henrietta Farrar quickly noticed the girl's musical talent as well as her dramatic impulsiveness. "Why do you use only the black keys?" she asked Geraldine as the child wildly improvised at the piano. "Because," came the reply, "the white keys seem like angels and the black keys like devils, and I like devils best."

One day a schoolboy whose attentions Geraldine had rebuffed drowned in an ice-skating accident. "Instantly I became a widow," she recalled. "Drama—real drama—had come into my life, and with all the feeling of an instinctive actress I played my role. I dressed in black; abandoned all gayeties; went to and from school mopping my eyes with a black-bordered handkerchief; and the other boys and girls stood aside in silence as I passed, leaving me alone with my grief." During another skating incident, when a lad named Clarence tripped her with his hockey stick, Geraldine tore three ribs from her umbrella and thrashed Clarence until his mother threatened to call the police. Henrietta learned not to interfere with her daughter's moods when Geraldine came home one day with a hideous pair of black-and-white-checked stockings and announced, "Mother, when I wear these stockings I want to be alone."

In 1894 Geraldine was selected to play Jenny Lind at the Melrose May Carnival. She sang Siebel's little ditty from *Faust* and "Home, Sweet Home," looking very seductive in her first low-neck dress—at twelve the future prima donna was already a beauty and mature for her age. The occasion attracted Mrs. J. H. Long, the best-known singing teacher in Boston, and she immediately agreed to give Geraldine lessons. Church engagements soon followed, and Henrietta began to keep a scrapbook of news clippings, which became increasingly complimentary. Local opera performances were also eagerly attended, and when the Metropolitan Opera came on tour with *Carmen* starring Calvé, the girl knew what lay in her future. "Then and there was born within me a fervent and earnest decision that, come what may, I too must some day sing Carmen with the most wonderful cast of grand opera artists in the world, and at the Metropolitan in New York." That was how Farrar described her resolution in the down-to-earth short autobiography written in 1916. Twenty-two years later, in the more flowery account of her life entitled *Such Sweet Compulsion*, she grandly spoke of Calvé as "the supreme and daring French woman never to be forgotten once heard," who inspired in her "a fire and urge to soar on wings of song to a delicious, dangerous, unknown adventure."

Geraldine may have been only fifteen, but she and Henrietta both felt it was not too soon to start the great "unknown adventure" by exploring the possibilities beyond Boston. Encouraged by praise from none other than Jean de Reszke and bolstered by a generous loan of $500 from Charles H. Bond, a Boston merchant, mother and daughter set out for New York City. There she began studies with Emma Thursby, an ironic choice considering that soprano's lack of theatricality and lifelong reluctance to set foot on the operatic stage. Even so, Farrar surely learned much from Thursby's classical training as well as benefiting from her connections—both Nordica and Melba heard her sing at the famous "Thursby Fridays," and the two divas' influence later came in handy. The young soprano also secured an audition with Metropolitan general manager Maurice Grau, who offered her a contract on the spot, a debut as Mignon opposite Melba. Gambling for larger stakes, Henrietta vetoed the idea of risking her daughter's future with an ill-considered brief flash of publicity. The Met debut would surely come, but only when Geraldine was fully trained and ready.

That meant, of course, European study. By 1898 both Mr. and Mrs. Farrar were convinced that the family's future lay in Geraldine's throat, and they were ready to give up everything to risk it. Sidney sold his store and hung up his baseball mitt, and Henrietta looked for a patron. She soon found one in Mrs. Bertram Webb, another wealthy Boston matron, who was prepared to loan the Farrars $30,000, her collateral being an insurance policy on Geraldine's life. With that, in September 1899, the three hopefuls set sail on a cattle boat for Paris.

Not surprisingly, Melba had encouraged the Farrars to seek out her old teacher, Marchesi, and even gave them a letter of introduction. If Mary Garden lasted just three weeks under the tutelage of the great Mathilde, Geraldine didn't even bother to call. "There was little to gain," she felt, "in submitting to a dazzling treatment whereby all voices were taught to shame the flute in impossible sky-rocket cadenzas or fall by the wayside when unable to do so. I had no true coloratura register and did not wish to change my own color in such mechanical attainment. I was even then aware of the monotony of beautiful even tones, when all dramatic expression was sacrificed to sound only. This seemed to prevail in the French school of that period." Instead, she followed Garden's example and went to Antonio Trabadello, although after eight months of lessons she was disappointed with her progress.

On the verge of moving on to Italy in the summer of 1900, the Farrars bumped into Nordica and her husband for the nonce, Zoltán Döme, who urged Geraldine to try her luck in Berlin with a Russian-Italian named Graziani, a teacher Döme swore by. Besides, he was a protégé of Herr Adolph von Rath, Berlin's leading banker, who, with his wife, had important social connections with dignitaries and officials of Kaiser Wilhelm's court. So off to Berlin they went, and it did not take Geraldine long to become the toast of the Von Rath's many supper parties, despite her bad German. At one of them she met Cosima Wagner, apparently in search of "an actual virgin of flesh and blood" to sing Eva in Bayreuth's upcoming production of *Die Meistersinger*. As far as anyone knew, young Miss Farrar still qualified, but after boldly registering her negative impression of the dominant "Cosima Wagner and that pallid, rather pathetic caricature of her great husband, her son Siegfried," Geraldine lost the job and future hopes of singing at the Wagner shrine.

Soon afterward, though, Farrar auditioned for the *Intendant* of the

Court Opera, Count von Hochberg—Elsa's Dream from *Lohengrin*, in German (the only German selection in her tiny repertory); Juliette's Waltz, in French; and Nedda's Ballatella from *Pagliacci*, in Italian. Hochberg was impressed—more by what he saw, one suspects, than what he heard—and he handed her a three-year contract, promising her that if she signed it she could sing all her roles in Italian while she learned German. "It will be a novelty," he said. "But the people here want one. You are very much of a novelty, quite different from the stout ladies who waddle about protesting their operatic fate to spectators who find it difficult to believe in their cruel lot and youthful innocence. In you I have discovered a happy combination of voice, figure, personality, and—eyes."

Farrar's debut—as Marguerite in *Faust* with Karl Muck conducting, her first performance on any stage—was scheduled for October 15, 1901. Von Hochberg was right. The audience did consider her a novelty, and soon the pretty nineteen-year-old *Amerikanerin* who sang in Italian was the talk of the town. Other roles followed, and not long afterward there were cries of *Skandal!* when the young Crown Prince began to take an interest in the new prima donna, attending all her performances and even coming to call. Even the Boston press took notice: GERMAN CROWN PRINCE LOVES MELROSE GIRL! screamed the headlines back home. The stories persisted until the Crown Prince eventually married Grand Duchess Cecile and the royal couple settled in the Marmor Palast in Potsdam. After that, Geraldine confounded the gossips by being a "frequent and informal guest on many a happy occasion."

If Farrar and the Prince actually did have a more serious romantic fling, the soprano took the secret with her to the grave, although some always insisted that Frederick carried a torch for the rest of his life. In 1937, when Risë Stevens was studying in Berlin, the young American mezzo and her teacher, Anna Schoen-René, spotted an elegant middle-aged lady having tea alone at the Hotel Continental. It was Farrar. "Those eyes," recalled Stevens, "were unbelievable, china blue, piercing. She was constantly looking toward the door of the hotel as we talked, and suddenly a huge cartwheel of a bouquet arrived. A few minutes passed, and a bellboy took the bouquet up the elevator. Farrar excused herself and went to the same elevator. And Schoen-René said to me, 'Keep watching the door.' I did, and a large man with a beard came in, and went immediately to the elevator. 'Do you recognize who that is?'

Schoen-René asked me. I said, 'Isn't that the Crown Prince?' Schoen-René nodded. 'Still following her,' she said."

Despite all the intrigue, Farrar's career at the Court Opera proceeded and prospered. Violetta, Nedda, and Juliette were her next roles, and after the latter she received the long-awaited invitation from Lilli Lehmann. One compelling reason to settle in Berlin had always been the possibility of studying with the great Lilli, but until now Farrar's letters had remained unanswered—Lehmann later said she never replied because the girl's handwriting was illegible. Once face to face, though, the two headstrong women seemed to get on famously, although Farrar knew her own limits. "She was a hard taskmaster and demanded the ultimate," Farrar remembered, "but found in me an energy equal to her own, if not quite to her physical resistance. I earned her respect much later. We argued frequently, for she often urged upon my vocal apparatus measures ill-suited to its particular reaction; where she would force obedience, I would obtain results by less strenuous efforts. Technical control to her meant everything, while emotional color was my natural asset and delight. We had to effect compromises, which in the course of time became my necessary response to her lofty ambitions for the art of song." One of Lilli's more drastic strategies to tame her rebellious pupil's overeager emoting was to have her sing with her hands tied behind her back.

Asked to perform the title role in the first Berlin production of *Manon* on December 1, 1903, Farrar went to Paris on May 26 to see Massenet. She arrived to find the composer in tears—it was the day of Sibyl Sanderson's funeral, and needless to say, Massenet was an emotional wreck. He had recovered a few days later, though, and the soprano received some lessons in French style that she always considered invaluable. Soon *die Farrar aus Berlin* was an operatic personality to conjure with throughout Germany and a much-wanted guest at other houses. In 1905 she traveled to Munich to sing in Auber's *Le Domino Noir* and Elisabeth in *Tannhäuser*, both conducted by Richard Strauss, who invited her to the premiere of his *Salome* in Dresden later that year in hopes of interesting her in the title role. When she sensibly demurred, the composer offered to make any changes in the vocal line to suit her, adding what the soprano seemed to consider a compliment: "You, Farrar, have such dramatic possibilities, can act and dance half-naked, so no one will care if you sing or not."

The year before, in 1904, she was invited to Monte Carlo, where she made her debut as Mimì in *La Bohème* opposite the Rodolfo of Caruso—the beginning of a partnership that would last until the tenor's death in 1921. During her three Monte Carlo seasons Farrar learned several rarities that she would never perform again: Mascagni's *Amica* and Saint-Saëns's *L'Ancêtre* (both world premieres), Verdi's *Don Carlos*, and Massenet's *Le Roi de Lahore*. This last opera featured an exotic young dancer named Mata Hari, who startled even Massenet by appearing topless at the rehearsals.

Among Farrar's first recordings in Berlin were an aria and two duets (with the tenor Wilhelm Grüning) from Leoncavallo's *Der Roland von Berlin*, an opera commissioned by the Kaiser to celebrate the Hohenzollern dynasty. The soprano's presence here is a bit of a mystery, since the role of Elsbeth at the 1904 premiere had been created by Emmy Destinn and Farrar never sang it—many years later she could not even recall making the discs. No doubt her favored status with the Kaiser and his family had something to do with this recording debut (coincidentally, she concluded her formal catalogue of operatic discs in 1920 with more minor Leoncavallo, an aria from *Zazà*). In any case, the overheated grandiosity of the music finds the twenty-two-year-old tearing into the material with the sort of hell-to-pay intensity that had already made her such a popular figure at the Court Opera.

The later Berlin discs show precisely what an unpredictable singer Farrar was to be throughout her career. Her basic sound is fresh and healthy, but a listener never knows quite what to expect from one note to the next. She recorded arias from *La Traviata*, *Manon*, *Le Domino Noir* (Auber), and *Roméo et Juliette* on what must have been a very good day—June 23, 1906—four selections that give a vivid portrait of a spirited young singer out to make an impression at all costs. The conclusion of Violetta's Act I scene tends to be a bit wild and messy, but the sheer manic ferocity of Farrar's abandoned singing is hard to resist. Occasionally, too, there are some amazingly deft technical touches—trills, shakes, and passagework—that might even have passed muster *chez* Marchesi. On the other hand, there is also much that is careless, while her expressive gestures are often haphazard and recklessly applied. One has the impression of an extraordinary natural talent on the edge and relying mainly on the inspiration of the moment. Voices of this sort frequently run out of steam early on, and Farrar's retirement at forty could hardly have come as a surprise to the veteran New York critics who had chronicled her ups and downs.

Meanwhile, Maurice Grau had not forgotten the pretty teenager whom he had wanted to cast as Mignon. By 1906 Grau had left the Metropolitan, but he advised his successor, Heinrich Conried, to scout out Farrar in Berlin and snare the now-celebrated young soprano. That, of course, is what Farrar and her mother had been aiming for all along, but the Met would have to take Geraldine on her terms. When he arrived, Conried rang her up and suggested that she come by his hotel and sing for him. Farrar cheekily replied that she was at home, and the impresario was more than welcome to call on her. Grau arrived and was a bit taken aback by the contract that mother and daughter had already outlined, full of explicit concessions regarding repertory, exclusivity, special appearances, and other emoluments. Conried listened, refused to commit himself, and departed. "Don't worry," Grau said when Farrar apprised him of the meeting, "he'll be back." Sure enough, a few months later Conried once again tracked down the young diva—on vacation in Franzensbad—and complied with all of her demands. "He said I knew more about protective paragraphs than any other star performer since the vigilant Adelina Patti," as Farrar proudly put it.

Her Met debut, as Juliette, took place on November 26, 1906. It was the opening night of the season, the only one that Caruso missed during his many years as the company's leading star—among Farrar's many demands was a stipulation that she would not make a debut with any tenor who might possibly upstage her (the French tenor Charles Rousselière sang Roméo). The next day the society columns spread the happy news that a new American prima donna had arrived on the scene: "First Opera's Farrar Furor Is Growing Yet!" "Her Whispered Waltz a Dream!" "The Little Star Drops German Court 'Curtsies' in a Tangle of American Beauty Bouquets and a Trooping of Foreign Colors!" "Such Lovemaking Not Seen Since Aunty Calvé, Such Joyous Grace Since Grandmother Sarah!" A new audience favorite had clearly come to town and the Farrar publicity machine had already sped into motion.

The music critics were impressed too, even if they were not quite ready to proclaim a new Patti in their midst. Nearly everyone had reservations about the technical quality of Farrar's singing—she would read mixed notices throughout her career, but they never had the slightest effect on her ability to sell tickets. Some of the older critics also vehemently complained about her acting, which struck them as excessively realistic. Good heavens, she had even sung much of the chamber scene between Roméo and Juliette lying down in her nightgown. Farrar defended herself on that score—she was a new kind of singer and the critics had better get used to it. "People are often shocked because when I sing in concert I don't wear gloves," she told Willa Cather, clearly intending to shock them some more. "I can't sing in gloves. I can't sing if I feel my clothes. I don't wear stays, and I would like to sing without any clothes, if I could. Fifty years ago a singer had nothing to do but nourish herself and sing; they had never discovered their bodies. But with a singing actress it's different; I sing with my body, and the freer it is, the better I can sing." The public loved her even more for such bold statements. They also loved her because she was a local girl who had won success the way Americans have always liked it: at an early age and through a rich natural endowment combined with sheer luck rather than dogged hard labor.

Although Juliette, with her roulades and coloratura, would not have been Farrar's first choice as a debut vehicle, she did give in to Conried on that point. Otherwise, her first season was cannily arranged to display her versatility, although few of the roles remained long in her Met repertory: the Marguerites of both Gounod and Berlioz, Nedda, Mimì, and Wagner's Elisabeth. Many felt that Farrar's Elisabeth displayed her best qualities, a ravishing creation in every respect. Ideally suited to flatter her essentially lyrical instrument, the music made no demands on her spotty bel canto technique, and of course she looked like an angel— "the finest creation of Miss Farrar's entire career," enthused Henderson. Astonishingly, and for reasons best known to Gatti, this artistic success was heard and seen at the Met for one performance only, with four more on tour.

Farrar was not inclined to complain, since she had been assigned one of the season's most eagerly awaited novelties, the first Met performance of Puccini's *Madama Butterfly*. Her colleagues were Caruso, Scotti, and Homer, and the composer himself had come to America to supervise the production. No one was more susceptible to a pretty face than Puccini, but he never could summon up much enthusiasm for the soprano's Butterfly. "Farrar doesn't satisfy me very much," he wrote to his publisher, Tito Ricordi. "She sings out of tune and forces, and her voice doesn't carry well in the large space." Even composers are sometimes wrong. Farrar's Butterfly must have had something, since it soon became the role that New Yorkers most identified with her. Over the next fifteen years she sang 139 Cio-Cio-Sans with the Met, accounting for a quarter of all her appearances with the company, and audiences adored her in the part. She also recorded most of Butterfly's music for Victor shortly after the premiere. The discs are among her best, and they remain good listening today. The voice is at its freshest and her honest interpretation effectively portrays both the little Japanese girl's delicacy and her passionate dilemma. Beyond that, one clearly hears a reflection of Lilli Lehmann's influence and training in the clean, fearless attack and sheer vitality of her singing.

Discophiles are still arguing over a small textual point in the *Butterfly* love duet with Caruso, where Farrar seems to substitute the words "He's had a highball" for "Sì, per la vita." The tenor, so the story goes, turned up several hours late for the recording session, and the impatient soprano got her revenge by inserting an impromptu suggestion to explain his tardiness. Caruso, not to be outdone by his partner's spur-of-the-moment invention, answers her with "Vieja [old woman in Spanish], vieni!" Questioned about this ad-libbing years later, Farrar vehemently denied everything and huffily replied, "Neither Caruso nor I were that kind of an artist." Oh, but they were. The tenor's penchant for practical jokes was chronic, and the pose of a hoity-toity grand dame in retirement that Farrar adopted late in life bore no resemblance to the impulsive, high-spirited young woman whose Butterfly enchanted Met audiences in 1907. In any case, what they actually sang is there for all to hear.

Farrar weathered the change in Met management in 1908, although the letter protesting the Gatti-Casazza–Toscanini appointment over Andreas Dippel—which she signed along with Caruso, Scotti, Sembrich, and Eames—was mostly her inspiration. Gatti never brought up that treasonous action in his later dealings with the soprano, but it's unlikely he ever forgot it. Her relationship with Toscanini was more tempestuous, and it began badly with their famous clash at a *Butterfly* rehearsal during the Maestro's first week at the house. The conductor must follow her, Farrar insisted, because she was the star. Toscanini shot back his reply, and it has become legendary: "The stars are all in heaven, mademoiselle. You are but a plain artist, and you must obey my direction."

Clearly the electricity they generated was not the usual sort that flowed between any ordinary ego-driven prima donna and headstrong conductor, and the atmosphere soon warmed up. Exactly when their affair began is uncertain (in 1908 Farrar was turning down Scotti's marriage proposals and would continue to do so for years), but later that season, on tour in Chicago, the two were definitely more cordial. During curtain calls the soprano could tell "from his warm hand-clasp that our sad differences were at an end." Whether or not Toscanini actually did leave the Met and America in 1915 after an either-me-or-your-wife ultimatum from Farrar is still a matter of speculation. They continued to correspond, though, and the Maestro was in the habit of absentmindedly leaving the soprano's letters in books or stuffed in his pockets to be discovered by his long-suffering wife, Carla. Farrar apparently also forgot a few things. Years later, when all the passions had subsided, Toscanini attended a dinner party at the retired diva's home in Connecticut. When caviar was served, the conductor suddenly became livid and whispered to his neighbor, "I slept with that woman for seven years. Wouldn't you think she'd remember that I hate fish?"

Now securely ensconced as a Met favorite, Farrar began adding new roles to her repertory: Micaela, Cherubino under Mahler, Manon, Charlotte in *Werther*, and her first Tosca. She had her heart set on creating Minnie in the world premiere of Puccini's *La Fanciulla del West* in 1910, but the composer remembered his displeasure with her Butterfly (as well as her refusal to sing his Manon during the Met's 1910 trip to Paris) and awarded the part to Emmy Destinn. A few weeks later, on December 28, Farrar took the lead in the Met's second world premiere of the season, Humperdinck's *Königskinder*. The opera never lasted in the repertory, but Farrar's Goosegirl is still fondly remembered as one of her most effective roles—her appearance as the innocent child at the city gates in Act II, a flock of live geese obediently following behind (Farrar had trained them herself), seemed like a fairy-tale vision come to life.

Other novelties followed—Dukas's *Ariane et Barbe-bleue*, Wolf-Ferrari's *Le Donne Curiose* and *Il Segreto di Susanna*, and Charpentier's *Julien*, a feeble sequel to *Louise*—along with bouts of poor vocal health. During a *Faust* in Brooklyn early in the 1913–14 season, her voice broke on a high B at the end of the Jewel Song, and to the audience's delight she angrily hurled Marguerite's mirror into the wings. The love duet in the Garden Scene was sung in half voice, the Church Scene declaimed, and the rest of the opera turned over to the Siebel of the evening, Rita Fornia. The remainder of the season was rocky for Farrar, but next year she was back in shape for her first Carmen, on November 19, a role she would sing fifty-eight times over the next eight years. At first many agreed with Aldrich, who found her Gypsy "interesting and in many ways charming," but missing "the smoldering Mediterranean fire that is an essential quality of the character." That fire was to be kindled when Farrar offered her new and improved impersonation a year later. In 1915 she spent the summer in Hollywood making a silent film of *Carmen* directed by Cecil B. DeMille, and when she returned to the Met that fall, many realistic touches had been added. The chorus girls in the Act I tussle may not have complained about being scratched and bit, but Caruso obviously did not appreciate getting the same treatment—in Act III he threw her to the ground with a vehemence that made the house gasp, and the next morning he marched into Gatti's office to register his distress in person.

That Farrar would eventually find her way to Hollywood and DeMille somehow seemed inevitable. The immediate impetus arose from the fact that the war in Europe prevented her annual summer trips back to the Kaiser's Court Opera—or anywhere else on the Continent for that matter. When an offer came in 1915 to make several films for Jesse Lasky and his Feature Play Company, Farrar seized the opportunity as both a convenient way of filling up the idle summer months and a chance to conquer a potentially even more glamorous world than opera. The success of her first Met Carmen (a hit with audiences if not the critics) made that subject a natural choice for her first vehicle, but DeMille also saw her potential in screenplays that bore no relation to opera.

Farrar arrived in Hollywood in a manner befitting the country's reigning diva, expecting—and receiving—star treatment. A private railroad car complete with a Bechstein grand piano had brought her and her current male interest—Jimmy Sullivan, a pop pianist of sorts—across the country. The studio provided her with a two-story bungalow fully staffed with maids, butlers, and cooks. A Hispano-Suiza limousine and chauffeur were at her disposal, and living expenses for everyone in her entourage were also fully covered by her contract. The working day was to last no longer than six hours, including a two-hour midday respite, and during the shooting a live orchestra was expected to play on the set and keep the star in the proper mood. As for billing, all promotional material had to refer to the leading lady as "Miss Farrar." *Photoplay* made merry, likening the notion of an opera singer in silent films to "the Mona Lisa without her smile, a Stradivarius without its strings."

Farrar may have made extravagant demands, but when she got down to work, no one had any complaints about her professionalism. Film techniques were still primitive in those days and many snags arose. The blinding klieg lights blotted out most of Farrar's teeth and those devastating "china-blue eyes," one of the singer's most seductive attractions, problems that were eventually solved by draping black velvet behind the camera. All the trouble must have been worth it, because the three films she made that summer—the other two were *Maria Rosa* and *Temptation* (the latter about an aspiring opera singer and a lecherous impresario who bore a passing resemblance to Gatti-Casazza)—were all popular and critical successes. The *New York Dramatic Mirror* proclaimed that Farrar "has proved herself one of the greatest actresses of all times. Her picture *Carmen* will live long after her operatic characterization has died in the limbo of forgotten singers." Perhaps the long-unseen Farrar films deserve a revival. Viewing *Carmen* seventy years later, the film historian David Groover found that little had dated, maintaining that "Farrar is luminous in a way that Garbo and Dietrich would later be—you can't take your eyes off her."

Back in Hollywood in 1916, Farrar tackled a project that later became her favorite film: a Joan of Arc extravaganza titled *Joan the Woman,* one of DeMille's first historical spectaculars. Farrar loved making the film, she bonded with her soldiers on the set (who affectionately dubbed her "Jerry-Joan"), and again the reviews were sensational. By now she was married to the actor Lou Tellegen, who had already worked with Lasky and DeMille as both actor and director, and turned out to be incompetent in both capacities. Despite Tellegen's bad credentials, Farrar demanded that her new husband participate in her upcoming projects, and DeMille refused. "Geraldine met me with the air of a lioness defending her young," he recalled. "She was magnificent, but I was firm. Both Geraldine and I have some small gift of forceful speech when aroused. All through the conversation, the subject of it lay blandly on his couch, letting Geraldine defend him."

In order to have Tellegen as her costar and director, Farrar signed up with Samuel Goldwyn, who agreed to the package. Weighed down by Tellegen's uninspiring presence and without DeMille's canny guidance, the diva's subsequent films turned out badly—even she later called them "tepid narratives," "lunatic fancies," and "irritations." Even worse, they were financial disasters. In 1920, with two years to run on her contract, Farrar tore it up, much to Goldwyn's surprise and relief. Her movie career was over—and soon her marriage to Tellegen would be as well. A weak character and a philanderer (apparently with both sexes), Tellegen was the most serious mistake Farrar made in a life that was otherwise managed with exquisite, almost cold-blooded, craft and care. When the actor committed suicide some ten years later, his ex-wife shed few tears. Upon hearing the news, she coolly summed him up: "Handsome and stupid, as long as physical appeal was seconded by youth, he typified romance and adventure to the casual eye. He could be charming and well-mannered when he wished, but had the perception of a moron, and no morals whatever . . . For him, it was only another glamorous episode, I suppose."

Farrar's last years in opera found her creating roles in several contemporary novelties at the Met each season, although only Puccini's *Suor Angelica* turned out to be an effective addition to her old standbys. Giordano's *Madame Sans-Gêne*, Leroux's *La Reine Fiammette*, Massenet's *La Navarraise*, and Mascagni's *Lodoletta* failed to capture the public's fancy, and, surprisingly, the soprano made less of an impression in *Thaïs* and *Louise* than one might have expected—perhaps New York's memory of Mary Garden in these two parts was still too fresh. In any case, Farrar must have sensed that time was running out. Her top notes were becoming increasingly unavailable after 1918, when she developed a node on her vocal cords and was unable to sing for six months. She recovered and continued to perform with undiminished frequency and vigor, but to some observers the deterioration was increasing.

Another warning sign came in 1921, when Maria Jeritza made her Met debut, clearly indicating that a younger and dangerously seductive prima donna had appeared on the scene. Farrar had survived the arrivals of Frieda Hempel, Lucrezia Bori, Claudia Muzio, and lesser lights without feeling threatened, but Jeritza's potent theatrical glamour was too close to her own for comfort. Farrar always claimed to be above petty professional jealousies, but she couldn't resist passing a catty remark about Jeritza's infamous flat-on-the-floor delivery of "Vissi d'arte" in Act II of *Tosca*. "From my seat," she wrote years later, "I obtained no view of any expressive pantomime on her pretty face, while I was surprised by the questionable flaunting of a well-cushioned and obvious posterior."

It was also clear that Gatti had begun to send those signals opera managers invariably do when they feel the time has come to ease out a fading but still popular diva. Not only had Jeritza been awarded some of Farrar's best roles, but Amelita Galli-Curci was chosen to open the 1921–22 season as Violetta in a new production of *La Traviata*—a sure sign, some felt, that Farrar was being edged toward the door. When as the season wore on and Gatti made no moves to renew her contract, Farrar told her manager, Charles Ellis, to arrange a concert tour for 1922–23. When Gatti's tardy contract finally did arrive, she sent it back and announced her retirement from opera. On the afternoon of April 22, 1922, she significantly refused to permit any eulogies from Met management, no farewell supper, no patronizing addresses, gold wreaths, cups, platters, or brooches. Like Emma Abbott fifty years earlier, Farrar offered her voice and persona to the public and she had complete confidence in their response. "I had loved them. They had loved me. And to them I wanted to address those last words. And so it was."

If she found it hard to let go, she never showed it. As with her opera and film career, Farrar's gradual withdrawal from public life was consummately orchestrated. She gave concerts, of course, and shortly after leaving the Met she toured the country in a condensation of *Carmen*, complete with costumes, scenery, and orchestra, giving 123 consecutive performances in 125 days. Similar fantasias were concocted for the three most popular Puccini operas, but the composer's publishers vetoed the plan. Farrar had to settle for a potted version of Lehár's *Romany Love* instead, but that unhappy project collapsed after a single out-of-town performance. In the fall of 1931 there was one last concert in Carnegie Hall, and then Farrar withdrew permanently from public performance to enjoy the rustic New England beauty of her Fairhaven estate in Ridgefield, Connecticut.

She briefly reappeared as a radio commentator when the Met began broadcasting Saturday matinees in the mid-thirties—no one seemed more genuinely surprised or excited than Farrar upon hearing the unheralded debut of Kirsten Flagstad as Sieglinde on the afternoon of February 2, 1935. Around the same time, she made some private song recordings, revealing that the attractive timbre of her middle register, always her strongest suit, had in no way deteriorated over the years. Like all true prima donnas, Farrar could not resist "setting the record straight" by offering the world the definitive version of her life, *Such Sweet Compulsion*, an often impossibly affected and highly selective memoir "concluded on a Sabbath Day, July, 1938." One oddity about the book is the division of narrative duties between herself and her mother (who died in 1923), an ingenious if excessively artful device that allows Farrar the luxury of paying herself some extravagant compliments as well as to pass critical pronouncements on the people on her enemies list. She also turned her hand to mystical poetry, embarrassing enough to read but intolerable when heard on the recorded readings she made in the late thirties. By the time Farrar died, on March 11, 1967, a stately if not starchy old lady of eighty-five, most of the original Gerryflappers were grown up and had forgotten all about her. By then, "Miss Farrar," as she still insisted on being addressed, seemed as though she had forgotten about herself as well.

Geraldine Farrar was lucky. Had she been born a generation earlier, when being an opera singer presupposed a secure command of brilliant fioriture and, as she once put it, a "dramatically quiescent" stage personality, it is doubtful she would have been more than a minor figure, despite her beauty. Had she come to the fore in the later years of the twentieth century, she would have met major competition from dozens of other attractive American sopranos whose vocal endowment and acting skills were equal to hers, if not superior, and whose ambition and industry were just as fierce. But when Farrar arrived on the scene, she was, as the Berlin *Intendant* who hired her in 1901 at the age of nineteen correctly observed, a novelty. Opera was still a creative force, new works were in demand, and composers produced vehicles that relied less on technical vocal display for their effect than on the force of a performer's personality. Farrar's singular combination of looks, brains, vocal honesty, and provocative stage presence was precisely what was needed to spread the gospel of Puccini as well as his lesser contemporaries.

Mary Garden shared the same characteristics, but she exuded a more exotic, otherworldly, even forbidden eroticism that set her apart. As Willa Cather pointed out, there was a wholesomeness about Farrar's all-American image, a naughty but nice free spirit that appealed to the country at large and permitted her the sort of Establishment success at the Met and in films that had eluded Garden, despite her notoriety. "I thought she was a marvelous and very well put together fake," the veteran Philadelphia music critic Max de Schauensee replied when he was once asked his opinion of Farrar. It was a perceptive observation and, in its way, a compliment. A thoroughly professional, consummately packaged, dazzling media figure rather than an artistic presence of overwhelming originality, Farrar was up to date and one of a kind. No wonder she never even considered teaching after her retirement, since what she had could never be taught. Like all startlingly new phenomena, she created her own traditions and became a dangerous role model, one whose style did not go unnoticed or unappreciated by the many ambitious American singers who succeeded her.

Fourteen

A Caruso in

Petticoats

~~~~~~~~~~~~~~~~

"Hey, *scugnizz'*. Do you know you look like me?" Enrico Caruso had just arrived at a Manhattan voice studio to audition a young vaudeville singer named Rosa Ponzillo. He probably did not expect much from her—a twenty-one-year-old whose career had so far been confined to a vocal act with her sister on the Keith circuit—but the face must have looked familiar and he couldn't resist passing a comment. Ponzillo, soon to be better known as Rosa Ponselle, was born in Meriden, Connecticut, but her parents came from Caruso's beloved Naples, where little moon-faced *scugnizze* (ragamuffins), many no doubt named Rosa and Enrico, still scampered up and down the narrow streets singing at the top of their lungs.

"I don't mind looking like you," Ponselle boldly replied, "if only I could sing like you." And with that, she launched into "Pace, pace, mio Dio," Leonora's great aria from the final act of Verdi's *La Forza del Destino*. By the time the last ringing high B-flat had died away, Caruso knew that he had encountered something more than the ordinary streetwise *scugnizz'*. "You'll sing with me, you'll see," he assured her.

Then, as Ponselle recalled many years later, Caruso "put his arm around me in a fatherly way and, letting his hand brush my throat, he said to me, 'You see, you have it there.' Next he pointed to my heart and said with a warm smile, 'And you have it there, too.' Lastly, he put his fingers to my temples and said, 'Whether you have it up there, only time will tell.' It was the finest appraisal any young singer could have been given."

That informal audition in the office of Ponselle's agent, William Thorner, took place in May 1918. The atmosphere may have been breezy, but Caruso had a serious reason to hear this young soprano, who, he had been assured, was something special. Although Ponselle claimed to be unaware of it at the time, Met general manager Giulio Gatti-Casazza and his star tenor were desperately searching for a soprano to sing Leonora in the first Metropolitan Opera production of *La Forza del Destino*, and the premiere was barely six months off. Why the role was not automatically awarded to Claudia Muzio, the company's leading Italian dramatic soprano in 1918 and who would surely have made an impressive Leonora, remains a mystery shrouded in ancient opera house politics. For whatever reason, Muzio was not in the running, and the war in Europe clearly limited Gatti's other options.

On Caruso's enthusiastic recommendation, Gatti quickly arranged to hear Ponselle. Even though nerves got the better of her and she fainted dead away in the middle of "Casta diva" from *Norma*, Ponselle still impressed Gatti mightily, and he agreed to take a chance on an unknown. The gamble paid off handsomely. On November 15, Rosa Ponselle made one of the great surprise debuts in Met history, and soon all New York was marveling over this unprecedented vocal prodigy who had come from nowhere, had generously been given her big break, and started triumphantly at the top. Not only had she never before sung an opera on any stage, but she had never even been to Europe—this superior vocal talent was definitely made in America. By the time Ponselle's first Met season was over, almost everyone agreed with James Huneker, who described her voice in the *Times* the day after her debut as "vocal gold," with "its luscious lower and middle tones, dark, rich and ductile," yet "brilliant and flexible in the upper register." Of course, Ponselle still had much to learn about style, method, and interpretation. The *Sun*'s exacting W. J. Henderson, too, was impressed by "one of the most voluptuous dramatic soprano voices that present-day operagoers have heard," and that exigent critic had heard every major singer at the Met since opening night in 1883. But his critique also contained the following drop of acid to put some perspective on the new vocal sensation: "Some day doubtless Miss Ponselle will learn how to sing, and then she will be an artist." Most Met patrons, for whom a glorious sound had always been paramount, could not have cared less about that. They were more than satisfied, and for them Ponselle was already "a Caruso in petticoats."

That prodigious vocal endowment, as well as the ability to use it properly at such an early age, seems to have been a genuine natural phenomenon. Unlike Patti, Ponselle was not born into a family of singers, nor did she pass her youth in an especially musical environment. Rosa was the third and last child of Benardino and Maddalena Ponzillo, who both grew up in Caserta, the capital of the district of Terra di Lavoro, part of the province of Naples. The young couple crossed the Atlantic during the summer of 1885, pausing briefly in Schenectady before settling permanently in Meriden, where Ben Ponzillo went to work in his older brother's saloon. Soon he owned not only the saloon but a neighborhood bakery, a grocery store, and a small farm as well. When Rosa was born, on January 22, 1897, the Ponzillo family life was one of hard work from morn till night, and music simply never entered the picture. Although he was making the American dream come true on a modest level and was financially comfortable by the time his youngest daughter had reached school age, Ben Ponzillo didn't even own a Victrola.

Rosa was five years old when sister Carmela, her elder by ten years (in her memoirs, Ponselle gives her sister's birth year as 1887), brought music into the household. Anna Ryan, the organist at the girls' parish church, heard Carmela's contralto voice in the choir, and she was impressed by its lush, dark coloring as well as by the instinctively musical way the girl used it. Piano and voice lessons began, and Rosa, who idolized her older sister and wanted to be exactly like her, demanded instruction as well. Miss Ryan obligingly took her on, and gradually realized that the younger sister was blessed with even more musical talent. At first Rosa concentrated on the keyboard, playing at sight and by ear with equal facility. Later she learned the rudiments of the violin and cornet, as well as singing for her own amusement. Both parents indulged their daughters' music-making without encouraging ideas of future careers, but the few musical events that Maddalena took Rosa to hear were choice and they made a big impact: local concerts by Ernestine Schumann-Heink, Nellie Melba, Luisa Tetrazzini, and Emma Calvé. Schumann-Heink impressed her most, largely because of the contralto's huge, seamlessly knit voice and total involvement with everything she sang—two qualities that would one day be so characteristic of Rosa Ponselle.

Maddalena Ponzillo was hardly cut out to be an ambitious and self-sacrificing stage mother along the lines of such formidable predecessors as Mmes. Kellogg, Hauck, Norton, and Farrar. But when Carmela turned twenty-one and announced that she intended to move to New York and break into the music business, her mother supported her plea despite Ben's predictable objections. Rosa was only eleven in 1908, when Carmela took the plunge, but she eagerly followed her big sister's progress as a café singer who did modeling on the side. For her part, Carmela pushed Rosa to realize her own musical ambitions, and found the girl a job as a song plugger in a Meriden dime store. Rosa also put her keyboard facility to good use at the neighborhood nickelodeons, and when she began to sing as well as play for the silent films, attendance picked up even more.

A local success, the teenager soon moved on to the "big time" at the San Carlino Theater in New Haven, where she was billed as Rosa Ponzillo, soprano. Her pièce de résistance was Ethelbert Nevin's "The Rosary," complete with a slide show in which the screen gradually turned a soft, pale rose color until the real-life Rosa was silhouetted against an oval picture of an American Beauty rose. By then the young singer even had a small orchestra to back her up, and she made her own arrangement of the sentimental ballad, complete with sweeping harp glissandos and chimes. There was no stopping her now. In 1916, nineteen years old, Rosa—surprisingly with Papa's blessings—moved to New Haven, first staying with a cousin of her mother's and later with one of Carmela's married friends. Both Ponzillo sisters were hard at work by then, Rosa singing in Mellone's, a New Haven nightspot popular with Yale students, and Carmela in Manhattan after her first break, a 1912 Broadway musical called *The Girl from Brighton*.

A few months later, Carmela came to hear Rosa at Mellone's, and after listening to her kid sister knock out the big arias from *Cavalleria Rusticana* and *Madama Butterfly* with ease, she got an idea. Her New York manager, Gene Hughes, had told her that sister acts were becoming increasingly popular on vaudeville bills. With their sultry Italian good looks and vibrant voices, Carmela figured, the Ponzillo sisters had to be a publicist's dream come true. When she brought Rosa to Hughes, the scenario, as Ponselle recounts it in her memoirs, played out like an old-fashioned one-reeler. Hughes had doubts at first—Rosa always had to struggle to keep her weight down, and she then weighed around 195. "Who the hell are you kidding?" Hughes remarked when he saw her. "Why, she must tip the scales at two hundred pounds. She's too big for the vaudeville stage." Carmela reassured him. "Just wait till you hear her sing." With that, Rosa sang the pop rage, "Kiss Me Again" from Victor Herbert's *Mlle. Modiste.* When she had finished, Hughes fairly leaped from his chair in delight. "I don't give a goddam *how* fat she is. When can she open with you?"

The answer was easy: Immediately. Opening night came just four days later, when "Those Tailored Italian Girls," as Carmela and Rosa billed themselves, made their bow on the stage of the Star Theatre in the Bronx. Their act began with the Barcarolle from *Les Contes d'Hoffmann,* followed by Carmela's rendition of Musetta's Waltz from *La Bohème,* with her sister providing the piano accompaniment. Then came another duet, "Comin' Thro' the Rye"; Rosa's big solo from *Mlle. Modiste;* "O sole mio" in Neapolitan dialect, and, as a grand finale, the trio from *Faust* sung in unison. The girls were an instant hit and in no time they were asked to appear at that vaudeville mecca in Manhattan, the Palace Theater at Broadway and Forty-seventh Street. A tour took them to Pittsburgh, then west to Topeka and Grand Rapids, where they sang the Flower Duet from *Madama Butterfly* dressed as geishas—"The costumes were mandarin," exclaimed an enchanted Michigan reviewer, "the voices golden."

Despite their lucrative vaudeville successes, both Ponzillo sisters still dreamed of an even grander, more glamorous future in opera—after all, their voices clearly pointed in that direction. Shortly after Rosa's success at the Met, the duo made four sides for the Columbia Phonograph Company and the results give an excellent idea of what their vaudeville act must have been like, as well as the reasons for its success. They blend ravishingly in "O sole mio" as one luscious voice enters after the other and joins in close harmony—a marvelous effect no doubt dreamed up by Rosa herself. Perhaps she also had a hand in devising the showy tour de force that concludes "Comin' Thro' the Rye," a cadenza far more elabo-rate than anything Bellini requires Norma and Adalgisa to sing.

Constantly performing and on the road, Rosa had little opportunity to see opera—before her Met audition she had been inside the house just twice, to see *Tosca* and *L'Amore dei Tre Re*, one with Farrar, the other with Muzio, and both with Caruso. But she avidly attended concerts by "legit" singers. One who fascinated her was Rosa Raisa, only four years her senior but already the star of the Chicago Grand Opera and the possessor of a dramatic voice that resembled the younger Rosa's to an uncanny degree. After a Raisa concert in New York, Rosa encountered a young Italian pianist, coach, and composer named Romano (Nino) Romani. Having heard Rosa in vaudeville, he thought her voice had even greater potential than Raisa's and he was determined to prove it. Romani brought both "tailored Italian girls" to William Thorner, one of the top entertainment managers in New York, who took them on immediately. At first Thorner seemed more impressed by the older, more experienced Carmela until one of the agent's card-playing cronies told him, "Can't you hear the difference? It's the other one whom the gods have smiled upon." That distinguished elderly gentleman should have known: he was Victor Maurel, Verdi's choice to create Iago and Falstaff, now retired and living in New York, where he enjoyed a late-blossoming career as a painter and set designer.

Thorner's career ambitions for the Ponzillos ran high. At first he insisted that they demand double their fee—an unrealistic suggestion, since the girls were already making $700 per week, top dollar on the Keith circuit. The strategy backfired, effectively pricing them out of vaudeville, and the sisters were reduced to café work until that fateful afternoon in Thorner's office with Caruso changed everything. When the exciting prospects of Gatti-Casazza's offer were translated into harsh reality, though, Rosa had a new set of problems to deal with. One was Carmela. The Met hired her in 1925, when Rosa had the star clout to insist on it, but Carmela never quite made the grade and the sisters' relationship would be strained for the rest of their lives. Another was a considerable reduction in earning power—the Met contract stipulated a weekly salary of $150 for no fewer than three and no more than four performances per week for the full season. And then there was a great deal of work to do. Since Rosa had never stepped on an operatic stage, she obviously knew no roles and had only weeks to learn what Gatti had assigned her. By November 11, 1918, she was expected to have prepared the leading soprano parts in *Aida*, *La Forza del Destino*, *Il Trovatore*, *Cavalleria Rusticana*, and the Verdi *Requiem*. Gatti also suggested that she change her last name to the more international-sounding Ponselle—Met audiences, he felt, were still more likely to think of Rosa Ponzillo as a two-a-day vaudeville performer rather than a glamorous diva.

Another problem was surely to some degree a psychological one. Like her girlhood idol, Ernestine Schumann-Heink, Ponselle had never received vocal instruction in any formal sense of the term. That must partly explain the almost pathological nervousness that beset her before every performance, as well as her decision to retire prematurely from opera in 1937. Despite her innate musicality and intelligence, good health, and glorious natural vocal endowment, Ponselle, one feels, never quite figured out how she made all those wonderful sounds. She could never be completely sure of herself or her instrument until actually singing onstage, and even then there could be sudden, inexplicable disasters. During her first-ever *Aida* with the Met, in Brooklyn on March 6, 1920, Ponselle lost the high C in "O patria mia," leaving her permanently terrified of a role that was otherwise ideally suited to her—after that initial unsettling experience, she sang just two Aidas with the Met on home ground, and only eleven more on tour. When top notes became increasingly troublesome during the thirties, her self-confidence often seemed to desert her altogether.

Asked to contribute to a book on the art of the prima donna, a few years after her Met debut, Ponselle remained typically vague about technical matters: "First of all, I regard singing as a mental operation—that is, the art of singing. For the girl who is a student of opera in the higher sense, mechanical exercises cannot be well advised, because vocal mechanics do not enter into singing as an art." She then went on to credit William Thorner as her teacher, proclaiming, "All that I may have gained in the way of voice production and flexibility, singing poise and tone development, I owe to him." Ponselle later came to regret that statement when Thorner actually started to advertise her as his student. In her memoirs she denied the claim and flatly contradicted herself: "And what angered me was that he had never once given me a voice lesson! In all my years with him he had done but one thing for me: he had made the right contacts with Gatti and Caruso so that I would be given an audition. Other than that, he had only collected his share of my paychecks."

Whatever the truth of the matter, one thing was certain: even before her Met debut, Ponselle relied entirely on Nino Romani, who acted as her musical adviser, second pair of ears, and coach if not actual voice teacher throughout her career. It was Romani who recommended repertory and taught her each new role—their relationship strikingly resembles the almost Svengaliesque rapport that existed between Richard Bonynge and Joan Sutherland a generation later, although of course Romani and Ponselle were not married. A romantic involvement was always assumed, but hard evidence is lacking and Ponselle devoted considerable space in her memoirs to denying that one ever existed:

If Nino's and my personal relationship was misread in those early years, so was our professional one—and it was partly my fault. For several years I agreed to let Nino advertise himself as "teacher of Rosa Ponselle." It began as a harmless practice in the early 1920s; he was conducting studio-recording sessions for the Columbia record company at the time, and was supplementing his income by teaching voice. But factually, Nino never taught me to sing. Nobody did, not even Miss Ryan. I was one of those fortunate few who are, I guess, just "born to sing."

Perhaps the geneticists can explain it; I know I can't. All I know is that from about age fourteen I had a fully rounded opera-like dramatic voice. As far back as I can remember, I never had what I would call a "girl's voice"—the light, breathy-sounding, high-pitched voice we normally associate with young children. My singing voice was always big and round, and even as a teenager I could sing almost three octaves. I never recall the slightest trouble swelling or diminishing a tone anywhere in those octaves.

But I wasn't a *perfect* singer—and this is where I learned a great deal from Nino Romani. Even though I was what you might call a "natural," I had a tendency to sing very high notes (say, the B natural, the high C, and the high D flat) incorrectly. Because I was essentially untrained (I had never had an actual voice lesson in my life), I tended to sing high tones a bit too brightly, not knowing how to "cover" them.

Although Ponselle was beset by fierce bouts of stage fright throughout her career, nothing quite equaled the nerve-wracking trauma of her debut. The summer had left her utterly exhausted. After learning the five roles Gatti had asked for, there was a sixth one to cram into her head: Rezia in Weber's *Oberon*, which she was scheduled to perform at the Met premiere on December 28. Gatti had also made her keenly aware that no other American singer had appeared at the Met in such an important, exposed starring role as Leonora in *La Forza del Destino* without previous operatic experience or European schooling. No wonder Ponselle felt such an enormous pressure to succeed and set a standard. Beyond that, Gatti's decision not to promote her in advance hardly bolstered her confidence. As the canny general manager explained to Ponselle, "Caruso believes you will sing beautifully, I believe you will sing beautifully, and so do you. But suppose something happens and you don't. Then what? If we have promoted you too much, your career will be over before it has time to get on its feet. We will have invited the critics to make headlines of a young girl's opening-night difficulties. But suppose the critics come to the opera house without knowing very much about you, and suppose you sing the way we all know that you can. Do you see what happens then? They, not we, will make you a star. They will have come with few expectations, but will have left with a new name to write about."

Gatti's reasoning was shrewd, but Ponselle took no comfort from it. The day before the big event she happened to read a devastating review of Giulio Crimi's Met debut, as Radamès on November 13, and went into shock. If the critics roasted a pro like Crimi, Ponselle figured, what would they do to her? After spending the rest of the day under sedation, she awoke the next morning a bundle of nerves. Even heavier sedatives were prescribed and the singer slept fitfully until it was time to leave for the opera house. Upon arriving, she made the mistake of vocalizing in her dressing room, little realizing that the heavy carpets and draperies absorbed the natural fullness and resonance of her voice. "Oh, God— now I've really done it!" she moaned. "I've completely lost my voice!" During the overture, while Ponselle sat onstage and fantasized about the headlines next morning—VAUDEVILLE SINGER DIES AT MET DEBUT—she knew that the first words she had to sing could hardly have better suited the occasion: "Oh, angoscia!"

Despite all the anguish and hand-wringing, Ponselle not only survived the evening but delivered the goods. Gatti could not have been more pleased with the results, and the Met's new star settled down to work, filling her first season with her contracted roles as well as the lead in the world premiere of an American opera, *The Legend*, by Joseph Breil. (An opera singer himself in his younger days, Breil was the principal tenor of Emma Juch's company in 1891.) The new work was a failure and Ponselle hated it so much she actually burned the score after the third and last performance. Breil's opera may indeed have been dreadful, but the soprano's avoidance of new music in general throughout her career was definitely a sign of the times. Young singers were more and more devoting themselves to operas from the past, and Ponselle was wholly typical in that regard. She sang a few other contemporary novelties— two by Montemezzi and one by her mentor, Romani—but mainly she concentrated on the great lyric-dramatic roles of the previous century, with the accent on Verdi. Although she met Puccini in Italy a few months before he died and recorded his most familiar arias, even that popular composer's operas played no part in her active stage repertory.

During the next five seasons Ponselle was heard in an extraordinary range of parts, all slowly and painstakingly learned under the tutelage of Romani: Rachel in *La Juive* opposite Caruso, Aida, Gioconda, Leonora in *Il Trovatore*, Maddalena in Giordano's *Andrea Chénier*, Elisabetta in the Met premiere of Verdi's *Don Carlo*, Selika in *L'Africana*, Elvira in *Ernani*, Margared in Lalo's *Le Roi d'Ys*, another Met premiere, and Matilda in *Guglielmo Tell*. Surely unique in the annals of diva memoirists, Ponselle quotes her bad reviews as generously as her good ones, showing just what a tough (and knowledgeable) crew New York's critics were in those days. Writing about *Don Carlo*, Henderson thought the Elisabetta of the evening to be "neither queenly nor tear-compelling, neither most musical nor most melancholy." When Ponselle sang Elvira in *Ernani*, Richard Aldrich wrote that she "sacrificed quality to power" and virtually "dismembered" the aria "Ernani, involami" "in an apparent attempt at dramatic expression." Obviously Ponselle was not at first unanimously greeted as the miracle of perfection that legend would later have us believe. Everyone agreed that the voice was astounding and the promise great, but the talent was still raw and it took several seasons for Ponselle to consolidate her gifts.

Some idea of her progress can be gleaned from the series of recordings Ponselle made for Columbia between 1918 and 1924—heard in sequence, the gradual improvement in poise, technical assurance, and matters of style is clearly audible. The soprano's first disc was a test record made in April 1918 and never meant for release—"Pace, pace, mio Dio" with Romani at the piano (the fact that Ponselle chose Leonora's aria from *La Forza del Destino* for her Columbia test and once again when she sang for Caruso a month later suggests that both she and Romani knew very well the high stakes they were playing for at a supposedly informal audition). Listening to it, one can better understand Henderson's concerns about what he heard as an essentially declamatory approach to a lyrical role, one that violated the basic principles of classical bel canto singing. Even the official version made with orchestra in July 1920 is only marginally more settled, an interpretation that probably struck some sophisticated operagoers of the time as provincial.

And yet, the sheer sound of the voice, its steady emission and wonderful repose, and the youthful spirit that propels the music in these early recordings are intoxicating. Vocal connoisseurs born later than Henderson were more tolerant of the occasional smeared portamentos, oddly prepared top notes, and dislocated phrase shapes, if indeed they heard such lapses as flaws at all. Writing in 1977 on the occasion of Ponselle's eightieth birthday, Walter Legge—record producer, husband of Elisabeth Schwarzkopf, and surely one of the most exacting amateur critics of his time—was uncharacteristically ecstatic:

For me, the revelation of first hearing Ponselle's 1919 records was akin to Saul's adventure on the road to Damascus. At last, here was a woman with a recognizably woman-sized voice not showing off how fast or how high she could sing, but communicating emotion in velvet magic. Her voice was, in retrospect, extraordinarily gramophogenic.

Those early Ponselle records have unique qualities. She was at the age of the characters she was portraying, in her impulsiveness (incredibly controlled by technique and taste), singing every note and emotion with the freshness of youth in life's spring. And this, with the most glorious voice that ever came from any woman's throat in the Italian repertory with a precocious sense of line, style and emotional honesty.

However one may disagree with this blanket praise, Legge's effusiveness is eventually justified as the Columbia series progresses and Ponselle grows and matures. By 1925, when the Met staged Spontini's La Vestale expressly for her, even Henderson had to admit that Ponselle had "ceased to content [herself] with splitting the ears . . . and has gone in for real singing." Although he considered the opera to be a dull example of outdated and musty classicism, Lawrence Gilman in the Tribune was more specific, rejoicing that "here was a 'youngest' Vestal who was obviously young. Here was a singer who could sing Spontini's long, gravely sculptured melodies with the required sense of line and dignity of style, and with the formal and somewhat stilted pathos that is their quaint and special mark." With *La Vestale*, the twenty-eight-year-old Ponselle had clearly reached a new plateau, demonstrating a vocal and musical artistry every bit as awesome as her God-given voice.

Despite Ponselle's rave reviews, *La Vestale* was a flop at the box office. Gatti didn't mind. In his view, the Spontini opera was just a warm-up for what he had long been hoping and planning for: Ponselle as Norma. The impresario had always dreamed of staging Bellini's bel canto classic at the Met, and he must have heard the potential in Ponselle's voice right from the first, even though the young soprano had passed out while singing "Casta diva" at her audition back in 1918. In those days, before the bel canto revival of the postwar years made *Norma* common coin once again, the title role was considered a Mount Everest even taller than Wagner's Isolde. No one had performed it at the Met since Lilli Lehmann in 1892, and everyone remembered Lilli's famous pronouncement that singing one Norma was more difficult than all three Brünnhildes combined.

Ponselle took a full two years to prepare Norma. The faithful Romani worked closely with her, of course (he even instructed her on the habits and customs of ancient Druids), but by now the soprano was also listening to Tullio Serafin, whose decade at the Met (1924–34) corresponded with Ponselle's greatest years. The conductor not only went over every detail with her but would also occasionally hit upon magical remedies that helped allay many of her fears and insecurities, especially regarding those terrifying high notes. "As a conductor," she recalled, "he made the orchestra 'breathe' with the performers. In rehearsals, he would make mental notes on a singer's breathing patterns, particularly on exposed high tones, by scrutinizing their attacks and approaches. He would practice breathing with them, and would pace the orchestra accordingly. This allowed him to give each singer maximum rein where a score might afford some flexibility with time values."

With Norma in 1927, Ponselle reached the apex of her career. Even the dreaded Henderson rewarded her—with perhaps the most extravagant praise he ever managed to summon up for a singer of her generation, calling her "Casta diva" a genuinely beautiful piece of singing. Although hardly an unconditional rave, that review gave Ponselle a special glow. "At last," she said after reading it, "I felt I'd made the transition from a singer to an artist."

After the critical and popular success of her Norma, Ponselle, it seemed, could have taken her career in any direction she chose. There were still many areas in which to venture—Puccini, Mozart, Wagner, even Strauss—but clearly Ponselle needed to be prodded. On her way up she seemed to rely on others to lead her, and she was lucky to have such wise or, at the very least, sympathetically concerned counsellors. Carmela, Romani, Caruso, Gatti, Serafin—each contributed positively to her ascendency, with the singer providing the voice, a willing spirit, and a capacity for much hard work.

The most obvious course in this case was not a new role but a new venue for her activities. So far Ponselle had been an exclusive Metropolitan artist, but her recordings had circulated overseas and the major European companies were definitely interested. She probably would have taken the plunge long before this had not that old devil stage fright kept her home. Eventually Serafin persuaded her that London would be safe—audiences there were far less harsh on newcomers than the hypercritical Italians—and Giovanni Martinelli, a much-admired visitor at Covent Garden, painted a rosy picture of an opera star's life in the English capital. Finally Ponselle agreed to take her Norma and Gioconda across the ocean for Covent Garden's 1929 spring season, rounding up an entourage of as many loyal friends as she could find to provide moral support. Serafin and Martinelli were correct—London audiences adored Ponselle the moment they heard her. And it was not just the voice they responded to but the total package. "Not only is her voice of great beauty," pointed out Ernest Newman in *The Times*, "but she also has the art of making it convey every nuance of the mind without its even for a moment losing its pure singing quality. The range of psychological inflection in it seems unlimited."

After reading reviews like that, Ponselle was encouraged to return to London for two more seasons, even trying out a new role the following year: Violetta in *La Traviata*. Another reason for introducing Verdi's consumptive courtesan away from home base was Gatti's doubts about the wisdom of such an experiment. The general manager needed Ponselle for weightier operas, and Met audiences were conditioned to seeing more petite Violettas with smaller voices, coloraturas like Amelita Galli-Curci or light lyrics like Lucrezia Bori. Perhaps to Gatti's dismay, Ponselle enjoyed yet another London triumph, and the critics warmed to the singer's "modern" approach. As Ponselle put it, "My Violetta . . . was one of much dramatic contrast: she would live hard, and would give up life unwillingly, not resignedly. To her last breath, she would fight for life." Once again, Newman was ecstatic, citing "the constant play of a fine mind upon the inner meaning of the music; her Violetta is so exquisitely sung because it is so subtly imagined. Even coloratura, as she sings it, ceases to suggest the aviary and becomes a revelation of human character."

After such a reception, Gatti had no choice but to offer Ponselle's Violetta to New York, on January 16, 1931. It was a critical disaster, and Henderson seemed especially eager to make up for the compliments he had paid about her Giulia and Norma. Ponselle, Henderson felt, had completely misconceived the musical nature of the work, forced a foreign vocal style on the opera, and in effect destroyed it. "The melodic character of the entire rôle of Violetta," he wrote, "is lyric . . . Legato singing must be the foundation of its interpretation." Ponselle disregarded that fact with her "spasmodic utterances," her "cold and heavy" treatment of the vocal lines, and for transforming a "plaintively pathetic conception into hard-breathed tragedy." Although Henderson never doubted Ponselle's artistic sincerity, he finally had to assume that "she has made a mistake about the possibilities of Verdi's Violetta. The public which, like the Athenians, incessantly clamors for some new thing, has made a sensation of it." Henderson always wrote circumspectly about Ponselle, but for him she clearly remained a provincial singer, despite her acclaim—and Met audiences did indeed find her Violetta a sensation.

Henderson's thoughtful reservations are worth pondering, even if from a later perspective they inevitably seem excessively purist—or at least they do on the evidence of a complete *Traviata* with Ponselle as broadcast from the Met four years later, on January 5, 1935. Possibly, by then, the soprano had taken some of Henderson's criticisms to heart. True, one can still hear the frequent distortions of rhythm, phrasing, and pure vowel sounds that apparently so troubled the venerable critic. And, exactly as Ponselle promised, her Violetta does not go gentle into that good night: Alfredo's denunciation in the gambling scene triggers an embarrassing outburst of wails and spoken protestations. Then, too, frequent transpositions testify to Ponselle's increasing concern about her top notes—"Ah fors' è lui" is taken down a half step and "Sempre libera" a full tone. But there are ample compensations. *Pace* Henderson, Ponselle's legato phrasing is often ravishing in its purling, velvety smoothness, the vocal colors are always warm and appropriately varied, the coloratura in Act I is gracefully negotiated, and not one note of this generous performance is without an exciting element of dramatic urgency.

No one had an inkling of it, but by the thirties Ponselle's operatic career was rapidly drawing to a close. There was one more happy season in London, in which she sang the only role she was never to offer Met audiences, the title part in *Fedra*, a feeble one-act opera by Romani (even Ponselle's star power could not influence Gatti to present that one). In 1933 the soprano was persuaded to make her one and only appearance on the Continent. It was Maddalena's dying wish that she sing in Italy, and so out of respect for her mother, Ponselle agreed to sing two performances of *La Vestale* at the Florence May Festival. She scored a grand success with the Italian public, and the occasion resulted in one of the most famous and touching incidents in the entire Ponselle lore. After Giulia's prayer "O Nume tutelar," pandemonium broke out along with insistant calls for an encore. The conductor, Vittorio Gui, had a firm no-encore policy, but just this once, to everyone's surprise, he broke it. "Do you know why I finally gave way and let them have that prayer again?" Gui confessed years later. "I heard a poor little voice behind me say, 'Who knows when we shall ever hear anything like that again?' and I thought, 'Who knows?— They shall have it!'"

That confidence-building triumph, plus a flattering personal audience with no less a fan than Benito Mussolini, very nearly encouraged Ponselle to accept further offers. Negotiations were opened with La Scala, but after attending a *Puritani* in Florence, she abruptly canceled them. She watched in horror as Giacomo Lauri-Volpi cracked on a high note in his entrance aria and unleashed a riot of whistles and catcalls from the audience. "That incident had a shattering effect on me," she wrote. "For the first time I saw what an Italian audience could do to one of its favorite tenors when, in a difficult moment, his technique failed him. The next morning, I cabled my feelings to Libbie [Miller, her manager] in New York. The message was simple: FORGET MILAN. ONLY IN AMERICA. ROSA."

Even in America, though, the days were numbered. After her triumph as Norma in 1927, Ponselle added only five new roles to her Met repertory during the next decade: Luisa Miller, Donna Anna in *Don Giovanni*, Violetta, the title role in Montemezzi's *La Notte di Zoraima*, and finally Carmen. By the time Bizet's Gypsy came into her life, Ponselle had further narrowed her scope, and her last two Met seasons consisted of little besides Carmen and a few Santuzzas. Everyone hoped that she would eventually return to her former glorious territory—Norma, Leonora, Aida, Gioconda—but even if she had elected to remain at the Met, it would probably never have come to pass. By 1935 Ponselle's fear of anything higher than a top A had become truly phobic. Her voice, in fact, seemed to be ripening into a rich mezzo-soprano, and a singer more career-driven and eager to perform would undoubtedly have taken the hint and made the switch. It was not to be, however, and one can only fantasize about tantalizing possibilities of a Ponselle Amneris, Azucena, or Eboli.

Surely the mixed reception given her Carmen, unveiled on December 27, 1935, helped spur her decision to retire. To say that her interpretation was controversial is to put it mildly—after the first performance Ponselle sat down to read the worst reviews of her career. Olin Downes in the *Times* was the most blistering: "We have never heard Miss Ponselle sing so badly, and we have seldom seen the part enacted in such an artificial and generally unconvincing manner." Even worse, wrote Downes, the whole performance "showed a cheerful disregard of good singing for which she has won richly deserved eminence." He also found her dancing acutely embarrassing, raising the question "whether Spanish gypsies preferred the Charleston or the Black Bottom as models for their evolutions."

Ponselle was devastated. She had spent two years preparing the role with her customary thoroughness, traveling to Paris to study the part with Mary Garden's old mentor and former Opéra-Comique director, Albert Carré, whose memories of *Carmen* dated back to the work's disastrous world premiere in 1875. Carmen, he said—and Ponselle agreed—should be patterned after the amoral, tough, dangerous seductress portrayed in Mérimée's original novella. Next Ponselle commissioned the flamboyant couturier Valentina to design her costumes—Carmen's matador outfit in the final scene created a sensation all by itself. (When Mary Garden saw that sassy male-female creation, she sought out Valentina and exclaimed, "If only I had known you when I did Carmen! My God, I never once thought of doing her in such a striking way in the last act!") Hardest of all, perhaps, Ponselle dieted herself down to 134, the slimmest she had ever been in her life.

Despite the critical drubbing, Ponselle's Carmen was a hot ticket for two seasons, in part because of the controversy it stirred up. If nothing else, the diverse reactions to her Carmen remind us that Ponselle onstage had always been a good deal more than just an extraordinary voice. She was also clearly a provocative dramatic presence who could excite an audience, even if the results sometimes turned out to be inconsistent, unconvincing, or completely misjudged. In any case, the Ponselle Carmen became sufficiently celebrated for Hollywood to become interested. Soon after her first Met performance MGM began to woo her, and in December 1936 she traveled west to make a screen test. Serious negotiations with Irving Thalberg and Louis B. Mayer were in progress until the soprano's outrageous demand for a quarter of a million dollars squelched the deal.

Two Met broadcasts of Ponselle's Carmen survive, and both tend to support Downes's dismay rather than the singer's apologists. When, in 1980, the Met released the performance from Cleveland on April 17, 1937 (Ponselle's unannounced final appearance in opera, as it turned out), the controversy started all over again, this time led by a generation of critics who had grown up admiring Ponselle's records but had been too young to see her perform. High Fidelity's longtime opera critic, Conrad L. Osborne, was appalled by what he heard and pronounced it "a thoroughgoing horror." Although Osborne noted that Ponselle had plenty of voice left, she vitiated everything with choices that were "invariably the most obvious and heavy-handed ones, and it is frankly hard to tell how much is the clumsy effort of an actress of little technique and taste, and how much the desperation of a performer who has a compulsion to be the center of attention . . ."

After this unfortunate swan song, Ponselle's Met career finally just petered out. She had always relied on others to make the big decisions for her, and by 1935 most of the important people who had taken her by the hand had dropped away. Romani played a negligible role in her life after 1936, when Rosa married Carle A. Jackson, the son of Baltimore's mayor. Few members of the Ponselle entourage approved of Jackson— the handsome young man was nearly ten years Rosa's junior and seemed far more interested in his horses than opera or his wife's career. The marriage soon led to a split with her longtime friend and secretary, Edith Prilik, and she had already been estranged from Carmela, increasingly bitter at having to play second fiddle opposite her famous sister. Worst of all, both Serafin and Gatti-Casazza left the Met in 1934. Although Gatti's successor, the Canadian tenor Edward Johnson, was an old friend and colleague, Johnson's rather casual management style hardly held out the strong guiding hand Ponselle needed to keep her happy and focused.

Johnson hoped she would return to her former repertory for the 1937–38 season. Ponselle, however, had set her heart on a revival of Cilèa's *Adriana Lecouvreur*—a favorite vehicle for divas with fading upper registers—but the project was vetoed as box office poison (even Caruso couldn't sell the piece in 1907).

Faced with so many changes, decisions, controversies, and uncertainties, Ponselle simply brushed them all aside. She soon settled into a conventional married life in Baltimore, where she and Jackson built a luxurious Tuscan-style mansion called Villa Pace, named after her good-luck aria from *La Forza del Destino*. There were occasional radio appearances during the late thirties, but after that she never sang in public again. Outwardly, Ponselle seemed like any other celebrity matron enjoying the local country-club society, but inner serenity apparently eluded her. Jackson enlisted in the navy the day after Pearl Harbor, and when he returned after the war, the marriage quickly disintegrated. Cast into a deep depression, Ponselle took an overdose of sleeping pills and spent the next four months in the hospital. Not long afterward, in 1949, Jackson walked out of her life forever.

After her marriage collapsed, Ponselle pulled herself together and turned once again to music for a bit of solace, even working to get her voice back in shape. There was never any suggestion of a comeback, but awed visitors returning from Villa Pace reported that Rosa Ponselle was singing again and she sounded as good as ever—perhaps even better. Encouraged, the soprano eventually allowed RCA Victor to come into her home and set up microphones, and in 1954 the company taped a collection of songs, enough to fill two long-playing records. The results astonished everyone. The voice had retained all of its lush, dark coloring in the middle octave, where the tone was now firmly centered, while her relaxed and assured interpretations were still quickened by the old Ponselle vibrancy. Her repertory was intriguing too, ranging from Schubert's "Erlkönig" to the latest show tunes from *South Pacific* and *Kiss Me, Kate*, as well as arias from operas she never sang: Saint-Saëns's *Samson et Dalila*, *Suor Angelica*, *La Cenerentola*, *Manon*, and—at last—*Adriana Lecouvreur*.

"In my long lifetime," Tullio Serafin once reminisced toward the end of it, "there have been three miracles—Caruso, Ponselle, and Ruffo. Apart from these have been several wonderful singers." Anyone who has heard even one Ponselle recording will know exactly what the conductor meant. But Ponselle's career, like her voice, was an anomaly that even the soprano herself could never quite explain. For a singer now regarded worldwide as one of the immortals, she had a limited and circumscribed exposure in opera. Mainly, her reputation around the world was built, and is sustained today, by her recordings. But then, virtually everything about Ponselle was unique, from her lack of technical schooling to her highly unorthodox Met debut. One wonders if Gatti-Casazza would have taken a chance by thrusting an untried twenty-one-year-old soprano into such a prominent role if circumstances had presented her to him while he was still head of La Scala. At that holy of holies such risks, even with a young voice as developed as Ponselle's, would have been courting disaster. But by 1918 Gatti knew his American audiences and how much the overnight success of one of their own would thrill them. It was the quintessential American success story, but one suspects it would have lasted longer and been even more productive had Gatti allowed Ponselle a year or two to study, understand her voice better, and acquire more self-confidence.

Then again, if Ponselle had approached singing with more circumspection, perhaps her vocal persona would never have been so exciting. The sheer voluptuousness of Ponselle's voice is both offset and complemented by an energy that seems to wrap the notes in a pulsating sound and galvanize everything she sings. It was very much her own performance style, and she never lost it, as her records amply demonstrate—despite the brevity of her stage career, recordings of Ponselle's voice cover a virtually unbroken span of nearly sixty years, from 1918 to her last private discs made at Villa Pace in 1977. What some heard as provincialism or a deficient classical technique, others heard as an exciting reimagination of old operas, a style that became a benchmark for every dramatic soprano who came after her. To Maria Callas, who had few kind words for any singer past or present, Ponselle was "the greatest singer of us all," and one she was happy to emulate. It hardly seems too much to say that the sound of Ponselle singing the Italian repertory became a paradigm for all sopranos who succeeded her—in that historical context she was indeed "a Caruso in petticoats."

Throughout the 1960s and '70s Ponselle served as artistic director of the newly formed Baltimore Civic Opera, where dozens of young singers came to be coached, including future stars like James Morris, Sherrill Milnes, Beverly Sills, and Lili Chookasian. And she never stopped singing, at least informally, right up to her death in 1981. Nor did she ever cease to astonish people with her voice, the first in this chronicle that I was fortunate enough to hear for myself. That occurred at a reception in a Baltimore hotel ballroom in 1976, the evening before the company's world premiere performance of Thomas Pasatieri's *Ines de Castro*. No one took much notice of the elegantly dressed elderly lady as she made a stately entrance down a staircase until the word "Pace" suddenly came out of her mouth, the first notes of that Verdi aria she had sung for Caruso nearly sixty years earlier. Everyone in the room turned toward her and visibly shivered. The liquid tone, the gorgeous *messa di voce* swell on the note, the exquisite portamento down to the F an octave below— it was unmistakably the same Ponselle voice of those scratchy old 78s, but miraculously here it was again. Ponselle was seventy-nine at the time, and clearly enjoying herself. At last, it seemed, she had found a way to conquer her nerves and enter singing.

Fifteen

⌣

Going on

Record

~~~~~~~~~~~~~~~~~~~~~~~~~~~~~~~~~~~~

For young American singers attempting to launch a career during the early decades of the twentieth century, the biggest obstacle was the lack of performance opportunities. Solo voices were always needed when the flourishing music societies in East Coast cities held their annual choral festivals, but that hardly amounted to a full-time occupation, and the soloists were usually big names imported for the occasion. Those hardy souls who aimed mainly for opera had the unpredictable, rough-and-tumble life offered by touring companies as their primary option, with the Metropolitan always looming as the ultimate, usually unattainable goal. Without that prestigious connection, it was scarcely possible to give concerts with any regularity, let alone break into the lucrative new medium of acoustic recordings, while radio was still in the future.

Despite those hard facts of life, it is astonishing how many Americans discovered their voices and pursued successful careers, either at home or abroad, and how many did reach the Met. Not all, of course, were as glamorous, famous, flamboyant, or quotable as Geraldine Farrar or Rosa Ponselle, but their presence added texture to the musical scene, and some made significant artistic contributions. There were even a few brave spirits who sensed that there were more important musical statements to be made than singing another Lucia or another rendition of "Home, Sweet Home." Most important of all, the increasing number of young men and women willing to take the plunge indicated that singing was finally perceived as a genuine profession rather than an eccentric whim or a rebellious gesture. Some music schools had even set up voice departments to help launch students into the hard, competitive world of professional music-making. Since few of them reached superstardom, these singers and the details of their lives are often shadowy, but in most cases their voices survive on disc, and a journey through their recordings tells its own colorful story.

In 1911 the idea of a contralto from Nashville singing music by the late Gustav Mahler must have seemed piquant, to say the least. But by the time Bruno Walter selected Sarah Jane Layton Walker (1870–1951) to participate in the posthumous world premiere of *Das Lied von der Erde* in Munich, Walker had left Tennessee far behind. There had been studies with Jean de Reszke in Paris, Gustav Walter in Vienna, and Amalie Joachim in Berlin, and she was already well known in prominent prewar European musical circles as Mme. Charles Cahier, having taken the name of her second husband. Mahler himself had engaged her to sing at the Vienna Hofoper in 1906, where her assignments included Carmen and several Wagner roles. In 1912 Mme. Cahier arrived at the Met for a brief stay—one performance each of Amneris, Azucena, and Fricka in *Die Walküre*—and the mild critical reception seemed to confirm the fact that her art was basically untheatrical and better suited to the concert stage.

The eight titles she recorded in the late 1920s bear this out: arias from *Carmen, Le Prophète,* and *La Favorite;* songs by Grieg, Sibelius, and Martini; and, most interesting of all, the "Urlicht" movement from Mahler's Second Symphony as well as the last of the composer's Rückert songs, "Ich bin die Welt abhanden gekommen." The rich, fruity voice is already threatening to become unglued, the tone lacks a secure center, and the stately manner hardly suits Carmen's seductive Habanera, but Mme. Cahier's approach to the Mahler songs is fascinating. Her measured, dignified performances contrast markedly with the hyperemotional anguish that singers would freely inject into Mahler two generations later, after his music had entered the standard repertory. It's more than likely that the composer instructed Mme. Cahier to interpret his music in just such a "classical" style, allowing the expressive power of the notes to register all the more forcefully. No doubt Stravinsky also appreciated the contralto's direct, concentrated style when she joined Leopold Stokowski and composer-pianists Alfredo Casella, Germaine Tailleferre, Georges Enesco, and Carlos Salzedo in the 1926 American premiere of *Les Noces*.

Concert work occupied Mme. Cahier for the rest of her career, and the programs she chose, always adventurous and forward-looking, were usually slanted toward contemporary composers. Perhaps in the end, though, she made her greatest contributions as a teacher and voice doctor. In 1916, while performing Azucena in Copenhagen, she was amazed to hear the young baritone who sang Di Luna help out a nervous Leonora by taking the soprano's high C for her. "But you are not a baritone!" she exclaimed to Lauritz Melchior after the performance. "I think that you are a tenor with the lid on." Mme. Cahier was right, of course, and she was the first to show Melchior how to take the lid off. A decade later, while on the voice faculty at the Curtis Institute in Philadelphia, she took Marian Anderson under her wing and instructed the girl in the Mahler style she had learned at the source, and the results are reflected in the younger singer's own nobly contained recording of the *Kindertotenlieder*. It was Mme. Cahier who passed on Arturo Toscanini's famous "voice of the century" comment to Anderson after the black contralto's breakthrough recital in Salzburg in 1935, an assessment that would soon be known and repeated the world over.

Like Mary Garden, Florence Easton (1882–1955) is claimed by both England, where she was born, and America, where she spent the most important and busiest years of her career. Taken to Toronto as a five-year-old, Easton returned to England in 1899 for study at the Royal Academy of Music, made her operatic debut with the Moody-Manners touring company in 1903, and married the American tenor Francis Maclennan a year later. After a dozen peripatetic years in London, Berlin, Hamburg, and Chicago, the couple eventually settled in New York, where Easton became such an integral part of the American musical scene during her best years that she would often even refer to herself as an American. Indeed, one wonders what Giulio Gatti-Casazza would have done without her. She spent thirteen seasons at the Metropolitan, demonstrating a versatility unmatched by any soprano since Lilli Lehmann. Easton made her debut on December 7, 1917, as Santuzza, later taking on Ah-Joe in Leoni's *L'Oracolo*, the title role in a rare staging of Liszt's oratorio *The Legend of Saint Elizabeth*, and the lead in Mascagni's *Lodoletta* when Farrar suddenly bowed out after one performance. The next year she was back to sing Nedda, Lauretta in the world premiere of Puccini's *Gianni Schicchi*, more Lodolettas and Ah-Joes, and the title role in the premiere of a short-lived American work, John Adam Hugo's *The Temple Dancer*.

Impressed by Easton's intelligence, musicality, capacity for hard work, and good notices, Gatti kept his new soprano busy with one assignment after another: Fiordiligi, Brünnhilde, Elisabeth, Carmen, Elsa, Fiora, Kundry, Tosca, Isolde, Turandot—the list goes on. Some roles she learned virtually overnight and performed only once or twice in emergencies. When it came to contemporary novelties, Easton could always be trusted with such roles as Dulcinée in Massenet's *Don Quichotte*, Pilar in Laparra's *La Habanera*, Anita in Krenek's *Jonny Spielt Auf*, and Aelfrida in Taylor's *The King's Henchman*. Once, during a two-week period in November 1927, the soprano sang Maddalena in *Andrea Chénier*, Gioconda, Rachel in *La Juive*, Butterfly, and the Marschallin.

A few months after that tour de force, she was asked by *Musical America* to prepare a list of her accomplishments. Running under the title "How Eighty-Eight Roles Are Sung," the article also noted that she had numerous other operas at her command that Met audiences had not yet seen—*Mignon, Les Huguenots, Fidelio*, D'Albert's *Die Toten Augen, La Fille du Régiment, Zazà, Rigoletto, Roméo et Juliette, Faust, La Fanciulla del West, Salome, Elektra*, Schreker's *Der Ferne Klang*. And, of course, she was prepared to sing several of these parts in three different languages. The conductor Karl Muck used to say that he could give Easton the score of an opera at eight in the morning and be confident she could sing the role at eight that evening. A colleague once remarked—some say it was Caruso—that "her head is a music box; she lifts off the lid, takes out one record and puts on another; that is the only way any singer could remember so many operas."

That comment perhaps provides a clue as to why Easton, for all her extraordinary industry and an extensive discography that attests to both her musical and her vocal excellence, has been largely forgotten. She adapted her voice and technique to so many different roles so successfully that she is remembered for none of them. Despite the enthusiasm of the New York critics, Easton's talents lacked strong individuality and vivid definition. For that reason her recordings also remain mostly un-reissued and unknown, despite the fact that they make better listening than those by many of her more famous contemporaries. "Un bel dì" is indeed ravishing for its focused tone, columnar security, musical honesty, and refusal to cover any vocal inadequacies with coy interpretive mannerisms. Indeed, Easton never had to resort to such tricks, even when singing such chestnuts of the era as "Kiss Me Again," "My Laddie," and "O Divine Redeemer." She had more than enough voice and technique to get the job done to virtual perfection, even toward the end— airchecks of Brünnhilde's entrance in *Götterdämmerung*, a memento of Liszt's *Saint Elizabeth* oratorio, and Strauss's florid song "Als mir dein Lied erklang," all recorded in the late thirties, are radiantly sung and show her voice virtually unimpaired. Easton may have been a victim of her own virtuosity, especially in an era when the cleverest opera singers recognized that making publicity had become an art in itself, but her records remind us of an important artist who was considerably more than just a "music box."

In addition to house sopranos who could step in as Aida at a moment's notice, opera companies have always needed versatile singers to fill a host of small roles. One of the Met's most treasured comprimarios during this period was Kathleen Howard (1880–1956), a contralto who hailed from the Canadian side of Niagara Falls. Another student of Jean de Reszke's, Howard had a busy career in Europe before she decided that her real forte lay in character parts and that the Met offered her financial security in that respect as well as plenty to do. Between 1916 to 1928 she sang more than forty roles with the company, from the crusty old grandmother in Janáček's *Jenůfa* to Magdalene in *Die Meistersinger* and Nicklausse in *Les Contes d'Hoffmann*, as well as Zita in the world premiere of *Gianni Schicchi*.

Even though Howard was never a headliner, she made a number of records, most often when a more famous singer required a companionable duetist. When she is paired with the charismatic Claudia Muzio, these two smoky voices blend in a deliciously insinuating rendition of the *Hoffmann* Barcarolle. The contralto's rather labored English-language version of Dalila's "Mon coeur s'ouvre à ta voix," on the other hand, shows the wisdom of her decision to stick to comprimario parts. But by 1928 Howard had become weary of playing second fiddle and embarked on a whole new career. Having already displayed another side of her talents ten years earlier in a racy memoir entitled *Confessions of an Opera Singer,* she launched herself as a journalist, first as a fashion editor for *Harper's* and, later in Hollywood, as a gossip reporter and feature writer for *Photoplay.* Soon she started acting herself, and between 1934 and 1950 appeared in around two dozen films playing an assortment of mothers, cooks, and housekeepers. Drawing on her long experience with operatic character parts, Howard once again delivered the goods, and her reviews were never better. "As the nagging wife," wrote the *New York Times* about her performance opposite W. C. Fields in *It's a Gift,* "Kathleen Howard is so authentic as to make Mr. Fields' sufferings seem cosmic."

The first Victor Red Seal artist to make a record that sold a million copies was Alma Gluck (1884–1938): "Carry Me Back to Old Virginny," released in 1914. Gluck's career was a short one—little more than ten years at its peak—but during that time she was probably America's most beloved concert singer, and her records, only slightly less popular than those of Caruso and John McCormack, made her rich. When Grace Moore was out driving with Gluck in a new Rolls-Royce, the younger soprano, who had ambitions of her own, couldn't resist asking, "It's such a lovely car. Does it cost much to get one?" Gluck astonished her companion by absently replying, "My dear, I just paid for it today with twenty thousand dollars which was part of a hundred-thousand-dollar check for royalties sent me by the Victor company."

The secret of Gluck's immense vocal appeal may be difficult to analyze today, but it was very potent in World War I America, and the success of her records was closely connected with her busy concert schedule and tours. Her daughter, the writer Marcia Davenport, thought it was the quality of intimacy in her voice, which in concert made each member of the audience think she was singing directly to him or her. "Musical snobs," said Davenport, "sometimes remonstrated with her for singing stuff like 'My Little Grey Home in the West' [which Gluck always referred to as "Little Grey Hole in My Vest"]. She had her reasons for what she did, in the faces of farmers and their families who drove fifty miles on dirt roads in model T Fords to hear her annual concert in the nearest town; and in letters from women who saved their egg-money and pin-money to buy her records."

This grass-roots audience must have also sensed that Gluck was one of them, a living symbol of the American success story who not only appreciated the fact but also positively radiated an "unabashed reverence for the ceremonies and sentiments of American tradition." Every Fourth of July she would gather the family together and read aloud the Declaration of Independence "with such sincerity that no eye was dry when she finished, herself in tears." Born Reba Fiersohn in Bucharest, Gluck passed the classic turn-of-the-century immigrant childhood in New York City, living humbly on the Lower East Side until she reached her teen years and found a job as a stenographer. Only after marrying Bernard Gluck, an insurance company employee, did she think of training her voice. Her fortuitous choice of a teacher was Arturo Buzzi-Peccia, the composer of many popular "Neapolitan folksongs" and a major figure in Milan's musical circles who had also recently settled in New York. One of Buzzi-Peccia's pals from the old days was Arturo Toscanini, and a not-so-chance encounter with the Maestro in the voice studio led directly to an audition with Gatti-Casazza, a Met contract, and a debut on November 16, 1909, as Sophie in *Werther* opposite Geraldine Farrar and Edmond Clément, at the New Theatre on Sixty-first Street and Central Park West—the Met's first attempt to find a smaller venue for intimate operas.

Gluck's Met career did not last long, despite the approval of audiences, critics, and management about her sweet lyric soprano, dark beauty, and sparkling presence. The soprano sang her first song recital a year after her operatic debut, and the experience convinced her that opera was just not for a singer who once remarked that her favorite role was the Forest Bird in *Siegfried*. "That's my idea of opera-singing," she said. "I go down to the opera house in a street dress, stand on a ladder backstage, sing on my cue, collect my money, and go home." In 1911 Gluck convinced the unwilling Gatti to release her from her contract at the end of the season, at which time she immediately went to Marcella Sembrich for coaching in the song repertory. A decade of tremendously successful and lucrative concert tours began, often in conjunction with her second husband, the violinist Efrem Zimbalist, whom she married in 1914.

Fragile health ended Gluck's career in 1924, but until then audiences up and down the land rejoiced in a voice that Richard Aldrich praised for its "aerial transparency and delicate lyrical quality," as well as the "use of legato, the finish of phrasing, the clearness of diction." She sang too much trash perhaps, but even this was graced with vocal skill and fine musicianship. And she was genuinely beloved. "When the First World War was over," reminisced Davenport in her memoirs, "some men brought my mother a battered record of 'Carry Me Back to Old Virginny,' framed like a picture, with a letter stating where the record had been carried and played, and what it had survived, during their unit's service in the trenches."

Another American soprano made her Met debut in *Werther* the same evening as Gluck—Anna Case (1889–1984), as Fritz, a role so tiny that it is not even listed in the score. She was still singing comprimario assignments two years later when an article in *Musical America* predicted great things for her while once again trolling the refrain, by now a familiar one, about the miracle of a young singer whose vocal studies had all taken place in America and who had never had even so much as a glimpse of Europe (hardly an unusual phenomenon for a young beginner by the time Case came along—Clara Louise Kellogg, old and forgotten by 1911, had done it all fifty years earlier). After praising Case to the skies, the enthusiastic reporter went on to say, "What if she has only sung Rhine maidens and flower maidens, little sandmen, little dewmen, royal pages and similar microscopic things? The time will yet come for the Butterflies, the Goose Girls, the Toscas, the Elsas, and who knows but maybe the Brünnhildes and Isoldes. It is all as inevitable as fate. If you don't believe it just wait and see for yourself."

With her small but penetrating soprano, Case herself could hardly have believed that fanciful prediction, but she never waited to find out. As early as 1914, just after she landed her first and last big assignment— Sophie in the Met premiere of Strauss's *Der Rosenkavalier*—Case ran into vocal trouble and no doubt had to agree with Aldrich's comment that "those who had admired her exquisite voice last season were disquieted to hear it so seriously affected by hard usage so soon." She eventually got her voice back together, but her operatic career had effectively come to an end. Thereafter, like Gluck, Case concentrated exclusively on concerts and making records. Thomas Edison was particularly fond of her voice and often used it in his famous "Tone Test" demonstrations. Setting up his playback apparatus on one side of the stage and a singer on the other, Edison invited the audience to guess when the machine left off and the real thing took over. It may strike us as incredible, but many listeners were actually unable to tell.

Case's records, although plentiful, were never as commercially successful as Gluck's, and the voice is not as attractive, but in many ways she developed into a far more interesting singer. On her earliest discs

the tone tends to be hard and uningratiating—a rather steely and charmless "Charmant oiseaux" from David's *La Perle du Brésil* recorded in 1915
suggests what a disappointing impression her Sophie must have made—
but matters obviously improved as time passed. Even Aldrich noted how
transformed her voice sounded in recital during the twenties: "a light
soprano of the most lyric quality, of delightful freshness and transparent
purity when it is heard at its best." Her interpretive approach also became more distinctive, and the electrical discs she made in 1931 are full
of character and vivid expressive gestures. That old Emma Albani chestnut, Handel's "Angels ever bright and fair," is delivered with uncommon
glowing intensity, and even a trifling novelty like Roland Farley's "Night
Wind," with its chillingly slithery portamento effects, fairly leaps out of
the speakers. Those discs were Case's swan song. In 1929 she had married Clarence H. Mackay, the millionaire telegraph king, and soon she
retired for good. She never forgot the first big break she got at the
Metropolitan, however, which must have been pleased and surprised
when, at her death in 1984 at the age of ninety-four, Case—who had, as
a girl, gone house to house selling soap to pay for her voice lessons—left
the company $1.2 million to be used for new productions.

The fact that Gluck and Case were more interested in concert work than
opera was definitely a sign of the times. It was much less time-consuming
and exhausting than opera, and the money was infinitely better. Nothing
matched a Met contract in terms of prestige and the possibilities it held
for future earning power, but the pay was pitiful for beginners, and
young singers were always put on a weekly salary of seldom more than
$50. Hulda Lashanska (1893–1974) was among the growing number of
singers who managed to avoid taking the operatic route entirely and yet
still had a distinguished career. That was all the more remarkable in
Lashanska's case, since her progress was frequently interrupted by yearlong pauses to enjoy marriage and a growing family.

   New York–born, Lashanska attended the city's Institute of Music and
Art and, like Gluck, went to Sembrich for finishing and repertory coaching. Her debut concert, arranged at Sembrich's own expense, took place
at the Lyceum Theater in 1909. That and a brief European tour were all
Lashanska needed to launch herself, and she soon became an audience
favorite as well as a much-in-demand soloist by two generations of distinguished conductors, from Walter Damrosch to John Barbirolli. The
sweet, pure, and immaculately groomed voice was even prettier than

Gluck's, and it never lost those qualities as the years passed. A recording of Louise's "Depuis le jour" from 1919 is exquisitely poised and floated, but so is Schubert's "Litanei" from 1939, accompanied by a million-dollar trio consisting of Mischa Elman, Emanuel Feuermann, and Rudolf Serkin. Lashanska could also let down her hair, as in her deliciously swinging 1927 rendition of the Nightingale Song from Zeller's *Der Vogelhändler*, complete with bird whistles.

Eva Gauthier (1885–1958) was another singer who avoided opera altogether after briefly flirting with the form in 1910. Although she was to become one of the great originals of her generation, Gauthier at first aimed for a conventional career, studying with an impressive series of mentors after leaving her native Ottawa in 1901: William Shakespeare in London, Jacques Bouhy in Paris, Giuseppe Oxilia in Milan, and Anna Schoen-René in Berlin—in London she even benefited from friendly coaching advice in coloratura matters from her fellow Canadian Emma Albani. All that was set aside when, during a European concert tour in 1911, she married a Dutchman, Franz Knoote, and followed him to his plantation in Java. The marriage ended in 1916, but by then Gauthier had discovered a new world of music and she was determined "to investigate the Javanese music, if it meant going to the Sultan himself. I journeyed to Solo, to the palace of the Sultan. I had all the necessary credentials and was kindly received. My request, to study the native music, was granted, and I was invited to live in the Palace—with the Sultan's four hundred wives."

After that revelatory experience, Gauthier moved to New York in 1915 and settled in Greenwich Village, ready to begin a career that was unprecedented, at least for a North American singer. For a number of years she made a specialty of singing the Javanese and Eastern music she had learned at the Sultan's palace, wearing native costumes and even taking her "act" into vaudeville houses when conventional concert venues hesitated to book her. Soon her curiosity about new musical sounds brought her into contact with contemporary composers and their songs: Ravel, Stravinsky, Bartók, Falla, Nin, Turina, Poulenc, Hindemith, Schoenberg, and a host of Americans from Griffes to Gershwin. It was Gauthier, in fact, who threw the famous dinner party that brought together those two mutual admirers Gershwin and Ravel.

By the 1930s Gauthier had become a New York legend. No one ever called the sounds she made beautiful, and her tough, often recalcitrant voice was hardly admired for its tonal quality. She probably encouraged the notion, soon to become a cliché, that only failed singers choose to specialize in new music. Perhaps, but her classical training and fierce musical spirit still shine through her recordings, which were often the first to document on disc much important new vocal music. Her recitals also expanded many young musical sensibilities with a philosophy that was as unconventional as it was totally uncommercial, a commitment to the new that she passed on to younger generations and that can be heard in the singing of her successors. Bethany Beardslee, Jan DeGaetani, and Dawn Upshaw are among her progeny, singers who also adopted Gauthier's simple credo: "My love for the old classics remains undiminished, but I believe that there is something good in modern music too, and the only way we can find out what is good is by giving it a hearing."

Several theories have been advanced to explain why Mabel Garrison (1886–1963) never quite lived up to her promise. It may have been bad timing. Frieda Hempel and Maria Barrientos were the reigning coloratura sopranos during Garrison's early Met years (her debut was in 1914), when she tended to such minor parts as Frasquita in *Carmen;* and by the time of her last season with the company, 1920–21, when she had graduated to Lucia, Adina, and Gilda, the even more sensational star of Amelita Galli-Curci was on the horizon. More likely it was simply a case of a pretty voice and a modestly pleasing stage personality that had gone about as far as it could. When Garrison got her first big break, as Urbain in an all-star revival of *Les Huguenots* (sung in Italian) in December 1914, Henderson politely complimented her singing but added that she was really "without the voice, the experience or the style demanded by the role."

Even at that, Garrison filled in capably when her betters were away, ill, or, in Hempel's case, squeamish about the Queen of the Night's high F's. Such notes held few terrors for Garrison, as can be heard on her accomplished recordings of Olympia's Doll Song, Lakmé's Bell Song, and Waldemar Thrane's "Norwegian Echo Song," an old Jenny Lind standby. There is also the rather horrid fascination of hearing the soprano's trickily warbled, almost manically driven renditions of such period pieces as "Dixie" and "Little Alabama Coon." All this technique was picked up, Garrison would invariably point out in her newspaper publicity, in America, first at the Peabody Conservatory in Baltimore, where she grew up, and later in New York. At Peabody she also met her husband, the conductor and pianist George Siemonn, who remained harmoniously at her side as principal coach and mentor until his death in 1952.

Since Garrison's voice still sounds fresh on her recordings made during the year she left the Met, one assumes that she headed off to sing with companies in Germany to avoid competition with Galli-Curci and in hopes of brightening her international image. Nothing special came of it, though. After returning to America, she offered two Rosinas in Chicago, in 1926, but her performances apparently added little spice or vocal glamour to a company whose sopranos that season included Rosa Raisa, Claudia Muzio, Edith Mason, Toti dal Monte, and of course the redoubtable Mary Garden. After that brief comeback, Garrison devoted herself to concerts and teaching, eventually becoming a professor of voice at Smith College.

By the time Garrison arrived in Chicago, Edith Mason (1891–1973) was the toast of the town, and had been ever since she created a sensation at her debut with the company, as Butterfly on November 16, 1921— Muzio came backstage to compliment Mason after the performance with tears in her eyes. She remained a Chicago institution for twenty years after that, and the city jealously guarded her as its very own prima donna. When, after an eighteen-year absence, she returned to the Metropolitan in 1935 to sing Violetta, Butterfly, and Marguerite, New Yorkers were also ecstatic and hoped she would stay—as one critic remarked, "I would bind Madame Mason with chains of gold if I were an opera manager." Some maintained that no American soprano of her generation had a lovelier voice, and her discography, infuriatingly small as it is, suggests that they may be right.

Perhaps if she had had a more extensive Met career, which would surely have brought with it a major recording contract, Mason would be better remembered today. But she was always an independent soul, offstage as well as on (her husbands numbered five, and she married the conductor Giorgio Polacco twice). Mason—the surname came from her first husband—always sang where she wished, and before she made Chicago her artistic home, she had traveled widely and always to acclaim. Born Edith Marjory Barnes to wealthy parents in St. Louis, Missouri, Mason was still at Boston's New England Conservatory of Music when she made her operatic debut, on January 27, 1912, in the time-honored operatic tradition as a last-moment replacement. "I had just coached Nedda at the conservatory," the soprano recalled, "when the Boston Opera's lyric soprano [Carmen Melis] got sick. My teacher told Henry Russell, the company's manager, that I could sing *Pagliacci* and suggested they try me. Friday afternoon I went over the score with a coach, Saturday morning I was fitted with a costume, and Saturday afternoon I went onstage."

Her success as Nedda, and later as Musetta, Zerlina, and Micaela, was sufficient for Russell to offer her a long-term contract, but after two seasons Mason was off to France to expand her horizons, studying with Edmond Clément and spending a short period with companies in Nice and Monte Carlo until the war in Europe sent her back home in 1915. Having just gained and lost the services of Elisabeth Schumann that year, Gatti-Casazza desperately needed a Sophie for the season's first *Rosenkavaliers*, and after basking in Mason's silvery soprano, few had any regrets about the replacement. For the next two seasons she was busily at work singing all the usual ingenues, but soon Mason was bored again and wanted to move on. Besides that, her extramarital affair with Polacco had created a mild scandal, and in 1917 the two joined the Bracale Opera Company for a tour of Central and South America. When the war ended, the couple based their activities for a while in Paris, where Mason sang at the Théâtre Lyrique, Opéra, and Opéra-Comique, specializing, like so many American sopranos before her, in Massenet's seductive heroines, specifically Manon, Thaïs, and Salomé in *Hérodiade*. The French adored her, invoking the still well-remembered name of Sibyl Sanderson.

In 1921 Mary Garden appointed Polacco Chicago's music director to succeed the late Cleofonte Campanini. Naturally it was understood that Polacco's wife would accompany him and sing with the company, but Mason never required that special connection to justify her presence. After her first deliriously received Butterfly, Edward Moore wrote bemusedly in the *Tribune*, "The chief duty in considering the performance is to sort out a set of superlatives and put them in the proper places. Looking back at it, one has a mild sort of wonder as to whether the opera was ever given in Chicago before." The public, Moore observed, applauded until "there were several thousand pairs of blistered palms in great need of cooling." And so it went, in role after role. In 1930, after Mason sang Iris, Mascagni's Japanese heroine, the *Tribune*'s critic had practically run out of superlatives. "Miss Mason," he finally wrote, "classifies among the company's golden throats, a gold that is close to being twenty-four karats fine."

Until she retired in 1942, Mason remained faithful to her Chicago public, occasionally venturing out of town to sing in select prestigious venues: La Scala in 1923, a *Falstaff* at the 1935 Salzburg Festival with Toscanini, a season at Covent Garden, and finally her triumphant return to the Met. When the time came to say her operatic farewell to her fans back home, it was as Mimì—which she agreed to sing, Mason said, only because her fifth and last husband, a prominent Chicago stockbroker named William Ragland, had never seen her sing an opera before. The house went wild, "and tossed her enough flowers to start a shop."

Considering how greatly she was esteemed and how well she knew her worth, Mason left an amazingly small recorded legacy of twenty-four titles (and many of those were duplications), fleshed out by only a handful of broadcasts. Even that gives just a sampling of her opera roles—Butterfly, Marguerite, Louise, Lady Harriet, Micaela, and Violetta—while the songs are mostly period potboilers such as "From the Land of the Sky-Blue Water," "Dreamin' Time," "Mighty Lak' a Rose," and "My Old Kentucky Home." For connoisseurs who prize a perfectly placed and classically organized voice that remains sweet and true throughout its range, not one of these precious discs is negligible. Butterfly was Mason's favorite role (she asked to be buried in her geisha robes), and we have her "Un bel dì" and two versions of the entrance music to understand why. Perhaps no other soprano who recorded this music—and they number in the hundreds—better resolves the musical paradox of Puccini's heroine, a fragile teenager whose tragedy must be expressed with the powerful instrument of a fully formed Italian dramatic soprano. Mason is irresistibly vulnerable and girlish, but how boldly she shapes each phrase and how thrilling the banked emotion she suggests as the voice opens up and soars without a blemish or trace of strain. Even a piece of treacle like Del Riego's "Oh, Dry Those Tears" seems ineffably moving as the soprano plays exquisitely with its rhythms and makes telling expressive points with her knowing command of portamento. For twenty years Chicago was indeed a very fortunate town to be able to enjoy the voice and art of such an enchanting singer.

Even though they never approached Mason in terms of vocal accomplishment or public favor, many other American singers found a home in Chicago during the teens and twenties, the only opera house in the country that could compete with the Metropolitan in terms of casts and repertory. In 1910, fifteen days after *La Fanciulla del West* had received its world premiere at the Met with Destinn and Caruso, Chicago saw the opera with a real American as the girl: Carolina White (1886–1961), the wife of an earlier Chicago Opera music director, Paolo Longone. Judging from the powerful and cutting top register she displays on her surviving discs, White must have been an imposing Minnie, even if the opera itself received only a polite reception. White's later roles, sung in quick succession, included the Countess in *Le Nozze di Figaro*, Massenet's Salomé, Giulietta in *Les Contes d'Hoffmann*, Manon Lescaut, Giordano's Fedora, Gioconda, Donna Elvira, Susanna in Wolf-Ferrari's *Il Segreto di Susanna*, Elsa, and Barbara in Herbert's *Natoma*. No wonder she often felt exhausted and in 1914 gave up opera and turned to the vaudeville circuit. Although we can't hear her, White still looks trim and pretty opposite Caruso in the 1918 silent film *My Cousin*.

Carolina Lazzari (1891–1946) from Milford, Massachusetts, made her operatic debut in Chicago in 1914, beginning in small roles but soon working her way up to Dalila opposite the burly Irish tenor John O'Sullivan. She came to the Met in 1920 to sing a single Amneris. Why she never appeared again seems odd, since she was well received and her records of the period reveal a singularly attractive and evenly schooled mezzo-soprano. Apparently her colleagues agreed, because for several years after that Lazzari toured extensively with Frances Alda, Charles Hackett, and Giuseppe de Luca, members of the Metropolitan Opera Quartet.

Florence Macbeth, Cyrena van Gordon, Chase Baromeo, Anna Fitziu, and Coe Glade were busy and valued singers in Chicago who never made much of an impact either east or west of the city, but for a while it looked as if Mary McCormic (1885–1981), a Garden protégée, might rival Mason. She also made her debut in 1920, ten days after Mason, as Micaela opposite Garden's Carmen. She sang, according to *Musical America*, "with limpid, colorful tones, warm, tender and powerful, with exquisite pianissimo shadings and an effortless swelling to her full voice." After a few seasons that garnered a sheaf of similar opinions, McCormic headed off to Paris, where audiences once again kissed their fingers over an American charmer, this time a dazzling blonde from Texas. In 1930 McCormic was back to ravish Chicago, even daring to make her *rentrée* in Mason's own *Madama Butterfly*. Once again Chicagoans were vanquished. Posterity has but four recorded titles by McCormic, all in execrable sound. Thaïs's Mirror Aria does give an idea of her urgent style, personal magnetism, and the appealing tug in her voice. The better-sounding duets from Massenet's *Manon* with Georges Thill are less flattering, suggesting that her rather pinched and vinegary tone was something of an acquired taste.

By the time Marguerite Namara (1888–1977) reached Chicago in 1919, she was already widely traveled and regarded as something of a character. Born Margaret Banks in Cleveland, she took her mother's maiden name, knocked off the unattractive Irish "Mc," and was known for the rest of her life, like Nazimova and Garbo, simply as Namara. Her singing career began with a *Faust* in 1908 in Genoa, followed by a period in Paris studying with Jean de Reszke. After a bit of time spent with an operetta troupe, she returned to America, made her first Met appearance in a 1913 Sunday night concert (there would be one more, in 1919), and then took to the road as a supporting artist in touring programs given by Caruso, Kreisler, and McCormack. Next she took up dancing and studied with Isadora Duncan, who declared Namara her finest pupil. After her 1919–22 stint in Chicago, with Thaïs as her most prominent role ("No more Thaïs for me; it's yours from now on," said Mary Garden, who would pass on similar improbable benedictions to Helen Jepson and Beverly Sills), Namara became a free spirit and did pretty much whatever entered her head. She turned up in Hollywood to make a silent film with Valentino and appeared in the first sound version of *Carmen*. On Broadway she starred in *Alone at Last* with John Charles Thomas and in several straight plays. Painting was also a passion (she claimed to have studied with Monet), and she presided over a number of one-woman shows. Whenever there was nothing better to do, she would take off on a concert tour and never seemed to have any trouble in attracting an audience. Despite being a singer with a reputation for never looking after her voice, almost all her recordings are full of zest, her reedy timbre skillfully employed for color and character. An especially provocative example is the set of three Chopin mazurkas arranged for voice and piano—Namara plays her own accompaniments—by another protean singer, Pauline Viardot.

With its shorter seasons and the breezy management style set by Mary Garden, the Chicago Civic Opera could accommodate colorful individualists like Namara and McCormic. For Giulio Gatti-Casazza at the Metropolitan, such risk-taking was considered imprudent, although he realized early on that encouraging and hiring American singers who took their profession seriously was not only a political desirability but also a practical necessity. Isolated from Europe's operatic mainstream, the Met had to maintain a core company of singers in all categories, and it only made sense to staff its personnel with native talent. By 1919 Americans easily dominated the roster, even if few ever became stars. A surprising number of now-forgotten names were given opportunities to appear prominently. Sometimes Gatti found himself in a bind and had no other choice, but there were singers with whom he took carefully calculated chances that failed to pay off. Sophie Braslau, for instance, was regarded as a promising young contralto (as well as being the mistress of the all-powerful manager Arthur Judson of Columbia Artists) when she made her debut in 1913 as the offstage alto voice in *Parsifal*. Gatti brought her along slowly, giving her increasingly larger roles and solo spots in Sunday night concerts, but it soon became clear that the spark was simply not there. Others—like Nina Morgana, Jeanne Gordon, Marion Telva, and Queena Mario—remained season after season, giving solid performances in leading roles—the sort of unspectacular but dependable work any impresario would appreciate.

Occasionally, too, a hot young singer simply self-destructed. When Ralph Errolle (1890–1973), born Ralph Smith in Philadelphia, arrived at the Met in 1924 after an apprenticeship in Chicago and Australia, hopes ran high. His debut role was Roméo opposite Lucrezia Bori, and he quickly proceeded from there to Léopold in *La Juive* with Florence Easton and Giovanni Martinelli, Almaviva with Amelita Galli-Curci, and eventually Offenbach's Hoffmann. A recording of the *Rigoletto* love duet with Anna Case shows that Errolle did indeed possess an attractive lyric tenor with an easy top and an unusually elegant manner. It all came to an end, literally overnight, when Errolle was caught by his wife *in flagrante delicto*, reported by the press in lurid detail. One night the tenor's wife tracked him to a ballet dancer's apartment, had the door forced, and found her pajama-clad husband trying to disappear into a cupboard. At the divorce proceedings Errolle admitted to philandering but pleaded poverty. "While it is a great asset to have a contract with the Metropolitan," he told the judge, "they pay me only $200 weekly for the season. Out of my earnings I have to pay for my wigs and costumes and a 10 per cent commission to an agent." That plea fell on deaf ears, and Errolle was ordered to cough up a yearly alimony of $3,900—and the current Mrs. Smith was already wife number three. Worse yet, the public scandal shocked the Met board—such things seemed to matter more in those days—and the company dismissed him on the spot.

From what one can tell by listening to Errolle's few records, America lost a potentially important singer. Others failed to have careers in their own country because they never even tried. One can only speculate why Arthur Krackman never sang professionally in the United States—although he was born in Chicago in 1893 and died there in 1975, Krackman spent his entire career in France, where he sang under the name Endrèze (taken from that of his maternal grandparents, Mr. and Mrs. Fredrick Endres). The reasons why the French so appreciated Endrèze are no mystery. Listening to his records, one would scarcely suspect a singer of American origins. Not only is his diction impeccable, but his understanding of how to shape the musical phrase to express the meaning of the words is also a classic Gallic trait. The rather dry timbre of the voice and its fast vibrato are two additional qualities which characterize French voices and which listeners in other countries often find unappealing.

While studying agronomy at the University of Illinois, Endrèze discovered his voice and was encouraged to take up singing by Walter Damrosch. The war intervened, but when the young baritone was demobilized, he decided to remain in France, attend the American Conservatory in Fontainebleau, and take lessons from Jean de Reszke. His operatic debut came as Don Giovanni in Nice in 1925, followed by further engagements in Cannes, where he was spotted by the composer, conductor, impresario, and confidant of Marcel Proust, Reynaldo Hahn. A fruitful relationship began, and Hahn helped ease his handsome young protégé into more prestigious engagements, as well as appearing with him as a pianist in joint recitals. In 1928 Endrèze made his Opéra-Comique debut, his first appearance at the Opéra a season later, and soon Paris had a new favorite. For the next twenty years he sang all the standard leading baritone roles, as well as participating in such important premieres as Magnard's *Guercoeur*, Milhaud's *Maximilien*, Sauget's *La Chartreuse de Parme*, and Honegger's *L'Aiglon*. In 1948 Endrèze returned to America and became a professor of singing at the University of Kansas, but Paris was in his blood and he soon moved back to enjoy his retirement years in the city that had become his true home.

It's only fitting to conclude this chapter with a brief tribute to a pair of American singers who seldom appeared onstage and whose activities were almost exclusively restricted to making phonograph records: Lucie Isabelle Marsh (1878–1956) and Olive Kline (1885–1976). Just as opera companies needed house singers, so did a busy phonograph concern like Victor, with the demand for home musical entertainment growing so rapidly that even so popular and prolific a recording balladeer as John McCormack could not make discs fast enough. In the recording studio, then as now, a small voice could come into its own, without needing to strain or force to fill a large opera house. Singing into the acoustic horn and later the micophone became an art in itself, one that both Marsh and Kline mastered to a high degree, as they retained their vocal freshness and technical finesse despite busy recording schedules.

After a brief time in Paris with Antonio Trabadello, Marsh returned to New York to establish herself as an oratorio singer, although there was a brief flirtation with opera at the Met: nine performances as a *Parsifal* Flowermaiden during the 1904–05 season (her one other operatic appearance was a concert performance of *Martha* in Schenectady in 1916). Marsh's soft-grained, limpid voice took especially well to the acoustical process, and record companies soon made capital of the fact. Although the numerous discs on which she purled out the songs of the day have long faded from fashion, the two operatic excerpts she recorded with McCormack—the Micaela–Don José duet from *Carmen* and the Tomb Scene from *Aida*—never disappeared from the catalogue for long and with good reason. Both singers would have been mad to attempt these roles onstage, but the duets are sung here as they are seldom heard in the opera house: by two beautifully tuned, ideally matched lyric voices that caress every gorgeous phrase.

Kline was even busier than Marsh, recording ballads and filling in whenever an extra voice was needed in an operatic ensemble. She also was not above singing the lowliest pop songs of the day with charm and vitality, although when she did so it was generally under one of her many *noms de disque* such as Alice Green. Kline achieved discographic immortality when she supplied the heart-tuggingly angelic offstage voice of Dulcinée in Chaliapin's famous two-sided 78-rpm discs of Don Quichotte's death from Massenet's opera. Although they were nothing if not professionals, both Marsh and Kline provide an echo of a previous and in some ways more civilized time, when young girls with pretty voices were always encouraged to polish their musical talents and sing for everyone's enjoyment at gatherings around the parlor piano.

Sixteen

The Glory

Road

*A*t last.
When Lawrence Tibbett triumphed at the Metropolitan Opera on the evening of January 2, 1925, America had been waiting a century to produce its first homegrown superstar male singer. And success came to Tibbett in time-honored fashion: overnight and by popular acclaim. Verdi's *Falstaff* was revived that night as a tribute to Antonio Scotti, the veteran Italian baritone who had sung the title role at the last Met performance in 1910, and the starry cast also included Lucrezia Bori, Frances Alda, Beniamino Gigli, and Adamo Didur. The role of Ford had been originally assigned to Vincente Ballester, but when that Spanish baritone fell ill, Giulio Gatti-Casazza decided to take another chance on an American, a twenty-eight-year-old whose Met roles since his debut on November 24, 1923, as the virtually invisible monk, Lavitsky, in Mussorgsky's *Boris Godunov*, had been little more than comprimario assignments: Fléville (*Andrea Chénier*), Schlemil (*Les Contes d'Hoffmann*), Morales (*Carmen*), D'Obigny (*La Traviata*), Marullo (*Rigoletto*), and, as a

token for being a good team player, the slightly more rewarding parts of Silvio (*Pagliacci*), the Herald (*Lohengrin*), and Valentin (*Faust*).

Even Met watchers who believed that Tibbett might one day move up to better things were astonished at what happened that evening as Act II, Scene 1, of *Falstaff* came to an end. Enraged by his wife's supposed indiscretion with the fat knight, the jealous Ford sings an aria that climaxes on the phrase "Laudata sempre sia, nel fondo del mio cor la gelosia," an octave-and-a-half ascent to a high G natural and a dramatic-musical effect calculated to bring down the house—old Verdi's last gift to a baritone with a healthy, ringing upper register and an ability to seize the moment. And Tibbett did precisely that. "I tore my heart out," he recalled with no false modesty in a candid memoir, published privately in 1933. "Some subconscious force lifted me up, cleared my throat, and my voice was never better . . . When I finished I knew that in my furious effort to make the audience pay some attention to me, I had acted the scene well and had sung, for me, superbly."

One eyewitness, the music critic and tireless chronicler of American singers Oscar Thompson, left a vivid description of the scene: "On the stage, behind his boscage of beard, young Tibbett took fire. The baritone sang like one possessed. He hammered the table against which he leaned, he flung a cup at it, he strode this way and that with an indifference to conductor and prompter that many veterans never acquire. Violent as it was, his acting rang true. And his voice, white-hot in the passion of his singing, startled and fascinated the audience the more because it scarcely knew the singer who stood before it." When the curtain fell for the scene change, that audience erupted. At first no one backstage quite seemed to realize why. Scotti went out for a solo bow, the other principals emerged, then Scotti and Tibbett returned together, and finally Scotti once again appeared. The uproar continued. Helen Noble, secretary to Gatti's assistant manager, continues the story:

> The house went into a rage yelling for Tibbett! Tibbett! At first, it seemed, Scotti didn't understand and kept going out for calls until finally someone told him they were calling for Tibbett. He then immediately went to his dressing room. As a young artist, Tibbett was not allowed to go out for a solo curtain call unless so ordered by the management. Gatti was standing on the stage that night, but for some unknown reason said nothing to Tibbett, so he too went off to his dressing room. But the applause

kept on, and the yelling for Tibbett until finally Angelo, the man who dressed the male artists, came running to Tibbett's dressing room and told him that Gatti wanted him on stage. When Tibbett got there Gatti merely beckoned him to go on out—all this after sixteen minutes of continued applause and yelling. Tibbett finally went out and took one curtain call. A little misunderstanding between a couple of baritones!

Even Larry Tibbett, a sheriff's son from Bakersfield, California, couldn't quite grasp what had happened. "Alone I stepped out in front of that audience," he wrote with wide-eyed wonderment, "the audience that had come to cheer Scotti. A thundering wave of applause and cheers smashed me in the face. I almost fainted. I still get goose flesh all over my body when I think of it. Thirty-five hundred persons had their eyes on me. They were cheering me! Not Scotti, nor Alda, nor Bori, nor Gigli, nor Kathleen Howard, but ME!" But there was the morning press to worry about, and Tibbett was hardly so young and inexperienced not to realize what the New York critics could do to a newcomer they felt still had a lot to learn about singing. "I hope they do more than to say I was 'adequate,'" Tibbett said after the performance while enjoying a bowl of soup at a neighborhood deli with his accompanist, Frank La Forge, both still a bit dazed. Not to worry. Tibbett's wife awoke him the next morning, shouting excitedly, "The hall outside is full of reporters and photographers! Look at the papers! On the front page! You were the hit of the performance!"

After that night Tibbett truly set off down "the glory road," to paraphrase the aptly titled spiritual that frequently appeared on the recitals he would soon be singing on radio and in concerts all over the country. Gatti—"my boss," as Tibbett liked to call him—immediately raised his weekly salary from $60 to $100, although the Met general manager proceeded cautiously with his new American star baritone. Many more Fords were in Tibbett's immediate future, but it would still be a few seasons before he began to assume the leading roles, mostly in Verdi's operas, that were to become so closely identified with him. Before long, though, by the 1930s, Tibbett was much more than a Met luminary. He was also the proverbial star of stage, screen, and radio, one of the country's most popular entertainment personalities.

In many ways, Tibbett became the male counterpart of his exact contemporary, Rosa Ponselle. Both grew up in the sort of middle-class surroundings that millions of early-twentieth-century Americans could recognize and identify with; both were abundantly blessed with a natural vocal endowment that they discovered almost by accident; and both became national celebrities whose careers burned out much too soon. As the daughter of immigrants and raised in an East Coast urban milieu, Ponselle had certain ethnic and cultural advantages that Tibbett lacked—Rosa Ponzillo may have been a total American phenomenon, but she still looked and sounded like an Italian dramatic soprano, Met audiences accepted her as such, and she had immediate access to a sophisticated opera public. Tibbett, on the other hand, was the typical all-round American boy from a White-Anglo-Saxon-Protestant background way out West, an image that he encouraged and one that helped him find his own audience as well as fueling his rise to fame and fortune.

Born in Bakersfield on November 16, 1896, Lawrence Mervil Tibbet (the extra *t* appeared on his name when the baritone made his Met debut—a typist's error that he liked and decided to keep) was the fourth and youngest child of William and Frances Tibbet. The family had arrived in California during the heady days of the 1849 gold rush, eventually moving south to Kern County, where William served as the local sheriff, obviously still a dangerous job. When Larry was seven, his father, "a God-fearing man with a large blond mustache," set off in pursuit of a bandit named Jim McKinney. "Father led the posse into the Chinese joss house where McKinney was hiding," recalled his son. "Father was too brave and too reluctant to kill. Instead of shooting on sight, he ordered McKinney to come out. McKinney killed my father with a shotgun and killed Jeff Packard, the sheriff, who came to my father's rescue. But my uncle Bert got Jim McKinney, with a shot right between the eyes."

Tragic as it was to lose his father so violently and at such a young age, Tibbett was able to draw on that memory many years later when he actually sang the part of a sheriff onstage—Jack Rance at the Met in Puccini's *La Fanciulla del West*. During rehearsals, as he was preparing to enter Minnie's cabin in Act II and conduct his search for the girl's bandit admirer, Tibbett was told by the director, one Ernst Lert, to come in crouching, with six-shooter held at arm's length. "This will never do," Tibbett complained. "The sheriff would enter standing erect, on the alert, with the gun held at his hip so he can swing it quickly to any part of the room."

"Poof!" cried Lert. "What does an opera singer know about sheriffs?"

Before he became a Met leading tenor and the company's general manager, Edward Johnson was a matinee heartthrob on Broadway in 1908 in Oscar Straus's *A Waltz Dream*. (HALL)

Johnson hoped to discover his own Rosa Ponselle in Dusolina Giannini, seen here as Tosca, but the soprano was more appreciated abroad than at the Met. (SCHMINDT)

Her voice deemed too small for the Met in 1937, mezzo-soprano Jennie Tourel went on to become one of America's most eloquent recitalists. (LUMIÈRE)

*B*efore she started "slumming" in the pop world and left opera behind, Helen Traubel kept the Met's romance with Wagner alive throughout the 1940s. (ALFREDO VALENTE)

A major Met Wagnerian presence from her debut in 1941 at age twenty-three, Astrid Varnay was also a leading exponent of Strauss's Elektra. (METROPOLITAN OPERA ARCHIVES)

Thanks to her glamorous Hollywood image and the astute career marketing of her husband, Walter Surovy, Risë Stevens became the Carmen of her generation.

Dorothy Kirsten checks out her pistol backstage at the Met before going on as Minnie in Puccini's *La Fanciulla del West.*
(METROPOLITAN OPERA ARCHIVES)

As the evil Ortrud, Blanche Thebom braided and wrapped her famous floor-length black hair around her neck like a muff. (METROPOLITAN OPERA ARCHIVES)

Mozart's Countess brought out the most ravishing tonal qualities of the young Eleanor Steber's luscious soprano. (METROPOLITAN OPERA ARCHIVES)

𝒜s well known for her pop-jazz vocal stylings as for her voluminous dramatic soprano, Eileen Farrell preferred to sing statuesque operatic heroines like Cherubini's vengeful Medea. (METROPOLITAN OPERA ARCHIVES)

𝒜ll American composers hoped that Jan DeGaetani—a protean mezzo-soprano at home in every kind of music, new or old—would sing their scores. (PHILIP WEST)

"Toscanini's tenor," Jan Peerce poses as Riccardo in *Un Ballo in Maschera*, a role he once sang and recorded with the legendary Italian conductor. (METROPOLITAN OPERA ARCHIVES)

Tenor Richard Tucker signs his tenth Met contract with Caruso's pen as general manager Rudolf Bing looks on approvingly. (METROPOLITAN OPERA ARCHIVES)

Famous for his deluxe baritone and ringing high notes, Leonard Warren first sang Macbeth in 1959, his twelfth and last Verdi role.
(METROPOLITAN OPERA ARCHIVES)

As a young baritone, Robert Merrill yearned to be a crooner, but soon found himself vocally overqualified for the job.
(METROPOLITAN OPERA ARCHIVES)

Amfortas in Wagner's *Parsifal* was among George London's signature roles after the young singing actor's sensational Vienna State Opera debut in 1949. (METROPOLITAN OPERA ARCHIVES)

Soprano Anna Moffo was noted for both her beauty and her Violetta, a role she is said to have performed more than eight hundred times. (METROPOLITAN OPERA ARCHIVES)

𝓑eginning at the Met with walk-ons, tenor James McCracken went to Europe and returned in triumph in 1963 as Verdi's Otello. (METROPOLITAN OPERA ARCHIVES)

𝓐 celebrity throughout America after her stunning Cleopatra at the City Opera in 1966, Beverly Sills made her bid for international stardom in 1969 as Rossini's Pamira at La Scala. (FOTO PICCAGLIANI)

When the young Leontyne Price sang at La Scala in 1960, the Italian critics were ecstatic, raving that "at last we have heard the true Aida, as Verdi probably imagined her." (FOTO PICCAGLIANI)

"General" Marilyn Horne specialized in bel canto warrior-heroes like Handel's Rinaldo, stunning audiences with her spectacular vocal technique. (WINNIE KLOTZ/METROPOLITAN OPERA)

Tiny but intense, soprano Teresa Stratas conducted a career on her own terms and was especially identified with Berg's free-living earth spirit, Lulu. (WINNIE KLOTZ/ METROPOLITAN OPERA)

Jon Vickers's plangent tenor never sounded more expressive than when singing tortured antiheroes like Britten's Peter Grimes. (METROPOLITAN OPERA ARCHIVES)

Baritone Sherrill Milnes raises a glass and prepares to add another name to his list of conquests as Mozart's Don Giovanni. (METROPOLITAN OPERA ARCHIVES)

Samuel Ramey's flexible bass made him in demand the world over for such virtuoso bel canto roles as Argante in Handel's *Rinaldo*. (WINNIE KLOTZ/ METROPOLITAN OPERA)

Grandeur, both physical and vocal, increasingly became Jessye Norman's trademark after her Met debut, as Berlioz's Cassandre. (WINNIE KLOTZ/ METROPOLITAN OPERA)

Soprano Kathleen Battle strikes a pert pose as Strauss's Zerbinetta, in happier days before the Met fired her for improper diva behavior. (WINNIE KLOTZ/METROPOLITAN OPERA)

$\mathcal{F}$rom the moment
Frederica von Stade
first sang Mozart's
Cherubino with her
tear-in-voice mezzo-
soprano, all hearts
were lost. (WINNIE
KLOTZ/METROPOLITAN
OPERA)

$\mathcal{S}$oprano Renée
Fleming makes her bid
for superstardom after
opening the 1995 Met
season as Desdemona
in Verdi's *Otello*.
(WINNIE KLOTZ/
METROPOLITAN OPERA)

Deborah Voigt, the great hope of Verdi-Wagner dramatic sopranos, took an impressive step forward after singing Sieglinde and Amelia (shown here) at the Met in 1996. (WINNIE KLOTZ/METROPOLITAN OPERA)

The international opera world is counting on Ben Heppner, here as Walther von Stolzing, to become the great Wagnerian tenor of the twenty-first century. (WINNIE KLOTZ/METROPOLITAN OPERA)

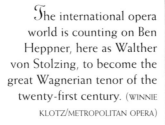

As the Baroque revival continues, America has lately become a rich source for such virtuoso countertenors as David Daniels, pictured here as Handel's Tamerlano.
(GEORGE MOTT)

"In the business of soaring—and diving deep," Lorraine Hunt as Charpentier's Médée definitely communicates a rare sense of danger.
(MICHAEL SZABO)

Baritone Thomas Hampson
may adore leading operatic roles
like Don Giovanni, but he feels
even more at home singing
songs on the recital stage.
(WINNIE KLOTZ/METROPOLITAN OPERA)

Soprano Dawn Upshaw, who
traded Mozart's Susanna for
Cherubino in 1997, wants it all
and seems to be getting it: opera
and song, new music and old,
classical and pop. (WINNIE
KLOTZ/METROPOLITAN OPERA)

Tibbett told him what he knew about sheriffs and played the scene his way.

Like most American children of his generation, Tibbett first discovered music on Sundays, in the Bakersfield Methodist church, where, at the age of six, he made his singing debut. The lad's vehicle was to be an a cappella rendition of "Jesus Wants Me for a Sunbeam," but the words flew out of his head, and after a bit of whispered advice from Mother, the youngster instead led the congregation in a rousing sing-along version of "The Star-Spangled Banner." After that, whatever future musical ambitions the family may have entertained for their son were set aside. After his father's death, Larry, it seems, was determined to be either an actor or a cowboy.

By the time the boy had reached his teens, Mrs. Tibbet moved the family to Los Angeles, where she kept the family together by running a boarding house. Larry attended the High School of Manual Arts between 1911 and 1915 and got caught up in many musical and theatrical activities, although no one, even the boy himself, was especially impressed by his abilities. "As I look back now," the Met star remembered at age thirty-six, "I often wonder why and how I ever kept at it. I was always struggling to get a part in a play or a place in a high-school concert. There was always somebody who undoubtedly was better than I. No matter how hard I tried in high school I never reached the top . . . Even now I am somewhat dazed by my success, and sometimes I feel that all this surely must be only temporary and that the next time I sing a high A flat my voice will shatter into a thousand pieces." Sadly, that was a prescient observation. Tibbett's eagerness to give unstintingly to an audience was one of his most appealing qualities and a likely reason why those high A-flats did indeed start to shatter much too soon.

After high school Tibbett began to find his voice, picking up odd jobs singing in church choirs and acting small parts, first at the Hollywood Community Theater and later in a Shakespeare company headed by Tyrone Power, Sr. ("I usually played old men with whiskers because I wasn't handsome enough to play heroes")—an early valuable experience in both music and drama that Tibbett shared with his Quaker-baritone predecessor, David Bispham. He also landed a part in a production of Horatio Parker's *Fairyland*, which brought him to the notice of Joseph Dupuy, a tenor and the leader of several local choral groups who eventually became the young man's first real voice teacher. In many respects, though, Tibbett remained an autodidact all his life, learning his craft through self-application and a healthy curiosity about everything that pertained to music or the stage—with the help of Berlioz's treatise on the subject, he even made a thorough study of orchestration.

In 1916, while trying out for a part in *The Mikado*, Tibbett met the star of the show, Basil Ruysdael. The American bass was nearing the end of his career at the Metropolitan, where, between 1910 and 1918, he sang some thirty-five roles great and small, his most frequent assignment being Hunding in *Die Walküre*. "Huge, hearty, blunt, with a torrid vocabulary," Ruysdael soon became the young baritone's next teacher, and he "changed my entire point of view toward music. He made an honest baritone out of me." Ruysdael did this by giving his new pupil a lesson in easy, natural verbal projection that Tibbett never forgot. Tibbett had been used to giving "high-class" pronunciations to common words when he sang—"wined" for "wind," "kees" for "kiss," "ahn-da" for "and," and so forth. Ruysdael had no patience for it.

> "Look here, young fellow," he said. "Singing is just speaking words to music. Try that song again. Sing it as you would tell me about it if we were sitting together at lunch—just speak the words on the tune."
>
> It was the best singing advice I ever had. It had never occurred to me that the best singing is the most natural singing.
>
> I tried again, and for the first time in my life sang "wind" instead of "wined," and pronounced naturally "love" and "God" and "kiss." When I finished I felt as stimulated as though I had taken a cold shower. The sham and the strut that I had believed to be a necessary part of Cultured Music were wiped right out of my technique. It was a tremendous relief to find out that it was all right for a singer to be himself.

Ruysdael's advice surely helped him focus his voice on precisely those qualities that he was to put to use so effectively and would be seized upon so gratefully by audiences of all kinds throughout the 1930s. Tibbett was positively driven by a need to communicate, with words as much as with his ravishing vocal sound, and few other Americans with classically trained voices reached a wider public, took such pleasure in singing, or offered their talents more generously.

Like Bispham before him, Tibbett was also a passionate advocate of singing in English. He, too, often sang Schubert lieder in translation without apology, and probably would have been more than content to perform his Verdi roles in English if the Met had let him. Yet there is nothing at all provincial about his style or vocal method. Dozens of recordings made in his prime, in the studio and from live radio broadcasts, testify to a refined musical spirit as well as a flawless technique. Most of all, though, Tibbett had reason to bless Ruysdael for inspiring his magnificent diction, a verbal mastery that invariably illuminated the musical shapes and sounds of an immense concert repertory that ranged from Elizabethan airs to musical comedy.

But Tibbett was still some distance from his big career, and in 1917 the war intervened. He enlisted in the Navy, and for the next two years, among other duties, he served aboard the SS *Iris* as a shipboard instructor, teaching rookie sailors how to row a boat, scrub decks, paint the ship, and tie knots. When hostilities ended, he was shipped off to Vladivostok in Siberia to help protect American interests in the Sea of Japan during the Russian Revolution. Four days after being discharged, on May 15, 1919, Tibbett married Grace Mackay Smith, whom he had first met in high school when the teenage girl was a boarder at his mother's rooming house.

Twin boys arrived less than a year later, and the young couple found themselves economically pressed, to say the least, living in a rented cottage some fifteen miles from Los Angeles. When he could not meet the monthly rent of $12.50, Tibbett would work off the debt in his landlord's vineyard, as well as helping himself to all the grapes he could eat. Occasionally a singing or acting opportunity came along to help ease the financial distress. One such gig was Iago in the Los Angeles Civic Repertory Company production of *Othello*, under the stage name of Lawrence Mervil.

Another of Tibbett's odd jobs was to provide the musical entertainment for several Los Angeles ladies' clubs. While performing one day at the Ebell Club, he met Rupert Hughes, a poet who also dabbled in composition. Tibbett sang a few of his songs and Hughes, impressed, urged him to risk it all and go to New York. Tibbett thought it over, decided to take the gamble, and approached James G. Warren, a wealthy businessman and president of the Orpheus Club, a men's choral group that the baritone had belonged to for several years. Warren promptly wrote out a check for $2,500, the first and far from the last financial assistance he was called upon to provide. Leaving his wife and twin sons temporarily behind, Tibbett, at the age of twenty-four, set off for New

York, promising Warren that if he was not a famous singer by thirty, he would return to Los Angeles and go into a friend's trucking business until he could pay back every cent.

Warren sent Tibbett to his daughter's voice teacher, Frank La Forge, whose connections in the "music center of the world" were extensive. Church work kept Tibbett busy at first, but soon La Forge directed him toward more prestigious engagements, one of them being the Metropolitan Opera Quartet, Frances Alda's touring group. Alda, at the time married to Giulio Gatti-Casazza, thought Tibbett "likeable," with "a good church voice" that "seemed promising." She took him on, even though the young singer resisted the suggestion, no doubt sensible at the time, that he change his name to Lorenzo Tibetto. The spoken theater still looked enticing, especially after he landed the part of Edgar in a Broadway revival of *King Lear*. The reviews were good enough for Tibbett to be offered a full-time contract, but he thought better of it and went back to singing.

After six months with the quartet, though, Tibbett had sufficiently impressed Alda with his progress that she suggested an audition for Gatti. Nothing was more easily arranged, and even when Tibbett's voice cracked on the top note of "Eri tu" from *Un Ballo in Maschera*, Alda's faith in the young man remained unshaken. She persuaded Gatti to hear him a second time a few months later, and after Tibbett poured it on for what must have been a white-hot rendition of Iago's "Credo," a Met contract materialized on the spot. "It's not enough," Alda said when she learned that her husband was offering her protégé a paltry $50 a week, "for a man with a good voice and a wife and two children to support. I'll phone Gatti." She did, and Tibbett's starting salary promptly rose to $60.

Since he was assigned tiny roles at first, Tibbett still had plenty of time to continue singing on Alda's tours. He was with the quartet somewhere in the Midwest during the fall of 1924 when Gatti sent his wife a telegram: "Do you think Tibbett could sing Ford?" Of course he can, Alda wired back, and immediately began to coach him in a part that, she confidently tells us in her memoirs, had been promised to Antonio Pini-Corsi before he had unfortunately fallen ill. (Usually a reliable observer for all her frequent bitchery, Alda was caught napping here. In 1924 Pini-Corsi, who created Ford in the world premiere of *Falstaff* back in 1893, was worse than ill; he had been dead six years.) When the couple arrived back in New York for rehearsals, Alda makes it clear just why Tibbett's triumph caught everyone at the Met by surprise.

There was no denying it, Tibbett was terrible. He was aware of how ill-prepared he was to sing the rôle. He was nervous, and he sensed the criticism of the other artists. Several of them, I remember, stood at one side of the stage and made frank and uncomplimentary comments of Tibbett's efforts as a singer and an actor. Fortunately for his composure, the remarks were in Italian, which he did not understand.

I understood them. I went over to the group.

"Oh, give the boy a chance," I protested. "He'll learn. He'll be all right."

And in English, to Tibbett: "That's fine. Go ahead. You're all right. You can do it."

The evidence may be only circumstantial, but one can't help wondering if Alda's interest in Tibbett ran deeper than merely that of a solicitous older singer looking out for the interests of a talented young colleague. After all, Alda was hardly noted for her goodwill or charitable deeds. Besides, her marriage to Gatti was well known to be an open one, and before Tibbett got his Met contract and brought his family east, he was living a lonely bachelor's life. The pianist André Benoist, who often accompanied Alda, gives the following description of her rehearsal methods when an attractive male was involved: "I arrived at her apartment at the Alwyn Court one fine October morning, and was, to my surprise, ushered into a charming bedroom. At the foot of a bed stood a small upright piano, and in the bed Madame was reclining comfortably, attired in a filmy nightgown. She informed me that she generally rehearsed that way as it gave her greater opportunity to rest. During this explanation, the filmy gown had a way of slipping out of place, thus sometimes revealing charms that would have proved more attractive in being divined than revealed."

If these charms had indeed been revealed to Tibbett, it may well be that he, too, eventually had to agree with Benoist. In any case, a few days after his first Ford, Tibbett sent word to Alda via the bass Adamo Didur that he would no longer be touring with the Metropolitan Opera Quartet. "Why should he do so," reported Didur, "now that he can make a thousand dollars a night, after all the publicity he has had out of the *Falstaff* incident?" Alda refused to rise to what she must have considered an ingrate's bait, remarking icily, "There the matter rested. I just went out and found another singer to take Tibbett's place on my program."

Tibbett and Alda still had to perform together at the Met, though, and a year later an onstage altercation during a performance of Giordano's *La Cena delle Beffe* indicated that some old wounds had not yet healed. Alda's role was Ginevra, Tibbett's faithless mistress, and "momentarily living the part," the baritone flew at her in a jealous rage, struggled furiously, and threw her violently to the floor. "Kerplunk," reminisced Tibbett with apparent relish, "flat on her back in the middle of the stage, feet flying, lay the outraged form of Madame Gatti-Casazza! My boss's wife! 'Oof!' was all she said then, but what she said at the end of the act was plenty!" After the performance, when he heard Gigli walk past his dressing room door whistling Chopin's Funeral March, Tibbett figured that he had gone too far this time and his Met career was effectively over. An armed truce was eventually declared, and luckily for Tibbett, Alda divorced Gatti soon afterward and left the Met for good.

Neri is the baritone lead in Giordano's opera, but even after his sensational Ford, Tibbett had to content himself with playing second fiddle to Titta Ruffo, who sang in the first performances with Alda and Gigli. And Ruffo was scarcely the only important baritone with whom Tibbett had to compete during the 1925–26 season, all of them assigned the roles that still lay in the younger man's future: Giuseppe Danise, Giuseppe de Luca, Antonio Scotti, Mario Basiola, and Clarence Whitehill. Although his comprimario days were behind him, Tibbett was being brought along slowly, and his new assignments—Mercutio, Kothner, Melitone, Ramiro in Ravel's *L'Heure Espagnole*—hardly presented him juicy opportunities to bring down the house once again. On tour that season and next, though, Gatti entrusted him with Tonio, Wolfram, and Germont, and it soon became clear to the impresario that Tibbett had qualities that should be nurtured.

A further indication came on the night of February 17, 1927, when Tibbett sang King Eadgar in the world premiere of Deems Taylor's *The King's Henchman*—"the most effectively and artistically wrought American opera that has reached the stage," opined Olin Downes in the *Times*. And the baritone loved singing Edna St. Vincent Millay's poetic text, even when he had to get his voice around such lines as "Come hither, Maccus, and slake thee! Thou hast a throat like a cornkiln, or I'm a Welshman! Hwita, a stoup here!" Still, it was in English, the audience seemed to like what it heard, and Tibbett was mightily impressed by the effect he made. It was, he later wrote, the first time that he had actually "felt the strong concentration of an audience on the story . . . It was the first time I ever sang in English at the Metropolitan, and at the end of the performance, I made up my mind that I would crusade actively all my life for opera in English."

As it turned out, Tibbett's crusade never got off the ground—his predecessors Clara Louise Kellogg, Minnie Hauk, and David Bispham were able to do much more, but even they never managed to convince Americans that opera sung in their own language was an acceptable proposition. At least Tibbett did his share to promote American opera. Enthused by the friendly reception given *The King's Henchman*, he gladly agreed to participate in several Met premieres over the next decade as Gatti continued his noble efforts on behalf of native opera: Taylor's *Peter Ibbetson* (1931), Louis Gruenberg's *The Emperor Jones* (1933), Howard Hanson's *Merry Mount* (1934), John Seymour's *In the Pasha's Garden* (1935), and Richard Hageman's *Caponsacchi* (1937). None became repertory pieces, but the best of them offered Tibbett plenty of scope to display his capacities as a singing actor when his voice was at the peak of its power, flexibility, and responsiveness. Indeed, when Gatti chose a new American opera, the idea could usually be sold to the board's production committee by pointing out that the work contained an important role for Tibbett.

Although neither was composed specifically for him, the Hanson and Gruenberg scores are essentially one-man operas, and in the surviving radio broadcasts Tibbett is in spectacular form, tearing into both roles with reckless abandon. As Brutus Jones, a black ex-convict whose self-proclaimed rule of a tropical island ends when he is hunted down and terrorized into suicide by his vengeful subjects, he alternates between speech and song in a dramatic crescendo that spirals to a climactic, impassioned rendition of the spiritual "Standin' in the Need of Prayer." Tibbett sang the role fifteen times with the Met, probably the most showy and physically taxing vehicle he ever tackled—a role of "pitiless exactions," as critic Pitts Sanborn styled it—and his impersonation was ranked by some as equal to Feodor Chaliapin's Boris Godunov. It's lucky that he soon put Brutus Jones aside, though, since the effort to sustain this tour de force must surely have cost him dearly in terms of his vocal capital. So did the killingly high tessitura of Hanson's Wrestling Bradford, the sexually repressed Puritan preacher who signs the Devil's Book and carries the innocent object of his lust, Lady Marigold Sandys, with him into hellfire. Needless to say, Tibbett did not spare himself, tossing off the role's high G's and A-flats thrillingly and without a care.

Tibbett seldom if ever sang much of the repertory for which he might have seemed preordained. Wolfram in *Tannhäuser* was his only major Wagner role, and he must have sounded ravishing in the part, to judge from the velvet legato and superb breath control of the "Evening Star" apostrophe recorded for Victor in 1934. He always called Hans Sachs his dream role and *Die Meistersinger* his favorite opera—"the purity, the mellowness, and the beauty of this masterpiece!"—but he only sang Act III in concert and left an exquisitely poetic 1934 radio performance of the Flieder Monologue, typically sung in English. Wotan might also have been an option, to judge from an imposing *Die Walküre* "Farewell," also recorded in 1934 with the Philadelphia Orchestra under Leopold Stokowski. Tibbett never sang a complete Mozart role, which seems a pity—a Don Giovanni or Count Almaviva from this suavest and most seductive of America's singing actors unfortunately remained a tantalizing fantasy.

Although he eventually fell heir to most of the major Verdi baritone parts (Di Luna in *Il Trovatore* and Renato in *Un Ballo in Maschera*, oddly, were not among them), Tibbett is most closely associated with Simon Boccanegra and Iago. Even when he was the Met's preferred Germont and Rigoletto, the baritone always had to contend with potent memories of the great Italians who preceded him in these roles, but when Tibbett took on Boccanegra in 1932 (the opera's American premiere) and Iago in 1937, he was free to create his own traditions in operas that were still largely unfamiliar to Met audiences. Most contemporary critics felt that the baritone's crowning achievement came in his impersonation of Verdi's agonized Doge, a performance that dominated the stage even in the formidable company of Giovanni Martinelli, Elisabeth Rethberg, and Ezio Pinza.

Excerpts from *Boccanegra* were recorded by Victor, but hearing him perform the complete part live during the Saturday matinee broadcasts in 1935 and 1939 reveals Tibbett's full command of the role's requirements—the declamatory authority, musical discipline, creamy legato phrasing, and heart-stopping *mezza voce* effects. One also hears an echo of Basil Ruysdael's wise advice to "speak the words on the tune." Here, as well as in his dangerous Iago, Tibbett used the marked personal character of his timbre to act with the voice and give each utterance a memorable dramatic inflection. Critics felt that his Iago looked rather hammy (this time Lawrence Gilman, perhaps influenced by the singer's green costume and feathered cap, was reminded of Robin Hood), but no one complained about the sting and power of his "Credo" or the sheer melting beauty of his voice as it sweetly poured pretty poison into Otello's ears in "Era la notte." According to the Met's leading comprimario baritone at the time, George Cehanovsky, Tibbett's "pianos were so delightful that even an Italian conductor like Serafin would just open his eyes and listen; he said, 'It cannot be better than that.'"

Tibbett's musical activities were hardly confined to the Met, and the moment his career took off, the rest of the country demanded to hear him. His opera appearances outside New York were confined mainly to Met tours and guest dates with companies in Chicago and San Francisco, but no other singer of his generation was busier on the concert circuit. The phonograph historian William J. Moran recalls attending a recital in San Francisco's War Memorial Opera House on April 19, 1937, when the baritone sang a program that attested to his wide-ranging musical tastes as well as his physical stamina. The first half alone consisted of an aria from Cesti's *Il Pomo d'Oro*; an aria from Mendelssohn's *Son and Stranger*; a group of songs by Schubert, Wolf, Rachmaninoff, Mussorgsky, and Deems Taylor; and arias from *Andrea Chénier*, *La Traviata*, and *Tannhäuser*. Part two contained many more songs, including "Shortnin' Bread," "Old Mother Hubbard," "The Water Mill" by Vaughan Williams, and a Shakespeare setting by Buzzi-Peccia. For encores, ten in all, Tibbett offered the Prologue to *Pagliacci*, "I Got Plenty o' Nuttin'," "Drink to Me Only," "De Glory Road," and finally "Long Ago in Alcala." "And this was not exceptional," writes Moran. "Tibbett never spared himself, and his public got full measure."

Records, radio work, movies—Tibbett was active in every medium. In part, he was making up for the reduced fees that the Metropolitan paid its artists in post-Depression America; during the 1932–33 season, even Ponselle was haggled down from $1,900 a performance to $1,000, while beginners like Rose Bampton were cut from $120 to $70 a week. Worse, the company also required its artists to pay a commission to the Met on their outside engagements. Tibbett often complained that the commissions the Met received on his radio and movie contracts totaled more than the house paid him for singing. The situation finally led the soloists to form the American Guild of Musical Artists in 1936, with Tibbett as its first president, a post he held until 1953. In 1937 he also helped organize the American Federation of Radio Artists and served in an executive capacity there as well until 1945. Needless to say, the Met was not at all pleased when its star baritone began messing around with labor unions. Even earlier, in 1935, he became concerned about the larger picture of the arts in America, and pressed Congress to pass legislation to create a cabinet-level Department of Science, Art, and Literature. Nothing ever came of it—the politicos in Washington paid as much attention to Tibbett as they had many years before to similar suggestions from Minnie Hauk and David Bispham.

The sensational "discovery" of Tibbett in 1925 fortuitously coincided with the advent of the electrical recording process, a new technology that revolutionized the way music was recorded and performed not only over the radio but also in films. Now that Hollywood had found its voice, the new medium naturally wanted to sing as well as talk. Suddenly the idea of filmed operettas looked very appealing, and a dashing young operatic personality as unmistakably and, indeed, irresistibly home-grown as Tibbett seemed just the thing to attract an audience. In the spring of 1929 he was summoned to Hollywood for a screen test that led to his first feature-length film, *The Rogue Song*, directed by Lionel Barrymore, with music adapted by Herbert Stothart from Lehár's operetta *Zigeunerliebe*. The plot featured Tibbett as a Russian bandit named Yegor who falls in love with one of his female captives, the Princess Vera, played by Catherine Dale Owen, while the roles of Ali-Bek and Maurza-Bek were played by two up-and-coming comics named Stan Laurel and Oliver Hardy.

When word got out that young Tibbett had been seduced by Hollywood, noses in New York were raised—how could such a fabulous vocal talent wreck his career before it had barely begun, travel to Tinsel Town, and sell himself for gold? Tibbett said he was only being practical. "I disarmed my advisers by confessing that perhaps I was money-crazy. I owed a good many thousands of dollars to friends who had financed my career, and here was a chance to pay back every dollar . . . It might seem to the public that I should have been rolling in wealth, but most of an opera singer's money goes for commissions to managers, musical coaching, traveling expenses, accompanists, wigs, advertising, entertaining, pianos, music, and heaven knows what else. The movies offered me a great deal of money, and I accepted."

Besides, the idea of making a film appealed to the actor in Tibbett, who felt he still had a lot to learn in that department. The experience, he always said, was invaluable and helped him considerably when it came to performing such demanding operatic roles as the Emperor Jones. But until he got used to the filmmaking process, now more complicated and even more demanding on performers than when Geraldine Farrar had made her silent movies ten years earlier, he wondered if perhaps he hadn't made a mistake after all: "The first voice tests were not so good. I sang so loud that I blew out a light valve in the recording apparatus . . . We got the sound straightened out, but the camera tests and the makeup almost caused me to run down to the ocean and drown myself in shame. They had to learn how to light me. They studied both sides of my face, from all angles and altitudes. I stood on a stage, while a dozen men and women, frowning and muttering, looked me over as though I were a horse. Electricians fussed with lights, cameramen held their hands in front of their faces and glared at me through spread-out fingers, now eying me from the floor, now from a perch on a chair, to see whether there was any way to shoot this guy so he'd look somewhat human . . ."

Tibbett made five more films, including Romberg's *New Moon* with Grace Moore, *Cuban Love Song* with Lupe Velez, and *Metropolitan*, the story of an American singer "trapped" in small roles at the Met due to the company's overwhelming European bias. They all achieved at least a modest success, although perhaps Tibbett's strong public identification as an opera singer prevented them from becoming box office hits outside urban centers (Tibbett once spotted a movie house in the Midwest playing *The Rogue Song* and was startled to see that the marquee read "Starring Laurel and Hardy"). He was soon eclipsed as a matinee idol by Nelson Eddy, also operatically trained but never a star in that high-class milieu and hence less threatening.

In 1932, shortly after marrying his second wife, Jennie Marston Burgard, Tibbett traveled to Europe for the first time. That honeymoon trip was purely for pleasure—Tibbett's first appearance outside the United States would not be until May 14, 1937, when he sang Scarpia at Covent Garden opposite Gina Cigna and Giovanni Martinelli. An immediate audience favorite, the baritone had less success with the London critics, who were frankly contradictory. Some thought his virile acting better than his singing, although others felt that he lacked Scotti's "refined mental sadism" and feared that such a vehement approach to the role would permanently damage his voice. His Iago, on the other hand, was considered to be dramatically unsubtle but consummately well sung. At least Tibbett had unequivocally impressed one British composer. Eugene Goossens became familiar with the singer's work during his stint as conductor of the Rochester and Cincinnati orchestras during the thirties, and insisted that no one else create the title role in his new opera, *Don Juan de Mañara*, which the baritone did on June 24. This time Tibbett earned full marks, the critics reserving most of their scorn for the work itself. From London Tibbett traveled to Scandinavia, Paris, Prague, Budapest, and Vienna before returning to New York in the fall to offer Met audiences their first view of his Iago.

The beginning of Tibbett's vocal decline is hard to pinpoint, and the reasons for it are even more difficult to trace. During the last twenty years of his life, Tibbett was known to suffer from acute alcoholism, a problem that some date from the rehearsals for Hageman's *Caponsacchi* in 1937. During a scuffle with the chorus, Tibbett, as the villainous Guido, lashed out with a knife and wounded a chorister. The gash was a severe one and the unfortunate man died a few hours later. Although the doctor in attendance assured Tibbett that death was due to coronary arrest and that the baritone was in no way responsible, he still blamed himself.

A year later, even though he was not yet experiencing serious vocal problems, Tibbett was clearly beginning to look over his shoulder. December 16, 1938 was to mark his first performance in the title role of *Falstaff*, and a promising young singer with an exceptional vocal endowment named Leonard Warren had been originally cast as Ford. Not long into rehearsals, though, when Warren was replaced by the much-less-glamorous-sounding John Brownlee, it was whispered that Tibbett insisted on the change. Whether he actually did is not certain, but Tibbett must have remembered all too well how another unknown had stolen the evening away from the great Scotti fourteen years earlier.

In September 1940 Tibbett fell prey to a mysterious throat ailment that forced him to cancel all his singing engagements for four months. The exact trouble was never satisfactorily explained, although one doctor who treated him reported several years later in *Newsweek* that the singer had suffered a severe case of "spasticity of the larynx muscle." Other theories were offered: a series of concerts sung through a heavy cold, the strenuous overuse of his voice, and alcohol abuse. Temptations in that direction no doubt only increased as a man who loved singing more than anything else in life watched his voice leaving him. Whatever the cause, Tibbett's rapid decline was all too painfully documented in the Metropolitan Opera broadcasts he sang throughout the decade—more and more during these years his place was indeed taken by the up-and-coming Warren. For radio listeners the first telltale signs came on a January 18, 1941, broadcast of *Otello*, the first after his four-month rest.

Here Tibbett's voice sounds uncharacteristically veiled and unwieldy, and what only two years earlier had been a subtly mercurial study in evil now emerges as obvious stage villainy. In November of that year his Germont is shockingly labored, and subsequent performances of new assignments—Don Carlo in *La Forza del Destino* (1943), Golaud in *Pelléas et Mélisande* (1944), Michele in Puccini's *Il Tabarro* (1946), Balstrode in Britten's *Peter Grimes* (1949), and Ivan in Mussorgsky's *Khovanshchina* (1950)— indicate that Tibbett should probably have retired gracefully early on rather than prolonging the agony. His almost legendary status at the Met and the faithful solicitude of Edward Johnson, one of the baritone's oldest stage colleagues, kept his name on the roster, a bit of charity that Johnson's successor, Rudolf Bing, felt no need to continue when he became general manager in 1950.

For a while rumors circulated that Tibbett himself might be named the next Met chief executive, but nothing came of it. Never one to remain inactive even when it was obvious that he had come to the end of "the glory road," Tibbett lost no time in finding work beyond the Met. In 1950 he appeared on Broadway in the Jan Meyerowitz–Langston Hughes opera *The Barrier*, and the following summer found him touring in a straight play, *Rain*. Like so many other opera singers in their twilight years, he also tried his hand at musical comedy, starring as Captain Hook in a 1950 *Peter Pan* with incidental music by Leonard Bernstein, and six years later taking over Ezio Pinza's role in Harold Rome's *Fanny*. Tibbett was last seen in public on March 2, 1960, applauding a Met performance of *Simon Boccanegra* starring Leonard Warren. Ironically, the two baritones died within a few months of each other, Warren on the Met stage during a performance of *La Forza del Destino*, just three nights after singing that final *Boccanegra*, and Tibbett on July 15 after surgery following an automobile accident.

Tibbett proved once and for all that not only could a singer be born and trained in America, but he could also reach the top of the operatic profession, which in his own country was still dominated and controlled by Europeans. He even proved that a native male singer could win over an audience that, for more than a century, had preferred to hear and applaud imported singers. Although he sang abroad more often than Ponselle, he was never accepted as a major figure in European opera centers and gained real respect from Continental vocal historians only after his death—the British, in fact, have since paid far more respectful attention to his recorded legacy than have Americans. Most commentators hear special qualities in Tibbett's voice and musical manner that are peculiarly American, and the singer himself attempted to describe them in an article published in *Pictorial Review* in 1933. Once again his words echo the wise advice he received long before from Basil Ruysdael: "What is the essentially American thing about a genuine American singer? I think, on the whole, it is greater directness and simplicity. I think it is honesty and sincerity of purpose. These qualities are not necessarily American. Any genuine artist may have them. But to the American artist I say emphatically: 'Be yourself! Stop posing! Appreciate the things that lie at your doorstep!' "

At least two other American baritones enjoyed important singing careers during Tibbett's glory days—Richard Bonelli and John Charles Thomas—although neither really challenged his supremacy at the Met. Bonelli, in fact, remained in Tibbett's shadow just as Riccardo Martin had in Caruso's a generation earlier. Born Richard Bunn in Port Byron, New York, on February 6, 1887, Bonelli discovered his voice at Syracuse University and promptly headed for Europe and studies with Jean de Reszke. Success in various opera houses abroad eventually brought him back to America, where he began his career in 1915 as Valentin with the San Carlo Opera at the Brooklyn Academy of Music. After appearing with other American troupes, most prominently in Chicago from 1925 to 1931, Bonelli finally arrived at the Met on December 1, 1932, as Germont opposite Rosa Ponselle's Violetta (he had made his company debut two days earlier in Philadelphia as Figaro in *Il Barbiere di Siviglia*), and remained with the Met until 1945. His lyrical voice as well as his dramatic presence seemed small and understated compared to Tibbett's generous persona, but he filled in honorably for his younger colleague, even in the killing part of Wrestling Bradford. Also like Tibbett, Bonelli looked good onstage, and he, too, was briefly tapped by Hollywood, making cameo appearances in a couple of films for Paramount between 1934 and 1941. They have vanished into obscurity, but one of them— *The Hard-Boiled Canary*—at least has an intriguing title. Bonelli died in Los Angeles on June 7, 1980.

John Charles Thomas (1891–1960) made more of a name for himself, but primarily as a concert singer, radio balladeer, and—fittingly, for the son of a Methodist preacher—a singer of hymns. By the time Thomas reached the Met in 1934, he was already a seasoned performer, having started out in prewar New York in operetta and serving his operatic apprentice years in Europe, primarily at the Monnaie in Brussels. Back home in 1925, Thomas quickly gained more renown as a recitalist than as an opera singer, until the Met beckoned; like Bonelli, he made his debut as Germont opposite Ponselle, on February 2, 1934. Thomas remained with the company for ten seasons, but he sang with it infrequently and increasingly turned his attention to the radio and recording studio, where his comfortable style, down-home tastes, and mellifluous baritone with its easy spin up top were put to good use singing the songs America loved best: "Darling Nelly Gray," "Where Is My Wandering Boy Tonight?," "Little Mother of Mine," and the like. And he sang them very well, with precisely the openhearted honest sentiment and common touch that Tibbett, with his more flamboyant operatic style and sophisticated manner, never cared to cultivate.

Seventeen

Black Gold

S he was not of vanity, nevertheless a child of nature, a *vis a tergo* controlled her being and taught her the true lessons of sublimity. Notwithstanding she knew the power of her voice, and the perfection of her attitude to command through curiosity, because of her formidable color, she heeded her inmost natural feelings and stood fair with all mankind."

Ah, most people would say upon reading that rather labored, flowery tribute—Marian Anderson, the first African American to break racial barriers and gain international recognition through the beauty and compelling artistry of her singing. Actually, these words were published in 1893 by a black physician named Monroe A. Majors, a reminder, to a world that had forgotten her, of Elizabeth Taylor Greenfield, known as "the Black Swan" during her brief years of celebrity in the 1850s. Nor was Greenfield the only black singer whose voice caught the attention of white audiences before and after the Civil War. Although each generation of American singers struggled to convince their compatriots that homegrown voices were worth listening to, black Americans had that much more to fight in terms of poverty, prejudice, poor education, and social rejection. That so many overcame these obstacles and were noticed at all is something of a miracle.

Monroe states the year of Greenfield's birth as 1809, but the later dates given in other biographical sources, between 1817 and 1820, seem more probable. In any case, she was born Elizabeth Taylor in Natchez, Mississippi, to slave parents—a full-blooded African father and a mother with white and Indian blood—owned by an elderly widow, Mrs. Jesse Greenfield. Taking her patroness's surname, Elizabeth was still a girl when she moved north to Philadelphia with Mrs. Greenfield, who had sold her Natchez property and freed her slaves, sending all those who wished to Liberia. It soon became apparent that young Elizabeth had musical talent, and Mrs. Greenfield did what she could to encourage its development. Formal instruction was, of course, out of the question, but one Philadelphia neighbor, "a physician, humane and courteous," was impressed by the girl's abilities and included her in his own daughter's musical activities. Soon Elizabeth had learned how to play the piano, harp, and guitar. Then one day "she sang; and before she had finished she was surrounded by the astonished inmates of the house, who, attracted by the remarkable compass and sweetness of her voice, stealthily entered the room, and now, unperceived, stood gathered behind her. The applause which followed the first trial, before this small, but intelligent audience, gratified as much as embarrassed her, from the unexpected and sudden surprise."

Meanwhile, Elizabeth remained with Mrs. Greenfield, tending to her needs as companion and nurse until the old woman's death in 1845. Luckily, Mrs. Greenfield had arranged for Elizabeth to receive $100 a year for the remainder of her life, and with that modest financial security, the young woman moved to western New York to stay with friends and cultivate her musical interests. Musicales in the Buffalo area spread her fame locally, and soon more patronesses materialized, leading to her first public recital, before the Buffalo Musical Association in October 1851. By then, like every other young American girl who dreamed of a life in music, Elizabeth had been dazzled by Jenny Lind, even if a similar career was clearly impossible. "We have it from her own lips," wrote Martin Robison Delany in 1852, "that not until after the arrival of Jenny Lind and [Teresa] Parodi [an Italian soprano who also toured the country widely] in the country, was she aware of the high character of her own talents. She knew she possessed them, because they were inherent, inseparable with her being. She attended the Concerts of Mad'll Jenny Lind, and Operas of Parodi, and at once saw the 'secret of their success'—they possessed talents, that no other popular singers mastered."

After her Buffalo concert, Greenfield began a tour under the management of Colonel J. H. Wood, taking her to Albany, Cleveland, Columbus, Detroit, Milwaukee, Chicago, Toronto, and Boston. The quality and range of her voice were always noted as unusual, and despite the obvious lack of technical finishing, she did not shy away from the identical operatic and concert repertory that Lind had just sung before an enraptured American public. "The compass of her marvellous voice," reported the *Daily State Register* in Albany, "embraces twenty-seven notes, reaching from the sonorous bass of a baritone to a few notes above even Jenny Lind's highest. The defects which the critic cannot fail to detect in her singing are not from want of voice, or power of lung, but want of training alone." A short, plain, thickset woman, Greenfield hardly cut a glamorous figure onstage, but apparently her gentle manner, coupled with the musical intensity of her interpretive powers and the rich, full resonance of her voice, provided ample compensations. Even at that, like others of her race who hoped to be taken seriously as artists in nineteenth-century America, she was considered little more than a curiosity. Even the most sympathetically disposed white audiences, while perhaps able to recognize an exceptional vocal endowment and willing to forgive unfinished technique and musicianship, could never quite accept the anomaly of a black woman attempting to sing the refined airs of European composers. Toward the end of her tour, on March 31, 1853, Greenfield gave a concert at Metropolitan Hall in New York, and the *Tribune* printed the following remarkable account of her reception—condescending in tone to our minds, but perhaps representing an "enlightened" view for its day:

> For our part we could not sympathize with the rollicking gaiety of a considerable portion of the audience in seeing her led forward on the platform. Her behavior was strictly in good taste, and gentlemen should not have laughed at her. Had her auditory been the English House of Lords they would have received her with marked respect . . . It is hardly necessary to say that we did not expect to find an artist on the occasion. She has a fine voice, but does not know how to use it. Her merit is purity and fulness, but not loudness of tone. Her notes are badly

formed in the throat, but her intonation is excellent. She sings, in a word, like a child . . .

What culture may do in the case in hand remains to be seen, but it is certainly a voice that ought to be cultivated in Europe, and ought to stay there. The bills of the Concert stated that no colored persons would be admitted, and a strong police was there in anticipation of riot, which did not happen. Under these circumstances we advise Elizabeth Greenfield to go to Europe and there remain. It may be added that she was encored in singing, and gave satisfaction to her audience, who appeared to recognize her musical position. That she has succeeded to the extent shown is evidence of intellect which merits development. She has had everything to contend against—an education neglected—a spurned thing in social life; but her ambition has thus far triumphed, and we hope to hear a good account of her studies in a country where Alexandre Dumas has learned how to read and write.

Whether the *Tribune's* critic knew it or not, Greenfield was in fact on the verge of following his advice. On March 7, 1853, back in Buffalo, her sponsors had arranged a testimonial concert to raise funds to send the Black Swan to Europe, and early in April she set sail for London. There she was treated with kindness and respect—England's image of blacks may not have been exactly enlightened, but at least those who aspired to artistic accomplishment were not automatically perceived as renegade slaves or buffoons—and one suspects that the year Greenfield spent abroad was the happiest period of her life. Practically upon arrival she had the good luck to encounter Harriet Beecher Stowe, who was visiting London and enjoying the international success of her new novel, *Uncle Tom's Cabin*. Stowe immediately introduced Greenfield to the Duchess of Sutherland, who presented the singer to London's musical elite at a concert on May 23 at Stafford House.

Greenfield continued to give concerts in England during the following year, which climaxed with an invitation to sing before Queen Victoria at Buckingham Palace on May 10, 1854. Despite that honor and the continued interest of the English public, the Black Swan never managed to generate sufficient means to support herself, and on July 15 of that year she sailed home to New York. There she sang a few more concerts, and at least one critic noted that she had benefited from her English experiences. "Her singing," he wrote in the October 7, 1854, issue of *Dwight's*, "is indeed a wonder, in which even fastidious ears may find pleasure; and her manner is simple and pleasing. She has profited by her stay in Europe. The Temple was about half filled by an audience composed in about equal proportion of whites and very respectable looking colored people . . ."

Elizabeth Greenfield may have worked hard to improve her art, but clearly America was far from ready for a classically trained black singer. Settling in Philadelphia, she soon gave up the fight, giving an occasional local concert and teaching voice privately until her death in 1876. Coincidentally that same year a young black woman named Marie Smith, also a native of Natchez, Mississippi, made her professional debut in San Francisco. A few years later, when a career seemed to be within her grasp, she changed her name to Marie Selika, a clever appropriation referring to the heroine of Meyerbeer's *L'Africaine*. Selika, or her managers, no doubt reasoned that if audiences were now ready to accept a black woman as the romantic lead in what had become a popular repertory opera, they might be prepared to extend that courtesy to the real thing.

It never quite happened, of course, but Selika (c. 1849–1937) had her brief moment. Details about her early years are sketchy, although she most certainly was a child of slaves before a wealthy white family took her to Cincinnati to be raised in freedom. After a peripatetic childhood, in 1873 Marie settled for a time in San Francisco, studying with a certain Bianchi until the year of her debut. Still on the move, the soprano turned up in Chicago a year later as a pupil of another Italian, Antonio Farini, before settling in Boston in 1878; there she adopted the name of Selika. At the time, there was even a report in the black press of her engagement at the Philadelphia Academy of Music to sing her eponymous role in *L'Africaine*, although whether the performance actually took place is unknown—an unprecedented event, if it did. By then, however, Selika was famous enough to be invited by President Rutherford B. Hayes to sing at the White House, where she shared a program with her husband, Sampson Williams, who sang under the name of Signor Velosko.

Four years later, in 1882, Selika and Williams traveled to Europe to give joint recitals. Far more poised and attractive than Greenfield, and rejoicing in what had been described as a sweet but brilliant coloratura soprano, Selika enjoyed considerable success, particularly with her scintillating rendition of Mulder's showy "Staccato Polka," a signature tune that earned her the sobriquet "the Queen of Staccato." During the couple's tour of European capitals, Williams sent letters back to James Trotter, telling the writer of enthusiastic audiences in England, France, Germany, and Belgium. Trotter passed on the news through the black newspaper *New York Age,* reporting on their Belgium engagement: "Here as elsewhere in the line of their travels, himself [Williams] and Madame Selika have never once been slighted on account of their color, and at the most elegantly appointed hotel in Brussels they could not have received more polite attention had they been Madame Patti and husband. What a lesson for our as yet uncivilized America!" Like Greenfield, Selika also received an invitation from the music-loving Queen Victoria, and sang her command performance in St. James Hall in 1883.

Finding the Continent far more hospitable than America, Selika and Williams based their careers there for the next ten years. The ever-alert Colonel Mapleson heard Selika in 1885 in Philadelphia and was taken by both her striking appearance and her voice. Nonetheless, even that bold entrepreneur felt unable to offer the soprano an opera contract. Back in America in 1893, Selika opened a music studio in Ohio and continued to concertize for the next eighteen years, as the country's curiosity to hear her sing gradually dwindled. When Williams died in 1911, she retired to teach in New York at the Martin-Smith School of Music in Harlem, where she remained an honored local celebrity until her death at the age of eighty-seven in 1937.

Just as Selika's star was setting, another black diva's was in the ascendant: Sissieretta Jones (1869–1933), soon to become universally known as "the Black Patti." Jones was born in Portsmouth, Virginia, to the Reverend Jeremiah Malachi Joyner and his wife, Henrietta, both former slaves. In 1876 the Reverend Joyner left the Reconstruction South for a church post in Providence, Rhode Island, where Sissieretta began studying voice and music at the Providence Academy of Music in 1883. That year, at the age of fourteen, she was also married to David Richard Jones, who worked as a newsdealer and hotel bellman. Apparently he also drank, gambled, and spent money freely, activities that did not lessen as he began to manage his young wife's career and business affairs. Despite that added impediment, finally removed by a divorce sometime between 1893 and 1898, Jones forged ahead with her music, studying privately at Boston's New England Conservatory of Music and with Louise Capianni in New York.

Even as a student in Boston, Sissieretta Jones began to make a local reputation with her voice, and soon after her New York debut in 1888 she was contracted to join a troupe of black musicians, called the Tennessee Jubilee Singers, to make several tours of the West Indies. By the time Jones returned, she found the press already referring to her as the Black Patti, a description that she had to live with for the remainder of her life. It always irked her, partly because she saw it as a sign of condescension and partly because she knew that it fueled the racism of many white audiences who considered the sobriquet exploitative, even offensive. Jones also realized that whatever her vocal talent, she could hardly compete with "the Queen of Hearts" and that their voices had very different qualities. Jones apparently excelled through the richness, range, and dramatic presence of her soprano, which was at its best in broad lyrical music rather than in Patti's coloratura repertory.

Still, people flocked to see and hear the Black Patti, especially after the widely publicized Grand African Jubilee held at New York's Madison Square Garden in April 1892. Having sung for President Benjamin Harrison earlier that year, Jones was a national celebrity, and for the next twenty-five years she traveled all over the country (although seldom in the South), as well as in England and on the Continent. Since she was prevented from pursuing a conventional singing career, Jones looked around for other options, eventually settling on a role as the singing star of Black Patti's Troubadours, a group of touring black entertainers, acrobats, dancers, and singers. A combination of vaudeville and minstrel show, the Troubadours' material was aimed at its predominantly white audiences and pandered to its interest in stereotypical "darky" humor and "coon songs." Although she could hardly have found the company an ideal showcase for her talents, the soprano created her own respectable artistic niche by confining her appearances to a series of "operatic kaleidoscopes": fully staged and costumed scenes from Lucia, Carmen, Martha, and other popular operas.

This mix of high and lowbrow entertainment proved to be immensely popular, and Black Patti's Troubadours enjoyed a twenty-year run before interest waned and the troupe disbanded in 1916. Life on the American road for a company of blacks was problematic, to say the least, and fraught with dangers. Racist groups might be encountered anywhere and most hotels were closed to the company, necessitating specially customized railroad cars that could serve as both home and refuge. And yet when they performed, the Troubadours were welcomed virtually everywhere north of the Mason-Dixon Line, although Jones clearly felt compromised.

She expected that Black Patti's Troubadours would detour her only temporarily from the concert stage, but the years passed and it soon became clear that no other performance options would open up for her. In 1916 Jones returned to Providence to look after her ailing mother and, aside from one concert in Chicago, she never sang in public again. Unlike the real Patti, who retired to her Welsh castle surrounded by wealth and cushioned by every creature comfort, the Black Patti spent her last years in poverty, a forgotten woman. Even so, she had made her statement and that, as well as the sheer quality of her voice, left memories. "I love to sing," she once said. "Singing is to me what sunshine is to the flowers; it is our life. The flowers absorb the sunshine because it is their nature. I give out melody because God filled my soul with it." A singer with such an appealing credo was bound to raise any audience's consciousness and perhaps even touch America's collective remembrance. If she found most conventional doors closed to her, Sissieretta Jones opened as many others as she could—certainly more than had been available to Elizabeth Greenfield fifty years earlier—and by doing so made a rough road just that much smoother for the next generation.

Several other black singers made a mark during the post–Civil War years—Flora Batson, Emma Azalia Hackley, Sidney Woodward, Hazel Harrison, Carl Diton, and the Hyers sisters (Anna Madah and Emma Louise)—but by the beginning of the new century whatever novelty they may have brought to the country's musical scene had pretty well dissipated. The cultural historian Eileen Southern offers one explanation: "The fickle public soon tired of black prima donnas. Although the singers were gifted, well trained, and fortunate in obtaining good management, their careers on the concert stage were relatively short, ranging from three or four years to a dozen or so in most instances. Their white impresarios staged concerts in the prestigious halls of the United States and Europe and arranged for command performances before important persons, but to no avail. By the mid-1890s the black prima donnas had almost disappeared from the nation's concert halls because of lack of public interest."

Since the small gains made by black singers had been effectively erased by the century's turn, it seemed necessary to begin the job all over again. When Roland Hayes first thought of pursuing a singing career as a teenager in the early 1900s, it must have seemed like sheer madness—few enough males took the plunge in those days, let alone black men. Eventually, though, Hayes not only succeeded beyond anyone's imagination but also broke through many barriers. Opera remained closed to him, but he was the first African American to perform with a symphony orchestra and the first to bring the spirituals of his people to the attention of concert audiences.

None of this was even a fantasy when Hayes was born to ex-slaves in Curryville, Georgia, in 1887. Hayes's parents were tenant farmers occupying a portion of the former Joseph Mann plantation, where the future tenor's mother, Fannie Mann Hayes, had worked as a slave. Fannie first encountered her husband shortly after the Civil War, trudging down the road from Atlanta to Chattanooga, with free-man documents in his pocket. Even William Hayes wasn't quite sure where he came from—he thought he might have been born in Illinois—but he was on his way south from Missouri to find work in Atlanta. An expert carpenter, craftsman, and hunter, the elder Hayes also had an ear for music, using his voice to lure deer, bear, and game birds as well as to teach his son how to identify birdcalls and attract them by answering back.

Hayes's mother was an even greater influence in his life, especially after 1898, when his father died and the family moved to Chattanooga, Tennessee, where Angel Mo', as he always called her, supported her children by doing laundry and ironing. Angel Mo' was a formidable matriarch, a deeply religious but unsentimental woman who cherished her sons' minds as much as their souls. Her dignity and practical focus instilled a deep sense of self-pride and responsibility in young Roland, as well as an urge to achieve, no matter what he set out to do. Compulsory church attendance also meant that even before his voice changed, Roland knew hundreds of spirituals by heart. But he also had to neglect his education and go to work early on to help support the family—in an iron foundry, where one day he was dragged through a conveyor belt, badly chewed up by the machinery, and briefly given up for dead.

By the time he reached sixteen, Roland and three other lads had formed a vocal group called the Silver-Toned Quartet. He also noticed the sweet voice of a friend, who instinctively seemed to sing in ways that Roland envied. "I knew nothing then of the middle voice, or mezza voce, although I had unconsciously acquired the first principles of its use from my father; but I said to myself that I wanted to be able to sing like that, to sing with beauty." He then approached Arthur Calhoun, an organist and choir director in Chattanooga, who gave the youngster lessons for fifty cents an hour. It was at Calhoun's that Roland got his first real taste of "white folks' music," and was entranced when he heard the voice of Caruso on a crank-up Victrola. Those golden sounds apparently clinched the matter. "I had not been studying with Calhoun for more than two or three months before I had privately resolved to make a career of my music. I set my heart on going to the Oberlin Conservatory, where my teacher had studied."

That dream never came true—by 1905, when Hayes gave up his job to study music full-time, his formal education had gotten no further than fifth-grade level. Instead, he settled for Fisk University in Nashville, where his musical talent rather than his academic credentials earned him admission, and odd jobs paid for tuition. Aside from his studies, Hayes spent most of his time singing with the Fisk Jubilee Singers—his tenor was in fact so valued that he continued to perform with them when, after his enforced departure from the university in 1911, the group visited Boston. Impressed by "the Athens of the Northeast" and its busy musical life, Hayes decided to remain, working as a page boy for the John Hancock Insurance Company and studying privately with Arthur Hubbard, a former Lamperti pupil. Apparently the lessons had to be held at Hubbard's home rather than at his downtown studio, in order not to embarrass the teacher and his white pupils.

Neither Hubbard nor Angel Mo', who had come to Boston to live with her son, had much faith that a black singer could ever make a concert career in white America. Hayes persevered, however, and his public appearances became increasingly frequent and successful over the next nine years as audiences, still in large part attracted by the novelty of a black concert singer, were won over by his personal warmth and the sheer beauty of his voice. A 1916 recital debut in tiny Jordan Hall turned out to be a financial disaster—no manager would agree to handle the event and Hayes had to promote it himself—but the critics were impressed. After a year of touring with a black baritone and pianist as part of the Roland Hayes Trio, the tenor had earned enough money to rent Boston's famed Symphony Hall for his next recital, on November 15, 1917. Vigorously promoted by Hayes and the many white friends he had made at John Hancock, the event sold out and the reviews bordered on the ecstatic. Hayes promptly set out on a cross-country tour, billing himself as "Roland W. Hayes, Celebrated Negro Tenor," and his hand-bills could quote a rave review from the New York Tribune comparing him to the great French tenor Edmond Clément.

By now Hayes had come to the conclusion not only that his skin was a different color but that his voice and the artistic spirit which made it live were also different. After those first recitals he realized that "I was unconsciously putting myself into competition with white singers, whose spotlight I wanted to share . . . I still had to be taught that I, Roland Hayes, a Negro, had first to measure my racial inheritance and then put it to use." One way to accomplish that was to include in his programs the spirituals he had learned as a child. Another was to de-velop the special texture of his voice, which the poet Hulda Hervin Newhouse had once described as "colored like old mellowed wine"—a simile that led Hayes to the conclusion "that even the voice I was born with was colored." No physiological proof exists for such a notion, but the idea appealed to Hayes and must partially account for the new focus and intensity that now fired his singing and spurred his career.

Hayes soon discovered the reality that, up to now, had eventually dawned on every American singer, black or white: acceptance as a con-cert or opera singer at home could come only after European success. So in April 1920 he sailed for London to concertize, work on his voice, expand his knowledge of European culture and classical composers, and improve his command of foreign languages. At first, as they had back home, people came to see and hear him out of curiosity, but Hayes didn't mind and he began to network. Soon he could number the pianist Myra Hess, poet Ezra Pound, and composer Roger Quilter among his friends. A year later the powerful London concert management of Ibbs and Tillett took Hayes on and presented him at Wigmore Hall, and two days after that warmly received concert he was commanded to appear before King George V and Queen Mary.

A busy decade had begun for the tenor as he consolidated his Lon-don reputation and toured the Continent, giving recitals in Berlin, Paris, and Vienna, as well as making later excursions to Italy, Spain, and Russia. Occasionally Hayes encountered hostile audiences. The worst must have been in 1924 in Berlin, where dangerous nationalistic sentiments were already rising and the prospect of an American black defiling Ger-man poets and composers threatened to start a riot even before Hayes stepped onto the stage. When he did, he decided on the spur of the moment to open the program with "Du bist die Ruh'," singing Schubert's invocation to peace with such melting tone and quiet invincibility that the audience suddenly became as still as the singer in the song. The French seemed to adore Hayes most of all—critic Paul Landormy wondered whether there was another tenor in all Paris who knew his métier as well. "Do not take M. Hayes for a savage," he wrote. "He could give points to the most refined musicians in our own civilization, in the way of spinning sound from the starting point of the melody to its finality." Even the aged Gabriel Fauré invited the tenor to his studio for personal coaching sessions, and André Messager was so enchanted by Hayes that he offered to write an opera especially for him.

Hayes was in his vocal prime during the 1920s, but unfortunately we have virtually no recorded evidence—he made a few discs for a small label, but they disappointed him and he personally destroyed them by cutting the matrices in two with a pair of shears. That he possessed a gorgeous lyrical sound that he used with exquisite refinement is still more than apparent on the records he did make many years later. One can easily imagine what so impressed Dame Nellie Melba in 1921 as she listened to Hayes give an impromptu rendition of "Una furtiva lagrima" from *L'Elisir d'Amore* at a garden party. As Hayes described the incident:

The air begins pianissimo on a high note. The attack must come without effort, like a breath out of the silence, with no indication of the vocal mechanics. What follows is written along a long, sustained vocal line which must remain intact, and at the end there is a cadenza which the voice has to carry without accompaniment.

I had not finished the first phrase, had scarcely sung two bars, when Melba jumped up from her chair and ran to me with outstretched arms.

"No one, not even De Reszke, has ever made such a divine entry into that song," she said.

Trying not to look distracted or embarrassed, I began the aria again and sang it through. I confess to a moment of great pleasure when I saw Melba dissolved in tears.

His European successes meant that Hayes could now include America on his itinerary. By the end of the twenties the tenor had won more gains than any black singer could have dreamed of a decade earlier. Hayes was now a rich man who owned a French villa, a house in suburban Boston, and—best of all—the Georgia farm in Curryville where his parents had been slaves and where he himself had been born into grinding poverty. An enthusiastic investor, Hayes suffered severe financial setbacks after the 1929 stock market crash, leaving him with little except his real estate and unrealized plans to establish a school for aspiring black musicians. Soon he also had to abandon his career in Europe, where the growing trend toward fascism made his presence impossible. From 1930 until his last concert, in 1972 at the age of eighty-five, Hayes devoted himself exclusively to America and increasingly to the spirituals he had done so much to popularize, especially a collection he had arranged into a unique cycle that traces the life of Christ. A ubiquitous presence on the concert scene, particularly in the Northeast, Hayes lived long enough to see an entire generation of black singers follow his example, not only on the concert stage but also in the opera house, which had been closed to him.

Right up to the end, Hayes's voice preserved much of the sweet tonal purity and aching expressivity that made such an impression on Melba. The late studio recordings, after 1939, and the live postwar recitals show him well past his vocal peak, but his art remained mesmerizing. On one disc, privately recorded in Boston in 1955, Hayes sings an unaccompanied rendition of "Swing Low, Sweet Chariot." Nothing could be more beautiful than the liquid sound of his voice as he tapers phrases that evaporate into silence, an audible reminder of the voice lesson he had learned so long ago from his father: how "the body must respond freely and newly to the mind's momentary act of recreation." But it was Hayes's own single-minded perseverance and generous spirit that led him to discover the singular quality which provided "the motto for my career: to understand the beauty of a black voice."

There's no telling in what directions that career might have turned had Hayes's skin been white—sometimes it must have seemed to him as though each recital was a fresh challenge to conquer his audience and overcome lingering prejudices. "It was not inspiring," he once wrote, drily recalling a concert in Kiev, Russia, "to sing to an audience of sniggering peasants who behaved as though they had come to inspect an African savage. I felt that they were resentful because I neither looked nor sang like an inhabitant of the jungle. The people out front were savages, actually, and I had to tame them." And of course treatment at home could be even more brutal. "Stones have been thrown through the windows of my house in Brookline; I have been refused a bed in a hotel in Tucson, a chair in a Seattle lobby, a meal in a restaurant in Duluth; and once, not so long ago, I was beaten and thrown into jail." But when a white minister in Duluth heard of Hayes's most recent indignity and promised that he would "take it up" with somebody, Hayes discouraged him. "There is nothing you can do," he said. "That is a job for me and my own people."

Hayes bore prejudice and did his "job" quietly and with grace. So did Marian Anderson, born ten years after the tenor, in 1897 (not 1902 as cited in biographical material during her life—even this modest woman thought it prudent to dock five years from her age). But unlike Hayes, whose name and career were largely forgotten soon after his death, Anderson played a key role in reversing the fortunes of black American singers, becoming a symbol that will surely remain as potent and unforgettable as the many recordings of her extraordinary voice.

Nothing in Anderson's youth prepared her for this extramusical role. She and her two younger sisters were raised in a lower-class section of Philadelphia in which white and black lived, worked, and played together with few signs of open racial discord. Like Hayes, she lost her father at an early age, and her view of the world was mostly shaped by the faith, discipline, and strict moral values of a strong mother. Everyone in the household worked hard, and when Marian decided that she wanted a four-dollar violin, she scrubbed neighbors' front steps for five cents until she had saved up the money.

The violin soon fell apart, but by then young Marian found that she enjoyed singing in the Union Baptist Church more—soon, in fact, the "baby contralto" was earning fifty cents, sometimes even a dollar, singing at local functions. It was at the Union Baptist—which like most Northern black churches had a rich and extensive musical life—that she first heard Roland Hayes sing, and the experience deeply impressed her: "His appearance was the highlight of the Philadelphia concert season. Mr. Hayes sang old Italian airs, German Lieder, and French songs exquisitely. Even people with little understanding of music knew it was beautiful singing, and they were proud that Mr. Hayes was one of their own and world-famous. But after a time a few grumbled that they did not understand what he was singing. And there were some who said, "If our Marian were on the program, we would understand what she was singing about." So eventually I was permitted to appear on his program and sing two or three numbers."

Slowly it began to dawn on the teenager that a lovely natural voice was not enough. She needed training, and obviously the place to get that was a music school. Encouraged by her mother and friends, Marian went to the nearest institution in downtown Philadelphia, only to be brusquely told, "We don't take colored." It was her first encounter with naked prejudice, and she was devastated: "I don't think I said a word. I just looked at this girl and was shocked that such words could come from one so young. If she had been old and sour-faced I might not have been startled. I cannot say why her youth shocked me as much as her words. On second thought, I could not conceive of a person surrounded as she was with the joy that is music without having some sense of its beauty and understanding rub off on her. I did not argue with her or ask to see her superior. It was as if a cold, horrifying hand had been laid on me. I turned and walked out."

After that discomforting revelation, Anderson resigned herself to private study, first with a local soprano, Mary Saunders Patterson, and later with Giuseppe Boghetti, a tenor and coach who remained her teacher on and off until his death in 1941. While Boghetti gave his new pupil valuable instruction in matters of technique and professionalism, Anderson continued to concertize, mainly in Southern black colleges and in the Philadelphia area. Eventually she felt ready to try her luck in New York City, with a recital in Town Hall on April 23, 1924. It was a disaster. The audience may not have laughed as they did some seventy years earlier when Elizabeth Greenfield ventured a program of art songs, but the reception was definitely chilly. Like Greenfield, Anderson impressed critics with her vocal endowment but also betrayed a grievous lack of experience, style, and finish—"Marian Anderson sang her Brahms as if by rote," complained one critic. The contralto returned to Philadelphia, discouraged and defeated. "The dream," she felt, "was over."

In fact, it had only been briefly interrupted. Anderson soon recovered her spirits, began to work on her voice again, and a little over a year later she was back in New York to collect her award for winning first prize in the Philadelphia Philharmonic Society's annual young artist's contest: a solo appearance at Lewisohn Stadium on August 26, 1925. This time the reviews were rapturous—"in high and low notes, there was a full rich quality that carried far," wrote the *Tribune;* "she is endowed by nature with a voice of unusual compass, color and dramatic capacity," echoed the *Times.* The notices caught the attention of the influential manager Arthur Judson, who engaged her on the spot. Encouraged by all the sudden flattery from high places, yet conscious of how much she still had to learn, Anderson came to the inevitable decision: only European finishing could bring her the necessary polish and culture that might, one day, put her in a class with Roland Hayes. A few months after that Lewisohn Stadium triumph, Anderson made her first trip abroad, where she was to spend the better part of the next decade.

After passing an uneventful year in London, Anderson went to Berlin, specifically to work on mastering German lieder, and there she impressed a young Finnish pianist named Kosti Vehanen. An artistic friendship was quickly established, and Vehanen persuaded her to tour Scandinavia, an experience that proved to be a turning point. Wholly unaccustomed to hearing black singers, the Norwegians at first marveled over her voice with a childlike delight that even Anderson had to admit expressed more wonderment than prejudice—one critic described her as "dressed in electric-blue satin and looking very much like a chocolate bar." But the enthusiastic reaction to her recitals was more important, since the sincere response "made me realize that the time and energy invested in seeking to become an artist were worth while, and that what I had dared to aspire to was not impossible." The Scandinavians loved her even more when she began singing the songs of their native composers and received the personal compliments of Jean Sibelius, Yrjö Kilpinen, and Edvard Grieg's widow, Nina.

Anderson's big international breakthrough, however, came in Salzburg during the 1935 summer festival. It was there, during the intermission of her recital, that Toscanini made his famous pronouncement about a voice such as one hears once in a hundred years. That comment seemed to circulate around the world the moment it was made—perhaps because in June of the same year the impresario Sol Hurok had heard Anderson sing at the Salle Gaveau in Paris, realized her potential as a "Hurok attraction," and signed her to an exclusive contract. From that moment, and for the remainder of her career, Anderson appeared under the aegis of Hurok, whose canny managerial style and showmanship equaled, and in some ways surpassed, that of P. T. Barnum himself. Hurok correctly sensed that now was the time for a triumphant homecoming concert, which took place on December 30, 1935, in New York's Town Hall, the very auditorium where she had suffered such a humiliating fiasco more than eleven years earlier.

Billed as "the American Colored Contralto," Anderson reappeared at the age of thirty-eight, a seasoned artist and her voice now in its glorious maturity. Her program included Handel airs, a group of Schubert lieder, a Verdi aria, some Scandinavian songs, and a choice collection of spirituals. "I will make no bones about the fact that the program was devised so that there would be opportunity to show whatever I was capable of doing, including low notes and high . . . Maybe there was something extra in all the spirituals at the end . . . When I reached them I felt as if I had come home, fully and unreservedly—not only because they were the songs I had sung since childhood but also because the program was almost finished, and I had survived." Anderson did much more than merely survive—the reviews were ecstatic and Howard Taubman's in the *Times* set the tone: "Let it be said at the outset: Marian Anderson has returned to her native land one of the great singers of our time."

The recordings and preserved broadcasts of the thirties and forties amply corroborate what Taubman heard. After Anderson had found her voice and self-confidence, she seemed to sing from the very center of her being, radiating a rocklike sense of security, not only in the technical management of her instrument but also in the emotional message she had to deliver. That registered most directly and powerfully in her performances of spirituals, always sung with eyes closed and hands clasped and creating an effect that seemed to remove barriers and erase racial lines every time, simply through the naked honesty, concentrated intensity, and sheer beauty of her singing. The voice during this period was at its richest and freshest, precisely tuned to every expressive need. Her German lieder interpretations are completely idiomatic, and it is difficult to believe that such immediate and spontaneous performances come from a singer who had once wrestled laboriously with the language.

Listening to Anderson, one inevitably has to wonder about the technical nature of such a singular voice. She herself always insisted she was a contralto, but in her prime the overall workable range was huge and resisted easy categorization. No one would question the contralto label while listening to the powerful, easily produced low chest register she uses to characterize a spiritual like "Tramping." But when Anderson sings a Sibelius song or a Handel aria, one hears an entirely different sound as she moves into head tones that take her without effort or undue pressure into soprano territory. Indeed, there are fascinating radio transcriptions of her ventures into the dramatic soprano operatic repertory—Verdi's "Pace, pace, mio Dio" and a bel canto test piece like Bellini's "Casta diva" raise speculations over what her operatic persona might have been like, had she been allowed to develop one. Perhaps the most telling example of Anderson's "different voices" is her recording of Schubert's "Der Tod und das Mädchen," in which her lightly inflected characterization of the dying maiden is so vividly contrasted with the seductive baritonal blandishments of Death, which ultimately descend to a striking and firmly placed low D. Could Elizabeth Greenfield have sounded something like this? Greenfield's critics also remarked wonderingly, if hardly flatteringly, about her extraordinary range, one that took her from the lowest tones of a bass up to high notes that were not even available to Jenny Lind.

The most famous event in Anderson's career, and the one that permanently turned her into a living symbol of racial equality, was her outdoor recital on Easter Sunday, April 9, 1939, in Washington, D.C., held in front of the Lincoln Memorial after the Daughters of the American Revolution refused to make Constitution Hall available to her. Like most legendary occasions, the exact facts of the matter are still hard to pin down. To this very day, representatives of the DAR maintain that the hall had been previously booked, although that claim has yet to be convincingly substantiated—most people remember what the manager of Constitution Hall, Fred Hand, said when pressed to explain the situation: "No date will ever be available for Marian Anderson in Constitution Hall!"

Even the inspired notion of having Anderson sing before the Lincoln Memorial is in dispute. Hurok, of course, claimed credit, although the impresario's biographer, Harlow Robinson, traces the idea back through Washington bureaucracy to an aide in the office of the Assistant Secretary of the Interior, Oscar L. Chapman, who brought the whole business before his boss, Harold L. Ickes. By the time Ickes approved of the concert venue, the press had made the dispute a national issue, particularly after Eleanor Roosevelt publicly resigned her membership in the DAR on February 27 in her widely read "My Day" column. On the big day itself, a crowd estimated at 75,000 came to hear Anderson sing "America," "O mio Fernando" from Donizetti's La Favorita, Schubert's "Ave Maria," and three spirituals. The recital was prefaced with a speech by Ickes in which he described a "great auditorium under the sky where all of us are free" and referred to Anderson as a living example that "genius draws no color line." Anderson herself typically took no part in the controversy, later remarking, "I could see that my significance as an individual was small in this affair. I had become, whether I liked it or not, a symbol, representing my people. I had to appear."

In many ways Anderson was uniquely qualified for the part. Her appeal had always been more direct and universal than the aristocratic, slightly aloof manner that Roland Hayes cultivated, and her serene simplicity conveyed a quiet, almost elemental dramatic force that audiences everywhere seemed to find utterly hypnotic. Even after the war and into the 1950s, when her three distinctive registers audibly began to separate, few could resist her eloquence. And in 1955, when Rudolf Bing decided that it was high time for the Metropolitan Opera to open its doors to black singers (many had been appearing regularly at the New York City Opera by then), the one to lead the way could only have been Anderson, even if her voice was now severely reduced and sounding increasingly tremulous. Her few performances over two seasons as Ulrica in *Un Ballo in Maschera* ushered in a long period of vocal decline that ended only when she gave her final, sentimental recital in Carnegie Hall on April 18, 1965. If her voice and presence were found to be disappointing, no one, as a spiritual she sang that afternoon tells us, said a mumblin' word.

Anderson lived on another twenty-eight years, loaded with honors as "the Lady from Philadelphia," America's traveling goodwill ambassador, a special United Nations delegate, the subject of numerous television documentaries, and a beloved icon. It is difficult now to separate the voice and the woman from the almost marbleized monument that Anderson became long before she died in 1993. Years earlier, Vincent Sheean took note of the poetic simplicity that emanated from her and characterized her life. During a chilly winter afternoon, writer and singer discussed the operas she had studied but never sung, how she first heard Roland Hayes sing in her hometown church, and her early experiences learning lieder in Berlin. While they talked, Anderson was occupied building a fire in the living room fireplace, and as the conversation progressed, a deeply moved Sheean recalled later in a letter to her, "the fire grew and blazed, and I declare to you that I have never seen a fire more beautifully built or more beautifully inflamed."

Eighteen

Glamour

Time

⁓⁓⁓⁓⁓⁓⁓⁓⁓⁓⁓⁓⁓⁓⁓⁓⁓⁓⁓⁓⁓⁓⁓⁓⁓⁓⁓⁓

*D*uring the 1930s it soon became clear that the biggest singing careers were no longer being made exclusively in the opera house. Records and radio could instantly spread the news about a scintillating new vocal talent around the world, but an even more crucial tool in creating stars was talking pictures. Although a few singers who enjoyed extensive film careers did have major voices—Beniamino Gigli, Jarmila Novotna, Josef Schmidt, Richard Tauber, Jan Kiepura—neither a prodigious vocal endowment nor a dazzling vocal technique was needed for success on the silver screen. Personal charisma and physical charm were the vital ingredients, especially since moviemakers were more interested in narrative stories embellished by music rather than filming full-length operas.

America produced its share of popular singing stars after Lawrence Tibbett made *The Rogue Song* in 1929 and suggested the tremendous commercial potential of movie musicals, ideal escapist entertainment during the Depression. None of the baritone's subsequent films fulfilled the promise of that box office bonanza—for Tibbett, making movies was an early sideline in a career that eventually fulfilled itself in more conventional ways. His second Hollywood project, though—*New Moon*—costarred him with Grace Moore, by then a veteran of both musical comedy and opera, a crossover artist before anyone had thought of the term. That movie created little excitement, but Moore was back in Hollywood four years later to make *One Night of Love*, a sensation that "catapulted me into a new world. I suddenly discovered I was listed second among box-office stars that year, voted one of the 'ten most beautiful women in the world,' awarded a fellowship and gold medal by the Society of Arts and Sciences for furthering the cause of good music in the films. Everywhere my face was known. I was sitting on top of the world and frightened to death."

Recounting the adventures of a struggling young opera singer and her romantic relationship with a Svengali-like voice teacher, *One Night of Love* follows the typical rise-to-fame trajectory of the musical biopic, a formula that soon went stale. In 1934, though, it all seemed fresh and new, and the perky blond persona of Grace Moore, whose pretty soprano seemed just as comfortable selling a pop song as an operatic aria, captivated a public that had never set foot inside an opera house. The film drew crowds everywhere—when first released in movie-mad Berlin, it played in forty theaters simultaneously. Londoners also flocked to see it, and when Moore's Covent Garden debut in *La Bohème* was announced later that year, the house sold out on the spot. Hardly "frightened to death," Moore relished every moment of her new celebrity, even though the classical-music world, suspicious of her populist appeal right from the start, could never quite take her seriously again. Sir Thomas Beecham stalked out of Covent Garden after she sang Mimì's first-act aria, and music critics were positively outraged when they attended a Moore recital, only to hear a voice from the balcony cry, "Come on, Gracie, give us 'Minnie the Moocher'!"

Emma Abbott, though, would have understood and approved. Moore not only possessed Abbott's common touch, but she also combined numerous other qualities that stamped her as a distinctly American phenomenon: Farrar's glamour, Garden's ambition, Kellogg's vanity and social aspirations, Eames's hard-nosed practicality, Sanderson's pleasure in being noticed, and Nordica's capacity for hard work were all part of her makeup. The ingredients she lacked that might have made her a more significant artist were Nordica's vocal splendor and the burning commitment of a Fremstad. The polar opposite of an obsessed "theater rat" like Fremstad, Moore loved to perform, but she enjoyed herself even more offstage and could honestly say that her life began only when the curtain came down—few singers ever wasted less time worrying about the judgment of posterity. Although she attained stardom, Moore never possessed the distinctive defining quality that would have made her a legend, and as a result she was soon forgotten after her death in 1947. The fact that she never created any roles of her own, apart from those eminently forgettable film ingenues, or even managed to give her operatic work a personal stamp, partly explains Moore's bland posthumous image. She did work hard to improve her vocal impersonations of Tosca and Louise, the two heroines that became most identified with her toward the end, but even then most operagoers associated both roles with her two predecessors, Farrar and Garden—still very visible living legends at the time Moore arrived on the scene.

And yet as a media figure who personified what could be accomplished by appearing at the right time and in the right place, Moore was definitely a force to reckon with. Even her birthplace sounds made up by a Hollywood publicist: Slabtown, Tennessee, where Mary Willie Grace Moore was born on December 5, 1898 (early on she exercised a prima donna's privilege and advanced the year to 1901—a small difference but one that had the psychological advantage of putting her squarely in the new century). Grace actually spent her schooldays in nearby Jellico, where her father was a partner in a dry goods firm before buying his own department store in Chattanooga (where, as fate would have it, a black teenager named Roland Hayes from the other side of the tracks was also dreaming of a singing career). Brought up in a solidly middle-class Baptist family, the always willfully independent Grace was a constant worry for her parents, especially when she became fascinated by music and the opportunities it offered for glamour and escape from small-town Southern living. After attending a concert by Mary Garden in Washington, Grace knew exactly what her future held. She went backstage, marched up to the soprano, and told her that she, too, intended to be a singer, blurting out, "You are my goddess!" Patting the acolyte's cheek and no doubt recognizing a bit of herself in this determined youngster, Garden "looked at me with a long, penetrating glance and said, 'We shall meet again one day.'"

After that, her father categorically forbade his recalcitrant daughter to entertain even secret hopes of a singing career. That was enough for Grace, who borrowed $300 from her current boyfriend, left school, and headed straight for New York City. There she took lessons from Mario Marafioti, got a job singing in a Greenwich Village nightclub called the Black Cat, and promptly lost her voice. Marafioti prescribed three months of absolute silence and then restructured her soprano from scratch. When the time seemed right, he finagled his pupil, by then penniless, into *Suite Sixteen*, a revue headed for Broadway but doomed to die on the road. Before it did, Grace impressed enough influential showbiz backers with her big moment, "First You Wiggle—Then You Waggle," to land parts in various other regional shows until one of them—the 1920 edition of *Hitchy-Koo*—finally brought her to Broadway. That hit served as Moore's entree into café society, where "life became a whirl of wonderful people and new friends." Now she began to hobnob regularly not only with the fabled Algonquin Round Table wits but also with magical names from the world of classical music like Jascha Heifetz, Efrem Zimbalist, John McCormack, and Alma Gluck. Soon Franklin P. Adams was referring to her in his daily newspaper column as his "dream girl, Gracie Moore."

All this attention was very well, but Moore still dreamed of a career in opera and she was determined to get it. Putting Broadway on hold for the moment, she headed off to Paris for further study, first with Antonio Trabadello, Garden's preferred teacher, who said he would need five years to "make a great star out of you." Grace found that leisurely timetable unacceptable, and decided instead to entrust her voice to the less exacting Roger Thiral. Mostly, though, she rejoiced in a social whirl populated by a whole new set of rich friends—Noël Coward, Bea Lillie, Elsa Maxwell, the Cole Porters, and Condé Nast—who clearly found this bright, spunky American showgirl a refreshing addition to their expatriate circle.

Moore may have been a hedonist and a snob, but she was no courtesan, so when money started to run low again, she returned to New York and took Irving Berlin's offer of the starring role in his *Music Box Revue* of 1923. Between shows, she continued working on her voice with Marafioti and made two unsuccessful auditions for the Metropolitan Opera. Undiscouraged, Moore pocketed her Broadway earnings and went back to France for more fun and work, finding plenty of both on the Riviera, where Garden had recommended study with her old coach, Richard Barthélemy. By now Moore's love life had become "enormously successful," as she coyly put it, and there would be many more affairs before 1931, when she settled into what seemed to be a happy marriage with the Spanish film actor Valentin Parera. One of the most heatedly discussed Moore scandals of the twenties, in private anyway, played a key role in realizing her big ambition to sing at the Metropolitan. The soprano first flirted with Otto Kahn, the all-powerful president of the Met's board of directors, at a dinner party in 1924, and the enchanted Kahn immediately arranged to introduce her to Giulio Gatti-Casazza. The Met general manager was unimpressed, but Kahn persisted until, in 1927, he thought he heard a tremendous improvement in her vocal method and again petitioned Gatti. "I believe she is now the most promising young American artist in the field," Kahn wrote to Gatti, "and worthy of your serious attention . . . Her voice has developed greatly, and she is getting to be a lyric-dramatic soprano. I hope very much you will surely hear her when you visit Paris."

Gatti finally granted Moore a third audition on July 27, 1927—although she had to travel to Milan for the honor—and the Met manager agreed, reluctantly one suspects, to schedule her debut early the following year. A diplomat as well as a shrewd impresario, Gatti knew it was politic to indulge Kahn, who was not only president of the board but owner of 84 percent of the opera company stock. Gatti also must have figured that Moore's showbiz aura would be useful in luring new audiences to the Met, as long as he felt certain there was enough voice to preserve the dignity of the house. He gambled correctly—on the showbiz part at least. Moore's debut, as Mimì in *La Bohème* on February 7, 1928, made the newsreels; an advance article in *Collier's* suggested that this typically American success story would make a fabulous movie; and the audience, including a delegation from Tennessee led by both the state's senators, gave her twenty-eight curtain calls. Cheering from the director's box, Kahn proclaimed it the most important Met debut since Rosa Ponselle's.

The critics, of course, were less euphoric. By now resigned to chronicling the end of the vocal world as he had always understood it, W. J. Henderson patiently wrote the next day, "This soprano has a pretty voice of lyric quality, the color tending toward mellowness and capable of more warmth than the singer knew how to evoke from it. The range was sufficient for Mimi . . . In the third act, when she had rid herself of the nervousness, she sang her upper tones with more freedom and something more like focus . . . Two or three constrained gestures used over and over and an alternation of facial expression from smile to no smile seemed to exhaust her pictorial resources."

Henderson must have known that any reservations he might express wouldn't matter in the slightest. Moore certainly paid no attention to the critics—her whole career, she once remarked, was based on bad reviews. After two Met seasons, Hollywood had heard all about the company's glamorous new soprano, inquired about her availability, and Moore headed West, "delighted with the promise of a glimpse at fairyland and hopeful for a nibble at the gingerbread house." Unfortunately, her first movie vehicle—*A Lady's Morals*—found her awkwardly trying to impersonate Jenny Lind, a disaster followed a year later by the equally disappointing *New Moon*. Even worse, those two career setbacks were not offset by appearances at the Met, where, after her much-touted debut, Moore made no further headlines.

By 1932, deciding that her operatic career had reached a standstill, the soprano returned to Broadway for a short run in an English version of Theo Mackeben's *Die Dubarry*, followed by a tour on the vaudeville circuit. She was not abandoning opera at all, Moore told the press, but only working on a long-range plan that would "develop the movement and finesse that should go with any successful operatic singing"—clearly a wise move. Henderson had not been alone in commenting about the narrow expressive range of her acting, and a clumsy presence was also cited as the main reason for her two film failures. By 1934 and after two years of intensive stage work, the new, improved Moore felt ready to take a second "nibble" at the goodies way out West, and arranged a well-publicized engagement at the Hollywood Bowl in hopes that the right film folk would take notice. In addition to satisfying her vanity, she admitted, "financially I needed another hypodermic, since most of my accumulated savings had gone, as had everyone's, in the crash. So I determined to make this trip West, the first since my previous picture venture, another movie try. I dieted all that summer, bought new clothes, and saved the most knockout dress of all for my Bowl appearance. The silken bait took."

Indeed it did. After her triumph in *One Night of Love*, Moore had no further career worries for the rest of her life. Five subsequent films followed and each was a solid success, her opera career flourished at home and abroad, audiences filled the house, and Moore relished every moment: "Opera at the Met, with all its intrigues and complications. The Opéra Comique in Paris; the opera houses of Liège, Deauville, Cannes, Rouen, and Bordeaux; Covent Garden in London. Concerts in Sweden, Norway, Denmark, Holland, Rumania, Poland, Mexico, Brazil, and other

South American countries. Impromptu concerts everywhere—harmonizing with Charpentier in Monmartre, with Noël Coward as my accompanist in Paris, with Heifetz playing the piano for me aboard ship, barbershop quartets with Alex Woollcott and Charles MacArthur and Scott Fitzgerald . . . I have an incurable love of living. It's an aberration I was born with in Tennessee. It looks, from the way I have lived my life, as if I shall never get over it."

And she never did until that final concert tour and a fatal plane crash in Copenhagen on January 26, 1947, put an end to it. Even then, they said, Grace would have enjoyed the eight-column newspaper headline (if not the gruesome photos of her charred body), and receiving top billing over the Swedish Crown Prince, who perished at her side. Even the obituaries were not especially kind about a woman who was largely superficial, no more than a generic talent, and a flawed singer who, as Vincent Sheean once remarked, "lived in terror twenty-five hours a day over her own shortcomings." Grace would have pooh-poohed all that, having orchestrated her career to meet the public demand rather than high artistic goals. As for the critics, she proved once again that living well is the best revenge. Underneath all the tinsel, though, there seemed to beat a truly good heart coupled with a generous spirit. Dorothy Kirsten was only one of the many beginners she befriended, advised, and helped ease into their own careers—before her first La Bohème in New York, with the San Carlo Opera in 1942, Kirsten found a picture of Moore on her dressing room table inscribed, "To the other Mimi, and may she be greater."

Moore was also thoroughly aware of her limitations and seldom pressed her luck. She may have dreamed about singing Violetta, on the surface an ideal role for her, but she realized that such a demanding part, technically and emotionally, was beyond her. She also dropped such showy heroines as Juliette and Marguerite early on to concentrate on a handful of personality roles that required little or no florid technique: Tosca, Louise, Mimì, Fiora, and Manon. Even at that, her commercial recordings, the opera arias in particular, betray a pretty if strangely impersonal voice that never quite gels or functions smoothly; and she never did get the hang of correct French and Italian pronunciation. The Metropolitan Opera broadcasts from the 1940s of Montemezzi's L'Amore dei Tre Re and Charpentier's Louise, music she had dutifully prepared under the guidance of the operas' composers, give some indication of her purely erotic appeal and even her dogged attempts at self-improvement.

In the end, though, all that didn't really matter. As a singer, Moore always remained a provincial from Slabtown, but as a thirties media package she was in a class by herself.

If Gatti-Casazza was hesitant to take a chance on Moore in 1928, it was probably because he feared the possibility of winding up with a second Marion Talley, possibly the greatest American embarrassment in Met history. The daughter of a Kansas City telegraph operator who had been a childhood pal of Walter Chrysler, the automobile tycoon, Talley was considered a local prodigy good enough to audition for the Met in 1922, at the age of fifteen. Sensibly told by management to go away and study, Marion went off to Europe for a bit but soon returned to New York and made her presence known. When stories began to appear in the newspapers about an extraordinary teenage coloratura sensation—a new Patti, a new Lind—Gatti, Kahn, and assistant manager Edward Ziegler called a top-secret conference, overheard and later recorded by Helen Noble:

> "Yes, she could study longer, I agree."
> "True, she's very immature, but that will help to make her a sensation."
> "Those people out in Kansas are putting pressure on us in several quarters. They are getting impatient."
> "We need more full houses."
> "Shall we risk it?"
> Finally the decision: "Well, let's debut her. After all she does have a fine voice. When that little girl comes out on the stage and sings as well as she does, it will take them by storm. We'll fill the house this season. Let next season take care of itself."

What a contrast to Gatti's sly tactics in 1918 when he eased the unknown Rosa Ponselle onstage to startle the public without advance fanfare—but then, this time the Met was not in control of the publicity machine. Talley's debut was arranged for February 17, 1926, as Gilda in *Rigoletto*. As insurance, Gatti did not stint on her costars—Giacomo Lauri-Volpi, Giuseppe de Luca, and José Mardones, with Tullio Serafin as conductor—and as the day approached, the press beat the drum more loudly than ever. On the morning of the seventeenth, the *Evening Journal* ran an ecstatic advance story, along with photographs of Calvé, Patti, Sembrich, Nordica, Ponselle, and Garden, over a headline that read

TALLEY SHARES HONORS WITH PATTI AND CALVÉ IN SINGING AT EARLY AGE. Not only that, she was "the Little Red Riding Hood of the Met" whose "only vice was candy." Not surprisingly, a curious mob gathered in front of the Met hours before the performance, disrupting traffic and hoping for a glimpse of the prodigy. Meanwhile, a special train had arrived with a local delegation from Kansas City, and those who couldn't make the trip relied on father Talley, who had set up a special telegraph line in the wings in order to relay the exciting events to the folks back home. Amid all the hoopla, few seemed to notice that a singer who would be far more important to the Met—Lauritz Melchior—had made his debut that afternoon, as Tannhäuser.

Nothing short of total disaster could have spoiled Talley's big night, and as it turned out, the honor of Kansas City was not disgraced. The packed audience gave her a heroine's welcome, although they were probably not pleased to read the next day that Henderson had found her something less than a sensation. No singer, Henderson pointed out, could ever live up to such advance publicity, not even Patti, "no more than a name to most of the chatterers," he growled, a great singer "who never got a whole column after any of her New York appearances." He then went on to catalogue Talley's vocal problems. The middle voice was consistently hollow, pallid in tint, and tremulous. The tone spread and lacked the firm and vital quality necessary for expression. The upper range was pinched, shrill, and piercing. Musically she didn't seem to have a clue about "Caro nome," singing phrases as if they were a mere succession of notes. Of course, Henderson wrote, "the entire matter will be settled in the end by the jury—namely, the public—the opera-going public of New York, not Kansas City. If opera-goers like Miss Talley it will make no difference whether her singing is good or bad. About this more will be known when she sings before audiences which have not been excited by passionate publicity."

Henderson's self-control was admirable, if the miserable singing one hears on the few existing recorded documents of Talley's voice fairly represent her. Still, over the next three seasons the public flocked to see the phenomenon sing more Gildas along with Philine, Lucia, the Queen of the Night, Olympia, and other coloratura parts, despite a press that was becoming increasingly hostile. Just when Met management cautiously decided that the company's artistic honor required a renewal of her contract on a limited basis, Talley surprised everyone by announcing that she was leaving to devote herself to study—and just as well too, since at the age of twenty-one her voice was rapidly shredding. After a few years on the concert circuit, a brief radio series sponsored by NBC, an unsuccessful film *(Follow Your Heart)*, marriage with her voice teacher, and a few abortive attempts at an operatic comeback, Talley finally just faded from sight, dying in Beverly Hills, California, on January 3, 1983.

At least Talley lived out her life, made a great deal of money, and, as far as anyone can tell, drew some measure of satisfaction from it all. The Met's third media star of the Roaring Twenties had an unhappier time of it: Mary Lewis, a former *Ziegfeld Follies* girl who made her debut on January 28, 1926, as Mimì in *La Bohème*, amidst a barrage of publicity that was surpassed only by the hullaballoo Talley's debut would create just three weeks later. When it came to beauty contests, though, neither Talley nor Moore could compete with Lewis, who was lovingly described by an ever-attentive press: "In her hair is the light of the sun's glow, wavy, abundant and becomingly dressed. Her eyes twinkle more beautifully than any stars above, and to the rosebud mouth are added teeth which look as though she held a string of pearls between ruby lips."

And she could sing a bit too, although voice and musical talent were the least interesting aspects of Mary Lewis's sad tale. Born in Hot Springs, Arkansas, on January 29, 1897 (like Moore, the soprano advanced her birth date into the new century, but was content to leave it at 1900), Lewis was never quite sure who her parents were. There never was any father in the picture, and the woman who claimed to be her mother placed Mary in an orphanage when she was still a tiny tot. The girl ran away to fend for herself, living in squalor until she eventually rejoined her mother in Dallas. Mary was soon "saved" from all this when a Methodist missionary couple, Rev. and Mrs. Frank F. Fitch, decided to save her soul, a process that involved a considerable amount of beating, and probably worse, but they did bring a bit of music into her life. It was here that Lewis's official account of her early life began, although she left out the part about being taken into the home of H. F. Auten, a wealthy land developer in Little Rock, after running away from the Fitches. Auten made it possible for Mary, now an extremely attractive teenager, to have voice lessons, hoping to groom her into a star. Ever rebellious, the girl seemed more interested in dating than vocal exercises, and in 1915, when she was eighteen, Auten married her off to one J. Keene Lewis.

Somehow Mary survived that loveless match for three years before running away once more, this time to join a touring company of *Reckless Eve*. The next two years found her wandering up and down the West Coast doing everything from jazz singing to violin imitations until she had finally saved enough money to get to New York in 1920. Once in the center of the real entertainment business, Lewis knew what to do, and her beauty as much as her voice quickly landed her a job with Ziegfeld. Like Moore, Lewis found an influential voice teacher (William Thorner, Ponselle's early mentor) and made sure she caught the eye of Otto Kahn while singing at a socialite party. Kahn whisked her off to Gatti-Casazza, who, along with everyone else, was getting used to Kahn's tasty discoveries (wondering why she couldn't appear at the Met too, Fanny Brice naughtily sang in her first sound film, "And if my high C don't hand Otto a thrill, / I think my tra-la-la will"). Gatti predictably suggested that some European experience might help, and Lewis, who by now also had contacts abroad and knew how to use them, agreed. During her two years in Europe she sang leading roles in Monte Carlo, Vienna, and London. Franz Lehár did not succeed in getting her for his next operetta, but Vaughan Williams was luckier—Lewis created the role of Mary in the professional premiere of *Hugh the Drover*, after an elocutionist managed to tame her Arkansas twang.

Lewis returned to America with genuine European credentials and the prospect of her Met debut. Needless to say, the occasion was a press agent's dream. "The house was sold out—and that without subscription," wrote *The Musical Courier*. "It was an unusual audience for the Metropolitan. Everybody on Broadway from Laurette Taylor down to the chorus of the *Vagabond King* en masse was there . . . They applauded at every opportunity, and there were many. Time after time Miss Lewis took curtain calls, with her fellow artists or alone. Among the audience was an entire corps of professional and semi-professional baseball pitchers to judge by the accuracy with which innumerable bouquets of violets were hurled onto the stage." Henderson, once again trying not to appear the old curmudgeon, wrote that this latest debutante was at least creditable and then passed the backhanded compliment that the Musetta, a certain Elizabeth Kandt and apparently truly dreadful, made Lewis seem "better than she was." Olin Downes, however, did not mince words and proclaimed that any singer who displayed a voice this uneven had a considerable distance to go.

Lewis, of course, never went the distance. Whatever else Grace

Moore may have lacked, she had the smarts and the emotional equilibrium to deal with success once she had it in her hand. Although she managed to last five seasons at the Met, adding Nedda, Giulietta, Marguerite, and Micaela to her list of meager accomplishments, Lewis never again found a way to capture major attention and sustain her career. In 1927 she astonished many by marrying the German baritone Michael Bohnen, ten years her senior. It was a match made in heaven and she intended to be an old-fashioned wife, Mary told the press in an article coyly titled "Mary Lewis Wants Babies." What she actually got, however, was more grief and spankings. When Bohnen decided to live with the dancer La Jana in 1929, Lewis sued for divorce on grounds of cruelty. In New York, she said, Mr. Bohnen had tried to make her jump out of a fourteenth-floor window; in Berlin he knocked her against a door so hard that the door burst from its hinges; in Los Angeles she was slapped and slammed up against a wall. Small wonder that, during a *Carmen* performance at the Met on April 12, 1930, Lewis, as Micaela, was reportedly "drunk as a lord, staggering all over the stage." Eight days after that debacle, Lewis appeared in a Met concert and then her operatic career was over. She next tried Hollywood, but nothing came of several announced film projects, and a trip back to Europe also led to a dead end. Her financial problems were temporarily solved by marrying Robert L. Hague, a marine architect for Standard Oil and a millionaire, but every attempt at a comeback—opera, concert, radio, and even nightclubs—never seemed to impress anyone. Soon she and Hague were separated, and Lewis staggered on to the end, dying in New York's LeRoy Sanatorium on December 31, 1941, from what was variously described as a throat tumor, a gall bladder ailment, and a heart attack.

Marion Talley and Mary Lewis were soon gone and forgotten, and Giulio Gatti-Casazza had become wiser in the ways of modern American publicity. When his next crossover sensation appeared on the horizon, he applied the sage theatrical rule he had followed when Rosa Ponselle made her unheralded Met debut: the public and the press like to make their own discoveries. With Lily Pons it worked again when she sang Lucia at a Saturday matinee on January 3, 1931. Pons achieved a genuine artistic triumph and the Met suddenly had a surprise star coloratura who could go the distance, arriving exactly when she was desperately needed. Health problems had forced the popular Amelita Galli-Curci into early retirement, Talley had self-destructed, Toti dal Monte was not to New

York's taste, and Lina Pagliughi's embonpoint made her an impossible option. An obscure soprano from the French provinces, Pons was not exactly a sure bet at first, but her petite figure (ninety-eight pounds), dark good looks, and vocal brilliance immediately enchanted nearly everyone. Even Henderson had good words to say about "Mr. Gatti's little Christmas gift from a kind providence," who rejoiced in "a voice of pure and pleasing quality and a technique far above the slovenly average of today."

Pons was so delighted by her reception that she made the Met her home base, becoming an American citizen in 1940 but never losing her accent or the glamorous *avoir du chic* quality that made her so adorable to her new compatriots—indeed, that was an important part of her mystique and, during the thirties at least, one reason why she fit in so easily and naturally. She inevitably followed Grace Moore to Hollywood in 1935, and made three films in three successive years, all carefully tailored to play up her Gallic coloratura charms: *I Dream Too Much, That Girl from Paris,* and *Hitting a New High.* If none of them rivaled Moore's in popularity—let alone those of Jeanette MacDonald, by then the film capital's own self-created and undisputed reigning diva—they definitely enhanced her box office appeal at the Met.

As Irving Kolodin drily observes in his history of the Met, the immense favor Pons found there "remained well after the reasons for it had departed." Even Rudolf Bing, who had managed to dispose of many aging company favorites during his first years, had to wait until 1960 before "Darling Lily" could be persuaded to quit the Met for good. An exact contemporary of Moore's, born in 1898, Pons always shaved six years off her age and could probably have gotten away with six more. According to Helen Noble, who was present at her audition with Gatti, she looked sixteen even though by then she was double that figure and already well past the age of most coloratura virtuoso debutantes.

Once established, Pons knew exactly how to capitalize on her advantage. Opera stars of the thirties were expected to be chic and glamorous, and she had the physical goods, as well as the intelligence and imagination, to make the most of her assets. A little less than five feet tall, she was "one of the first to prove that a huge cage is not always necessary to hold a singing bird." That "cage" was always impeccably robed and coiffed, and the bound programs documenting her tours record the gown she wore at each concert: Valentina pink and red for Los Angeles, the brown and orange Schiaparelli for a *Telephone Hour* broadcast, the ivory Balenciaga for Portland and Seattle, a Ricci of white satin and black lace for Denver and St. Louis. On one of those early jaunts she was ostentatiously accompanied by a pet jaguar named Ita, which she later donated with great fanfare to the Bronx Zoo (and was much put out when the curator informed the press that the animal was really an ocelot). Her fame was such that a town in Maryland was renamed Lily-pons in her honor, and each Christmas she made sure that her cards were mailed from the hamlet carrying the proper postmark. Sometimes she would even grace Lilypons herself, driven to town in a limousine with custom license plates that read LP13, her lucky number. In 1938 she confounded the pundits by marrying pop-concert conductor André Kostelanetz—hardly a love match the gossips said, pointing instead to the fact that their joint appearances attracted even greater crowds and commanded huge fees. A doting press recorded her every move and the public eagerly lapped it all up. Risë Stevens, a young newcomer in the late thirties, recalls that Pons singlehandedly made life at the Met "a glamour time, when everyone dressed and was bejeweled. You were expected to be very glamorous. And we were."

Of course, the voice was also there, even if some heard it as only a decorative flourish. The tone may have been small, but its bright, pin-point focus—typically French in its metallic clarity and lack of vibrato—penetrated the huge Met auditorium right up to the top of the Family Circle. The upper register was especially brilliant (Pons always sang Lucia's Mad Scene transposed a tone higher for extra éclat), and that trait rather than her tippy-toe fioriture and attempts to cultivate a trill stirred Met patrons to a frenzy. Connoisseurs complained about her monochromatic tone and narrow emotional range, drawbacks that prob-ably explain why Europeans never really took to her, even when she was a youngster singing in her native France. The expressive monotony of her singing never troubled most Met audiences, for whom the gut appeal of sheer sound was always more important than interpretive niceties. Then, too, Pons was an excellent musician—as a girl her first ambition had been to be a pianist—and colleagues respected her for that.

Like Moore, Pons also had the wisdom to limit her repertory to what she did best. Lucia was her most frequent assumption—she sang the role no fewer than ninety-three times with the company—and in the early days her portrait of the mad Lucy was always delicate and precisely etched, for all of its one-dimensional character. During her twenty-nine seasons at the Met, Pons sang only nine other roles, and even her most ardent admirers began to tire of them, even when she went on the road. Appearing at the San Francisco Opera in 1946, she must have been distraught to open the *Chronicle* one morning to read a billet doux from the paper's music and art critic, Alfred Frankenstein: "I love you. My wife loves you. Everybody in San Francisco and the wife of everybody in San Francisco loves you like anything." But, the letter continued, "we want you to learn another role to replace that of Lakmé." Pons eventually complied six years later by offering her first Violetta anywhere to her San Franciscan fans, stunning them with four gorgeous gowns that reputedly cost $20,000. Significantly, she never sang the part anywhere else. Twenty years earlier Pons had wisely refused Gatti when he asked her to prepare *La Traviata* for her first Met season, well aware that the large-scale emotional response required for Verdi's consumptive heroine was beyond her.

Pons preserved her characteristic vocal quality right to the end of her life, but like all fashion plates, she eventually went out of style. By the fifties and the arrival of Maria Callas, Pons's canary-bird ways began to sound quaint in the bel canto repertory, and operas like *Lakmé*, perhaps her most successful vehicle, were no longer taken seriously. It seems unfair that memories of her Lakmé center mainly on her bare midriff—a "costume that left off at the delicate rib cage and resumed at the hips"—instead of how she sounded. Rather than her terminally chirpy Lucia, the various Met broadcasts of Delibes's opera remain the most flattering documents of her singing, as well as showing a response to a fragile heroine with whom Pons clearly felt an identity. The showy tintinnabulations of the famous Bell Song were of course what her fans waited for, and the energy, sparkle, and spot-on accuracy of her singing invariably brought down the house. Even more memorable, though, are the many bewitching cantabile passages, caressingly phrased and bewitchingly turned by a French-born singer still at least marginally in touch with her musical roots and an opera whose mood she perceptively felt as "one of mist and tenderness, of delicacy and withering ecstasy."

There is nothing more delicious than when glamour girls, especially those whose charms have been dignified by opera, let down their hair and behave naughtily. Pons understood that when she agreed to perform a pas de deux with Lauritz Melchior at a "Grand Operatic Surprise Party" for the departing Gatti on March 31, 1935, she dressed as an apache dancer and the hefty heldentenor in a tutu. As an encore, Pons was joined by two curvaceous colleagues, Gladys Swarthout and Helen Jepson, in a number titled "Woodman Spare That Trio," which actually turned out to be—yes—an all-star rendition of "Minnie the Moocher." For a moment it looked as though the blond and beauteous Jepson might join Pons and Moore as one of the Met's crossover queens, but her modest talents never quite pushed her far enough. Swarthout, on the other hand, would follow Pons to Hollywood that summer, and while the petite coloratura was on the RKO set making *I Dream Too Much*, the sultry mezzo-soprano was busy over at Paramount putting the finishing touches on *Rose of the Rancho*. Four more films followed in as many years—*Give Us This Night, Champagne Waltz, Romance in the Dark*, and *Ambush*—and by then Swarthout had joined an elite company as one of the Met's biggest moneymakers.

From this distance, the reasons for her celebrity seem a bit obscure until one sees her press photos as Carmen and Mignon or how provocative she looks in the trouser roles that showed off her figure, Siebel (*Faust*), Nicklausse (*Les Contes d'Hoffmann*), Stéphano (*Roméo et Juliette*), Pierotto (*Linda di Chamounix*), and Frédéric (*Mignon*). Swarthout was perhaps the most photogenic of them all with her large brown eyes, delicately shaped cheekbones, and raven hair parted in the middle and framing the face of a Ghirlandaio angel. Early on she, or more likely her managers, had the wisdom to choose Valentina to dress her exclusively, and no one, not even Pons, appeared in public looking more exquisitely gowned. Few seemed to mind that she lacked temperament or that her voice, although attractive and tastefully used, had no special distinctive character. Patti, according to Henderson, may have turned Carmen from a cat into a kitten, but Swarthout's Gypsy, noted Virgil Thomson, "never left the country club."

But then, Swarthout was basically a quiet, unassuming woman, and that quality was mirrored in her performing persona. If Pons and Moore determinedly orchestrated their own careers, the former with Gallic cunning and the latter with sheer gall, Swarthout more or less left the decision-making to others. Unlike many failed singers who take charge of their wives' careers, Frank Chapman was a master of commerce and publicity, and Swarthout adored him—not since Louise and Sidney Homer was there a happier operatic marriage. Born on Christmas day in 1900 in Deepwater, Missouri, the mezzo must have seemed like a bit of a mouse before Chapman came along. Even her debut role during the

1924–25 season with the Mary Garden–Cleofonte Campanini company in Chicago was the shepherd boy in *Tosca*, sung offstage. Still, she was a pretty mouse, and Garden, as usual, must have sensed something special, even if Mary couldn't quite put her finger on what it was. "Swarthout!" she suddenly cried one day at rehearsal for no apparent reason. "Where's Swarthout?" The young singer rushed in and meekly prepared to be scolded for God knows what. Ripping her mantle in two and extending half of it to the trembling tyro, Garden grandly proclaimed, "You shall be the next great Carmen!" Even with that confident prediction, Swarthout waited another fifteen years before making the attempt, logically enough back in Chicago, where she had started out. What Garden thought about the beautiful but bland Gypsy that finally did succeed her is not on record. She no doubt took note of the general public approval and held her peace.

That was in 1939, when Swarthout had already been at the Met for a decade and was at the peak of her popularity, although the country at large considered her mainly a screen star and a radio and concert personality. The canny management of Chapman would account for that— he knew very well where the big money was—not to mention Swarthout's diffidence about opera and her reluctance to experiment with roles she sensed were beyond her, another trait she shared with Pons and Moore. "Although there were many opportunities offered to me to sing roles such as Amneris and Santuzza, I always declined," she once said, looking back shortly before her death in 1969. "Anyhow, I did not have either the chest tones or the temperament for them. One must know one's own limitations, and in that era far more singers did." She even hated every moment of making films, and kept at it, presumably, for the boost it gave her career.

Like Ponselle's Carmen, Swarthout's was also costumed by Valentina, who certainly knew how to dress her divas in accordance with their impersonation. In contrast to Ponselle, a spitfire provocatively clad in masculine bolero trousers, "Miss Swarthout," the couturier recalled, "gave an image of tender and lovely femininity which led me to follow her type and personality." Tender and lovely is exactly how she looks in her immaculately tailored two-piece Gypsy ensemble, the perfect pictorial complement to the luscious sounds she makes on the March 15, 1941, Met broadcast of the opera. It's a gorgeous piece of singing, as are the highlights recorded commercially for RCA five years later, where the voice is always warm, pliant, and smoothly consistent. But Thomson was right. This well-bred Carmen could possibly be tempted by another martini, but never by Don José.

Moore, Pons, and Swarthout were made-in-America singers, no longer the anomaly such a phenomenon had been barely a generation earlier. Their glamorous images made them easily recognizable as such, and perhaps for that reason all three remained essentially local celebrities. Despite their fame and earning power at home, not one was successfully able to export her talents. As she readily admitted, Swarthout didn't even try—with her sharp understanding of her limitations, she must have known that what played well at home was strictly an American brand of glamour unlikely to appeal to Europeans. Just as much as the more flamboyant Moore and Pons, though, she was a crossover personality who moved comfortably between serious and popular culture in ways that would never be quite as available to American singers again. But for those attracted to the life, things were getting easier. By the 1930s, to become a classically trained singer was no longer quite the heroic gesture it had been for Farrar and Garden, let alone for Nordica and Kellogg. With the repertory now frozen and precedents set, a volatile and risky career choice was beginning to settle down into a profession.

The Yellow

Brick Brewery

~~~~~~~~~~~~~~~~~~~~~~~~~~~~~~

fter Caruso's death in 1921, no one of comparable vocal splendor appeared from across the sea to set the tone and influence the country's perception of what a "real" singer should be. True, the Metropolitan Opera was still filled with famous European stars who sang regularly and to great acclaim—Gigli, Martinelli, Jeritza, De Luca, Galli-Curci, Bori, Chaliapin, Rethberg, Melchior, Scotti, Pinza, Lauri-Volpi—but none captured the general public's attention as Lind or Caruso had. Indeed, the times seemed to indicate that the Met's crossover personalities now were Americans like Ponselle, Tibbett, and Moore, singers who not only had impeccable operatic credentials but also sang popular songs of the day in English, talked and acted like down-to-earth Americans, and cultivated a wide nonoperagoing public through radio and films.

There were definitely changes afoot, but only the Met's notoriously shabby yellow-brown exterior of dirty bricks suggested that it was still anything other than a glamorous European cultural citadel, both in spirit and in its daily operation, and as such not really available to ordinary folk. Even though the Met had been built on American soil, with American money, and for the pleasure of the wealthy Americans who paid for the privilege, the institution retained its sense of European exclusivity and remoteness. Ponselle, Tibbett, and, to a lesser degree, Moore proved that an exceptional American vocal personality could make an impact, but they were exceptions. The Met was still, in essence, a "European" opera company. Giulio Gatti-Casazza had been in charge since the board brought him from Milan's La Scala in 1908, and yet right up to the day of his departure in 1935, few had ever heard him utter a word of English. To ensure that he held the upper hand in artistic negotiations, all communication had to be made in either Italian or French, although it was generally suspected that Gatti understood and spoke English perfectly well and missed little, whatever the language. Even to his closest associates, the Met's immaculately dressed, sad-eyed general manager remained a man of mystery as he inconspicuously glided from one appointment to the next. No one dared question his authority, and why should they have? Under Gatti's aegis, not only did opera at the Met continue to glitter, but, until the crash, it also actually made money— the 1927–28 season was the all-time top, showing a profit of $141,000.

Gatti was never one to discuss his style of opera house management—even his memoirs, written in the 1940s, long after he had put New York behind him, are maddeningly tight-lipped—and much about the man and his long Met reign remain, if not a mystery, at least misperceived and misunderstood. A practical creature of the theater, Gatti had known Verdi and fully endorsed that composer's famous dictum that opera houses were meant to be full and not empty. Although many aspects of America's cultural scene must have puzzled him, he was hardly unaware of the country's musical potential and that tapping into it was not only a duty but also a necessity if a full-time, seven-days-a-week opera company isolated from the European mainstream was to function smoothly. Gatti never initiated a formal program to recruit American singers, but he hired dozens of them and heard hundreds more. "Perhaps you think it was difficult to get an audition at the Met?" asks Helen Noble, who helped field Gatti's correspondence. "Not at all. You had only to write a letter; you'd get a reply, a date would be set, and when you arrived the topmen of the Opera House were waiting to hear you."

Perhaps it was never quite that simple—obviously some sort of weeding-out process had to be established—and Gatti dealt ruthlessly with those who were given a chance but quickly indicated that further prominent exposure would be pointless. When Kathryn Meisle (1899–1970) arrived for her audition on Friday afternoon, December 20, 1929, no doubt some around the house hoped that the mezzo might one day succeed the beloved Louise Homer. Meisle had sung leading roles with the Chicago Civic Opera since 1923, her national reputation was growing, and she had a sheaf of glowing reviews from critics across the country. Despite all that, the anonymous Italian comment on her audition sheet—not in Gatti's hand (possibly written by Tullio Serafin or Vincenzo Bellezza)—is curt: "Good voice in the lower register, but of little extension—is more a contralto than a mezzo-soprano. Little temperament, mediocre diction." Eventually the Met decided to try out Meisle in 1935, after she had sung a bit in Europe, but not much came of it. After one Amneris, two Azucenas, and a handful of low-voiced Wagnerian goddesses, Meisle left the company to finish her modest career singing in less prestigious surroundings.

By the 1920s all aspiring singers like Meisle had two professional tools that the previous generation lacked, assets guaranteed to get people's attention if not necessarily the big career: enthusiastic press-agentry and heavy promotion from artists' managements. Even the humblest beginner had a specially prepared pressbook to help sell the goods, and the career director everyone wanted to be in charge was Arthur Judson, whose firm, Columbia Concerts Corporation, would later metamorphose into the all-powerful Columbia Artists Management, Inc. (CAMI). And of course the Met connection, if the singer was lucky enough to have even a tenuous one, was emphasized as often as possible. Meisle's 1935 pressbook is typical, containing a host of biographical articles that, hopefully, busy editors across the country would refer to and possibly even reprint in their newspapers when the singer came to town. In it we learn that Meisle is known to her public as "America's beloved singer"; rises daily at seven-thirty and likes long walks; attributes her success to four letters, W-O-R-K; is an enthusiastic fisherman and does surf-casting in hip-length rubber boots; likes gangster movies; enjoys housekeeping and admits that her Philadelphia pepper pot is hard to beat; often sings with and is a great friend of soprano Kirsten Flagstad (a clever stroke—Flagstad's 1935 Met debut was still hot news); and is "vibrant," "fascinating," and "radiating a warmth which makes audiences feel immediately at home."

None of that helped Meisle become a second Louise Homer, but she was positively a major player at the Met compared to some of her more obscure compatriots who were brought in toward the end of Gatti's regime, and always with great press fanfare. In January 1935, in the *New York World-Telegram*, a feature writer named Douglas Gilbert took note of the many new American faces in the country's premier opera house and decided that the phenomenon merited a series. Under the banner THEY MADE THE MET, he led off with Myrtle Leonard, "a sunny blonde, with a trim figure and a cello voice" and about to make her debut as La Cieca in *La Gioconda*. Gilbert was apparently unaware that young Leonard's role was that of an old blind woman, remarking that the company's latest discovery "represents, fetchingly, the modernistic trend opera is taking—easy-to-look-at singers. It is a curious and an interesting method of reviving a tottering art form." Leonard could not have hoped for a more flattering spread, although the grand predictions about her future never came true. She survived at the Met for two seasons, making a minuscule contribution: one more La Cieca, a Maddalena in *Rigoletto*, four performances as a minor Valkyrie, and a few concert appearances.

The next day it was Mary Elizabeth Moore's turn to be profiled in the *World-Telegram*, "a new coloratura and our own Lily Pons." The article describes her as a colleen of Cork ancestry, "a normal young woman" of twenty-two fond of simple pleasures like hiking around the Central Park reservoir. How Moore got a Met contract at all seems to puzzle even a drum-beating columnist like Gilbert, since her experience had been restricted to a few unremarkable performances with local opera companies. "There can't be anything to say about me," the soprano confides. "I have no background. I haven't sung in Europe. I wish I could say I had. I wish I could say that I'd sung about the country. I haven't. Everything in my life, practically, has taken place almost within a radius of thirty New York blocks." Despite her modest credentials, the terms of her "agreement with Gatti-Cassazza [sic] bind him to present her only in stellar roles—no walk-ons for Mary." Reading between the lines, Moore's friendship with Billy Guard, the Met's formidable press director, and the fact that Bruno Zirato, Caruso's former secretary, was her manager may help explain her good luck. Who knows what Gatti thought about it all, but he did honor the terms of Moore's contract. There were no walk-ons for Mary, but there were no leading roles either. After participating in three concerts during March 1935, her Met career was over.

Many other American singers came and went during Gatti's long tenure. Some, like Leonard and Moore, no doubt made it to the Met through personal connections, and few besides their patrons ever expected them to amount to much. Others, like Meisle, who had solid training and operatic experience, were put onstage in hopes of a miracle à la Flagstad or Pons. A select few stayed on and proved to be useful house singers, even if they never became stars. One of the most stalwart was the tenor Frederick Jagel (1897–1982), who made his debut as Radamès on Election Day, 1927, and remained to sing thirty-four more roles until retiring in 1950. Gatti first heard Jagel when the young tenor from Brooklyn was singing in Italy under the name Federico Jeghelli. "The Sphinx of Opera," as the Jagel family used to call him, presented a contract on the spot and was willing to wait a year until Jagel had worked off his European obligations. Gatti surely had no delusions about what he heard, but he likely knew how valuable such a voice might turn out to be: a lyric tenor with spinto potential whose sturdy, muscular vocal quality may not have been especially attractive but clearly promised staying power and reliability. Indeed, Jagel's moment of glory came during a 1938 Saturday matinee broadcast of *Aida* when Giovanni Martinelli suddenly succumbed to food poisoning in the middle of "Celeste Aida." Jagel, who was listening at home, instantly hopped into a cab and headed for the Met, stepping onstage as Radamès to pick up where Martinelli had left off less than twenty minutes earlier.

For all the American singers he may have auditioned and hired over the years, Gatti probably never expected them to compete seriously, or at least in quantity, with the stars he imported from Europe. After paying token homage in his memoirs to the few native artists who did make it big before and during his regime, Gatti concludes with one of his typical laconic comments: "I have found that American singers are full of good will and ambition." What Gatti actually seems to be saying is that singers like Lawrence Tibbett and Grace Moore may have meant more to the country at large than Beniamino Gigli and Maria Jeritza, but their fame had only a passing relevance to real opera, an art form that remained essentially European. Gatti surely left the Met even more convinced about that fact than when he arrived—after all, he had presented no fewer than fourteen American operas, more than any other Met general manager before or since, and not one had a lasting success.

When Gatti's chosen successor, Herbert Witherspoon, dropped dead in his office just months after taking up his duties in the spring of 1935, the Canadian tenor Edward Johnson suddenly found himself in the general manager's chair, and he was determined to carry out Witherspoon's dream of "Americanizing" the Met's roster. And to a large extent he succeeded. In achieving that goal, Johnson was greatly helped by the reduced fees the company now paid—Gigli was only the most prominent foreign star who refused to take a salary cut and returned to Italy—and, a few years later, by World War II, which effectively put a five-year moratorium on importing new singers from Europe.

Born in 1878 in Guelph, Ontario, Johnson was probably the most famous tenor that North America had produced to date, although one suspects that his success had more to do with vigorous industry, musical intelligence, a strikingly handsome presence, and a personable nature (everyone always called him Eddie) than a glorious vocal endowment. His first big success came in 1908 as Niki in a Broadway production of Oscar Straus's *A Waltz Dream*. Johnson could easily have continued as a musical matinee idol, but opera was his goal and he set off for Italy, where he made his debut in Padua in 1912 as Andrea Chénier, singing under the name Edoardo di Giovanni. The Italians were delighted, and quickly put him to work learning and singing a huge repertory that included most of the standard Verdi-Puccini roles as well as a host of novelties and world premieres. His most prestigious success was as Parsifal in the first Italian production of the opera, at La Scala in 1914.

In 1919 Johnson returned to make his American opera debut in Chicago, where he spent three seasons sparring with Mary Garden, who declared war by refusing to sing Mélisande opposite the Pelléas of "that young Canadian upstart from Italy." In 1922 Johnson began his long association with the Metropolitan as Avito in *L'Amore dei Tre Re*. He impressed Richard Aldrich as "a tenor who is something more than a voice, who is an artistic personality." Over the years Aldrich tempered his praise somewhat, and probably got closer to the truth when he observed, "If his singing does not at all times show all the refinements of vocal art, his straightforward and energetic style, his discernment of the emotional and dramatic significance of the music he deals with and his skill in presenting it impressively make his performances interesting and often engrossing." The tenor's recordings from this period are neither plentiful nor especially distinctive—clearly, during his thirteen seasons as a Met leading tenor, Johnson was valued for getting the job done crisply and professionally, but he lacked the vocal flair and personal magnetism to become the tenorial equivalent of a Ponselle or a Tibbett. His best role was considered to be Pelléas (*pace* Garden), which he sang thirty-two times between 1925 and 1935 opposite the

Mélisande of Lucrezia Bori. As long as that attractive team appeared in it, Debussy's notoriously hard-sell opera very nearly became a Met repertory piece.

When the Met fell into his care, Johnson was further encouraged to Americanize his new charge by a three-year $150,000 guarantee from the Juilliard Foundation. Among its stipulations, the grant required the establishment of a supplementary spring season of opera in English at popular prices, performances that would give young American singers the opportunity of appearing on the Met stage. Johnson embraced that idea enthusiastically—he even hoped to develop a touring company to bring opera to the heartlands, a project eventually deemed impractical due to the Met's precarious financial situation. The founding of the Metropolitan Opera Guild in 1935 and its numerous "Save the Met" campaigns over the next decade also gave the company an increased national profile, as did the continuing Saturday afternoon broadcasts and the annual Metropolitan Opera Auditions of the Air, inaugurated in 1937 and soon to produce important talent.

American singers may have been a priority during the fifteen-year Johnson regime, but in other areas the company left much to be desired. There were seldom more than two new productions each season, the sets of existing operas became threadbare, stage direction was virtually nonexistent, and the general manager himself, although popular with most everyone around the house, could hardly be called a skilled administrator. Like many singers who try to run opera companies, Johnson had difficulty saying no to old colleagues, or even taking a strong stand on issues that would be in their own best interests—Ponselle's Met career might well have been extended or eased into new directions had Johnson known how to handle this delicate temperament. Instead, "Eddie" smiled at everyone and left Edward Ziegler, a holdover from the old regime, to do the hatchet work. "You could hardly get a definite Yes or Nay out of Eddie," recalled one associate. "He was charming, charming at all costs—too damned charming!"

Johnson's lackadaisical management style may have infuriated many, and day-to-day performance standards could be alarmingly impromptu, but American singers were now gaining access to the Met more than anyone had ever dreamed possible. The 1935–36 season began, typically, with a sequence of nine different operas in seven days—one wonders how any kind of quality control could be applied under such a crushing production schedule—and Johnson filled the casts with Americans that Gatti had bequeathed to him, as well as introducing several of his own choosing. The new production of *La Traviata* on opening night featured Richard Crooks and Lawrence Tibbett (Lucrezia Bori, of course, sang her signature role of Violetta), and making her debut as Flora was Thelma Votipka, the first of 1,420 performances with the Old Met until that institution retired in 1966. The next evening Crooks traveled with the company to Philadelphia for a Cavaradossi in *Tosca* with John Charles Thomas as Scarpia. The first *Faust* of the year was distinguished by Charles Kullman's debut in the title role, with Edith Mason as Marguerite and Richard Bonelli as Valentin.

Others who set the American tone of Johnson's first week were Frederick Jagel and Helen Gleason in *La Bohème;* Queena Mario as Gretel; Julius Huehn as the Herald in *Lohengrin* and Chase Baromeo as Ramfis in *Aida,* both house debuts. Just to drive the point home, the traditional Sunday night concert that week was an all-American affair with the exceptions of Carlo Morelli and Marjorie Lawrence, an Australian soprano who had just made an impressive debut as Brünnhilde in *Die Walküre*—even Myrtle Leonard was given another break, singing Dalila's "Mon coeur s'ouvre à ta voix." Other Americans who appeared later in the season to begin respectable careers at the Met and elsewhere included Josephine Antoine, Dusolina Giannini, Norman Cordon, and Sydney Rayner. The names of Natalie Bodanya, Lucielle Browning, Hilda Burke, Susanne Fisher, Emily Hardy, Anna Kaskas, Ruby Mercer, Helen Olheim, Maxine Stellman, Charlotte Symons, Rosa Tentoni, Joseph Bentonelli, Wilfred Engelman, Dudley Marwick, Nicholas Massue, Hubert Raidich, George Rasely, and Joseph Royer—all debutants in 1935–36—are more or less footnotes to Met history, but their presence testifies to Johnson's determination to give the company a strong American vocal character.

One singer during the new general manager's first years at the helm came closer than Johnson himself to becoming the tenor counterpart of Ponselle and Tibbett: Richard Crooks (1900–72) from Trenton, New Jersey. He never quite evolved into the same sort of megastar, mostly because of his modest manner and a stage presence that was more pleasant than dramatically riveting—from his photographs at least, Crooks always gave the impression of a friendly insurance salesman. But the voice was by far the most attractive among the American tenors of his generation, combining the sweet Irish lilt of a John McCormack with the weightier accents of a German lyric. Indeed, it was in Germany that he began his operatic career in 1927 after several busy concert seasons as a promising young oratorio and song recital specialist in New York, where he was a favorite with Toscanini, Walter, and Mengelberg—under the latter's baton, Crooks participated in the American premiere of Mahler's *Das Lied von der Erde*.

Crooks did not arrive at the Met until 1933, when he made his debut as Des Grieux in *Manon* and, according to a newspaper report the next day, the sheer beauty of his voice won him an unprecedented thirty-seven curtain calls. The Massenet opera was the tenor's most frequent assignment during his eleven Met seasons, with Faust, Alfredo, and Don Ottavio not far behind. Crooks was often asked but he was far too sensible to gamble his voice on Wagnerian roles such as Lohengrin, Walther, and Parsifal in a house as large as the Met—and he agreed to risk Cavaradossi on just two occasions. He might have gotten away with more, since his tenor was "notable for its mingled sweetness and virility," as one critic accurately described it, although there were limitations at both ends and ringing top notes were always a problem until Crooks learned how to produce them as cleverly mixed head tones. Like his slightly older contemporary John Charles Thomas, Crooks became a national celebrity mainly through his huge number of ballad recordings and hundreds of radio broadcasts, especially as a regular guest on *The Voice of Firestone* beginning in 1932. It was during a 1945 Firestone program that Crooks lost a top note—muscular support had become increasingly difficult after a series of operations for peritonitis—and he retired on the spot.

Charles Kullman (1903–83) was another American tenor who got his start singing the standard repertory in German translation between 1931 and 1936, first in Berlin and later at the Vienna State Opera. He also shared much of Crooks's lyric repertory, including Mahler's *Das Lied von der Erde*, which he sang and recorded under Bruno Walter. By the time he reached the Met in 1935, though, Kullman had already lost much of the radiance and flexibility that had made him such a favorite in Vienna, qualities abundantly evident on a series of discs he made there for the Columbia label in the early thirties. Even as his voice became grainier and more opaque over the years, Kullman was appreciated for his musicianship and dependability. He remained a useful member of the company for twenty-five seasons, first in roles ranging from Faust and Rodolfo to Walther von Stolzing and Don Ottavio, and later as a character tenor content to swap Pinkerton for Goro and, in *Boris Godunov*, Grigori for Shuisky.

Three important American singers who came to prominence during the early Johnson years never quite thrived at the Met to the degree that their talents might have suggested. The initial stumbling block facing Rose Bampton (1909–   ) was one of voice register. While puzzling out whether she was a soprano or a mezzo, Bampton spent her first five years with company singing lower parts—her debut was as Laura in *La Gioconda* on November 28, 1932. Despite warm praise from Henderson, who heard a "rich, powerful, sensitive mezzo-soprano . . . with a delightful smoothness throughout the scale," the only big role to come her way was Amneris and she felt underemployed. Besides, at the back of her mind was a comment Serafin had made after her Met audition: "Rose, when you are going to do Aida, no matter where you are, you must come to me to prepare it." A few years later Bampton took Serafin up on his offer, traveling to London to learn the role with the Maestro. After that, the Met put her right to work.

At first it was hoped that Bampton might help fill the breach left by the departure of Ponselle and, later during the war years, of Flagstad. That was a great deal to expect of any singer, and soon Bampton found her vocal talent being spent recklessly, another besetting sin of the Johnson era. In January 1940 she was called upon to sing Aida on the nineteenth and Amneris on the twenty-sixth. During the first months of 1943 she was thrown on the stage to sing Elisabeth, Elsa, and Kundry, Wagnerian parts she was performing for the first time. Small wonder that her voice began to sound thin and pinched up top, while the richness and smoothness Henderson noticed in her lower register had long since departed—the decline is documented on recordings she made as early as 1940. Perhaps Bampton was unwise to make the switch at all, but the Met's irresponsible exploitation of a potentially valuable singer could only have exacerbated her vocal problems. The fact that her husband, Wilfrid Pelletier, was a house conductor throughout her seventeen Met seasons only makes the situation all the more deplorable.

It has been said that when Dusolina Giannini (1902–86) finally arrived at the Met to sing Aida in 1936, the bloom was off her voice, which critics faulted for having an unpleasant edge and quaver. Perhaps so, but since Giannini continued to be extravagantly admired by vocal connoisseurs right up to her farewell recital tour in 1956, there must have been another reason for her inability to impress New Yorkers, and it probably arose from Met audiences' traditional preference for the sort of plush sounds produced by Flagstad and Ponselle. Johnson was surely aware of that fact, but he was eager to discover his own Rosa Ponselle, and Giannini, although already well known and experienced by 1936, looked promising and came from a similar Italian-American background. But Ponselle, whose family was not musical, more or less stumbled into a singing career and conducted it mainly by instinct, while Giannini inevitably grew into hers while obtaining all the sophisticated technical and musical grooming her older colleague lacked.

Both Giannini's parents were musicians and she took her first voice lessons from her father, who ran his own small opera company in Philadelphia and cast Dusolina as La Cieca in *La Gioconda* when she was barely twelve years old. It was Ferruccio Giannini, the singer explained, who taught her how to place her voice forward in the sinus cavities (or the "mask" in vocal parlance) to give the tone maximum presence, definition, and resonance. That, and subsequent technical polishing with Marcella Sembrich, resulted in a sound as grandly scaled and wide-ranging as Ponselle's but much brighter and more sharply etched—no doubt one explanation for the "quaver" and "edge" critics thought they heard in her 1936 Aida. And yet Giannini's rendition of "Ritorna vincitor," as sung on a February 16 radio broadcast four days after her Met debut, is imposing precisely because of its secure attack, controlled line, and fierce commitment.

Johnson must have been disappointed by the lukewarm reaction to Giannini, especially since he wanted to revive *Norma* and had no one to sing it—Flagstad had learned the role but decided that Bellini's Druid priestess was not for her, and Ponselle's top could no longer be trusted. Giannini, he thought, would save the day, but the performances were canceled at the last minute, apparently because of rehearsal disagreements between the soprano and the conductor, Ettore Panizza—a shame, considering the stunning "Casta diva" she recorded in 1931, so different from Ponselle's in its steely glint and smoldering intensity. Giannini's Met career never amounted to much—five performances each of Aida, Santuzza, Tosca, and Donna Anna over six seasons, and to small acclaim. Elsewhere, though, she was better appreciated, especially at the

Salzburg Festival (Don Giovanni under Walter and Falstaff with Toscanini), as a welcome guest in opera houses throughout Europe, a star of the first New York City Opera season in 1944, and as a recitalist in Germany before and after the war. German lieder, in fact, had long been a Giannini specialty, one that she cultivated with impeccable musicianship, sophistication, and expressive intelligence.

Jennie Tourel (1900?–73) had an even briefer Met career than Giannini's—in fact, her major contribution to America's musical life was not to be in opera at all and will be considered elsewhere. No one really knows for sure the details of Tourel's origins and upbringing—the singer herself enjoyed giving conflicting accounts—but the generally accepted theory was that she was born Jennie Davidovich in Vitebsk, Belorussia, and fled from the Revolution in 1918. Her family eventually settled in Paris, where Jennie studied with Reynaldo Hahn and Anna El Tour (surely the source of her professional name, although Tourel always denied it), and appeared at the Opéra-Comique as Carmen, Cherubino, Charlotte, and Bizet's Djamileh. In the mid-1930s worsening conditions in Europe brought Tourel to the United States via Canada, and North America became her home base for the rest of her career.

When Tourel made her Met debut on May 15, 1937, as Mignon— the second and last special spring season designed to try out new American talent—she was clearly no beginner. Nor does she sound like one. Some said that the voice seemed small for the house, and perhaps it was, but an aircheck of the occasion reveals a thrilling piece of singing. The vibrant voice, with its familiar intriguing tang and pungency already securely in place, ranges seamlessly and easily over more than two octaves—Tourel takes all the soprano options, with stunning results—and in every measure there is the distinctive musical and interpretive intelligence that discerning American audiences would soon learn to treasure. She gave only a handful of performances with the company over the next decade—as Rosina, Carmen, and Adalgisa—which perhaps reflects more on Met management policies than the worth of a singer soon to be recognized as a very singular artist.

There was another debut that spring season—on May 12, three days before Tourel's—and by a soprano who was to become far more important to the Met. Helen Traubel, in fact, was one of the first singers to be known later as a "Johnson Baby," an odd way to think of Traubel, perhaps, already a very large woman with a very large voice when she sang

Mary Rutledge in the world premiere of Walter Damrosch's eminently forgettable *Man Without a Country*. But she introduced a generation of important American singers who centered their activities around the Metropolitan Opera and would dominate the musical scene for more than two decades.

Nineteen

Johnson Babies: I

~~~~~~~~~~~~~~~~~~~~~~~~~~~~~~~~~~~~

*B*y the end of World War II, Johnson had achieved his goal to Americanize the Met, if only by default. Due to wartime realities, the roster was now overwhelmingly dominated by American voices, versatile singers who could move easily from one *Fach* to another. And most had learned their craft without making the obligatory trip to Europe for artistic finishing. Indeed, there was no longer any need to. Once a singer had been signed up by the Met, the company's musical staff of European refugees provided all the necessary background instruction. Never before had the company been blessed with such a density of distinguished conductors—Bruno Walter, Sir Thomas Beecham, Fritz Busch, and George Szell were only the most prominent—and a Met contract guaranteed coaching with an array of musicians versed in European operatic traditions and styles. It was a unique moment in Met history, and unfortunately one destined not to last.

Of course, any American who expected a Metropolitan engagement to be a passport to riches was soon disabused of the notion. When twenty-three-year-old Astrid Varnay arrived in 1941 to sing a steady Wagnerian diet of Sieglindes, Brünnhildes, Elsas, and Elisabeths, she started out with a weekly salary of $75. Only established box office draws received the top fee of $1,000 a performance, and even singers who qualified for that princely sum could scarcely live extravagantly if they sang only at the Met—few made more than twenty appearances during the course of a thirty-week season, including the annual spring tour. Despite the bad pay, the prestige of the Met was still crucial if a singer hoped to make up the difference by breaking into the lucrative concert-and-radio circuit, and later television. Most took full advantage of their opportunities to do so, none more eagerly or more controversially than Helen Traubel. In fact, the Met—or, more accurately, its new general manager in 1950, Rudolf Bing—eventually decreed that her "slumming" tarnished the dignity of the house and was no longer to be tolerated. A later generation may wonder what all the fuss was about when Traubel began to sing in nightclubs and perform comic routines on the radio with Jimmy Durante, or, after putting opera behind her, played a heart-of-gold madam in Rodgers and Hammerstein's *Pipe Dream* on Broadway and camped it up in a Hollywood film opposite Jerry Lewis. Later opera stars would move easily between pop and classical genres without the Met so much as raising an eyebrow, but for Traubel that crossover dream, along with a waning ability to sustain the heroic repertory that had always been her specialty, led to the end of her opera career.

Had she handled herself differently, Traubel might have had the best of both worlds, but she was a complex woman whose motives were never entirely clear, not even to herself. Few singers with a comparable vocal endowment—and few would deny that this voice ranks among the great Wagnerian sopranos of the century—have ever moved quite so slowly into the limelight. By the time Traubel sang her first Wagner role at the Met, Sieglinde in 1939, she was already forty and had been singing in public for nearly twenty-five years, mostly in her hometown of St. Louis. During that time, friends, family, and admirers continually urged her to move forward more aggressively, but Traubel always gave the same response: "I'm not ready." Some would cite her attitude as that of a sensible singer who knows her voice and how to pace it, but on closer examination one begins to see a woman whose lack of ambition and chronic indolence dictated her career moves rather than shrewd self-management. "Her favorite posture was sitting and her favorite activity was eating," sourly observed Erich Leinsdorf, who conducted many of her 168 Wagner performances with the Met.

"I knew what I was," Traubel writes early on in her autobiography, *St. Louis Woman*. "I knew what I wanted to be; and I knew what I hoped to become and what I would work myself to death to become. I was to be a singer. Not particularly a great singer, perhaps, but one to whom everyone would be glad to listen and from whom the world could draw some happiness." That, more or less, states the whole truth of the matter, but one does wonder if Traubel ever knew what she really wanted. She was an extremely stubborn woman, but the trajectory of her career hardly resembles the ferocious goal-oriented paths of such ambitious earlier American singers as Nordica, Farrar, and Moore.

Singing always came easily and naturally to her as a girl in South St. Louis, where she enjoyed a happy but unremarkable childhood living over her father's drugstore in the city's German section. She may never have had a career at all had she not fallen into the hands of Mrs. Louise Meyerson Vetta-Karst, a birdlike woman with an explosive temper and locally famous as the most exacting singing teacher in town. At first Vetta-Karst charged the Traubels $5 a lesson to train their daughter, but soon, after she realized the vocal potential in the youngster's throat, the lady refused to take a cent—and not because the family was needy. "Clara," she told the girl's mother, "I want to control Helen. I want a hold over her. If she feels she is obligated to me, I can hold her better . . . It will be a very long pull before she can sing—I mean, before she can sing the way I want her to." Vetta-Karst was right. Traubel took a lesson with her mentor almost daily for the next seventeen years and she rather seemed to enjoy being kept on a short leash. "My God, you big cow," the teacher once shrieked at her teenage pupil, already a buxom lass, "how can you do that? Don't cocky-doodle-doo!" Helen would often dissolve in tears, sobbing, "I can never satisfy you!" but Vetta-Karst always shot back, "When you can satisfy me you won't need me any more!" It's doubtful that Traubel ever satisfied such a taskmistress, who was still looking after the singer years later in the 1940s, when Traubel had become the Met's indispensable Wagnerian soprano.

Traubel's formal debut took place in 1923, singing the finale of Mahler's Fourth with the St. Louis Symphony led by Rudolph Ganz, and she soon was a local celebrity. Two years later, when Ganz was engaged to conduct a concert at New York's Lewisohn Stadium, he brought Traubel along to sing the Liebestod from *Tristan und Isolde.* Her voice so impressed conductor Walter Damrosch and manager Arthur Judson that they urged her to study in Europe. Traubel not only declined that suggestion but also refused to audition for Giulio Gatti-Casazza when the call came. Instead of seizing her advantage, the soprano returned to St. Louis to continue her comfortable life of song in the city's churches, synagogues, and concert halls, earning $3,600 a year, with an occasional extra $100 for singing at funerals. There was also a husband, a car salesman named Louis F. Carpenter, whom Traubel had wed in 1922, but apparently the marriage had long since cooled into habit and friendship. In any case, it was back home in St. Louis that Damrosch discovered her for a second time, in 1934, when he arrived to conduct the city's orchestra and once again Traubel's Liebestod amazed him. Damrosch was composing his Met commission, *The Man Without a Country,* and although the cast was originally all-male, he decided to write in the part of Mary Rutledge especially for Traubel—who of course told him that she wasn't ready (by then she was thirty-five). Two years later, when the opera was finished, she reluctantly agreed to come to New York for a read-through of the score and a formal audition for Met management with arias from *Lohengrin* and *Tannhäuser* ("Good voice but it diminishes in top register" was the comment—a short top was in fact Traubel's bane throughout her career and must partially explain her chronic lack of confidence). Damrosch's opera was found acceptable, the Met was willing to hire his protégée to sing in it, and Traubel's major career looked as if it had been launched at last.

But no. It was clear to all even then that Traubel was fated to sing primarily Wagner, and in 1937 the Met's needs in that area were already sufficiently tended to by Kirsten Flagstad, with the able assistance of Lotte Lehmann, Marjorie Lawrence, and Elisabeth Rethberg. After four performances of Mary Rutledge in Damrosch's tepidly received opera, no further calls from the Met were forthcoming. This time, though, Traubel did not head straight back to St. Louis. In 1936 she had met her future second husband, William Bass, a happy-go-lucky sort who later became his wife's business manager and whose temperament matched hers to a tee, and New York was beginning to look like home. After securing divorces from their respective first mates, Bass and Traubel were married in Weehauken, New Jersey, in October 1938, and found themselves flat broke with no prospects—typically, the soprano had torn up a $10,000 contract for radio appearances on NBC because, she said, "I loathed the way I sounded."

By 1939, even Traubel must have decided that, at long last, she was ready. She rented Town Hall, hired the distinguished pianist Coenraad Bos, bought a $16 dress, learned a program of songs and arias, and gave a recital. The next morning all the papers contained raves—"one of the finest voices to be heard anywhere today" was the general tenor of the reviews—and by 11 A.M. Traubel had received a call from Edward Johnson, who had a Met contract waiting for her in his office. When she learned that her formal Wagnerian debut was to be Venus in *Tannhäuser*, Traubel said "No, thank you" and walked out—a love goddess who wears diaphanous gowns and exercises power over men, she correctly reasoned, was not for her. A week later she sang the Liebestod under Fritz Reiner's baton on *The Ford Sunday Evening Hour* radio program, and a few days after that the Immolation Scene with John Barbirolli and the New York Philharmonic, also broadcast. By now the press was in an uproar. "Why isn't Traubel at the Met?" the critics screamed. There was another call from Johnson, who offered Venus once again and with even greater enthusiasm. Traubel said no again and with even greater firmness, demanding Sieglinde for her "real" Met debut—it was, in fact, the only Wagner role she knew, and Johnson was well aware of it. "You don't seem to understand, Helen," Johnson purred in his most charming manner. "All I have to do is ring bells and I would have six Sieglindes in here in a moment. Why should you be the seventh?" Traubel insisted. Soon, even Johnson lost his temper, and the interview ended when Traubel told him, "in furious and level tones," exactly what he could do with the Metropolitan Opera. Since it was clear by now that Traubel would have to sing *something* at the Met, and soon, a third-party mediator was summoned and the stubborn soprano finally got her way: Sieglinde it was to be, on December 28, 1939, with Kirsten Flagstad, Lauritz Melchior, and Friedrich Schorr.

Despite good notices, Traubel made little progress during her first couple of Met seasons, but in 1941 all that changed. In April, Flagstad returned to Norway to be with her husband for the duration of the war. Two months later Marjorie Lawrence was stricken with polio while singing in Mexico City. Lehmann and Rethberg were clearly reaching the end. For the next dozen years Traubel sang all the most strenuous Wagnerian roles—Isolde, Brünnhilde, Elsa, Elisabeth, and, briefly, Kundry—

with only young Astrid Varnay to spell her. The top Met fee of $1,000 was hers, *Time* put her on its cover in 1946, Adrian of Hollywood designed all the flowing robes she wore onstage ("We attract as little attention as possible to her bust," said Adrian; "her great bulk is disguised by making lines run up and down"), recording and radio dates were plentiful, there were frequent invitations to the White House to hobnob with fellow Missourian Harry Truman—Traubel even acted as an advisor to the President's vocally undernourished daughter, Margaret, in her pathetic attempts to launch a singing career. Traubel's public fight with Bing in 1953 made the front pages ("Nobody knows the Traubel I've seen," the Met's general manager wryly observed to the press) and helped launch her new pop career with great fanfare and higher fees than the Met could ever hope to offer. With all this attention, the thought of singing opera in Europe never tempted her, and throughout her life Traubel remained essentially an American phenomenon.

Traubel's posthumous image is not a flattering one. As an opera singer she, possibly more than any other American who found national success in the genre, helped create the popular image of the enormously fat, winged-helmeted Valkyrie as a symbol of grand opera in all its silliness. That, perhaps, was not entirely her fault, but after she left the Met and plunged deeper into lowbrow entertainment, Traubel started looking even more ridiculous as she mocked her own operatic past in her nightclub acts, on television with Jimmy Durante, and as a regular on radio's comedy show *Duffy's Tavern.* Nor did playing Katisha opposite Groucho Marx's Ko-Ko in *The Mikado* on television and "ballin' the jack" with José Ferrer in the 1954 film *Deep in My Heart* add much distinction to her legend—other older opera singers made the transition into pop culture with far more grace and dignity and still reached a broad-based audience. Beyond that, although there was plenty of voice left, at least in the middle register, Traubel never really showed such a natural affinity for delivering a pop song as did her younger colleagues Risë Stevens, Eleanor Steber, and Dorothy Kirsten. Her films are not especially amusing either, even as quaint period camp, and her performance in Rodgers and Hammerstein's *Pipe Dream* skirted disaster. *Variety* found Traubel's work in the 1955 musical to be "hearty and modestly amusing," but she "never establishes the sort of theatre-electrifying magnetism expected of a major star." She also took a positively perverse pleasure in posing for embarrassing publicity shots—the worst must be the series of photos that show the aging Traubel dusting off the plate and standing "at bat" for one of her favorite hometown baseball teams, the St. Louis Browns. It's hardly surprising that after the publication of *St. Louis Woman* in 1959—a diva apologia whose special pleading reveals more damaging information about the singer than she perhaps realized—Traubel and Bass simply faded away into the obscurity of their Santa Monica, California, retirement home, where the soprano died in 1972 at the age of seventy-three.

Luckily, for Traubel and for us, many of her Met broadcasts from the forties survive. On virtually all of them she sounds spectacular, and the best indicate exactly why wartime audiences still clamored for Wagner despite the absence of Flagstad and the presence of considerable anti-Axis feeling (Puccini's *Madama Butterfly*, after all, had been banned for the duration). Met coaches may have despaired while pounding these parts into her head, and Traubel may have been the ultimate phlegmatic stand-and-deliver Wagnerian soprano. She also may have truly believed it when she said that opera bored her, that it was just a job, and that the nine roles she learned (apparently the Damrosch opera never counted) were all she ever cared to know—surely few other singers with a comparable vocal gift had a more limited imagination, about their own potential as well as the art they had chosen to pursue. And yet many of those Isoldes and Brünnhildes are thrilling for the sheer sound of the voice, a column of glowing tone that could ring out with imperious force just as easily as it could be spun down to a fine silken thread.

Nor does Traubel sound emotionally uninvolved, and she outdid Flagstad in expressing the full range as well as the nuances of Isolde's rage, despair, sarcasm, and sexual abandon. The top always was a problem, and it became more of one as time wore on—her final Isolde in March 1953 finds anything over G something of an adventure, and most of the highest notes are simply left out, as they had been for several years. Their long unavailability even led Traubel to the disarmingly equivocal statement that the top notes of a woman's voice had always been unpleasing to her, including her own. After that unconvincing confession, Traubel went on to compare her voice and Flagstad's candidly, concluding with an observation no one is likely to quarrel with: "Flagstad was better than I in the high register in several ways; I think I can take the honors from her in the over-all performance of warmth and dramatic intensity."

In making that comparison, Traubel, of course, was talking about vocal character, not acting. In that respect, both she and Flagstad would soon be outdone by a younger soprano who shared the Wagner repertory with Traubel in the forties and went on to become a founding pillar of Wieland Wagner's new Bayreuth in the fifties and sixties: Astrid Varnay. Met patrons could hear and see the promise in Varnay's surprise debut as Sieglinde on December 6, 1941—the very same matinee in which Traubel was singing her first *Walküre* Brünnhilde, although both performances were overshadowed by the events of Pearl Harbor on the following day. The two sopranos may have at first shared the same Wagnerian repertory, but Varnay soon ventured off on her own path and into an operatic career that far outstripped Traubel's, both in terms of repertory and duration, one that began in 1941 in America and ended fifty-five years later in Europe.

Varnay first came to Johnson's attention in 1940, when George Szell suggested to her coach—Hermann Weigert, head assistant conductor for the Met's German wing—that she should sing for Edward Johnson, purely to get his opinion and advice about future study and repertory. An informal audition was arranged for July 10, and Johnson's scribbled notes read, "Good material, excellent German and Italian, musical, worthy of attention." He then invited Varnay into his office for a chat, which ended when the general manager asked her for a letter giving him the basic facts about who she was and what she had to offer. A week later a letter arrived containing the following information. Name: Violet A. Várnay. Age: 22. Born: Stockholm, Sweden (Hungarian descent). Education: elementary; high school (completed); private musical college (eight years as a piano major). Languages: English, German, Italian, French, Hungarian. Vocal training with her mother. Repertory studied with Hermann Weigert. Her repertory list included most of the major Wagner roles: Senta, Elsa, Elisabeth, Eva, Sieglinde, the three Brünnhildes, Gutrune, and the Third Norn; she was still working on Isolde. In Italian she was prepared to sing Aida, Desdemona, Santuzza, and the *Forza* Leonora, with more to come. "The immediate reaction when this letter hit Mr. Johnson's desk," Varnay later recalled, "was unbridled hilarity. The general manager thought he was being subjected to some kind of hoax on the part of Weigert, who had a bit of a reputation as a quick-witted scamp when it came to wise cracks, but never, never ever in musical matters. Could this pupil of Weigert's really have put thirteen of the toughest soprano roles in her brain and throat at the tender age of 22? And what other 'parts' were left for preparation? The whole idea was most inconceivable, but, as Mr. Johnson confessed many years later, he thought this audition might be good for a laugh, to pass the time away on an otherwise dismal November afternoon. It would be interesting, he thought, to put the claims in the letter to the test."

By the time Johnson and his staff heard the young soprano's formal audition—which included bits and pieces of nearly everything on her repertory list—it was clear that Violet Várnay was no hoax (the girl's given Hungarian name of Ibolyka had been Anglicized to Violet early on by a practical first-grade teacher). "Ought to engage," wrote Johnson on the audition card, and, as he later said to Weigert, "I don't know what in blazes to do with the girl, but I've got to have her in the house." He was soon to find out just how useful she would be. On December 6 Lotte Lehmann called in sick and Varnay was quickly readied for an unexpected debut as Sieglinde, her first appearance of any significance on any operatic stage. Six days later, when Traubel came down with the bug, Varnay once again stepped into *Die Walküre*, this time as Brünnhilde. On January 9, 1942, the day originally scheduled for her debut, she sang Elsa in *Lohengrin*, and shortly after that Elisabeth in *Tannhäuser* and Telea in the world premiere of Gian Carlo Menotti's short-lived *Island God*. It may not have been Ponselle all over again, but the critics were impressed—in fact, said *Time*, they "all but ho-yo-to-hoed" after her debut as Sieglinde. According to the *Times*, she was "thoroughly at home on the stage, acting with sensitivity and imagination and singing with unforced, secure tones."

The fact that Varnay arrived at the Met so well prepared was no accident. Both her parents were Hungarian-born opera singers, Alexander Várnay and Mária Jávor, who met onstage at the People's Opera in Budapest in 1911 during a rehearsal of Jean Nouguès's *Quo Vadis?* Soon after his marriage, Alexander gave up singing for the more stable career of a stage director, and the couple promptly relocated to the Royal Opera House in Stockholm, where Ibolyka Astrid Mária Várnay was born on April 25, 1918. Mária continued to sing leading coloratura roles with the Royal Opera, bringing little Ibolyka along with her and tucking the baby into one of the lower drawers of the makeup table in her dressing room while she sang Gilda. At times the child would be looked after by another young soprano who was singing soubrette roles with the company, Kirsten Flagstad.

In 1923 the Várnay family made what they at first thought would be a brief sojourn in the New World: a summer engagement in Buenos Aires followed by a turn through New York in hopes of promoting Mária at the Metropolitan. Once settled in town, Alexander took a job directing productions at the Manhattan Opera House, but Mária had little luck in interesting the Met—Galli-Curci was the reigning coloratura at the time, and Lucrezia Bori had a firm grip on the lyric repertory. Just as the family was about to move on again, tragedy struck: Alexander suddenly fell ill and died from kidney poisoning. Mária settled down to raise her daughter as best she could, taking odd jobs and singing for the local Salmaggi Opera. That colorful troupe eventually even provided her with another tenor husband in the person of Fortunato De Angelis, who briefly became a second father for little Violet.

The new family made its home in an Italian neighborhood in Jersey City, where Violet grew up in modestly appointed urban surroundings. She attended William L. Dickinson High School, studied piano (the first movement of Beethoven's *Pathétique* was her party piece), and, in 1932 at the age of fourteen, went to her first opera at the Met: *Simon Boccanegra* with Maria Müller, Giovanni Martinelli, Lawrence Tibbett, and Ezio Pinza. Müller especially fascinated her. "Seeing opera for the first time in these lavish surroundings," she recalled, "was thrilling enough, but the great voices of the two protagonists [Müller and Tibbett] made it even more exciting. As I leaned over the railing of the gilded box to admire this unusually attractive young singer, I felt the same sensation other American kids my age might have experienced in those days watching Greta Garbo in the movies. It was very glamorous, and I was glad to be a part of it, if only vicariously." Varnay could scarcely have guessed at the time that, less than twenty years later, she would be on the Met stage singing the same role and in the same production.

Despite her fascination with Müller—not to mention daily exposure to her mother's voice students and frequent visits to the Met as a standee—Varnay was still focused on becoming a pianist. Graduation from high school in 1935, though, meant making some kind of contribution to the household budget, particularly after Mária's second husband packed up and went back to Italy for good. Violet took various jobs, as a typist and a clerk in a bookstore, but her musical ambitions were getting stronger and the voice had gradually begun to take precedence. And, of course, there was an excellent teacher right at hand. By the time Violet's true vocal placement had been discovered, there was a fond reunion with Flagstad. Now a big Met star, Flagstad recommended sending the baby she once tended in a drawer at the Stockholm Royal Opera to Weigert. It was a fateful meeting, and with Weigert's help Varnay learned not only the notes but how to "develop the skill of taking on another personality and building my own actions and reactions on the logical response of that individual to the motivations at hand. In short, I wasn't merely learning music, or just checking fine points in the score. Under the tutelage of this brilliant pedagogue, I was slowly forming my own approach to the craft of being a professional opera singer. And I loved it!"

Varnay was destined not to spend the major part of her career in the country where she was reared, but it hardly seems likely she would have been quite the same sort of artist had she been brought up in Europe. The Metropolitan desperately needed her to spell Traubel in the forties, and that reality provided her with the sort of on-the-job training available to few young singers at the time, certainly not to budding Wagnerians—by 1950 she had sung fourteen Wagner roles at the Met, all the major heroines save for Brünnhilde in *Götterdämmerung*. Luckily, Varnay possessed the vocal stamina and technical background not only to sustain a punishing schedule but also to grow and thrive on it. And, of course, there was the inspiration of Weigert, whom she married in 1944. He continued to be her coach as she branched into different repertory, most notably such strenuous Strauss assignments as Salome, Elektra, and the Marschallin. The Met was reluctant to cast her in Italian parts— Santuzza and Amelia in *Boccanegra* were her only assignments—but by 1951 she had sung Aida, Gioconda, and Desdemona in Mexico City, and Lady Macbeth at the Florence May Festival. That year also found her singing at the postwar opening of Bayreuth, the beginning of a long association with the festival where her Wagner interpretations would mature under the watchful eye of Wieland, the composer's grandson.

In fact, after a final Kundry at the Met in 1956, Varnay headed off to Europe, where she would spend the best twenty years of her career—by the time she returned to the Met, in 1974 as Kostelnička in *Jenůfa*, she had already dropped the big *hochdramatische* parts and turned to character roles. It was America's loss, but in retrospect her choice made sense. By the mid-fifties, Met management had come to take her for granted. The initial excitement over her youthful debut had long since cooled, and Varnay's soprano—with its reedy texture and laserlike intensity—was not calculated to please a larger public that had swooned over the velvet-voiced Flagstad or basked in the warm glow of Traubel. And, needless to say, Varnay's more subtly conceived Wagner heroines were simply lost on most Met audiences, who responded mainly to beautiful sounds. This must also partially explain why Varnay, alone among her Met colleagues at the time, never made much of an impact on radio or television, let alone in films. She was always a creature of the operatic stage, and would remain so.

There were other strong lures that took Varnay to Europe. Wagner began to play an increasingly small role in Rudolf Bing's plans after 1950, and the new general manager clearly felt that her voice was unsuited to the Italian repertory that was his own personal preference. Even in Wagner, Bing had Varnay pigeonholed as little more than a useful house soprano, and he seemed incapable of seeing her potential— but then, he always regarded the soprano's great Bayreuth colleague and most admired Wotan of the day, Hans Hotter, as little better than a comprimario. Weigert had died in 1955, and Varnay, still dependent on him for guidance, was emotionally at sea. There were too many memories in New York, and Europe—Bayreuth especially—offered an opportunity for new directions and, as it turned out, vocal and artistic fulfillment. Once again, America had ironically provided the training ground and launching pad for an important singer whose full worth was realized and recognized only in Europe.

Traubel and Varnay were able to prolong the Met's 1930s romance with Wagner through the next decade before the tradition eventually expired under Bing. Both sopranos served honorably and with distinction, although the aura conjured up by the legendary Flagstad-Melchior partnership could never be recaptured. Between them, Risë Stevens and Dorothy Kirsten created a similar feeling of fin de siècle: the American opera singer as a national symbol of glamour and media crossover. That phenomenon had definitely begun to wane, and neither Stevens nor Kirsten was destined to be as celebrated in their day—or as mythic after they left the scene, for that matter—as Garden and Farrar had been. For one thing, the possibility of capturing the country's attention by making a Hollywood film was becoming harder as the industry developed its own singing personalities. And although both Stevens and Kirsten appeared briefly in the movies—and Stevens's two vehicles, *The Chocolate Soldier* and *Going My Way*, advanced her career spectacularly—the demand for filmed operettas starring singers with operatically trained voices was declining. Beyond that, opera itself had lost much of its exotic appeal, new works were no longer wanted, and singers found themselves in direct competition, not so much with each other as with memories of an earlier generation that had sung the same roles. Kirsten, in fact, could never quite shake the notion that she was merely a smartly turned-out blond clone of her mentor, Grace Moore.

At first Stevens had the still active Gladys Swarthout to contend with, although the latter's reluctance to pursue her career with vigor made the younger mezzo's mission a bit easier. Besides, if Swarthout had a husband who guided her affairs with calculated astuteness, Stevens had one who proved to be a genius at career management. Perhaps Stevens's greatest triumph was to convince an entire generation that she and the role of Carmen were virtually synonymous—no small feat considering how the same trick had been turned by an unbroken line of such potent American predecessors as Ponselle, Farrar, Garden, De Lussan, and Hauk, not to mention the most celebrated Carmen of them all, the French soprano Emma Calvé. When Stevens was finally asked to present her interpretation to Met audiences, on December 28, 1945 (significantly ten months after Swarthout sang her final Carmen with the company), she had her own ideas about the role, but the goods had all been cunningly packaged to guarantee a presold success by her husband, Walter Surovy, who started laying the groundwork two years earlier. "They've been futzing around at the Met for years about letting you do *Carmen*," he told her, "but they never get around to it. We'll *make* them do it." And in effect that's precisely what he did.

The first shot in Surovy's campaign came during the filming of *Going My Way* in 1943, when he insisted, against much protestation from the production team, that Risë sing the Habanera as her big number in the movie. ("Noble," remarked costar Bing Crosby. "Not the sort of thing the old Bingeroo digs with pleasure, but noble. You wouldn't want to do 'Because' instead, would you?") The film was a huge commercial success, and Stevens's sashaying rendition of the Habanera suggested that she had been singing Carmen all her life, an impression reinforced that same year when she was pictured in Chesterfield cigarette ads in magazines across the country costumed as the fiery Gypsy, throwing one hand ecstatically aloft and clenching the de rigueur flower between her teeth. ("In my day," Geraldine Farrar acidly commented, "artists became Carmen by singing *Carmen*.") Next Columbia Records released a bestselling album of excerpts, and Surovy saw to it that his wife programmed at least one of Carmen's arias at every concert and on every radio broadcast in which she appeared. By the time that Met debut in the role finally arrived, the first performance of 124 with the company, Stevens was already the most famous Carmen of her generation, completely eclipsing Swarthout before she even set foot onstage.

Risë Stevens provided an echo of old-time opera-star glamour, at least at the beginning, but her career also looked to the future. She was packaged as a product to be marketed and sold to American tastes, but her made-in-America celebrity image did not lead to triumphs abroad. Puzzled Europeans, if they were aware of her at all, never entirely understood what all the fuss was about on her brief sorties to Glyndebourne, Paris, and La Scala. Like Swarthout before her, Stevens wisely stuck close to home, where she was perceived as a star and where every move to keep her one could be controlled by Surovy.

Before Surovy, though, two controlling forces helped shape Stevens's life and career. The first was her mother, Sadie, who like so many of the strong matriarchs we have already met in this chronicle was convinced that her daughter's voice would take her straight to the top. There wasn't much money in Stevens's mixed-parentage household— Sadie's folk were Jewish and Risë's father, Christian Carl Steenberg, came to the Bronx as a child from Norway—but as in most immigrant New York family circles, there was plenty of discipline and lots of determination to succeed. "She'll be BEST!" screamed stage-mother Sadie to her doubting husband before taking little Risë downtown for a tryout on Orry Parado's *The Children's Hour* on radio station WJZ. After she outgrew Parado's program, Risë was avidly looking for performance opportunities, eventually finding plenty of work as well as valuable experience with the quaintly named and short-lived New York Opéra-Comique, Inc., which operated for a couple of years out of Brooklyn.

Soon another familiar type of authority figure materialized in the person of Anna Schoen-René, one of the best-known vocal pedagogues in New York, who zeroed in on Stevens in much the same way Louise Vetta-Karst embraced Traubel. "If you weren't good, you wouldn't be here," she announced to a trembling Stevens when she presented herself for lessons. "I don't have failures in my class; I get rid of them. Now, do you want to work, or is singing merely a fad with you?" The girl obeyed, and prospered under Madame's strict tutelage while making ends meet by singing for $80 a week on *The Palmolive Beauty Box Theatre*—not bad pay for radio work in the early thirties.

Eventually the time came when Schoen-René insisted that an American singer could consider a serious career only after the proper vocal finishing abroad. Indeed, Stevens was the last major American singer to have the opportunity to study and gain valuable early experience at provincial opera houses as they existed and functioned in prewar Europe. That took place during the late thirties at the New German Theater in Prague, where she first tested several of the roles that would later become identified with her—Octavian, Carmen, Orfeo, and Mignon—as well as some Italian roles that she tried out once and immediately and permanently put aside. Like Traubel, Stevens may have been easily influenced by stronger people in her life, but she was a stubborn woman and knew her limits. "You can throw me to the crocodiles of the Nile," she once remarked after singing her first and last Amneris, "but I'll never do that part again." Not long after settling in Prague, she met Surovy, a young Hungarian-Viennese actor in the local theater company. It was a stormy stop-and-start romance, but after many delays due to prewar political complications, Surovy finally arrived in America to marry Stevens after she had established herself at the Met in 1938.

In a new country, struggling with a new language, his own career taken from him, his managerial instincts aroused, Surovy threw himself into managing his wife with a vengeance. "Star roles only, Sadie," he promised his approving mother-in-law. Sure enough, after working off a few yeoman assignments early in her Met days—Laura, Fricka, Marina, Erda—Stevens got pretty much what she wanted until she gracefully departed in 1961. Not only were they star roles, but whenever possible Surovy saw to it that they were title roles: by singing Carmen, Mignon, Dalila, Orfeo, and Octavian, Stevens was guaranteed the coveted last bow at the end of the performance.

Not only was Surovy a master tactician, but he also knew the value of diplomacy, now that the days when prima donnas could dictate their wants to operatic management were over. Although Surovy made certain that Stevens was well treated (she was the first mezzo to get the top house fee of $1,000, after starting out in 1938 at $200 a week), he was never greedy, a fact gratefully noted by Rudolf Bing, who especially appreciated the mezzo's professionalism and lack of star temperament. After Stevens's early flirtation with Hollywood, there were no more films, even though Louis B. Mayer was apparently determined to wean her away from opera and turn her into a full-time screen actress. "You're great in opera," growled Walter, "and that's where you belong." Risë agreed—perhaps they both saw that the day of the opera singer as a movie star was coming to an end, and besides, those two smash-hit films had more than served their purpose. So Stevens remained the Met's leading mezzo in a narrow repertory of prominent roles, a busy recitalist on tour, and an increasingly visible presence on television, all the while enjoying a stable domestic home life with Surovy and their son, Nicky, born in 1944. It was a safe career and artistically a restricted one, but few American singers ever rejoiced in a more consistent or untroubled professional life.

Like Traubel, Stevens also strayed from "high art" to dabble in low-brow shenanigans on radio and TV, as well as recording a fair amount of pop material, greatly broadening her national name recognition beyond the narrow confines of opera. If Bing disapproved, he never made an issue of it. When Risë Stevens burlesqued *Carmen* with Fred Allen, performed parodies with Eddie Cantor and Jack Benny, or sang duets with Frank Sinatra and Jack Haley, it always seemed more like a glamorous class act graciously letting down her hair and innocently having a good time.

Stevens left the Met just in time. By the late fifties it was clear that her voice was aging rapidly, that the registers had begun to separate. Her basic repertory was obviously now best entrusted to younger singers, and of course, any move down to character roles was out of the question. There were a few brief appearances in a couple of musical comedy revivals, but in 1964 at the age of fifty-one she officially retired. Stevens never severed her ties with the Met, becoming director of its short-lived national touring company, remaining on after that as an active board member and an advisor to the company's various young artists programs. She also took a brief, if largely symbolic, fling at higher education, as president of the Mannes School of Music from 1975 to 1978.

Risë Stevens clearly had something to offer her generation: a consummately packaged star quality that was hard to resist. But it was basically a comfortable vocal persona based on conventional glamour and unthreatening entertainment values calculated to appeal to a rattled postwar society that had already been sufficiently challenged. In its prime, the voice was pleasant and reliable if of unremarkable quality, a smoothly managed instrument that was seldom asked to address music that might expose its limitations or venture into areas where the artistic risks might be high. Such restricted talents seldom resonate through the ages, and looking back, one now better understands why this career, which seemed so big to Americans at the time, remained essentially parochial and unexportable. Her many Met broadcasts and recordings, the two films, and all the *Voice of Firestone* programs and other television appearances reveal an immaculately groomed, slightly superficial, even artificial persona who makes all the correct musical and theatrical gestures without suggesting an original vocal imagination at work.

In most important respects, Dorothy Kirsten (1910–92) was Risë Stevens's soprano counterpart, although she had a more independent streak and never entirely delivered herself or her career into anyone else's hands. And she was even more fastidious about her image and priorities, which tended toward grandeur. "A prima donna," she once told a fan, "is the woman onstage at the end of the opera." To another she confessed, late in life, "Singers aren't idols anymore. They're too close to the public. When they go on the talk shows, they become too familiar, too much the good Joe and the girl next door. I've tried to maintain the image of the prima donna all through the years, wherever I was." And she did, rigorously. Dorothy Kirsten may have worshipped the memory of her benefactress, Grace Moore, and their operatic repertories were very nearly identical. But, ironically, Moore herself looks very much like the happy-go-lucky girl next door compared to Kirsten, whose disciplined lifestyle and carefully cultivated public image permitted few of the carefree self-indulgences so characteristic of her you're-only-human-once mentor.

But Kirsten possessed a superior voice and, where they can be compared, used it with far more skill and musical sophistication than Moore. The last American soprano to prepare Louise under the guidance of Gustave Charpentier, then eighty-seven, Kirsten respectfully postponed singing the role at the Metropolitan until more than a year after Moore's untimely death, but there is little question whose broadcast performance takes the palm. The younger soprano's crystalline tone, easy top, finely chiseled phrases, and idiomatic French on her 1948 performance all outclass Moore's 1943 effort, which sounds amateurish in comparison. Moore's "and may she be better" inscription on the autographed photograph she presented to Kirsten on the occasion of the young soprano's first Mimì in 1942 was both a gracious gesture and a wish that came true. Even when singing lighter music, Kirsten was not only more adept than Moore in adjusting the weight and color of her soprano to suit the material, but she delivered it with a more easy, natural swinging charm.

She could also have given her other Met colleagues lessons in how to inflect and color the show tunes of Gershwin and Kern. One of her more formidable rivals in this repertory, Dinah Shore, went so far to exclaim, "It just isn't fair that anyone who looks that lovely can hit a really high note dead center and hit a golf ball the same way. It just isn't fair, Dorothy Kirsten." With her versatility, strong sense of self, and vocal gifts, Kirsten might have had a crack at an international career, but like most Americans of her generation she seldom strayed far from home after peace came to Europe, and mostly out of choice.

A native of Montclair, New Jersey, Kirsten was born in 1910, a fact that only emerged after her death in 1992 and much to everyone's surprise—early on she advanced her birth date seven years and got away with it to the end, sporting a face and figure as carefully preserved as her voice. It was a necessary fiction at first, since the soprano got a late start. Most of her Met contemporaries were already working hard at their careers by the late thirties, when Kirsten quit her job as a secretary for the Jersey Bell Telephone Company to try her luck as a "girl singer" in Manhattan. Up to that point there had been little serious vocal training, and the teacher Kirsten found in New York apparently proved to be of small value, although he never actually harmed her voice. He even offered to teach her for free if she would double as his "secretary." As Kirsten delicately puts it in her memoirs, "That arrangement worked out fine for a while, but when other duties were forced upon me it was very uncomfortable." Even then, the blond soprano was, as they said in those days, "quite a looker." Luckily, two radio personalities befriended her, Grace and Eddie Albert (the latter just at the beginning of his big stage and screen career), and an audition as a singer for radio station WINS won her a weekly fifteen-minute solo spot. Soon she was noticed by the gossip columnist Dinty Doyle, who was so struck by her physical and vocal resemblance to his pal Grace Moore that he arranged a meeting on the spot. Moore was interested in hearing her "kid sis" sing, but not her pop radio repertory—she asked Kirsten to prepare two Puccini arias, even though the budding soprano hadn't yet sung a note of opera. Two months later the Mimì and Musetta arias were in her voice, and Kirsten sang them for Moore on May 31, 1938. Obviously impressed, the diva proclaimed, "We'll make her a star. She has it!"

Generously financed by Moore, Kirsten promptly set sail for Italy to study with Astolfo Pescia, Beniamino Gigli's old teacher, who successfully enlarged her soprano and brought it into sharper focus. The time abroad, though, was all too short, and the imminent threat of total war sent Kirsten back home a year later. Thanks to Moore's influence, there was a spot waiting for her at the Chicago Opera Company, where she made her operatic debut as Pousette in *Manon* on November 9, 1940. Other comprimario roles followed, but Kirsten was soon promoted to Musetta and Micaela. The next step up was to the recently formed New York City Opera, where the soprano offered her first Violetta and Manon Lescaut in 1944. The following year she reached the top: debuts at both the Metropolitan and the San Francisco Opera, which would provide her with a secure home base on both coasts for the next thirty years—even longer at the Met, where Kirsten, nearing seventy, sang one last Tosca in 1979. "Doorootee, wheen weel you queeet?" chirped Lily Pons wickedly some years before that valedictory performance. "Neeveer, Leelee," came the sweet reply. And for a while it seemed as though she meant it, right up to one final "Un bel dì" in 1986 at a fundraiser for the French Foundation for Alzheimer Research. Kirsten had established the foundation and ran it herself with tireless energy soon after her third husband, the noted brain surgeon Dr. John Douglas French, died of the disease.

Kirsten's longevity was based on a secure technical method that never deserted her, one that grew from a naturally comfortable voice placement and the good singing habits instilled by Ludwig Fabri, her only teacher after 1941. From Fabri she learned what it means to sing an even scale, that a good forte tone is developed only out of a properly executed pianissimo, and how to pass the voice over its entire range without any detectable register changes. The basic tonal quality of her soprano remained bright, lustrous, even girlish throughout her career, and can even be heard in excellent estate on live recordings as late as 1975. The other factor Kirsten always said contributed to her good vocal health was her firm belief in the word "No." Although most of the heavier Puccini heroines were comfortably in her voice right from the start, she shied away from anything that might cause strain, and her active repertory, while hardly as limited as Traubel's, was even more carefully chosen and monitored than Risë Stevens's. Very likely many of her decisions on that score were dictated less by vocal prudence than by personal taste and a suspicion that certain roles were not suitable for a prima donna. Rudolf Bing asked her in vain for Fiordiligi, Elisabetta di Valois, Barber's Vanessa, Marie in Berg's *Wozzeck*, and Liù, most of them viable for her voice, although she did stretch her repertory in San Francisco by performing Walton's Cressida and Poulenc's Blanche in *Dialogues of the Carmelites*. She also turned down Cole Porter's request that she appear in *Kiss Me, Kate* when she realized that he had Bianca in mind for her rather than the title role. That she ultimately regretted, as well as never finding the opportunity of singing such tempting star parts as Adriana, Thaïs, Boito's Margherita, and Desdemona.

Even with her busy schedule in opera, Kirsten never stopped singing popular music, and she continued to be a regular vocal presence on radio, where she shared the microphone with America's best: Frank Sinatra, Bing Crosby, Al Jolson, Nelson Eddy, Gordon MacRae, and Perry Como. For two years in the late forties Kirsten and Sinatra sang together on NBC's *Light Up Time*, allowing the soprano to learn all there was to know about timing, phrasing, microphone technique, and pop rubato from the master. There were also two films in the fifties—*Mr. Music* with Crosby and *The Great Caruso* with Mario Lanza—but despite the commercial success of the Lanza film, Kirsten found herself in Hollywood a decade too late to take advantage of film as a career-building vehicle— one reason why her national profile never matched Risë Stevens's, let alone Grace Moore's. There were also too few recordings, due more to bad luck and how the industry was structured in the forties and fifties than to any reflection on her vocal abilities or sales potential. Kirsten shuttled back and forth between America's two big classical labels, recording her favorite arias and a plentiful amount of pop material, but Columbia never had much interest in recording her or anyone else in complete operas, and RCA's major work in that field began only in the sixties, when the soprano's star was shining less brightly.

"Never compromise on the big things, but be ready to do so on the less important ones." That was just one important bit of advice that Kirsten often heard from Moore and took to heart. Another wise tidbit she never forgot came from Mary Garden, ever ready to pass on her secrets to yet another generation. "Dorothy," Garden once told the young soprano, "that first impression is very important. Exude confidence and let your bosoms lead you." Kirsten took heed of both suggestions, incorporating an awesome self-confidence and refusal to compromise into a no-nonsense performing persona that was determined to keep up prima-donna appearances at all cost. That combination, so effective in many ways, also set a limit on her appeal—there was always a hard-edged, calculating side to her singing as well as to her coolly assured stage impersonations, which lacked spontaneity and inner conviction. Impeccably groomed offstage and on, Kirsten kept track of her Jean Louis gowns just as religiously as Lily Pons or Gladys Swarthout, but the time had passed when such surface finery impressed the fans. Even her chic, smartly tailored Minnie in Puccini's *La Fanciulla del West*, for all its vocal éclat, looked more like a New York socialite weekending on an upstate dude ranch than an innocent girl tending bar for a rough crew of California forty-niners. Showbiz operatic glamour may have been going out of style, but at least Dorothy Kirsten showed it to the door with class and vocal distinction.

One glamour girl "Johnson Baby" could legitimately lay claim to the title: Patrice Munsel, who made her debut as Philine in *Mignon* on December 4, 1943. Munsel had won the Metropolitan Opera Auditions of the Air earlier that year, and on the night she claimed her prize she became, at seventeen, the youngest singer ever to appear in a leading role at the Met. The audience was enchanted by her perky apple-pie charm and pluck, but for most of the critics it was Marion Talley all over again, and one of the Johnson regime's crassest bids for publicity. Now that the venerable W. J. Henderson was no longer around to blow the whistle (perhaps having heard enough, that long-suffering critic had put a bullet in his head in 1937), Virgil Thomson simply flung his hands up in horror. After complimenting the two Thomases of the evening—the composer and the conductor, Sir Thomas Beecham—he summed up an otherwise all-American affair as "amateur night at the Met." In the title role, Risë Stevens "forced and misplaced her beautiful voice in a most irregular fashion and mugged around the stage for all the world as if the audience were a camera-man come to photograph her teeth." James Melton's vocalism as Wilhelm "as always, was naif and his dramatic performance vague." Norman Cordon as Lothario "sang with constricted throat and stalked about stiffly." As for Munsel, Thomson was appalled by her "unschooled voice . . . If she continues to abuse it in public as she did last night, it may in short time turn into a cracked whisper . . . The idea that any female voice at seventeen is ripe for big time is the sheerest folly to entertain."

Still, Thomson grudgingly admitted that Munsel had potential—a "young woman of phenomenal talents" who might possibly have a great singing career if she ever learned how to use her voice properly. He also perceptively took note of the teenage debutante's exuberant theatrical personality—her personal radiance and a stage quality permeated by real temperament. The package had a certain appeal, at the very least suggesting that here was a born performer who, despite premature exposure, might escape the fate of a vocal personality as pallid as Talley. And she did, although Munsel never became an important singer, and in retrospect it seems astonishing that even a nonchalant manager like Johnson continued to allow her to grow up singing leading coloratura roles on the Met's stage. After a rocky beginning (her Lucia a year later was panned even more mercilessly—Lily Pons could hardly have felt threatened), Munsel eventually became a useful company member during the early Bing years. She hit her stride as a saucy soubrette in several of the new general manager's biggest Broadway-flavored hits: Adele in the Garson Kanin–Howard Dietz version of Johann Strauss's *Die Fledermaus* in 1950, Despina a year later in Alfred Lunt's English-language production of Mozart's *Così Fan Tutte*, and the title role in Offenbach's *La Périchole* in 1956 with Cyril Ritchard, also sung in English.

Such a light repertory seemed to indicate that perhaps "Princess Pat," as her vigorous fan club dubbed her early on, had always been meant for musical comedy, especially since her continued attempts to make an impression in the bravura coloratura repertory—Gilda, Rosina, Lakmé, and Juliette, as well as more Philines and Lucias—never amounted to much. And the film producer who thought that the sparky Spokane-born Munsel was the right singer to cast as Nellie Melba in a biopic of the legendary Australia diva must have been slightly daft. *Melba*, a box office disaster in 1953, effectively marked the end of Hollywood's interest in opera stars. The soprano found a more congenial venue two years later at the New Frontier Hotel in Las Vegas, where, according to one admiring showbiz critic, "she stripped behind a screen from a bouffant black and white gown to $1,400 pink satin, jeweled toreador pants and a low-top halter top. Then she stretched out on a couch and swung her shapely legs while she sang. Interspersed were a few bumps and grinds that astonished the crowd." Even Helen Traubel hadn't gone that far. Munsel's usefulness as an opera singer had clearly come to an end by 1958, when, getting on at age thirty-three, she briefly experimented with a heavier repertory—one unsuccessful Mimì—and left the Met for good. With the theatrical spunk and zest noted by Thomson apparently undiminished, she then plunged full-time into musical comedy and nightclub work, specializing in an endless succession of Dollys and Mames in summer stock and regional theaters around the country, a busy second career that lasted more than thirty years.

During the seventeen seasons between 1944 and 1961 that Blanche Thebom and Risë Stevens overlapped at the Metropolitan, it probably seemed to most observers that the younger mezzo was completely over-shadowed by her more colorful colleague. And so she was in terms of publicity and media razzle-dazzle. For those who could look far enough back and remember such things, it must have seemed ironic that Thebom's principal teacher and coach in New York after arriving from her hometown of Canton, Ohio, in 1939 was Edyth Walker, a mezzo who had similarly found herself playing second fiddle to Louise Homer at the Met many years earlier. The daughter of Swedish immigrants—her father and two older brothers worked the steel mills in Pittsburgh and later Canton—Thebom was on board ship in 1938 with her family, returning from a visit to the Old Country, when her vocal talents were first heard by Marian Anderson's Finnish accompanist, Kosti Vehanen. His letter of encouragement impressed the young woman's boss back in Ohio, who offered to underwrite his twenty-one-year-old secretary's vo-cal education in New York. The gamble paid off quickly. After a year working on her voice in Manhattan, Thebom attracted a manager, started giving recitals, and was soon appearing in orchestral concerts conducted by Ormandy and Mitropoulos. Like so many American sing-ers who captured the Met's attention in the early forties, she made her operatic debut without previous stage experience—where was an Ameri-can to find that at home, let alone in Europe, during wartime?—and Johnson was content to let her learn her craft on the job.

If it appears that Thebom never threatened Stevens's position as the Met's prima-donna mezzo, appearances are deceiving. Though she con-ducted her career more quietly and seldom got a chance to sing the three flashy roles that Stevens virtually monopolized—Carmen, Dalila, and Mignon—Thebom made her own statement. For one thing, the two singers' voices were entirely dissimilar. Thebom's dark, imperious colum-nar sound lacked the sensual warmth that made Stevens's basic tonal coloring so attractive, and, truth to tell, those three French heroines didn't really suit her anyway. It was Amneris, the one role Stevens re-fused to touch again after her early disaster with the part in prewar Europe, that was Thebom's principal property during the fifties, and she sang Verdi's Egyptian princess eighty times with the Met—not, perhaps, with the chesty flamboyance or throat-tearing intensity of a typical Italian dramatic mezzo, but with more than sufficient fine-tuned theatrical point and vocal security. She also kept the Wagner roles in her repertory, Brangäne and Fricka especially, long after Stevens had renounced them, and there were excursions into other areas that her less musically adventurous "rival" never cared to explore: Stravinsky's Baba the Turk, Bellini's Adalgisa, Mozart's Dorabella, and Verdi's Eboli. Thebom's musical curiosity, versatility, and sheer love of performing also led her to character roles when the time came: Strauss's Herodias and Adelaide, Berg's Countess Geschwitz, and the Baroness in Barber's *Vanessa*.

Although Thebom did her share of radio and television work—she even accepted a bit part in *The Great Caruso* when a mezzo was needed to film the *Lucia* sextet—she never went out of her way to cultivate a media image, and her flirtation with pop music remained just that, an occasional operetta or "dignified" musical comedy like *The King and I* or *Song of Norway* on the summer circuit during her later years. Thebom was a handsome woman, but her only apparent vanity was her voluminous floor-length black hair (Milton Cross, the announcer for the Met's broadcasts, was often instructed to inform the radio audience on Saturday afternoons that Miss Thebom's hair was indeed all her own). Having no interest in conjuring up whatever vestiges were left of old-time operatic glamour, Thebom preferred to spend her time away from the Met touring for the State Department's cultural relations programs, lecturing for educational organizations, encouraging composers to write works for her concert use, and, even when her own career was at its height, establishing a scholarship foundation to help launch young professionals. Like most of her contemporaries, Thebom sang little opera abroad, but the British seemed to appreciate her one Glyndebourne appearance in Mozart, as Dorabella, more than Stevens's Cherubino. Certainly, being chosen to sing Dido in preference to a British mezzo in John Gielgud's production of Berlioz's *Les Troyens* at Covent Garden in 1957 was a prestigious coup for an American, as was her participation in the classic Furtwängler-Flagstad recording of *Tristan und Isolde* made in London in 1951.

Like Astrid Varnay, Regina Resnik (1922–   ) started out at the tender age of twenty-two as one of Johnson's youngest and busiest workhorses. Later as a mature artist, again like Varnay, Resnik found herself more appreciated in Europe, although she never completely severed ties with the Met. She further complicated her progress in mid-career by making the change from dramatic soprano to mezzo-soprano, which in part explains why her up-and-down work list during thirty Met seasons looks positively schizophrenic: from Musetta to Carmen, Aida to Amneris, Donna Anna to Donna Elvira, Alice Ford to Dame Quickly, Chrysothemis to Klytämnestra, Leonora to Azucena, Rosalinde to Prince Orlofsky. It is amazing that Resnik survived all the vocal wear and tear of her early years, with even enough voice left at the end to sing Madame Armfeldt in Stephen Sondheim's *A Little Night Music* at the New York City Opera, a return engagement more than fifty years after appearing in small roles during the company's 1944 inaugural season. In the same year Resnik won the Metropolitan Opera Auditions of the Air, launching her Met career on the spot. Like Varnay, she was immediately thrown onstage, with just twenty-four hours' notice and under crisis conditions, when Zinka Milanov found herself unable to sing Leonora in *Il Trovatore* on December 6. Three days later Resnik appeared in her scheduled debut role, Santuzza, and less than a week after that performed Aida—three demanding Italian dramatic soprano roles in ten days.

By the time Resnik reached her thirties, she should have been hitting her stride. Instead, she faced a vocal crisis as her instrument, darkly textured even for a dramatic soprano, became increasingly heavy and more covered. After much anguished soul-searching, she went to the retired baritone Giuseppe Danise, who restructured and recentered her voice as a mezzo-soprano. But the change did not impress Rudolf Bing, who said he couldn't hear the difference—in his opinion, Resnik had now been reduced from a useful house soprano to a great character actress, and, among other "plums," he offered her Marcellina (*Figaro*), Magdalene (*Meistersinger*), and Geneviève (*Pelléas*). Resnik begged to differ, and it took another impresario—David Webster of Covent Garden—to help realize her potential. With Webster's encouragement and connections, she became a favorite singer in London and Vienna during the early sixties, although even then her Continental reputation left Bing unimpressed. "I would come away from London," she recalled, "having sung a great part like the Prioress in the first *Dialogues of the Carmelites* there, and then Amneris and Carmen, then fly to Vienna for Fricka and in the Festwochen Klytämnestra and the whole *Ring*, Herodias, Carmen,

Amneris and then Eboli at Salzburg—and come home to face Marcel-lina!"

Resnik might have become the Met's preferred Carmen after Stevens gave up the role—and her tough-as-nails, thinking man's Gypsy did offer a refreshing alternative to Stevens's glamour—but Bing gave her few opportunities to prove herself in the part. More "character roles" were offered, and only a handful of the leading parts Resnik had sung in Europe with so much distinction. Once again a valuable American vocal talent suffered from double Met mismanagement: dangerous early over-exploitation by Johnson, followed by almost complete indifference from Bing. By the sixties, in fact, Bing's clear European bias had become a fact of life that many American singers engaged by his predecessor had to face, particularly those possessed with strong egos or difficult personali-ties that required special handling. Resnik kept busy and sang a great deal during a long career, but as an artist of superior musical and dra-matic intelligence—not to mention a singer whose vocal gift was so imposing, especially during her mezzo-soprano period—she never re-ceived proper recognition at home.

More docile and less high-profile singers tended to fare better under both Johnson and Bing when it came to steady employment. Margaret Harshaw traveled in the opposite direction taken by Resnik, arriving at the Metropolitan in 1942 as a mezzo—such roles as Amneris, Ulrica, Quickly, Azucena, and Fricka—and departing in 1964 after more than a dozen years of heavy duty as a Wagnerian soprano. In both capacities she proved to be an immensely useful artist, particularly in helping to keep the Wagnerian repertory alive with distinction after Varnay left the company and before Birgit Nilsson appeared on the scene. A solid and dependable singer, Harshaw enjoyed an even more important career after she left the Met to become one of the country's most effective and influential voice teachers, based at the Indiana University School of Music.

Many lyric sopranos came and went during the late Johnson years, but few attained prominence or lasted for long. One who did was Na-dine Conner, who sang for eighteen seasons between 1941 and 1960. Susanna, Marguerite, Mélisande, Sophie, Micaela, Pamina, Gretel, Zer-lina, and Mimì—these tender creatures all sounded better to Met regu-lars when graced by Conner's sweet soprano and winning stage personality. There were others who shared her repertory and took on heavier assignments—Frances Greer, Mimi Benzell, Florence Quartararo, and Polyna Stoska—but one rejoiced in a ravishing lyric soprano and generous musical personality that outshone them all: Eleanor Steber. Only after her career was over and could be properly assessed did a wondering posterity realize that Steber was by far the most prodigiously gifted singer of her generation. With her diversity of striking vocal talents, she seemed poised to join the world pool of great singers and establish a truly American vocal style at last. The fact that Steber failed to make that leap and become the international artist she could and should have been is one of the saddest tales in the annals of the American singer.

Twenty

If I Could

Tell You

~~~~~~~~~~~~~~~~~~~~~~~~~~~~~~~~

*T*o put it mildly, Miss Steber committed herself to sing one of the most foolhardy recital programs of modern times. And, being Eleanor Steber, she planted her feet on the stage and sang it!"

That critic was not exaggerating. On the evening of October 10, 1958, in Carnegie Hall, Eleanor Steber was once again presenting one of those vocal marathons that, by then, were her specialty. Most of her friends and close colleagues knew why Steber was periodically compelled to send a message to a musical establishment that often seemed to take her for granted—especially Rudolf Bing's Metropolitan Opera. Ever since Bing became general manager in 1950, Steber felt, sopranos from Europe were being given the attention (and higher fees) that she had rightfully earned after eighteen years of performing leading roles with distinction and rushing to the rescue as the company's "fire horse": the singer who was always on call and ready to leap into the breach to save the Met in a crisis. Full points for an exceptional American singer who had worked hard and deserved proper recognition was what she mostly craved. "Here it is—all I can do, the best I can do," she seemed to be saying in Carnegie Hall that night. "Now somebody top it!"

One wonders if anyone could have topped her that evening, faced with such a challenging program. Always renowned for her Mozart, Steber began with three contrasting dazzlers by that composer: the brilliant "Alleluia" from the motet *Exultate, Jubilate*, Ilia's melting "Zeffiretti lusinghieri" from *Idomeneo*, and Constanze's vaulting "Martern aller Arten" from *Die Entführung aus dem Serail*. Next came Berlioz's *Nuits d'Été* song cycle—a repertory work today but virtually unknown when Steber recorded it with Dimitri Mitropoulos in 1954—followed by the florid bel canto Mad Scene from Bellini's *I Puritani*. The second half of the program opened with the Empress's two big solo scenes from Strauss's *Die Frau ohne Schatten*, also a rarity for New Yorkers at the time and a role Steber had sung in concert at her Vienna debut in 1953. After that strenuous sequence she turned to Samuel Barber's *Knoxville: Summer of 1915*, which the soprano had commissioned and first performed in 1948 and quickly became an American classic. Still not finished, she topped off the evening with arias from *Ernani*, *Louise*, *Tosca*, and *Madama Butterfly*. All the music on this virtuoso tour de force had been closely associated with Steber over the past twenty years, and the audience, definitely a partisan group that had come to cheer, was well aware of the fact. When the entire extraordinary concert was released on compact discs in 1992, two years after the singer's death, another generation could share in the occasion and better understand why it may well have been the moment that crowned the singer's entire career. As Steber recalled the night: "The truth was that I loved singing tours-de-force, and I enjoyed every minute of that concert. I'd have to or I wouldn't be a singer. No one would. It's too dangerous, because all of you is out there on the edge every time. But you see, there's something that happens when you sing—and I don't know if people who don't sing can imagine it—but there is an exaltation to the point of pure ecstasy, when singing takes you out of yourself, and music takes you over. And for me, in the act of singing—for that brief time—I transcend my mortal self."

None of the important singers from Steber's generation ever talked like that. But, then, none was ever quite like her. When Steber stood before an audience, she was not there modeling gowns, massaging her ego, or hoping to catch the eye of an influential angel. She had come to sing, and the sheer love of that physical act seemed to radiate from her and out into the hall as a welcoming embrace. No wonder she was one of the most frequent guests on *The Voice of Firestone* when that popular radio program began to be televised in 1949. Steber participated without apology or condescension, even in the quaintly dated "production numbers" that make the surviving kinescopes of the Firestone series such endearing artifacts of early television. Both her voice and generous spirit are irresistible. She seemed to be in love with every aria, old chestnut, and pop novelty that she was asked to sing on those shows—even "If I Could Tell You," a sentimental ballad by Idabelle Firestone that each guest, by sponsor decree, had to sing before the program could begin (only Joan Sutherland ever refused, although she did agree to perform a wordless vocalise over a chorus). No one spun out that treacly signature tune with more enthusiasm or sheer vocal beauty than Steber, and she became so identified with it that, after *The Voice of Firestone* went off the air, she even included the song in her concert recitals.

One moment in those Firestone telecasts (all performed live) sums up the special nature of Steber's vocal alchemy, and it came on the evening of February 1, 1950. During one solo sequence she is "wearing what looks like a quilt and posing in front of a wrinkled backdrop of Tara," wrote an awed Albert Innaurato, playwright and vocal connoisseur, after seeing the video in 1992, "but it doesn't matter. Her singing of 'Carry Me Back to Old Virginny' has the spontaneity and naturalness, the easy sweetness for which Patti was famous, and which we can hear from Melba. The endless breath and firm 'piano' singing of the refrain are feats but don't seem so. Steber is living the song, and the miracles seem as natural as breathing."

Such a rare combination of vocal radiance, technical mastery, and personal charisma should have made Steber at least the leading American singer of her generation, if not one of the greatest the country had ever produced. Some thought so then, and even more do now, but despite her busy career and many achievements, Steber was never quite perceived that way during her lifetime. And toward the end of it, in a moment of introspective honesty that rarely comes to any prima donna, she perhaps put her finger on the reason. It was not just prejudice toward American singers—too many important careers had been made by then to fall back on that convenient excuse.

"I look back over that first 25 years of my career," Steber wrote in a memoir published after her death, "and I can see that much of what happened to me I brought on myself, because in my strongwilled, dramatic way, I wanted to have it all, and I didn't want to wait for anything. Perhaps if I had taken time to think a bit, I might not have charged in so quickly where 'Angels fear to tread'—but if it had been any other way, I might not have been the kind of artist I am." She even forgave Rudolf Bing for the failure of her Met career to fulfill itself when her voice was at its peak in the fifties. Bing, Steber admitted, showed extraordinary patience toward a singer who was often infuriatingly impulsive, unpredictable, and unthinking, even when her own best interests were at stake. "Somebody once labeled me as 'the prima-tive donna'—and that's what I am: a prima donna with a small town kid inside. I've been a maverick all my life, and the establishment has often lost patience with me." In many respects, Steber was her own worst enemy. Had it not been for her love of singing, general good health, optimism, tenacity, and amazing resiliency, she might not have accomplished as much as she did.

Both sides of Steber's family came to America from Germany in the 1800s and settled in Wheeling, West Virginia, where Eleanor arrived on July 17, 1914—born laughing, she was told, and, at nine pounds, already with a weight problem. The girl's first musical memory was the sound of her mother singing soprano solos in St. Matthew's Episcopal Church, and the image never left her. Like so many other mothers in this narrative, Ida Nolte Steber was the dominant force in the household, and she took her daughter's musical ambitions very seriously, making sure that whatever musical instruction Eleanor desired would be the best she could afford. Ida had a fine natural voice, and whatever unconscious yearnings she may have had for a career were clearly passed on to Eleanor. Piano and voice lessons, home musicales, community sings, school shows—the girl was encouraged to make music everywhere. One of Ida's favorite stories depicted her exuberant little daughter singing the long octave drop on the opening phrase of Leonora's "Pace, pace, mio Dio" from Verdi's La Forza del Destino while sliding down the banister—"not a bad way to learn to sing a portamento line," Steber later recalled.

All through childhood and adolescence, Eleanor fairly bubbled with energy and seized every opportunity to perform, since that seemed to be the quickest way to earn parental approval and get her own way. After high school graduation, though, when the time came to think about more serious training, William Steber rebelled at the thought of his daughter going on the stage in any professional capacity. So Ida dipped into her own savings and badgered friends and relatives until she had raised enough capital to send Eleanor off to the New England Conservatory of Music in 1933—"because," Steber guessed, "it was farthest from home, and she knew that if I studied in Boston, she'd eventually get to visit the city herself."

Steber originally entered the conservatory as a piano major, but her voice teacher, William Whitney, heard gold in the girl's throat. He was determined to mine it and convinced her to make the switch by dangling the prospect of a full five-year scholarship. Although not a professional singer himself, the seventy-two-year-old Whitney had made a thorough study of vocal methods, undoubtedly influenced by his father, Myron Whitney, Boston's most celebrated opera and oratorio singer in the latter half of the nineteenth century (see Chapter Six). Both father and son had studied in Florence with Luigi Vannuccini, and the younger Whitney passed this classical bel canto training on to Steber—in certain respects more successfully than he had forty years earlier when, as a young man, he taught an aspiring young mezzo-soprano from Pennsylvania named Louise Homer. Steber once described how Whitney drilled her in basic vocal disciplines, and from her account one can easily understand why this luscious instrument functioned so superbly in its prime years.

> Slowly and methodically he subdued my enthusiastic but undisciplined vocal delivery. He taught me to "mount the breath," which means bringing support up under a phrase and keeping it there so that the sound is riding *on* the breath. It is the breath, vibrating as it passes through the vocal cords and resonating against the mask (the face and its resonant cavities), which produces the quality of tone. With hundreds of exercises, many of them his own creation and others by Panofka and Vaccai, he eased my voice down to the essential core of my middle range, then gradually extended it in either direction, letting it grow naturally in strength and quality.
>
> My Maestro's approach was completely classical . . . He taught me to float a tone and to perfect the fine art of "messa di voce" (a tone beginning pianissimo, gradually swelling to forte

and just as gradually decreasing to the ultimate pianissimo). He drilled me in coloratura, cadenzas, appoggiaturas and embellishments until they were my second nature. He taught me to use my voice like an instrument.

The right chemistry, when it exists between student and teacher, can be mysterious, even inexplicable, and Steber sensed instinctively that Whitney and his methods were right for her. She put complete trust in them for the next six years, soon realizing that when Whitney said, "Pretty good, Steber," she had come up to his highest standards. The soprano never needed another teacher, and she regularly checked in with Whitney even when he was in his late eighties and her career was in high gear. It seemed to do her good to hear that familiar twangy New England voice asking, "Can you still sing, Steber?"—and proving it to his satisfaction, even if that meant only vocalizing over the phone.

Steber performed in as many of the conservatory's musical presentations as she could cram in, while taking the inevitable church jobs to augment her meager allowance. It was in the choir of the Union Congregational Church in February 1934 that she met Edwin Bilby, a recent Harvard liberal arts graduate with vague ideas of becoming a singer himself but no firm career prospects in sight. Less than a year later the couple became formally engaged, much to Ida's dismay—Edwin struck her as an ineffectual young man, even though he seemed more than ready to devote himself completely to Eleanor's musical future. Meanwhile, in 1936, Steber felt she was ready to make her operatic debut in a WPA Opera Project production of *The Flying Dutchman* in English—a bold choice for a twenty-one-year-old lyric soprano, but Whitney eased her carefully into Senta and made sure she did nothing to harm her voice. As with Risë Stevens and Dorothy Kirsten in New York, Steber found useful exposure on radio. Even before graduating, she landed a job as a featured singer on the I. J. Fox Fur Trappers radio show, where she picked up valuable pointers on microphone technique from pop singers Morton Downey and Frank Parker.

In the spring of 1938 Steber got her diploma and that fall she and Edwin were married. Although she stayed on in Boston for a time, Whitney finally pushed his fledgling out of the nest, and she and Edwin moved to New York. It took a couple of years of garret living, lots of auditions, and frequent church singing, but on March 9, 1940, Whitney's teaching and faith paid off. Steber had made it to the finals of the

Metropolitan Opera Auditions of the Air, and two weeks after she had sung that important date, conductor Wilfrid Pelletier phoned to tell her she had won a contract (at $75 a week), and her debut was scheduled for December as Sophie in *Der Rosenkavalier*. When the news broke, Ida saw to it that "Eleanor Steber Day" was promptly declared in Wheeling, a gala occasion that featured a parade through town, signs and billboards on the storefronts, crowds jamming the sidewalks, and a sold out "Homecoming Concert"—the first in what would be an annual event.

Although she was kept busy recording, concertizing, and singing on the radio for the next decade, Steber made the Met the center of her activities. Like all her American colleagues, she knew that the prestige more than made up for the miserable wages, and for this self-confessed "natural born ham," the opera stage would always be her first love. In addition to Sophie, the young soprano was entrusted with Micaela along with the usual lesser Wagnerian maidens, both Rhine and flower. Soon, however, Mozart came into her life—modestly at first, as the First Lady in *Die Zauberflöte*—and he never left it. During Edward Johnson's last decade as general manager, Steber was particularly identified with the Countess in *Le Nozze di Figaro*, but she also sang numerous Donna Elviras and Paminas, and, in 1946, she became the Met's first Constanze in *The Abduction from the Seraglio*. Later, under Rudolf Bing, she added Donna Anna and Fiordiligi to the list, and by the time she left the company in 1966, she had sung more performances of more Mozart roles than any singer in Met history. Steber was only twenty-eight when she sang her first Countess, and the ravishing photographs of her in the role, coupled with recordings of the arias, indicate the enchanting impression she must have made. Her soprano, youthful and shimmering, does indeed float magically on the breath as Whitney had taught her. The long vocal lines are exquisitely shaped, the musical instincts sovereign, and the voice has that special urgency that Steber could, when at her best, control and manipulate to make the most compelling expressive effects.

Johnson knew what a jewel he had in Steber, and other roles quickly came her way: Marguerite, Antonia, Alice Ford, Violetta, Eva, Manon, and Mimì—exactly the right repertory for a young lyric voice, and this time Johnson did not recklessly overuse a valuable budding talent, although Steber never seemed to run out of steam and was always ready for more, outside as well as inside the opera house. There was a war on, of course, and Edwin was away serving in the armed forces, but one gets the impression that Steber didn't miss him a great deal. As Whitney had observed early on, when his pupil was once caught sneaking into a New England Conservatory dorm window well after curfew, "Steber works hard, so let her play hard"—and she did. There may not have been extramarital affairs, at least at first—Ida Steber impressed the morals of a Puritan into her ebullient eldest daughter as well as fierce career ambitions—but Steber was never one to say no to food, drink, and a good time. All three would eventually play a part in creating problems for her in the 1950s. One can almost see it all beginning to happen before our eyes on those early *Voice of Firestone* videos. Just by looking at her live on camera, one has a fairly good idea when a program was probably made after a night of heavy partying, although the singer's voice and professionalism never suffer. Even Steber's weight, always one of her biggest battles, seems to fluctuate from one month to the next.

After the war ended, Steber joined most of her more prominent American colleagues in gingerly testing performance opportunities abroad. The first offer came from the Glyndebourne Festival, always eager to welcome American talent. In 1947 the soprano was invited to sing her Mozart Countess, not during the Sussex festival itself, but on a Glyndebourne visit to the newly founded Edinburgh Festival, an enterprise masterminded by an Austrian impresario named Rudolf Bing. Neither knew what stormy disagreements lay ahead at that time, of course, and Steber had a warmer memory of the effusive compliments about her Mozart singing from no less a longtime secret admirer than the great pianist Artur Schnabel, who was also performing at the festival. There were other sporadic European appearances in the 1950s—Vienna, Bayreuth, Florence—but this career, like those of most American singers of Steber's generation, was conducted mostly at home.

Clearly it was also time to branch out into new repertory, so Steber accepted an offer to sing Madame Butterfly at a staged performance in the Hollywood Bowl on September 3, 1948. Judging from an aircheck of the occasion, the performance was a rocky one. Steber's colleagues are dependable enough—Jan Peerce is Pinkerton and Richard Bonelli, coming to the end of his career, sings Sharpless—but Eugene Ormandy, who rarely conducted opera, is barely in control and more than one scene threatens to come completely unglued. It also indicates that Bing may have been correct about Steber on at least one point. She never did sound quite right in the Puccini idiom, despite her later partiality for Tosca and Minnie. Her voice was simply too rich, with its plush vibrato and throbbing overtones, to give a Puccinian phrase the proper sharply focused thrust, while the composer's heated emotionalism only encouraged her tendency to hyperventilate and overindulge the melodrama of the moment. Like many highly strung singers, Steber was usually at her best singing composers like Mozart and Strauss, who, in their very different ways, successfully challenged her to discipline her impulsiveness while encouraging her deepest expressive instincts.

Steber may have also considered her Bowl date as a chance to explore the possibilities of making a film, but she came along too late for Hollywood, although a "starlet contract" was offered: no studio guarantee for specific projects, a salary that came nowhere near to matching her recital and radio fees, only six weeks off for concert and opera, and—worst of all—an order to diet, although by then she was down to a size 14 dress and about as petite as she was ever going to be. Needless to say, Steber quickly headed back East.

In 1949, on the opening night of Edward Johnson's last season, Steber sang her first Marschallin in *Der Rosenkavalier*—Johnson's crowning gift to her, she said, and the only opening night she was ever to have at the Met. But it was televised, and except for Irving Kolodin, who felt she was too young for the part (at thirty-five she was almost exactly the age Strauss and Hofmannsthal stipulated for the Marschallin), the critics complimented her for style, grace, tenderness, and sensuous charm, as well as for a voice that had matured into a responsive lyric instrument of unusually warm, voluptuous tonal beauty. Steber had been a happy, hardworking singer under Johnson, but with the advent of Bing the picture clouded over almost instantly. As Steber sourly observed, "The opera company, which had become almost 60 percent American, once more began to call heavily on the pool of European-born or trained singers."

Beyond that, Steber's hearty, blunt manner and earthy lifestyle inevitably clashed with Bing's Old World hauteur, no matter how much he may have admired the soprano's vocal quality and usefulness. The rift between them was sealed during the winter of 1953–54, a period when Steber's troubled marriage to Bilby was reaching its rocky conclusion and her professional life had never been more hectic or pressured. It was especially at such times that Steber tended to overindulge, and she did so to excess one night in January, arriving the next morning at a special stage rehearsal of *Figaro* "still feeling my drinks. I made it to the Met all right, but when I got on the stage, I got lost in the scenery. I couldn't remember my entrances or a single word of the text. I tried, but I was gone." Soon after that embarrassing incident, Bing called her into his office and pointed out the dangers of an artist's personal problems spilling into her work and firmly suggested that she do something to straighten out her life.

To a certain extent she did, working and singing—and playing—harder than ever. Some four years later, on the eve of that 1958 marathon concert in Carnegie Hall, it would have seemed to most casual observers that Steber had little to be unhappy about, either with her past accomplishments at Rudolf Bing's Met or with her career activities outside it. In 1951 she scored a great success when Bing cast her as Fiordiligi in the Alfred Lunt English-language production of *Così Fan Tutte*. Later in the same season she made front-page headlines by singing a "doubleheader" on February 9: Desdemona at the matinee and Fiordiligi that evening. Early the following year she took on another major Wagner heroine, Elsa in *Lohengrin*, and was invited to sing and record the same role at Wieland Wagner's "new" Bayreuth that summer. In 1955 she sang the title role in the Met premiere of Strauss's *Arabella* when she was at the peak of her vocal form—the Saturday afternoon broadcast of the opera that year is perhaps the most glorious representation of Steber's voice in its glowing maturity. Yet in spite of all these prestigious career advancements, Bing still refused to increase her performance fee from $800 to $1,500, by then the regular starting rate for what Steber drily called "recent imports" (no doubt a reference to the mid-fifties arrival of Tebaldi and Callas, among others).

Friction with Bing came to a head just before the 1956–57 season when the general manager offered Steber just one role (a repeat of Strauss's Arabella). The soprano said no thank you and went off on an extensive tour of the Far East—with fateful results in Saigon, where she met and fell in love with the man who would soon become her second husband, Major Gordon Andrews. But the soprano settled her differences with the Met and for a while it seemed that all was well again. Steber returned the following season when Bing agreed to let her sing Donna Anna in an all-star new production of *Don Giovanni* and create the title role in Samuel Barber's new opera, *Vanessa*, when Sena Jurinac bowed out at the eleventh hour. Steber had less than six weeks to learn the part, but once again the critics loved her, and even had kind words for the opera. On the strength of that personal triumph, as well as her much praised Donna Anna, she wrested Tosca out of Bing at last. Also during that season, while with companies in Chicago and Philadelphia, she ventured roles that New York seldom, if ever, saw her sing: Maddalena in *Andrea Chénier*, Violetta, Manon Lescaut, and Marguerite. Meanwhile, there was the usual number of recitals and orchestra concerts, not to mention marriage to Gordon Andrews the moment her divorce from Edwin Bilby became final.

But when the Met season began in 1958, the soprano was once again distressed to learn that Bing had assigned her only one new role, Marie in the Met's first presentation of Berg's *Wozzeck*. Steber was not averse to taking on such a challenging assignment, but she expected more. When she heard the news, "I listened in bitter silence, my bel canto soul crying out, 'Why?'" Her marathon recital in October that year was clearly meant to be an answer and a challenge. Later that season she did manage to retain Vanessa and Donna Anna, while holding Bing to an old quid pro quo to give her the Tosca broadcast late in the season, but by now Steber knew that in any future battles she would surely be the loser. Worse, Andrews had now become an active participant in them, and only the soprano herself, still infatuated with her new husband, seemed unaware that Met management considered him a meddling, ignorant boor. When Steber arrived to sing Act II of *Tosca* at a gala performance of opera excerpts the week before her broadcast and found Albanese listed as the heroine, she exploded. So did Gordon Andrews, who became abusive in public with Robert Herman, Bing's assistant manager, an argument that continued "to the front of the house where it was overheard by too many people. There had actually been some shoving, if not actual fisticuffs. The degree of violence hardly matters. I will never know how seriously the battle affected my future; but it seriously damaged, and maybe destroyed, the remaining good will between management and myself."

Steber was right. After that, any hopes she had of singing her beloved Minnie in the Met's long-awaited new production of *La Fanciulla del West*, scheduled to open the 1961–62 season, were dashed. Steber's meager Met assignments over the next couple of years consisted of a few more Annas and Maries, until Bing bluntly suggested that she might be happier pursuing a concert career. The hint was taken, but Bing had to call upon the old fire horse to rush to the rescue one last time: a Met Minnie, finally, was hers on January 17, 1966, as a last-minute replacement when both Dorothy Kirsten and her cover fell ill. "Hello, Steber!" cried the miners—and even some members of the audience—when the soprano burst into the Polka Saloon, six-guns blazing. For more objective viewers, even those of us who had long treasured a great singer more than the Met often seemed to, there was a distinct bitter edge to this triumphant homecoming. By then Steber's aging soprano had begun to unravel, and she now looked distinctly blowsy after years of high living. Beyond that, since she had not sung the role in almost ten years, bits of the score had to be pasted on parts of the scenery. Franco Corelli, who sang Johnson, lasted for one act of this unhappy farce. The tenor pleaded illness, was replaced by the tiny Gaetano Bardini, and the performance stumbled on to the end. Steber, however, seemed oblivious to how pathetic she appeared, even to her most ardent partisans. She was back at the Met, on center stage performing a favorite role, loving every minute of it, and the audience was clearly on her side—"I was so happy, I didn't believe anything could spoil the moment." One person could, though. As she was walking to her dressing room, she spied Bing leaving for home. "He glanced up at me rather obliquely and murmured coolly, 'Good show, Steber.' That was all—not a 'thank you'—not anything!" Bing was obviously grateful, but hardly taken in by the sentiment of the occasion. Steber's Met career, which had begun so rosily twenty-five years earlier, was over.

Even before that unexpected Met farewell, the soprano had begun to channel her restless energies into other activities. The biggest—and, in the end, most disastrous—was establishing and attempting to manage her own record label. Although Steber made as many commercial recordings as most of her American contemporaries, she had the misfortune to live at a time when the country's two premier record companies, RCA Victor and Columbia, were still hesitant to make complete operas. She did participate in a few—performances of *Faust*, *Madama Butterfly*, and *Così Fan Tutte* for Columbia, whose brief flirtation with the Metropolitan during the early fifties yielded ten full-length recordings—but like her colleagues she mostly had to settle for the occasional aria recital and a generous amount of bestselling light music. To rectify that situation, at least partially, Steber and her husband launched ST/AND Records, shorthand for Steber/Andrews, in 1958. Complete operas were out of the question, of course, but studio recordings of the soprano's huge concert repertory and tapes of her recitals would provide the chief source of material, along with albums featuring young instrumentalists and singers playing unusual repertory. At first it looked as though this risky venture might actually work. The idea of a Metropolitan Opera soprano turning herself into a recording entrepreneur was news, and the first batch of releases captured a lot of attention. The initial publicity gave the project a tremendous boost, and the records sold briskly when put on sale at Steber's concerts and in a few selected book and record stores around New York City.

Perhaps this mom-and-pop operation might eventually have succeeded if it had continued to be conducted on a small scale—Steber and Andrews did all the work, right down to stuffing the discs into their jackets. But Andrews unwisely wanted to expand ST/AND into a nationwide operation and Steber soon found herself in deep trouble. The house of cards collapsed, and when the soprano examined the wreckage, she discovered that she had lost $100,000 on the venture, money she had managed to put aside after twenty-five years of hard work. The sorry situation also helped open her eyes to her husband, who had power of attorney and signed the checks, leaving Steber with no idea where most of her money went. Except for an untouchable annuity, her home, and the other properties she insisted on keeping in her own name, everything soon vanished. Down at the Columbia Concerts office, Steber eventually discovered, they didn't speak of "Col. Andrews" by name; he was referred to as "the Chocolate Soldier."

Worse discoveries were to come. During Steber's absences on tour, Andrews had turned Melodie Hill, their Port Jefferson home on Long Island, into a pleasure palace with "the Chocolate Soldier" as the resident Don Juan. By 1966 the marriage had fallen apart, Steber was practically bankrupt, and her career was in shambles. In that sad state the soprano prepared to bid a bittersweet adieu to the Old Met, a token appearance during a gala concert on April 16 prior to the company's move uptown to its glamorous new home at Lincoln Center. Despite frantic last-minute efforts to save the building, the Yellow Brick Brewery on Broadway and Thirty-ninth Street was soon to be demolished, and one can imagine Steber's feelings that evening when her trembling voice launched the quintet from Samuel Barber's *Vanessa*: "Let me look around once more. Who knows when I shall see this house again! To leave, to break, to find, to keep, to stay, to wait, to hope, to dream, to weep and remember."

Ever resilient, Steber picked herself up and went back to work. For three years she and Blanche Thebom, ideally teamed as blond-brunette sisters in the Met's 1951 *Così Fan Tutte*, gave nostalgic joint recitals around the country, singing popular songs, opera duets, and specialty numbers, including a rousing encore of "Bosom Buddies" from *Mame.* She happily took on supporting roles in revivals of *Where's Charley?* and, at New York's City Center, *The Sound of Music.* Still eager to sing before any audience that wanted to hear her, even if that meant shocking the establishment, in the fall of 1973 Steber gave a heavily publicized poolside recital at a popular Manhattan gay bathhouse—the event was even issued on discs by RCA.

By now Steber was in serious danger of becoming a camp caricature of herself, but teaching helped restore her dignity, as well as recoup her financial losses. She began a happy nine-year association with the Cleveland Institute of Music, and through her own Eleanor Steber Music Foundation, established in 1973 with gifts from fans, friends, and colleagues, she further aided the career progress of young near-professionals.

That year also saw one last Steber marathon: a series of three concerts in New York's Alice Tully Hall, one devoted to German lieder, another to American song, and the third to favorite opera selections. "A full-blown, gutsy comeback at 56," wrote the *New York Times* (she was actually fifty-eight), "by an artist who has not only worked hard, but, by her own admission, has lived hard." By then, in fact, she was probably lucky there was any voice left to sing those concerts. Having grown up with the sound of Steber in my ears, I was saddened by the state of her voice for the second recital, the one devoted to American song (thirty songs by twenty-eight composers), but as an apprentice *Times* reviewer I was determined to be gallant. "It would be impossible not to capitulate to Miss Steber's warm presence, the hearty charm of her pre-song commentaries, her sheer pleasure in singing, and her artistic sensitivity, which seems even keener now than during her prime. In the upper register from about C to G, the voice is often as lovely as ever; elsewhere tremolo and register breaks were evident, but Miss Steber shrewdly minimized these problems whenever possible."

Steber never lost the luscious quality of those five notes in her upper octave, and they were there the last time I heard her sing—the Countess's first aria, "Porgi amor"—in a studio at New York radio station WNCN more than a decade later. Another observer found her at the Opera Theater of Saint Louis in the summer of 1988 giving a master class for young singers, and he was astonished by that apparently indestructible top register. "She was then age 74. She wobbled through some Mozart, pointlessly, but *miracolo!* she essayed 'Marietta's Lied' from

Korngold's *Die Tote Stadt*, with its repeated pianissimo high B-flats and, by God, they were there—gorgeous, floating, spinning sound. Christine Brewer, who was there for coaching in the aria, sat by listening to Steber at more than twice her age sing those purling high soprano tones. Brewer glared, jaw dropping, at Steber, then mouthed to her friends: 'I *hate* her!' "

Those Indian-summer high notes were another testimony to the teaching of William Whitney, but the hard facts of the matter are that the overall reliability of the instrument he had so lovingly fashioned at the New England Conservatory during the late thirties began to fail almost immediately after her 1958 Carnegie Hall triumph. With the successes of Vanessa and Donna Anna behind her, Steber, some thought, might have branched out into even more challenging repertory, had Bing been interested or willing to indulge an artist who was obviously not as emotionally stable or professionally organized as Risë Stevens and Dorothy Kirsten. But by 1960, when Steber was forty-six and should have been at her peak, the voice was no longer viable for operatic performance. The same admirer who heard her float those pianissimo high B-flats in 1988, and had known the voice and the woman since the mid-forties, admits that she could no longer even sing Donna Anna in key. "If the voice had been spared the Maries, the Vanessas, and the Wagner—and especially the vodka—Steber's career climax might have been a memorable Norma. Instead it was a sad ending." She proved it in 1960 with a raw, overdriven Cassandre in a Carnegie Hall concert performance of Berlioz's *Les Troyens*. Bing may not have handled the Steber problem very diplomatically at the end, but under the circumstances there was little else he could do for her.

Steber never quite left the public eye, but during the last thirty years of her life, those lucky enough to have shared all or part of the previous twenty could only prop her up and be thankful for the memory. Living in Boston, I was able to experience prime-time Steber during the fifties, often in such unusual roles as Eva and Manon—no one seduced Des Grieux in Saint-Sulpice more vigorously or with more voluptuous tonal beauty. When Steber sang Marguerite in Berlioz's *La Damnation de Faust* with such heartbreaking beauty at Tanglewood in the summer of 1954, few in the audience could have guessed that "the performance was sheer torture of heart and mind." The fated marriage to Bilby had reached its most painful stage, and singing that performance "with and for people from Boston with whom Edwin and I had grown up musically, and with whom we shared our early hopes and dreams," was more than she could bear. And yet even when this difficult evening came to an end, Steber's sense of occasion did not desert her. When leaving the stage for the final time, the conductor Charles Munch accidentally trod on her trailing gown, which ripped off and fell to the floor. Unfazed, Steber bent over, picked it up, waved the remnants at the audience, and merrily danced off.

Like many people still full of life when they near the end, Steber began to believe in reincarnation, and one wonders if, before she died in 1990, she ever pondered the remarkable similarities between herself and Lillian Nordica. Although Steber never went on to the heavier Wagner roles, as Nordica did, both sopranos rejoiced in a healthy, well-trained, gleaming voice that could handle a wide-ranging repertory from lyric-coloratura to spinto-dramatic; both learned how to sing at the New England Conservatory; both were inspired to pursue their careers by overachieving mothers; both enjoyed their biggest European triumph as Elsa at the Bayreuth Festival; both had miserable bad luck with the men in their lives; and, most of all, both worked hard and sang to the end, not because the voice was still there but because they had to. And like Nordica, Steber found complete fulfillment only when she was standing onstage and singing for an audience.

No one realized that better than Steber herself when she wrote, "For me, singing is life! When I am singing, then I am a unified spirit. I have had to accept the fact that I was incapable of expressing myself fully except through my voice. The warmth and love that is 'me' show through consistently in my art; it is the only way I can fully share what I am." The miracle of Eleanor Steber is that every golden note of that appealing credo shone through her art, even as she took her dangerous lifestyle and "prima-tive donna" compulsions to extremes, compromising her voice, art, career, and personal happiness.

None of the singers bred in Edward Johnson's "cradle" at the Metropolitan had a major global career, at least in the sense we understand the term today. But many could well have taken their voices around the world if there had been more regional opportunities to grow at home and if the structure of Rudolf Bing's Met had not become so increasingly Eurocentric. No one was better equipped to succeed than Steber, potentially the greatest of them all and proof that the country could now produce prodigiously gifted singers prepared to compete at the highest international level. Her failure to do so with any consistency when her vocal powers were at their glorious maturity is tragic and a sad reflection of the country's inability to nourish or nurture such a treasure. Her story is also a cautionary tale—the American singer clearly still had a great deal of growing up to do.

Twenty-one

Johnson Babies: II

~~~~~~

When Edward Johnson found it necessary to search out fresh young American voices for the Metropolitan's European-depleted roster during World War II, he could pick and choose among many promising sopranos and mezzos. Repopulating the company's male contingent posed a tougher problem, even with the Metropolitan Opera Auditions of the Air acting as a valuable conduit for new talent. Although Lawrence Tibbett and several other useful voices had appeared during the twenties and thirties, never had there been an entire generation of male American singers to match the quality, let alone generate the box office appeal, of a seemingly inexhaustible stream of heavily promoted vocal sensations from Europe. This was about to change.

The fact that the four Johnson tenor and baritone "discoveries" who enjoyed the most important careers—Jan Peerce, Richard Tucker, Leonard Warren, and Robert Merrill—were children of Ashkenazic Jewish immigrants from Eastern Europe and brought up in New York City is significant and not entirely coincidental. From the early twenties through the war years, the fields of vaudeville, Broadway, radio, film,

early television—indeed, the entire spectrum of the American entertainment scene, behind the curtains as well as in front of them—were filled
with young Jewish talents, many of them nurtured in New York's flourishing immigrant communities, particularly on the Lower East Side. Opera would also eventually benefit from this prodigious explosion of performing talent, but that was still in the future. The idea of singing
leading tenor roles at the Metropolitan was hardly considered an option
when Jacob Pincus Perelmuth, later Jan Peerce, began to think about
musical studies as a child on Lower Manhattan's Orchard Street.

Peerce's parents came from the Jewish towns—shtetls—of Russia.
They were already married and the parents of a son, Mot'l, when they
arrived on the Lower East Side around 1902 and Louis Perelmuth found
work in a local sweatshop as a garment presser. "Back when I came to
America," Perelmuth would recall in later years (he was nearly ninety
when he died in 1963), "you could get a good meal in a restaurant on
Essex Street for six cents. But the trick was, where did you get those six
cents?" The couple's second son, Jacob Pincus (Pinky to his chums,
Pinye or Pinyele at home) was born on June 3, 1904. Tragically, he
became the eldest son in 1907, when six-year-old Mot'l hooked a ride on
the back of an ice wagon, jumped off, and was struck by a horse-drawn
trolley. The family mourned his death for years, but Pinky soon had
other brothers and a sister to take Mot'l's place.

Like many Jewish mothers who grew up in Eastern Europe, Anna
Perelmuth considered music a cultural necessity rather than a mere social
ornament, and she expected that her first child born in the New World
would at least become conversant with a musical instrument if not a
prodigy on it. Since a parlor piano was an unaffordable status symbol,
Anna settled for a fiddle. To pay for it and Pinky's lessons, she promptly
opened a private restaurant in the family apartment, charging twenty or
twenty-five cents for a five-course meal. "Her customers were mostly
shopgirls and single men who came recommended," according to Peerce.
"Often they were Chasidic Jews wanting good kosher food, and always
they were decent people struggling to live on measly salaries, for whom
my mother was a godsend. I can't remember a family dinner without at
least eight paying guests." Even that extra income was not enough to pay
for the only teacher Anna considered good enough for her son, H. M.
Shapiro on 110th Street—a lordly three dollars a week for the lessons,
not to mention an extra dime for the round-trip ride to Shapiro's uptown
studio. So Anna took in boarders, and soon a steady stream of lodgers

joined Anna and Louis, Anna's parents, Pinky, his two brothers, and a sister in their five-room apartment.

Like so many other children of his generation in all parts of America, Peerce was first exposed to music where his family worshipped. "I never discovered my Jewish identity," he said. "I always had it. I can't think of a time when I wasn't going to synagogue. I must have started at the age of two." And it was certainly in the synagogue where Peerce, and his future Met colleagues bred in the same environment, heard the cantor and took him as a vocal role model. In Judaism, the possession of a sweet voice is regarded as a heavenly gift that belongs in the synagogue—not always a tenor voice, perhaps, but as Peerce observed, "The most exciting voice in which to worship God is the tenor. It just seems to have something more to say to God." The great cantor of Peerce's early years was Yossele Rosenblatt, and the cantorial style practiced in those days, as imported from Europe, was one of high intensity and unbridled emotionalism. To both Peerce and Richard Tucker, it must have seemed a short distance between Caruso's unbuttoned approach to Italian opera and the cantor's fervent avowal of religious faith, an outburst of song colored by all the physical suffering, loss, grief, and passionate devotions of the psalmists. Although the two tenors developed individual vocal personalities, both instinctively identified Jewish liturgical music with the arias of Verdi and Puccini, and one can hear the crossover at work in their recordings.

Although Peerce began vocal studies soon after his voice broke, he was still more serious about his violin. After all, there was ready money in it, especially after the Perelmuth family expanded Anna's at-home meals into a full-time catering business. Soon Peerce had organized four other neighborhood lads into Pinky Pearl and His Society Dance Band to play at social functions at four dollars a man plus tips. When summer arrived, the group moved up to the Catskills, where Peerce began to throw in some well-received vocals with his fiddling. He had toyed with medical school, but that plan was set aside in 1928, when he and his longtime girlfriend, Alice Kalmanowitz, decided to get married. For the next several years Pinky Pearl played and sang up and down the borscht circuit from New Jersey to the Catskills until an influential fan heard him sing and arranged an audition with Earl Carroll—a powerful Broadway impresario whose *Vanities* revues in those days were comparable to the *Ziegfeld Follies.*

It was a sobering audition that came to naught when Peerce had the nerve to ask Tom Rooney, Carroll's chief talent booker, for $125 a week.

Rooney laughed in his face. "Kid," he said, "if you were as tall as I am, if you looked more like me, if you had a good profile, and if you didn't have to wear those big thick eyeglasses, and if you were handsomer, instead of having that big chest and even bigger stomach, and if you weren't short and stocky, then you could name your price with Earl Carroll, because the boss is wild about your pipes." Peerce admitted that he had always had a complex about his appearance, and Rooney's unflattering description was all too accurate. Still, he had Alice, whose constant encouragement, shrewd business sense, and ability to keep Peerce's often explosive temper in check and career goals in perspective were probably his most valuable lifelong assets, aside from his voice.

Soon after that debacle, Peerce came to the attention of another Broadway pioneer, Samuel L. "Roxy" Rothafel, whose main ambition in life was to mix good music with showbiz entertainment and bring both to the masses—New York's famous Roxy Theatre was only one of his monuments. The tenor also knew he had found another ally, second only to Alice, when Roxy told him to throw away his fiddle and concentrate on a voice that was bound to make him rich. "You just sing, sing the best you can," Roxy shouted, "and you'll be beautiful! You study and you sing and you'll be even taller and handsomer and more good-looking than you are now!" With that, Roxy found Peerce a teacher, promptly renamed his protégé John Pierce, and gave him a permanent spot on the popular *Radio City Music Hall of the Air* program. Soon after the Music Hall itself opened in 1932, Peerce appeared regularly in that show palace's extravaganzas, as well as the stage-and-screen shows produced by its smaller neighbor, the Center Theater at Sixth Avenue and Forty-ninth Street.

For the rest of the decade Peerce was one of the busiest singers in town, particularly on radio, where his unromantic image was irrelevant and his voice would impress listeners all over the country. In 1934 he could be heard singing every Monday night on *The A & P Gypsies,* and the following year he added a weekly stint on *The Chevrolet Hour.* Sundays were especially busy. Peerce had his *Chevrolet Hour* commitment to fill as well as rehearsals and a performance on the Music Hall's live radio program; as Jascha Pearl in the WEVD studios on Forty-sixth Street, he sang Yiddish, Hebrew, and cantorial music on *Forverts,* a program sponsored by the newspaper *Jewish Daily Forward;* and sandwiched in between there were four stage shows at the Music Hall. It was there in 1936 that Peerce first sang "The Bluebird of Happiness," which, more than any opera aria or cantorial selection, became his signature song for the rest of his life. And by the end of the decade he was singing under the name Jan Peerce, another Roxy invention, which both men felt to be a more appropriately cosmopolitan professional alias than John Pierce.

Peerce was thirty-four when he took his first step into "legit" classical music. The catalyst was none other than Arturo Toscanini, who heard the tenor on a Radio City Music Hall broadcast singing, of all things, the first act of Wagner's *Die Walküre*. The great conductor decided that here was precisely the voice he needed for an upcoming performance of the Beethoven Ninth Symphony with his NBC Symphony Orchestra—the beginning of a fifteen-year association that yielded broadcasts and recordings of Puccini's *La Bohème*, Beethoven's *Fidelio*, and Verdi's *La Traviata*, *Un Ballo in Maschera*, and the last act of *Rigoletto*. "After the Ninth Symphony went well," said Peerce, "I was 'Toscanini's tenor.' What he came to like especially when we did Verdi and Puccini was my pronunciation of Italian. In fact, when he found fault with some of his Italian singers' pronunciation, he would say to me, 'Peerce, you show them.' I used to feel terrible when this happened, and of course the Italians felt worse."

"Don't make too many commitments," Alice Peerce began telling her husband in the late 1930s. "We must leave time open for the Metropolitan." Peerce had already dipped a toe into opera, singing selections and staged scenes at the Music Hall and sharing the spotlight with Robert Weede and James Melton in the touring Columbia Opera. By 1939 Peerce had been studying with Giuseppe Boghetti, and it was this connection with Marian Anderson's teacher that brought him to the attention of Sol Hurok and the Metropolitan. Peerce sang a few arias for the impresario, who immediately said, "All right, Pirs, you'll be my artist." That was that, and the spoken contract—20 percent for concerts and 10 percent for records and radio—remained unchanged for over four decades. Hurok moved his new artist slowly toward opera, since they both agreed that the "slow career"—one that grows gradually but lasts for many years—was best.

Peerce made his San Francisco Opera debut on October 19, 1941, as the Duke in *Rigoletto*, and was a hit. "Such was my ovation that Tibbett [who sang the title role] made me take an extra solo bow, something to which, as a newcomer, I had no right." The tenor thanked Tibbett for letting him have all the glory, but the baritone shrugged and wistfully remarked, "Listen, kid, why shouldn't I? First of all, you deserve it. Second of all, didn't somebody do the same for me?" Two weeks later the call came to audition for Edward Johnson. Peerce was annoyed to hear Hurok talking in the auditorium during his second rendition of "Una furtiva lagrima," but all irritation vanished when his manager told him what the discussion had been about. He was now a member of the company.

Peerce made his Met debut, as Alfredo in *La Traviata*, on the afternoon of November 29. No one had the nerve to tell the tenor that the conductor he had briefly rehearsed with, Gennaro Papi, had dropped dead in his bathroom an hour before curtain time; but despite that unsettling incident, Peerce once again achieved a popular and critical success. Best of all, that Saturday matinee performance, with Jarmila Novotna and Tibbett, was broadcast and preserved, and it shows Peerce's vocal traits as they would remain, more or less unimpaired, for the rest of his life. The basic tonal quality is bright, ringing, and firmly focused on the note, although the overall texture tends to be a trifle dry—for some tastes, the comparative shallowness of the tone, its lack of juicy resonance and its monochromatic coloring, always presented something of a listening block, especially when heard against the rounder, richer tenor sound of Richard Tucker, to whom Peerce would soon inevitably be compared. The superior diction that Toscanini so admired is abundantly audible, as is the elegant musicianship and fervent declamation. Most striking of all, this debutant exudes an infectious self-confidence and absolute security in his vocal personality, virtues that cannot be taught. All those years of performing before audiences at the Music Hall and on radio had obviously not been wasted.

It was a busy decade for Peerce at the Met as he added roles to his repertory: the Duke, Edgardo, Cavaradossi, Riccardo (*Un Ballo in Maschera*), Rodolfo, and Pinkerton—all carefully chosen not to strain Peerce's basically lyric voice. Like most singers, though, Peerce eventually experienced a midlife vocal crisis. Toward the end of the 1940s, after comfortably coasting for fifteen years, Peerce was distressed to hear the bad news from Alice one night as she drove him home after a performance. "Your projection was bad," his severest critic finally summoned the nerve to tell him. "Your intonation has been better. Your phrasing wasn't what it could or should be. Your intensity tonight wasn't what it was a year ago." Alice never got any further because Peerce exploded, probably because he knew that his wife was right. "Only the fact that she was driving kept me from hitting her on the head in traffic and

killing us both. Instead I just yelled and screamed and called her names."
After he calmed down, the tenor had to admit that he had indeed been
slipping into bad habits and disregarding the natural voice placement
that had apparently come to him instinctively when he began singing in
the Catskills as Pinky Pearl. After looking around for a dependable pair
of ears to put him back on the right track, Peerce eventually began
listening to advice from his old pal the baritone Robert Weede, who had
already successfully acted as voice doctor for many of his colleagues.

As with other Johnson Babies, Peerce sensed trouble with Rudolf
Bing right from their chilly first meeting. Although he remained with the
Met until 1968 and left only because of deteriorating eyesight, the
tenor's appearances during Bing's administration were sporadic. The general manager did not appreciate him, Peerce felt, "probably because I was
such a credit to his predecessor. But I was riding high and involved in a
career that was blooming in spite of him."

And it was. Like all his colleagues, Peerce needed the Met for prestige purposes, but the big money lay elsewhere and the tenor was busily
providing generously for Alice and their three children. In addition to
radio, television, recitals, and concert work all over the country, Peerce
recorded most of his major operatic roles as well as an enormous amount
of popular and classical songs and much Jewish liturgical music. There
were even a couple of films, cameo appearances in *Carnegie Hall* and
Tonight We Sing, and a nonsinging role in *Goodbye, Columbus*. The latter was
directed by his son, Larry, who by then had become a successful Hollywood film director, and Peerce and his brother Mac displayed their flair
for comedy by playing two waggish uncles in the carpet business. It was
a healing gesture too, since Larry had been disowned by his father when
he married a Gentile, and it took nearly five years, as well as all of Alice's
best diplomacy, to repair the breach. When Peerce and the Met finally
parted company for good, the tenor followed many singers of his generation into musical comedy, making his Broadway debut in 1971 as an
especially authentic Tevye in *Fiddler on the Roof*. His vocal technique
never again deserted him after that crisis around 1950, and he remained
recognizably the same singer right up to his death in 1984 at age eighty.
The "long career" decided upon by Peerce and Hurok had come to pass,
mainly through shrewd vocal management.

From 1951 to 1964 Peerce toured annually with the Bach Aria
Group, and there were frequent trips to Europe—mostly for concerts,
although he did appear at Moscow's Bolshoi as Alfredo in 1956, with

side trips to Kiev for *Un Ballo in Maschera* and Leningrad for *Rigoletto*. The Russian cultural elite adored him, but for Peerce the great moment of that trip was singing a service in the Great Synagogue of Moscow at a time when such things involved considerable political risk. "I had my own skullcap. The rabbi and the *shamus* handed me a big prayer shawl. I put it on, walked slowly to the altar, and began to sing. For once in my life, the first phrase was one that I had to work hard to get out. Emotionally, it was a very trying moment. My eyes filled with tears as I looked upon this place filled to overflowing by the Jews of Moscow who had come to hear me pray. But once that wall of emotion was penetrated, I gathered strength and sang my heart out for them . . . To this day, I could walk into that synagogue—as I did seven years later—and be recognized and greeted as if I'd been living there all my life. The Jewish community of Moscow and I shared a great moment together."

When Peerce did return to the Great Synagogue of Moscow in 1963, the *New York Herald Tribune* reported on the occasion, an editorial that was read into the *Congressional Record*. Of Peerce's singing of the Thirteenth Psalm—"How long wilt thou forget me, O Lord? Forever? How long wilt thou hide thy face from me?"—the editorial writer commented, "These questions have been weighing for decades on the hearts of Russian Jews. But none would dare voice his complaints to the Lord in public for fear of punishment by the lords of the Kremlin. It was the son of a Jewish emigrant from Russia who was able to do it for them—Jacob Pincus Perelmuth, better known as Jan Peerce. And the reason he could raise the questions without fear of reprisal by the Kremlin is that his father left Russia so that he might be born on Orchard Street."

Simply by the nature of their voices, proximity in age, and choice of repertory (both operatic and cantorial), Jan Peerce and Richard Tucker were probably fated to be rivals, but not, perhaps, bitter enemies who avoided each other even at important family functions. They were, in fact, brothers-in-law—Tucker married Peerce's only sister, Sara, in 1936, and that may have been a contributing factor to the feud. Peerce honorably refused to discuss the situation in his book, since by then (1976) Tucker had been dead just a year and was unable to answer back. Eight years after Peerce's autobiography appeared, though, a family-authorized biography of Tucker by James A. Drake spoke up for him, and by then Peerce was dead. According to Drake, each tenor had his own view of the situation. Peerce apparently saw Tucker as an intolerable narcissist with an intelligence and social demeanor distinctly below his own. It's also clear that Peerce considered Tucker an ingrate who neither acknowledged nor repaid favors done for him early in his career. Tucker, in turn, saw Peerce as a spiteful, jealous man who hid petty hatred under the cloak of religion. "I don't go showing my dirty laundry in public," Tucker said in his oral-history interview for the American Jewish Committee. "But when people ask the question, 'How is it you two brothers-in-law don't get along?' I say it's simple. There's one word—jealousy. This man can't take it when anybody surpasses him."

Tucker always considered himself the singer with the superior voice and more important career, and he wasn't shy about saying so. When people called him "the American Caruso," and the epithet often arose toward the end of his life, Tucker fervently believed it. (Perhaps Peerce was taking another swipe when he observed, "To this day, whenever I hear someone described as 'a second Caruso' or 'the second Gigli,' I think to myself: Maybe second fiddle?") Certainly Tucker was one of the few American singers with little to complain about at the Met after 1950. He thrived under the Bing regime until the day he died, at age sixty-one in 1975—no small achievement, considering the competition during his thirty-one Met seasons ranged from Ramon Vinay to Luciano Pavarotti and in between included Giuseppe di Stefano, Jussi Bjoerling, Ferruccio Tagliavini, Mario del Monaco, Nicolai Gedda, Carlo Bergonzi, Sándor Kónya, Franco Corelli, Jon Vickers, Alfredo Kraus, and Plácido Domingo. But if Tucker did have the voice to compete, he also knew how to protect his interests. When Di Stefano and Tagliavini arrived at the Met in the late forties to threaten young Tucker's gains, the tenor blithely informed his wife not to worry: "I'm gonna be around long after people forget how to spell their names."

Like his brother-in-law, Tucker radiated self-confidence, not only about his singing but also about in his day-to-day living. More than Peerce, though, Tucker was driven by a sense of personal mission that Drake has interpreted as an extension of his Jewish identity, as one of the Chosen People and the recipient of a God-given gift that had predestined him for an extraordinary life. It all began on August 28, 1913, when Israel and Fannie Ticker produced their sixth and last child, Rubin—long after he became Richard Tucker, the tenor was always "Ruby" to friends and family. The Tickers came to America from a shtetl in the Carpathian Mountains near Rumania, and eventually settled in the Williamsburg section of Brooklyn—a tough, urbanized immigrant neighborhood that bore little resemblance to the genteel, almost rural community of 11,000 that Emma Thursby had grown up in seventy years earlier. Not long after arriving, Israel changed his first name to Sam, and found a niche as a middleman in Lower Manhattan's fur industry, selling cutter remnants to be stitched into cheaply made gloves, hats, and other articles of apparel. A devout and observant Orthodox Jew, Sam Ticker noticed his youngest son's remarkable alto voice when the boy was six and immediately placed him in the care of Cantor Samuel Weisser of the Tifereth Israel synagogue on Allen Street on the Lower East Side. There Ruby remained for seven years until his voice changed, during which time Cantor Weisser carefully nurtured the lad's talents: his plummy and evenly produced tone, rock-solid sense of pitch, and complete lack of nervousness when brought forward for a solo.

Otherwise, Ruby led a conventional boyhood, excelling in athletics and impressing his pals with his eagerness to take almost any risk and make it pay off. Aside from singing in the synagogue, Tucker paid little attention to music and sought no formal instruction aside from voice training. Throughout his life, in fact, singing remained strictly a profession, and his family claims he almost never sang at home, even in the shower. Unlike most opera singers of his generation, Tucker took almost no interest in pop music or show tunes—for Tucker, singing was always a matter of hitting home runs, not singles, and home runs meant opera. It was well into their courtship before Sara Perelmuth even realized that her husband-to-be had a voice at all, a fact revealed when the twenty-year-old tenor took the girl to a Rumanian café and serenaded her with "One Night of Love." When the flabbergasted Sara returned home, she burst into her mother's kitchen and exclaimed, "Ruby *sang* for me tonight, Mama! Why, he sings just like Jan!" Some months later, when the couple became formally engaged, Tucker assured Sara that he intended to be not just an opera singer but an opera *star*. "Ruby, have you ever *seen* an opera?" she asked. Tucker shook his head no, but he didn't see why that minor omission should dampen his ambition.

Stardom in opera must have seemed a long way off when Richard and Sara were married in 1936. At the time, Tucker was earning $25 a week as a salesman in the fur business and picking up small change by singing at weddings and bar mitzvahs to finance his voice lessons with Cantor Joseph Mirsky. As was the custom in Orthodox Jewish families, the new bride and groom were expected to live with Sara's parents, who became increasingly fond of their new son-in-law and involved with his career ambitions—no doubt another source of friction with Peerce, who by then was out on his own with Alice and a singing star himself at the Music Hall and on radio. Peerce did help open doors for his brother-in-law, but always begrudgingly and apparently with strongly expressed reservations about Tucker's abilities to make a career as a cantor, let alone as an opera singer—after all, Tucker was a musical illiterate who could not play an instrument or even read notation, and his as yet underdeveloped voice still needed much work. Peerce probably did his biggest favor for Tucker by bringing him to Paul Althouse, who was enjoying far more success as a singing teacher than he had during his modest Metropolitan career competing with Caruso and later with Melchior. Althouse and Tucker hit it off instantly, a fruitful teacher-pupil relationship in which the older singer instilled a lifetime of good vocal habits into his impetuous young charge and gradually built a rather small but securely placed voice into a brilliant lyric tenor of operatic proportions.

Soon after Peerce made his Met debut, as Alfredo in the fall of 1941, the ever-competitive Tucker not coincidentally made his first appearance in opera in the same role, although necessarily under more humble conditions—with the rough-and-ready local Alfredo Salmaggi touring troupe at Manhattan's Al Jolson Theatre. Even Tucker's limitless self-confidence must have been sorely tested—the performance clearly indicated how much he still had to learn compared to Peerce, by then a polished, mature artist. There are no reviews of this debut, but one friend who was there reported that the fledgling opera star "was so stiff he looked like he had rigor mortis. I don't think he moved three feet during any of the acts!" Tucker would only marginally improve his stolid stage presence, a familiar complaint throughout his career, although he soon acquired a better command of idiomatic Italian style after intensive coaching with Angelo Canarutto. Against Althouse's wishes, he felt ready to try out for the Metropolitan Opera Auditions of the Air in 1942, but it was too soon and he lost out to an obscure coloratura named Virginia Card. After that setback, Tucker returned to his cantorial job and, with a loan from Peerce that must have stuck in his craw, decided to bide his time and support his growing family by launching his own business in the fur trade.

The Met may have rejected Tucker for the time being, but the company's talent scouts had hardly written him off, and they quietly kept tabs on the tenor's whereabouts and activities. In 1943 Tucker had begun to be a prominent radio presence on *The Chicago Theatre of the Air* and *Music from the House of Squibb,* while, as the newly appointed cantor of the Brooklyn Jewish Center, his voice was heard in New York weekly by hundreds of wealthy, socially prominent people. Not surprisingly, it was not long before Edward Johnson came to the Center to hear the much-praised tenor for himself. Impressed, Johnson urged Tucker to forget about his failure with the Met Auditions and come down to the house for a personal tryout on the stage. "My boy," he exclaimed, "if you can satisfy the critical ears of two thousand people in this prestigious temple, you can satisfy any audience at the Metropolitan Opera House." A firm offer was made on the spot, but all of Johnson's smooth talking could not disguise a contract that stipulated mostly comprimario parts and cover assignments, with a debut in the five-minute role of the Italian Tenor in *Der Rosenkavalier.* "Talk about *chutzpah,*" Tucker, the born gambler, recalled. "I gave the word a new meaning. I looked Eddie Johnson, Frank St. Leger, and the others right square in the eye and I told them I wasn't going to do *Rosenkavalier* and I wasn't going to be anybody's cover. I said that when I would come to the Metropolitan, I was going to come through the front door, not through the back."

Poor Johnson. It must have seemed like Helen Traubel all over again, and once more he surely realized that he must bow to the inevitable. The Met needed Tucker. Not only had radio exposure already brought his ardent young voice to national attention, but the Met's roster of lyric tenors for the 1944–45 season sorely needed a bit of beef. After the tenor's successful debut, as Enzo in *La Gioconda* on January 25, 1945, Johnson was no doubt grateful that Tucker had forced his hand. "When Tucker finally decided to give his major effort to opera," concluded Irving Kolodin in his history of the Met, "the Metropolitan acquired its most beautiful tenor voice since Gigli's."

That comment was made at a time, long since vanished, when most important singers were considered members of a permanent ensemble rather than corporations of one who negotiate with dozens of opera companies and, during the course of a season, fly around the world from one prestigious engagement to another. The Met remained Tucker's home until the day of his death, even when his European commitments picked up during the last decade of his life. Indeed, when Bing arrived in 1950, Tucker was one of the few American singers bequeathed to him by Johnson who remained a top priority—for fear that, as Bing wrote in his first autobiography, "someone in Europe would hear this remarkably beautiful voice and steal the man away." Bing also appreciated Tucker's professionalism, vocal dependability, and sense of fair play—most startlingly demonstrated early on when the tenor suggested that they toss a coin to decide whether he was to receive $700 or $750 a performance (Tucker lost). "Shall we say it was the most unorthodox negotiation I can recall?" said Bing years later. "I don't believe Richard ever asked me for another increase. If we differed, it was basically over repertoire, and even that was not very often. He was very easy to deal with—especially when compared to some of the other tenors, who were next to impossible at times—and he always gave his best when he performed." As for Tucker, he could assess his relationship with Bing after the general manager retired as "cordial, wonderful, never a harsh word between us. I sang in all his best productions, I had eight opening nights under him [*sic*—it was actually seven], and he put me with the greatest directors and finest maestros the Met ever had. Let's say I did well by him, and he did well by me."

While consolidating his position at the Met, Tucker made just two important extracurricular ventures: his debut in Italy at the Verona Arena in 1947—again as Enzo, opposite a young beginner named Maria Callas—and as Radamès in Toscanini's *Aida* broadcast two years later (Peerce, still "Toscanini's tenor," wouldn't touch the part, even in concert; Tucker himself only sang the role onstage for the first time in 1965). Otherwise, New Yorkers—and the rest of the country through Met broadcasts and tours—watched and listened approvingly as the tenor added one role after another to his repertory. And the sheer sound of this seemingly infallible voice was invariably glorious, blessed with many of the same features so admired when he sang in the synagogue as a boy alto: the unblemished, evenly produced, and effortless tone, along with an unfailing sense of accurate intonation. The basic texture became somewhat darker and even more vibrant as he aged, but the essential lyrical quality never departed, possibly lubricated by the florid cantillations of Jewish liturgical music, a genre that Tucker continued to cultivate enthusiastically throughout his operatic career. That also may be the root of certain provincialisms and odd tics that the tenor never quite erased from his style: an annoying habit of articulating double consonants in Italian by inserting a tiny pause ("Gli oc—chi belli"), sharpening a climactic note for unnecessary extra emphasis, and a lachrymose overuse of glottal catches. The latter lapse did tend to be corrected as time passed—compare the all-too-evident self-pity of his Alvaro in the

1954 EMI recording of *La Forza del Destino* with his far more nobly sculptured remake for RCA a decade later. All in all, though, Tucker gave the
Met nearly thirty years of amazingly consistent vocal excellence.

Tucker managed to make more recordings than many of his contemporaries, but there could and should have been more. Early on he was
hampered by an exclusive contract with Columbia after that company
gave up its brief commitment to record complete operas with the Met in
the mid-fifties. He wriggled out of that hole when RCA began to record
in Rome around 1960, but after making several opera sets, that lucrative
relationship ended abruptly when Tucker briefly interrupted the *Forza*
sessions to fly to New York to attend the bris of his first grandson.
Furious, RCA dropped him for a decade. Luckily, he lived well into the
era of the "pirates," and there is scarcely a role in his repertory that is not
documented by one or more live recordings.

More determined than most of his colleagues to be an international
operatic figure, Tucker began to set his sights on Europe in the late fifties
with debuts at the Vienna State Opera and London's Covent Garden in
1958. In Vienna he gave what he always considered the greatest single
performance of his career. That did not take place in the opera house,
but as with Peerce in Russia, it occurred at a synagogue, and apparently
Tucker had never sung the music of his ancestors with more power or
emotion. As described by Nathalie Eisenstadt, a friend from the tenor's
Brooklyn days who accompanied the family to Vienna, the scene was
even more dramatic than Peerce's moving moment in Moscow. "The
elderly people, especially, sat in their seats and cried. For nearly twenty
years, they had not heard the prayers of a *hazzan* like Richard Tucker.
They were so moved by his singing that they surrounded him like a
king, hoping to embrace him and thank him personally. As Sara and I
and the rebbitsin left the upstairs gallery, we saw elderly women actually
kneel down and kiss Richard's feet, they were so moved."

As he grew older, Tucker's "Caruso complex" became more pronounced. He was just forty-eight, Caruso's age at his death, when he
opened the 1961–62 Met season in Puccini's *La Fanciulla del West* sporting
the same leather jacket worn by Caruso at the world premiere. A year
later Tucker was briefly sidelined by a severe heart attack, and although
he typically responded to his illness with total denial, part of him must
have recognized that time was getting short. In 1960, after all, both Jussi
Bjoerling and Leonard Warren had suddenly succumbed to cardiovascu-
lar disease at the age of forty-eight, and another favorite colleague,

Dimitri Mitropoulos, had collapsed and died on the podium of La Scala. Despite warning signs, Tucker gradually began to add all the stressful Caruso dramatic roles to his repertory—Manrico, Radamès, Canio, Samson—and his performances took on a new vocal intensity. Irving Kolodin once wrote him a note after a particularly searing *Pagliacci*, pleading with the tenor to go easy—surely a unique example of solicitation for a singer on the part of a music critic.

At the time, Tucker was also facing the one truly dangerous rival in his career. Franco Corelli was now on the scene, a huge box office draw who had clearly become a special pet of Bing's. Not only could the younger Corelli compete with Tucker note for note in the same repertory, he also had matinee-idol looks—critics never stopped complimenting Tucker on his voice, but his stocky stage presence continued to have all the allure of a bank president. The rivalry, if there ever was a serious one, never came to a head. Soon after his arrival at the Met, Corelli approached Tucker and asked if he could watch him sing a tricky passage in the last act of *Tosca* and perhaps learn something. "To sing it right, Franco," the surprised Tucker replied, "you have to be Jewish." After that, the two tenors roared with laughter, fell into each other's arms, and became cautious friends.

During his last decade Tucker campaigned tirelessly for a Met revival of Halévy's *La Juive*. Not only had Éléazar been Caruso's last role, but clearly the part of a Jewish goldsmith driven to use his foster daughter as an instrument of revenge against his Christian oppressors had a special resonance for Tucker. The opera itself may be of only spotty musical quality, but Éléazar is a powerfully dramatic figure whose apostrophe to his daughter, Rachel, in the fourth act has an eloquence missing elsewhere in the score. Bing thought *La Juive* a bore and continually refused to consider mounting it, but Tucker finally wrested the promise of a production from Bing's successor, Schuyler Chapin. On New Year's Day, 1975, Chapin phoned Tucker to tell him that the funding had been all but guaranteed for the next season, and his colleagues would include Beverly Sills, Nicolai Gedda, and Paul Plishka, with Leonard Bernstein in the pit. A week after receiving that happy news, Tucker was in Kalamazoo, Michigan, on a concert tour with Robert Merrill when he suffered a massive coronary and died in his hotel room.

At least Tucker died at the top of his profession and he knew it. One night when he and Maria Callas were sharing an ovation after her 1965 return to the Met in *Tosca*, the soprano—just another girl from Washington Heights to Tucker, who called her Mary—wondered why she always felt so good when she sang with him, ever since that *Gioconda* in the Verona Arena so long ago. "It's simple, Mary," Tucker replied. "When you're singing with me, you're in the big leagues."

When Peerce and Tucker arrived at the Metropolitan during the war years, their competition could hardly have been called fierce. Leonard Warren, on the other hand, had the daunting figure of Lawrence Tibbett before him when he made his debut in 1939, as Paolo in *Simon Boccanegra*, with the older baritone in the title role. That season Tibbett also offered his Iago, Germont, Falstaff, Scarpia, Rigoletto, and Amonasro, all parts that would one day be associated with Warren, who probably never dreamed how quickly he would inherit them. Tibbett, it must have seemed at the time, surely had many good years ahead of him, and Warren, for all his vocal promise, lacked Tibbett's dashing stage charisma. The young baritone was not entirely unaware of the impression he made, on both Met management and the public. In 1956, at the peak of his powers, Warren admitted to *Variety* that his road to the top couldn't have been duller:

> Determined on a singing career in the face of my family's disapproval of anyone mad enough to want it, I got a job in the Radio City Music Hall chorus. I had a couple of sustaining radio programs on WOR, sang at weddings and funerals and generally was proving my family's point by the complete lack of distinction in my alleged career, when I was accepted for the Metropolitan Auditions of the Air. When the Music Hall refused me a few weeks off to prepare for it, I quit. I was one of the winners, but at the time I had only the arias I'd sung at the Auditions, so that summer I went to Italy to get some roles under my belt and learn the small part I was to debut in. There I met a charming blonde American voice student, and later we were married. So far you see, it's like many a movie script. It doesn't get any more startling, either.

What was startling was the voice. Born in the Bronx on April 21, 1911, Warren was the son of Russian immigrants named Warenoff, and he fully expected to follow his father in the fur business or take up some other trade. No one in the family had the slightest interest in music, and the future baritone just seemed to drift in that direction when he discovered singing to be more pleasurable than dealing in fur. "I was very much to myself, the dreamer type," Warren once told an interviewer trying hard to pry some colorful background from a man of few words. After a boring year as a business major at Columbia University, he quit to study voice at the Greenwich House Music School and supported himself with various odd jobs, including grease monkey at a local service station. The only encouragement from home apparently came from his grandfather, who, said Warren, "was a frail old man, something of a philosopher, and he used to sit me on his knee and feed me raisins and say, 'You know, Leonard, we all carry a sample case as we go through life. One of these days you're going to be carrying that sample under your arm and you're going to have to show it. When the time comes, be prepared to *deliver.*' " It was a homely piece of advice, but it seemed to stick. Warren surely must have remembered it when he started to deliver all those easy A-flats from the Met stage with a trumpetlike brilliance many of his tenor colleagues envied.

Before the sample case could be displayed, though, it had to contain some wares. During a visit to Radio City Music Hall in 1935, Warren was impressed by how Robert Weede sounded onstage and decided to take the plunge himself, but he only won a spot in the chorus—like Tibbett at the Met, Weede was the Music Hall's star baritone of the moment and not easily dethroned. At the time, Jan Peerce may have been singing songs and arias for Music Hall patrons unseen behind a screen, but Warren never got even that much exposure—in three years he never once had a solo turn. In despair, the baritone went back to his devout grandfather for solace, complaining that "I'm floundering. I'll never get anywhere." This time the sage response was more laconic, but once again it gave Warren something to chew on. "A goal never comes to a man," quoth the old man. Reflecting on that bit of wisdom, Warren decided his fate was indeed in his own hands, and he went off to study with his first important teacher, Sidney Dietch. "When I first heard the voice," Dietch remembered twenty-five years later, "it was of very fine basic material but the quality was not so good. A little rough. I would never have expected him to make the career he has made. But all of a sudden, after two years or so, the voice grew in size, got its characteristic color, and I realized it was a great organ." Warren, too, had grown in size. By the time his voice was fully developed, his unexpanded chest measured fifty-one inches, his abdomen was generously proportioned and his head massive, he took a size 17½ shirt collar, and his weight clocked in at well over two hundred pounds—an impressive torso supported by two thin, spindly legs. Like Peerce and Tucker, Warren hardly cut a glamorous figure onstage or before a camera, and fame came to him almost exclusively through a remarkable vocal endowment.

No major singer, not even Ponselle, arrived at the Metropolitan with less advance fanfare or experience. By the time he won the Met Auditions, Warren had seen just one opera—*La Traviata* at the Met ("I cried like a baby," he said)—and his "sample case" of operatic material contained just five arias and "an inkling" of *Rigoletto*. Up till then his only stage appearance had been back in high school, when he played an Indian in a drama about Daniel Boone. But the voice he and Dietch were working on must have been there, even if no one at the Music Hall wanted to hear it. When Warren sang his first aria at the Auditions, conductor Wilfrid Pelletier rushed into the auditorium to check that someone was not substituting a recording by Ruffo or De Luca. The baritone won a contract on the spot and was sent to Italy for the summer for coaching with Riccardo Picozzi in Milan. There he learned five roles in seven months: Germont, Count di Luna, Ford, Tonio, and his debut role in *Boccanegra*—clearly Met management knew right away what repertory their new find would excel in. The "charming blonde" Warren came home with, Agatha Leifflen, was a voice major from Juilliard studying in Milan. The fact that Agatha was a Catholic posed no problems. Unlike his tenor colleagues, Warren never felt drawn to or defined by his Jewish identity, and he converted to his wife's faith. "Any religion that would claim Agatha," he once confided to Blanche Thebom, "was the one for me."

For once the Johnson team did not seize upon a fresh young voice and misuse it. Still very much the awkward novice when he returned from his crash course in Italy, Warren was brought along slowly. Even before his formal debut, on January 13, 1939, he was eased onstage during Sunday evening concerts, including scenes from *Pagliacci* and *Rigoletto* in costume. Other, more traditional apprentice roles quickly followed Paolo—Valentin, the *Lohengrin* Herald, Escamillo, and Alfio—and later on the high priests in Gluck's *Alceste* and Saint-Saëns's *Samson et Dalila* and the role of Ilo in the premiere of Gian Carlo Menotti's *The Island God* with Astrid Varnay. The role of Ford in *Falstaff*, which he had also prepared for that first season, never materialized—clearly Tibbett had no intention of letting history repeat itself. After Tibbett's vocal crisis of 1940 and the onset of his slow decline, Warren soon found himself stepping into the older baritone's roles more frequently—indeed, he sang his first Rigoletto as a last-minute substitute for Tibbett on a Saturday matinee in December 1943, the day after performing Renato in *Un Ballo in Maschera*. The other big Verdi roles came quickly after that, and during Johnson's last season Warren stepped up from Paolo to sing his first Boccanegra—by then he was the Met's leading Verdi baritone, and destined to play a key role in Rudolf Bing's future plans.

That relationship got off to a bad start. Bing wanted Warren to open his first season, as Rodrigo in *Don Carlo*, but the baritone, by then comfortable with the impromptu style of the Johnson regime, objected to the unprecedented three-week rehearsal period that Bing demanded in his quest for more integrated dramatic productions. The role went to young Robert Merrill, but whatever ill will the incident generated was quickly smoothed over, and soon Warren became an indispensable element in Bing's seasonal planning. During the next decade he added Gérard (*Andrea Chénier*), Scarpia, Carlo (*Ernani*), and Macbeth to his repertory, and appeared in eleven new productions. Although he made a few forays outside the Met during the forties and fifties—in *Il Trovatore* in Mexico City (his only appearances opposite Callas), *Rigoletto* in Buenos Aires, and with the companies in Chicago and San Francisco—Warren seldom ventured far from home thereafter, except to make a La Scala debut in 1953 and a Russian tour in 1958. It was a quiet career, and one of slow, methodical, even dogged progress as the singer worked to improve his vocal style and his dramatic presence while carefully nurturing his voice. Indeed, the most dramatic moment of Warren's life came on the very last night of it, during a performance of *La Forza del Destino*, just three days after he had starred in a new production of *Simon Boccanegra*. The baritone was about to launch the rousing cabaletta to Don Carlo's aria, which begins "Morir, tremenda cosa" ("To die, a momentous thing"), when he pitched face-forward to the floor. A few minutes later he was pronounced dead of a massive cerebral vascular hemorrhage, and the rest of the performance was canceled. Warren was only forty-eight, and looking forward to adding more Verdi roles to his repertory—he had already been hard at work preparing Nabucco for opening night of the 1960–61 season.

Perhaps Warren was not as stolid and even-keeled as he sometimes seemed on the surface. Even his closest colleagues never knew he had been receiving treatment for high blood pressure, and his personal physician, seated in a box next to Agatha, watched him die onstage. Then, too, just the previous week there had been a tremendous blowup during a rehearsal preceding the *Boccanegra* opening when Warren engaged in a heated dispute with the conductor, Dimitri Mitropoulos. The entire orchestra felt demeaned by Warren's verbal onslaught, and only after a personal apology could the rehearsal continue. Less than five months before that tragic night of March 4, 1960, a profile of Warren appeared in the *Times* indicating that however bland the baritone may have appeared from a distance, he was in fact a rather difficult character who "tells other singers how to sing, conductors how to conduct, directors how to direct, photographers how to photograph, recording engineers how to engineer and costumers how to costume; and, they say, if Verdi were around he would tell him how to compose."

Another profile, in *Opera News* much earlier in his Met career, perhaps got at the truth when it described him as a man who "takes his art without levity." "One of his favorite gags," wrote a newspaper columnist, was "to confuse unsuspecting victims by referring to Giuseppe Verdi, his favorite composer, as Joe Green . . ." And that's about as uproarious as it got from a man who had no children and whose main pastimes were playing gin rummy and adding to his miniature railroad collection, a hobby his doctor had advised him to take up when the strain of learning so many roles back in the summer of 1938 for his first Met season brought him close to a nervous breakdown.

But there was that voice—and the spirit of a perfectionist that motivated it—to make him a crucial element in Bing's ensemble. Bing summed up his debt to the baritone: "Warren's death was a terrible blow to the musical quality of our Italian wing: his was a unique voice of great beauty and power, perfectly placed for Verdi. Never an actor, he worked hard at everything he did, and invariably improved his dramatic performance from year to year. I honored him especially, perhaps, for the care he took of himself, not racing around to parties or to perform in far places, making sure he would be in the best possible condition for every performance at the Metropolitan."

The rich, rounded, mellow quality of this voice, fairly bursting with resonant overtones, may not have been to every taste, particularly those preferring a narrower baritonal focus that "speaks" more quickly on the note. But by any standards it was a deluxe, quintessentially "Metropolitan Opera sound," one that seemed to take on a special glow and lustrousness as it opened up and spread itself generously around the big auditorium. And of course the easy top was its special glory—when relaxing with friends Warren would often tear into tenor arias like "Di quella pira" and toss off the high C's that many tenors lacked. He could have, but never did, overindulge that applause-getting facility, and a careful listening to Warren's recordings and live performances reveals just what a thoughtful singer he really was, especially when he is heard polishing his roles over the twenty-year period of his professional activities. His Iago grew into a particularly fascinating vocal creation, even more suave and insinuating than Tibbett's. Warren could also be melodramatically flamboyant when the occasion demanded—listen to his lustful slavering after Gioconda at the end of Ponchielli's potboiler and the crazed rage that follows when she robs him of her body by stabbing herself. Most of all, though, Warren excelled in projecting the musical line and sustained mood of such nobly contained Verdi arias as Germont's "Di Provenza," where, the baritone once remarked, "you have a simple melody and an even simpler accompaniment. It is the voice which must speak, emote, gesture and move. Through voice alone the artist can construct his portrayal."

Nor was Warren quite the stiff, unresponsive actor that history seems to remember. He hardly illuminated character subtleties with the swift, rapierlike precision of a Tito Gobbi, but his impersonations were thoughtfully conceived, effective, and dynamic. He saw Tonio in *Pagliacci*, for instance, not only as a neurotic personality who cannot bear a rebuff but also as a natural actor who can mask his seething emotions under the guise of a seemingly harmless simpleton. When Warren came to study Scarpia, he spent two weeks simply trying to determine the Roman police chief's manner of walking: "Traditionally he carried a cane but he was not lame. The cane, which I did not use, seemed almost a potentially ominous weapon, not an assistance. He was a menacing man, then. He was also, we knew from the script, an aristocrat, a politician, powerful, cruel, suspicious. Such a man would have walked with purpose and authority but also with abrupt changes of pace; periodically he would have stopped suddenly to look back over his shoulder, perhaps to see that his orders were being obeyed, perhaps to observe the effect of his last verbal thrust on the object of his displeasure or of his fancy. The result was a walk of sinister threat."

After he had sung the role for a bit, Warren discovered that Scarpia was Sicilian, so he decided to add an appropriate touch to his costume: long black stockings ornamented with the tiny design of a red clock.

"Those are the kind of stockings that a man of that type would wear. He is so vain, so powerful, that he has to have a touch of color even though he dresses entirely in black. The red clock, I think, allies Scarpia to the Sicilians."

A singer who ponders his roles this closely would inevitably show signs of temperament and impatience with the system, and Warren had worked too hard and achieved too much to suffer fools gladly. With an instrument more refulgent than either Bispham's or Tibbett's, Warren might eventually have won a reputation as singing actor to equal or even surpass his predecessors' had he lived to develop his talents into the final, third phase of his career. This self-made artist was always growing, his goals clearly in sight, and, true to his grandfather's wise words, he definitely delivered.

Although the first fifteen years of Robert Merrill's Metropolitan career coincided with Warren's glory days, the younger baritone never played Tucker to the older man's Peerce. For one thing, there were no family tensions to aggravate any potential feelings of jealousy or rivalry, and the two singers more or less staked out their own turf. Merrill's first signature role was Figaro in *Il Barbiere di Siviglia,* a part that Warren himself realized was physically unsuited to him. Other early Merrill specialties included Enrico Ashton, Escamillo, the *Samson* High Priest, and Marcello—roles that Warren had mostly begun to put aside—as well as Rodrigo in *Don Carlo,* which he never sang. There were, of course, overlaps—Germont, for example, Merrill's debut role on December 15, 1945, and which he continued to perform regularly during his thirty-two Met seasons, 132 times in all. Only after Warren's death did he move into the heavier Verdi repertory, and even then the difference between the two baritones' voices and methods seldom caused Met old-timers to make comparisons or weigh the vocal values of one singer against the other.

Merrill's father, Abraham Millstein, was an apprentice tailor in a little store in Warsaw when he fell in love with the boss's daughter, Lotza, and decided to emigrate to America. He became Abe Miller at Ellis Island when an impatient official simplified his name, and after Lotza arrived they were married. Their first son, Moishe, was born on June 4, 1917, soon followed by a second, Gidalia. Moishe Miller, later Robert Merrill, never looked back on his youth in Williamsburg with the nostalgia that colored Peerce's and Tucker's comparable memories. "It was a filthy, roach- and baby-infested, chalk-marked block," as Merrill recalled his neighborhood, "that got the sun for a few minutes at high noon and for the rest of the day lay in shadows as if under a cloud. It was ugly, gray, and foul, and across its face in colored chalk was a scrawled message to its inhabitants: 'Drop dead!' "

Nor did Merrill draw much strength from his Jewish heritage. He was mostly an unhappy little boy, grossly overweight and afflicted with a stutter, but also with a lovely treble voice that excited his mother no end. Back in Warsaw, young Lotza had been admired for the beauty of her pure soprano but to little avail—the fact that her family never permitted her to study or pursue a career was a canker that gnawed away at her until her death. But she would eventually find consolation in her eldest son, and once again we meet a powerful mother figure determined to propel her offspring to vocal glory. "God gave you a voice and you gotta use it," Lotza insisted. "You walk on your feet, you sit on your *tuchis*, and you'll sing with that voice." As Merrill put it, "From the first time I yelled 'Momma' from the courtyard on South Second Street, Momma was sure of *my* future and called me 'singer mine.' "

Actually, along with playing baseball, young Moishe liked to sing. He never stuttered when he did, and he admired Bing Crosby—or "Pink Cruspy," as Lotza called him after deciding that a pop crooner as a vocal role model was better than nothing: "A Rosenblatt he's not. A Caruso he's not. But it's not such a bad sound when you get used." All that changed when young Moishe reached his teen years and began working as a dress-rack pusher on Eighth Avenue in the garment district. One day he was idly passing the rear of the Metropolitan Opera House while the scenery was being removed from the previous evening's performance, and he wandered in. There was a rehearsal of La Traviata in progress, and the baritone's voice sounded familiar—it was his new idol, Lawrence Tibbett, whom he had recently seen in the movies. Now here was Tibbett in person and singing Germont opposite the beauteous Lucrezia Bori. It was an ecstatic impromptu moment rudely interrupted when some stagehands hastily expelled the intruder. "I couldn't articulate it then, but somehow I knew that inside there was form and that here in the street was only chaos. Inside the theater a beautiful world was in the making; outside it was a jungle. I will never forget the shock of reality when I saw daylight and the sinking feeling when I saw that damned dress rack." When he told Lotza about his revelation, she was overjoyed—her son had received the true calling at last. "Moishela!" she cried. "Tomorrow we make an appointment during your lunch hour with Samuel Margolis of the Metropolitan Opera Building!"

One of the city's leading voice pedagogues, Margolis loved what he heard when Merrill arrived at his studio, and even agreed to teach him free of charge until, as he told the delighted Lotza, "he becomes a star." There were to be many ups and downs in Merrill's career before that, but once he settled into a teaching routine with Margolis, he never broke it and never ran into serious vocal problems. Obviously the technique he gained was precisely the correct one for what must have been a naturally healthy, perfectly positioned baritone voice—even when he left the Met in 1976, it was hardly because the instrument was failing him. Margolis eventually got the lad and his mother free tickets for their first opera—a Saturday matinee *Il Trovatore* on February 15, 1936, with Rethberg, Martinelli, Meisle, and Bonelli—and Merrill was stunned by another American baritone. "He wasn't just singing, making melody; his soaring voice was expressing not only the character he was playing but my own unformed feelings and thoughts. He sang for *me*, and I seemed to be singing through him. That night [*sic*] Richard Bonelli changed me from a confused, stagestruck kid to a true opera student."

Merrill's own Di Luna at the Met was still nearly a dozen years in the future, and there was still a long apprenticeship ahead, in some ways similar to Peerce's in its route from weddings and bar mitzvahs to variety acts on the borscht circuit and finally into opera. By now he was calling himself Merrill Miller, having turned from a shy, insecure adolescent into a smug, arrogant young man very sure of himself and his exceptional vocal gift. It was a sobering moment when, in 1941, he tried out for the Metropolitan Opera Auditions of the Air with Figaro's "Largo al factotum"—and lost. "Totally unprepared," he later admitted, "I showed not one bit of musicianship or discipline. Wit became slapstick; I threw my gift in their faces like a custard pie." Back in the Catskill hotels, the baritone had plenty of time to reconsider his attitude until he met "an agent *and* a gentleman" named Moe Gale, who prodded him into more prestigious venues such as H. Leopold Spitalny's *NBC Concert Orchestra* program, Lewisohn Stadium, and Radio City Music Hall. Now renamed Robert Merrill, he made an opera debut at last: Amonasro in a thrown-together *Aida* in Newark, New Jersey, opposite Gertrude Ribla and Giovanni Martinelli. The aging tenor must have liked what he heard, since he asked young Merrill to sing a first Tonio opposite his Canio in another provincial production, in Worcester, Massachusetts. By 1945 Gale felt Merrill was ready for another try at the Met Auditions, and this time his "vital but disciplined" rendition of Figaro's entrance aria, along with Gérard's "Nemico della patria" from *Andrea Chénier* and Iago's "Credo," won him the top prize and a contract.

Although considered not much better than a stick onstage (next to Merrill, Warren could sometimes seem like Laurence Olivier), the debutant won rave reviews for his fresh, resonant, secure voice, and new roles came quickly. But Merrill still restlessly felt the lure of "show biz" and yearned for even wider celebrity. After all, he was earning only $125 a week at the Met, while his radio engagements netted him $2,000 a week. Beyond that, his bestselling disc of "The Whiffenpoof Song" rose to number one on the Hit Parade, was playing in jukeboxes all over the country, and brought him a six months' royalty check of $45,000. On top of all this was the prestigious connection with Toscanini, who had summoned Merrill to sing Germont in his 1946 NBC Symphony Orchestra performance and broadcast of *La Traviata*. "It marked an association that added a few cubits to my stature as a singer," Merrill admitted. "It added nothing, however, to my gray matter and erased any humility I might have had. Now a favorite of Toscanini, I might just as well have been knighted. My feet never touched the ground, and Sir Moishe began flying in and out of the Metropolitan, barely bothering to rehearse properly." This, Merrill recalled, was his "champagne period": night clubs, flashy girls, fan mail, and claques, but no time to study.

Soon, though, Merrill noticed that Edward Johnson's early fatherly affability toward him had cooled to glacial neglect, and he began to wonder why. "You've asked me to clear the air," Johnson finally told him, "and I will. I have lost all respect for you." The general manager went on to point out the baritone's ill-preparedness, his flippancy at rehearsals, and insensitivity to other singers. Briefly abashed, Merrill vowed to reform, especially since Rudolf Bing, a new, even stricter boss, was on the horizon. Although Bing quickly moved the baritone into his 1950 opening production of *Don Carlo* after Warren bowed out, there was trouble ahead when Merrill signed a contract with Paramount Pictures several weeks into the opera season—the prospect of $65,000 for a few weeks' work on a musical film with Dinah Shore and the possibility of realizing his old dream to become another Bing Crosby proved irresistible. Unfortunately, the filming schedule coincided with the Met's 1951 spring tour, but Merrill blithely set out for Hollywood, certain that Bing would release him from his Met obligations. He was wrong. Citing breach of contract, the general manager fired him on the spot. Worse, *Aaron Slick from Punkin Crik* turned out to be a disaster for all concerned, sending Dinah Shore back to radio and Merrill back to New York, wondering whether he would ever sing opera again. After months of public penance and open letters of apology to the Met, Merrill was reinstated when a forgiving letter from Bing was widely published in the press: "To admit one's mistakes the way you have done is a sign of moral courage and decency. I shall be willing to forget the past." In private, Bing "thawed further, although his index finger was like an icicle pointing at me. 'You'll be a good boy now, Merrill?' " The penitent replied, "I will be a good boy, Mr. Bing."

After that sobering incident, Merrill's career continued smoothly and without dramatic events or interruptions for the next twenty-five years. His three-month marriage to twenty-two-year-old Roberta Peters in 1952, two years after her Met debut as Zerlina, was perhaps his last big mistake ("Roberta was a kid; that's her excuse. I was an idiot; that's mine"). Soon after that brief interlude, he settled into a happy second marriage and a relatively untroubled life that kept him busy singing a conventional repertory (mostly Verdi) at the Met and making occasional guest appearances abroad, along with a generous number of recording dates, television appearances, and concerts. Merrill had learned at last that he was, in fact, no Bing Crosby and never could be—not only was he vocally overqualified for the job, but he possessed little of the easy charm and stage presence to succeed as a pop musical personality. Even his modest leading-man looks—he certainly had far more to offer in that department than Peerce, Tucker, and Warren—were insufficient to make him a bobby-sox idol.

Merrill sang steadily, but by 1976 he finally just wandered away from the Met. It seemed as if he had become bored with the limited repertory he was given, but he made no serious efforts to broaden his artistic horizons. There didn't seem to be anything left to discover in Germont, which by then he had sung more than five hundred times at the Met and elsewhere, a stolid portrait that never varied in any significant way—Alfredo's troubled, bumbling, but loving father had more or less just stood there for thirty years, posing for his own effigy. After hearing the young singer's callow but vocally imposing audition, Toscanini had vowed to "make you a father, *caro,*" but that goal was largely unsuccessful. But then, Merrill's Scarpia never amounted to much more than a cipher, his Count di Luna stalked the stage stiffly, and his Iago emerged as a ludicrous study in silent-movie villainy—a televised rendition of the "Credo" on *The Voice of Firestone* in 1963 is positively hilarious. One can understand why Merrill loathed the virtually invisible Enrico in *Lucia di Lammermoor*—"the lousiest baritone role ever written," he always said—but one can also see why the Met would be so often tempted to cast him in such a faceless but vocally crucial part.

After all, he had that extraordinary sound, and it never failed to fill the house. For sheer vocal quality, Merrill was doubtless the most prodigiously endowed of all the American "Verdi baritones" who graced the international operatic scene during an unbroken sixty-year span from Lawrence Tibbett to Sherrill Milnes. The voice rang out with firm, secure tonal authority over nearly two octaves, and the dynamic range, always under perfect control, was enormous. For those who found Warren's velvet sounds too thick and spongy, the perfect focus of Merrill's no-nonsense, right-on-the-mark attack and lean, columnar tone provided a refreshing alternative. But it was never an art that bore close scrutiny or sustained listening. In fact, there was little evidence that anything much was transpiring behind that impressive, virtually flawless wall of sound. Merrill limited his armory of expressive effects to the mechanical basics, while his habit of attempting to raise the dramatic temperature by applying a sudden "woof" to convenient syllables, whether they required special emphasis or not, quickly degenerated into a meaningless, irritating mannerism. Even so, many of the more sophisticated European baritones who came to the Met during Merrill's prime would stand in the wings and marvel whenever he sang. The sheer beauty of sound that issued from the throat of Lotza's "singer mine" was unparalleled.

Peerce, Tucker, Warren, and Merrill effectively eclipsed most of their lesser male colleagues, who mainly served as useful house singers. For eight years after his Met debut, as Tamino in 1942, James Melton (1904–61) tended to a half dozen or so light lyric roles such as Wilhelm Meister, Massenet's Des Grieux, and Don Ottavio. His late operatic arrival at age thirty-eight was preceded by a decade as one of radio's most popular singing personalities. In fact, Hollywood typecast him in 1935 as the lead in *Stars over Broadway*, the tale of a radio singer who has a spectacular Metropolitan audition, turns his back on opera at the urging of a money-conscious manager, loses his radio audience, and battles his way back to triumph on the Met stage—virtually a capsule of

Melton's own career, except that his busy radio career was never in jeopardy. And, one would have to say, his time at the Met was never one of continual ovations and critical approval, although the more susceptible matrons on the Met board must have been disarmed by seeing such a wholesomely handsome tenor onstage. Like Peerce, Melton got his start at Roxy Rothafel's Roxy Theatre in 1927, where his boyish charm and good looks advanced his career as much as his sweet Irish-style tenor. That pretty much sums up the cosmetic surface appeal of Melton's tiny talent, although at least one critic thought he could have become "a brilliant concert artist if he took himself a little more seriously." It was not to be, however, and in later years Melton was as famous for his extensive collection of antique cars as for his bland singing.

Eugene Conley (1908–81) took on a more strenuous repertory during his seven-year stint at the Met beginning in 1950, although when he was singing Cavaradossi, Faust, Turiddu, Rodolfo, and Alfredo, audiences were inclined to miss Tucker, Bjoerling, or Tagliavini all the more. The most impressive part of Conley's voice was its easy upper extension, which probably explains why he was found at La Scala in 1949 singing Arturo in what was, for those days, a rare revival of Bellini's *I Puritani*, and two years later appearing opposite Maria Callas in *I Vespri Siciliani*. The Italians went wild over the tenor's high notes, and his success in Milan no doubt explains why Johnson immediately tapped him for a quick debut as Faust. He sings the part on the Met's 1951 recording with Eleanor Steber and Cesare Siepi, again providing impressive sounds above the staff but little sense of the music's elegance and lyrical grace. Perhaps Conley's most prestigious moment came when he sang Tom Rakewell in the 1953 American premiere of *The Rake's Progress*, but neither Stravinsky's opera nor its hero's rather pallid performance was much admired by Bing or the New York critics.

Although Brian Sullivan (1917–69) first captured attention on Broadway in 1947 as the juvenile lead in Kurt Weill's *Street Scene*, he sang Florestan in *Fidelio* that same year in Central City, indicating a young American tenor with definite heroic possibilities. His Met bow came a year later, as a much-admired Peter Grimes, followed by Tamino and Don José as he worked his way up to Lohengrin (1953) and Parsifal (1957). Both Wagner roles were sung with earnest concentration and thoughtful lyricism, even if to these ears Sullivan's basically attractive tenor always seemed bottled and rather stiffly managed. New York critics of the day, though, were more impressed, especially after having suffered the long drought that followed Melchior's departure in 1950. For Howard Taubman, Sullivan's Lohengrin was blissfully free of the barking and wobbling usually offered up by provincial German tenors, and Harold C. Schonberg found his singing of Parsifal brushed with "more vibrancy and color than almost any heroic tenor since Melchior."

After reading reviews like that, Sullivan must have felt that it was time to branch out, especially since it was clear by then that, despite the good words in the press, Rudolf Bing had lost interest in him. Karl Böhm, however, thought enough of the tenor to bring him to Vienna in 1959 for Erik in a new production of *Der Fliegende Holländer*, and Sullivan innocently walked right into one of the city's notorious opera scandals. The critics and audiences loathed everything they heard and saw, Sullivan most of all. Such a second-rate tenor, they claimed, could only have been imported by Böhm so he could curry favor in American opera circles. Not much happened after that debacle, although by the late sixties Sullivan had recovered his confidence sufficiently to assay respectable interpretations of Otello and Herod back home on the West Coast. On the basis of those comeback performances, he felt ready to sing his first *Götterdämmerung* Siegfried in Geneva during the spring of 1969. Perhaps Sullivan was unaware that he had been hired only to cover another American tenor, Claude Heater, or perhaps other misunderstandings and disagreements developed after he arrived. At any rate, Sullivan never did get to sing the role and apparently the whole experience devastated him. He disappeared several days after all chances of performing onstage had evaporated, and, according to various conflicting newspaper reports, his body later turned up in Lake Geneva, in the Rhône River, or near an iron grid on a bridge that spans the river.

The baritones of the Johnson era achieved a good deal more success, and they lasted longer. We have already met Robert Weede (1903–72), Peerce's colleague at the Roxy Theatre and Radio City Music Hall in the thirties. Born Robert Wiedefeld—Roxy Rothafel also gave Weede his professional name—he was still singing at the Music Hall when he appeared as Tonio in 1937 during one of the Met's short-lived spring seasons. The baritone's official debut with the company came as Rigoletto in 1941, but his sturdy, penetrating baritone lacked Warren's heady appeal and individual timbre, and despite a consistently good press, the Met called upon Weede only sporadically. He was actually a more important presence in Chicago (he sang in *Il Trovatore* there with Callas in 1955) and San Francisco, where, after seeing him as Verdi's Macbeth,

Frank Loesser asked Weede if he would be interested in the lead of his new "through-composed" Broadway musical, *The Most Happy Fella* (1956). Weede was most definitely interested, and the role of Tony Esposito, certainly as strenuous in its vocal demands as Rigoletto, brought him far more fame and popularity than any of the Verdi roles in his repertory. In fact, those who saw him in both genres were astonished at how much more dramatically alive and vital he seemed on the Broadway stage. Although he never entirely phased out opera, Weede continued to thrive in leading musical comedy roles after that debut, most notably Jerry Herman's *Milk and Honey* (1961), with Molly Picon and, in 1970, Mitch Leigh's *Cry for Us All*, which earned him a Tony nomination.

Like Warren, Mack Harrell (1909–60) died too soon and with much more to offer. Although he proved useful to the Met during his thirteen seasons (on and off from 1939 to 1958), his refined voice and art somehow seemed out of place in a busy repertory opera company. He was used most frequently as a polished Kothner in *Die Meistersinger*, a quicksilver Masetto in *Don Giovanni*, and a host of smaller roles, but his most memorable characterization was surely his elegantly voiced Nick Shadow in *The Rake's Progress*. He also sang Wozzeck in the New York Philharmonic's famous 1951 concert performance of Berg's opera conducted by Dimitri Mitropoulos, later released on disc by Columbia Records. His success with those two pioneering roles indicated where Harrell's musical sympathies truly lay, and it was his bad luck that New York's opera public was unable to appreciate either work, let alone the artist who interpreted them so eloquently. Mostly, though, Harrell excelled as a singer of songs, and the special beauty and quiet glow of his baritone sounded particularly ravishing in German lieder. Unfortunately, concert audiences of the time were not much interested in hearing them either.

Frank Valentino (1907–91) inaugurated his twenty-one Met seasons in 1940 as the loathed Enrico in *Lucia di Lammermoor*, afterward tending to other unglamorous baritone roles no one else wanted to sing much, such as Marcello and Sharpless, while filling in whenever Warren or Merrill were unavailable. After Merrill defected to Hollywood, Valentino got his biggest chance, Rodrigo in *Don Carlo*, although he was soon asked to relinquish the part when the prodigal son returned home. Born Francis Valentine Dinhaupt in the Bronx and raised in Denver, Colorado, the baritone became Francesco Valentino when he set off to Italy in 1927. His operatic debut was in Parma that year, launching a busy European career that might have gone on indefinitely had not the war broken out. He found plenty of work back home, though, even if neither his career nor his sturdy if throaty voice ever generated much special luster.

Frank Guarrera (1923–   ) traveled a similar path after winning the Metropolitan Opera Auditions of the Air in 1948, just two weeks after graduating from the Curtis Institute of Music in Philadelphia, where he studied with Richard Bonelli. That piece of luck initiated a long and honorable period of service to the Met that included 676 performances of thirty-five roles and lasted until 1976. Toscanini, an inveterate radio listener, also heard young Guarrera sing his winning selections, and four days later the baritone was off to La Scala to perform Fanuel in the Maestro's upcoming revival of Boito's *Nerone*. If that represented something of an early peak not to be topped—unless one counts his performance of Ford in Toscanini's 1950 *Falstaff* broadcast—Guarrera still proved his usefulness to Rudolf Bing in numerous ways. Merrill might have been the general manager's obvious choice for Alfred Lunt's English-language production of *Così Fan Tutte*, but that baritone was still in the doghouse in 1951. Besides, Guarrera was just as good-looking as Merrill and a far better actor. Later, the versatile baritone became invaluable after Warren died, and if the rougher nap of his voice could hardly hope to compete in terms of vocal glamour, his Boccanegra developed into a rounded, moving characterization of considerable dramatic stature. Mostly, though, Guarrera looked after the likes of Escamillo, Valentin, Amonasro, Sharpless, Silvio, and Ping, along with the occasional reward of a Germont, Rigoletto, or Scarpia. More prominent assignments might have come his way in the sixties, but by then Bing was looking toward Europe for Warren's successors. So he sang the big-league roles elsewhere on the growing American regional circuit—in San Francisco, Washington, Philadelphia, Central City, and Cincinnati—which was surely delighted to have the services of such a personable and vocally reliable baritone.

The only American bass of consequence to arrive during Johnson's era was Jerome Hines (1921–   ), who started out as a student of chemistry at the University of California, Los Angeles. He had gingerly tested out opera before then—a Monterone in *Rigoletto* in 1941 with the San Francisco Opera—and soon he was encouraged to pursue singing full-time. Like Guarrera, Hines was just twenty-five when he made an inconspicuous Met debut on November 21, 1946, after winning the Caruso Award: the Police Sergeant in *Boris Godunov*, a role he soon set aside as he

progressed up to Pimen and later the Tsar himself. Hines sang uninter-
ruptedly at the Met for nearly forty years, and in 1996 he could still be
found on the regional circuit offering an occasional Méphistophélès or
King Philip in *Don Carlo*. In between, most of the great bass roles were
his at the Met and elsewhere, a huge repertory that included Basilio,
Don Giovanni, Wotan, Gremin (Tchaikovsky's *Eugene Onegin*), Arkel,
Gurnemanz, Fiesco, King Marke, Sarastro, and dozens of others in operas from Handel to Stravinsky. Hines's world-class bass was heard more
extensively abroad than the voices of most of his American contemporaries during the fifties and sixties—Glyndebourne, Rio de Janeiro, Buenos Aires, Mexico City, Bayreuth, Milan—and he even sang Boris at the
Bolshoi. He also expressed his born-again Christian beliefs in an opera
of his own, *I Am the Way* (he tailored the role of Christ for himself), and
in 1968 he published his autobiography, *This Is My Story, This Is My Song.*

Obviously Hines was a man of parts and his voice was definitely a
deluxe instrument: weighty, wide-ranging, smoothly produced, amazingly flexible, and utterly dependable. He was also an imposing figure
onstage, well over six feet, athletically trim, and a competent, thoughtful, if not especially imaginative actor. Such assets ensured a long, continually active career, but the star quality that came easily to Met contemporaries who shared much of his repertory—Cesare Siepi, for
example—eluded Hines. Beyond that, he made very few commercial
recordings—strangely, since his vocal prime coincided with the early
days of LP and stereo, when record companies began to produce complete operas in quantity and might have gratefully made extensive use of
his mellifluous bass. For those who were there, though, the facts made
the situation a little less mysterious. When Hines stepped up to sing
King Philip after Siepi, the effect was rather like that of some suburban
father caught in the middle of a trivial family melodrama rather than a
complex monarch tortured by political and emotional forces beyond his
control. By the same token, when Hines relinquished the role of the
ninety-year-old Grand Inquisitor in the same opera to Hans Hotter or
Hermann Uhde, one suddenly saw how terrifying this cameo could be,
even when delivered by a less vocally gifted but more theatrically imaginative interpreter. Hines's vocal quality took him around the world, but
in many respects he was a pioneering example of the busy but bland
professional American singer, a breed that was destined to multiply.

Twenty-two

Job Hunting

*R*udolf Bing never considered artist development to be a proper Metropolitan Opera function, let alone a necessity. Although he made what he considered appropriate use of the Americans brought along under Johnson, Tucker and Warren especially, Bing "discovered" and promoted few native singers who had not first proven themselves at home and abroad—the exceptions of Roberta Peters, Mildred Miller, Lucine Amara, Rosalind Elias, Martina Arroyo, and Teresa Stratas just about exhaust a meager list. Besides, now that the war was over and foreign talent available once again, Bing felt it imperative to draw upon that resource and reassert the Met's position as the most important international company in the world.

So another ironic turnabout occurred. As a select coterie of celebrated European stars once again descended upon the United States, fledgling American singers began to flock to Europe in search of a career. Most of the Continent's opera houses had survived the bombings, but young native singers to fill them were in short supply and audiences hungered to have their musical culture restored. Meanwhile, America had not as yet developed its regional opera stages, and opportunities to sing at home were no more plentiful than they had been before the war. It soon became obvious to ambitious Americans where the big careers beckoned, and with the help of family money, GI grants, Fulbright scholarships, and any other financial assistance aspiring singers could lay their hands on, one hopeful after another crossed the Atlantic. Most headed for Germany, where there was an opera company in every major city and jobs were especially plentiful. Those whose voices were trained and ready quickly signed up with foreign agents, auditioned, and immediately found work, while others established themselves as students in the principal *Musikhochschulen*—mainly in Berlin, Munich, Hamburg, and Stuttgart—where they could get their bearings, put a foot in the door, and, with luck, be successfully launched.

And for at least a decade the demand seemed insatiable. In the 1950s, German opera houses were crowded with Americans, fresh young voices that had matured after the war and, in most cases, had been taught back home by European immigrants. No wonder they were far better prepared, technically and musically, than their still war-shocked young German counterparts, a fact that became increasingly clear as they aggressively made their presence known. When the Stuttgart Opera gave a new production of *Il Trovatore* in 1959, the local newspapers headlined their reviews EIN AMERIKANISCHER *TROUBADOUR*, and they were correct—the cast featured Astrid Varnay (Leonora), Grace Hoffman (Azucena), Eugene Tobin (Manrico), and Raymond Wolansky (Count di Luna); even the conductor, Armando Aliberti, was an American. Germany's musical honor may have been wounded, but if strong Verdi voices were wanted, hiring Americans seemed the only answer. Varnay, of course, was already a star throughout Germany by then, her early Met career as well as her New World roots almost entirely forgotten. Hoffman (1921–) had arrived in Stuttgart from her native Cleveland in 1955, made the German city her home thereafter, and applied her reliable mezzo-soprano to a great variety of leading roles, from Kundry and Kostelnička to Brangäne and Amneris. Although Hoffman made guest appearances with other companies and even sang briefly at the Met, Tobin (1922–) confined his career to Europe with few exceptions and remained virtually unknown to his countrymen. His repertory in Stuttgart consisted mainly of the major Verdi and Puccini tenor roles, which, during his best years in the late fifties, he sang with remarkable ringing power and security—a major vocal endowment that probably would have traveled further in a different time and place. Wolansky (1926–) was only twenty-six when the Stuttgart Opera engaged him in 1952, and his sturdy baritone eventually took him all over Europe as well as to Covent Garden and Glyndebourne—again, an important voice that Americans seldom heard.

At the same time, another American community sprang up in Munich, its most prominent members being soprano Claire Watson (1927–86), tenors Howard Vandenburg (1918–) and David Thaw (1928–), and bass Kieth Engen (1925–). Only Watson (who was married to Thaw) made much of a name for herself beyond Bavaria, but she never strayed long from Munich, where she was especially prized for the clarity of her soprano, personal warmth, and patrician musical instincts—in Mozart and Strauss particularly, but also in a large repertory that stretched from Handel to Britten. Born Claire McLamore in New York City, Watson got a late start, and her route to Europe was circuitous to say the least. While studying at the Eastman School in Rochester after the war, she married a doctor of biophysics named Michael Watson, and soon realized that her husband was serious when he once told her, "The best way to keep a woman out of trouble is to keep her pregnant." Three children soon followed to prove that Dr. Watson meant what he said. The soprano still kept up her vocal studies, and in New York she was heard by Elisabeth Schumann and Otto Klemperer, who, in 1951, urged her to accept an engagement singing Desdemona with the Graz Opera. She did, and that success quickly brought her offers for Micaela, Freia, and the *Figaro* Countess—until she was summoned home, eventually to produce child number four. After scattershot appearances in the New York area over the next few years, she auditioned and was accepted by the Frankfurt Opera, then headed by the young Georg Solti.

Still, there were family commitments to consider, so Watson compromised: to sing with the Frankfurt Opera twice a year for two periods of three months each and to be a housewife for the other six. That worked out for a while, but when Munich made a tempting offer in 1958, she decided to burn her bridges, get a divorce, and become what her ambitions and natural vocal timbre had always seemed to indicate: an authentic *jugendlicher Sopran*, one whose shimmering, virginal timbre traditionally appealed to German taste—"it had that phosphorescent top register," as she once described it, "and those pianos and pianissimos that could be heard over the orchestra." And there she stayed to pursue a rich, fulfilling career until her retirement in 1976. Named *Kammersängerin* by the Bavarian government in 1962, Watson was never again even tempted to leave her home base, although there were frequent guest appearances in London and Vienna, as well as an occasional foray to San Francisco, Chicago, Pittsburgh, and New Orleans. Even the Metropolitan made overtures, but Bing's offers to sing an Italian repertory did not strike her as appropriate for her voice.

Claire Watson's conscious choice to become an expatriate American soprano was surely the right one for a singer whose special vocal gifts were, in the fifties, more marketable abroad than at home. There were others prominently at work in Germany—Arlene Saunders (1935–   ), Edith Lang (1927–   ), and Norman Mittelmann (1932–   ) in Hamburg; Donald Grobe (1929–86) and Barry McDaniel (1930–   ) in Berlin; Sylvia Stahlman (1929–   ) in Frankfurt—while some tried their luck in Italy. Here there was less demand for imports, partly because Italy's musical life had not been quite so disrupted as Germany's and partly because the American temperament naturally seemed to fit in more comfortably up north. Even so, some found a modest success. Anne McKnight (1926–   ), for example, arrived in Italy with Toscanini's imprimatur after singing Musetta in the Maestro's 1946 NBC performances of *La Bohème*. After changing her name to Anna de Cavalieri, the soprano soon demonstrated that native Italians had nothing on her when it came to charged theatrics or emotive melodrama, and for a while she found her Aida and Turandot in demand up and down the country until the wear and tear began to tell. A more demure vocal personality, Margherita Roberti (1928–   ), specialized in Verdi during the late fifties and sixties, while her modest but idiomatic command of Verdi style even brought her to the Met in 1962. She hardly created much excitement in New York, but the few who heard her one Aida and two Toscas were probably unaware at the time that they were actually listening to Margaret Roberts from Davenport, Iowa.

Some Americans even made it into the sacred precincts of the Vienna State Opera, where it was perhaps hardest to adapt to local traditions, since the war had not seriously disrupted that distinguished house's tightly knit core ensemble. One American who succeeded was Teresa Stich-Randall (1927–   ) from West Hartford, Connecticut, whose instrumentally oriented vocalism and refined musicianship won her the title of Austrian *Kammersängerin* in 1962. Another young soprano who had the good fortune to catch Toscanini's ear, Stich-Randall was barely out of Columbia University (where, as Teresa Stich in 1947, she sang Henrietta M. in the world premiere of Virgil Thomson's *The Mother of Us All*) when the Maestro heard her over the radio and was captivated. After singing the Priestess in the conductor's 1949 broadcast of *Aida* and, a year later, Nannetta in *Falstaff*, Stich-Randall was virtually assured of a career. Armed with a Fulbright, she left for Europe, winning the 1951 Lausanne Singing Competition and making her debut in Weber's *Oberon*—as a mermaid splashing about in a pool at Florence's outdoor Boboli Gardens. From there she moved quickly on to more prestigious engagements at the Salzburg Festival, reaching Vienna in 1952 as Violetta.

The Austrian public took to Stich-Randall instantly, and from her recordings, surviving broadcasts, and memories of her performances, it is not difficult to understand why. Again, the voice is tuned to a special taste, but its narrow, piercing attack and tightly coiled vibrato were calculated to enchant a Viennese audience that had grown up doting on sopranos with identical vocal characteristics, prizing them particularly in the Mozart repertory that Stich-Randall would soon make her own. Indeed, the fierce intensity of her expressive mannerisms tended to be even more extreme than those of such local favorites as Lisa Della Casa and Elisabeth Schwarzkopf. Although she appeared with some frequency on the international scene over the next twenty years and briefly became a familiar Donna Anna at the Met in the early sixties after Eleanor Steber had departed, Stich-Randall never achieved equivalent success elsewhere, and, like Watson in Munich, she more or less remained a local celebrity. Many ears found her hard-edged tone rather unpleasant, while her typewriterish execution of coloratura sounded distinctly unstylish, if not comical, next to Callas or Sutherland. Phyllis Curtin, a soprano with a rather different voice and technique, as well as musical priorities, once told a tale of how she continually failed to please conductor Josef Krips, definitely a Stich-Randall partisan. Nothing seemed to be going right during rehearsal and finally the impatient conductor asked Curtin flat out why she could not sing Mozart like Frau Stich-Randall. "Because," came the exasperated reply, "I have vocal cords in my throat, not two wires."

Singers who took the European route during the fifties and sixties understandably found it prudent to become part of a permanent ensemble, which offered not only professional security but such not-to-be-scorned middle-class attractions as a pension and health benefits as well. Those who tried to make a go of it as freelancers more or less had to live by their wits, and many simply fell by the wayside. Nan Merriman (1920–), though, had her select circle of admirers and seldom found herself unemployed despite never belonging to any European company. Once again Toscanini provided the initial boost to propel a young singer on her way. That the Pittsburgh-born Merriman arrived in New York after a brief career of supplying background vocals for Hollywood films hardly prejudiced the conductor, who simply liked her warm musical manner and the appealing smoky sound of her mezzo-soprano. In fact, Toscanini used Merriman in more NBC broadcasts than any American singer other than Jan Peerce, casting her as Maddalena in the last act of *Rigoletto*, Meg in *Falstaff*, Emilia in *Otello*, Orfeo in Act II of Gluck's opera, and in Beethoven's *Missa Solemnis*. She also won the approval of Toscanini protégé Guido Cantelli, who engaged her to sing Dorabella in *Così Fan Tutte* at the Piccola Scala in 1955–56. By then Merriman was already well known in the part—two years earlier she had recorded it with an all-star cast under Herbert von Karajan.

After that high-profile success, she was kept busy for the next ten years in Europe—Aix, Glyndebourne, Vienna, Paris—a singer who chose her dates and repertory with care in order not to strain a smallish voice that would never have suited a conventional operatic repertory in large houses. The incisive attack, throbbing vibrancy, and wide expressive range of her voice were probably heard to best advantage in the song literature. EMI recorded her in two LP discs of French and Spanish music during the mid-fifties, records that never lasted long in the commercial catalogues but soon became collectors' items among vocal connoisseurs. Presumably satisfied with a quiet yet fulfilling career, Merriman retired in 1965, her voice and artistry still in peak condition.

Some singers never made it to Europe, or remained there only briefly, and looked for work wherever they could find it at home.

For a brief time after the war, it seemed as though opera might make a go of it on Broadway, attracting new audiences and creating its own singing stars. Gershwin's *Porgy and Bess* of 1935 provided a prologue of sorts, but the trend really began in 1947 with Weill's *Street Scene*. Despite a disappointingly short Broadway run (only years later would *Street Scene*, like *Porgy*, find its real home in the opera house), the show did help launch the careers of Brian Sullivan and Polyna Stoska (1911–). After performing her brief Broadway stint, the soprano followed Sullivan to the Met, where they shared the stage in *Peter Grimes*. From what little one can hear of her on recorded excerpts from the Weill opera and a few Met broadcasts, Stoska had a strong voice and temperament to match, qualities that should have taken her further.

As a Broadway opera composer, Gian Carlo Menotti had more luck than Weill did. His 1947 double bill of *The Medium* and *The Telephone* was a huge hit, so much so that he followed that success with *The Consul* (1950) and *The Saint of Bleecker Street* (1954). It soon became clear that the commercial music theater and the world of opera would not mix, but at least each new Menotti work introduced one high-powered vocal personality: Marie Powers (1910–73) as the haunted Madame Flora in *The Medium*, Patricia Neway (1919–   ) as the doomed Magda Sorel in *The Consul*, and David Poleri (1921–67) as the incestuous sinner in *The Saint of Bleecker Street*. With acting skills to match their aggressive vocalism, both Powers and Neway may have sounded as if they were made of iron and steel, but the impression was deceptive and their voices soon collapsed after nightly appearances in Broadway runs of such strenuous music. Poleri's ringing Italian-style tenor, on the other hand, survived longer, and he might even have gone on to a more important career had not his unpredictable behavior proved to be his undoing. Once, while singing *Carmen* with the New York City Opera on tour in Chicago, the temperamental Poleri reached the final scene, dropped his knife, shouted "Finish it yourself!" and marched off the stage, leaving a perplexed Carmen, Gloria Lane, to stab herself to death. After that, Poleri was not surprisingly viewed as a bad risk. The tenor did make a glorious sound, though, one that was prematurely silenced when he died in a helicopter crash in Hawaii.

By far the largest group of singers who found themselves more or less on their own at this time and looking for ways to use their voices was the generation of black Americans born shortly after the turn of the century and who overlapped with Marian Anderson. Paul Robeson (1898–1976) was her contemporary, and had society been structured differently or had his musical inclinations led him in other directions, he might have been her male counterpart. As it turned out, Robeson's career, important as it was in theater, films, and politics, takes him outside the scope of this chronicle, although the wine-rich beauty of his bass-baritone and the power of his interpretive personality could surely have made him one of the outstanding opera and concert singers of the interwar years.

As an actor, Robeson often performed Eugene O'Neill's *The Emperor Jones*, but when the Metropolitan decided to produce Louis Gruenberg's operatic setting in 1933, no one thought of engaging him to sing the title role. That prestigious assignment automatically went to Lawrence Tibbett, who blackened his face and body for the part, and enjoyed one of his greatest dramatic triumphs. Robeson did sing excerpts from the opera in 1940, with the Philadelphia Orchestra under Eugene Ormandy, and eight years before that he had sung chunks of *Boris Godunov*, again in concert, at New York's Lewisohn Stadium. But it was too soon to ask for more, and all an approving critic like Olin Downes could do was lament that such "an exceptional endowment as a singer and dramatic inter- preter" would never be heard and seen as Boris, Méphistophélès, or the Emperor Jones. Perhaps it could never have happened anyway, since Robeson's priorities lay elsewhere. "I am essentially a folk song singer," he once said when asked why he seldom strayed from the repertory of spirituals in which he specialized. "I am not especially at home with Brahms or Schumann." Posterity will always most closely identify this resonant voice with "Ol' Man River" from *Show Boat*, a song that Jerome Kern wrote specifically with Robeson's rolling tones and expressive in- tensity in mind.

Two significant events occurred during the thirties that paved the way for the acceptance of black singers as operatic artists: the first per- formances of the Virgil Thomson–Gertrude Stein opera *Four Saints in Three Acts* and Gershwin's *Porgy and Bess*. When *Saints* had its world pre- miere in February 1934, it was generally considered a wild avant-garde novelty, not only for its free-associative libretto and "white-key" hymn tunes but because Thomson had cast the entire opera with black singers. There was no inherent reason to do so, other than the fact that Thom- son liked the way blacks sounded when they sang his music. No one in the original *Saints* cast ever found a way to pursue a career of national prominence, but at least for the first time in America a group of black singers could find employment in a musical context that did not depend on their ethnicity.

The opera was sufficiently noteworthy for RCA Victor to record about half the score, and the voices as preserved there support Thom- son's initial instincts and later enthusiastic approval. Beatrice Robinson- Wayne's soprano is especially attractive in its gleaming, diamondlike brilliance, in perfect contrast to Edward Matthews's plangent baritone, and virtually every other member of the cast possesses not only real vocal quality but also an assured technique. The country could certainly have used a lyric tenor as polished and elegant as Charles Holland (1909–87), who sang St. Chavez on the recording and sounds ravishing in the role. Although he later sang on radio and in black musicals, Holland felt underused at home and in 1949 went to Europe, where, like blacks from Elizabeth Greenfield to Roland Hayes, he found a more welcoming atmosphere. After making his debut at the Paris Opéra in 1954, as Mozart's Tamino, Holland pursued a successful operatic career throughout Europe for the next twenty years, singing a wide range of standard-repertory operas unavailable to him in America, including *Carmen*, *Faust*, *Boris Godunov*, *Les Pêcheurs de Perles*, and, in London, an English version of *Otello*, which must have sorely taxed this lyrical voice. The tenor did not return home until the age of seventy-two, when he gave an emotional recital in Carnegie Hall before an audience that had cause to regret not only his long absence but also the reasons for it.

Many *Saints* cast members went on to sing in *Porgy and Bess* the following year, although the work itself was mostly dismissed by "serious" music critics, who perceived *Porgy* as some sort of strange halfbreed spawned of opera and musical comedy—even Thomson scorned the piece at first as "crooked folklore and halfway opera, a strong but crippled work." Still, this "folk opera," as Gershwin termed it, gave black singers additional exposure and helped weaken barriers, even if it hardly removed them. The original Bess, Anne Brown (1912–   ), eventually found racial prejudice in America intolerable, and in 1948 she settled in Norway, where she married a Norwegian lawyer and Olympic athlete named Thorleif Schjelderup. Shortly before leaving the country, however, Brown recorded much of the role that made her famous, revealing a lovely soprano so easily produced and securely managed that one wonders where it would have taken her had she been born a decade or so later. Brown told her story in a moving autobiography, *Sang fra Frossen Gren* (*Song from a Frozen Branch*), which became a bestseller in Norway but, typically, was never translated or made available in the United States.

When the first Porgy, Todd Duncan (1903–   ), reluctantly showed up at Gershwin's apartment to audition for the role, he apparently did not place that composer's music high on his career agenda. As Duncan later recalled, "I knew he was big on Broadway. But I thought of him as 'Tin Pan Alley,' so I wasn't really interested." At the time, the young baritone was basking in excellent reviews for singing Alfio in *Cavalleria Rusticana* with the Aeolian Opera Association, an all-black company that briefly performed at New York's City Center, and he was aiming for more serious things. After hearing Duncan sing about ten bars of Giuseppe Sarti's bel canto aria "Lungi dal caro bene," Gershwin interrupted him, offered him the part on the spot, and the surprised singer accepted. Apparently the composer wanted a Porgy who possessed Duncan's vocal personality—sweet, dreamy, aristocratic—rather than that of the more burly-voiced baritones who later became associated with the role. Those qualities are certainly evident in the recordings Duncan made, of Porgy's music as well as of numerous spirituals.

In any case, Duncan became identified with *Porgy* and stuck with the show even after its initial Broadway run of 124 performances, appearing in the revivals of 1937 and 1942. He also went on to perform in three musicals, the London production of Kenneth Leslie-Smith's *The Sun Never Sets* (1938) and on Broadway Vernon Duke's *Cabin in the Sky* (1940) and Kurt Weill's *Lost in the Stars* (1944). Although the event never quite received the publicity of Marian Anderson's Met debut in 1955, Duncan's engagement as the first black singer to perform with the recently established New York City Opera in 1945—as Tonio in *Pagliacci*—represented a major breakthrough that probably would not have been possible without the international fame he had won as Porgy. But it was still too soon, and Duncan never became a prominent member of the company. During the previous year he gave a well-received recital debut at Town Hall—the same stage on which Anderson had astonished New York concertgoers in 1935—and, like Roland Hayes, the baritone spent the rest of his career as a concert singer, chalking up more than two thousand recitals in fifty-six different countries before retiring to his Washington, D.C., studio to teach the next generation.

That Dorothy Maynor (1910–96) never sang in opera may have had less to do with racial issues than with a singer whose temperament was not in the least bit theatrical and whose tiny but plump physique discouraged stage acting. Standing at less than five feet and weighing over two hundred pounds, Maynor was once described in *Collier's* by Howard Taubman as a "pint-sized and serious Aunt Jemima"—such a condescending if not racist remark in an otherwise laudatory article was apparently considered a sign of affection for a black artist in 1940. The soprano was born in Norfolk, Virginia, the daughter and granddaughter of ministers, and quietly pursued her musical education until she sang informally for Serge Koussevitzky in August 1939 at Tanglewood, the Boston Symphony's summer home in the Berkshires. The conductor was overwhelmed by the purity and beauty of her voice, and after making his famous pronouncement—"Her voice is a miracle, a musical revelation that the world must hear"—he immediately summoned the press. The critics agreed, filled the papers with praise, and that November all New York was primed and eager for Maynor's recital debut at Town Hall.

Olin Downes was ecstatic. "She proved that she had virtually everything needed by a great artist," he wrote. "The superb voice, one of the finest that the public can hear today; exceptional musicianship and accuracy of intonation; emotional intensity, communicative power. Her breath control is extraordinary, and it enables her to phrase with wonderful beauty and distinction of melodic line, and to maintain an exquisite pianissimo." It's hard to believe that Maynor was quite that good, and one gets the feeling that Downes was attempting to right more than a century's worth of discriminatory wrongs in one review. There was bound to be a backlash, and Virgil Thomson provided it a year later, just two weeks after he became music critic of the *New York Herald Tribune*, when he wrote that Maynor was hardly in full control of her voice and sounded "immature vocally and immature emotionally." The outcry that followed nearly cost Thomson his job, since by then Maynor was, if not a symbol of black achievement like Anderson, a much-beloved figure.

Actually, the truth probably lay somewhere between Downes's effusive praise and Thomson's doubts. Maynor's voice, despite its real technical limitations, had an irresistible silvery sheen, and her musical personality, if not the most sophisticated, was always welcoming and urgent—qualities that definitely transcended race and were best savored in her signature piece, Charpentier's "Depuis le jour." That aria from *Louise* ended nearly every Maynor recital and brought out all the shimmering radiance and floating tones of her top register. That gorgeous sound alone made the soprano a popular musical figure during a busy concert and radio career that lasted until 1961, when she retired to devote the rest of her life to her noble pet project, the Harlem School of the Arts, which she founded in 1963. Throughout the forties and fifties, Maynor complemented Anderson's regal, wrapt spirituality with her more approachable beaming presence—two great voices that helped make the aspirations of America's next generation of black singers more attainable.

Many other blacks of Maynor's generation might have had more prominent careers in a later period. One notable voice belonged to Ellabelle Davis (1907–60), who was actually working as a dressmaker in

New York City when a wealthy client heard her singing an aria by opera's most famous seamstress—Louise's "Depuis le jour"—and whisked her off to a voice teacher. Impressed by her performance in a New York revival of William Boyce's eighteenth-century opera *The Chaplet* in 1941, Thomson opined that "she may well become the next great Negro singer." After her recital debut in 1944, he was even more enthusiastic. But Davis was never able to achieve Maynor's fame or popularity, though, let alone Anderson's. An Aida in Mexico City in 1946 launched a brief career that took her Aida to La Scala, but mostly she gave recitals until her untimely death from cancer at fifty-three.

Also appearing with Davis in the Boyce opera was Carol Brice (1918–85), and Thomson raved about her as well, marveling over her "rich and round mezzo voice of wide range." Although also championed by Koussevitzky, who helped spur her career in 1946 by presenting her privately to a group of influential Boston Symphony patrons, Brice never found ways to fulfill her promise. After a decade of concert work and supportive reviews, her voice began to fail her, and the rest of her career was limited to musical shows and the occasional revival of *Porgy and Bess*.

Well before Anderson broke the color barrier at the Metropolitan, blacks were gradually becoming familiar presences at the New York City Opera following Todd Duncan's pioneering appearance in 1945. A year later Camilla Williams (1922–   ) arrived to sing Madama Butterfly, a role especially suited to her vibrant soprano and generous temperament. "Already she is one of the great Butterflys of our day," a great Butterfly of another day, Geraldine Farrar, told *Newsweek* after Williams's debut. In 1948 Lawrence Winters made his City Opera debut singing Amonasro to Williams's Aida at a time when casting even these two roles with black artists was unprecedented. That baritone's sturdy voice and dynamic presence did not go unnoticed, and he soon was entrusted with such roles as Escamillo, Tonio, the *Hoffmann* villains, and Rigoletto. Without fanfare, Winters achieved the distinction of being the first black singer to perform standard-repertory roles on a regular basis with an American opera company. Another potentially valuable baritone, Robert McFerrin, appeared in the City Opera's world premiere of *Troubled Island* by the black composer William Grant Still on March 31, 1949. It was a modest warm-up for a more important engagement when McFerrin sang Amonasro at the Metropolitan on January 27, 1955, the first black male to sing with the Met, just three weeks after Marian Anderson's debut. Nearly two years later Mattiwilda Dobbs was singing leading soprano roles with the company, and another major hurdle had been vaulted. By 1961, when Leontyne Price took full possession of the Met stage as Leonora in *Il Trovatore*, the black singer's long battle for recognition seemed unequivocally won at last.

Not every American singer who joined a European company after the war was absorbed into the regional musical culture to remain more or less a local celebrity. A select few made the initial journey abroad, found success, and proceeded to win international stardom, and one of the first was George London (1920–85). In fact, London's triumph, swiftly achieved with the Vienna State Opera at the Theater an der Wien in 1949, no doubt encouraged others that the postwar situation in Europe was so favorable for American vocal talent that such success could happen to anyone. But of course not every singer who tried had this bass-baritone's vocal equipment, dark good looks, imposing physique, iron determination, and disciplined approach to his craft.

London was also fortunate enough to arrive early in the game. Beyond that, he was just plain lucky. When he reached Paris in June 1949, he had few contacts, but one of them was a Viennese agent named Martin Taubman, brother of his American-based coach and accompanist, Leo Taubman. Martin Taubman suggested that they travel immediately to Brussels, where the Vienna State Opera was giving a series of guest appearances. Although exhausted after a long *Figaro* rehearsal, the conductor Karl Böhm agreed to hear London, who launched into the Toreador Song from *Carmen*. After about ten measures, the entire *Figaro* cast—key members of the famous Vienna Mozart ensemble, including Sena Jurinac, Irmgard Seefried, Paul Schöffler, and Erich Kunz—returned to the rehearsal room, and when London was through, the singers gave him what Taubman correctly described as "the greatest ovation of your career to date." He then sang aria after aria until the Opera's director, Franz Salmhofer (who was seen shaking his head throughout the whole audition, mumbling "What a voice! What a voice!"), offered him a contract on the spot. London had been in Europe barely a week, and already he was scheduled to sing at the Vienna State Opera on September 3, a date less than three months off.

London's debut was to be as Amonasro in *Aida*, "a role which I had never sung in my life before, but since my repertoire sounded pretty sparse at the time they had asked for it, I just mentioned it as a part I knew." Here was another brazen but typical American maneuver of those days, and one to be used by many other singers with varying degrees of success. At least London had the whole summer to study Amonasro, which is a short role, but since all his future colleagues had performed in the production many times, there would be no stage rehearsals and the twenty-nine-year-old debutant would have to go on cold. "You dog," one admiring old-timer told London backstage during the ovation that followed his major scene, "you could only have done that with your American nerves." More than merely surviving a risky gamble, the bass-baritone immediately became Vienna's new darling. "After the third act," wrote critic Joseph Wechsberg, "during which Amonasro is seen for the last time, Set Svanholm, who was singing the part of Radamès that evening, pushed London out from the wings to take a solo bow, and the response of the opera-loving Viennese made it clear that in this man who could act as well as sing they had found a new star, whom they would long remember."

Vienna's new toast of the town had been born George Burnstein in Montreal, the only child of Jewish-Russian immigrants who had met in New York and become American citizens before moving to Canada to start a millinery business. As a youngster growing up in the mid-thirties, London was among the first generation of American singers initially attracted to opera by the Metropolitan's Saturday afternoon broadcasts, which he tuned in religiously after 1935, when the Burnstein family, still suffering from the 1929 crash, moved to hoped-for greener pastures in Los Angeles. There young George was sent off to Hollywood High, where he developed a crush on a classmate named Lana Turner, then a devastating brunette, and discovered his voice—an impressed neighbor heard him singing in the shower one day and suggested voice lessons. When he entered Los Angeles City College, London enrolled in one of the first opera workshops to be established in America, presided over by Dr. Hugo Strelitzer, a fugitive from Nazi Germany and a prominent choral director in Berlin. It was Strelitzer who gave the budding singer a solid grounding in music theory and vocal style, and pointed him toward his first performance opportunities. Soon London, already focused and dedicated, was polishing the rough edges of his vocal technique and building up his scrawny six-foot-two frame into the body of a muscular athlete—both a healthy voice and a strong physique would be essential, he quickly realized, for that dynamic combination of singing and acting he hoped to achieve.

Few budding opera stars who arrived on the international scene in the 1950s had a more unorthodox practical training. There were to be many different theatrical adventures between 1941, when George Burnson first appeared onstage at the Hollywood Bowl (virtually unnoticed as Dr. Grenvil in *La Traviata* with Jarmila Novotna and Jan Peerce), and 1949, when George London emerged triumphantly at the Vienna State Opera. He took on the usual church jobs, civic choral presentations, and local operetta productions, but London also turned up in the chorus of the *Ice Follies*, and he can also be spied in a few frames of the classic Bogart-Bergman film, *Casablanca*, singing "The Marseillaise." Gradually more important engagements materialized, most crucially in a touring company of Romberg's *The Desert Song* in 1946. When the show arrived for a brief run in New York, his performance as Ali-Ben-Ali caught the attention of Columbia Artists' Arthur Judson.

Now that he had concert management, London embarked on his most colorful pre-opera experience. Just before Judson took the bass-baritone into the fold, he had signed up "a young tenor by the name of Mario Lanza and he didn't know what to do with him at the time. And he also had a young soprano by the name of Frances Yeend from Vancouver, a girl with a glorious voice. Somebody in the corporation got the bright idea to put these three youngsters together, and they dubbed us the Bel Canto Trio. We toured the U.S., Canada, and Mexico for one entire season. I couldn't tell how many concerts we did, I could not believe it possible, but when you are that young and that ambitious, nothing is too difficult. At the end of that tour Mario went into the movies, he was snapped up immediately. Frances went on to other operatic activities, and I decided that the time had come to get down to serious work on my operatic career . . ."

Before heading off to Europe in 1949, London spent a year working on his voice with Paola Novikova, a retired Russian-American soprano, and studying the key roles that he had a hunch might come in handy one day with another Russian-American: George Doubrovsky, a former baritone colleague of Feodor Chaliapin. He was also advised by Léon Rothier, a retired French character bass and a Metropolitan institution for years, to specialize in a few roles and never let himself be taken for granted, as Rothier himself had been. London agreed, and he immediately began to concentrate on the star parts that would soon make him famous, especially Scarpia, Boris Godunov, and Méphistophélès.

London's Vienna debut seemed like a storybook success, but it wasn't, really—despite his unorthodox training and limited operatic experience, the baritone had never wasted a moment, he knew all about the rigors of performing under pressure, and he was more than ready. After Amonasro, he sang Méphistophélès and the four *Hoffmann* villains at the State Opera, also to great acclaim, followed by his first solo recital. Rudolf Bing saw London in *Hoffmann* during his second Vienna season, and the Met's front door instantly swung open for a debut on opening night of the 1951–52 season, once again as Amonasro. The next morning Virgil Thomson wrote in the *Tribune*, "Last night [London] took his place among the greatest singing actors we have any of us known"— a judgment subsequently confirmed when London offered Met audiences his Don Giovanni, Boris, Scarpia, Count Almaviva in *Figaro*, Mandryka in *Arabella*, Golaud, and the Dutchman. Wieland Wagner had also taken notice of the new American sensation, and felt he had found his ideal Wotan for the Bayreuth Festival's grand reopening in 1951. London didn't yet feel ready for that challenge, but he did accept Amfortas in *Parsifal*, another role that became identified with him. Salzburg and other major companies all over Europe soon beckoned. As early as 1951, Columbia Records had signed him up and released his first solo recording, and by 1953 George London was an operatic celebrity in demand everywhere.

Although Leonard Warren and Robert Merrill had to some degree filled the void left by Lawrence Tibbett, neither baritone projected an equivalent dynamic stage presence. London did, and in that sense he was Tibbett's true successor, even though the only operatic parts they shared were Amonasro, Wolfram, Scarpia, Escamillo, the *Hoffmann* villains, and Golaud. They also differed to the extent that Tibbett sang just one Wagner role and avoided Mozart, while London sang virtually no Verdi, aside from his signature role of Amonasro, and had little taste for taking on new operas (Menotti's *The Last Savage* as the one not so notable exception). But both singers worked diligently on the total package until they became masters of stagecraft—not only in how they presented themselves, in concert as well as opera, but also in the inventive ways they used their voices to create dramatic personalities. Perhaps London's more thickly textured instrument lacked Tibbett's vocal suavity and quickness of articulation, but its dark, virile beauty, billowing tonal amplitude, and easy flexibility—remarkable in a voice of such deep-centered resonance—encompassed an astonishing range of expressive colors and nuances. It was uniquely adaptable to explore in detail the emotional lives of the two Mozart noblemen that he sang so incomparably, but perhaps this voice never sounded more haunting than when London applied it to the music of Wagner's two cursed antiheroes, Amfortas and the Dutchman. The latter role, especially when ignited by Leonie Rysanek's demonic Senta, developed over the years into a portrait of truly frightening intensity. Surely London would have become the Wotan of the age had not fate cruelly stepped in not long after he sang his first complete *Ring* cycle in Cologne in 1963.

Despite his busy professional life, London always prided himself on being the most careful of singers—about diet, health, exercise, and vocal maintenance—once his career settled into a comfortable groove; like Jan Peerce, he intended to be in there for the long haul. And yet it all lasted barely fifteen years. Not long after his triumph in Russia—on September 16, 1960, he became the first American to sing Boris at the Bolshoi—London began feeling uncomfortable at the top of his range, and in 1963 he was diagnosed as having a paralyzed nerve on the right vocal cord. At first there were no serious consequences, but soon London's ever-attentive wife, Nora, "could tell that some high notes were becoming increasingly difficult, and then little by little I noticed that he did not have the customary thrust in the voice."

The situation slowly degenerated, and by the end of 1964 every performance had become an ordeal. The agony was prolonged until one final Amfortas at the Met on March 10, 1966. There was a brief remission, but a year later London decided never to sing in public again. Worse tragedies were to come. In 1977, after more than a decade of directing opera and holding various posts in artistic administration, London suffered a heart attack. That, coupled with a stroke, left him virtually immobile and literally voiceless until his death eight years later. Long before that, this noble singer wrote his own simple artistic epitaph in a letter to his wife after his last concerts in Germany. The audiences were enthusiastic, but London was dissatisfied and he knew that the time had come: "When I sing it must be representative of my best standards. Otherwise I harm my inner self even if the public buys it."

Many younger singers would be inspired by London's dynamic artistry and commitment, none more so than the soprano Teresa Stratas when she summed up his legacy: "George London? The sheer virility of his sound? The genius of his musical imagination? His brilliant acting? No. It was more than that . . . It was as if you were in the presence of a great lifeforce. There was always that feeling of danger."

Europe was still hungry for voices from the New World when Anna Moffo (1932–), fortified with a Fulbright scholarship, set off for Italy in 1955 to make her fortune. A shoemaker's daughter from Wayne, Pennsylvania, Moffo naturally headed for the land of her ancestors when it became clear to her that she might be happier as a singer than as a nun, the family's ambition for young Anna. When she got her career, and a big one it was for a while, perhaps few were more surprised than the folks back home. During her four years as a scholarship student at the Curtis Institute of Music in Philadelphia, Anna worked hard, studied piano and viola in addition to voice. She impressed everyone as a devastatingly attractive girl, but also as a good student who absorbed everything from her Curtis mentors, then including some of the best in the country. There was an inkling of what lay ahead when Anna won the Philadelphia Orchestra Young Artists Auditions in 1954 and Eugene Ormandy said, "It is impossible for anyone that beautiful to sing, so I closed my eyes and she won on merit." Once Moffo arrived in Rome, she blossomed further under the tutelage of the fabled coach Luigi Ricci and the soprano Mercedes Llopart, who at the time was also working on the voices of Renata Scotto and Fiorenza Cossotto.

There was more competition in Italy than in Germany, and the musical life down south, opera in particular, was typically disorganized. Still, Moffo had special qualities to offer. Her youthful lyric soprano encompassed both coloratura agility and the dramatic *slancio* necessary for heavier parts. She was also, one suspects, far better trained than her Italian colleagues, not only in vocal technique but also in other musical disciplines—few Italian singers in those days, she soon discovered, were even taught to read music. Besides, the girl who once caught Ormandy's eye had developed into an exceptionally glamorous young woman, so it was probably a sign of the times that she got her first big break in a 1956 televised production of *Madama Butterfly*. That exposure instantly propelled her to a major career, and soon all her professional activities were being closely supervised by her new husband, Mario Lanfranchi, who had directed the *Butterfly* production.

"Suddenly I was interviewed five times a day, my picture was in every magazine," Moffo recalled years later. "Right away they started to nail me with 'The New Callas' title, and I didn't want that." Lanfranchi apparently did, and he soon edged Moffo into Callas's bel canto repertory of Lucia, Amina, Elvira, Violetta, and Gilda. Italy continued to be her home base, but by 1957 she was securely launched on a busy international itinerary that, over the next few years, took her to London, Paris, Salzburg, Vienna, and back home to Chicago and the Metropolitan. There were also hundreds of TV appearances and numerous Italian films—in Europe during the fifties and sixties, Moffo was as famous for her movies as her operatic performances. *Una Storia d'Amore* in 1970 became the most notorious, mainly for what everyone thought was a nude scene. "If I had known that this would make more news than if I had done *Salome* . . ." Moffo sighed. "In the film I am in the shower, and I am not nude. I. Am. Not. Nude. It was a closed set, and one Italian creep photographer got in there. In the angle he got of me, I *look* nude, but I'm not. I am *not.* It was all hype, phony. But anyway, it was very, very upsetting. This was one of the things that began the steady decline of my marriage."

Husbands of opera singers are a breed apart. The benign ones offer unconditional love and support, managing such harmless details as travel arrangements and the diva's fans while leaving the important career matters to professionals. Others take complete charge for better or worse, and in Moffo's case Lanfranchi may have done her irreparable harm during their marriage, when she was young, eager for fame, and her voice was functioning at its very best. Thinking back on it all while vainly struggling to recover from a vocal crisis in the mid-seventies, Moffo knew that something had gone wrong, even though she was never more in demand. "I did an average of twelve new roles a year for the first four years of my career," she said. "They were all star parts. The smallest role I ever sang was Micaela. Then there were more roles because of recordings and movies. To date [1977] I've done 136 altogether. I was working too hard and traveling too much. I got mixed up in TV, films, things like that. Psychologically I was miserable, *always* away, *always* alone. But I don't think I was singing *that* badly until I reached a point where I was just *so* tired."

Until she reached that depressing point, though, Moffo gave much pleasure to audiences and won general critical approval, even during the competitive years when her repertory overlapped with such goddesses as Callas and Tebaldi on the one hand and a vocal phenomenon like Sutherland on the other. Violetta became the role most closely associated with her (by 1990 she claimed to have sung it 877 times), a rather soft, pastel interpretation when compared to Callas's searing intensity, perhaps, but still touching in its genuine vulnerability and skillful vocalization, sung in lovely, unblemished tones brushed with a delicate pathos.

And of course she looked ravishing. After her Metropolitan debut, as Violetta in November 1959, Richard Rodgers rushed backstage and offered to write a Broadway musical version of *Camille* if only Moffo would take nine months off to star in it. Lanfranchi may have been tempted, but by then he could not find a way to interrupt this busy operatic career, even for such an alluring commercial project, and for most of the sixties Moffo continued her progress around the globe. Her complete recordings from that period—*La Traviata*, Verdi's *Luisa Miller*, *Lucia di Lammermoor*, Puccini's *La Rondine*, *La Bohème*, and *Le Nozze di Figaro*—may not reveal an arrestingly original vocal talent, but they continue to make highly enjoyable listening. Most interesting of all, they display Moffo's appealing vocal endowment in its all-too-brief prime, a lyric soprano with easy coloratura facility but also with a dramatic edge that made such Puccini roles as Butterfly, Mimì, and Liù available to her. No wonder Violetta became her best role as some murmured about a "second Callas." No wonder, too, that it was all over too soon.

Some singers enter their prime when they reach forty, but Moffo was more or less a wreck by then, physically and emotionally. As early as 1968 she fainted onstage during a *Traviata* performance in Berlin, and when it happened again in Venice, the press began to suspect that perhaps the swooning had less to do with nervous exhaustion than with a vocally troubled diva's hunger for publicity. There was an infamous Met broadcast of *Lucia* on February 1, 1969, now considered something of a party item, when Moffo's voice was in such parlous condition that Rudolf Bing was apparently prepared to ring down the curtain rather than risk having her Mad Scene beamed out across the country. In an attempt to get her voice and career back together, Moffo finally removed herself from Lanfranchi's influence, divorcing him in 1972, but it was too late, and there were worse professional embarrassments ahead. In 1974 the soprano married Robert Sarnoff, RCA's chairman of the board, utterly enchanted to have such a glamorous opera singer for his new wife but oblivious to her vocal troubles. Although Moffo's voice was pretty well shot by then, neither she nor Sarnoff seemed to notice, and RCA launched a huge campaign to publicize her latest recordings, principally a complete performance of Massenet's *Thaïs*. The reviews were devastating.

Eventually even Sarnoff and Moffo herself suspected that perhaps she wasn't singing quite as well as she used to. The New York voice doctor and teacher Beverley Johnson was called in, and she reported her diagnosis of Moffo's problems to the press: "It's just that somebody along the way forgot to tell her that you can't run a Rolls-Royce without gas in it. Anna had one of the really naturally beautiful voices, like Tebaldi. But she never had any true physiological technique to fall back on. She had no breath support; there was no resonance in the middle and lower voice. Only air was coming out. So what we've been trying to do for the past two years is wash away the crud and build up her stamina. A singer, like an athlete, has to have every workable muscle trained."

That sounded like a reasonable, if crude, analysis of the situation, but even after working with Johnson, Moffo never regained more than a fraction of the original vocal quality that her new teacher had correctly identified, nor did she really succeed in restructuring her voice in purely technical terms. Moffo's story is the classic cautionary tale of too much too soon. She became one of the first mid-twentieth-century singers whose voice was completely used up, not so much through a faulty technique but by ambitious managers, media hype, bad advice, and frantic jetting about the globe. Although the soprano's high-profile international career was effectively over by the mid-seventies, she never quite seemed to accept the fact. As late as 1990, when Moffo was nearing sixty, a cruel cover story in the journal *Opera Monthly* painted a pathetic portrait as she talked of such dubious upcoming projects as the Marschallin, Aida, and Norma. "And of course, I'm still going to sing *Traviata* and *Lucia* and *Puritani* and that kind of thing forever," she promised. If these performances actually took place, no one seems to know where or when. Perhaps her fans, friends, and even a merciful press have ignored it all, preferring to remember that brief moment when Anna Moffo was one of America's loveliest and most engaging lyric-dramatic sopranos.

The list of performances given by James McCracken (1926–88) at the Metropolitan makes strange reading. Between the time he made his debut in 1953, in the tiny part of Parpignol in *La Bohème*, and his death thirty-five years later, he had sung both the Messenger and Radamès in *Aida*, Roderigo and the title role in *Otello*, a messenger and Samson in *Samson et Dalila*. There are numerous anonymous walk-on parts—heralds, servants, retainers, and such—but interspersed among them are also some of the heaviest roles in the dramatic tenor repertory: Canio, Tannhäuser, Don José, Florestan, Calaf, and Don Alvaro. McCracken accomplished what many at the time would have thought impossible. He began on the bottom rung in the country's premier opera house during the early Bing years, and he might well have remained there. Instead, after a few frustrating seasons he took himself to Europe and returned in 1963 to initiate his second Met career as Otello. That phase of his Met life may not always have run smoothly, but when McCracken died, his obituary in the *Times* could accurately state that he was "the most successful dramatic tenor yet produced by the United States."

McCracken's burly voice must have been the main reason why he was signed on by Bing's talent scouts, who apparently heard only a sturdy comprimario who could give solid day-in, day-out service in small roles. Indeed, McCracken's two similarly endowed contemporaries, Robert Nagy and Charles Anthony, did precisely that for many seasons. At first the young tenor was elated. "If I don't become a fine singing actor, it won't be the fault of the Metropolitan," he said in 1953 when asked about all the training and onstage experience the Met was giving an operatic novice whose main exposure up to then had been solo stints at the Roxy Theatre and on Broadway as a chorus boy in the musical version of *A Tree Grows in Brooklyn*. Such gratitude quickly ceased when McCracken found himself going nowhere. He soon realized that "in one of the world's great opera houses, a person in my voice category sings either the messenger or the lead. There are almost no small roles—like there are for a mezzo—that give my kind of tenor the chance to grow within the company."

Finding himself a young tenor with a big voice and big ambitions trapped in a big rut, McCracken and his second wife—Sandra Warfield, a mezzo-soprano who was also toiling as a Met comprimario and hoping for better things—turned their backs on New York and job security, and left for Europe. They eventually got lucky, but not lucky overnight like George London. The next six years were full of poverty, rejection, and disappointment, but by 1959 both singers had found a sympathetic ear in Herbert Graf, the new chief administrator at the Zurich opera house, who heard the tenor's potential. It was in Zurich that McCracken began singing major roles with regularity and where, in 1961, Bing finally heard his erstwhile comprimario perform Otello, which by then he had sung all over Europe. Arrangements were immediately made to bring the tenor back to the Met in a new production of Verdi's opera, and on March 10, 1963, when McCracken made his second debut, Otello's ringing cry of "Esultate!" never sounded more authentically triumphant.

The next years were busy ones, capped at the Met in the seventies when McCracken starred in new productions of Otello, Carmen, Aida, Le Prophète, and Tannhäuser.

Even during his most active period, McCracken created controversy with his voice—both its unusual texture and his vocal method were not to all tastes. The intensely pressurized tone and prominent vibrato relaxed only when he carried the voice over into a detached falsetto to achieve a pianissimo that some never accepted as a legitimate device. And yet no one ever said that McCracken could not be heard, and his ringing tones carried easily over the loudest orchestral onslaughts. An imposing man, larger even than Leonard Warren, the five-foot-ten singer's weight varied between 240 and 270 pounds, and his chest expanded to fifty-four inches—eight inches more, it was said in Time magazine in 1963, than the boxer Sonny Liston's and twelve more than the ample bust of actress Jayne Mansfield. Despite his enormous girth, McCracken could still give committed performances of consistent high energy and dramatic power, although perhaps his physical presence was a factor in his next Met fight, first ignited after two telecasts of Otello were taken from him. McCracken accepted the first loss stoically but took the next one as a personal slap. In the fall of 1978 he gave two weeks' notice, and left the company scrambling to fill some of the hardest-to-cast tenor roles in the repertory. Nor was this his first professional blowup. In 1964 the tenor had signed an exclusive contract with Decca Records stipulating a whole series of complete operas that never materialized. Since McCracken felt he could have recorded them with competing labels while Decca failed to act, he claimed that the situation had damaged his career, sued the company for $120,000, and won.

In all these battles one is inclined to sympathize with a basically decent man who often seemed to be fighting internecine music-business politics for what he believed to be only right and fair. And he eventually got what he wanted. A third Met career began in 1983, when he participated in the company's centennial gala singing Otello's "Dio mi potevi scagliar." That was followed, at last, by a Live from the Met telecast on January 3, 1985, when McCracken sang Radamès opposite Leontyne Price's final Aida. Unfortunately, it was too late by then. When he left the Met in a huff, the tenor was probably at the peak of his career, but time had caught up with him seven years later and his valedictory Radamès sounded dry, colorless, and too carefully husbanded. Undaunted, McCracken continued to sing to the end, dying from a stroke in April 1988 before he could fulfill his Met commitments as Manrico in *Il Trovatore* that month.

Evelyn Lear (1926–) and Thomas Stewart (1928–) were married in 1955 and left for Europe a year later, both with Fulbright scholarships to the Berlin Hochschule für Musik. Unlike McCracken and Warfield, neither had the prestige of having sung even tiny roles at the Metropolitan Opera, and their performance history up till then had been typically improvisatory. Stewart had come to New York's Juilliard School from San Saba, Texas, after a brief army stint at the end of the war. There he met Lear, a fellow Juilliard student and a divorcée struggling to raise two small children but still determined to make a career. After graduation, reality set in with a vengeance for both of them, although Stewart sang bass roles briefly with the Chicago Lyric and the New York City Opera. "They were shaky times," Stewart later said. "We were kicked around, scrounging here and there. It's disgusting what you have to do—churches, borscht belt, choruses, television, capsule operas, everything. I even won a TV contest and appeared with Mae West at the Latin Quarter!"

Lear was not doing much better. There was a Concert Artist's Guild Award in 1955, a Town Hall recital, and a lead role in Marc Blitzstein's *Reuben, Reuben*, which folded in Boston during its out-of-town tryouts. None of that seemed to be leading anywhere, nor did all the summer-tent work and musicales for Hadassah and ladies' clubs. She came within a hair of playing the lead in *West Side Story*, but was deemed too old for Maria. "Our world was at rock bottom," said Stewart, who was finally persuaded by Frederic Cohen, director of the Juilliard Opera Workshop, that both singers should try their luck in Europe. "I was pessimistic, fed up with the whole thing. It's a hell of a lot of hard work and few make it to the top . . . or even manage to hold their own. So I . . . made an appointment with IBM in New York, and they offered me a job in Poughkeepsie. Just then the Fulbrights came through—so fate decided the rest of my life. It was the last grasp at a life vest by a drowning man."

It was the late fifties and gifted American singers were still in demand—Stewart needed only two weeks before he was accepted as a lead baritone at the Berlin Städtische Oper, where he made his debut as the Minister in *Fidelio* in 1957. Lear had to wait a bit longer, but her turn came in 1959 at the same house, as the Composer in Strauss's *Ariadne auf Naxos*. "Our secret was that we never said no," she recalled in the seventies. "Whatever it was, we could do it. We learned and faked and kept our heads above water." Lear's nerviness paid off when, in 1960, she agreed to substitute for Helga Pilarczyk in Berg's *Lulu*—a concert performance only three weeks off, and she had never even heard the opera, let alone looked over the music. When the score arrived, the soprano was horrified: "I almost dropped dead, because it was the most difficult thing I'd ever seen in my life." But she survived, flourished, and in 1962 sang the role onstage at Vienna's Theater an der Wien. Many thought they knew the opera well by then, but Lear left audiences with the impression of hearing the full vocal implications of the music for the first time. Perhaps the ultimate compliment came from Elisabeth Schwarzkopf, who pronounced the performance as "one of the supreme achievements of the operatic stage anywhere in the world."

Capitalizing on their gains, Lear and Stewart made Germany their home base of operations for the next few years. The baritone's most prestigious engagements were at Bayreuth, where he took over Amfortas and the Dutchman from George London and Wotan from Hans Hotter. Later he became Karajan's preferred Wotan at Salzburg, while Lear sang Mozart at the festival—Cherubino, Fiordiligi, and the Countess—as well as being the first American to give a lieder recital in Salzburg. Both yearned to return home, but even in the sixties it was still difficult for an American singer, even one of international stature, to survive in the States. The Met offered Stewart a $300 weekly contract to sing *Figaro* and *Pagliacci*, which he not surprisingly rejected. He waited, and it paid off. Eventually Stewart made his Met debut in 1966, at top dollar as Ford in *Falstaff*, and Lear arrived the next year for the world premiere of Marvin David Levy's *Mourning Becomes Electra*.

Lear had been back home for hardly a year before she ran into the vocal crisis that seems to strike so many singers in their early forties (although at the time she was passing for thirty-seven). The soprano laid the blame on Lulu, Marie in *Wozzeck*, Lavinia in Levy's operatic setting of the Eugene O'Neill trilogy, and all the other new music she had been singing. Speaking on behalf of his colleagues, Ned Rorem wasn't buying that excuse, and he had an answer for all singers who insist on making the composer a scapegoat for their vocal troubles: "Evelyn Lear, biting the hands that fed her, repeatedly states: 'Thank God my coach forced me to give up modern stuff, it almost ruined my voice. Composers should take lessons if they want to learn to write grateful vocal music.' But Callas and Tebaldi ruined *their* voices on standard stuff. Meanwhile, that tiny handful of specialists—Beardslee, Curtin, Gramm, Wolff—sound better than ever after decades of singing contemporary music along with their 'grateful' programs. That's because they don't treat modern music as modern music, but as music. No music of any period, if a singer believes in it, can harm the voice." In any case, the American half of Lear's career was only a pale reflection of her European successes, when her voice was fresh and responsive and her interpretive powers at their peak.

Stewart's career, however, continued uninterrupted, and whenever possible the two appeared together, in opera and recital. Although no two singers had ever managed a more successful marriage—something of a miracle in such an ego-driven field—they made an odd musical couple whose temperaments were opposite; perhaps that was the secret of their happy life together. An honest, forthright singer, Stewart used his muscular baritone with intelligence and care to create portraits of Wotan, Golaud, Ford, and the rest that would always leave audiences well satisfied, even if they were not hearing an especially glamorous voice or a compellingly original musical imagination at work. Lear, on the other hand, was a much more complex singer, who, when at her best, commanded a wide range of vocal colors that she applied craftily. She almost invariably animated lieder texts with unusual sensitivity for their emotional content, and few Americans living in Germany at the time responded more eagerly to the language or sang it so idiomatically—no wonder Schwarzkopf was so impressed with her Lulu. Unfortunately, by the time Lear came home, she had lost much of that inner spirit along with her vocal confidence, and by the seventies her style, possibly to compensate for her vocal difficulties, had become impossibly arch and mannered. Perhaps Schwarzkopf would have approved of that too.

One of Stewart's frequent tenor partners at Bayreuth was Jess Thomas (1927–93) from Hot Springs, South Dakota. Thomas reached Germany in 1958 after a brief apprenticeship at the San Francisco Opera, where he sang such tiny roles as a Major-Domo in *Der Rosenkavalier* and Malcolm in *Macbeth*. The tenor wanted more intensive operatic experience and that is precisely what he got in his first job at the Staatstheater in Karlsruhe, where he sang thirty-eight different roles in as many months. His clear, unpressured lyric voice and vigorous, unaffected style already suggested a singer ready for heavier duty, and after impressing Wieland Wagner with his Bacchus in *Ariadne*, Thomas began to ease himself into the Wagner repertory, first as Parsifal and Lohengrin at Bayreuth and later in the principal operatic capitals as Tannhäuser, Siegfried, and finally Tristan. During his first weeks at the Met, as a sudden replacement, Thomas even sang Radamès in German—save for "Celeste Aida," the only part of the opera he then knew in Italian. The tenor's good looks and heroic bearing certainly helped his progress—this romantic Swan Knight truly seemed to have stepped from an illustrated storybook—and for a while Wagnerians everywhere held their breath, hoping he would develop into the heldentenor the world had been waiting for. It never happened, though—by the early seventies Thomas's voice had thickened and its youthful ring had vanished after a decade of strenuous use.

Although he lacked the young Jess Thomas's vocal and physical glamour, James King (1925–   ) lasted longer—he was still singing such character roles as Aegisth in Strauss's *Elektra* respectably at age seventy—possibly because his Wagnerian adventures seldom extended further than Siegmund, barring the occasional Walther von Stolzing, Lohengrin, or Parsifal. Originally trained as a baritone, King reached Europe in 1961, and soon afterward began his tenor career at the Deutsche Oper in Berlin. His easy top, firmly focused tone, and stylistic versatility were instantly appreciated, and offers quickly came from all over Germany, leading to a Metropolitan debut in 1966 as Beethoven's Florestan. Along with Leonie Rysanek, Christa Ludwig, and Walter Berry, under Karl Böhm's direction during the sixties and seventies, King was a key member of the famous *Frau ohne Schatten* ensemble that helped bring world popularity to Strauss's complex fairy-tale opera, making it a repertory piece at the Met, Covent Garden, and the Paris Opéra.

Like James McCracken, Jean Madeira (1918–72) came to the Metropolitan early in her career and was immediately typecast as a useful comprimario whose main duties consisted of Berta, Mercedes, Suzuki, Maddalena, Marcellina, and small bits in Wagner whenever a low voice was needed. The occasional Carmen and Amneris did come her way, but usually only on tour or at student matinees, and so in 1955 Madeira correctly sensed that she would be better appreciated in Europe. Soon she was a prominent interpreter of all the parts the Met seldom offered her: Carmen, Klytämnestra, Dame Quickly, Dalila, and Erda. Although she never completely severed her New York ties, Madeira was always denied the réclame at home that she enjoyed in Vienna, Bayreuth, Salzburg, Munich, Aix, and London. Part of the reason for her vogue abroad must have been Madeira's unusually deep-centered voice—she was that rarity, a real contralto—coupled with her theatrical flamboyance. At the Met, Madeira may have been perceived as a rather blowzy, even vulgar singer of bit parts, but on the Continent she remained a star right up to her untimely death from cancer.

Theodor Uppman (1920–) enjoyed his greatest moment of glory in Europe: at Covent Garden in 1951, when he created the title role in Benjamin Britten's *Billy Budd*. Britten liked to write for specific singers, but he had searched in vain for a baritone to sing Melville's epitome of goodness and innocence, finding the California-born Uppman only at the last minute—at thirty-one, this handsome curly-haired blond with a high, lightly textured baritone and athletic build must have seemed sent from heaven. It wasn't exactly all downhill from there, but Uppman never again found such a congenial role or so much international acclaim, although the Met kept him busy for many seasons singing the limited repertory that best suited his attractive voice and sunny presence in that vast house: Pelléas (under Monteux), Papageno (under Walter), Gabriel von Eisenstein, Guglielmo, Paquillo in *La Périchole*, and Harlekin in *Ariadne auf Naxos*. At another time and in another place this appealing vocal talent would surely have been more widely appreciated.

On his artist's questionnaire when he joined the Metropolitan in 1955, Giorgio Tozzi (1923–) answered the question "Are you a citizen of the U.S.?" with a "YES!!!!" By then, even many of his American colleagues must have thought that Tozzi, who had been performing mostly in the country of his immigrant parents since 1950, was a native Italian. Before that, though, this Chicago-born basso had followed a by-now-familiar route to Europe. Army service had interrupted his education, but when peace came, musical ambitions had replaced Tozzi's original intention to be a biologist, and while studying with Giacomo Rimini in his hometown, he grabbed at whatever performance opportunities came his way—nightclub dates, singing in the chorus of the *Chicago Theatre of the Air*, and local musical shows. His first important break came in New York when Broadway once again flirted with opera: Britten's *The Rape of Lucretia*, which had a brief run at the Ziegfeld Theater in 1948 with Tozzi singing Tarquinius opposite Kitty Carlisle's Lucretia. That prominent exposure was followed by an engagement that took Tozzi to London, where he played a prizefighter who falls in love with a princess in Sir Charles B. Cochran's musical comedy *Tough at the Top*. When that extravaganza folded, Tozzi headed for Milan and operatic experience in the Italian provinces, radio performances on RAI, and finally a 1953 La Scala debut with Renata Tebaldi and Mario del Monaco in Catalani's *La Wally*. Two years later he reached the Metropolitan as Alvise in *La Gioconda*, and during the next twenty seasons the company cast him in a wide-ranging repertory, German as well as Italian: Ramfis, Basilio, Colline, King Philip, Don Giovanni, Silva, Gremin, Méphistophélès, Rocco, Daland, Raimondo, Banquo, Plunkett, Hans Sachs, Pogner, Figaro, Gurnemanz, Arkel, Fiesco, King Marke, Sarastro, and the Doctor in *Vanessa*.

Nothing if not a useful and appreciated presence around the house, Tozzi still never quite achieved the star status of George London, Cesare Siepi, and others who shared many of these roles with him at the time. Although a resourceful actor, Tozzi failed to project the former's stage magnetism, while his light bass (which always betrayed its baritone origins) lacked the depth, richness, and creamy sonority of Siepi's instrument. And yet he was seldom idle, and at the height of his Met activity Tozzi could still be found from time to time in Europe, prominently in La Scala's all-star revival of Meyerbeer's *Gli Ugonotti* in 1962. He even risked introducing his Hans Sachs to a discriminating German audience in Hamburg, and the production was filmed (not perhaps the most flattering document of his art—seen up close, Tozzi's rather manic cobbler-poet bears an unsettling resemblance to Groucho Marx). Tozzi also enjoyed doing musicals before and after his opera career. He supplied Rosanno Brazzi's singing voice in the 1958 film of *South Pacific* while simultaneously appearing in a staged production with Mary Martin in Los Angeles. Toward the end of his career (like Robert Weede, who created the role), the bass found one of his most congenial vehicles as Tony Esposito in Loesser's *The Most Happy Fella*.

Throughout the sixties most Americans continued to find that a base in Europe was practically the only way to launch an operatic career, whether they remained a local celebrity or later blossomed into international prominence. Soon, though, the competition on the Continent became more vigorous as a new generation of European singers matured and opportunities for green interlopers from across the Atlantic shrank. The days were gone when Nell Rankin (1926–   ), a mezzo-soprano from Montgomery, Alabama, could arrive in Zurich in 1949 at the age of twenty-three, make a debut as Ortrud, sing 126 performances during her first season, and be summoned to pursue a modest but busy Met career two years later. Irene Dalis (1925–   ) from San Jose, California, was also lucky to get a Fulbright scholarship when she did. Dalis chose to study in Milan in 1952, quickly obtained a contract with a provincial opera house in Germany (Oldenburg), soon graduated to the Berlin Städtische Oper, and from there went to the Met in 1957, with which she chalked up sixty-seven Amnerises, twenty-six Azucenas, twenty-three Brangänes, and many other mezzo-soprano leads over nineteen seasons. Eventually it took more than a Fulbright or the GI Bill to set such a career in motion—or, for that matter, simply to exist as the European economy gradually recovered and the cost of living abroad mounted for impecunious young Americans. Nor did the doors to foreign opera companies abroad swing open in the seventies quite as readily or as often as they had in the past. But the scene was beginning to change in America as well, and if the traditional visit to the Continent never actually ceased to be an option for advancement, it was certainly not the only one.

La Divina

$\mathcal{L}$ ike Adelina Patti, Maria Callas may be claimed by many countries. Although her home until the age of thirteen was New
York City, where she was born on December 2, 1923, Callas received
most of her vocal training and early performance experience during the
war in Greece, the birthplace of her parents, George and Evangelia
Kalogeropoulos. She returned to New York for a short period after the
war, but launched her international career at the Verona Arena in 1947,
opposite Richard Tucker in *La Gioconda*. Based in Milan in the fifties with
a husband many years her senior, a prosperous brick manufacturer
named Giovanni Battista Meneghini, Callas was perceived as an Italian
diva as her fame grew throughout the world. Estranged from Meneghini
during the next decade and hoping to marry shipping magnate Aristotle
Onassis, she took Greek nationality in 1966. With the collapse of the
Onassis affair and her voice in ruins, Callas ended her life as a homeless
spirit haunting a lonely apartment in Paris, where she died on September
16, 1977. America played only a small role in Callas's adult life and
during the all-too brief prime years of her career, but occasionally her

New World roots surfaced in unexpected ways. It could only have been one tough cookie from Washington Heights who once turned on a horde of photographers and journalists at a New York airport and yelled, "Lay off me, will you!"

And yet Callas's impact on American singers was enormous—indeed, her influence affected singers the world over. Along with Enrico Caruso and Feodor Chaliapin, she is named by voice historian Michael Scott as one of the century's three greatest opera singers, artists who altered the history of singing through a combination of vocal and musical genius that excited audiences everywhere. As Scott persuasively argues, Callas was instinctively drawn to resuscitate the early-nineteenth-century bel canto composers, who celebrated the voice while finding compelling musical ways to express a character's internal emotion. Although Tosca was one of Callas's most famous roles, particularly toward the end as her voice became increasingly recalcitrant, it was never one of her favorites. It was in the operas of Rossini, Donizetti, Bellini, and early Verdi, where the singer is the center and raison d'être of the entire musical-dramatic fabric, that her art found its fullest expression during the decade when her voice was at its peak.

Callas hardly initiated the bel canto revival of the 1950s singlehandedly, and her finest achievements during those years could only have been accomplished through collaborations with such distinguished conductors as Serafin, De Sabata, Giulini, Gui, Gavazzeni, Kleiber, Bernstein, and Karajan, not to mention designer-directors like Visconti, Zeffirelli, and Wallmann. But it was the haunting expressive quality of her voice and her riveting musical perceptions that revitalized a repertory that had fallen into neglect and abuse, and this was her true legacy. Sutherland, Caballé, Sills, Gencer, Horne, and many others who followed Callas and sang her repertory would have used their voices in quite different ways without her example. As Scott puts it, "It is impossible to believe that she could ever have doubted her ultimate success; she worked ceaselessly on honing her instrument, so that it became for her consummately expressive. At her best, in the early 1950s, she was a great singer because her prodigious technical skill enabled her voice to reveal every nuance she desired to effect, articulating easily the most formidably intricate music. This makes her unique among sopranos this century."

Few who knew Mary Kalogeropoulos as a girl in New York, even her own family, could have predicted that. Evangelia—Litza to the family—

was already pregnant when she and George Kalogeropoulos arrived in New York from Greece four months before the birth of their second daughter. A druggist by trade, George eventually secured a license to open his own store, but that enterprise survived only briefly before the 1929 crash swept it away. Looking for work, George took a job as a traveling salesman for a drug company, and for a while he was constantly moving about the city—Mary had already attended six different public schools by the time the family finally found a permanent home in Washington Heights.

The girl was drawn to opera early, an interest stimulated by the Metropolitan's weekly broadcasts, recordings from the local public library, and Litza herself, for whom opera represented a "golden world" of escape from household drudgery and a troubled marriage. For Mary, short-sighted, overweight, and painfully shy, opera also served as an entree into a delicious fantasy world, but one that she already sensed had its own rules and practical realities—while listening to Lily Pons warble Lucia over the air on a Saturday afternoon, the girl announced that one day she would also sing the role, but in tune. When a neighbor actually overheard ten-year-old Mary singing and recommended lessons, Litza sent her younger daughter off to a voice teacher on the spot and encouraged her to perform at every opportunity. A year later Mary participated in a radio contest for children, emceed by Jack Benny, but she lost out to an accordion player. By now Litza was pushing the girl vigorously toward a career, and after much nagging she persuaded George to let her take Mary back to Greece, where voice lessons were considerably less costly than in New York. No doubt relieved to be rid of his wife, George agreed, and mother and daughter departed for the Old Country in February 1937.

If Callas's girlhood experiences in New York significantly shaped her musical personality and artistic outlook, the evidence is well hidden. Self-consciousness over her physical appearance kept her close to home, which hardly seems to have been a welcoming haven of warmth, understanding, and support despite Litza's interest in the girl's voice. One suspects that Mary Kalogeropoulos, who felt unattractive and unloved as a child, would have eventually become Maria Callas no matter where she grew up, given a proper exposure to music. In any case, the budding soprano, now called Marianna, applied herself to her vocal studies with ferocious dedication, first with Maria Trivella as a scholarship student at the National Conservatory in Athens and later with the retired Spanish coloratura Elvira de Hidalgo. When De Hidalgo first heard Callas sing, she was astonished, recalling the effect as "a violent cascade of sound." A fellow pupil, Arda Mandikian, describes Callas at the time as "a fat, tall girl with beautiful eyes and great self-assurance. Judging by her appearance, I didn't think she would be able to sing. But when she opened her mouth . . . my mouth fell open too. It was an amazing voice." The choice of De Hidalgo as a teacher was fortuitous, since it was in her studio that Callas received her basic training in the bel canto techniques and musical disciplines that would soon have the world by the ear. The distinctive qualities that made her unique, however, Callas developed herself, and she could never articulate them. The series of master classes she gave at the Juilliard School in 1972 were revelatory only when Callas used the remnants of her voice to demonstrate points that her verbal analysis failed to clarify.

While living and studying in Greece during the war, Callas sang in opera for the first time as a member of Athens's Olympia Theater troupe—Santuzza in 1939—and later, with the Lyric Theater Company, she sang Tosca, Martha in D'Albert's *Tiefland*, Santuzza again, and Beethoven's Leonore. Already a perfectionist with little patience for singers who gave only their second-best, Callas soon alienated virtually everyone in the company, and her contract was not renewed. Now that the war was over, she decided to return to her father back in New York and launch her career from there. It was a frustrating two years as she auditioned and received little encouragement and even fewer opportunities to perform. There was a Met tryout, but the tale that she turned down Edward Johnson's offer to perform *Madama Butterfly* (she felt too fat for the role) and *Fidelio* (she wouldn't sing Leonore in English) is apparently yet another fictitious bit of Callasiana, and one that the soprano herself circulated toward the end of her life. Her Met audition card merely reads, "Good material. Needs work on her voice." Soon after that she came to the attention of the aging tenor Giovanni Zenatello, founder of the summer opera seasons at the Verona Arena and looking for a soprano to sing Gioconda in August 1947. He was considering Zinka Milanov and Herva Nelli, but they proved to be too expensive. As Meneghini later described it, Zenatello "saw that she was down and out so he offered a hangman's contract"—a measly 40,000 lire (about $60) a performance. Callas seized her chance, went to Italy, and immediately began, as she later put it, the "big" career.

When the slimmed-down soprano returned to make her debut in the country of her birth, as Norma with the newly formed Lyric Opera of Chicago seven years later, she was at the summit of her vocal powers and the world's eyes were upon her. It had all happened quickly, thanks largely to the careful coaching of Tullio Serafin. In 1949 Callas's "volcanic" soprano may not have astonished the venerable conductor as Ponselle's molten-lava tone had twenty-five years earlier—even Callas, who admired Ponselle above all her predecessors, bowed before that phenomenon. But who in those postwar days had ever heard a voice and a musical intelligence that responded with equal authority to the eloquent coloratura filigree of Bellini and the dramatic lyrical rhetoric of Wagner? It was probably Callas's feat of singing Brünnhilde in *La Valchiria* on January 8, 1949, and Elvira in *I Puritani* eleven days later, both at Venice's La Fenice and both conducted by Serafin, that alerted Italian operagoers, at the time a musical lobby with much international influence, to the arrival of an exceptional talent.

An excited press delegation met Callas at the Chicago airport, and if there were any old-timers among them who remembered Mary Garden's flamboyant arrival in town forty-four years earlier, they must have been taken aback by a diva who behaved with unexpected modesty, despite one whom all Italy now called "La Divina" and whose fiery temperament promised hot copy. Instead, she thanked the reporters for coming, politely introduced her husband, and immediately wanted to meet her conductor (Nicola Rescigno) to discuss rehearsal schedules. Once settled in her hotel, she shopped at the local supermarket and cooked for Meneghini—by then her manager, although, since he knew no English, Callas had to deal with the Lyric Opera management herself. Rescigno was astonished at the first rehearsal. "I sat down at the piano in front of her and played through the whole of *Norma*. I wasn't a Serafin, or any of those great conductors. It was a test, Maria said she would feel more comfortable. She had such integrity that if I hadn't been up to par then, she wouldn't have made any bones about it. She was by far the easiest singer I have ever conducted because of her musicality. Her sense of everything that makes a performance vital was instinctive."

This is not the image of Callas that would soon be familiar to Americans: the capricious prima donna raging at the press, hastily fleeing an opera house in mid-performance, attacking Rudolf Bing after being fired from the Metropolitan for breach of contract, and, as a darling of café society, relishing Elsa Maxwell's weeklong parties or extended yacht cruises as Onassis's mistress. All these things and worse did happen, but only after her marriage with Meneghini collapsed and her technique had begun to disintegrate. But when Callas first arrived in Chicago in 1954, her vocal estate would never be better, and the critics were ecstatic. For Claudia Cassidy, a Callas partisan to the bitter end, her Norma was "wand slim and beautiful as a tragic mask . . . Her range is formidable, and her technique dazzling." Callas's Violetta and Lucia were received with even greater enthusiasm, and from James Hinton, Jr.'s comments in *Opera* one can gauge just how startling she must have sounded to American ears in such familiar "canary-bird" roles: "After having heard Miss Callas in this performance I cannot imagine why anyone would [prefer the traditional Lucia], except out of sheer perversity. It was not so much the mere size of the voice that told . . . It was the play of color and the sense of reserve power that could be brought to bear . . . in climaxes. The effect was far less that of a dramatic soprano with an exceptional top than it was a huge soprano leggiero with great variety of color and practically unlimited dynamics."

It was somehow appropriate that the scene of Callas's most imposing American triumphs should have been Chicago, already known as "La Scala West" due to the company's preference for importing the latest Italian sensations, often before the Metropolitan. Indeed, a contract with the Met was still pending by the time she returned to the Windy City a year later for what would be her final stage performances of *I Puritani* and *Il Trovatore* as well as her only Butterflys. It was after her third and last Butterfly that the bomb exploded. A process server confronted her backstage and presented her with a summons—a suit by a would-be impresario named Eddie Bagarozy with whom she had made a loose contract back in 1947 and who now demanded $300,000, what he calculated was 10 percent of her earnings over the past eight years. The lurid photograph of the scene appeared in newspapers everywhere: a frightened marshal in full retreat with Callas about to pounce and shrieking (said the photo captions), "No man can sue me! I have the voice of an angel! Chicago will be sorry for this!" From that moment, in America at least, Callas ceased to be an arts-page phenomenon and became a front-page news personality.

A few weeks before the *Butterfly* scandal, the American papers printed a more benign photo from Chicago, but less prominently: Rudolf Bing pictured backstage following *Il Trovatore*, kissing Callas's hand after she had signed a contract to sing at the Met the next season. To some ears, by the time she offered her Norma to New Yorkers on October 29, 1956, the soprano was already sounding less happy in the role than she had two years earlier in Chicago. The city went wild anyway. From the moment she arrived in town for rehearsals, the daily press detailed her every movement. A *Time* cover story appeared on the day of her debut, an article that once again recounted the real or imagined Callas-Tebaldi feud, the outrageous size of her fee (actually a modest $1,000 a performance, substantially less than the $2,500 Caruso had received forty years earlier), her temper tantrums, and all the other "human interest" touches. By far the most damaging revelation was a quote from a letter Callas had written in 1951 to her mother, who had by then applied for welfare: "I can give you nothing. Money is not like flowers, growing in gardens . . . I bark for my living. You are a young woman [Litza was fifty-two] and you can work. If you can't earn enough to live on throw yourself out of the window."

That set the seal on Callas's image as the ultimate operatic *monstre sacré* as far as the American public was concerned, particularly among those less interested in the realities of operatic life than in tabloid dirt. As Irving Kolodin drily remarked in his history of the Metropolitan, "Among Americans conditioned to a belief that motherhood is even more sacred than country . . . this aroused antagonism where nothing else—professional rivalries, personal animosities, artistic differences— would have." In fact, nothing Callas sang during her brief Met career, good or bad, generated as much comment as her personality and stormy behind-the-scenes activities. Her three seasons in the house were among the least noteworthy events in her career, amounting to only twenty performances of four roles, all from the standard repertory and performed, with minimal rehearsal, in some of the Met's oldest, most tattered productions: *Norma, Tosca, Lucia,* and *La Traviata.* Callas might well have achieved a genuine Met triumph with the new production of Verdi's *Macbeth* that had been planned for her in 1959, but she and Bing disagreed over scheduling. The soprano continued to put off signing her contractual agreement, finally balked over the arrangements, and eventually Bing fired her. Such things occur regularly in operatic life without remark, but by then Callas was news whatever she did, and the fracas generated international publicity. In retrospect, Bing has generally been portrayed as the heavy in the *Macbeth* contretemps, an impresario just as egocentric and jealous of his prerogatives as any diva. But Scott sees other forces at play during this crucial period in Callas's career, and he feels that the soprano virtually provoked the general manager into firing her. "What none of Callas's disputants, in Rome, San Francisco or Milan, took into account," says Scott, "was that she may well have been greedy, even capricious, but these factors were less significant than her fast-fading vocal powers and consequently her lack of nerve. Her powers were slipping steadily from her, tempting her to endless procrastinations over her contracts."

By 1960 Callas's importance as a singer was effectively over. Even during the previous year—concert tours of America and Europe, a concert version of Bellini's *Il Pirata* in Carnegie Hall, and staged performances of *Lucia di Lammermoor* and Cherubini's *Medea* in Dallas and London—her voice was in a state of terminal deterioration. Her only operatic appearances in 1960 were as Norma in the ancient auditorium at Epidaurus and one final new role at La Scala, Paolina in Donizetti's *Poliuto*, significantly an opera in which the tenor has the more prominent part. America heard her in opera once more only, in March 1965, after she made up with Bing and, with barely a thread of a voice, sang two deliriously received Toscas at the Met. Then came the Juilliard master classes in 1972, and a truly pathetic final world concert tour with her old colleague, Giuseppe di Stefano, who by then was as vocally ravaged as his partner. Audiences went wild even so, but like Marilyn Monroe and Judy Garland, Callas had long since degenerated into a cult figure whose art, for those who remembered and understood it, had totally receded into the background. Heaven only knows what went through her head during those last wretched years, although she dropped a hint in a sad remark to Di Stefano when he visited her shortly before the end: "Each day is one day less." Olive Fremstad would have understood.

As a live stage personality, Callas reached only a fraction of the Americans who might have wanted to experience or be enriched by her singing firsthand. Instead, she performed mostly for the high-society worlds of New York, Chicago, and Dallas, audiences who responded more to her celebrity than to her art. Lind, Patti, and Caruso were all heard by a wider general public as they restlessly toured the country, became figures of national prominence, and influenced musical tastes wherever they went—even Malibran touched more true music-lovers within America's narrowly circumscribed musical world of 1825. Most people who read the news about Callas scarcely thought of her as a singer at all but as the quintessential flamboyant, bitchy, self-absorbed, even slightly crazed opera diva—a caricature that long survived and resurfaced as late as 1995 in Terence McNally's egregious Broadway potboiler, *Master Class*, a trivialized portrait of Callas based on her 1972 appearances at Juilliard.

For those who took opera seriously, Callas exercised her main influence posthumously through her live and studio recordings, which document nearly every important role she sang after 1949, often in multiple versions. What initially struck many listeners, as Hinton noted when he heard her Lucia in Chicago, was how completely she reimagined Lucia, Gilda, Amina, and Elvira, roles that for decades had been primarily associated with such soprano leggeros as Pons, Galli-Curci, and Tetrazzini. Callas discovered an emotional weight and expressive depth in her musical characterizations of these heroines that most singers—and audiences too—had forgotten even existed. No wonder when Callas sang Norma and Anna Bolena, some historically aware connoisseurs felt that they were hearing these roles interpreted with the same passion and musical precision originally conjured up by Pasta and Malibran. Callas's revivals of other, long-unheard operas by Donizetti, Rossini, and Bellini proved to be even greater revelations, which led to a worldwide exploration and reappreciation of early-nineteenth-century Italian opera. The movement soon grew and inspired an investigation of even more obscure operatic byways from the past, the Baroque era in particular. It is no exaggeration to suggest that the generation of singers who trained their voices to revive and perform the operas of Handel, Lully, Rameau, and their contemporaries so stylishly in the 1980s and '90s are Callas's direct descendants. Many vainly tried to copy her manner and inimitable vocal gestures when they sang the operas specifically associated with her voice, and most failed to grasp the simple lesson that Callas taught: these works can be reanimated only through the basic virtues of technical discipline and musical integrity. The rest—her genius—died with her.

Twenty-three

Homemade
Goods

~~~~~~~~~~~~~~~~~~~~~~

While little Mary Kalogeropoulos was finding fault with Lily Pons's Lucia over the radio in the mid-1930s, an even younger, less critical Pons fan in Brooklyn had also tuned in and was listening attentively. Soon she got the opportunity to see her idol, as Lakmé in 1938, and when she did, Beverly Sills, aged nine, made her decision. "I just sat there quietly and completely transfixed. Pons was beautiful, a Dresden doll come to life. Her voice was exquisite. That was going to be me . . . Whatever she sang, I wanted to sing."

Some thirty years later, when she finally achieved stardom, Sills had heard Callas and changed her priorities—not so much about the repertory she wanted to sing but about the way in which she intended to sing it. "There are two schools of opera singing," Sills later maintained. "One is concerned exclusively with making beautiful sounds . . . The other school features equally talented singers, who, in certain instances, will sacrifice a beautiful sound in order to make a dramatic point in an opera. Maria Callas was such a singer." Callas, one suspects, might have disagreed with that simplistic analysis of her intentions—Sills was hardly the first or last singer who failed to appreciate the purely musical basis of Callas's expressive art and, while imitating her manner, fell short of the model. Still, such statements always played well in the post-Callas era, and Sills consciously opted for that "other school" when she began to perform the bel canto vehicles associated with her predecessor—Lucia, Elvira in *I Puritani*, Anna Bolena, Norma, Rosina, Violetta, Gilda, Fiorilla in Rossini's *Il Turco in Italia*—as well as roles that Callas never sang, such Donizetti heroines as Queen Elizabeth, Maria Stuarda, Lucrezia Borgia, Norina in *Don Pasquale*, and Marie in *La Fille du Régiment*. The results were controversial, but for a brief time Beverly Sills was famous throughout the land, a populist prima donna firmly in the tradition of an American soprano from an earlier century, one whose name she had probably never heard: Emma Abbott.

Although Sills was only six years younger than Callas, she had never been a direct competitor, and her career did not really gather momentum until Callas's great days were behind her. In the fall of 1966, after performing Handel's Cleopatra in the New York City Opera's glamorous new Lincoln Center home, Sills was suddenly propelled into national prominence and her reputation grew quickly—indeed, it took off like a skyrocket, a phenomenon that no one could have predicted. From the time of her City Opera debut in 1955, as Rosalinda in *Die Fledermaus*, Sills had spent more than a decade as a hardworking house soprano for New York's second company, appreciated but hardly perceived as having superstar potential. Several reasons might explain her slow progress, the bad timing of her arrival on the scene almost certainly being one of them.

For Americans just starting out on a singing career as the fifties came to an end, the opportunities that had seemed so plentiful at the beginning of the decade, when the Met was filled with native talent, were once again depressingly reduced. For one thing, job openings in Europe for young unknowns had dwindled. The musical scene abroad had recaptured much of its prewar vigor, a new generation was securely in place, and opera houses were no longer as eager to hire foreigners—the day when George London could arrive and immediately establish himself as a star in Vienna was definitely over. The situation back home, on the other hand, had changed little—indeed, in many ways it had even deteriorated. Recordings had replaced live music-making on radio, once such an important showcase offering singers national exposure and attention. Classical music was never destined to become a major presence on commercial television, and the few programs that managed to survive seldom featured unestablished vocal personalities. The explosion of regional opera was still more than a decade off, and to singers who aimed for a stage career—and few still thought of anything else—Rudolf Bing's Metropolitan Opera must have looked like an unassailable citadel, populated by entrenched Americans from the Johnson era and the emerging big names of Europe.

One bright spot in the picture, and a sign of things to come, was the New York City Opera, which since 1944 had already welcomed dozens of young American singers. The company's original mandate was drawn up when the City Center of Music and Drama was established by the city of New York. The City Opera was to be a major constituent of the new arts center, which made its home in the Mecca Temple, a mosque-like structure on Fifty-fifth Street between Sixth and Seventh avenues. And its purpose was clear: not only to provide high-quality opera for less affluent New Yorkers but also to create a troupe of American singing actors who would perform a varied repertory of music theater, old and new, in innovative ways—in other words, a feisty young company to complement the costly and conservative Metropolitan. Unfortunately, the City Opera could not afford the luxury of full seasonal employment—during the fifties performances took place over the course of four or five weeks in the fall and for another month in the spring. But that was enough time to get noticed, gain valuable experience, and establish credentials to find concert work during the off-seasons. By mid-decade the roster already boasted names that would later become well known around the country. Some even advanced to the Met and on to international careers, but that was still in the future. In its early days the City Opera was very much an ensemble troupe with a core group of regulars.

The City Opera's most famous product, and that by a considerable margin, was to be Beverly Sills. At the height of her national celebrity, Sills not only epitomized the company's plucky made-in-America spirit, she apotheosized it. Aided by the media and Sills's own irrepressible personality, her long struggle to reach the top and the "overnight" success that had made her a star intrigued the American public to an unprecedented degree. During the seventies nearly every man in the street knew who she was, even those without the slightest interest in opera or music. It could not have been entirely coincidental that when the time came to establish her nationwide image as Supersills, the soprano hired Lily Pons's former press agent, Edgar Vincent, to handle her publicity.

The basic facts about Sills's background and early family life as a native New Yorker will by now have a familiar ring. Born Belle Silverman on May 26, 1929, Sills came from Eastern European Jewish stock—her father's people had emigrated from Rumania in the late 1800s and her mother came to America from Odessa in 1917—and she grew up with her two older brothers in comfortable middle-class surroundings in Brooklyn. Once again a strong mother provided the initial impetus toward music and singing, especially when Shirley Silverman noticed that her little daughter had memorized all the arias on her precious collection of Galli-Curci records. Although Bubbles, as the family called her, was barely four years old, Shirley knew talent when she heard it, and she marched the girl down to Bob Emery, host of radio station WOR's kiddie program, *Rainbow House*. After three years with "Uncle Bob," she graduated to Major Bowes's *Capitol Family Hour*, renamed herself Beverly Sills, and took home $65 a week for chirping out the whole Pons–Galli-Curci repertory to a nationwide audience that already seemed to adore her. Determined to replace the $5 spinet piano Shirley had given her, the resourceful ten-year-old took matters into her own hands, recorded a widely played radio commercial for the Rinso laundry-soap manufacturers ("Rinso white, Rinso white, happy little washday song"), and bought a $1,000 Baldwin with her earnings.

Obviously a singing teacher was now required. Shirley noticed a picture of Estelle Liebling on the cover of a music magazine and discovered that this former Marchesi pupil had recently nursed her favorite singer, Galli-Curci, through a patch of vocal troubles. That was recommendation enough, and Liebling immediately took on the tiny tot, remaining Sills's only teacher until she died in 1970. Sills has spoken little about her work with Liebling, but the remarkable technique the soprano commanded in her best years clearly indicated that she was thoroughly drilled in Marchesi principles. Sills scarcely sang in public at all after she began studying with Liebling, and not until after seven years of steady work was the soprano ready to think about resuming her serious career as a very mature teenager. At nearly the same age, Adelina Patti had already made her New York debut in opera and become an instant star, but Sills was destined to soldier on for another twenty years before her turn would come.

The first sortie in the campaign was humble enough, a Gilbert and Sullivan tour in 1945 that hit all the major Shubert theaters of the East and Midwest. That was followed by a decade of fly-by-night tours with the Charles Wagner company, singing on cruise ships, solo dates in high schools, appearances on the borscht circuit in the Catskills, and even a stint in an after-hours social club called The Hour Glass. Meanwhile, there had been titillating encounters with fabled prima donnas from an earlier era to remind Sills of the goal ahead, including a few coaching sessions on Manon and Thaïs from Mary Garden. Even Sills admitted that Garden's glamour secrets would never work for a soprano who always tended to be buxom, but at one point in her autobiography she reports, "Mary gave me the tiara she'd worn during the years when she alone owned that opera [Thaïs] . . . 'From now on,' she said, 'nobody but you can wear this crown.' Coming from her, that was the most thrilling compliment I'd ever received." Perhaps Sills would have been less thrilled if she had known how fond La Garden was of impulsively distributing her relics and anointing such inferior successors as Marguerite Namara and Gladys Swarthout (Garden even once pronounced Helen Jepson's pallid Thaïs superior to her own). Sills did sing Manon under Rosa Ponselle's tutelage in Baltimore, but advice from a singer so unversed in Massenet style seemed even less appropriate than Mary's, and the performance was not a success. She did learn a thing or two about music criticism, however. One night the talk turned to Ponselle's premature retirement from the Met—it had nothing at all to do, Rosa insisted, with Olin Downes's devastating review of her Carmen. Then, after a few brandies, she took Sills down to the basement and showed her cartons and cartons containing Downes's critique, "as if Rosa had tried to buy up all the issues the Times had printed that day so that nobody could read the scathing review. I urged her to destroy them."

Although consistently busy in the boondocks, Sills soon saw that it was all leading nowhere, and by 1951 her dreams of becoming the next Lily Pons had pretty much faded. There were a few performances with the San Francisco Opera, a nibble from Georg Solti (then director of the Frankfurt Opera), constant tryouts for Joseph Rosenstock at the City Opera—all to no avail. Then, exasperated when she learned that Rosenstock felt she had no personality, Sills decided to correct that impression, even if that meant being shown the door for good. She stormed into her eighth audition "in a jumper—but without a blouse underneath. I bought myself a pair of black mesh stockings and the highest heels I could find. I'd always tied my hair back in a bun; this time I let it hang all the way down my back. When I came out onstage that day, Dr. Rosenstock addressed me directly for the first time. He walked down the aisle and said, 'Vell, vell, vot have ve got here?' " Sills then proceeded to sing the heaviest, most inappropriate aria for her voice she could think of—"La mamma morta" from *Andrea Chénier*—and the astonished Rosenstock hired her on the spot.

Wearing a white stole that her mother had bought for $5 at the Ritz Thrift Shop, Sills made her City Opera debut as the glamorous Rosalinda and pocketed just $75 for her work. The reviews were good, though, and other roles soon came her way, a reflection of the company's eclectic repertory in those days as well as Sills's versatility: Oxana in Tchaikovsky's *The Golden Slippers*, Madame Goldentrill in Mozart's *The Impresario*, Philine in *Mignon*, Violetta, Sonia in *The Merry Widow*, Douglas Moore's Baby Doe, the Coloratura in Hugo Weisgall's *Six Characters in Search of an Author*, Milly Theale in Moore's *The Wings of the Dove*, Louise, Donna Anna, Marguerite, and the *Hoffmann* heroines. If there was any hint of what to expect in the future, it could be heard in the florid éclat of Sills's Philine and even more so in her adorable Baby Doe. "Miss Sills," the composer presciently complimented her after hearing her audition for the part, "you *are* Baby Doe." Sills did indeed make this cuddly, self-sacrificing gold digger—a real-life character from America's colorful Wild West past—very much her own. Best of all, her fresh, young lyric-coloratura soprano sounded ravishing in Moore's attractively tuneful music, tailor-made to display her remarkable breath control as well as her skill in sustaining long, arching lines and spun pianissimos. Sills, in fact, may have been the last American singer to find a role in a new opera that not only was popular with the public but also effectively defined and flattered her entire vocal personality. Meanwhile, the soprano's personal life took a happy turn when, during a City Opera tour to Cleveland in 1955, she met Peter Greenough, a wealthy newspaper man. After marrying Greenough, Sills was relieved of all financial pressures and she could relax on that score—it looked as if the rest of her singing career would be conducted more or less as a hobby.

Sills herself had probably never really given up hope of being a star. Perhaps the diva in her sensed that the City Opera's upcoming production of Handel's *Giulio Cesare* at the new State Theater in Lincoln Center would be the rendezvous with destiny that it in fact turned out to be. In any case, her campaign to sing Cleopatra was conducted with a ruthlessness that any great prima donna would have applauded. Julius Rudel, the company's general director, had promised the role to Phyllis Curtin, in all but name the City Opera's leading soprano since her debut in 1953.

Curtin had missed few seasons since then, performing a variety of such standard roles as Rosalinda, Salome, Violetta, Alice Ford, Antonia, Mozart's Countess, Constanza, and Fiordiligi, as well as many contemporary novelties, including a demanding triple role in Gottfried von Einem's *The Trial*, William Walton's *Cressida*, and three operas by Carlisle Floyd. Indeed, Curtin was as closely identified with Floyd's *Susannah* as Sills was with Moore's *The Ballad of Baby Doe*, two of the most successful American operas ever written. While it's true that by the mid-sixties Curtin was also singing at the Metropolitan and in Europe, it took an amazing amount of gall for Sills to storm into Rudel's office and accuse him of unjustly assigning Cleopatra to a soprano she airily labeled an "outsider." Brazening it out to the end, Sills told Rudel that if she didn't get the role, she would quit the City Opera and use her husband's money to hire Carnegie Hall for a recital that would feature all of Cleopatra's arias— "and you're going to look sick." Rudel was probably already looking a bit ill by then, but since Sills was a key factor in his future Lincoln Center plans, there was little he could do except cave in. Curtin seldom talked about this back-stabbing incident in later years, but except for one guest *Figaro* Countess in 1976, she never sang at the City Opera again. Dripping honey, Sills sweetly curtsies to Curtin after airing all this dirty linen in her memoirs: "We did stay friends. Phyllis is quite a lady."

Sills may have acted shamelessly, but after the night of September 27, 1966, she could have borrowed Sibyl Sanderson's words when that determined careerist introduced herself to Massenet: "If they blame me for it, after I have succeeded I shall reply that success excuses everything." And perhaps in this case it did. Curtin would surely have sung a distinguished Cleopatra, but Sills sang a sensational one. Seldom does everything come together so happily for a singer at precisely the right time. The voice so carefully trained by Liebling had matured into a flexible, responsive instrument that not only rippled and shimmered through Handel's florid arias but also reflected every emotional nuance of Cleopatra's alluring personality. Rudel had prepared a freely arranged performing edition that enraged Handel scholars, but it was craftily organized in order not to tax the patience of an audience still unused to leisurely Baroque operatic conventions, and the production had been given a flashy staging by Tito Capobianco. Act II ended with Cleopatra's great lament, "Se pietà," and Sills dispensed with false modesty when summing up her achievement: "When I began 'Se pietà,' an absolute hush came over the audience. People were hanging on every note. I think 'Se pietà' was the single most extraordinary piece of singing I ever did. I know I had never heard myself sing that way before. It was very different from the usual coloratura fireworks—it was all control and pianissimo singing. When I finished the aria, I saw Gigi [Capobianco's wife] in the wings. She was weeping. The curtain began coming down very slowly, and the deathlike silence continued—and then a roar went through that house the likes of which I'd never heard . . . What happened is simply that the role of Cleopatra was tailor-made for me. Vocally, there were just no hurdles in it that I couldn't handle, and handle brilliantly. And I knew it."

Sills wasted no time in maximizing her gains—in addition to repeats of Cleopatra, her six-week season that fall also included Mozart's Donna Anna, Queen of the Night, and Constanza, as well as the *Hoffmann* heroines. Over the next four years, every new role—Rimsky-Korsakov's Queen of Shemakha, Manon, Marguerite, Lucia—seemed to reveal another unexpected facet of her improved vocal skills, and she brought to each part a radiant stage presence that now positively glowed with personality and self-confidence. The media were also becoming increasingly interested, and Sills, a nonstop talker and potent charmer now that she had found an audience willing to listen, always provided good copy. Her against-all-odds rise to the top inevitably appealed to the American press, and there were plenty of extras to add color and poignancy to the story, which Sills, irrepressibly jolly and plucky despite personal tragedies and tardy recognition of her talents, was always ready to tell in her inimitable Brooklyn-girl-from-next-door style. After cover stories in *Time* and *Newsweek* and frequent appearances on widely watched television talk shows, American families soon knew all about Sills, her professional struggles, her happy marriage, her charities, her two handicapped children, and her inability to impress that Eurocentric villain Rudolf Bing, who stubbornly refused to open the doors of the Metropolitan to her.

When she sang her first Lucia in the fall of 1969, Sills had already decided where her career was headed next: into the bel canto repertory that had become fashionable once again and had made international stars of Callas, Joan Sutherland, and Montserrat Caballé. The tantalizing prospect of joining that select company must have seemed like a real possibility after Sills made her widely covered European debut earlier that year at La Scala as a replacement for Renata Scotto in a revival of Rossini's *L'Assedio di Corinto*. Sills never cared for the role of Pamira, which was too dramatically passive for her taste, but now that she had finally arrived at what she called *"the* official shrine of international opera," she decided that it was time to flex a bit more of the diva muscle that had so effectively removed Curtin from the scene. When the costume designer ignored her requests to replace the gold costume originally made for Scotto (it clashed with the substitute soprano's strawberry blond hair), Sills calmly snatched a pair of scissors that the woman wore around her neck and cut the gown in half. Then there were fights with her costar, Marilyn Horne, who must have realized that she had met a formidable rival when it came to getting press attention. After Scala officials told Horne that Edgar Vincent was busily sorting through pictures of the production and throwing out all the ones with the mezzo in them, she stormed into Sills's dressing room, and, according to the soprano, "called Edgar a son of a bitch and threatened to punch him in the face if my picture appeared in *The New York Times* and hers didn't." But Sills felt she could afford to be forgiving, since Marilyn Horne, poor thing, "has a *great* voice, but never has gotten the attention she deserves." Besides, she continues in her memoirs, "it was fun to take on that public and show them a thing or two about singing Rossini." Apparently Sutherland's wildly acclaimed Semiramide at La Scala seven years earlier—a success soon to be shared with Horne in Chicago—didn't count.

Sills may have become slightly intoxicated with her newfound celebrity status, but not everyone agreed that her plans to move into the more stressful bel canto territory were wise or carefully thought through. Sills admits that her decision to plunge forward "greatly displeased Miss Liebling. She wanted me to stick pretty much to French repertoire like *Manon,* and told me that way I'd be able to save my voice. But what was I saving it for? Better to have ten glorious years than twenty safe and ultimately boring ones." So Sills rashly gambled her voice, and she did manage to survive the wear and tear for ten years—barely. But what had started out as a decade of glorious artistic fulfillment quickly degenerated into a crescendo of media razzle-dazzle on the one hand and precipitous vocal decline on the other. At least Liebling was spared the pain of hearing it all happen. When her teacher died on the night of September 25, 1970, Sills, still in prime condition, was singing Massenet's Manon, one of the roles that had always best suited her voice and temperament but among those she would soon leave behind.

Sills herself insisted that her peak came as Donizetti's three British queens, in the so-called Tudor Trilogy at the City Opera: *Roberto Devereux* (1970), *Maria Stuarda* (1972), and *Anna Bolena* (1973). Even the soprano's most uncritical fans had to admit that these three ferociously difficult bel canto roles made dangerous demands on her voice, particularly Queen Elizabeth in *Roberto Devereux*, which Sills labeled "the greatest artistic challenge and the finest achievement of my career." It wasn't, really. Sills's light soprano never had sufficient weight or coloristic range to deal with the role's vaulting musical lines and dramatic rhetoric, while her stagy impersonation of the aging Elizabeth seemed based mainly on campy mannerisms borrowed from old Bette Davis movies. Norma came next, although Sills never had the opportunity, or perhaps the nerve, to expose herself to New Yorkers in a role that lay so far outside her capacities. Small wonder that her disastrous recording of Bellini's Druid priestess never circulated outside the United States. If Sills's worldwide reputation eventually failed to equal that of Sutherland or Caballé, let alone Callas, her disappointing recordings made during these years explain why. Even as her vocal powers waned, though, Sills's fame and influential position in America continued undiminished. Caballé once expressed an interest in performing the three Donizetti operas at the Metropolitan, but Bing reluctantly had to veto the idea. As he later observed, "We finally accepted the fact that Beverly Sills of the City Opera, having been born in Brooklyn, was entitled to priority in the portrayal of British royalty." That was an unnecessarily catty remark, but Bing later gave a more honest explanation of why he never hired Sills, an opinion shared by many others in the international opera world at the time. "I simply did not care very much for her," Bing wrote in his second book of memoirs. "For her somewhat off-the-beaten-track repertory, I had Sutherland and Caballé whom, quite frankly, I thought were better."

Meanwhile, there were increasingly audible reasons for Sills's inability to realize her global ambitions, since by the early seventies her voice had already begun to show signs of deterioration. The lovely tonal sheen was rapidly wearing away, while the top notes became tight, strident, and marred by an unpleasant beat. The technique and musicianship largely survived, and her stage presence was, if anything, more assured than ever, but the freshness and spontaneity that had characterized her Manon, Baby Doe, and Cleopatra were gradually being usurped by her need to be a prima donna. Even sadder than her vocal decline was the brittle, hard-edged, and self-regarding persona that had replaced a once captivating performer. Three years after Bing's retirement, in 1975, she was finally invited to join the Met, but it was already too late. By then her transformation into a calculating media darling was complete.

What actually happened onstage had become irrelevant—audiences no longer came to applaud Beverly Sills, but her success.

Andrew Porter tersely summed up the depressing situation in *The New Yorker* when Sills sang Thaïs at the Met in 1978, a performance that surely would have caused Mary Garden, had she been alive to see it, to demand her tiara back: "*Thaïs* is a pretty opera, and very skillfully written, but it was a mistake to essay it without a heroine more alluring of voice and more secure on exposed, sustained high notes above the staff than Beverly Sills was. Moreover, Miss Sills was histrionically unconvincing. She seemed too refreshingly sensible and self-aware to have or to inspire any questioning belief in her portrayal, and instead invited the audience to enjoy watching her play at playing Thaïs." This was the diva that Europeans saw and heard in the seventies, and most came away wondering why Americans were making such a fuss over so little. Both Anna Moffo and Sills recorded *Thaïs* around this time, and perplexed British critics "found it hard to decide who was the less persuasive, the near voiceless Anna Moffo sexily crooning on RCA, or EMI's shrill and wobbly Beverly Sills." Never having experienced Sills during her brief glory years a decade earlier, operagoers abroad were just puzzled. Back home, though, Sills's fame, as Irving Kolodin had once observed about Lily Pons's, remained long after the reasons for it had departed.

Even Sills must have realized that the time was getting short and that she had better make a graceful exit as soon as possible. Claiming that she had always intended to quit opera at the age of fifty, the soprano sang her farewell performance at the City Opera in the fall of 1979 as the mad Queen Juana in *La Loca*, a dramatically feeble, musically vapid vehicle concocted for her by Gian Carlo Menotti. After that, Sills promptly plunged into a new career as Julius Rudel's successor at the City Opera, a rocky ten-year reign beset by financial crises and spotty artistic achievement. Inevitably, Sills was also asked to write an official account of her life, but it came out as an outrageously self-serving document, even when measured against other diva apologias. An extensive and varied enemies' list ("I *do* hold grudges") is drawn up and old scores are settled. If Sills did have trouble establishing an international presence, she says, there were dark reasons: Sutherland fans conspired against her at Covent Garden; anti-Semitism did her in at the Deutsche Oper in Berlin; Rolf Liebermann's personal animosity kept her away from the Paris Opéra; after her "sensational" debut in *L'Assedio di Corinto*, La Scala would offer her only tacky, second-class productions, which she had to refuse. Forgetting about Carol Fox and Ardis Krainik of the Lyric Opera of Chicago, Sills proclaims herself a female pioneer in operatic administration; her failures, if any, were only in the imaginations of antifeminists. Most disingenuously of all, Sills inflates her own importance, creating the impression that until she came along and changed everything, American singers were invariably treated as insignificant nobodies.

By the time she came to write this peevish book, Sills was still a visible and influential figure in New York's musical life, as a board member, fund-raiser, and society matron. But as a singer she had already been largely forgotten, and she probably suffered from that knowledge as she so vigorously promoted the legend. The ultimate indignity came in the mid-1990s when La Gran Scena, a popular transvestite opera troupe based in New York, had to consider dispensing with its hokey, fast-talking hostess—"Sylvia Bills, America's most famous retired diva"—because the audience no longer got the joke. The handful of recordings and videos that remained, all made much too late, scarcely gave an adequate explanation of why there had once been a truly magical opera singer called Beverly Sills. At some point long before that, even Super-sills herself seemed to have forgotten why.

On some level, Sills must have realized that during her relentless campaign to become Maria Callas, Lily Pons, and America's operatic sweetheart all in one, she succeeded only in losing her voice. And when she began to believe in her own publicity, she lost something even more precious. So shrewd and worldly a woman could scarcely have failed to grasp what had happened to her, and perhaps that explains the sour woman who emerges in her autobiography. Phyllis Curtin, so coolly outmaneuvered by Sills in 1966, had far more cause to be bitter, but as Curtin told an interviewer six years later, "Bitterness is a useless condition because it only hurts the person who is bitter." Even so, she still felt considerable pain over her experience with the City Opera, which she called "the only heartbreaking thing in my career." When she first joined the company in 1953, the sense of family unity was strong. After Erich Leinsdorf's financially disastrous 1956 season, there was talk that the Met might absorb the City Opera, but Curtin and her colleagues banded together and convinced the board to appoint Julius Rudel general director. As Curtin recollected,

We saved the City Opera. Now, I would think that a company would find it unique that it was saved by its artists, *not* by its board of directors . . . Then came *Julius Caesar* in 1966. That's when the knife went into my back. Julius Rudel had asked *me* to do it, and I wanted to very much. My whole fall schedule was booked solid, and it took some doing, but my management moved all the dates they could, and when they called to say I was clear, they were told, "Oh, we've already got Miss Sills to sing the part."

I was so stunned! After my life at the City Opera, which had always been so successful for me and the company, I simply couldn't believe that my family would do that to me . . . I lost a stage, and a stage I believed in.

By then, perhaps as a consequence of its move to Lincoln Center, the City Opera had begun to develop its own stars rather than remaining the closely knit ensemble family Curtin had joined in 1953. It was the sort of operatic environment that a singer like Curtin, who never aspired to be a "star" in the Sills sense, thrived in and one she would never find again—"a company full of wonderful individuals," as she remembered it, "but individuals who cared deeply about each other, and our work enhanced each other's. *That's* what makes good theater, not a series of star turns." Not surprisingly, Curtin's appearances at the Metropolitan were sporadic, and she never received any special favors. Although Bing may have responded to her coolly aristocratic manner more readily than he did to Sills's brasher urban persona, apparently his admiration stopped there—"Rudolf Bing enjoyed me as a luncheon companion," Curtin once wryly commented. He also told her that "you'll never sing Tosca here because you're not Italian" (the year after Bing's departure Curtin finally did get to sing three Met Toscas, but only in the city's parks).

Still, it was a busy career elsewhere—in fact, by the time she was finessed out of the City Opera, Curtin had already made her European debut singing Susannah at the 1958 Brussels World's Fair, soon followed by Manon at Buenos Aires's Teatro Colón, Violetta and Salome at the Vienna State Opera, and Fiordiligi at La Scala. There were plenty of concerts and recitals as well—Curtin always had a keen sense of musical adventure, maintaining an interest in the song literature throughout her career as well as an avid curiosity in what new composers were writing. Her voice may have lacked the immediately identifiable timbral characteristics that all the greatest singers have, but its intonational purity and attractive silvery sheen adapted to an amazing variety of styles and the secure technical base of her method never deserted her, right up into her mid-sixties.

Even before that, Curtin had become one of the country's most sought-out teachers of singing, passing on a lifetime of practical musical and career advice to a distinguished student list that included Dawn Upshaw, Cheryl Studer, Sanford Sylvan, and John Aler, among many others. What she had learned herself originated in the 1940s as she began to sing in Boston-area churches and new-music concerts, as well as in her first operatic performances with Boston's indefatigable opera-singer trainer, Boris Goldovsky. For those who had the opportunity to follow Curtin from those humble beginnings through her City Opera and Met years, and then to savor her rich concert/recital repertory, the musical perceptions she instilled into her best pupils came as no surprise. As their teacher perhaps told them, "Throughout my entire singing career, I was always listening to my colleagues, noticing what worked for them and what did not. I was interested in technique, but not as an end in itself but as a support for what I wanted to do. You should go for everything you can imagine artistically, and the technique must be adequate to service it . . ." As Sills once correctly observed, quite a lady— and indeed, quite a classy singer.

After Sills's triumph in *Giulio Cesare*, many felt that her costar in the title role, Norman Treigle (1927–75), would soon be every bit as famous. It never happened, although at the City Opera Treigle always enjoyed a special position with management and the public, as the list of roles during his twenty years with the company indicates: Julius Caesar, Boris Godunov, Don Giovanni, the Father in *Louise*, Mephistopheles (Boito and Gounod), the *Hoffmann* villains, Rimsky-Korsakov's King Dodon, Gianni Schicchi, Figaro, Escamillo, and many parts in contemporary works, most famously Olin Blitch in Floyd's *Susannah*. The frightening intensity of Treigle's performance as Blitch, the tortured preacher who rapes Susannah and repents too late, was surely in part drawn from his own Southern background and devoutly religious nature, not to mention his frustrations over a career that never developed in ways he had hoped.

Treigle came to the City Opera in 1953 after schooling and local operatic work in his native New Orleans. It took him only a few seasons before he was entrusted with the major bass-baritone roles, each one stamped by a theatricality that always created a vivid effect, even if it sometimes verged dangerously toward broad staginess. Treigle used his voice with flair and imagination, but its penetrating tonal quality was not to everyone's taste, a tightly focused, sinewy bass that lacked conventional beauty—no doubt Bing felt he had no need for such a rough diamond at the Met when he could draw on the velvety lower voices of Cesare Siepi, George London, and Nicolai Ghiaurov. The one role that Treigle made completely his own—in an opera that had not been seen in New York since the days of Chaliapin—was Boito's Mefistofele. Tito Capobianco's 1969 production was consciously designed to take full advantage of the bass's cadaverous physique and athletic performing style. Treigle's snarling vocal delivery was also complemented by his viciously witty conception of Boito's flamboyant spirit of denial, a role he played in a striking skin-tight body stocking that never quite fit comfortably over his less rail-thin successors.

For all his popularity at the City Opera, Treigle continued to yearn for wider acclaim, and it must have irked him to watch Sills's career take off while his remained parochial. Many in the company sympathized with his discontent, including Sills herself. On the other hand, nearly everyone at one time or another had been irritated by Treigle's high opinion of himself and unpredictable behavior. After singing his first Boris, he wrote a letter to Julius Rudel referring to himself as the world's finest exponent of the role, and included a list of operas he was studying. Among them were *Mefistofele*, Massenet's *Don Quichotte*, Verdi's *Attila* and *Don Carlo*, and he demanded that the company stage at least two. Even the one that Rudel agreed to do—*Mefistofele*—did not launch the bass on his hoped-for world career despite much local praise. Finally Rudel agreed to one more Capobianco production conceived to spotlight Treigle's special performing qualities: a new staging of *Les Contes d'Hoffmann* with Sills, who says she deliberately played down her approach to the four heroines—at least at first—in order to give her colleague a star turn as Hoffmann's four nemesis figures. Apparently Treigle seized his big chance with a vengeance. According to Sills, "Norman turned in the most extraordinary, egotistical, self-serving performance I've ever seen on an opera stage. He wasn't merely being a ham and upstaging everybody by doing cheap schlocky stuff. Norman was doing all kinds of inventive balletic movements and was never where he was supposed to be . . . when the curtain came down, I knew I'd seen an astonishing performance. Crazy, yes, but definitely astonishing."

As it turned out, that 1972 new production was the bass's last at the City Opera. He left the company determined to go after the elusive big career in earnest, and for a while it seemed that it might be within his grasp. During the next two years there was a Covent Garden debut as Gounod's Méphistophélès, an EMI recording of Boito's *Mefistofele*, and engagements in Hamburg, Buenos Aires, and San Francisco, but soon it was all over. In February 1975, at the age of forty-seven, "this brilliantly talented, tortured man," as Sills records in her book, "died alone in his New Orleans apartment." Just how tortured Treigle really was, or even how he died, may never be known. After his death many private recordings were found among his belongings, mostly of hymns, spirituals, and oratorio arias. One song was by Treigle himself: a harsh country-and-western lament with a pounding rock beat and sung in a raspy pop voice that only faintly resembles the bass's familiar commanding vocal presence. The chilling refrain pleads for somebody to help him find the way—perhaps he meant the words to be his epitaph.

Although most sopranos at the City Opera during Sills's hegemony were necessarily overshadowed, Patricia Brooks (1937–93) had her ardent admirers. One of them was Frank Corsaro, who directed her in a production of *La Traviata* that had its premiere just a month after Sills's triumph in *Giulio Cesare*. A product of Lee Strasberg's Actors Studio, Corsaro brought "the method," popularized in the fifties by the likes of Marlon Brando and Montgomery Clift, to Verdi's opera and staged it with searing realism. After her guests had left the party in Act I, this Violetta stood for a full half-minute in silence with her back to the audience—a dangerously long pause in any opera—her thoughts clearly on Alfredo; when she at last turned to begin "Ah, fors' è lui," a brittle courtesan had suddenly melted into a sick, vulnerable young girl who probably had never really been in love before. This dying Violetta did "not go gentle into that good night," but, in a burst of bitter rage, hurled a crucifix across the room, only to crawl in horror after it.

Brooks brought off Corsaro's conception with magnificent precision and clarity—the director compared her to Marietta Piccolomini, one of Verdi's favorite Violettas, whose performance was considered at the time as shocking for its explicitness. When Sills was not singing Manon, Brooks usually filled in for her, offering an entirely different characterization but one that was equally absorbing, an intriguingly frail but voluptuous Lulu-like figure straight from Pandora's box. Of course, there was no real vocal competition with Sills. Brooks's rather thin, thready soprano could effectively illuminate a select repertory, but this was obviously not a voice for export. Still, for a while, the City Opera counted itself fortunate to have so affecting a *seconda donna* and one who commanded such an extraordinary expressive range.

Maralin Niska (1930?–   ) was another resourceful singing actress who graced the company in those days. Although her voice was scarcely more glamorous than Brooks's, it had enough thrust, staying power, and versatility to take its owner a bit further—even to a modest career at the Metropolitan, where the soprano spent a few seasons singing mainly cover assignments and lots of Musettas. Niska arrived at the City Opera in the fall of 1967 as Mozart's Countess, followed by Violetta, Butterfly, Susannah, and later—in a rather delirious tour de force—Donna Anna sung in Italian and, five nights later, Donna Elvira in English. None of this stirred up any special comment, but in the fall of 1970 Niska found the role of her life as Emilia Marty in *The Makropoulos Affair*, another successful production staged by Corsaro. There was always a quirky aura of mad grandeur about Niska's stage presence that never quite suited Mozart or Puccini, but it gelled perfectly as Janáček's 334-year-old heroine, especially in a smoke-and-mirrors production that so cleverly combined the opera's elements of science-fiction fantasy with its humanistic message. Niska relished inhabiting both worlds, and in no other opera she sang in New York did her cool, steely soprano sound more eloquent or articulate.

It was the City Opera's good luck to have the fresh, young voices of Plácido Domingo and José Carreras on hand to provide vocal glamour opposite its leading ladies during the late sixties and early seventies, but such rising stars would clearly soon move on to more prestigious stages. The company's other tenor discoveries could never boast equivalent quality, but several provided honorable service while in residence, Americans all despite their Italian names. Michele (Mickey) Molese (1936–89) was one of Sills's frequent hardworking partners between 1964 and 1977, and his rather squeezed but always sturdily dependable voice did yeoman service in virtually the entire standard repertory. Like most company workhorses, Molese felt underappreciated, and a fit of pique abruptly terminated his City Opera career, at least for a while. At the second performance of a new staging of *Un Ballo in Maschera* in 1974, after receiving a tepid review from the *Times* for his first Riccardo, the tenor turned to the audience at the conclusion of the tenor-soprano duet in Act II and announced, "That high C was for Harold C. Schonberg!" On hand to spell Molese and take up the slack after his sudden departure were Enrico di Giuseppe (1938–   ) in the lyric repertory and Ermanno Mauro (1939–   ) in the more strenuous spinto parts.

John Alexander (1923–90) appeared on the scene earlier and stayed longer, proving his worth as a quick study at the City Opera (1957–77), in regional companies around the country, and at the Metropolitan (1961–85). His enormous repertory encompassed practically every style expected of a tenor, from Baroque (Handel's *Rinaldo*), the major Mozart roles, bel canto (Bellini's Pollione was one of his specialities), and the standard lyric Verdi-Wagner-Puccini heroes, to novelties by Korngold, Massenet, Menotti, Barber, and dozens of others. Like so many singers who can apparently sing anything, Alexander never found a way to define himself, and as a result he spent most of his career typecast as a pinch hitter. Whenever he did appear, though, audiences could always count on fervent delivery, solid musicianship, and a secure, ringing top. Another longtime City Opera family member who perhaps never received her due during nearly thirty years as the company's resident mezzo-soprano was Frances Bible (1927–   ). Although she excelled in trouser roles (Hansel, Cherubino, Octavian), the two parts most closely associated with Bible testify to her versatility: a charmingly vulnerable Cenerentola in Rossini's opera and as the flinty Augusta Tabor in *The Ballad of Baby Doe*.

Because of the City Opera's strong commitment to performing contemporary operas, by European composers as well as Americans, Bible and her colleagues were always kept busy learning new music as well as singing much of the standard repertory in English. When one thinks back to the company's original ensemble priorities—before Sills and Treigle were touched by stardust and the search for vehicles began—that twin fact might explain why its singers at the time were considered so personable, versatile, musically quick, and adept at acting. As Curtin put it, "When the audience understands every word you are singing straight out of your mouth, out of your whole being, the entire evening changes. You can't get that from reading a précis flashed up over the stage."

This ensemble principle especially favored the company's baritones and basses, notably John Reardon (1930–88) and Donald Gramm (1927–83), whose voices never really suited the glamorous roles from the nineteenth-century German-Italian repertory. Their careers got an early boost from the City Opera—Gramm joined in 1952 and Reardon in 1954—and soon they were in demand all over the country as the regional scene gathered momentum in the sixties and seventies. Gramm developed an especially beneficial relationship with Sarah Caldwell's Opera Company of Boston from 1958 to his death, and both singers were regulars at Santa Fe, where new operas were performed with frequency each summer. Even the Met eventually called upon them, albeit mainly for character parts. As a singer who started out in musical comedy, Reardon found himself completely at home on the stage, creating roles in new operas by many leading contemporary composers. Gramm was also an inventive singing actor of exceptional grace and imagination, but his attractively grainy bass-baritone, superb diction, and musical intelligence made him a mesmerizing singer of songs as well. Although at home in the European literature, he preferred to work with the music of his countrymen and the sounds of his own language. Many lucky composers heard Gramm sing their songs for the first time, but Ned Rorem was perhaps the most fortunate and most grateful. After hearing Gramm's recording of his *War Scenes*, Rorem wrote, "The result is satisfying to the point of tears: I've heard no better performance of any of my music by anyone ever, nor can it—need it—be surpassed."

There have always been important singers who never cared to establish a mutually beneficial affiliation with any opera or concert group, and preferred to conduct careers on their own terms. Eileen Farrell (1920–   ) was the most prominent American voice to follow that route after World War II. Farrell's vocal endowment was second to none, but many regretted the fact that the soprano so infrequently put it to use in the music nature seemed to indicate. It was a huge sound when fully unleashed. Franco Corelli, who often sang in Puccini's *Turandot* with Birgit Nilsson and matched her trumpeting soprano decibel for decibel, appeared with Farrell in Philadelphia, in *La Forza del Destino*, and reportedly rushed off stage screaming, "Ma, chi è questa donna? Lei m'assordava!" (But who is this woman? She has made me deaf!) But Farrell could also tame the volume and pare it down to an intimate but firmly spun thread of sound, particularly when she sang pop and jazz. Early on she not only showed a preference for the idiom but also demonstrated to her operatic colleagues who dabbled in it how to retune a classically trained voice to sing proper pop style. Her scale was as seamless as Nordica's, her middle register as solid as Traubel's, and her versatility as impressive as Steber's, according to Albert Innaurato, who heard her frequently in her prime and was especially struck by the subtle tonal effects she could produce when singing Wagner in concert: "Her piano and mezzo-forte were—paradoxically—softly immense, and the big soaring phrases literally lifted some of the audience out of their seats."

Farrell's parents were both singers and she had always sung at home in Willimantic, Connecticut, but when the time came to think about a career, she naturally gravitated to radio. Perhaps that had something to do with her figure, not as ample as Traubel's, but close. She had her own program on CBS for seven years starting in 1940, and by the time she decided to move on, Farrell had already won national name recognition. A concert career seemed destined for a singer whose temperament lay mainly in her voice and whose chief priorities remained with her husband, a New York City policeman, and their two children. Always practical and unassuming, Farrell neither wished to be an international celebrity nor did she entertain romantic notions about herself or her voice. "I just sang," she told Innaurato. "I was always a dramatic soprano, period. I never had registers. My mom used to say if you don't have a sound at the bottom, you won't have any at all at the top. Nobody ever mentioned a middle register. Later on people would ask me about my break. I'd say, what the hell do you know about my arms and legs? Then I realized they meant some weird thing in my voice. I never had it. Coloratura? Well, I was a big girl but I could still climb the stairs fast if I had to run for the bus. The voice has to be the same."

In 1951 Farrell sang a searing Marie in Dimitri Mitropoulos's famous concert performance of Berg's *Wozzeck* with the New York Philharmonic—at the time the opera was still considered outrageous cacophony in conservative New York—and the subsequent release of the recording immensely enhanced her prestige. Farrell's major breakthrough, though, came when she provided Eleanor Parker's singing voice in the 1955 film *Interrupted Melody*, the story of Marjorie Lawrence and her battle with polio. It was a tour de force that ran from Brünnhilde's Immolation to "Waltzing Matilda," and Farrell sounded sensational in all of it. The soundtrack album made her voice even more famous, and two years later her debut in staged opera came at last, as Santuzza in Tampa, Florida, and a few months later she appeared at the San Francisco Opera in *Il Trovatore* opposite Jussi Bjoerling. She reached the Metropolitan, as Gluck's Alceste in 1960, but relations with the house were sporadic and uneasy during the five seasons she sang there. Rudolf Bing no doubt felt acutely uncomfortable dealing with the sort of earthy American prima donna who once looked down into the orchestra pit during a rehearsal, spotted conductor Thomas Schippers, and loudly remarked, "Ah, I see that Pippers is in the shit again!"

In opera, Farrell sang mainly the Italian repertory, although her soprano seemed more suited to the heroic German roles. To the eternal regret of those who valued this remarkable voice, she never sang the great Wagner heroines during the years of her vocal prime, except in concert. By the mid-sixties the top had lost some of its brilliance and security, and Farrell turned increasingly to the pop-jazz literature that she had always projected with such ease and naturalness. There had been many operas and art songs left unsung, but during her best years this independent spirit still outsang most of her contemporaries and left few who heard her unaffected. When she finally called it quits after making her last record of popular songs in 1993, on the eve of her seventy-third birthday, Farrell bade farewell in typically down-home fashion: "Look, maybe I had some kind of gift, or was just lucky. But I realized from the get go, that there would be somebody listening, maybe by accident to the radio or a record, or maybe standing at the concert hall. And you could change their life, give some joy, maybe just for a couple of seconds. If I've done that for a handful of people then I'm happy."

Farrell was only the most prominent singer to move between opera and concert without typecasting herself as a specialist in one field or the other. Maureen Forrester (1930–), although a contralto, was in many ways Farrell's Canadian counterpart. Her voice was as voluminous as her figure, and it proved to be the ideal instrument to assist the Mahler boom that grew rapidly during the late sixties. Soon Mahler and recital work, along with endless Beethoven Ninths, began to seem too limiting, so Forrester ventured cautiously into opera. Thanks to her numerous concert appearances, she was actually more famous than either of her colleagues when she shared the stage with Sills and Treigle in the 1966

City Opera *Giulio Cesare*. After that successful experiment, she became a busy singer of character roles, from Klytämnestra to Mistress Quickly, with regional companies all over the continent.

Illness rather than career priorities limited the progress of Judith Raskin (1928–84), a favorite of many exacting conductors (Szell, Bernstein, Böhm) and Stravinsky's choice to sing Anne Trulove in his second recording of *The Rake's Progress*. Those who still remembered Elisabeth Schumann liked to compare Raskin's silvery soprano and polished musicianship to that paragon, whose concert and Mozart-Strauss operatic repertory she shared. When Raskin had to leave the scene much too early, Benita Valente (1934–   ) was there to replace her, a pupil of Lotte Lehmann, who had clearly passed on many of her secrets about refined Mozart singing and German lieder interpretation. Valente's interests soon branched out from there, particularly into new music. Although never a strict specialist in that area either, Valente easily proved that singing the most demanding contemporary works could never damage a healthy voice whose prime assets were its lustrous sheen, instrumental purity, and technical security.

Some singers did prefer to devote themselves almost exclusively to new music, a decision that automatically doomed them to national obscurity, at least during the years immediately following World War II. That was pretty much the fate of Nell Tangeman (1917–65), although for a while she sang prominently due to the enthusiastic championship of several eminent composers. As early as 1946 she gave the first New York performance of Olivier Messiaen's *Poèmes pour Mi*, a prestigious event in the new-music community that led to other important world premieres: Aaron Copland's *In the Beginning* (1947), Mother Goose in *The Rake's Progress* (1951), and Dinah in Bernstein's *Trouble in Tahiti* (1952).

Her most enthusiastic fan, however, was Ned Rorem, who wrote dozens of songs with her voice in mind and left a glowing tribute to her art: "So far as my own music went, Nell Tangeman's wise, lush contralto became the defining instrument. During her brief peak, from 1948 to 1954, hers was the one 'real' voice doing new repertory. All I wrote then was for her, and by extension all I write now comes from what I learned from her." At her recital debut in Town Hall on October 24, 1948, Virgil Thomson concurred, heralding the arrival of "an artist right off the top shelf . . . with brains, beauty, and skill." Recordings of her voice are scarce—new music, never plentiful on discs, was even less so in those lean days—but a performance of Schoenberg's massive *Gurrelieder* made it to the record shops in the early days of LP, and Tangeman's singing of the Wood Dove's narrative confirms Rorem's description of her voice, even if it could not conjure up her physical presence: "Her handsome appearance, her violet eyes, her aggressively passive delivery and opal-colored décolleté dress (gowns, as singers call them) were balanced by a brand of vocalism that no longer exists: a true contralto that passes from a velvet growl to a clarion purr, or descends from a heady altitude to a golden chest-tone, all in the space of a breath." Apparently by 1954, most of those remarkable qualities were already beginning to desert her. Tangeman soon vanished, only to resurface eleven years later when her broken body was found in a Washington, D.C., apartment, several days after a stranger she had brought home left her for dead. "Who besides a few old acquaintances," wrote Rorem, long out of touch when he heard of her death, "remembered her as the most interesting mezzo-soprano of our mid-century?"

Cathy Berberian (1925–83) from Attleboro, Massachusetts, captured wider notice, partly because the new-music world had developed more muscle by the time she arrived and partly because of her highly theatrical performance style. She had also married Luciano Berio in 1950, having met the composer soon after coming to Milan on a Fulbright for vocal study with Giorgina del Vigo, and Berio's influence on her proved to be enormous. During their sixteen years of marriage, he wrote many pieces especially designed to highlight her special gifts, and her fame in new-music circles grew with his. Perhaps the most striking Berio score to utilize all of Berberian's musical wit, intelligence, and vocal virtuosity was Circles, based on poems by e. e. cummings. The piece is an especially brilliant example of the "new vocalism," using unorthodox and more traditional vocal techniques that treat words as both vehicles of meaning and phonetic sounds. During the course of the performance, Berio asks the singer to join the instrumental ensemble in moving about the stage, creating a fascinating abstract mini-opera from concentrically evolving musical and physical gestures.

Other composers eagerly took advantage of Berberian's unusual musical, dramatic, and vocal talents. John Cage provided her with Aria with Fontana Mix, a spectacular aleatory mad scene and a virtual textbook of the flashy avant-garde vocal techniques that composers were experimenting with in the fifties. Even the aging Igor Stravinsky was intrigued by Berberian, and he styled the vocal lines of his Elegy for J.F.K. specifically for her smoky mezzo-soprano, which could also be put to more conventional uses. Berio arranged an exquisite suite of folk songs for her, and even Marlene Dietrich could scarcely have bettered her suggestively sinuous renditions of the two gorgeous torch songs he inserted into his ballet *Allez-Hop*. After the marriage broke up in 1966, Berberian found herself somewhat at sea for the rest of her too-short life, as she looked for other avenues to explore. Those included several Monteverdi opera productions under Nikolaus Harnoncourt and an entertaining program of salon *morceaux* prepared for the Edinburgh Festival (ranging from Griepenkerl's vocal version of the *Moonlight* Sonata to the Beatles' "Ticket to Ride"). She even turned to composition—her *Stripsody*, a sound collage of familiar onomatopeic comic-strip explicatives, contains much of the same inventive genius Berberian had brought to other composers' music.

Berberian conducted her career mostly in Europe. Back home in America, the leading new-music singer of the day was Bethany Beardslee (1927–   ), who over a span of nearly four decades virtually defined the native art song for two generations of composers. Not only did Americans of every stylistic persuasion clamor for her services, but she also introduced an entire repertory of important European vocal music to the country, including works by Stravinsky, Schoenberg, Berg, and Krenek. Although Schoenberg's *Pierrot Lunaire* had been a locus classicus of twentieth-century vocal music ever since 1912, it was Beardslee's performances fifty years later that made many listeners appreciate the poetry in this moon-drenched expressionistic music for the first time. Few singers before or since better grasped what the composer meant by the term *Sprechstimme*, which stipulates precise observation of rhythms and indication of pitch while "speaking" on the note. Beardslee possessed the necessary awesome musical skills and ability to tune notes accurately and conquer the most difficult scores, while her pure lyric soprano demolished the cliché of the voiceless new-music singer. Not only that, she brought a throbbing sensualism to everything she sang, even a score as rarefied as Milton Babbitt's *Philomel*, in which the voice flutters in concert and in competition with the ethereal sounds of a synthesizer. Like many singers who eventually tire of being pigeonholed as specialists, Beardslee later combined her work in new music with performances of older music—German lieder and French songs especially—forming fruitful partnerships with pianist Richard Goode and composer-pianist Robert Helps.

If new music—song in particular—gradually became a more welcome presence in the mainstream of America's musical life as the century marched to its end, Jan DeGaetani (1933–89) could surely take much of the credit. Actually, DeGaetani was never a specialist—she simply sang music, and her involvement with the new was a natural extension of her love for the old. Both nourished her spirit and sharpened her musical instincts, and probably contributed to the repose and concentration that radiated from her whenever she sang. By 1958, when DeGaetani moved from Ohio to base her musical activities in New York, a "new virtuosity" was in the wind as a whole generation of musicians reinterpreted the classics of early-twentieth-century music with unprecedented passion and insight, which in turn inspired composers to exploit their skills with fresh challenges. Indeed, the defining piece for DeGaetani was George Crumb's *Ancient Voices of Children*, which she premiered at the Library of Congress in Washington in 1970, a compelling theatrical score whose glowing mystery was further enhanced by her meticulous musicianship and expressive power. DeGaetani's subsequent performances and Nonesuch recording made the work an instant contemporary classic. As critic David Hamilton wrote of her performance, "She can 'tune' a timbre as accurately as she can tune a pitch, make a *messa di voce* on changing vowels, sing the most elaborate melismas, interspersed with tongue-clicks and flutter-tonguing . . . She can, in fact, do just about anything."

Composers did not consider DeGaetani so much a performer as a collaborator. Critics who felt she was a "cool" singer were probably not listening hard. Her personality never got in the way of the music, but neither was it absent, either in her engagement with the text or in the ways she found—with the bittersweet timbre of that limpid, perfectly tuned mezzo-soprano—to make the music express the exact meaning of the words. Once she had the attention of a wider audience, DeGaetani immediately set out to demonstrate that neither her interests nor her communicative powers were restricted to new music, or even to the conventional concert repertory. She surprised everyone by taking up the songs of Stephen Foster, savoring their period humor as well as freshening every delicate twist in the melodic line of a touching ballad like "Ah! May the Red Rose Live Alway." DeGaetani was also the definitive Ives interpreter, conveying more of the composer's transcendental spirit, quirky humor, hard-cider tang, and sheer cussedness than most of her predecessors. When it came to German lieder, she was also supreme, particularly in such demanding material as Hugo Wolf's *Spanish Songbook* collection, in which mystical meditations of painful religious ecstasy alternate with adorable songs that describe the bristling love banter between a typical *maja* and her *majo*. They are devilishly difficult—Wolf's greatest challenges to a singer—and rarely performed. But DeGaetani's voice serenely conquered all, and each song she sang glowed with a polished tonal precision that left no emotion unsung. Typically, although she knew she was mortally ill with leukemia in 1989, she learned several songs by Berg, Webern, and Zemlinsky to include on her final recital at Brandeis University.

When DeGaetani was drawn to the songs of Cole Porter, the consensus seemed to be that a versatile musician, whose only other known misjudgment was to attempt Wagner's Erda, had made a serious error. Years later, replaying the recording she made of nineteen Porter songs, the error seems ours, not hers, as she puts new musical perspectives on these American classics. By the final chord of "At Long Last Love," she has made it clear that this is no cute specialty number but a disturbing love song of striking musical beauty and depth. Only the greatest singers can turn a listener's head and heart around like that.

Twenty-four

~

At the Top

~~~~~~~~~~~~~~~~

*C*onsolidating the gains made at home and abroad during the 1960s, the American singer was by the end of the decade emerging as a global presence that would continue to grow right up to the millennium. If the previous generation, the Johnson Babies of the forties and fifties, was content to make a comfortable home base at the Metropolitan and seldom stray from it, the new stars of opera and concert were eager to sing everywhere—and they did. More than ever before, the music world was becoming internationalized, and important American voices were being added to the mix in increasing numbers. One of the first to make a major impact in the sixties was Leontyne Price, and her rapid ascent to the top must have been a source of great satisfaction to many. Not only was she an American with a superior vocal endowment, but she was also the first classically trained black opera singer to attain worldwide stardom.

When Price made her Metropolitan Opera debut, as Leonora in *Il Trovatore*, on January 27, 1961, most of the audience left the house in a state of dazed elation, having just given the soprano a forty-two-minute ovation. With its glinting whorl of colors and fascinating smoky vibrato, this distinctive voice would have commanded rapt attention under any circumstances. But there was much more to admire on that night—the thrilling vibrancy, shining tone, and sustaining power of the upper register; the complementary ability to spin out the sweetest and softest high tones; the classic nobility of utterance and expressive urgency that drove every note. One hardly had to be a vocal connoisseur to realize that a major talent had arrived, and with her the hope that the great Verdi soprano roles would be in safe hands at the Met for the next twenty years. It didn't quite work out that way, partly because the realities of global operatic life would soon change everyone's expectations, and partly because Price, like all important singers, developed a career according to her own priorities and personal needs.

Having already sung in Milan, Vienna, Salzburg, London, San Francisco, Chicago, and Verona, the thirty-three-year-old soprano hardly burst upon the New York scene unheralded. One of Rudolf Bing's least-remarked-upon but canniest tactics in those days was to intentionally delay contracting the newest vocal sensation in order to heighten the suspense. By doing so, the eagerly awaited first appearances of Birgit Nilsson, Maria Callas, and Renata Tebaldi, as well as Price, cleverly reinforced the perception that a Met debut was indeed the last and most important step up the international ladder, both a fulfillment and an anointment. It certainly worked out that way for Price, and she was ready to make the most of it. During her first two months at the Met she followed Leonora with Aida, Madama Butterfly, Liù, and Donna Anna, each role earning her more critical accolades than the last and bringing with it nationwide recognition and a *Time* cover story in March. Even if she had retired after her first Met season, Price would be remembered as one of America's most famous singers.

As the press breathlessly recounted it in those days, Price's rise to prominence could hardly have proceeded more steadily, serenely, or inevitably. The daughter of a midwife and millworker in Laurel, Mississippi, Price had been blessed by poor but strong, supportive parents and a wealthy patroness, Elizabeth Chisholm, who first encouraged the girl's interest in singing, financed her early musical studies, and provided the wherewithal to send her to the Juilliard School for voice training with Florence Page Kimball. It was at Juilliard in 1951 that Virgil Thomson spotted her as Alice Ford in a student production of *Falstaff* and whisked her into a prominent revival of his *Four Saints in Three Acts*. The Broadway producer Robert Breen was also impressed by Price in *Falstaff*, and signed her to sing Bess in a two-year world tour of Gershwin's opera that set out in 1952.

After the *Porgy and Bess* tour, Price quickly moved onward, boosted by NBC's short-lived interest in televising its own live opera productions in the mid-fifties. "My name, whatever it is," Price could truthfully remark a few months after her Met debut, "was made by the TV *Tosca* in 1955. There was a lot of controversy about that which made it interesting"—an understatement to say the least, since the notion of a black Tosca in 1955, on national television no less, was still unprecedented. But it led directly to Price's formal operatic debut two years later in San Francisco, as the Second Prioress in the American premiere of Poulenc's *Dialogues of the Carmelites*, followed by Aida.

By then she had also caught Herbert von Karajan's ear at a casual audition in Carnegie Hall—the conductor was so excited by what he heard that he pushed aside the accompanist and took Price through Leonora's "Pace, pace, mio Dio" himself. Now a favorite of Europe's *Generalmusikdirektor*, then at the height of his power and influence, she found the doors of the Vienna State Opera, the Salzburg Festival, and La Scala quickly thrown open. And Price soon proved to all that Karajan's enthusiasm was not misplaced. The Austrians marveled over her command of Mozart style, a Donna Anna who not only burned with dramatic fire but also rejoiced in uncommon vocal richness and easy flexibility. She applied the same sterling qualities to Aida, which La Scala audiences found close to perfection—"At last we have heard the true Aida, as Verdi probably imagined her," wrote one Italian critic. There were very few sour notes struck during this rapid ascent, although one came in 1959, and it should have sounded a warning bell about certain roles that even this protean young singer might have been well advised to avoid: *Thaïs* in Chicago, sung in front of the same sets that had served Mary Garden nearly fifty years earlier. Claudia Cassidy, in one of the kinder reviews of Price's courtesan, complained that "she knows only the surface of the role, and she has been miserably coached. It is often hard to know what she is impersonating, unless it might be the Statue of Liberty."

Most singers would agree that getting to the top of their profession is far easier than staying there, a reality that must also have occurred to Price as she collected one plum after another on her way to the Metropolitan. Despite emerging triumphantly from her Met debut, the ten-

sions could only have mounted as she tested her voice and inner resources while delighting Met patrons during those busy months early in
1961—even then, few opera stars would have dreamed of risking such
heavy exposure by singing five roles for the first time in New York over
so short a period. But Price delivered the goods so successfully that Bing
rewarded her with Minnie in next season's opening night new production of La Fanciulla del West with Richard Tucker as her costar. That laid
another weighty responsibility upon Price—no one of her race had ever
before been the centerpiece of that glittering event, traditionally one of
more social than artistic significance. Even Price may have doubted that
the gun-slinging, poker-playing Minnie suited her voice and temperament any more than Thaïs had, but there was no way to refuse the
honor. Needless to say, the experiment was not a success, although the
critics offered Price their sympathies. After the opening night performance, many others seemed to agree with the witchy Broadway columnist Dorothy Kilgallen, who, in those politically incorrect times, could
tell her readers that she had just been to the Met and seen the most
peculiar Italian opera in which a Jewish cowboy falls in love with a black
cowgirl. During the second performance Price lost her voice and had to
be replaced in Act III by Dorothy Kirsten. A virus infection was cited as
the cause, but it seems more likely that her frantic Met schedule of the
past year—exacerbated by having to sing an exceedingly uncongenial
role—had finally caught up with her. Price immediately took the first of
what would soon be many long rests.

A dozen years later, when her infrequent Met appearances had become a subject of worried conjecture, Price frankly confessed that the
cost of fame had been considerable during those early days, the pressures on her as much racial as artistic: "My career was simultaneous with
the opening of civil rights. Whenever there was any copy about me,
what I was as an artist, what I had as ability, got shoveled under because
all the attention was on racial connotations. I didn't have time to fight
back as an artist except to be prepared and do my work and take that
space because I was the only person allowed the opportunity. That is
what it meant being black then . . . If you get in the door, you have to
accept and almost gobble up everything that comes with it. With it, in
my case, was pressure."

Those words were spoken in 1973, and by then Price had experienced several other unhappy nights. After three months' rest following
her Minnie debacle, she was back at the Met in April as, said the Times, a

"rather tentative and careful" Tosca, "more a series of poses than a finished conception." Even though her Tosca would continue to remain just
that—an uncomfortable fit for a voice that had always lacked a working
chest register and an interpreter whose strengths lay in communicating
generalized nobility rather than etching out specific character or emotions—Price refused to leave the role alone. The next few seasons found
her miscast as Elvira in *Ernani*, Tatiana in *Eugene Onegin*, and Fiordiligi in
Così Fan Tutte, new roles that flattered neither her voice nor her limited
acting abilities. Then, in 1966, came a greater honor and an even greater
fiasco than *Fanciulla*: Samuel Barber's *Antony and Cleopatra*, commissioned
to open the Met's new home at Lincoln Center. This time, at least, Price
emerged from the wreckage with her voice and honor intact—most of
the critical scorn was reserved for Franco Zeffirelli's overdecorated production, which effectively buried the opera and the cast. Still, the
wounds remained and they never seemed to heal entirely. Nine years
later, while attending a revised and more sensibly scaled version of the
opera at the Juilliard School, Price confided to a friend that she had
broken out in a cold sweat upon hearing the first notes.

After *Antony*, Price further removed herself from the stress of the
opera stage and found a more comfortable, less challenging and emotionally draining environment on the lucrative concert circuit. Only
rarely could she be lured back into the opera house, usually for one of
the three Verdi heroines that had always sat so comfortably in her voice,
the two Leonoras and Aida. But even those classic assumptions had
gradually become little more than carefully preserved, marbleized interpretations unaltered in any significant way since she first sang them.
When Price added Puccini's Manon and Strauss's Ariadne to her repertory and discovered that neither one pleased the critics or the public,
she quickly dropped them and stopped learning new roles altogether.

By the time she officially bade the opera stage farewell with one last
Aida at the Met in January 1985, Price had long been a legendary figure
beyond criticism, and few had the nerve to point out that most of Aida's
music was no longer hers to command. By then she was reduced to a
collection of desperate whoops, careening roller-coaster portamentos,
and wild register shifts—one was left with the queasy sensation of Aida
sung by a nightclub singer. And yet the upper half-octave retained much
of its former gleaming tone, and she made capital of that fact throughout
the next decade on her recital programs, which she was still singing as
late as 1996 at age sixty-nine. Her signature tune on nearly all these

occasions was the high-lying "Chi il bel sogno di Doretta" from Puccini's *La Rondine*, with its perfectly placed C generously projected from right to left over an adoring audience. The other rewards on her concert programs were mostly of a nostalgic and symbolic nature, favors mostly distributed in provincial towns and cities where Price would not have to bear hard critical scrutiny.

For those who were there to experience it from the beginning, Price's career in the opera house can scarcely help but leave the troubling perception of a fabulous vocal gift that went largely unfulfilled. Her recordings, however, tell a different story. If Price felt more comfortable on the concert stage, she was clearly even more at ease in the recording studio without having to face a live audience. It is Price's large discography rather than her disappointing stage career that surely accounts for her posthumous and unassailable reputation as one of America's greatest and most prodigiously endowed singers. There are many complete opera recordings from 1961 onward to prove it—the *Aida* of that year shows best how much vocal gold was in her throat right at the beginning—but an even more revealing set of discs are her five *Prima Donna* albums made between 1966 and 1980. The repertory here consists mainly of arias from roles Price never sang onstage, and the range is astonishing, from Gilda and Isolde to Norma and Turandot, from the Baroque (Handel) to the contemporary (Britten). Again, the earliest discs are the best—the signs of failing vocal powers inevitably become more evident as the series progresses, and the studied interpretations seldom say very much about character or situation. Even at that, the sense of adventure created by this journey hints at what was lost as the soprano's live performances during these years became increasingly self-conscious, emotionally confined, and infrequent. Price gradually turned herself into a symbol and as a consequence left music and the opera singer she might have been far behind. Perhaps that fate would have inescapably befallen anyone who assumed the heavy and perhaps impossible social responsibility of being the world's first black operatic superstar. If so, the rest of America must share the blame for the disappointingly restrictive nature of Price's art as it developed after that magical night in 1961.

"Of the two most beautiful voices in America, one belongs to Leontyne Price, the other to Marilyn Horne," veteran critic Louis Biancolli wrote in 1964, following the mezzo-soprano's first solo recital in New York. "It is a voice of ravishing beauty, molded by nature as a thing of unblemished purity and schooled to preserve it whatever the demands imposed upon it." Horne herself might have disagreed with that extravagant assessment and deferred to a singer whose natural vocal endowment even she could not match. "All my life," Horne admitted, "great singing has knocked me out; I don't care if the artist is my biggest rival, I *adore* great singing. For one singer to be moved to tears by another is very rare, and Leontyne has touched me that deeply. In Vienna, after Price had finished singing in the 'balcony trio' [in 1959, while recording Donna Elvira in *Don Giovanni*], I turned to Martin [Taubman] and said, 'I quit.' She was so fabulous I didn't even feel qualified to squeak in her presence."

Horne probably never "squeaked" in her life—few other American singers had ever been so obsessed with vocal mechanics, her own in particular. In interview after interview during the seventies, when Horne was at the peak of her technical virtuosity, she talked of little else. But then, why not? Beverly Sills to the contrary, Horne was the American singer at the forefront of the international bel canto revival during those years, the lower-voiced counterpart of Joan Sutherland, who was her frequent partner, most famously in *Norma* and *Semiramide*. The excitement they generated was even remarked upon with characteristic hyperbole in the entertainment trade sheet *Variety* after Horne's Met debut, as Adalgisa, in 1970. In the "New Acts" column under the heading of "Chix Clix," we read: "This is a hot 'New Act' comprising Joan Sutherland, audience-wowing coloratura from Australia, and Marilyn Horne, a local thrush in all ranges who's been around the concert big time for some years. Pair have been selling out at the Met doing standards from Bellini's *Norma* with accompaniment by Dick Bonynge and his pitmen. The girls can play anywhere to good results. They solo socko and unite in the duet department for the best close harmony act of the century. They tore the house down after each belting, at show caught."

Despite Biancolli's encomium, Horne's voice was not, like Price's, notable for voluptuous texture or seductive tonal beauty. Having considered its nature long and hard throughout her career, Horne could talk about its special qualities with an objectivity that escapes most singers, whose egos usually preclude useful self-analysis. "It's this peculiar darkness of my voice," she once explained, using a paradoxical equation, "with this gleam, this brightness. And then there's that dramatic thrust to it, a rhythmic thing that gives my singing its strength, its force." Also, Horne might have added, that dark, gleaming brightness she could summon up shone brightest whenever she sounded the firmly anchored fundamental tones of her lowest register, which possessed an ease and power that excited audiences as much as Lily Pons's high E-flats once had. They went especially wild when Horne tossed off one of her celebrated two-octave drops, descending precipitously from an unforced silvery high B-flat to a trumpeting low B-flat—an effect that some considered a vulgar circus trick, but one Rossini often invited a singer to perform, if she could. Mostly, though, it was her bravura technique that astonished the fans, an awesome coloratura agility and her ability to spin out long, seamless *mezza voce* lines. With Horne, beauty of individual sound definitely took second place to dazzling pyrotechnics.

Horne had several mentors over the years, beginning with her father, Bentz J. Horne, back in her hometown of Bradford, Pennsylvania, where she was born in 1934. In 1945 the family moved to Los Angeles, where Horne worked with the vocal pedagogue William Vennard, who provided the technical basics that would serve her well for her whole career. The third and perhaps most important influence was that of her husband, conductor Henry Lewis, whose encouragement and coaching in the bel canto repertory was as important to Horne as Richard Bonynge's was for Joan Sutherland. "Vennard," said Horne, "is incredible for building the low voice in females. But it was my husband who gave me the courage to use it."

While studying with Vennard at the University of Southern California, Horne developed a working range that extended from low E to high C, but it was only much later, after she had learned about such great nineteenth-century prima donnas as Pasta, Malibran, and Viardot, that she realized the possibilities opening up for her—"I'm a throwback to another age," she eventually discovered, "a soprano with mezzo qualities, or a mezzo with soprano qualities." Even then she sang most anything that came her way, which in Southern California in those days included solos with the Roger Wagner Chorale and singing for Hollywood's most famous musical resident, Igor Stravinsky. Horne must have impressed the composer, since he dedicated his last completed work to her, orchestrations of several Hugo Wolf lieder. Like Eileen Farrell, Horne also made a famous ghost-singing appearance in a mid-fifties hit film: Otto Preminger's *Carmen Jones*, in which she supplied the singing voice for Dorothy Dandridge—a light, lyric soprano that later fans of her voice would scarcely recognize.

In 1956 Horne decided to follow the many other young American singers who had gone to Europe, spending three years in the drab industrial city of Gelsenkirchen. It was her period in the galleys, but Gelsenkirchen gave her opportunities to learn the craft, as well as a secure base from which to branch out and sing elsewhere in Europe. Her role list in Germany, mostly in soprano territory, shows both a singer of extraordinary versatility and one who was still uncertain about what direction to take: Mimì, Minnie, Giulietta in *Les Contes d'Hoffmann*, Tatiana, Amelia in *Simon Boccanegra*, and Marie in *Wozzeck*. And that eclectic assortment only scratched the surface. Berg's heroine, in fact, became Horne's debut role at the San Francisco Opera upon her return to America in 1960, while her other assignment that year was, characteristically, the deep contralto part of Zita in *Gianni Schicchi*. A year later she reached New York and joined voices with Joan Sutherland for the first time, in a concert performance of Bellini's *Beatrice di Tenda*. It was Sutherland's New York debut, and few took much notice of Horne in the *seconda donna* role of Agnese. Richard Bonynge did, however, and he called up Terry McEwen, artists and repertory director for London Records, Sutherland's exclusive label. "You *must* come over here," he said. "There's a girl here sounds like Rosa Ponselle." McEwen hastened down, and although he may well have disagreed with the Ponselle analogy—Horne had closely studied the great Rosa's records, but her sound could not have been more dissimilar—he did give Horne a contract. It took a while for the public to catch on, but after Sutherland and Horne tore the house down in the American Opera Society's presentation of *Semiramide* in 1964, the mezzo's musical future seemed clear.

Not that Horne specialized exclusively in bel canto after that, but in no other areas of the literature did she seem quite so effective. Her flouncy, braying Carmen was truly vulgar and self-indulgent, and what should have been one of her triumphs—the great Viardot role of Fidès in Meyerbeer's *Le Prophète* at the Metropolitan in 1977—was compromised by an extended bout of bad health. For a moment in the late sixties it seemed she might follow Christa Ludwig's example and explore the dramatic soprano repertory, but after a few concert experiments with Brünnhilde's Immolation Scene and the like, that dangerous route was sensibly sealed off. And although she hated to admit it, Horne also realized that her voice never sounded quite right in the big Verdi mezzo roles of Azucena, Amneris, and Eboli, and she explained why in 1981. "With Amneris, I have to compensate a little too much. I'm better off doing *Tancredi*, and *Barbiere* and *L'Italiana*. And I hate this, because I like being versatile. It's a shame I have to stay away from them, but on the other hand it's probably smart. With the bel canto roles the middle voice is lightened, you don't have to sing this incredibly big middle register, so you can open up freely on top. In Verdi, you have to support and carry the full weight up to the top, bringing this column of sound up with you. In Verdi, I have to move the center of my voice . . . I have to gear myself, in a way, for singing like a soprano, if that sounds possible, in spite of the fact that the parts are low."

Horne also had her limits in the bel canto repertory. The reedy quality of her midrange and the aggressiveness of her basic vocal personality limited her expressive power, particularly in Rossini's delightfully feminine comic roles such as Rosina, Isabella, and Angelina. "That voice, it is to die," a colleague once accurately remarked, "but she has no charm." No, she didn't, but "General Horne" excelled in Rossini's great warrior-hero roles like Arsace, Tancredi, Malcolm, Neocle, Calbo, and Falliero, as well as similar characters in the Handel and Vivaldi operas. For articulate clarity, breathtaking bravura, and sheer physical zest, nothing like it had been heard for over a century—and even back then, one suspects, an American mezzo-soprano like Adelaide Phillipps would hardly have been able to compete.

"My voice," Teresa Stratas has said, "is an extension of my soul." Few singers would ever have been caught making such a grand observation, even in an epoch more prone to flowery self-analysis than the late twentieth century. For one thing, it carries with it the hint of an apology for something less than a first-class voice, unnecessary in this case. While Stratas never claimed to be a vocal prodigy, her soprano was both distinctive and more than suited to her purposes. Despite her five-foot stature and birdlike physique, Stratas resisted being typecast in the fragile Mimì-Violetta-Mélisande roles, although she did sing them to great effect. Like Mary Garden, she also looked past her apparent physical and vocal limitations to perform heavier heroines—Butterfly, the Composer in Ariadne auf Naxos, Dvořák's Rusalka, Tchaikovsky's Lisa, and even Salome, if only on film. More important, she found at least two roles she could make completely her own: Berg's Lulu and Weill's Jenny in Mahagonny. Now that the standard repertory had become more or less fixed, it was nearly impossible for singers to find effective parts that lacked famous predecessors, and Stratas was among the last to do so. Toward the end of her career, in 1991, she even offered one vivid world-premiere creation at the Metropolitan: Marie Antoinette in The Ghosts of

Versailles, the single memorable ingredient in a trivial pastiche by composer John Corigliano and playwright William H. Hoffman.

Most of all, though, Stratas had the courage to present herself as a complete original, an independent spirit at a time when opera singers the world over were beginning to appear distressingly interchangeable—the dreaded phrase "cookie-cutter singer" originated around this time and it was being applied most often to Americans as they proliferated in the global operatic community. In fact, Stratas was so reckless in her career decisions, famous for canceling performances at the last minute and removing herself from the scene for long periods, that she could honestly say in the middle of it all, "I've ruined my career over forty times according to some, but I go along and do what I have to do." She also admitted to being "a self-styled iconoclast, admitted schizophrenic with tendencies to manic-depression, a recluse and a free spirit." As if to prove it, in 1982 and at an age (forty-three) when most singers are preparing to enjoy their best years, Stratas simply turned her back on the opera world. Instead, she took time out to reeducate herself by reading Gide, Wedekind, Whitman, and dozens of other deep thinkers. She backpacked around India, winding up in Calcutta to help out in Mother Teresa's hospice. She spent a year back in her native Toronto, taking care of her own manic-depressive father during his last year with Alzheimer's disease. When the Ceauşescu regime fell in Rumania, she went there to work in orphanages with AIDS-infected children. Briefly, in 1986, Stratas interrupted this torturous odyssey to appear in a short-lived Broadway musical by Charles Strouse, Stephen Schwarz, and Joseph Stein that had caught her fancy: *Rags*, the story of a sorely beset but indestructible woman who arrived in America in 1910 at the height of the great wave of immigration from Eastern Europe.

Perhaps the show reminded Stratas of her own childhood, when she lived over a Chinese laundry in the tenements of Toronto. Herself the daughter of Greek immigrants, she was born on the dining room table in her parents' hole-in-the-wall restaurant, where she helped out as a girl, occasionally singing for the clientele. One night a drunken customer unable to pay for dinner offered the sixteen-year-old Teresa a pair of tickets to a touring Met performance at the Maple Leaf Gardens: *La Traviata* with Licia Albanese, Jan Peerce, and Leonard Warren. Enchanted, Stratas suddenly knew exactly what she wanted to do with her life—at least in the immediately foreseeable future. She promptly began vocal studies at the University of Toronto with former Met dramatic soprano Irene Jessner, eventually making her debut as Mimì with the Canadian Opera. Stratas had just turned nineteen when she applied for the Metropolitan Opera Auditions of the Air, still "a greenhorn who knew nothing." Yet there must have been something about this tiny girl with a big spirit and a surprisingly ample voice that impressed Bing and his staff. As Stratas recalled in a 1978 interview, "I gave Bing my note, he asked what I wanted to sing and I said 'Pace, pace,' and they laughed. I sang it and they didn't laugh, and they asked for another, and I did 'Sola, perduta' [from Puccini's *Manon Lescaut*] and then the 'Addio' from *Bohème*. Then Bing asked for some Mozart, and I told him I didn't like Mozart, and they were shocked—today he's my favorite composer. Then someone made a joke which I didn't understand—something about asking her to sing Isolde. Someone said, 'Ask her to sing Tristan and she wouldn't know the difference,' and they all laughed. It was true—I didn't know the difference."

Despite all the hilarity, Stratas eventually won a contract to make her debut as Pousette in *Manon*, which led to similar humble assignments. Everyone knew that Bing tended to typecast singers once they got into the Met, and at first it seemed that Stratas was permanently doomed to walk-ons, but apparently a special bond had sprung up between the intense little soprano and the austere general manager. "I always had gone to Mr. Bing with my problems," she said, "and people just didn't do this, but he would always see me." Perhaps Bing sensed her special qualities and was just waiting for the right moment to test them. In any case, on the morning of March 9, 1961, he rang up Stratas and told her that if she wanted to prove herself, she could do so that night by singing Liù in *Turandot* with Birgit Nilsson and Franco Corelli. Stratas sang, the audience loved her, and the reviews were fabulous—"it was an overnight success story. I was too dumb to be terrified."

For a while Stratas was content to enjoy her new opera-star status, not to mention the amorous attentions of the glamorous young Zubin Mehta—at least until the soprano discovered that Mehta "wanted me to give it all up and be Mrs. Conductor." Like so many successful but thoughtful singers whose art is basically instinctive, Stratas soon began to fret, not only about the why of what she was doing but also about the how. A confidence crisis ensued, but again "it was Rudolf Bing who got me through this with long talks. He said most artists suffer, wondering if they are good enough." (The soprano would repay her mentor with faithful visits when the nonagenarian Bing, suffering from Alzheimer's, languished virtually forgotten in a Bronx nursing home.) By the 1970s Stratas was secure enough with her unusual talent and equally unpredictable career priorities to make her own rules. That fact in part may explain her strong identification with Lulu, an interpretation that reached its definitive form in the 1979 Boulez-Chéreau production in Paris, the first performance of the complete three-act score. Not only did Stratas's voice, with its brightly piercing small-bore beam of sound, encompass all the fearsome demands of the score with spot-on accuracy, but her interior persona and this free-living earth spirit became closely entwined in Act II, when Lulu looks deeply inside herself and sings to Dr. Schön, "I never wanted to be anything but what I've been taken for, and no one has ever taken me for anything but what I am."

That central feature of Stratas's offbeat vocal personality made her elusive performance style hard to resist but difficult to analyze. The power of her interpretations did not arise so much from telling vocal inflections, subtle musical perceptions, or special refinements of physical detail. Those elements were always present in everything she sang and she could manipulate them with exceptional intelligence—early on her nickname of "Baby Callas" had been honestly earned. More striking, though, was the degree of inner conviction and raw emotional intensity she could generate with a physical presence and vocal equipment that deceptively suggested vulnerability and fragility. During her best years that combination paradoxically communicated indomitable strength rather than weakness. And although vocally diminished when she returned to opera after seven years' absence in 1989, as the three heroines in the Metropolitan's revival of Puccini's *Il Trittico*, Stratas could still accomplish amazing feats of vocal legerdemain. Typically, she had planned the evening as a pathological study of how love changes the lives of three very different women, and the most searing panel in this triptych was Suor Angelica. For some hard hearts, Puccini's little nun, driven to suicidal madness by the death of her illegitimate son, is a figure of intolerable operatic sentimentality. For Stratas, however, Angelica represented "the cry of those thousands of women in Lebanon or wherever, who have lost their child. It's all these women, from ancient times to the present—all one and the same woman—speaking from their souls. And the music takes over where the words fail." And, one might add, when the music failed, Stratas took over, offering her vision of everywoman with the probity of an opera singer who had lived a real life.

It's odd that this remarkably self-aware singer did not know when to stop. In 1994, with even less voice and too much mannered attitude, she finally went over the top as the sorely beset heroines of *Il Tabarro* and *Pagliacci,* testing the patience of even her most loyal partisans. After that, it seemed best to remember a singer whose fierce individuality and luminous vocal integrity once cut through the politics and artificial trappings of a profession that was becoming increasingly bland and publicity-oriented.

"The day of the ad man has taken over," fumed Jon Vickers in a 1974 interview, warming to one of his favorite subjects. "A man who sings is judged not by his artistic ability but by his ability to get himself in the right newspaper with the right quotes. Contrary to what anybody thinks, I never had any burning ambition to be a singer. I never drove or forced myself into a career. And I have never paid for a line of publicity. If I had been that intense on having a career, I would certainly have tried to capitalize on everything I have done. But I don't have a publicity agent, and I am violently opposed to them. I think they are corrupting our art form." Like his fellow Canadian Teresa Stratas, Vickers had more than a touch of the preacher about him when artistic matters were at stake, and he remained a purist about such things—even Stratas hired a publicist at one point. No doubt this burly tenor from Prince Albert, Saskatchewan, came by his evangelical fervor legitimately—he was the son of a Presbyterian lay minister—and he lived by his strict principles rigorously throughout a forty-year career, thirty-two of them singing a carefully chosen heroic-tenor repertory in which he had few rivals, especially as Otello, Berlioz's Énée, Peter Grimes, Samson (Saint-Saëns and Handel), Canio, Don José, Siegmund, Parsifal, Florestan, and Tristan.

Inevitably Vickers clashed with colleagues who found his moralistic views a bit much. Those who did not measure up to his standards received his scorn—Franco Zeffirelli, for instance. There were fierce arguments during rehearsals for a revival of the designer-director's decorative production of *Otello* at the Metropolitan in 1972, and they began when Vickers pointed out the absurdity of Otello's first entrance, standing on the poop deck of a ship that docks backward. There were dozens of other touches that struck the tenor as outrageous, but worst of all, Zeffirelli's direction, he said, showed a basic lack of understanding about the dynamics of the male-female relationship. Vickers quickly emphasized that he was not complaining for himself; what really suffered, he felt, was the work at hand. "It's a great privilege to be at the service of Boito and Verdi and *Otello*. What a privilege even to open the bloody score."

Vickers illustrated his high artistic ideals by investing his vocal style with a dynamic interior life and smoldering expressive intensity that powerfully reflected his convictions. And the fact that he avoided publicists and seldom granted interviews hardly seemed to impede the progress of a busy career that began with his first international success in 1957, as Énée at Covent Garden, and ended thirty years later as Saint-Saëns's Samson at the Metropolitan. If he had had to wait until he was thirty to achieve major attention, that was at least partly due to the huge size of his voice, which needed time to mature and settle. "When you've got a big voice when you're young," Vickers correctly observed, "it drives you crazy because it's very difficult to control and you crack a lot, and it becomes a terrible embarrassment and a terrible fear, too." Then, too, midwestern Canada offered minimal musical opportunities to a boy who had to spend more time pitching hay, sowing crops, and tending cattle than singing in his father's church with his seven brothers and sisters.

In 1950 Vickers had won a scholarship to study with the baritone George Lambert, who was teaching voice at Toronto's Royal Conservatory. By the time four years were up, Vickers had the technique that would serve him for the rest of his career, along with dozens of operas, oratorios, and songs at the ready, all performed either at the Conservatory or on CBC-TV. The videos still exist, bits of Manrico, Cavaradossi, and Des Grieux, roles that he would hardly sing again, if ever. These mid-fifties performances already show the elements of his characteristic vocal personality firmly in place: the fierce concentration and dignity of feeling, the broadly cushioned heroic tone, and an absolute certainty of musical and emotional purpose. After watching them, one easily understands why Vickers could arrive in London in 1957 and immediately be signed up to sing prominent leading roles at Covent Garden.

He soon found himself in demand everywhere—appearances in Bayreuth, Vienna, Salzburg, New York, Milan, and San Francisco followed his Covent Garden debut—and Vickers chose his roles with care. His roomy tenor lacked the focused thrust and *squillo* that the Italian repertory required, but he still made Otello and Canio very personal, theatrically gripping statements—it was probably the *in extremis* nature of those two cursed figures that especially attracted him. No tenor in the latter half of the century communicated Otello's agony with more heartbreak or tragic nobility than Vickers. He did the same for Peter Grimes, which he always denied explicitly expressed Britten's sense of community rejection for being homosexual—the role went further than that. "I believe Benjamin Britten saw an opportunity here: in his anxiety to win sympathy and compassion for the homosexual world, he plunged into the whole psychology of human rejection, and I believe the whole opera, not just the role of Peter Grimes, is an in-depth study, and a magnificent one, of the whole psychology of human rejection. Britten was so intense about it, searching the depth of his feelings, that he fell into the trap, in a way, of holding the lens so close to his eyeball that he blotted out the universe. And in so doing he created a work of art so great that to continue to portray it in this cameo, almost chamber-like way, limiting it to the experience of one man in a situation, was not doing the work justice." Britten disagreed—the composer apparently loathed Vickers's half-crazed fisherman—but this mesmerizing interpretation was in large part responsible for making the opera a worldwide repertory piece during the 1960s and '70s.

That sort of introspection also led Vickers to reject certain roles that he might otherwise have performed superbly—Siegfried, for instance. The older hero of *Götterdämmerung* intrigued him, but not enough to study the role, while the young Siegfried merely struck him as a cardboard figure, and he would have nothing to do with him. Then there was Tannhäuser, which he learned in 1977 and was scheduled to perform at Covent Garden and later at the Met. The buzz around the opera world was that Vickers suddenly withdrew because he realized his voice might never survive this proverbially killing role; but the tenor had another explanation, and to judge from all his public statements, it rings true. The whole philosophy of the opera, he said, had finally sickened him, the idea "that a human being can make an approach to eternity by being such a blackguard . . . Tannhäuser's abuse of Elisabeth's good will and his expectation that the pope should forgive him for his behavior—that doesn't go down with me." Luckily, such high-minded scruples did not prevent Vickers from delving into Siegmund and Parsifal, two Wagnerian heroes who also might not bear close moral scrutiny but whose music did lie lower and in the most effective part of his voice. Indeed, his Parsifal in Bayreuth during the 1964 festival ravished the ear—listening to an aircheck of a performance, one can actually hear the audience gasp at the honeyed beauty of his *mezza voce* singing as he caresses

Parsifal's visionary phrases in the Good Friday Spell with Gurnemanz and Kundry.

As Vickers aged, his voice showed few signs of deterioration, but his expressive devices—the crooning, dynamic extremes, exaggerated portamentos and verbal effects—could sometimes degenerate into mannerism. Fortunately, his unannounced Metropolitan farewell as Samson in 1987 avoided all that, and for one last time an audience could marvel at the penetrating vocal and physical expressive gestures of a singer fired by his fierce convictions. After that special valedictory performance, his work done, Vickers quietly left the scene and vanished from public sight.

Rudolf Bing was correct about Leonard Warren. The baritone's sudden death in 1960 was a terrible blow to the musical quality of the Metropolitan's Italian wing, but Bing's desperate rush to fill the void by bringing in one mediocre Italian baritone after another was premature. Indeed, by 1970 it must have seemed that the line of American "Verdi baritones" founded by Lawrence Tibbett had not been broken after all. Robert Merrill continued to be an important vocal presence, soon to be joined by Cornell MacNeil and, in 1965, Sherrill Milnes. Indeed, it would not be long before MacNeil and Milnes would dominate the international scene as the rediscovery of Verdi's early operas gathered momentum. Both singers participated prominently in that important movement, on the world opera stages and in the recording studios, the preferred baritone standard for *Nabucco, Ernani, Macbeth, Alzira, Attila, Giovanna d'Arco,* and *Luisa Miller* as well as all the more familiar Verdi operas.

Like Vickers, both MacNeil and Milnes were farm boys. MacNeil (1922–) grew up in Minnesota, outside Minneapolis, but as the youngest of three sons and relegated to such lesser chores as snapping beans and separating milk and cream, he soon took off for the big city to become a singer while supporting himself as a machinist. Even though still in need of training, his burly voice landed him a small role in a 1947 Broadway revival of *Sweethearts* with Bobby Clark, an experience that encouraged him to seek out serious vocal study with Friedrich Schorr at the Hartt College of Music in Hartford. When Gian Carlo Menotti chose MacNeil to sing Patricia Neway's husband in the 1950 Broadway premiere of *The Consul,* the young baritone's rounded, richly textured, firmly focused voice was singled out for special praise. MacNeil spent the rest of the decade moving up the professional ladder from national touring companies to the New York City Opera (1953), and subsequently to San Francisco (1955), Chicago (1957), and Mexico City (1957), reaching the top in 1959 when he sang Don Carlo in *Ernani* at La Scala on March 5 and Rigoletto sixteen days later at the Metropolitan. Although it was a struggle even for an exceptional voice to find experience, get noticed, and make it big in America during the 1950s, it could be done occasionally, and soon the opportunities would become even greater.

MacNeil was essentially a vocal phenomenon. He lacked Tibbett's dashing stage presence, London's acting skills, and Milnes's matinee-idol looks, but the voice equaled theirs and in some ways surpassed them. None had a more secure or powerfully ringing top register, an essential requirement for a Verdi baritone, and he retained that asset virtually intact, even after the voice's overall tonal quality had deteriorated, right up to his retirement in 1987 at the age of sixty-five. Nor did the athletic reliability of his basic instrument diminish or weaken throughout its two-octave working range—during his prime years such a secure technique would surely have permitted him a greater variety of expressive options had he cared to exploit them. Indeed, MacNeil was as blunt and direct in his singing as he was in conversation, a practical man of few words but strong beliefs. Like Tibbett in his later years, he became deeply involved in the musicians' union as head of AGMA (American Guild of Musical Artists), and as such wielded considerable influence on working conditions behind the scenes at the Met, especially during the company's periodic labor problems. Even though MacNeil's voice eventually coarsened and developed a wide beat, the Met continued to cast him in prominent roles, a fact that some suspected had more to do with backstage politics than art. In any case, no one messed with "Big Mac," as he was known about the house, and everyone remembered the famous Parma incident back in 1964, when, annoyed with a noisy audience's rudeness toward the soprano during *Un Ballo in Maschera*, MacNeil shouted "Basta, cretini!" from the stage and stalked off to his dressing room in mid-performance. There, in the ensuing scuffle, the baritone traded blows with the Teatro Regio's staff and its director, Giuseppe Negri. Somehow the fracas seemed entirely appropriate, quite in tune with the baritone's typical sock-it-to-'em delivery of a Verdi aria.

"Sherrill Milnes," wrote actor and opera fan Tony Randall in 1979, "is an Italian baritone. He was born in Downers Grove, Ill., in 1935, worked on the family farm, sang in the church choir, attended Drake and Northwestern Universities, studied to be a high-school music teacher, decided to try singing, and last year sang some 60 operatic performances at about $7,000 each. This places him in the superstar class of only a few tenors and sopranos like Pavarotti and Sutherland, and would seem to make him the current King of Italian Baritones." Randall's biographical sketch was entirely accurate, even that paradoxical bit about Milnes being an "Italian baritone." At the time, Milnes was in demand everywhere Verdi's operas were sung, even in Italy. But then, since the once flourishing breed of Italian baritone (as well as the Italian soprano, mezzo, tenor, and bass) seemed in danger of becoming a threatened species, he had little competition abroad.

Although the big juicy Italian roles of the Romantic/verismo repertory were his specialty and he sang them with the idiomatic and unbuttoned *slancio* of a native, Milnes still knew his roots and where they were planted. In 1977, when he was never busier, he told an interviewer, "I try to divide my time among about fifteen places, but I'm an American singer, and I like to sing in cities like Cincinnati. I intend always to be an American singer who goes to Europe to sing occasionally—I'll never live there. I love America. America allowed me my career, in the sense that I established it here first and went to Europe as a leading singer. I didn't have to fight over there." Milnes's musical identification with his homeland lay not so much in new music—the only major premiere he sang came in 1967, the role of Adam Brant in Levy's *Mourning Becomes Electra* at the Met—but in the music he had learned as a boy, the country's Protestant hymns, ballads, and patriotic songs, all of which he unabashedly offered in recital and recorded prolifically. Early on he also devoted himself to such good causes as Affiliate Artists' development program for young American singers, hoping to remove "this tremendous gap where the middle of the profession ought to be; can you think of any other profession where a really capable, hard-working person can't earn some kind of living?"

Milnes could afford to be generous with his vocal capital, especially during the early years of his career—like Tibbett, in fact, he may have been excessively prodigal. His rounded, full-bodied, resonant baritone ascended easily to high A, and he would often join the tenor on that note at the end of their Act II *Otello* duet. He once described tossing off those thrilling high notes as his greatest physical pleasure, next to sex, and Milnes probably overindulged—in high A's at least. Luckily, this clean-living, regular guy was spared Tibbett's sad fate and his voice never gave out entirely—he could be found singing Falstaff with his alma mater, the New York City Opera, as late as 1996. But there had been an unsettling vocal problem some fifteen years before that, and even after hard work to rebuild those money notes up top, they never rang out so freely or so often again. He also must have had to reconsider an artistic philosophy that he and many other in-demand artists subscribed to as global opera flourished and increasingly became a lucrative singers' market, especially for personable, bright, ambitious, fresh-voiced young Americans like Milnes. "It may sound crass to talk about opera in terms of fees and tickets and publicity," he once confessed when the money was rolling in, "but part of being an opera singer is marketing a product. I sell a commercial product in the opera world. I sell a sound that is, by normal standards, a pleasant sound, not an offbeat one that requires an offbeat repertory. I can sing all the standard Italian and French things . . . I simply try to do what dozens—no, hundreds—of baritones have done over the years, except that I try to do it better."

Perhaps that packaged-product attitude explained the curiously bland, all-purpose quality of Milnes's singing, despite the energy and physical drive that propelled it. When his virile young baritone was in optimum condition, the sheer sound of the voice, of course, could always be enjoyed as a thrilling aural sensation. It resembled Warren's to the extent that the basic quality was uncommonly plush and full of overtones, a distinctly glamorous sound but one that lacked the sharp edge needed for shaping a legato phrase as a cleanly defined sequence of centered tones. Despite that drawback, Milnes was a consistently musical, well-coached singer. Still, he always seemed more in love with the sound of his voice and his rather antiseptic all-American-boy image than with the expressive specifics of the characters he played. One unkind but not inaccurate critic once characterized his Don Giovanni as having all the aristocratic bearing and dangerous erotic appeal of an Iowa college frat-house stud. Milnes could indicate all the right emotions efficiently enough, but since they lacked dramatic specificity and tension, his generalized performances seldom amounted to more than one-dimensional vocalized portraits.

In certain respects, Milnes became a more interesting singer after a reduction in his resources forced him to tone down the vocal swagger, curtail the heavy schedule of international appearances, and put an end to the many complete-opera recording projects that kept him spinning around the world in the 1970s. After the great Verdi roles had to be put aside, he began investigating Saint-Saëns's Henry VIII in San Diego,

Thomas's Hamlet at the New York City Opera, and Puccini's Jack Rance and Cilèa's Michonnet at the Met, parts that required—and received—a degree of refined detail and nuance Milnes had seldom offered in his days of youthful bravado.

Dozens of other Americans arrived at Rudolf Bing's Metropolitan Opera to perform leading roles during the general manager's long reign. These singers never formed a tightly knit community like the generation Johnson had fostered—even the least of them, due partly to increasingly aggressive artist managers, were able to pursue active careers in other parts of the country and in Europe. Only a select few ever became glittering international stars, but all functioned at the top of their profession. Two of the most durable made debuts in Bing's first season: Lucine Amara (1927–) and Roberta Peters (1930–). At twenty-two, Amara made a modest bow—an invisible one, in fact, as the Celestial Voice in *Don Carlo* on November 6, 1950—but it was the new boss's own debut and definitely a prestigious event. After that, Bing gave Amara every opportunity to shine. Early on the soprano garnered leads in new productions of *Les Contes d'Hoffmann, Eugene Onegin* (both opening nights), and *Pagliacci,* as well as a huge variety of important roles over the years: Aida, Ariadne, Fiordiligi, Marguerite, Elsa, Butterfly, Desdemona, Ellen Orford, and many others. Europe also seemed genuinely interested in her at first, with appearances at Glyndebourne and the Vienna State Opera in the fifties, and there were a few recordings for major labels. The soprano even had her own fan club, which regularly kept its members up to date with the young diva's doings in a breezy publication entitled *Lucinerama.*

Amara never seemed to click with the public, though, and eventually even Bing stopped accommodating her with important premieres, although he knew he could always count on her "to manage at least acceptably most of the soprano roles of the Italian repertory" despite the fact that she "never acquired the projection of a star." And yet Amara most assuredly possessed a quality instrument, a cool, strong soprano that readily adapted itself to nearly everything, if without much dramatic urgency, individuality, or special defining characteristics—the same problems that had apparently tended to depersonalize the versatile Florence Easton a generation earlier. So along with other pinch hitters like Herva Nelli, Mary Curtis-Verna, and Elinor Ross, Amara remained a dependable house soprano and cover artist until, when she was forty-nine, a new management felt that her usefulness had come to an end. It was then, in 1976, that the singer made the biggest waves of her career by suing the Met for age discrimination, winning her case in 1980. During the long legal process she engaged the sympathies of the press in an attempt to prove that she was singing better than ever. Richard Dyer, music critic of the *Boston Globe* and longtime Amara watcher, sat with the soprano as she played a recent tape that featured her singing Weber's soaring aria "Ozean, du Ungeheuer." The singer Dyer heard that day displayed a boldness and vigor, he said, that was no part of the Amara he knew. "Certainly as I sat there watching her eyes flash and her voice rise in anger and break into laughter as she discussed her case, I felt I was watching Lucine Amara's most charismatic performance." Amara had proved her point, but it was too late to do much about it. She returned to the Met as Amelia in *Un Ballo in Maschera* in 1981, offered her usual dependable performance, and went on for several more seasons, still failing to stir up much excitement.

Roberta Peters was only nineteen when she made her Met debut, as Zerlina, eleven days after Amara, as a last-minute substitute for Nadine Connor. "She was a sensation, a *Wunderkind*," remarked Eleanor Steber, who sang Donna Elvira that night. "It was as if she had done it a thousand times. We were astounded." Even Bing was impressed with Peters, more so in the long run, it seemed, than with Amara: "Few artists have survived being thrown on the Metropolitan stage without warning," he later wrote in his memoirs. "Miss Peters became a star." Well, yes—not of the "super" variety, perhaps, but this career lasted more than thirty-five years at the Met and even longer on the recital and summer-tent circuit.

Her youth, pert good looks, and light coloratura voice placed Peters squarely in the none-too-distinguished Met tradition of Marion Talley, Mary Lewis, and Patrice Munsel, but this soprano rose above her models and outlasted them by some margin—and that in an age when such "canary bird" voices definitely sounded passé next to the weightier sounds produced by Callas and Sutherland. In fact, Peters's first solo disc, recorded in 1953, billed her as the "Youngest Member of a Great Tradition" as she competed with the likes of Tetrazzini, Galli-Curci, and Pons. Peters may never have quite matched the first two for sheer panache or the third for media glamour, but she had her own charm and a technique second to none. And she had worked hard to attain it. Indeed, with the consent of her parents, she quit school at thirteen and for six years took the subway from the Bronx to Manhattan every morning for a voice lesson with William Herman, who had also been Munsel's teacher—perhaps Herman was determined that his new protégée would not make the same mistakes. Those six years consisted of little else other than vocal study, and by the time Peters reached the Met, she already knew twenty operas by heart. There were also lessons in ballet, languages (she was devouring Dante in the original at fourteen), and acting, all with the best teachers in New York. No wonder she coolly performed Zerlina like a pro at her Met debut, adding the Queen of the Night and Rosina with equal aplomb within the next three months.

Peters was the youngest and last member of that generation of American singers who considered the Metropolitan home base and the occasional appearance in Europe as icing on the cake. One of Peters's earliest and most prestigious forays abroad was as Arline in a revival of Balfe's *The Bohemian Girl* in 1951 at Covent Garden under Sir Thomas Beecham's direction, but she made few efforts to cultivate a career on the Continent. She also participated in one of Hollywood's last flirtations with classical music, appearing with Jan Peerce in the life story of her own manager, Sol Hurok: *Tonight We Sing.* Peters's Met repertory included twenty-four roles, few of them venturing beyond such lyric-coloratura staples as Gilda, Lucia, Adele, Adina, Susanna, Norina, and Despina. In the seventies there were out-of-town experiments with Violetta, Mimì, and Manon, but this most sensible of singers quickly pulled back and returned to what she did best.

Without question, the most impressive emergent American voices to sing both at the Metropolitan and on the international circuit during and after the Bing regime belonged to black women. None ever possessed young Leontyne Price's special vocal radiance or attained her prestige, but Martina Arroyo (1936–   ), Grace Bumbry (1937–   ), and Shirley Verrett (1931–   ) came close. Their careers were even more extensive and varied, even if, like Price, they never fully realized their potential. Arroyo and Bumbry each captured major attention at the Metropolitan Opera Auditions of the Air in 1958, but like many of their compatriots, both decided that European experience would give them a better chance at major careers than performing small roles at the Met. Arroyo learned the hard way after a few seasons of comprimario work. Five years and many European performances later, after she made a successful return as

Aida, one headline proclaimed MARTINA ARROYO LOOKS LIKE MET'S NEW NE-GRO DRAW. "I'm the other one," Arroyo would good-naturedly say to fans when they approached her backstage after performances and asked "Miss Price" for her autograph.

A droll, merry-andrew sense of humor was, in fact, a keynote to Arroyo's character. After wearing an unbecoming brown dress as Elisabetta in *Don Carlo*, the soprano managed to secure a substitute gown by sweetly complaining, "But Mr. Bing, my mother couldn't even see me on stage in that dress until I smiled." Such sassy one-liners came naturally to her, and for a while they helped make her a regular on *The Tonight Show*; such exposure did no harm in furthering "Madame Butterball's" career (a large woman, Arroyo also had no hang-ups about her weight). Over the next dozen years she was favored by Met management with three opening nights, most of the repertory that Price might have sung had she made herself more available, plus such spinto heavies as Gioconda, Lady Macbeth, Maddalena, and Santuzza. Arroyo also took an interest in new music, from the neoromantic lyricism of Samuel Barber's heated concert piece *Andromache's Farewell* (which she introduced in 1963) to the complex avant-gardism of Karlheinz Stockhausen's *Momente*.

In the end, Arroyo failed to stir up much long-lasting excitement, and finally, in 1978, weary of being taken for granted at the Met, she returned to Europe's opera houses and pursued a full schedule, with only occasional visits back home for concerts. Those, and sporadic operatic recordings from the Continent after 1980, suggested that the rich texture and columnar security of her wide-spanning voice had already begun to depart. Even during her best decade, 1965–75, Arroyo disappointed those who hoped for more than conventional vocal posturing from such a deluxe instrument. Beyond that, her sparkling offstage personality seldom registered in the opera house, where her stolid presence projected dignity but minimal dramatic involvement.

At least Arroyo never elected to play the old-fashioned prima donna. That role was assumed by Grace Bumbry, who relished the grand-diva pose throughout her career. Bumbry had been in Europe just three years after sharing the spotlight at the Met Auditions with Arroyo in 1958 when her big break came, and it generated tremendous publicity. Despite sinister wartime associations with Hitler and all that that implied, the Bayreuth Festival had always welcomed minority singers, but never before a black. So when Wieland Wagner chose Bumbry to sing Venus in 1961, and in a production of *Tannhäuser* that positively celebrated her blackness and youthful beauty, the glamorous American "Schwarze Venus" made headlines around the world. She immediately warmed to the diva's role, and as her reputation as an intractable, competitive colleague grew, she came to be known as "Her Grace" and "La Bumbarina." By then Bumbry was no longer the earnest young Lotte Lehmann protégée who had spent her student years humbly studying voice and lieder interpretation at the foot of the beloved soprano in her classes in Santa Barbara. At the peak of her career, when confronted with her grand ways, Bumbry gave the standard prima-donna reply: "I was pushing a *career* then, *now* I am being an artist. What people took as being difficult was a certain integrity."

Even though there was always considerable debate about the depth of her artistry, Bumbry still circled the world in triumph with Carmen, Amneris, Eboli, and other showy parts. Like so many mezzos with a secure, ringing top register, she began to convince herself that perhaps she really was a soprano, and that with a bit of vocal restructuring, the entire dramatic-soprano repertory would be available to her. She even added a racial dimension to her argument by suggesting that black women had almost always been stereotyped as lower-voiced "motherly" singers whatever the natural placement of their vocal apparatus. Marian Anderson, Bumbry insisted, was really a dramatic soprano, although the musical culture of those days never permitted her to develop that part of her voice—a controversial statement, but careful reassessment of Anderson's vocal endowment in her prime years suggests that such an assertion is not at all far-fetched. In any case, Bumbry made the transition, via such bridge roles as Lady Macbeth and Santuzza, and soon she was just as much in demand for her Salome and Tosca as she had been for her Amneris and Carmen. When she pushed herself further to try out such demanding bel canto roles as Norma and Verdi's Abigaille, the wisdom of her choices could be questioned, but few would deny the sheer amount of voice she summoned up to get the job done.

It was a splendid sound in its youthful prime, large, rich, and ductile. Bumbry succeeded up to a point when she began to expand her soprano ambitions, but history will surely best remember the aggressive young mezzo-soprano whose energy and vocal generosity swept all before her—well, almost all, since her interpretive ideas, perhaps best described as explanatory underlining, seldom came across as either especially personal or emotionally convincing. Then, of course, there was her voluptuous beauty, a physical presence that made her a Salome any Herod would slaver over or a Carmen well calculated to drive Don José to sexual madness and murder. On the whole, Bumbry's soprano adventures yielded mainly undisciplined performances, a prodigious expenditure of physical energy unleashed in a stylistic vacuum without a true vocal or dramatic focus. As her career began to wind down, Bumbry sensibly scaled back and looked for more reasonable options, such as Stravinsky's Baba the Turk and Massenet's Hérodiade.

Shirley Verrett presents a bit of a puzzle. Voice, intelligence, musicianship, beauty, stage presence—Verrett had them all, and on any number of occasions it seemed as if she were on the verge of being propelled right up there with the greatest names of her generation. Verrett was a late starter whose only wish at first was to be a concert singer like Marian Anderson or Dorothy Maynor. When her opera career finally got under way with a much-noticed appearance as Carmen at the 1962 Spoleto Festival, Verrett was suddenly appearing all over Europe, particularly at Covent Garden, where she sang most of her major mezzo roles for the first time. She finally brought her Carmen to the Metropolitan in 1968, but relations with Rudolf Bing and his staff were never comfortable—the mezzo, not unreasonably, felt that their offers of roles ranging from Erda to the Priestess in *Aida* were eccentric, and she was immediately pegged as a "difficult" artist. The post-Bing regime proved more welcoming, and Verrett created a sensation at the company's premiere performance of Berlioz's *Les Troyens* in 1973 when, due to Christa Ludwig's sudden indisposition, she sang Didon as well as Cassandre. Europe also seemed to be at her feet after her 1975 Lady Macbeth at La Scala— the acclaim was such that the management presented her with a blank contract and told her to write in any role she wished.

Even after all that excitement, not a great deal happened and Verrett was unable to build on her gains. "Miss Verrett still hovers on the very edge of that hysterical breakthrough that turns a career into myth," wrote one admiring but puzzled fan in 1977. "Storybook things have happened to her, yet left her less than legend." Like Bumbry, Verrett thought she had found the right path after deciding that the nature of her voice opened up soprano possibilities, although she never explored them with any consistency. For the rest of her career Verrett veered back and forth between soprano roles like Norma and Beethoven's Leonore on the one hand and equally demanding contralto parts like Donizetti's Léonor and Saint-Saëns's Dalila on the other—in 1976 she even sang both Norma and Adalgisa separated by only a few weeks. That only confused the public, and there was also a toll being taken on her voice, as Verrett's once creamy-smooth instrument began to separate into three very distinct registers, none seeming to have much in common with the others and severely compromising the technical quality of her work. Then, too, there was a chronic health problem, resulting in frequent cancellations, a condition finally identified as an allergy to mold spores that clogged her bronchial tubes. Mainly, though, Verrett was most likely paying the price for not heeding the sage advice offered her by Giulietta Simionato, Italy's premier mezzo-soprano, at the time of her 1962 Carmen in Spoleto: "Shirley, don't ever let them talk you into being a soprano. You've got the high notes. Keep them there; that's your reserve. What we should call ourselves is a mezzo-soprano *lunghi*."

Verrett always preferred to call herself just a "singer" and echo Olive Fremstad, another "mezzo-soprano *lunghi*" whose range and soprano abilities were often disputed, by saying that whatever a role called for she would produce. The only reason she became pegged as a mezzo, she said, was that years before, as a young singer on Arthur Godfrey's *Talent Scouts* show, she had replaced her scheduled aria, Elisabeth's "Dich, teure Halle," with Dalila's "Mon coeur s'ouvre à ta voix" because the low-lying Saint-Saëns aria had been recently turned into a pop tune and might capture more attention. That rationalization hardly seems worthy of Verrett, who might have channeled her ambitions into better things than futile attempts to sing Norma or Fidelio. She was a winning, musically inquisitive recitalist in her younger days, when the rich texture of her voice so expressively illuminated the heartbreak of Brahms's "Mainacht" or the sensuality of Granados's "Maja" songs, but she soon put aside those early ambitions to be a concert singer and never really returned to them. In any case, by the late seventies it was already too late, and the gamble on superstardom never did pay off.

By the seventies it seemed as if racial barriers had been broken everywhere. Arroyo, Bumbry, and Verrett were the most highly profiled black American singers at work, but artists like Mattiwilda Dobbs, Reri Grist, Gloria Davy, and Felicia Weathers had also pursued prominent careers, albeit mainly in Europe. Black males making a name for themselves were much scarcer, a situation paralleled a century earlier when nearly all the famous American singers were women. One who did rise to what must have seemed a rather lonely prominence as a leading operatic tenor was George Shirley (1934–   ), and in 1971 he pondered the situation:

I have been lucky. I came into opera at just the right time, after the ice had been broken. All my experiences before I joined the Met [as Ferrando in *Così Fan Tutte* in 1961] were congenial—with the Turnau Opera Players in Woodstock, at Tanglewood with Boris Goldovsky, in Florence and Milan as a winner of the American Opera Auditions, with the Amato Opera in New York City, at the New York City Opera. After I won the Met's Auditions in 1961, I felt a little distance between me and some of my new colleagues. Was the reason ethnic, I wondered, or the usual reception by established artists to any newcomer? Whatever was the case, this was soon to wear off. I was told, however, that a certain singer from the South voiced dislike for me, but in a later engagement in another company we got along well—perhaps a growth of mutual respect, perhaps just the passage of time, perhaps the discovery that I was not a monster after all. Pockets of prejudice remain, and some companies (mostly in the South) still will not engage me.

Shirley never became a megastar, but he covered a great deal of ground, fit in comfortably wherever he sang, and performed the lyric tenor repertory prominently in America and England: Don Ottavio, Roméo, Alfredo, Pinkerton, and Almaviva at the Met; David (*Die Meistersinger*), Pelléas, and Loge at Covent Garden; Tamino, Idomeneo, and Percy (*Anna Bolena*) at Glyndebourne; and, in Santa Fe, more unusual roles such as Cavalli's Egisto, Alwa (Berg's *Lulu*), Apollo (Strauss's *Daphne*), and Leandro (Henze's *The Stag King*). Shirley brought a bright-toned voice brushed with an attractive huskiness to all these parts, along with a dignified presence and musical sophistication that especially endeared him to the British. When he began to curtail his appearances in the mid-seventies, it was certainly due more to the vocal problems that began to erode his upper register rather than to any extramusical causes. Even Shirley is hard-pressed to explain why so few black males followed his lead, since he arrived at a time when the doors were swinging wide open for all American singers, whatever their ethnicity.

Twenty-five

The End

of the

Adventure

~~~~~~~~~~~~~~~~~~~~~~~~~~~

*B*y the end of the twentieth century American singers were working prominently in every part of the globe that had developed a taste for Western music, opera in particular. But then, so were singers from England, Scandinavia, Russia, Eastern Europe, and Asia— voices in quantity from everywhere, it seemed, except Italy, France, and Germany. The nations that had produced the core vocal literature since 1600 were no longer providing a rich supply of voices to sing it, and what had once seemed a bottomless pool of talent showed dangerous signs of drying up. Many factors contributed to this unfortunate state of affairs, but among the most important was the sad reality that opera and song, in the form in which they had been continuously practiced by European composers for 350 years, had lost their creative vitality, and as a consequence the national vocal schools that rose to perform this music died out along with it. Meanwhile, a large repertory from the past continued to be in demand and in need of fresh voices to perform it.

Without long-entrenched creative musical traditions of their own to keep them anchored within a consistently evolving vocal style, Americans had learned how to adapt successfully to whatever kind of music came their way, no matter what the country of origin. Partly as a result of that, by the 1980s American singers' reputation for versatility, thorough preparation, dependability, and eagerness to do whatever it takes to get the job done had become proverbial. No wonder they were so busy, on opera and concert stages everywhere. As the traditional European performing styles gradually blended and disappeared, the rootlessness, directness, and practicality of the American approach to singing— more a set of behavioral patterns than of musical characteristics, as conductor-musicologist Will Crutchfield has perceptively identified it— came to be professional assets that singers in other countries began to envy and emulate. This chameleonlike ability to sing anything efficiently and plausibly became the true American style by the end of the twentieth century, and it dominated the international scene.

Of course, there was a price to pay. As the art of singing became increasingly generalized, the new voices that practiced it inevitably tended to lack expressive flavor and character—and generalities, as Phyllis Curtin once drily pointed out to a pupil who said she had "a general idea" of a song she was about to sing, do not make great art. On the other hand, for managers and impresarios, singers who prized smart efficiency over individual temperament greatly facilitated the increasingly complex business of opera, which by the century's end had turned into a thriving—if still often dangerously risky and disheveled—global enterprise. And for that very reason, ever-ready Americans were in demand the world over, triumphantly moving through this milieu as consummate professionals, a state that had been achieved, as professionalism often is, at the loss of considerable imaginative vitality. In 1990 the idea of encountering exciting, outsized egocentric personalities such as Geraldine Farrar and Olive Fremstad at smartly run, fresh-scrubbed opera festivals like those at Santa Fe and Glimmerglass was inconceivable. Most American singers had probably never even heard of Farrar, Fremstad, or any of their important predecessors. Indeed, few showed an interest in vocal or performance history of any kind, let alone the fact that they might be part of a rich tradition.

"Honestly, I don't know who sang [Donna Anna] before," Cheryl Studer commented blithely in a 1991 singers' roundtable that included Dawn Upshaw and Patricia Schuman as the three sopranos prepared to sing Don Giovanni at the Metropolitan.

"I really don't think about history," chimed in Upshaw. "Just recently

I went out with some people whom I would call opera buffs, and they talked about this and that singer and what they had sung. It was fascinating, but it's not something I know much about."

"I agree," said Schuman. "I'm not really up on that sort of thing. I know Schwarzkopf sang Elvira, but I don't think about that. I wonder if the audience really cares."

"You just have to work on your own role and build your own concept," concluded Upshaw. "I never listen to recordings of someone else doing the role."

An eavesdropper on that extraordinary conversation would have to conclude that smug self-satisfaction was also a characteristic trait of American singers of the nineties as they diligently learned role after role and rushed from one engagement to another. No wonder so many functioned in an artistic vacuum, applying their craft in ways that struck many as generic and faceless. It's all very well to prepare an interpretation of an operatic role without being influenced by famous singers of the past or copying their manner, but to be completely ignorant of the traditions of one's own profession—and proudly boast of the fact—just seems self-defeating.

No doubt such a blinkered attitude was one inevitable by-product of the growing tendency to view operatic production as a tightly run business, a fact of life on the international scene by 1990 and one that American singers could respond to and make work to their advantage. Yet, whether they were aware of it or not, they all sang the repertory of their predecessors, and as such would inevitably be compared to singers who had participated in a vital performing tradition that stretched back more than 150 years. If the current crop of stars seemed to shine less brightly, that had little to do with technical training or basic vocal endowment—the physiological features of the human body that determine a healthy and pleasing voice had certainly not changed, and the quality of musical education then available to young Americans was perhaps the best in the world. The problem was deeper and more subtle, one that revolved mainly around questions of feeling and perception rather than technique.

It's a cliché: old-timers will always complain that the vocal standards of their youth have deteriorated. When W. J. Henderson found the singers of his old age technically inferior and less well prepared than those of his youth, he was right—or at least consistent with his understanding of the rules of good singing. After all, the artists he faulted, from Farrar to Moore, were interested mainly in performing the music of their own time, and the criteria for excellence as a Puccini or Massenet or Strauss interpreter were not the same as those required to sing the bel canto specialties that Patti warbled so incomparably in the 1880s. But when late-twentieth-century critics carp about young singers, their objections are not necessarily about declining vocal quality or slipshod preparation. On the contrary, something more intangible is missing in the work of these smartly trained paragons as they recycle the past, and the British critic Norman Lebrecht tries to identify it in his apocalyptic study of classical music in crisis at the century's end: "This was supposed to be a golden age of American singers, but it would take a consultant laryngologist to distinguish between Carol Vaness and Cheryl Studer, Dawn Upshaw and June Anderson, Deborah Voigt and Susan Dunn. Raised by superteachers and agents to be ultraprofessional and free of obvious fault, young performers shed whatever color and fire they once possessed and settled into dread conformity. Many were, beyond doubt, better technicians than the divas of yesteryear, but who would not give all the faked orgasms of the modern model-vocalists for one half-shriek from Callas?"

Lebrecht has a valid point, however he may overstate it. When the current generation's contribution to singing can be assessed more objectively, some truly original vocal personalities may possibly emerge from the crowd of determined professionals, deftly maneuvered about the world by managers who consider "difficult" artists with original temperaments disruptive and bad for business. But on their road to global success American singers have certainly lost something—not one, after all, has captured the public's imagination to the degree that Farrar, Ponselle, Tibbett, or even Grace Moore did when they were at the height of their careers. Catherine Malfitano (1948–   ), for example, can be seen as a direct descendant of Farrar. Not only has she sung many roles once associated with Farrar—Tosca, Butterfly, Violetta, Mimì, Manon—but she, too, began with such lyric-coloratura parts as Gounod's Juliette before successfully extending a light voice of no special quality to take on heavier dramatic parts that required less vocal allure. Early in her career Malfitano also took a healthy interest in singing new operas, although none had the class or sustaining power of the Puccini works that Farrar "created" for the Met. Both were intelligent, ferociously ambitious women who knew exactly what they had to do when onstage, and they managed their career moves shrewdly, sizing up the available opportunities and seizing the moment. Neither lacked an audience—Malfitano has even reached a world stage through jet travel, recordings, and opera videos in ways that Farrar could never have conceived.

And yet where Farrar was glittering and charismatic, almost everything about Malfitano has seemed manufactured and hard-edged, from her gritty industry and wiry soprano to her well-calculated, cleverly packaged interpretations. While some also dismissed Farrar as "a very well put together fake," at least there was a genuine fascination about her glamorous persona, and a wide public adored her. More a crisp businesswoman than a provocative entertainment personality, Malfitano has not been able to conjure up the same mystique, onstage or off. Indeed, how unthinkable the scenario of Malfitano announcing her unexpected retirement from the opera stage in 1998 (at age fifty), as Farrar did at the Met in 1922 (at age forty). One can scarcely imagine the audience sobbing "No! No!" or a farewell performance capped by a mob of frenzied fans dragging the departing diva's limousine through Lincoln Center. The more likely reaction: a collective shrug of the shoulders, with management lining up the next efficiently trained, eager American soprano to step in, carry on, and get the job done.

At least Malfitano, after she traded Lucia and Susanna for Lulu, Fidelio, Salome, and other punishing personality roles, has been able to keep her voice in more or less respectable shape for a longer time than her critics ever thought possible. Maria Ewing (1950–   ), also promoted as a potent singing actress, has managed the trick less successfully. After spending a few years using her light mezzo-soprano as nature intended, singing such Mozart parts as Cherubino and Dorabella, she "restructured" her vocal equipment and reemerged to tackle such dramatic soprano roles as Tosca and Salome. Perhaps to cover up an inability to deal adequately with the music and disguise a rapidly deteriorating voice, Ewing presented herself as a troubled but "interesting" singer who, presumably like Callas, was such a riveting, dynamic singing actress that her vocal flaws were irrelevant in the face of such mesmerizing burnt-earth interpretations. For many, though, Ewing's bizarre onstage behavior has been just as eccentric and unmusical as her singing. At the Met in 1986 she portrayed a cartoon Carmen, a loopy Gypsy who might have just landed from the moon as she lurched spastically from one scene to the next without allure, consistency, credibility, or vocal distinction. That Ewing continued to be taken seriously over the next decade in the face of ongoing vocal collapse, whooping and scooping through one part after another, only indicated how decadent the Farrar-Garden tradition had become. Many audiences—and conductors as well—seemed to have stopped listening.

As the millennium approached, opera companies everywhere desperately searched the world for spinto sopranos qualified to sing the popular Verdi-Puccini operas, but found only stopgaps. America offered several candidates, but none could measure up to the standards set three decades earlier by the young Leontyne Price, let alone Rosa Ponselle in 1918. For a few moments during the eighties it looked as if Aprile Millo (1958–   ) might provide some relief from the drought—not only did her voice possess a warmth and depth that reminded some listeners of Renata Tebaldi's, but Millo also seemed dimly aware of the vocal gestures and expressive devices that had once made that beloved Italian soprano's Verdi singing so arresting. But it soon became apparent that Millo was merely pasting on the manner rather than drawing it from any inner conviction or true understanding of the style, and her performances soon degenerated into irritating, mannered artifice. Worse, the voice itself ran into technical troubles early on, and soon it became increasingly doubtful that Millo's promise would ever be realized.

Others shared the stage with Millo, most of them with superior vocal endowments—Leona Mitchell (1949–   ), Sharon Sweet (1951–   ), Alessandra Marc (1960–   ), Andrea Gruber (1965–   ), Susan Dunn (1954–   )—but they showed even less musical and dramatic imagination, and the public soon seemed to lose interest. By the mid-nineties Deborah Voigt (1964–   ) had positioned herself to fill the vacuum, singing the heavier Wagner-Strauss repertory as well as Verdi operas. With a healthy voice of superior quality and with little competition on the horizon, from the United States or anywhere else, a rosy future was virtually guaranteed, even if Voigt's work up till then had displayed little temperament or special character.

Always more populous even in the worst of times, the line that descended from Nordica through Steber—lyric sopranos who excelled in Mozart and as the lighter Wagner and Strauss heroines—offered more than a glimmer of hope. For a few years Cheryl Studer (1955–   ) was the most impressive of all, displaying a versatility that took her from Wagner (Elsa, Elisabeth, Eva) and Strauss (Salome, the Empress, Chrysothemis) to Mozart (the Countess, Elettra, Donna Anna, the Queen of the Night, Constanze) and such old bel canto favorites as Lucia, Semiramide, and Violetta—Studer's role list, when she was at her busiest during the late 1980s, made her seem like Nordica redevivus. Alas, it was only an illusion, and one created mainly on recordings. When Studer first burst on the scene in Germany, where the virginal purity of this streaming, typically Teutonic soprano was sure to appeal, her phonogenic voice could be heard on dozens of complete opera recordings, and its spotless clarity and silvery radiance made for pleasant home listening. When encountered in person, however, Studer proved to be less interesting, a singer whose attention span seemed more suited to short recording takes than sustaining a whole role over a long evening. By the early nineties, Studer was suddenly laid low by vocal troubles, her furious recording schedule abruptly came to a halt, and another American dream seemed over.

With similar vocal equipment, Carol Vaness (1952–   ) proceeded more cautiously, avoiding even the lighter Wagner and Strauss heroines as she gradually worked her way up through America's regional companies to become a world presence. At first Vaness was in demand mainly for Mozart heroines, and at her best she came very close to duplicating Steber's vocal excellence and technical expertise, even if the older soprano's warm inner glow was not part of her tightly clenched vocal character. Once she had the ears of international audiences in the early eighties, Vaness branched out, singing Leonora (*Trovatore*), Anna Bolena, Tosca, and eventually Norma. Except perhaps for the Bellini role, all these adventures were honorable stabs, although they hardly displayed a soprano with compellingly original views on such oft-performed diva vehicles. Vaness had found a comfortable niche as a Mozart specialist, but it soon became clear that she lacked both the vocal means and the inner resources to stretch her talent in the directions she hoped to travel.

By 1996 Renée Fleming (1959–   ) had become the new darling of the day. Like Vaness, she also started out on the regional circuit as a Mozart singer, gathering experience and winning high-profile awards. She even substituted for Vaness as Desdemona at the Met in 1994, achieving the attention-getting success that solidified her reputation. Her luscious soprano had by then bloomed into an ample, smoothly textured sound with an easy flexibility that made both Mozart's Fiordiligi and Rossini's florid Armida available to her. Suddenly a hot property, Fleming found herself in demand by such star conductors as Georg Solti and James Levine. She opened the Met's 1995–96 season as Desdemona, Decca/London signed her to an exclusive record contract, and a Bayreuth debut as Eva in *Die Meistersinger* came in the summer of 1996. By then she was booked solid for the next five years, her engagement calendar crammed with important performance and recording dates worldwide. As she rose to prominence, the soprano exhibited stunning vocal potential but conventional career priorities, a New Age diva poised to enter the twenty-first century doing only the most predictable things, whatever the system required. While hoping for Fleming to surprise the musical world and prove herself an artist of spirit and imagination who made her own rules, opera fans held their breath and prayed that, at the very least, this deluxe lyric-soprano voice would last the course. And yet one wondered how long even that might be. At the same age Fleming burst into prominence, in her mid-thirties, Steber had already accomplished far more, and Farrar was only a few years away from retirement.

American leggeros in the Pons-Munsel-Peters mold never sounded quite the same after Callas and Sutherland. Indeed, when June Anderson (1952–   ) arrived at the New York City Opera in 1978 to sing the Queen of the Night, Gilda, Lucia, and Elvira in *I Puritani*, she was mostly likened to the Australian diva, whom she resembled both physically and in size of voice. After four seasons of hard work singing the old Sills repertory at the City Opera, Anderson headed for Italy, where her major career really began. From there she took the once-again fashionable Rossini-Bellini-Donizetti repertory around the world, made a slew of recordings—mostly bel canto vehicles and rarities from the French repertory, works such as Bizet's *La Jolie Fille de Perth* and Auber's *La Muette de Portici*—and eventually returned home to New York and the Metropolitan as Semiramide and Lucia. By then Anderson had become a useful participant in the continuing bel canto revival, but for all the considerable vocal éclat she generated, her piercing tone, glaring top register, mechanical fioriture, and chilly stage manner were distinctly off-putting.

For those who found Anderson's hard-edged brilliance too icy and her no-nonsense bel canto heroines too mean-spirited, Ruth Ann Swenson (1959–   ), a cuddly Swedish-Italian blonde from Long Island, soon appeared to offer an alternative. Sutherland was again the model rather than Callas, but one could also detect an attempt to incorporate the lovable lyrical personae of Mirella Freni and Bidú Sayão as Swenson sang her preferred repertory of Zerlina, Gilda, Juliette, and other ingenues. Actually, when the opera business decided that the time had come to promote Swenson as a major player, the soprano she most closely resembled, at least in her early choice of repertory, was Emma Eames. After establishing her credentials in San Francisco and the Metropolitan,

Swenson made a glossy EMI recital disc in 1994 to display her strengths to an international audience, and the coloratura chestnuts she chose were mainly right out of Mme. Eames's songbook. Comparative listening even shows Swenson handling the florid passages of Juliette's Waltz rather more crisply and cleanly than Eames on her two versions recorded in 1905–06, but it is the older soprano who suggests the young girl's excitement and pleasure at finding herself at her first ball. Already thirty-four when her big career was launched (Eames was just twenty-three when she made her bow, as Juliette, at the Paris Opéra), Swenson must surely have been at her vocal peak and unlikely to develop much more interpretive character or expressive range in a repertory that relied mostly on youthful freshness and spirit. Her debut disc revealed these qualities in quantity, but it also prompted reviewers once again to sing the dreaded but familiar refrain: "A want of really distinctive individuality."

After Grace Bumbry and Shirley Verrett, the principal mezzo-soprano of the day was Tatiana Troyanos (1938–95), one of the Met's most versatile house singers until her untimely death from cancer. Troyanos seemed prepared to sing it all, and, unlike Bumbry and Verrett, she was content with her mezzo-soprano lot. At the Met her roles ranged from Verdi's Amneris and Eboli through Wagner's Kundry and Brangäne to Mozart's Sesto and Idamante, Richard Strauss's Octavian and Composer, Massenet's Charlotte, Stravinsky's Jocasta, Bellini's Adalgisa, Berg's Countess Geschwitz, Handel's Giulio Cesare, Humperdinck's Hänsel, Berlioz's Didon, Johann Strauss's Prince Orlofsky, and Philip Glass's Queen Isabella in *The Voyage*. Elsewhere she explored Purcell's Dido, Donizetti's Giovanna Seymour, Bernstein's Anita in *West Side Story*, and Penderecki's Jeanne in *The Devils of Loudon*, as well as a host of concert works including Schoenberg's *Gurrelieder*. Only Carmen eluded her—it was a part that Troyanos recorded superlatively, but playing the role of a sexy vamp onstage did not come naturally, even to this protean mezzo.

Although she was awarded many new productions and television galas at the Met, no one could accuse Troyanos of being accorded favoritism or special treatment—the voice, along with the keen musical intelligence to drive it, was present in abundance. Its dark, burnt-amber texture was distinctive and alluring, smoothly consistent from the lowest contralto depths to a stunning high B-flat, and the security of her method allowed her to excel in both Mozart and the Baroque repertory.

Possibly, like so many other singers who set few limits on themselves, Troyanos's versatility often prevented her from bringing her operatic characters to life with much specificity. Her generous performances were distinguished mostly by an excess of nervous energy, which she only occasionally disciplined and channeled to produce precise, genuinely exciting results. Berlioz's Didon, as preserved on a Met video of a performance in 1983, shows Troyanos at her best, presenting a wonderfully focused, three-dimensional character, hopelessly caught in a classic queen-versus-woman dilemma.

For all her apparent ability to sing everything, even Troyanos never quite sounded right in the ever-popular Verdi operas, but help was soon at hand. "I went in green and came out Verdi," joked Dolora Zajick (1959–   ) about her first major performance in opera—in San Francisco in 1986 as Azucena—and she did not exaggerate. After that revelation, Zajick was in demand everywhere for the big Verdi mezzo-soprano roles, and critics soon began to call her "the reigning dramatic mezzo of the age." And indeed that seemed to be the case, an imposing vocal presence with a huge, powerful columnar sound and a working range from the C below middle C to the Queen of the Night's stratospheric high F. "She has a voice on which one could raise whole temple complexes," a German reviewer marveled after hearing her sing Amneris in 1995.

Just as Marilyn Horne had once pretty much monopolized the lower florid bel canto and Baroque roles, Zajick has suddenly found herself the preferred singer of parts that had once been the property of such celebrated Italian mezzos as Ebe Stignani, Bruna Castagna, Giulietta Simionato, and Fiorenza Cossotto. There seemed no one else around to do the job, and Zajick, a voice-technician freak like Horne, could explain exactly how she did it: "You should be able to bring the head voice down to a third below the top of the chest voice. It will be weak, but it will be there. And you should be able to bring the chest voice at least a major third above the break where the chest voice ordinarily ends. This gives you strength in both directions. You should be able to go from above the break to below and back on all vowels, without a break. When you can do this, you've mastered technique. You can choose." And, given her basic equipment and the worldwide need for the sounds she had to offer, Zajick knew she would choose Verdi, with future options on Ortrud, Santuzza, Dalila, Marfa (*Khovanshchina*), Tchaikovsky's Maid of Orleans, and Meyerbeer's Fidès. But not Carmen—"I'm an actress," she explained, "not a dancer." As she approached mid-career, that candid admission perhaps suggested the reasons for the limitations of Zajick's dramatic imagination and the curiously abstract effect of her awesomely efficient Amneris, Azucena, and Eboli. With an equally secure technique, Horne may have been just as obsessed with her voice, but at least she communicated a zest and physical exhilaration that always brought her stage characters to life. With Zajick, it has so far been all voice and little personality.

No American tenor appeared to pick up the torch dropped by Richard Tucker, although for a time Neil Shicoff (1949–) seemed as if he would be a natural successor. As a boy, this son of a New York cantor received a voice lesson a week from his father, and the cantorial tradition that had formed the basis of Tucker's style—and Jan Peerce's—was clearly audible in the younger tenor's exuberant singing and eagerness to communicate. Shicoff's voice was also blessed with ringing metal and attractive plangency, pointing him directly toward the Verdi-Puccini repertory in which Tucker had excelled. By his late twenties he was already at the Met tossing off Puccini's Rinuccio and Verdi's Duke with amazing confidence and focused energy—a generously endowed tenor who meant it when he admitted that "what really turned me on [about singing opera] was the idea of becoming famous." That also suggested a tenor with attitude problems, and soon the impression of Shicoff as "a high-strung loner method-acting his way across the stage, skulking like an operatic Al Pacino" became part of his offstage persona as well, and it seldom worked to his advantage. Once, after reading a *New York Times* review mildly critical of his Hoffmann, he impulsively sent the offending reviewer a terse telegram that read "Fuck you!" Eventually the Met lost patience with him and Shicoff soon disappeared from the company and America, leaving his wife, the soprano Judith Haddon, and their adopted daughter behind. His career continued in Europe, although by the time he had sorted out the legal problems of his divorce and could return to the Met in 1997, as Lensky in *Eugene Onegin,* he was forty-seven, his voice a trifle thicker but his art no deeper. Perhaps Shicoff was a troubled egomaniac, but he was also the most vocally gifted tenor of his generation. The world of opera had once been able to accommodate and nurture such difficult personalities, but the kind of behavior Shicoff indulged in was now considered "unprofessional" and few managements were willing to tolerate it.

More malleable American tenors quickly appeared on the scene, but they, too, flourished only briefly, competing vainly for the coveted, if pointless, title of "fourth tenor" after José Carreras, Plácido Domingo, and Luciano Pavarotti formed their famous pop trio and made a fortune. Among American contenders with sufficient vocal metal to make a grab for the crown have been Richard Leech (1956–   ) and Michael Sylvester (1951–   ). Leech's lovely lyric voice was strengthened by secure top notes and ringing spinto potential, which he perhaps overestimated and overindulged. The simple adjusting of vocal dynamics soon became a chore, and eventually the sound of his unmodulated, inexpressive *forte* began to strike even his earliest boosters as monotonous and charmless. Sylvester's quality *tenore di forza* made him an even more valuable future property as Radamès, Manrico, Calaf, and the rest of the Italian *squillante* heroes who had gone begging after the disappearance of the likes of Del Monaco, Corelli, and Tucker. But by the time he reached forty-five, Sylvester was still struggling to get his voice and career into focus.

During the mid-eighties the Met began to groom another tenor, Gary Lakes (1950–   ), as its answer to the heldentenor drought. Hampered by his considerable bulk, and a grainy, guttural voice that was neither especially attractive nor pliant, Lakes never got beyond Parsifal, Siegmund, and Erik, while proving himself of limited use in other areas of the repertory. He was soon displaced by someone far more promising: the Canadian Ben Heppner (1956–   ), another bear of a man, but one able to move gracefully and use his sweet yet powerful tenor with unusual musical refinement. A distinguished Lohengrin and Walther von Stolzing at thirty-five and scheduled to sing Tristan by the time he turned forty, Heppner tried to keep himself from being typecast as a Wagnerian specialist, but the possibility that North America might have at last produced a world-class heldentenor has proved too tempting for opera companies—or Heppner himself—to resist.

Possessed of a lighter, more lyric voice than Leech, Sylvester, Lakes, or Heppner, Jerry Hadley (1952–   ) has also found more options while wisely avoiding the "fourth tenor" promotional trap. In opera, he has placed himself directly in the Gedda-Kraus-Wunderlich tradition and has seldom strayed from it, at the same time frequently addressing a wide-ranging popular repertory: American musicals, Neapolitan songs (Hadley's mother was of Italian descent), Paul McCartney's *Liverpool Oratorio*, and old-time hits from the turn of the century. Perhaps Hadley should have gone entirely pop, since he has always seemed more involved and engaging as Gaylord Ravenal in *Show Boat* or Bernstein's

Candide than as Nemorino, Tom Rakewell, or Rodolfo. Like the American tenor he most resembles, James Melton—another lyric with barrels of boyish charm and more at home singing light music on the radio than Mozart in the opera house—Hadley possesses an attractive yet small vocal talent that can take him only so far.

Some singers gravitated toward a specialized repertory because their unusual voices more or less led them in that direction. The success enjoyed by Rockwell Blake (1951–   ) and Chris Merritt (1952–   ) has stemmed from an uncommon agility and range that made them indispensable when a virtuoso tenor was needed to sing the Rossini-Donizetti-Bellini operas on the Continent and, to a lesser extent, back home. Blake's rather squeezed, bleaty sound, in particular, was an acquired taste that Europeans seemed ready to cultivate more than Americans, but no other singer at the time could negotiate the florid twists and turns of a Rossini line more easily or accurately or with such bravura flair. The basic sound of Merritt's voice was not much more attractive, but he was equally adept in fioritura, and critics often compared him to the great Andrea Nozzari (1775–1832), who created the vertiginous tenor roles that Rossini had tailor-made for him in *Otello*, *Armida*, and *La Donna del Lago*. Of course, there was no way of telling whether Merritt approximated Nozzari's method, let alone his texture or timbre. But the younger singer fearlessly trod in his predecessor's footsteps while producing a surprisingly substantial sound that earned him the sobriquet "the Heroic Bel Canto Tenor." As his voice became increasingly juiceless, Merritt eventually branched out into unrelated but equally difficult areas. Indeed, at the 1996 Salzburg Festival, he went about as far afield from Italian bel canto as possible by singing Aron in Schoenberg's twelve-tone masterpiece *Moses und Aron*.

Although there was no nationwide scarcity of lower male voices, the unbroken line of distinguished American "Verdi baritones" that stretched from Lawrence Tibbett to Sherrill Milnes had clearly come to an end. Light-voiced lyrics like Gino Quilico, Dale Duesing, Dwayne Croft, Richard Stillwell, Rodney Gilfry, and Mark Oswald now dominated the scene—baritones who sensibly directed their attention mainly toward a less demanding repertory: Mozart, Rossini, French opera, and the occasional contemporary novelty. The two leading names of the period were actually lyric basses, James Morris (1947–   ) and Samuel Ramey (1942–   ), and each filled an important vacuum. After a modest Met apprenticeship singing mainly cameo roles, Morris stepped in as a substitute Don Giovanni in 1975 and scored a big popular success, as much with his dashing all-American braggadocio as with his mellow bass-baritone. Better still was his sinister Claggart in Britten's *Billy Budd* three years later, a dangerously handsome portrait in evil all the more chilling for its understatement.

Morris never built on that impressive achievement, but aimed his sights on a more prestigious future. In 1984 he sang his first Wotan, in Baltimore, and suddenly found himself in demand as the preferred interpreter of the role at every opera house that performed Wagner's *Ring* cycle except, strangely, Bayreuth. And few Wotans could ever have made a more glamorous sound or voiced the god's anger, love, and frustrations so firmly or with more tireless energy. Certainly there was no contemporary competition in that respect, although Robert Hale (1937–)—another American bass-baritone, one with less beguiling vocal equipment—made an honorable substitute when Morris wasn't available. Of course, nitpickers were quick to point out that, for all its deluxe surface sheen, Morris's Wotan seldom gripped the imagination or revealed the role's more subtle, deeply troubling dramatic aspects. After singing the part for more than a decade, Morris gradually added more detail, nuance, and verbal point to his concept, but by then the bloom had begun to fade, the recordings were made, the videos filmed, and the original, stolid interpretation preserved. During the latter years of his career Morris made a few tentative ventures into baritone territory, mainly Scarpia and Iago, but they added little to his prestige. Lacking the vocal, expressive, and theatrical range to deal effectively with such high-lying roles, he merely seemed miscast.

For the sheer quality of his vocal endowment—smooth, mellow, and resonant over a two-octave range—Ramey outshone most all of his competitors, singing just about everything except Wagner: the big Verdi and Mozart bass parts, Boris Godunov, Mephistopheles (Gounod, Boito, Berlioz), Stravinsky's Nick Shadow, French opera of all kinds (Meyerbeer, Offenbach, Saint-Saëns, Bizet, Massenet, Thomas), musical comedy, and American art songs. But what made Ramey special was his skill with florid music—unheard from an American bass since Myron Whitney impressed New Englanders with his superior Handel singing a century earlier—and that made him an invaluable figure in the bel canto revival. The son of a meatcutter from Colby, Kansas, Ramey hardly seemed destined for the job, and it was only a chance hearing of an Ezio Pinza recording well after his voice changed did the idea of becoming a singer even occur to him. In fact, the first opera he ever saw was from a vantage point in the chorus at the Central City Opera in Colorado, where he took due note of the Don Giovanni sung by Norman Treigle, who immediately became an idol and role model.

Not long afterward, in the mid-seventies, Ramey found himself at the New York City Opera, where he quickly moved up to Treigle's parts after the older singer had left the company. Unlike that ill-fated bass, Ramey went on to become world-famous, although it took a surprisingly long time considering his vocal quality was pretty much there right from the start. As so often in the past, Europe embraced an important American voice long before the Metropolitan, which often felt disinclined to hire stars discovered and nurtured by its neighbor across Lincoln Center Plaza. Then, too, Ramey was never one to push himself forward, and offstage he always seemed the embodiment of a simple, shy country boy from the Midwest—a fact that may also partly explain the rather laconic nature of his performing persona, which remained one-dimensional for all its tonal glamour and bare-chested swagger. But by the mid-eighties, his silken bass was in demand everywhere as Don Giovanni, King Philip, Don Quichotte, and Attila. In all those roles Ramey sounded beautiful if bland, but when it came to tossing off virtuoso Rossinian coloratura, he had no equals.

Although he has never enjoyed the fame or prestige of Morris and Ramey, Paul Plishka (1941–   ) has been no less valuable to the Met, singing dozens of bass roles since his debut with the company in 1966. As a twenty-fifth-anniversary gift, a grateful management rewarded him with the baritone role of Falstaff—more suitable to his cherubic physical presence than to a roomy deep bass with a Slavic buzz that testified to the singer's Ukrainian ancestry. Plishka also recorded prolifically and occasionally appeared in Europe, but mainly he seemed content with his lot as a Met house singer. Once, when bluntly asked if he resented the term, the bass admitted that the subject was a delicate one and, yes, he did get a little upset at being taken for granted. Then, in an equivocation that only a singer could make, Plishka continued, "When you try to make yourself into a superstar, you develop a superstar's personality. So then when you go onstage as all these different characters, you're never credible. If you can retain some kind of anonymity, some kind of blandness to your own personality, I think it's easier for you to make these characters more acceptable to the audience." With that, Plishka, inadvertently perhaps, summed up his modest career, and why the Met has found this dependable but unremarkable singer so indispensable.

Obviously the times were not favorable for old-fashioned ego-driven divos or divas, however older opera fans may have missed the glamour and excitement the breed once provided. One or two still managed to surface, although their attempts to cultivate the role eventually backfired. Before that happened to Jessye Norman (1945–), the soprano flourished, from the moment she set foot on an opera stage—as Elisabeth in *Tannhäuser* at the Deutsche Oper Berlin in 1969—and she continued to command wide attention of one kind or another even as both the century and her vocal powers began to wane.

Americans first saw her in opera at the Metropolitan in 1983, as Cassandre in *Les Troyens* and later as Didon—on two occasions she sang both roles in the same evening. With her imposing presence and rhetorical majesty, she presented an awesome figure of doom as Berlioz's tragic seeress while pouring out a flood of glorious sound. That startling transformation began a decade earlier as an already ample physique grew still larger, and a somewhat tentative performing persona suddenly blossomed into a singer as comfortable with her earth mother appearance as with her artistic priorities. Even with her new self-confidence, though, it looked as if Norman would limit herself to the concert stage, especially after she stopped performing opera in Europe in the mid-seventies. It was only a brief sabbatical, however. By 1980 this remarkable voice—which seemed equally comfortable as a contralto or a dramatic soprano—was fully settled, firmly in place, under complete control, and ready for anything. Perhaps Marian Anderson would have sounded something like this if she had been allowed to develop her full potential.

Even at that, Norman proceeded with care, cannily choosing operatic vehicles and concert situations that would always be certain to showcase her as the centerpiece of a genuine occasion, unconventional fare like Rameau's Phèdre, Gluck's Alceste, Janáček's Emilia Marty, and a one-woman theater piece conceived by avant-garde director Robert Wilson called *Great Day in the Morning*, based on her repertory of spirituals. It did not take long for the Met to be sufficiently convinced of her drawing power to present her in a double bill of Bartók's *Bluebeard's Castle* and Schoenberg's *Erwartung*, a hard-sell evening that could only rise or fall on the strength of her presence. There was more Wagner—Kundry and Sieglinde—and many felt that the Isolde everyone had been waiting for

was just around the corner. Meanwhile, the concerts and recitals continued apace, and if a presenting organization needed a soloist to lend
celebrity tone to an opening night or gala event, Norman was one of the
few classical musicians left with the name recognition to guarantee the
proper aura. And she seldom failed to provide it. By then most audiences
were fascinated by her surface appeal: the opulence of her multitextured
voice and exotic, larger-than-life presence.

Soon the manner began to dominate, even obliterate, the music. As
the years passed, Norman's *grandezza* increased alarmingly until even her
most ardent fans were put off by a performing persona that eventually
degenerated into empty pretentiousness and posturing. When she sang
her first Met Kundry in 1991, Norman put no limits on her overbearing
attitudinizing and exaggerated vocal mannerisms—an opera singer who
seemed to be writing her own roles. The solo recitals, too, had become
ego trips, almost religious rites with Norman as the officiating high
priestess. Her treatment of the song literature, once so natural and in-
ward, was now vitiated by stagy poses and calculated expressive gestures. When encountered offstage, she also seemed like a diva descended
from another planet, couching her conversation in what was variously
interpreted as "an outrageously affected, received British pronunciation"
or as some sort of no-man's-land mid-Atlantic patois. "The critic's legitimate question," asked one sympathetic interviewer, finally exasperated
after wondering what to make of an increasingly unreal creature, "is
whether the artifice necessary to sustain the outer shell will also lock up
the characters a great artist must develop onstage." Soon that question
became academic as the all-too-human goddess's voice began to suffer
and unravel. By then any hope of a complete Isolde—or even a decent
performance of a Schubert song, for that matter—had to be abandoned.

Norman's pretentious posturing and sad decline corresponded with
that of another one-time favorite, Kathleen Battle (1948–   ). Battle's
diva behavior even became too much for the Metropolitan. General
manager Joseph Volpe fired her in 1994 for "unprofessional actions,"
which included arriving late, leaving early, and not showing up at all for
rehearsals of *La Fille du Régiment*, most arranged to suit her convenience, as
well as being "very nasty" to members of the cast when she did deign to
appear. It seemed that Battle had turned herself into the world's most
difficult diva with an unprecedented ability to alienate an entire industry.
Tales of her bizarre antics were legion and widely reported in the press.
Riding in her chauffeured limousine, she purportedly rang up her New

York management via cellular phone and demanded that someone from the home office call the driver on *his* cellular phone and tell him to slow down. At one rehearsal she unsettled colleagues by angrily accusing them of staring at her mouth while she sang. After chewing out the Met's lighting crew for some real or imagined offense during a *Nozze di Figaro* rehearsal, she suddenly found herself without a follow spot during the performance and singing Susanna's last-act aria in the dark. The irate employees of the San Francisco Opera ordered a run of "I Survived the Battle" T-shirts after the soprano's offstage tantrums threatened to sabotage their revival of *La Fille du Régiment.* Old-fashioned diva temperament had apparently gotten out of hand and strayed into the realm of dysfunctional behavior.

By the time she reached this sorry pass, Battle was scarcely recognizable as the beautiful and delightful young woman who fifteen years earlier had disarmed audiences as one of the classical music world's most adorable celebrities, whose pure lyric soprano was matched by a fresh, spontaneous, giving musical presence. Even though all those enchanting qualities had disappeared and her operatic career seemed over after the Met scandal, Battle continued her mannequinlike progress across the world's concert stages for several more years almost as a curiosity, still a certified moneymaking celebrity attraction to be summoned whenever a glamorous name was needed, no matter how much she continued to irritate colleagues or bore listeners who still cared about music. But the old magic was clearly gone, and no one could explain where or why it went—a stupid and tragic waste of a wonderful talent.

Part of the opera world mourned the dearth of larger-than-life personalities, but the type of singer Battle and Norman came to embody was clearly not what they missed. They yearned for what these sopranos had been a decade earlier: personable, immensely talented singers who enjoyed their work, communicated naturally, excited large audiences, and earned their fame. The mini-affair that Battle generated when she was dismissed from the Met was front-page news everywhere, but the country at large only regarded the scandal as further proof that the tiny closed world of classical music was populated mainly by eccentric creatures who bore little relation to real life. No one really gained from such negative publicity. While the grand poses affected by Norman and Battle added spice to a bland opera and concert scene, their preposterous behavior hardly advanced the cause of music, changed ideas about singing, or influenced anyone's opinions about the works they chose to sing.

Amid the larger picture, Norman and Battle loomed only as anomalies. The old-fashioned prima-donna behavior they affected set them apart from, but hardly above, their hardworking colleagues, who were never busier or more in demand. American singers had traveled far since the difficult days of Eliza Biscaccianti and Elizabeth Greenfield, Annie Louise Cary and Clara Louise Kellogg, Lillian Nordica and Olive Fremstad. But as the parade of confident, crisp professionals prepared to cross over triumphantly into the millennium, the song they sang was becoming increasingly elusive, dispiriting, and, in too many cases, boring. The spark that had lit such bright fires under earlier generations of singers now flickered only fitfully—so faintly, in fact, that some must have occasionally paused to wonder why they had ever troubled to learn how to sing in the first place. The exciting American adventure inspired by Maria Malibran, the adored "Signorina" back in 1825, seemed over, and nothing symbolized that more vividly than the next European singing sensation to wash up on America's shores.

~

Life After the

Three Tenors

~~~~~~~~~~~~~~~~~

Many famous European vocal paragons had become stars in the United States over the past 175 years, making fortunes beyond the wildest dreams of hardworking American singers, but the Three Tenors outstripped them all, a phenomenon conducted with a cynical commercial cunning that made Barnum's efforts on behalf of Jenny Lind seem positively chaste. The first get-together featuring José Carreras, Plácido Domingo, and Luciano Pavarotti was a comparatively low-key affair in Rome in 1990, planned mainly as a lark to celebrate the World Cup soccer finals and to salute Carreras, who had recently made a miraculous recovery from leukemia. Indeed, the trio took a flat fee for the event and donated most of their earnings to charity. But when the concert was later released on disc and surprised everyone by hitting the pop charts to become the biggest bestselling classical record ever made, a reunion was obviously in order. And this time the tenors were determined not to make the same investment errors. To be held during the next World Cup playoffs four years later in Los Angeles, the Three Tenors II was conceived as a coolly arranged business deal to guarantee the star attractions $1 million each, plus the all-important royalties they had waived the first time around. When the second megaconcert turned out to be another moneymaking triumph, plans were immediately laid for a 1996–97 world tour that would increase the singers' take-home pay tenfold. "Good money, eh?" Pavarotti salivated as he explained all this to a *New York Times* journalist. "By God, it's good money!"

It certainly beat performing in the opera house, where, for a night of hard work, the fee never exceeded five figures, even for superstars. Casually addressing a program of easy-listening favorites, the electronically amplified tenors hardly had to strain their million-dollar voices. Each concert followed the same format, a winning formula of such chestnuts as "Granada," "La donna è mobile," and "Vesti la giubba," followed by a pop medley of "My Way," "Moon River," "Singin' in the Rain," and the like. "Nessun dorma" from *Turandot*, with its concluding cries of "Vincerò!"—the perfect grand finale for an athletic event—climaxed the evening as the three traded off phrases of the Puccini aria until they reached an earsplitting climax on a unison high B. What had started out innocently in 1990 had become a Frankenstein monster, an event without soul or conscience. To paraphrase *The Message Bird*'s sour comments heralding the much-anticipated 1850 arrival of Jenny Lind: if Carreras, Domingo, and Pavarotti had died on their way to their next big arena concert, their skins, properly stuffed, would have been nearly as successful.

Pavarotti functioned as the group's lead singer, and he had no illusions about what he was doing. "There is nothing left for us to do except to be clowns," he had once idly remarked to Beverly Sills many years earlier in San Francisco while facing a crowd of screaming fans who demanded a third encore. Pavarotti did indeed go on to play the clown, and probably surprised even himself at what a success he made of the role. He never deserted opera, which gave legitimacy to his low-brow activities, but his cynical arena attitude was deplorable. Here was a prodigiously gifted singer who turned slovenly, unmusical, and uncaring whenever he stooped to entertain the masses—one can scarcely imagine Caruso so demeaning his art or profession as he brought his voice to the people. But Pavarotti gleefully reaffirmed a truth that Barnum had discovered long ago: Americans will indeed flock to "culture" as long as it is presented with showbiz flair and remains unthreatening. And no one had to tell the Three Tenors that a sucker is born every minute.

There was no way that native-born singers could compete with this sideshow, however dazzled they may have been by the box office receipts. But the virus it unloosed proved all too infectious as many rushed to adapt the downscale recipe to serve their own ends—an even tackier, minor trio of operatic talents materialized, billed as the Three Sopranos. With opera singers already in danger of turning into automatons, this depressing spectacle of music used solely for commercial exploitation set only one more bad example by further deflecting attention from the expressive potential of a classically trained voice raised in song. Indeed, the further singers could distance themselves from the Three Tenors syndrome and the increasingly machine-driven world of opera, the better the chances were for their song to become real and eloquent once again. And a small number did grasp that fact. When one sifts through the dozens of Americans active at the end of the century, the most compelling and original artists have not locked themselves into conventional operatic careers but looked for other options, even if those offered no guarantee of large-scale success or big money. While American singers may not have been reinventing themselves en masse, some independent spirits still found ways to work within the system and make individual, creative statements—and survive.

Most quickly learned that singing music outside the mainstream operatic repertory had one great benefit: there were no shadows from the past to compete with—inevitably so when bringing a contemporary score to life, but also when investigating long unperformed works, particularly those of the seventeenth or eighteenth century. These new pioneers also profited from performing conditions far less pressured than those that prevailed in opera houses, a working environment that encouraged thoughtful preparation with colleagues who shared in the excitement of discovering and singing new music as well as old. Most of all, they were fired by the simple urge to communicate directly to audiences, a need that led to a renewal of a genre long given up for lost: the song recital. Jennie Tourel had noticed that the spirit was leaving the song as long ago as the 1960s, when she sensed that American singers were in danger of losing something very precious. "When I was young and first came to this country and sang concerts, even in America's smallest towns," Tourel once told an interviewer, "I didn't want to go down to the public; I wanted the public to come up to me . . . I wanted to bring my heart to the audience, sing out my heart. And I never cared how big or small the audience was—when one heart speaks to another it is understood . . . It's a give-and-take thing. But right now, the young people just want to take. They don't want to give anything."

Tourel could eloquently translate that artistic ideal into music, even when it seemed that the song recital really was dying out. I first heard her vocal alchemy for myself in a Boston concert hall in the mid-fifties with a tiny audience of no more than twenty or thirty people. After glancing at the disappointing turnout with the slightest hint of resigned dismay, Tourel proceeded to sing a program of art songs and arias with the I'm-here-for-you generosity so typical of her, while applying an extraordinary range of vocal colors and expressive dynamics, illuminating every emotion from Gretchen's heartbreak to Périchole's tipsy joie de vivre. For a teenager experiencing his first vocal recital, Tourel's vivid communicative powers were potent but also misleading—all singers, I figured, must surely conjure up the same magic. They didn't, of course, and even those few Americans who cultivated the art of the song during the sixties and seventies risked being ignored by managers and publicists as well as by large audiences. This began to change toward the end of the century as an increasing number once again delved deeply into the literature and, like Tourel before them, found it possible to reawaken a give-and-take relationship with audiences, even if the financial rewards remained meager compared to those on the big-time opera circuit.

Arleen Augér (1939–93) was among the first to take a lead in bringing American singers back to song. Until she returned home to give her first New York recital in 1983 after fifteen years based in Europe, Augér was virtually unknown here except as a soprano whose attractively phonogenic voice could be heard on a vast number of opera and oratorio recordings. Unwilling to be typecast and anxious to transfer her career back home, Augér was determined to explore the full range of possibilities available to her. Even at that, four Marzellines in *Fidelio* at the Metropolitan in 1978 seemed to indicate that, like Claire Watson before her, Augér would probably not be comfortable singing in the vast expanses of the Met, let alone trying to create the requisite "glamour identity" necessary to succeed in that world. Besides, critics were already beginning to rave about her song recitals, and the beauty, freshness, and grace her voice brought to the literature. Augér concentrated mostly on German lieder at first, but she quickly broadened her scope to include songs from all countries, and even began commissioning American composers to provide her with new material. Before long she was giving recitals all over the country, receiving more invitations than she could accommodate, and welcoming younger singers who flocked to her for coaching and advice. Who knows what more she might have accomplished had not cancer struck in 1991, when her voice was still in its prime and her career flourishing. But by then dozens of singers had either studied with her or been inspired by her example to make the singing of songs a top priority. If Barbara Bonney, John Aler, Roberta Alexander, Helen Donath, Barbara Hendricks, Stanford Olsen, Vinson Cole, Kurt Ollmann, William Parker, and others hardly renounced the operatic stage, they found that performing recitals had become a luxury they could indulge and profit from.

As musicology and musical performance became increasingly interwoven, singers drawn to the older repertory suddenly found themselves in demand as never before. Baroque music performed on authentic instruments of the period had long ago exploded into a worldwide craze, and it seemed only a matter of time before that era's vocal music would regain currency. When it did, America was ready to meet the demand: Julianne Baird, Howard Crook, Lisa Saffer, D'Anna Fortunato, Dana Hanchard, Juliana Gondek, Jan Opalach, Jill Feldman—dozens of singers whose smallish voices and refined musicianship would have been lost in the Metropolitan or large European opera houses were now put to use singing Handel, Rameau, Lully, and Charpentier in intimate venues and with exquisite results.

Along with the Baroque revival came a voice type that had never flourished in America before: the countertenor. For many years the lone practitioner of any note had been Russell Oberlin (1928–   ), a founding member of Noah Greenberg's famous New York Pro Musica and a leading exponent and popularizer of early music at a time when anything composed before Bach was considered arcane and unapproachable. By the century's end it must have heartened Oberlin to see so many young countertenors participating in the Baroque-opera revival, with its stylish productions and recordings. Taking the lead in this important movement were Jeffrey Gall, Drew Minter, Derek Lee Ragin, Brian Asawa, Randall Wong, and David Daniels, countertenors with strong, flexible, high-placed voices that they used with unparalleled technical virtuosity. They also took to the operatic stage with an uninhibited theatricality determined to sweep aside any lingering doubts that American audiences were not ready to appreciate the sound of a male alto/soprano as Handel's Giulio Cesare or Monteverdi's Nero—or, for that matter, as Britten's Oberon, one of the great countertenor roles of the contemporary repertory and one that Oberlin himself sang at Covent Garden soon after the opera's premiere.

When David Daniels (1966–   ) won the Richard Tucker Foundation's top award of $30,000 in 1997, some conservative souls feared that the "American Caruso" would surely start spinning in his grave. The folk in America's heartlands who never went to the opera may have loved watching Pavarotti sing trash on television, but how would they react to a falsettist caroling Handel on the foundation's annual televised opera gala? Obviously the jury that chose Daniels didn't consider this a problem, a panel comprised of the country's most influential opera impresarios and myself as the lone music critic. Besides, among the two dozen or so finalists, there was no question about who was the most compelling young vocal personality on the list, a singer whose stage presence and dramatic flair invariably excited audiences wherever he appeared. Daniels's big, beautifully produced, amazingly secure voice easily sailed through the most florid Baroque arias with show-stopping bravura, while his command of style and color also made the song literature available to him—here was a countertenor of such extraordinary musical gifts and versatility that one actually yearned to hear him sing the great song cycles of Schumann and Schubert. Many other future options also seemed possible. Now that Marilyn Horne had retired the heroic Rossini warrior-hero roles from her repertory, an intriguing and worthy successor had arrived. One opera director was clearly putting no limits on this talent when he opined that Daniels "could probably sing the hell out of Charlotte in *Werther*." If, as Richard Tucker once said, singing was a matter of hitting home runs, Daniels had only just stepped up to the plate and he was already batting 1.000.

Some singers, even those lacking unusual vocal placements or special agendas, managed to carve out careers in opera and song completely on their own terms—and at that, without establishment assistance from the Metropolitan, the New York City Opera, the regional opera circuit, or provincial German opera houses. Sanford Sylvan (1953–   ) grew up in New York, attended the Manhattan School of Music, earned his way by ushering at the Met for five years, and launched what looked like a conventional career until he began to question his role in the system. To find out, he traveled to a colony in Finland to meditate, and reordered his priorities:

I didn't sing for nine months. I didn't vocalize. Nothing. It was wonderful. I had started singing when I was very young and have been in love with singing since I was a child. I needed to find out who I was when I wasn't a singer. I had to take that time to do it myself, so I stopped. And it was a great thing. It helped me to understand that it's my choice—that we can't become victims of a system that we think owns us. Now I sing because I choose to, and my career goes the way it goes because I make the choices. I choose the music I want to sing and the people I want to sing with. I've committed myself to that music and those people . . . To think you're not doing what your heart's desire is, that is a terrifying prospect. I think that's what selling out really means—achieving something and then losing sight of what it is that you want to be doing.

Sylvan was blessed with an attractively warm, flexible baritone and exceptional musical intelligence to back up his independent spirit. He was also fortunate early on to strike up a beneficial association with the director Peter Sellars, who gave Sylvan's special talents prominent exposure in his controversial productions of Mozart's three Da Ponte operas at New York's PepsiCo summer festival, performances later released worldwide on video. After that came two even more widely seen and much discussed new operas by John Adams: *Nixon in China* (with Sylvan as Chou En-lai) and *The Death of Klinghoffer*. His work in those operas caught the attention of Nonesuch Records, an adventurous New York company that released both Adams works on disc and recorded the baritone in a series of song recitals, most notably an achingly beautiful rendition of Schubert's *Die Schöne Müllerin*. When not on the road with a Sellars production, giving recitals, or making records, Sylvan has made his home in Boston, participating in that city's rich musical life of early music, oratorios, and concerts—obviously a singer fulfilled and functioning happily out of the international rat race.

Another maverick, Lorraine Hunt (1954–) also worked with Sellars, and she found the experience a liberating one as she tapped into a singular musical persona and intensity that struck many as positively mesmerizing. Hunt sang Donna Elvira in Sellars's *Don Giovanni*, a provocative production that relocated the opera in New York's Spanish Harlem. Her appearance at the window during the great trio in Act II as she confronted the faithless Giovanni was heart-twisting—the image of a humiliated, brokenhearted woman made all the more moving because the music was being sung with such exquisite purity, control, and expressive point.

Sellars discovered Hunt while directing a production of Handel's *Orlando* in Cambridge, Massachusetts. She was playing viola in the orchestra, and when Sellars learned she also sang, he asked to hear her. "She started singing," the director recalled with awe, "and you were in the middle of this raging forest fire." After that, Sellars cast Hunt as often as he could and rekindled the fires every time—most memorably as Sesto, the tortured adolescent son of the murdered Pompey in his updated vision of Handel's *Giulio Cesare*, set poolside at the Cairo Hilton. In opera, Hunt's choices over the next decade continued to be mainly in the Baroque and Classical repertory, especially when she could work with directors like Sellars and conductors like William Christie, who drew out her deepest feelings but also managed to tame the wilder side of her performing spirit when it threatened to go over the top. By 1996 Hunt seemed to have gotten that under control too. As Irene in Sellars's production of Handel's *Theodora* at the Glyndebourne Festival, she bowled the director over once again, especially by how much her art had deepened. "The poise and centeredness of the character and the music just came together in a way that made you gasp," he said. "The word is devotion. What the Hindus call *bhakti*—this tremendously deep, devotional quality to Lorraine's work, which moves ego directly out of the way and pours her whole being, as a kind of offering, into her role, into the music. And I mean your own sense of vocation is deepened and altered when you're in the presence of that." The British critics also capitulated, singling out Hunt for her "voluptuous, keenly articulated singing," which "confirmed her reputation as the outstanding Handelian mezzo of today."

After that international success, it seemed as though Hunt might be able to do, and get, almost anything she wanted. Whatever that might turn out to be, it was unlikely that she would opt for the sort of conventional career pursued by her contemporary Jennifer Larmore (1958–   ), who also was singing Handel and Mozart on an international level and with considerable vocal flair but without comparable expressive intensity or creative imagination. In 1995 Larmore boasted that she had sung Rossini's Rosina more than 250 times in opera companies large and small all over the world—a feat that would scarcely have occurred to Hunt as ever a good thing to do. Rather than become a highly paid headliner at the Metropolitan or the Salzburg Festival, this original had a different future in mind: "I'm in the business of soaring. And diving deep. And I'd like to play with people who want to do that too." As it had been with George London and Teresa Stratas, Hunt always communicates that sense of danger.

If Sanford Sylvan and Lorraine Hunt are radicals who refuse to compromise their ideals to accommodate the Establishment, others work within it and, by making judicious adjustments, still find ways to diversify their musical activities, keep their priorities clear, and win the respect of both connoisseurs and a broad public. International opera, recitals, new music and old, pop crossover, media recognition on television and records— some wanted it all in wide-ranging careers that would bring artistic satisfaction as well as fame. Only a few had the necessary combination of talent, charisma, and backbone to get all that, and among the first was Frederica von Stade (1945–   ). Known to everyone by her childhood nickname of Flicka, Von Stade was, in fact, beloved by nearly all who saw and heard her, a singer whose appealing image seemed to generate instant affection. It was a vocal personality that projected strength as well as delicacy—a modesty and candor that, some said, even expressed moral character. "I don't want to be Flicka's lover," one admirer once commented. "I want to be her brother."

Von Stade's gracious image was further enhanced by the fact that she never seemed to go after her career aggressively—everything came naturally and as if by right to a girl whose aristocratic family pedigree stretched back to America's colonial era. Along with inborn elegance and breeding, the voice was always there, a beguilingly velvety mezzosoprano with a tug and a tear in the tone, qualities that were put to expressive use with an instinctive musicality even though Von Stade had never received formal lessons as a youngster. She still couldn't even read music when, deciding that it was time to take her voice seriously, she enrolled in the Mannes College of Music and the school's opera workshop program. There Von Stade found the only voice teacher she ever seemed to need, Sebastian Engelberg, who remained her mentor until his death in 1979. "He set to work on my bad habits," the mezzo recalled the next year, "moving the voice upward from a low alto to where I had a high C, showing me how to put my will on the vocal machinery.

He gave me not only a cupboardful of technique but also a delight, a sense of joy."

It was Engelberg who persuaded his protégée to audition for Rudolf Bing, ever on the lookout for useful young Americans to give yeoman service in tiny roles, and the Metropolitan general manager hired her on the spot in 1970 for a modest debut as a Genie in *Die Zauberflöte*. Von Stade caught more than a few ears and eyes as she gamely tended to Mercedes, Wowkle (*La Fanciulla del West*), Suzuki, Lola, Maddalena, Flora Bervoix, and such until she was noticed by Rolf Liebermann, visiting New York and scouting talent to launch his regime at the reborn Paris Opéra. He immediately signed Von Stade to sing Cherubino in the opening production of *Le Nozze di Figaro* conducted by Georg Solti, directed by Giorgio Strehler, and given at Versailles in 1973. The event received international attention, and everyone who saw a performance came away in love with Von Stade. Writing in *Newsweek*, Hubert Saal could not remember "a Cherubino more breathlessly young or more passionate, or one who poured out her love in such sweet and liquid accents."

Mozart's page boy became Von Stade's signature role for the next twenty years, a focal point from which the mezzo quite literally radiated to explore an operatic repertory carefully chosen to flatter her distinctively honeyed mezzo-soprano and patrician musical character as well as her glowing stage presence: Rosina, Charlotte, Octavian, Mélisande, Cendrillon, Cenerentola, and Mignon. The first four roles were offered to Metropolitan operagoers, but Von Stade was always seen and heard to better advantage in smaller houses, where the fine points of her essentially intimate vocal personality could better be savored. "From the beginning," she once frankly admitted, "I knew I was going to have to chase after the lyric roles wherever they were being done, and the Met has never been a big Rossini house. I can't do Eboli and all the Verdi ladies. I'm a person of very modest vocal means. Charlotte was a stretch. Octavian was a stretch." And, she might have added, attempting Adalgisa in *Norma* at the Met was a downright mistake, one of this scrupulous singer's few miscalculations.

Since she conducted her career so quietly, Von Stade scarcely attracted any special attention when she began to diversify her activities and take advantage of the options that were beginning to be available to any American singer with the curiosity to investigate them. On the one hand, she was among the first with an international reputation to plunge into the Baroque repertory, correctly sensing that the expressive declamation of Monteverdi's *Il Ritorno d'Ulisse in Patria* and Rameau's *Dardanus* would suit her better than the florid arias of Handel and his Italian contemporaries. At the other end of the musical spectrum, Von Stade also gladly performed in new operas, showing a preference for the conservative lyrical works of Thomas Pasatieri (*The Sea Gull*), Dominick Argento (*The Aspern Papers*), and Conrad Susa (*Les Liaisons Dangeureuses*). In this last opera, she even confounded those who had long ago typecast her as the lovable prima donna from next door by playing her first operatic villainess, the Marquise de Merteuil.

As a schoolgirl, Von Stade had idolized Ethel Merman, although even then she knew that her delicately textured voice could never belt out show tunes with similar power and gusto. That hardly stopped Von Stade from eagerly exploring a repertory that would soon provide younger singers with a rich and rewarding source of material: the classical American musical comedy. Her activity in this field began in mid-career and it was mainly conducted on records and in television specials rather than in onstage productions. The 1988 EMI recording of *Show Boat* conducted by John McGlinn revealed just how seriously the genre was now being taken. Every scrap of music Jerome Kern wrote for the musical's various stage and film versions was included. It was a scholarly enterprise that never sounded like one, featuring Von Stade as a meltingly vulnerable Magnolia, Teresa Stratas as Julie, and Jerry Hadley as Gaylord Ravenal—operatic voices to be sure, but each one perfectly restyled and retuned to fit the idiom with a lilting naturalness. By 1996 Von Stade had starred in concert versions and recordings of *The Sound of Music*, *On the Town*, and *Anything Goes*, as well as solo discs devoted to a variety of pop material from Richard Rodgers to Dave Brubeck. Such risky crossover ventures by classically trained singers had been infrequent since the days of Dorothy Kirsten and Risë Stevens, but Von Stade helped show the right way back by treating a distinctly American art form with easy grace, charm, and musical sophistication.

Sherrill Milnes's successor as the country's premier baritone was Thomas Hampson (1955–   ), a different sort of singer altogether—the line of dramatic "Verdi baritones" that began with Lawrence Tibbett had definitely come to an end with Milnes, at least temporarily. By the mid-nineties, Hampson had sung Germont and Rodrigue in *Don Carlos* (significantly in the original French), with Di Luna as a possible future option, but clearly his priorities lay elsewhere. In any case, his voice was better suited to other enterprises, as its owner knew very well. "I'm mad about Monteverdi," Hampson burbled to an interviewer just as his career was getting into high gear, "and I love Hugo Wolf's and Cole Porter's songs equally. I guess it's my own kind of schizophrenia. Whether I enjoy practically every genre because of my superficiality or my depth, I can't decide."

Audiences seldom seemed troubled by such questions and simply enjoyed Hampson's purling voice in whatever he chose to sing, his graceful six-foot-four frame and dark good looks, and, as one admiring British critic observed, "the sort of complete openness and zest for life that tired old Europeans think of as typically American, and West Coast American at that." Raised in Spokane, Washington, Hampson enjoyed "a tremendously normal childhood," playing baseball and entertaining thoughts of a future in engineering or politics until, at age twenty, he encountered a nun named Sister Marietta Cole, who had once studied with Lotte Lehmann down the coast at Santa Barbara. Sister Marietta heard Hampson sing and promptly decided his future. "Young man," she said, "God made you a singer, and you have the responsibility to be one. When you're ready to accept that responsibility, call me." With that, she produced a record of Gerhard Hüsch singing a Schubert lied, said "have a listen to this," and the young man's mind was made up on the spot. Later he went to Santa Barbara himself to study with the retired French baritone Martial Singher. It was a stormy relationship, but Hampson learned much from Singher's Old World aesthetic, especially about what would be his primary love, the song literature.

It was this thoughtful singer who won the Metropolitan Opera Auditions in 1980, but Hampson turned down a chance to enter the company's apprentice program, preferring to get experience in the time-honored way in a small German opera house. He headed for Düsseldorf and was instantly hired to sing mostly a slew of nameless heralds, gendarmes, and sergeants. In 1984 he moved on to Zurich, where Nikolaus Harnoncourt put him to work as a leading baritone in the Mozart-Monteverdi-Rossini operas and had him helping out in the Concentus Musicus's ongoing project to record the complete Bach cantatas. Soon Hampson was back in America singing at the St. Louis and Santa Fe opera festivals while waiting for the Metropolitan to open its front door for a debut as Mozart's Count Almaviva. By the time that happened, he was already noted for his thoughtfully programmed song recitals and a rapidly growing discography.

Well before he turned forty, Hampson let everyone know that he, too, intended to have it all—an insatiably curious singer who couldn't possibly live long enough to explore every piece of music that interested him. If Hampson agreed that a reputation for careerism and even haughtiness often preceded him, he has laid all that to his impatience with the business rather than to egomania: "It's frustrating and overwhelming. It can get me going sometimes and make me seem more aggressive than I am. I'm often untactful and seem arrogant, [but] I'm not at all taken with triumphs. I think I've done good work, but I don't think the world is waiting for Thomas Hampson." Actually, it sometimes seemed as if the world had indeed been waiting to hear him sing whatever he wanted. In opera there were the conventional roles available to his sunny, smoothly textured, small-bore baritone—Rossini's Figaro, Don Giovanni, Onegin, Marcello. But there were also less obvious choices, such as Thomas's Hamlet, Roland in Schubert's *Fierrabras*, the Dark Fiddler in Delius's *A Village Romeo and Juliet*, and Handel's *Giulio Cesare*. When newer operas catch his attention, Hampson has been eager to investigate them too, such as the title role in Henze's *Der Prinz von Homburg*, Britten's *Billy Budd*, the romantic lead in Susa's *Les Liaisons Dangereuses*.

But mostly Hampson has put his heart into song, and whatever fame and fortune he might win in opera has been partly in order to have the luxury of giving recitals. As he put it in a 1989 interview, "If you could make $8,000 a night singing a Liederabend and knew people would be out there screaming and hollering because they had just seen the light on a Goethe poem, you'd see a lot more people singing lieder." And his appetites in this area have been varied and vast. The changes Hampson rings on German lieder seem endless, with programs organized around poets, instructive chronologies, approaches to the same poems by different composers, or a program of songs set in German by early Americans. Sometimes he finds two composers who were exact contemporaries but complete opposites—Rossini and Meyerbeer—and juxtaposes their seldom-heard songs. Another favorite Hampson evening consists of kindred spirits, vocal and instrumental, exploring the musical landscape of America in the mid-nineteenth century via the popular songs of Stephen Foster. And, on disc, the baritone has vigorously indulged his love of theater music from Porter and Kern to Lloyd Webber. Everything

Hampson sings he researches and annotates himself, and in concert he sometimes even instructs audiences from the stage about the finer textual points. Such didacticism often threatens to give his music-making a studied, even mannered quality, but that breezy West Coast informality noted and appreciated by "tired old Europeans" usually steps in and rescues the moment.

No, it is not Milnes, Warren, or Tibbett that Hampson recalls, but an American baritone of a century earlier, one who also loved to tell his audiences stories in song and who also had a touch of the schoolmaster about him: David Bispham. That "Quaker Singer" would have immediately recognized Hampson as a brother in song when the young baritone once breathlessly blurted out his credo: "I know what's important to me, and it's not dollars. What's important is what I do—to be taken seriously, to be asked to sing songs, to try to excite someone to literature, poetry, to thoughts—almost like a priest—to be able to convey that to someone, to reach them—that makes it all worthwhile."

As Hampson pursues that noble goal, his admirers pray that he can curb his inclination to adopt airs of self-regarding pomposity, an alarming trait that sometimes threatens to transform him into the male counterpart of Jessye Norman. In that respect, he stands in marked contrast to William Sharp (1951–   ), another superior but far less famous American baritone, who closely resembles Hampson: his voice is just as beguiling and evenly schooled, his onstage presence is no less attractive, and his musical intelligence and sense of adventure are equally keen. If this engaging singer maintains a distinctly lower career profile, it must surely be his choice, a clear preference for the concert and recital stage rather than the high-pressured world of opera, which would help spur him on to world stardom. But like Sanford Sylvan, Sharp seems perfectly content doing precisely what he wants, and that with rare musical excellence.

"See," Dawn Upshaw (1960–   ) pointed out to an interviewer marveling at her presumably charmed career, "you *can* have it all! You know who told me that? It was Jan DeGaetani—yes, really, I can hear her now. And, you know, Jan spoke with great authority."

Actually, if measured in terms of star power, Upshaw has gathered quite a bit more than DeGaetani, whose neglect of opera prevented her from achieving the international fame that might have been hers. Otherwise, both pretty much did have it all: exceptional vocal talent, uncompromising musical values, critical respect, and a supportive family. Upshaw frequently went to DeGaetani for coaching, and the older singer not only instilled the younger with a lifelong curiosity for the music of living composers but also the idea "that singing should express the experience of life, and that sometimes involved emotions that are not attractive." It was a piece of sound advice that no doubt helped the soprano eventually find the emotional center of her voice, as well as adding an edge to a musical personality that could sometimes seem just too serene and sensible—and, as we've already seen regarding her predecessors on the operatic stage, a trifle smug.

In an *Opera News* profile by Brian Kellow, Upshaw's smooth ride to the top was aptly likened to the untroubled progress of a Manhattan taxicab that manages to hit all the green lights from 125th Street down to the Bowery. And so it seemed, a happy trip that began with a contented childhood in a Chicago suburb as a charter member of the Upshaw Family Singers—the whole household liked to sing when Dawn was a girl, and the folksy repertory was heavily weighted toward the likes of Peter, Paul, and Mary. From there the young soprano quickly branched out to pursue basic musical training at Illinois Wesleyan University before heading east to study with Ellen Faull at the Manhattan School of Music. It was there in 1983, in a triple bill staged by the school's opera workshop, that I first saw Upshaw, cast against type as the heroine of Hindemith's lurid one-acter, *Sancta Susanna.* If the role of a sex-starved nun who tears the loincloth from a crucifix somehow seemed inappropriate for this proper Upshaw family singer, there was no mistaking the shining clarity of her soprano, her concentrated musicianship, her pleasure in facing up to a tough challenge, and her sheer determination to succeed. This girl, I thought, will go far, and sure enough, only a year later she was already on the fast track—a week after graduation, Upshaw found herself courted by two influential New York talent boosters, Young Concert Artists and the Metropolitan Opera Young Artist Development Program. After three years on the YCA's busy regional recital circuit and profiting from intensive opera training at the Met, Upshaw had made powerful friends in the business. They especially admired her ability to understand and adapt instantly to the realities of the profession while simultaneously projecting a polite but provocative musical persona that promised to defy the status quo in unexpected ways. To everyone's surprise, it seemed that for once the system had actually worked: an enormously talented young singer had eagerly taken full advantage of every useful career-building tool, but in the process sweetly refused to sacrifice the musical priorities that made her so special.

Upshaw continued to base her operatic activities at the Met, where James Levine had become an important ally, but as with Von Stade, her voice and delicate charm would be better appreciated in smaller houses. It did not take long for Europe to beckon, and soon the soprano was singing her charming "ina" roles (Despina, Pamina, Adina, etc.) around the world. Upshaw could have left it at that, enjoying uninterrupted success and big money by specializing in a dozen adorable soubrettes, especially now that Kathleen Battle, her chief rival in that repertory, had self-destructed. But opera was only one part of her agenda, and it served mainly, as with Hampson, as a prestigious bargaining chip that would give her access to less commercial projects. Also like Hampson, Upshaw felt that a recital program should be more than a miscellaneous collection of songs designed to show off a singer's voice, versatility, and ego. In pursuing her ideas on that score, she was more than likely influenced by the ingeniously organized programs the Swedish soprano Elisabeth Söderström sang when she visited New York in the eighties: a sequence of songs by many different composers on the same subject matter, but arranged in such a way that each successive item was suggested by the one that preceded it.

Upshaw developed that string-of-pearls concept even more vigorously, particularly in an ambitious 1996 three-concert series called "Voices of the Spirit," music that set out to examine "the path of the human spirit" and explore "a framework of common spiritual development." The trilogy was a startling musical mix, with songs, cantatas, dramatic monologues, and arias by Bach, Fauré, Purcell, Messiaen, and Wolf among others, as well as contemporary scores commissioned for the occasion. The first program functioned as a call to the spirit, the second dealt with crises of faith, and the conclusion was a lofty epiphany—a journey that struck some ecumenical souls, especially those who feel that the devil always gets the best tunes, as excessively rarefied and arty. Nor, in fact, did Upshaw's fresh-scrubbed earnestness seem especially spiritual—certainly not as "spiritual" was understood and projected by Eleanor Steber, for whom "in the act of singing, for that brief time, I transcend my mortal self." But few could deny the focused intensity of

Upshaw's commitment to her vision, the chaste purity of her voice, and her patrician musicianship—not to mention the sheer nerve of offering such a high-minded musical experience to jaded New Yorkers.

Upshaw pondered the form and content of her recorded programs just as carefully. Most of her discs contain an hour or so of tightly connected works on single subjects, integrated collections that, she hoped, would be listened to almost as a single musical statement. One consisted of songs in English about mysterious moon-drenched nights, another of German lieder to texts by Goethe, yet another of sensuous songs by turn-of-the-century French composers and others influenced by them. When the time came to venture into the classical-pop repertory, Upshaw also did it with class, much hard thinking, and on her terms. Her first crossover album consisted of songs by four Broadway composers, kindred spirits who found different ways to reinvent and elevate the musical theater through dramatic song: Kurt Weill, Marc Blitzstein, Leonard Bernstein, and Stephen Sondheim. After that came a Rodgers and Hart collection that fully explored the bitter and the sweet elements of that unique collaboration. With those albums, both huge commercial successes, Upshaw at last put the dutiful "good girl" image behind her to release the expressively urgent, heart-melting singer that some felt had been there all along. Since she had already sung so much American-English vocal music, new and old, Upshaw automatically projected the verbal subtleties of these songs more vividly than most of her colleagues, many of whom seemed innocent of what words mean, no matter what the language. The enchanting effect of Upshaw's pop singing was also due to her grasp of the technical adjustments that must be made when addressing this repertory: a more forward placement, breathier production, reduction of vibrato, and colloquial diction.

Perhaps, as she continues her avid investigation of new scores, this singer of uncommon musical principle and vocal allure will eventually find one that will do for her what Barber's *Knoxville: Summer of 1915* did for Eleanor Steber or Crumb's *Ancient Voices of Children* for Jan DeGaetani— or, for that matter, what Debussy's Mélisande did for Mary Garden. When that happens, Upshaw will indeed have it all.

Coda

*I*t would be overly optimistic to conclude that adventurous singers like Dawn Upshaw, Lorraine Hunt, Thomas Hampson, David Daniels, and Sanford Sylvan herald the arrival of an entire new generation of exciting young Americans, original vocal talents with thrilling voices that have the world by the ear, who sing important new music that audiences everywhere demand to hear, and whose unique artistry is changing the way we listen to music of all kinds, from the past as well as the present. Sad to say, no such phenomenon is in sight. And yet there is no dearth of vocally gifted Americans to address most areas of the repertory, which they do with technical competence and musical assurance in opera houses and on concert stages all over the globe. Through their vigorous efforts to turn an unruly and unpredictable adventure into an orderly and well-regulated profession, American singers have reached a pinnacle of sorts, but their position at the top is an ironic one. After spending so many years trying to crash the party, they have finally earned an honored spot on the guest list, only to find the hour late and the festivities cooling off.

Now that the world of classical music has become completely internationalized, its creative juices flow sluggishly, and musicians—busy
singers in particular, and from every corner of the globe—function
mainly as efficient custodians rather than as active participants in a continually evolving repertory of new work. And as such, Americans play a
leading role—in fact, they had to deal with borrowed goods from the
very beginning, and they became increasingly adept at the task as time
passed. With that in mind, looking back at the statements by Clara
Louise Kellogg and Beverly Sills which introduced this chronicle makes
the complaints of those two quintessential American prima donnas seem
even further off the mark. Each was convinced that America's age-old
preference for European singers stood in their way as they battled to
establish themselves as important artists in their own country. While
that familiar refrain is trolled continually throughout the history of
American singing, it is actually a scapegoat that disguises a far more
significant reality: the sense of cultural inferiority that has always
haunted this country. It's ironic that Kellogg and Sills, had they been
born in Europe, would surely never have won the fame and prestige they
managed to gain in America, for all their laments about a system dominated by foreigners. Both possessed the driving ambition that anyone
must have to achieve stardom, and their efforts paid off handsomely at
home, where they were celebrated as heroines of American musical culture from coast to coast. But Kellogg never had the vocal quality to
compete on the highest international level, and Sills always remained
parochial despite her attempts to establish herself as an important figure
in Europe. One hard fact of life seemed to escape these otherwise
shrewd American prima donnas as they grasped for the stars. The greatest singers with the greatest voices, when they appear at the right time
and in the right place, will always be given preference, whatever their
nationality. Rosa Ponselle could tell us that. So could Leontyne Price,
Lillian Nordica, Lawrence Tibbett, Richard Tucker, and George London.

Those and all the other indisputably great American voices faced a
far tougher challenge than competition from abroad. Without roots in a
clearly defined musical culture, they had to make themselves up as they
went along. Ponselle was perhaps the most striking example, a singer
who quite literally came from nowhere and never truly understood how
she made all those glorious sounds. The fact that she had no formal
voice lessons at all, let alone direct contact with a long-standing vocal
tradition that came to Europeans as part of their birthright, surely con-

tributed to her fears, insecurities, and too-early retirement. Nordica became an international figure at the turn of the century, but her triumph
was due as much to dogged hard work at self-improvement as to her
magnificent vocal endowment. It was the cantorial music he heard as a
child, not opera at the Metropolitan, that inspired Tucker to become the
operatic star he yearned to be, even before he had seen an opera onstage. And who could have predicted London's overnight success with
the notoriously exacting Viennese opera public in 1949, after a decade
of "training" in the *Ice Follies*, operetta road shows, and cross-country one-
night stands with the Bel Canto Trio? Singing in church choirs and high
school pageants as a boy in California during the early years of the
twentieth century prodded Lawrence Tibbett to a career in song and
opera. Price's first step on her way to the world's great opera stages was
taken in the black Baptist churches in Laurel, Mississippi. Each great
American singer, it seems, was self-invented by a singular personality
with a prodigious vocal gift, a fierce individualist fired by the burning
creative imagination to make the dream come true. Beyond that, the
history of American singers, as their life stories tell us, consists largely of
a collection of fortuitous accidents.

Small wonder that a school of American singing, with its own defining stylistic traits and musical characteristics, never developed, and even
now can scarcely be said to exist. Before today's well-organized profession crystallized, Americans who aspired to a singing career more or less
had to rely upon their own ingenuity, and that was what gave their art—
and their lives—such character, color, energy, and texture. Since opera
and concert singing could never develop here as it did in Europe over
the centuries, as a response to a steady stream of new music provided by
composers of originality and genius, the story was one mainly of imitation and assimilation as the country's classically trained singers looked to
Europe for songs to sing. As a result, they inevitably had to follow rather
than take the lead, at least at first. The early pioneers—Wheatley, Biscaccianti, Phillipps, Hensler, and the rest—could scarcely have been
expected to match the expertise, réclame, and earning power of such
sensational visiting stars as Malibran, Lind, Mario, Grisi, and Patti. As
the leading voices of the day, those singers were quite simply the best in
the world, and American audiences understandably wanted to hear
them—and not necessarily because of snobbish prejudice for things European. Without proper technical training or stylistic grasp of the Italian
bel canto operas that dominated the repertory, America's first singers

could hardly have hoped to attain the same level of technical or artistic accomplishment as their Continental counterparts, and the country's audiences at the time were hardly so naive as to think that they could.

In some respects, the next generation had even greater challenges to face, and they were only slightly better prepared to meet them—no wonder their adventurous lives often seemed more interesting than their purely vocal achievements. Kellogg and Hauk doubtlessly sang lyrical and—by the time they learned them—old-fashioned bel canto heroines like Linda, Lucia, and Amina more comfortably than their predecessors, but these post–Civil War divas soon found themselves tackling the rigors of Wagner and late Verdi, most certainly compromising and overextending their voices by singing such demanding contemporary music. Their successors were luckier. By the turn of the century, New World society was sufficiently settled and structured to produce artists better able to compete internationally. The formidable triumvirate of Nordica, Eames, and Fremstad mingled comfortably with the European elite and did not suffer in comparison. Since they had studied and thoroughly absorbed the classical vocal traditions of Europe, their manner and method became virtually indistinguishable from those of their Continental colleagues. A generation later, when the "modern" musical dramas of Puccini, Strauss, Massenet, and their lesser contemporaries became the latest fashion, America was ready for that development too, supplying colorful theatrical personalities like Farrar and Garden to help carry the message of such provocative heroines as Salome, Butterfly, Tosca, and Thaïs around the country. And as the twentieth century progressed, many other American singers soon discovered precisely what was needed in order to become major players on the international scene as they transformed themselves into cosmopolitan vocal personalities.

An accident of global warfare Americanized the Metropolitan's roster by necessity in the 1940s, and for a brief moment it seemed as if the country was on the verge of developing a national vocal school at last, especially in the wake of Giulio Gatti-Casazza's noble attempts to cultivate native opera during the twenties and thirties. But that proved to be a deceptively brief interlude. Edward Johnson failed to build on Gatti's achievement, Rudolf Bing even less so, and one can understand why. By aping already outmoded European operatic styles, twentieth-century American composers showed little feeling for the operatic stage and even less musical originality. If the flawed works by Deems Taylor, Howard Hanson, Louis Gruenberg, and the rest never added up to a significant body of work, they did produce an ardent advocate in the vibrant voice and theatrical persona of Lawrence Tibbett. As he avidly added new works to his repertory and eagerly sang operas and songs in English, Tibbett developed into the most quintessentially "American" opera and concert singer the country had ever produced. But even his example failed to take root. Today Tibbett is primarily remembered as America's first "Verdi baritone," a title his successors—Leonard Warren, Robert Merrill, and Sherrill Milnes—inherited proudly as they distanced themselves even further from the music of America.

The internationalization of American voices continued as they secured a dominant role in keeping alive a magnificent repertory of opera and song from the past. In the process, whatever special musical or vocal qualities that could even be faintly labeled as distinctly "American" have by now been absorbed into the global mix—soon only an expert linguistician or phoneticist will be able to identify the differences between an American, Italian, German, Icelandic, or Korean tenor. What distinguishes American singers today is not their vocal individuality or creative fantasy but their craftsmanship and relentless industry. Inquiring singers like Von Stade, Hunt, Upshaw, and others continue to investigate a diversity of music in order to find their own special voices, and no doubt they will have successors. And yet it is more difficult than ever for such mavericks to make their way in a music world that prizes conformity above all and, as a result, becomes increasingly homogenized. It is also unrealistic to expect that the complex and expensive apparatus needed to support the continuing performance of classical music—at least as we have always understood it—will survive indefinitely as new social and economic realities alter our culture. After all, the royal European courts that sustained a glorious repertory of medieval music for centuries have long vanished, and the world, while looking for new songs to sing, has spent little time in mourning the loss. Good things need not always last forever.

No doubt American composers will one day write those songs, and wonderful American singers will sing them. Although new native operas have once again begun to reach the stage in quantity, few have offered music that inspires the voice to what it can do best. Only music of a lyrical, expressive eloquence that invites singers to participate actively in bringing a work of musical theater to life can reanimate the age-old, mutually beneficial relationship between singer and composer. This has not yet happened in America, at least in the conventional world of opera, which depends less and less on the contributions of exciting vocal personalities. Maria Callas, Jon Vickers, or George London could never have become important singers by performing *The Ghosts of Versailles, Einstein on the Beach,* or *Nixon in China.*

Other composers will try harder, other voices will appear to take up their challenges, and American singers will reinvent themselves yet again. Perhaps when they do, a truly distinctive school of American singing will arise at last. If that ever happens, the story as told in this book will be just the beginning.

𝒩otes

INTRODUCTION

1 "In my own country": Sills, pp. 57 and 129.
1 "The Italians of the chorus": Kellogg, pp. 40–41.
5 "Girls, I've made up my mind to go on the stage!": Ibid., p. 21.

PRELUDE

8 "highest and most costly entertainments": New-York American. April 15, 1825; quoted in V. B. Lawrence, p. xliv.
10 "How an opera is to be got up": Harmonicon, October 1825, p. 194; quoted in Bushnell, pp. 18–19.
10 "Never before within the walls": New-York American, November 30, 1825; quoted in V. B. Lawrence, p. xlvii.
11 "In what language": New-York Evening Post, November 30, 1825; quoted in Mattfield, p. 14.
11 "The style of singing": New-York Literary Gazette and Phi Beta Kappa Repository, December 17, 1825; quoted in Mattfield, p. 15.
12 "Signorina García, of the Italian Opera": New-York Mirror, December 3, 1825, p. 50; quoted in V. B. Lawrence, p. xlix.
12 "But how or in what language": New-York Review and Atheneum Magazine, pp. 80–81; quoted in V. B. Lawrence, p. xlix.
13 "Here they are already half crazy": Quoted in Bushnell, p. 25.
13 "It's only García": Quoted in Pougin, p. 17.
14 "On Saturday you are to appear": Ibid., p. 29.
14 "Papá, papá, por dios": Ibid., p. 32.
14 "In the chamber scene": New-York Evening Post, February 9, 1926; quoted in Bushnell, p. 25.
14 "an overflowing audience": Ibid., October 2, 1826; quoted in Bushnell, p. 34.
15 "There is no instance": Ibid., October 9, 1827; quoted in Bushnell, p. 41.

CHAPTER ONE

17 "The auditorium was different": Ritter, p. 208.
17 "The opera, they say": Hone diary entry for September 15, 1833; quoted in Krehbiel, CO, p. 21.
18 deficit of $29,275.09: Ritter, pp. 211–12.
18 "The faces of artists": Ibid., pp. 198–99.
19 "Now grown up": Quoted in Thompson, p. 31.

20 "The young debutante": *Morning Courier & New-York Enquirer*, November 26, 1834; quoted in Thompson, p. 36.

21 "But, the young lady": J. Price, *A Life of Charlotte Cushman* (1894); quoted in Thompson, p. 36.

22 "With the Maeders": Emma Stebbins, ed., *Charlotte Cushman: Her Letters and Memories of Her Life* (1878); quoted in Thompson, p. 36.

22 "no breath of scandal": *Notable American Women*, Vol. 1, p. 424.

22 "I listened and gazed": Quoted in ibid., p. 423.

22 "fine baritone-contralto voice": Kellogg, p. 52.

23 "Signora Biscaccianti made her debut": *Morning Courier & New-York Enquirer*, December 15, 1847; quoted in V. B. Lawrence, pp. 462–63.

24 "the young lady has undoubtedly": *Evening Mirror*, December 9, 1847; quoted in V. B. Lawrence, pp. 464–65.

25 "One set have put her down": *New-York Herald*, December 9 and 17, 1847; quoted in V. B. Lawrence, pp. 465–66.

25 "Who, upon hearing thy song": Quoted by Pauline Jacobson in *San Francisco Bulletin*, May 5, 1917.

25 "embodied grace": "Pioneer Prima Donnas," p. 20; San Francisco Opera archive.

26 "People went about": *The Alta California*, March 24, 1852.

26 "Every piece sung by our accomplished townswoman": *Dwight's Journal of Music*, February 5, 1859.

27 "in a fog of tobacco fumes": "Pioneer Prima Donnas," p. 28.

27 "she was young, beautiful": Quoted in Thompson, p. 39.

28 "The honors of the day": *History of the Handel and Haydn Society of Boston, Massachusetts*, Vol. 1, p. 53.

29 "If the current anecdote": Ibid., p. 62.

INTERLUDE ONE

30 "her rooms were thronged": Barnum, p. 333.

31 "Her fears of the water": *The Message Bird*. November 15, 1849, p. 135; quoted in V. B. Lawrence, p. 617.

31 "JENNY LIND does not return": *Punch*, Vol. 19 (1850), p. 146; quoted in Maude, pp. 159–60.

32 "as significant an event": Quoted in Wagenknecht, p. 10.

32 "Mr. Dodge is a fool": Quoted in Field, p. 220.

33 "was a woman": Werner, p. 188.

33 "First, the face": Brown, p. 202.

33 "There was always a pathos": *Baltimore Sun*, September 28, 1920; quoted in Wagenknecht, p. 99.

34 "The dream-like echoes": H. R. Haweis, "Jenny Lind," *Contemporary Review*, Vol. 59 (1891), p. 908; quoted in Wagenknecht, p. 100.

34 "I become a different thing": Quoted in Brown, p. 207.

34 "When every day": Holland and Rockstro, Vol. 2, p. 438.
34 "To a mind eminently sensitive": *New York Home Journal,* March 23, 1850.
35 "as stingey as a hive of wasps": Quoted in Pleasants, p. 202.
35 "something as entire": Ibid., p. 204.
35 "She is as great an artist": Holland and Rockstro, Vol. 1, p. 5.
35 "An approximate imitation": Quoted in Pleasants, p. 203.
36 "It can now": Chorley, pp. 195–96.
36 "You see that boy?": Quoted in Liza Lehmann, p. 33.
37 "a remarkable artist": Pleasants, p. 198.
37 "without disparagement": Wagenknecht, p. xii.
37 "There is always a peculiar interest": Ibid., pp. 185–86.
37 "The Swedish Swan": Faner, p. 62.

CHAPTER TWO

39 "the Grand Opéra at Paris": *Dwight's Journal of Music,* March 4, 1854, pp. 170–71.
40 "Mlle. Nau, who was of course": Ibid., November 25, 1854, p. 62.
42 "young and attractive": La Fama, Brescia, December 1853, as translated in *Adelaide Phillipps: A Record* (1883) by Mrs. R. C. Waterston; quoted in Thompson, p. 45.
43 "Among a large number": Quoted in Thompson, p. 40.
43 "One other person in the company": Kellogg, p. 41.
44 "is so fat that she can only stand still": Quoted in Thompson, pp. 47–48.
46 "*petite* Sontag": *Dwight's Journal of Music,* May 3, 1856, p. 35.
46 "a teacher and composer of high repute": Ibid., June 10, 1854, p. 70.
46 calm, collected, dignified manner: Ibid., p. 79.
48 "Sig. Squires": Ibid., May 20, 1854, p. 54.
49 "excellent figure, brown hair": Ibid., p. 359.
49 "has had the advantage": Quoted in Thompson, p. 63.
50 "For a long time": Quoted in *Dwight's Journal of Music,* October 18, 1856, p. 22.
51 "the defects of a thin, cold voice": Quoted in Thompson, p. 68.
51 "magnificent soprano voice": Ibid., p. 69.
52 "foremost in the very respectable list": Ibid., p. 69.

CHAPTER THREE

Unless otherwise indicated, all quotes in this chapter are taken from Kellogg.

57 "Miss Kellogg's impersonation of Martha": *Dwight's Journal of Music,* December 7, 1861, p. 287.
59 "The Margaret was beautiful": Quoted in ibid., April 16, 1864, p. 220.
65 "the greatest living contralto": Quoted in Thompson, p. 83.

66   "Fancy Kellogg": *Dwight's Journal of Music*, December 7, 1878, p. 349.
66   "If the voice": Quoted in Thompson, p. 77.
66   "Her best friends": Quoted in Odell, Vol. 11, p. 615.

CHAPTER FOUR

Unless otherwise indicated, all quotes in this chapter concerning Abbott are taken from S. E. Martin; concerning Thursby, from Gipson; concerning Albani, from Albani.

69   "Oh dear. Another one to tell": Kellogg, p. 272.
69   "very unattractive, exceedingly plain": Ibid., p. 272.
70   "the one girl in ten thousand": Ibid., p. 273.
70   also outfitted the girl: Ibid., p. 273.
71   "young and attractive": Odell, Vol. 9, p. 235.
71   "I have wept such gallons of tears": Quoted in Gipson, p. 97.
74   "Emma Abbott did appalling things": Kellogg, p. 274.
81   "a sensible American girl": Quoted in *Notable American Women*, Vol. 3, p. 460.
83   "voice of exquisite quality": Quoted in Scott, *RS—1: to 1914*, p. 24.
83   "Her singing is perfect": Quoted in Thompson, p. 153.
83   "Rarely has the Academy of Music": Ibid., p. 153.
84   According to Klein: Klein, *GWSMT*, p. 106.
86   "Now I understand why I am Patti": Quoted in Ronald, pp. 103–4.

CHAPTER FIVE

Unless otherwise indicated, all quotes in this chapter are taken from Hauk.

87   "dusky daughter of the sun": *Dwight's Journal of Music*, October 26, 1878, p. 325.
88   "Mon Dieu!": Ibid.
88   "All the songstresses": Ibid.
91   "Her first note convinced": *New York Times*, December 1, 1866; quoted in Thompson, p. 99.
91   "include in her general haul": Kellogg, p. 103.
91   "Minnie Hauk was very pushing": Ibid., pp. 103–4.
95   "But one must be just": Lilli Lehmann, p. 253.
96   "stating he would do anything": Mapleson, pp. 116–17.
96   "was simply delighted": Klein, *TYMLL*, p. 86.
97   "strong sensual suggestion": Quoted in Thompson, p. 108.
97   "an undulating seductive creature": Henderson, p. 372.
98   "I therefore had to commence": Mapleson, p. 122.
99   "What could the public think": Ibid., p. 264.
101 "somehow its rather thin": Quoted in Thompson, p. 118.

CHAPTER SIX

Unless otherwise indicated, all quotes in this chapter are taken from Bispham.

102 "Miss Katie Smith": *Dwight's Journal of Music,* January 10, 1874, p. 156.
105 "truly beautiful and well nursed vocal means": Quoted in *Dwight's Journal of Music,* August 31, 1867, p. 95.
106 "a man of imposing stature": Lahee, *GOA,* p. 324.
107 "with the *bâton* grasped in his right hand": Mapleson, p. 308.
108 "is really superb": Quoted in *Dwight's Journal of Music,* January 10, 1874, p. 156.
108 "the demon's sardonic humor": Ibid., p. 156.
112 "There was about it an element": Klein, *TYMLL,* p. 338.
112 "His voice was of a real ugly, harsh quality": Wood, p. 81–82.
112 " 'What have you been doing with your voice?' ": Ibid., p. 82.
113 "They are possibly proud of him": Shaw, Vol. 2, p. 380.
114 "His gift of versatility is extraordinary": Klein, *TYMLL,* p. 338n.
115 "to emphasize every characteristic touch": Aldrich, p. 291.

INTERLUDE TWO

Unless otherwise indicated, all quotes in this chapter are taken from Cone.

120 "Well, let him sing!": Quoted in Scott, *RS-1: to 1914,* p. 21.
120 "correct breathing, scales": Klein, *GWSMT,* p. 37.
122 "By whom is this aria": Quoted in Weinstock, p. 276.
122 "most heavenly and touching": Klein, *RP,* p. 174.
122 "sublime effect": Conati, p. 51.
122 "tone formation, portamento": Hanslick, *VGYM,* pp. 206–7.
123 "There is only one Niagara": Quoted in Klein, *RP,* p. 381.
124 "Long before daylight": Mapleson, p. 198.
125 "quite the most remarkable singer": Kellogg, p. 130.

CHAPTER SEVEN

Unless otherwise indicated, all quotes in this chapter are taken from Glackens.

129 "It is wonderful how Mme. Nordica": *New York Daily Tribune,* November 28, 1895, p. 7.
133 "We have always been good friends": Kellogg, p. 309–10.
136 "She is competence itself": *The Pall Mall Gazette,* March 14, 1887.
137 "Miss Nordica turned Elsa of Brabant": *The Star,* May 31, 1889.
140 "Those who have seen Nordica": Ibid., July 21, 1894.
142 "I was a fool": Melba, p. 163.
143 "duped, betrayed, deceived": Quoted in *Notable American Women,* Vol. 2, p. 635.
143 "Her voice was huge": Finck, p. 232.

144 "Nordica was not tempestuously temperamental": Henderson, p. 494.
145 "Madame Nordica was determined and brave": Bispham, p. 359–60.
146 "She did her damnedest": Pleasants, p. 268.

CHAPTER EIGHT

Unless otherwise indicated, all quotes in this chapter are taken from Eames.

148 "Last night there was skating": Quoted in Scott, *RS—1: to 1914*, p. 34.
148 "Whoever has not seen Miss Eames": *The World*, June 20, 1894.
149 "very flexible": Radio broadcast, February 2, 1939; reproduced on IRCC LP 3142; Romophone CD 81001-2.
154 "When Eames entered in the first act": B. Marchesi, pp. 50–51.
155 "charming, but not a great artist": Quoted in Davis, *OC*, p. 54.
156 "Miss Eames is not a great artist": *New York Daily Tribune*, December 15, 1891.
156 "There is no blood in her performance": Quoted in Kolodin, p. 154.
157 "Oh, I did not resent it": Quoted in E. Lawrence, p. 132.
161 "The days of resurrection": Quoted in Eaton, *BOC*, p. 166.
161 "its individual, unique, crystal clearness": Ibid., p. 167.
162 "To a sensitive person": Radio broadcast, February 2, 1939.
162 "absolutely in time": Ibid.
163 "We were driving": Quoted in notes to Cantilena LP 6221.
164 "Emma is impossible": Ibid.
164 "Melba didn't care": Ibid.
164 "What is so remarkable?": Ibid.

CHAPTER NINE

Unless otherwise indicated, all quotes in this chapter are taken from Cushing.

166 "A great tragic actress": Cather, p. 46.
167 "longingly into the forest": Quoted in Christiansen, p. 187.
168 "My work is for serious people": Quoted in Cather, p. 42.
168 "Mme. Fremstad's voice": Aldrich, p. 200.
168 "sensitive to the point of being quixotic": Gatti-Casazza, p. 196.
172 "I will never come here again": Quoted in Bispham, p. 304.
172 "Nonsense! We were all worms": Quoted in Thompson, p. 224.
173 "a delight with small alloy": *New York Times*, November 26, 1903, p. 4.
173 "Mme. Fremstad's Kundry": Cather, p. 47.
174 "She is a trained Wagnerian": *The Sun*, December 1, 1904.
174 "I do not claim this or that": Cather, p. 46.
174 "left the listeners staring at each other": *New York Daily Tribune*, January 23, 1907.

174 "But in the galleries": *New York Times*, January 23, 1907.
178 "Well, why not ask it": Gatti-Casazza, pp. 198–99.
180 "There was a time during the War": Letter in Metropolitan Opera Archives.

CHAPTER TEN

183 "not only gained a lot": Mathews, p. 222.
183 "a little too Londonienne": Quoted in Thompson, p. 185.
183 "spoiled child": Ibid., p. 186.
184 "and was, in consequence": Lahee, *FSTY*, p. 216.
184 "as if in mute": Quoted in Thompson, p. 186.
184 "I believe the ringleaders": *The Musical Record*, Boston, May 1885.
185 "She was a small, graceful woman": Odell, Vol. 15, p. 118.
185 "She was a kind-hearted": B. Marchesi, p. 53.
185 "Dear Master": Quoted in Massenet, pp. 175–76.
186 "What a fascinating voice!": Ibid., p. 176.
186 "ideal": Ibid., p. 179.
186 "A painful evening last night": Harding, p. 89.
186 "there was a gasp of adoration": Garden and Biancolli, p. 24.
187 "to see Mademoiselle *Seinderson*": Quoted in Harding, p. 108.
187 "Of Miss Sanderson's performance": *New York Daily Tribune*, January 17, 1895.
188 "Massenet was breathing heavily": B. Marchesi, pp. 54–55.
189 "Don't you think you should smoke": Garden and Biancolli, p. 57.
189 "I'm glad": Ibid., p. 58.
189 "I thought I never would": Ibid., p. 59.
189 "about an inch long": Quoted in Thompson, p. 144.
189 "A slim, graceful, sprightly little lady": *Spirit of the Times*, July 28, 1888; quoted in Thompson, p. 144.
190 "looked the part well": *The Star*, July 9, 1888.
190 "the hackneyed and trivial Carmen": *The World*, August 5, 1891.
190 "does not grow more interesting": *The World*, May 13, 1891.
190 "she has gained much": *New York Daily Tribune*, November 27, 1894.
191 "the Queen's own": Quoted in *Notable American Women*, Vol. 1, p. 458.
191 "grieved my mother deeply": B. Marchesi, p. 55.
192 "Although my mother spoke": Ibid., p. 56.
192 "It was only after the five years": Ibid., p. 56.
192 "one of the latest illustrations": *New York Daily Tribune*, January 5, 1897.
193 "In order to conciliate the offended prima donna": Mapleson, p. 239.
194 "the pious belief that every soprano": Quoted in *Notable American Women*, Vol. 2, p. 618.
194 "not like the usual tiny miserable squeaks": B. Marchesi, p. 53.
195 "Opera is very hard work": Antonio Altamirano; quoted from notes to Yaw recital on Pearl LP GEMM 239.
196 "gifts and training commensurate": Quoted by Philip L. Miller in notes to Cantilena LP 6228.

196 "resided in halls half a tone lower": Ibid.
196 "an earnest, honest, soulful": Ibid.
196 "a cheerful, merry person": Ibid.
198 "as pretty and dainty as a Dresden doll": Quoted in *Notable American Women*, Vol. 2, p. 632.
198 "A mobile face": Eaton, *TBOC*, p. 36.
200 "harassing her with annoying imitations of odd voices": Quoted in Street, p. 102.
202 "owing to the super sensitiveness of one vocal cord": Quoted in Kolodin, p. 370.

CHAPTER ELEVEN

Unless otherwise indicated, all quotes in this chapter are from either Anne Homer or Sidney Homer.

205 "Domesticity is not a role": Cather, p. 34.
207 "one of nobility, dignity": Quoted in Thompson, p. 215.
209 "a contralto of great purity": Ibid., p. 82.
209 "It was the most beautiful voice": Ibid., p. 82.
210 "one of the noblest contralto singers in the world": Quoted in *Notable American Women*, Vol. 1, p. 298.
211 "delicate artificial refinements": Shaw, Vol. 1, p. 177.
217 " 'Come on in and sit down' ": Cushing, p. 172.

CHAPTER TWELVE

Unless otherwise indicated, all quotes in this chapter are taken from Garden and Biancolli.

220 "remains immortal": Alda, p. 20.
221 "She hardly moved her hands": Quoted in Christiansen, p. 277.
225 "slender, agile, unsophisticated": Quoted in Cone, *OHMOC*, p. 113.
225 "It was, however, the conception": Ibid.
225 "There [was] no reason": Garden, "My Life," *Hearst's International*, Vol. 45. (February 1924), p. 73; quoted in Cone, *OHMOC*, pp. 108–9.
227 Press quotes from Cone, *OHMOC*, pp. 130–32.
228 "I know full well": Quoted in Cone, *OHMOC*, pp. 133–34.
229 "When Mary Garden came to New York": Ibid., p. 134.
230 "somewhat bewildered": Massenet, pp. 237–38.
231 "to bend over": Reginald de Koven, *New York World*, January 29, 1909.
231 "Miss Garden has realized a conception": *New York Daily Tribune*, January 29, 1909.
231 "Although I might have continued": Quoted in Cone, *OHMOC*, p. 219.
232 "I'm wondering, Miss Garden": Quoted in Alda, p. 20.
233 "Chicago's just going to love *Salome*": Quoted in Davis, *OC*, p. 83.

233 "The door of her bedroom jerked back": Ibid.

234 "It was disgusting": Ibid.

234 "Performances like that of *Salome*": Quoted in E. Moore, p. 75.

234 "I don't know just what could be done": Quoted in Davis, *OC*, p. 90.

234 "tedious, stupid": Ibid., p. 130.

235 "We want to go out in a blaze of glory": Ibid., p. 133.

235 "It's going to be an American opera company": Ibid., p. 134.

235 "It was a remarkable opera season": Quoted in Christiansen, p. 280.

236 "Even to eyes susceptible to her usual magic": Quoted in Davis, *HOAW*, p. 116.

236 "She wore a close-fitting hat": Horgan, pp. 56–57.

238 "Well, boys": Author's memory of a radio news item, circa 1960.

INTERLUDE THREE

241 "Caruso, the new tenor": Quoted in Scott, *GC*, p. 70.

241 "lacked aristocratic flavor": *New York Evening Post*, December 3, 1903.

241 "bourgeois": *New York Sun*, December 3, 1903.

241 "Before Caruso came": S. Homer, p. 191.

242 "His is the performing style": Scott, *GC*, p. xviii.

242 "My emotions got all tangled up": Quoted in Scott, *GC*, p. 74.

244 "I feel a role too much": Quoted by Bruno Zirato; MS in Francis Robinson Collection, Vanderbilt University, Nashville, Tennessee.

244 "fortissimo and in full verismo style": Scott: liner notes to *The Complete Caruso*, RCA 60495-2-RG, p. 79–80.

245 "I strain myself": Quoted in Scott, *GC*, p. 197.

CHAPTER THIRTEEN

Unless otherwise indicated, all quotes in this chapter are taken from Farrar's two autobiographies.

246 "Has George Cohan stopped crying?": Quoted in Kolodin, p. 305.

247 "Children, this is no occasion": Ibid.

247 "What is a Gerryflapper?": *New York Sun*, November 20, 1920.

248 "The scores of the older repertory": Quoted in Martens, pp. 92–93.

252 "Those eyes were unbelievable": Quoted in Mayer, pp. 145–46.

256 "People are often shocked": Cather, p. 38.

256 "the finest creation": Henderson, p. 313.

256 "Farrar doesn't satisfy me very much": Quoted in notes to MET CD 705.

258 "I slept with that woman": Quoted in Groover and Connor, pp. 142–43.

259 "interesting and in many ways charming": Quoted in Kolodin, p. 250.

259 "the Mona Lisa without her smile": Quoted in Groover and Connor, p. 201.

260 "has proved herself": Quoted in ibid., p. 194.

260 "Farrar is luminous": Ibid.
260 "Geraldine met me with the air of a lioness": Quoted in ibid., p. 200.
263 "I thought she was a marvelous": Quoted in Mayer, p. 136.

CHAPTER FOURTEEN

Unless otherwise indicated, all quotes in this chapter are taken from Ponselle.

265 "vocal gold": New York Times, November 16, 1918.
265 "one of the most voluptuous": New York Sun, November 16, 1918.
270 "First of all, I regard": Quoted in Martens, pp. 233–34.
273 "neither queenly": Quoted in Kolodin, p. 294.
274 "For me, the revelation of first hearing": Opera, January 1977.
277 "The melodic character": Henderson, pp. 402–8.
280 "a thoroughgoing horror": High Fidelity, March 1980.
281 "In my long lifetime": Quoted by Walter Legge in Opera, January 1977.

CHAPTER FIFTEEN

286 "But you are not a baritone!": Quoted in Emmons, p. 12.
287 "How Eighty-Eight Roles Are Sung": Musical America, April 21, 1928.
287 "her head is a music box": Quoted by John Stratton in The Record Collector, Vol. 21, No. 9.
289 "As the nagging wife": Clipping in Metropolitan Opera Archives.
289 "It's such a lovely car": G. Moore, p. 27.
289 "Musical snobs sometimes remonstrated": Davenport, p. 64.
290 "unabashed reverence": Ibid., p. 19.
290 "That's my idea of opera-singing": Quoted in ibid., p. 45.
290 "aerial transparency": Aldrich, p. 518.
290 "When the First World War was over": Davenport, p. 112.
291 "What if she has only sung": Musical America, December 10, 1911.
291 "those who had admired": Aldrich, p. 410.
292 "a light soprano of the most lyric quality": Ibid., p. 510.
293 "to investigate the Javanese music": Quoted in notes by Philip L. Miller on Town Hall LP TH-003.
294 "My love for the old classics": Ibid.
294 "without the voice": Quoted in Kolodin, p. 252.
295 "I would bind Madame Mason": Quoted in liner notes by Edward Hagelin Pearson on Romophone CD 81009-2.
296 "I had just coached Nedda": Quoted in Opera News, March 18, 1967.
296 "The chief duty": Quoted in Davis, OC, p. 136.
296 "Miss Mason classifies": Ibid., p. 185.
297 "and tossed her enough flowers": Ibid., p. 219.
298 "with limpid, colorful tones": Ibid., p. 137.

299 "No more Thaïs for me": Quoted in liner notes to International Record Collectors' Club LP L-7009.
300 "While it is a great asset": Newspaper clipping in Metropolitan Opera Archives.

CHAPTER SIXTEEN

Unless otherwise indicated, all quotes in this chapter are taken from Tibbett, *The Glory Road,* as reprinted in Farkas.

304 "On the stage": Thompson, p. 365.
304 "The house went into a rage": Noble, p. 173.
310 "likeable": Alda, p. 255.
311 "There was no denying it": Ibid., p. 256.
311 "I arrived at her apartment": Benoist, p. 172.
311 "Why should he do so": Alda, pp. 257–58.
312 "the most effectively and artistically wrought": *New York Times,* February 18, 1927.
313 "pitiless exactions": *New York World-Telegram,* January 8, 1933.
315 "pianos were so delightful": Mayer, p. 151.
315 "And this was not exceptional": Quoted in Farkas, p. 10.

CHAPTER SEVENTEEN

Unless otherwise indicated, all quotes in this chapter concerning Hayes are taken from Helm, concerning Anderson from her autobiography.

322 "She was not of vanity": Majors, p. 155.
323 "a physician, humane and courteous": Ibid., p. 156.
323 "she sang": Ibid., p. 156.
323 "We have it from her own lips": Delany, p. 121.
324 "The compass of her marvellous voice": Quoted in Majors, p. 161.
324 "For our part": Quoted in *Dwight's Journal of Music,* April 9, 1853, pp. 2–3.
326 "Her singing is indeed a wonder": Ibid., October 7, 1854, p. 6.
327 "Here as elsewhere in the line of their travels": Quoted in Story, p. 29.
329 "I love to sing": Ibid., p. 19.
329 "The fickle public": Ibid., pp. 35–36.
339 "No date will ever be available": Quoted in Robinson, p. 230.
340 "the fire grew and blazed": Quoted in Story, p. 42.

CHAPTER EIGHTEEN

Unless otherwise indicated, all quotes in this chapter concerning Grace Moore are taken from her autobiography.

345 "I believe she is now the most promising young American artist": Quoted in Kobler, p. 196.

345 "This soprano has a pretty voice": Quoted in Tuggle, p. 211.

347 "lived in terror twenty-five hours a day": *Opera News*, December 20, 1969, p. 15.

348 "Yes, she could study longer": Noble, p. 142.

349 "no more than a name": *New York Sun*, February 20, 1926.

350 "In her hair is the light": Quoted in Dougan, p. 33.

351 "The house was sold out": *The Musical Courier*, February 14, 1926.

352 "Mary Lewis Wants Babies": Clipping of magazine article in the Metropolitan Opera Archives.

352 "drunk as a lord": Quoted in Dougan, p. 34.

353 "Mr. Gatti's little Christmas gift": *New York Sun*, January 4, 1931.

353 "remained well after": Kolodin, p. 356.

353 "one of the first to prove": Eaton, *MM*, p. 230.

354 "a glamour time": Quoted in Mayer, p. 171.

355 "I love you": Quoted in Davis, *HOAW*, p. 104.

355 "costume that left off": Eaton, *MM*, p. 230.

355 "one of mist and tenderness": Quoted in Rasponi, p. 429.

356 "never left the country club": Quoted in ibid., p. 412.

357 "Swarthout! Where's Swarthout?": Quoted in Davis, *OC*, p. 155.

357 "Although there were many opportunities": Quoted in Rasponi, p. 411.

357 "Miss Swarthout gave an image": Quoted in *Opera News*, March 10, 1941.

INTERLUDE FOUR

360 "Perhaps you think it was difficult": Noble, p. 135.

361 "Good voice in the lower register": Kathryn Meisle's audition sheet, dated December 20, 1929, six o'clock, in the Metropolitan Opera Archives.

361 "America's beloved singer": Quotes from Kathryn Meisle's Columbia Concerts Corporation pressbook in the Metropolitan Opera Archives.

362 "a sunny blonde": *New York World-Telegram*, January 7, 1935.

362 "a new coloratura": Ibid., January 8, 1935.

363 "I have found that American singers": Gatti-Casazza, p. 205.

364 "that young Canadian upstart from Italy": Quoted in Mercer, p. 94.

364 "a tenor who is something more": *New York Times*, November 17, 1922.

364 "If his singing": Aldrich, pp. 636–37.

365 "You could hardly get a definite Yes or Nay": Quoted in Eaton, *MM*, p. 274.

367 "notable for its mingled sweetness and virility": Raymond Ericson, *New York Times*, March 27, 1966.

368 "rich, powerful, sensitive mezzo-soprano": Quoted in Kolodin, p. 373.
368 "Rose, when you are going to do Aida": Quoted in McGovern and Winer, p. 123.

CHAPTER NINETEEN

Unless otherwise indicated, all quotes in this chapter concerning Traubel, Varnay, and Kirsten are taken from their autobiographies; concerning Stevens, from Crichton.

374 "Her favorite posture was sitting": Leinsdorf, p. 104.
374 "My God, you big cow": Quoted in *Time*, November 11, 1946.
375 "Good voice but it diminishes in top register": Audition card in Metropolitan Opera Archives.
377 "We attract as little attention as possible to her bust": Quoted in *Time*, November 11, 1946.
377 "Nobody knows": Author's recollection from news reports of the time.
377 "hearty and modestly amusing": *Variety*, December 7, 1955.
380 "all but ho-yo-to-hoed": *Time*, December 22, 1941.
380 "thoroughly at home on the stage": *New York Times*, December 13, 1941.
388 "A prima donna": Quoted in notes by Bruce Burroughs to MET 217 CD.
388 "Singers aren't idols anymore": Quoted by Robert Jacobson in forward to Kirsten.
389 "It just isn't fair": Blurb on Kirsten dust jacket.
392 "amateur night at the Met": *New York Herald Tribune*, December 6, 1943.
393 "she stripped behind a screen": *New York World-Telegram and Sun*, October 4, 1955.
396 "I would come away from London": Quoted in *Opera News*, December 8, 1984.

CHAPTER TWENTY

Unless otherwise indicated, all quotes in this chapter are taken from Steber.

399 "To put it mildly": Quoted from notes to Video Artists International CD VAIA 1005-2.
401 "wearing what looks like a quilt": *Opera News*, October 1992.
412 "A full-blown, gutsy comeback at 56": *New York Times*, October 11, 1973.
412 "It would be impossible not to capitulate": Ibid., March 29, 1973.
412 "She was then age 74": James A. Van Sant, letter to the author.
413 "If the voice had been spared": Ibid.

CHAPTER TWENTY-ONE

Unless otherwise indicated, all quotes in this chapter concerning Peerce and Merrill are taken from their autobiographies, those concerning Tucker from Drake.

423 "To this day": Peerce, p. 119.
423 "These questions have been weighing for decades": *New York Herald Tribune*, May 14, 1963.
427 "When Tucker finally decided": Kolodin, p. 452.
427 "someone in Europe would hear": Bing, *5NO*, p. 147.
431 "Determined on a singing career": Quoted in *Variety*, December 12, 1956.
432 "I was very much to myself": Quoted in *New York Times*, October 25, 1959.
432 "was a frail old man": Quoted in *Opera News*, December 1, 1956.
432 "I'm floundering": Quoted in *Daily Mirror*, January 20, 1956.
432 "When I first heard the voice": Quoted in *New York Times*, October 25, 1959.
433 "I cried like a baby": Ibid.
433 "Any religion that would claim Agatha": Walter Price, author of an unpublished biography of Leonard Warren, in conversation with the author.
435 "tells other singers how to sing": *New York Times*, October 25, 1959.
435 "takes his art without levity": *Opera News,* undated clipping the Metropolitan Opera Archives.
435 "One of his favorite gags": Undated and unidentified clipping of a newspaper article by Bill Young in the Metropolitan Opera Archives.
435 "Warren's death": Bing, *5NO*, p. 263.
436 "you have a simple melody": Quoted in *Opera News*, April 9, 1956.
436 "Traditionally he carried a cane": Quoted in *Theatre Arts*, April 1956.
437 "Those are the kind of stockings": Quoted in *New York Times*, October 25, 1959.
443 "a brilliant concert artist": Quoted in Melton's obituary in the *New York Herald Tribune*, April 23, 1961.
444 "more vibrancy and color": Quoted in Sullivan's obituary in the *New York Times*, June 18, 1969.

CHAPTER TWENTY-TWO

450 "The best way to keep a woman out of trouble": Quoted in Rasponi, p. 394.
450 "it had that phosphorescent top register": Ibid., p. 401.
452 "Because I have vocal cords": Anecdote told to the author by Richard Dyer.
455 "an exceptional endowment": Quoted in Abdoul, p. 92.
455 "I am essentially a folk song singer": Ibid., p. 94.
456 "crooked folklore": Quoted in Story, p. 67.
456 "I knew he was big on Broadway": Quoted in *Modern Maturity*, June–July 1983.
457 "pint-sized and serious": Quoted in Story, p. 77.
458 "Her voice is a miracle": Ibid., p. 79.

458 "She proved that she had virtually everything": Ibid., p. 81.

458 "immature vocally": Ibid., p. 77.

459 "she may well become": Ibid., p. 88.

459 "rich and round mezzo voice": Ibid., p. 85.

459 "Already she is one of the great Butterflys": Ibid., p. 75.

460 "the greatest ovation": Quoted in *The New Yorker*, October 26, 1957.

460 "a role which I had never sung": London, p. 35.

461 "You dog": Ibid., p. 35.

461 "After the third act": *The New Yorker*, October 26, 1957.

462 "a young tenor by the name of Mario Lanza": London, p. 30.

463 "Last night [London] took his place": Quoted in *The New Yorker*, October 25, 1957.

464 "could tell that some high notes": London, p. 160.

464 "When I sing": Ibid., p. 169.

464 "George London?": 1997 brochure of the George London Foundation for Singers, Inc.

465 "It is impossible for anyone": Quoted in the notes to Angel LP 35861.

465 "Suddenly I was interviewed five times a day": Quoted in *Opera Monthly*, September 1990.

466 "If I had known": Ibid.

466 "I did an average of twelve new roles": Ibid.

468 "It's just that somebody": *New York Times*, May 15, 1977.

468 "And of course, I'm still going to sing": *Opera Monthly*, September 1990.

469 "the most successful dramatic tenor": *New York Times*, May 1, 1988.

469 "If I don't become a fine singing actor": Quoted in *Opera News*, December 14, 1953.

469 "in one of the world's great opera houses": Quoted in *Ovation*, September 1985.

471 "They were shaky times": Quoted in Jacobson, p. 232.

471 "Our world was at rock bottom": Ibid.

471 "Our secret was that we never said no": Ibid., p. 233.

472 "I almost dropped dead": Ibid., p. 111.

472 "one of the supreme achievements": Elisabeth Schwarzkopf to Paul Hume in the *Washington Post*, May 23, 1965.

472 "Evelyn Lear, biting the hands that fed her": Rorem, *AG*, p. 162.

475 "Are you a citizen": Giorgio Tozzi's artist's questionnaire in the Metropolitan Opera Archives.

INTERLUDE FIVE

Unless otherwise indicated, all quotes in this chapter are taken from Scott, *MMC*.

479 "Lay off me": Jellinek, p. 283.

481 "Good material": Callas's audition card in the Metropolitan Opera Archives.

481 "saw that she was down and out": Meneghini, p. 21.

483 "wand slim": *Chicago Tribune*, November 2, 1954.
483 "After having heard Miss Callas": *Opera*, March 1955.
484 "I can give you nothing": Quoted in Evangelia Callas: *My Daughter Maria Callas*, p. 141.
484 "Among Americans conditioned to a belief": Kolodin, p. 576.
485 "Each day": Di Stefano in the film documentary *Maria Callas, Life and Art* by Tony Palmer.

CHAPTER TWENTY-THREE

Unless otherwise indicated, all quotes in this chapter concerning Beverly Sills are taken from her autobiography.

493 "If they blame me for it": Massenet, pp. 175–76.
496 "We finally accepted the fact": Bing, *5NO*, pp. 300–1.
496 "I simply did not care very much for her": Bing, *KO*, p. 65.
497 "*Thaïs* is a pretty opera": *The New Yorker*, February 6, 1978.
497 "found it hard to decide": *The Gramophone*, July, 1996, p. 104.
498 "Bitterness is a useless condition": Quoted in *New York Times*, May 14, 1972.
499 "We saved the City Opera": Ibid.
499 "a company full of wonderful individuals": Quoted in *Opera News*, November 1990.
499 "Rudolf Bing enjoyed me": Ibid.
499 "you'll never sing Tosca": Quoted in *New York Times*, May 14, 1972.
500 "Throughout my entire singing career": Quoted in *Opera News*, November 1990.
501 world's finest exponent of the role: Pointed out in Sokol, p. 174.
501 "Norman turned in the most extraordinary": Sills, p. 242.
502 "this brilliantly talented, tortured man": Ibid., p. 244.
504 "That high C was for Harold C. Schonberg!": Author's memory of the occasion.
504 "When the audience understands": Quoted in *Opera News*, November 1990.
505 "The result is satisfying to the point of tears": Rorem, *FD*, p. 315.
505 "Ma, chi è questa donna?": Notes to Testament Farrell recital CD SBT 1073.
506 Her scale was as seamless as Nordica's: Ibid.
506 "I just sang": Ibid.
507 "Ah, I see that Pippers": Sills, p. 179.
507 "Look, maybe I had some kind of gift": Quoted in liner notes to Testament Farrell recital CD SBT 1073.
508 "So far as my own music went": Rorem, *ST*, p. 263.
508 "an artist right off the top shelf": Quoted in Rorem, *KWS*, p. 345.
509 "Her handsome appearance": Rorem, *KWS*, p. 344.
509 "Who besides a few old acquaintances": Ibid.
511 "She can 'tune' a timbre": *High Fidelity*, August 1971.

CHAPTER TWENTY-FOUR

515 "My name, whatever it is": Quoted in *New York Times*, October 15, 1961.
515 "At last we have heard the true Aida": Ibid.
515 "she knows only the surface of the role": Quoted in Davis, *OC*, p. 256.
516 "My career was simultaneous": Quoted in *New York Times*, September 16, 1973.
517 "rather tentative": Ibid., April 2, 1962.
518 "Of the two most beautiful voices": *New York World-Telegram and Sun*, April 23, 1964.
519 "All my life, great singing has knocked me out": Horne, p. 111.
519 "This is a hot 'New Act' ": *Variety*, September 23, 1970.
519 "It's this peculiar darkness of my voice": Quoted in *Opera News*, February 14, 1981.
520 "Vennard is incredible for building the low voice": *New York Times*, January 17, 1971.
520 "I'm a throwback to another age": Quoted in *Opera News*, February 14, 1981.
521 "You *must* come over here": Quoted in *New York Times*, January 17, 1971.
521 "With Amneris, I have to compensate": Quoted in *Opera News*, February 14, 1981.
522 "That voice, it is to *die*": Quoted in *New York Times*, January 17, 1971.
522 "My voice is an extension": Quoted in *Opera News*, December 9, 1989.
523 "I've ruined my career over forty times": Quoted in *Opera News*, December 2, 1978.
524 "I gave Bing my note": Ibid.
524 "I always had gone to Mr. Bing": Ibid.
524 "it was an overnight success story": Ibid.
524 "wanted me to give it all up": Ibid.
524 "it was Rudolf Bing": Ibid.
525 "the cry of those thousands of women": Quoted in *Opera News*, December 9, 1989.
526 "The day of the ad man has taken over": Quoted in *Opera News*, March 16, 1974.
527 "It's a great privilege": Quoted in *Opera News*, March 1, 1986.
527 "When you've got a big voice": Quoted in *Ovation*, October 1986.
528 "I believe Benjamin Britten": Quoted in *Opera*, August 1984.
528 "that a human being": Quoted in *Saturday Review*, March 18, 1978.
530 "Sherrill Milnes is an Italian baritone": *New York Times*, January 14, 1979.
531 "I try to divide my time": Quoted in *Opera News*, January 1, 1977.
531 "this tremendous gap": Quoted in undated and unidentified clipping from article on Milnes by Conrad L. Osborne in Metropolitan Opera Archives.
532 "It may sound crass": Quoted in *Opera News*, January 1, 1977.
533 "to manage at least acceptably": Bing *5NO*, p. 201.
534 "Certainly as I sat there": *Boston Globe*, February 11, 1979.

534 "She was a sensation": Quoted in *Opera News*, November 1985.
534 "Few artists have survived": Bing, *5NO*, p. 160.
536 MARTINA ARROYO LOOKS LIKE: Undated and unidentified clipping in the Metropolitan Opera Archives.
536 "I'm the other one": Overheard backstage at the Met by the author, circa 1965.
536 "But Mr. Bing, my mother couldn't even see me": Quoted in *Jet*, May 4, 1967.
537 "I was pushing a *career* then": Quoted in *Opera News*, October 1981.
538 "Miss Verrett still hovers on the very edge": *New York Times*, January 30, 1977.
539 "Shirley, don't ever let them talk you into being a soprano": Quoted in *Opera*, July 1973.
540 "I have been lucky": Quoted in *Opera News*, January 30, 1971.

CHAPTER TWENTY-FIVE

542 more a set of behavioral patterns: *Opera News*, July 1991.
542 "Honestly, I don't know": Quoted in *Opera News*, February 2, 1991.
544 "This was supposed to be a golden age": Lebrecht, p. 284.
545 "a very well put together fake": Quoted in Mayer, p. 136.
549 "A want of really distinctive individuality": *Gramophone*, May 1996.
550 "I went in green": Quoted in *Opera News*, July 1988.
550 "the reigning dramatic mezzo": This and all subsequent Zajick quotes are from *Opera News*, March 2, 1996.
551 "what really turned me on": Quoted in *Opera News*, December 3, 1977.
551 "a high-strung loner": *Opera News*, January 21, 1984.
555 "When you try to make yourself": Quoted in *Opera News*, March 30, 1991.
557 "an outrageously affected": *Opera News*, February 18, 1984.
557 "The critic's legitimate question": Ibid.
558 Old-fashioned diva temperament: The tales of Kathleen Battle's strange antics, on and offstage, were legion in the business before her dismissal from the Metropolitan. After that, journalists began printing them nonstop. "Battle Royal" by Annalyn Swan in *Vanity Fair*, May 1994, is one of the most thorough documentations.

POSTLUDE

561 "Good money, eh?": Quoted in *New York Times*, March 24, 1996.
561 "There is nothing left for us to do": Quoted in Sills, p. 247.
562 "When I was young": Radio interview in Dallas, 1960, with John Ardoin, reproduced on Eklipse CD EKR 55.
565 "could probably sing the hell out of Charlotte in *Werther*": Quoted in *Opera News*, July 1996.
566 "I didn't sing for nine months": Quoted in *Opera News*, August 1991.
567 "She started singing": Quoted in *Opera News*, November 1996.

567 "The poise and centeredness": Ibid.

567 "voluptuous, keenly articulated singing": *Opera*, festivals issue, 1996.

568 "I'm in the business of soaring": Quoted in *Opera News*, November 1996.

568 "I don't want to be Flicka's lover": Quoted in *Ovation*, May 1983.

568 "He set to work on my bad habits": Quoted in *Opera*, January 1980.

569 "a Cherubino more breathlessly young": Quoted in *Opera*, January 1980.

569 "From the beginning": Quoted in *Opera News*, April 1, 1995.

571 "I'm mad about Monteverdi": Quoted in *Ovation*, October 1986.

571 "the sort of complete openness": *Opera*, June 1996.

571 "a tremendously normal childhood": Hampson quoted in ibid.

571 "Young man, God made you a singer": Quoted in ibid.

572 "It's frustrating and overwhelming": Quoted in *Opera News*, February 4, 1989.

572 "If you could make $8,000 a night": Quoted in ibid.

573 "I know what's important to me": Quoted in ibid.

573 "See, you *can* have it all!": Quoted in *Musical America*, January 1991.

574 "that singing should express the experience of life": Quoted in ibid.

575 "in the act of singing": Steber, p. 203.

Bibliography

Abdoul, Raul. *Blacks in Classical Music*. New York: Dodd, Mead, 1977.

Albani, Emma. *Forty Years of Song*. London: Mills & Boon, 1911.

Alda, Frances. *Men, Women and Tenors*. Boston: Houghton Mifflin, 1937.

Aldrich, Richard. *Concert Life in New York*. New York: Putnam, 1941; reprinted by Books for Libraries (Freeport, N.Y.), 1971.

Aloi, Richard. *My Remembrances of Rosa Ponselle*. New York: Vantage, 1994.

The American History and Encyclopedia of Music: Musical Biographies. Vols. 1 and 2. Compiled by Janet Green; edited by W. L. Hubbard. New York: Irving Square, 1908.

Anderson, Marian. *My Lord, What a Morning: An Autobiography*. New York: Viking, 1956.

Annals of the Metropolitan Opera: The Complete Chronicle of Performances and Artists: Chronology 1883–1985. Edited by Gerald Fitzgerald. Boston: Hall, 1989.

Armstrong, W. G. *A Record of the Opera in Philadelphia*. Philadelphia: Porter & Coates, 1884.

Barnum, P. T. *Struggles and Triumphs: or, The Life of P. T. Barnum*. Edited by George S. Bryan. New York: Knopf, 1927.

Bauer, Roberto. *Historical Records, 1898–1908/9*. London: Sidgwick & Jackson, 1947.

Benoist, André. *The Accompanist . . . and Friends: An Autobiography of André Benoist*. Neptune City, N.J.: Paganiniana, 1978.

Biancolli, Louis. *The Flagstad Manuscript*. New York: Putnam, 1952.

Bing, Sir Rudolf. *5000 Nights at the Opera*. New York: Doubleday, 1972.

———. *A Knight at the Opera*. New York: Putnam, 1981.

Bispham, David. *A Quaker Singer's Recollections*. New York: Macmillan, 1920.

Brown, Horatio F. *John Addington Symonds: A Biography*. New York: Scribners, 1895.

Buffington, Judith. *He Loves Me When I Sing: Remembering Eleanor Steber*. Eastham, Mass.: Judith Buffington, 1993.

Bulman, Joan. *Jenny Lind*. London: Barrie, 1956.

Bushnell, Howard. *Maria Malibran*. University Park, Pa.: Pennsylvania State University Press, 1979.

Calvé, Emma. *My Life*. Translated by Rosamon Gilder. New York: Appleton, 1922.

Carner, Mosco. *Puccini: A Critical Biography*. 2nd ed. London: Duckworth, 1974.

Cather, Willa. "Three American Singers: Louise Homer, Geraldine Farrar, Olive Fremstad," *McClure's Magazine*, Vol. 42, No. 2, December 1913.

Chase, Gilbert. *America's Music from the Pilgrims to the Present*. 2nd ed., rev. New York: McGraw-Hill, 1955.

Chorley, Henry. *Thirty Years' Musical Recollections.* Edited by Ernest Newman. New York: Knopf, 1926; reprinted by Vienna House (New York), 1972.

Christiansen, Rupert. *Prima Donna: A History.* New York: Viking, 1985.

Conati, Marcello. *Encounters with Verdi.* Ithaca, N.Y.: Cornell University Press, 1984.

Cone, John Frederick. *Adelina Patti: Queen of Hearts.* Portland, Oreg.: Amadeus, 1993.

———. *Oscar Hammerstein's Manhattan Opera Company.* Norman: University of Oklahoma Press, 1964.

Corsaro, Frank. *Maverick: A Director's Personal Experience in Opera and Theater.* New York: Vanguard, 1978.

Crichton, Kyle. *Subway to the Met: Risë Stevens' Story.* New York: Doubleday, 1959.

Cushing, Mary Watkins. *The Rainbow Bridge.* New York: Putnam, 1954.

Damrosch, Walter. *My Musical Life.* New York: Scribners, 1926.

Davenport, Marcia. *Too Strong for Fantasy.* New York: Scribners, 1967.

Davis, Ronald L. *A History of Opera in the American West.* Englewood Cliffs, N.J.: Prentice-Hall, 1965.

———. *Opera in Chicago.* New York. Appleton-Century, 1966.

Delany, Martin Robison. *The Condition, Elevation, and Destiny of the Colored People of the United States.* Philadelphia: published by the author, 1852; reprinted by Ayer (Salem, N.H.), 1988.

Dizikes, John. *Opera in America: A Cultural History.* New Haven: Yale University Press, 1993.

Dougan, Michael B. "An American Tragedy," *Opera News,* July 1984.

Drake, James A. *Richard Tucker, A Biography.* New York: Dutton, 1984.

Dwight's Journal of Music. Edited by John Sullivan Dwight. Boston, 1852–81. Reprinted by Johnson Reprint (New York) and Arno (New York), 1967.

Eames, Emma. *Some Memories and Reflections.* New York: Appleton, 1927.

Eaton, Quaintance. *The Boston Opera Company.* New York: Appleton-Century, 1965; reprinted by Da Capo (New York), 1980.

———. *The Miracle of the Met: An Informal History of the Metropolitan Opera 1883–1967.* New York: Meredith, 1968; reprinted by Da Capo (New York), 1978.

———. *Opera Caravan: Adventures of the Metropolitan on Tour, 1883–1956.* New York: Metropolitan Opera Guild, 1957; reprinted by Da Capo (New York), 1978.

Eisler, Paul E. *The Metropolitan Opera: The First Twenty-Five Years, 1883–1908.* Croton-on-Hudson, N.Y.: North River, 1984.

Elson, Louis C. *The History of American Music.* New York: Macmillan, 1925.

Emmons, Shirlee. *Tristanissimo: The Authorized Biography of Heroic Tenor Lauritz Melchior.* New York: Schirmer Books, 1990.

Faner, Robert D. *Walt Whitman & Opera.* Philadelphia: University of Pennsylvania Press, 1951.

Farkas, Andrew, ed. *Lawrence Tibbett: Singing Actor.* Portland, Oreg.: Amadeus, 1988.

Farrar, Geraldine. *Geraldine Farrar: The Story of an American Singer.* Boston: Houghton Mifflin, 1916.

————. *Such Sweet Compulsion.* New York: Greystone, 1938; reprinted by Da Capo (New York), 1970.

Field, George T. *Memories of Many Men and Some Women.* New York: Houghton Mifflin, 1931.

Finck, Henry T. *My Adventures in the Golden Age of Music.* New York: Funk and Wagnalls, 1926; reprinted by Da Capo (New York), 1970.

Garden, Mary, and Biancolli, Louis. *Mary Garden's Story.* New York: Simon & Schuster, 1951.

Gatti-Casazza, Giulio. *Memories of the Opera.* New York: Fifth Avenue Bank of New York, 1941; reprinted by Vienna House (New York), 1973.

Gipson, Richard McCandless. *The Life of Emma Thursby, 1845–1931.* New York: New-York Historical Society, 1940; reprinted by Da Capo (New York), 1980.

Glackens, Ira. *Yankee Diva: Lillian Nordica and the Golden Days of Opera.* New York: Coleridge, 1963.

Groover, David, and Conner, C. C. *Skeletons from the Opera Closet: An Irreverent Appreciation.* New York: St. Martin's, 1986.

Hanslick, Eduard. *Vienna's Golden Years of Music, 1850–1900.* Translated by Henry Pleasants. New York: Simon & Schuster, 1950.

Harding, James. *Massenet.* New York: St. Martin's, 1970.

Hauk, Minnie. *Memories of a Singer.* London: Philpot, 1925.

Helm, MacKinley. *Angel Mo' and Her Son, Roland Hayes.* Boston: Little, Brown, 1942.

Henderson, W. J. *The Art of Singing.* New York: Dial, 1938; reprinted by Da Capo (New York), 1978.

Henschel, Sir George. *Musings and Memories of a Musician.* New York: Macmillan, 1919; reprinted by Da Capo (New York), 1979.

Heylbut, Rose, and Gerber, Aime. *Backstage at the Opera.* New York: Crowell, 1937.

Hines, Jerome. *Great Singers on Great Singing.* New York: Doubleday, 1982; reprinted by Limelight Editions (New York), 1984.

Hitchcock, H. Wiley. *Music in the United States: A Historical Introduction.* Englewood Cliffs, N.J.: Prentice-Hall, 1969.

Holland, Henry Scott, and Rockstro, W. S. *Jenny Lind the Artist, 1820–1851.* London: Clowes, 1893.

Homer, Anne. *Louise Homer and the Golden Age of Opera.* New York: Morrow, 1974.

Homer, Sidney. *My Wife and I: The Story of Louise and Sidney Homer.* Macmillan, 1939; reprinted by Da Capo (New York), 1978.

Horgan, Paul. *Tracings: A Book of Partial Portraits.* New York: Farrar, Straus & Giroux, 1993.

Horne, Marilyn (with Jane Scovell). *Marilyn Horne, My Life.* New York: Atheneum, 1983.

Horowitz, Joseph. *Wagner Nights: An American History*. Berkeley: University of California Press, 1994.

Howard, John Tasker. *Our American Music: A Comprehensive History from 1620 to the Present*. 4th ed. New York: Crowell, 1929, 1965.

Hurok, Sol (with Ruth Goode). *Impresario*. New York: Random House, 1946.

Irvine, Demar. *Massenet: A Chronicle of His Life and Times*. Portland, Oreg.: Amadeus, 1992.

Jackson, Paul. *Saturday Afternoons at the Old Met*. Portland, Oreg.: Amadeus, 1992.

Jacobson, Robert. *Reverberations: Interviews with the World's Leading Musicians*. New York: Morrow, 1974.

Jellinek, George. *Callas: Portrait of a Prima Donna*. New York: Dover, 1986.

Johnson, H. Earle. *Musical Interludes in Boston, 1795–1830*. New York: Columbia University Press, 1943; reprinted by AMS (New York), 1967.

Jones, F. O. *A Handbook of American Music and Musicians*. Canaseraga, N.Y.: F. O. Jones, 1886; reprinted by Da Capo (New York), 1971.

Kellogg, Clara Louise. *Memoirs of an American Prima Donna*. New York: Putnam, 1913; reprinted by Da Capo (New York), 1978.

Kirsten, Dorothy. *A Time to Sing*. New York: Doubleday, 1982.

Klein, Herman. *The Golden Age of Opera*. London: Routledge, 1933.

———. *Great Women Singers of My Time*. London: Routledge, 1931.

———. *Musicians and Mummers*. London: Cassel, 1925.

———. *The Reign of Patti*. New York: Century, 1920.

———. *Thirty Years of Musical Life in London: 1870–1900*. New York: Century, 1920; reprinted by Da Capo (New York), 1978.

Kobler, John. *Otto the Magnificent: The Life of Otto Kahn*. New York: Scribners, 1988.

Kolodin, Irving. *The Metropolitan Opera, 1883–1966: A Candid History*. New York: Knopf, 1966.

Krehbiel, Henry Edward. *Chapters of Opera, Being Historical and Critical Observations and Records Concerning the Lyric Drama in New York from its Earliest Days Down to the Present Time*. New York: Holt, 1909; reprinted by Da Capo (New York), 1980.

———. *More Chapters of Opera, Being Historical and Critical Observations and Records Concerning the Lyric Drama in New York from 1908 to 1918*. New York: Holt, 1919.

Kutsch, Karl J., and Riemens, Leo. *Grosses Sängerlexikon*. 2 vols. Bern: Francke, 1987.

———. *Grosses Sängerlexikon, Ergänzungsband*. Bern: Francke, 1991.

———. *Grosses Sängerlexikon, Ergänzungsband II*. Bern: Saur, 1994.

Lahee, Henry C. *Famous Singers of To-Day and Yesterday*. Boston: Page, 1898.

———. *Grand Opera in America*. Boston: Page, 1902.

———. *Grand Opera Singers of To-Day*. Boston: Page, 1912.

Lauw, Louisa. *Fourteen Years with Adelina Patti*. Translated by Jeremiah Loder. New York: Norman L. Munro, 1884; reprinted by La Scala Autographs, 1977.

Lawrence, Edward. *A Fragrance of Violets: The Life and Times of Emma Eames.* New York: Vantage, 1973.

Lawrence, Vera Brodsky. *Strong on Music: The New York Scene in the Days of George Templeton Strong, 1836–1875, Vol. 1: Resonances, 1836–1850.* New York: Oxford University Press, 1988.

Lebrecht, Norman. *When the Music Stops . . . Managers, Maestros, and the Corporate Murder of Classical Music.* London: Simon & Schuster, 1996.

Lehmann, Lilli. *My Path Through Life.* Translated by Alice Benedict Seligman. New York: Putnam, 1914.

Lehmann, Liza. *The Life of Liza Lehmann.* London: Unwin, 1919.

Leinsdorf, Erich. *Cadenza: A Musical Career.* Boston: Houghton Mifflin, 1976.

Levine, Lawrence W. *Highbrow/Lowbrow: The Emergence of Cultural Hierarchy in America.* Cambridge: Harvard University Press, 1988.

London, Nora. *Aria for George.* New York: Dutton, 1987.

Lowens, Irving. *Music and Musicians in Early America.* New York: Norton, 1964.

Majors, Monroe A. *Noted Negro Women: Their Triumphs and Activities.* Chicago: Donohue & Henneberry, 1893; reprinted by Ayer (Salem, N.H.), 1986.

Mapleson, James Henry. *The Mapleson Memoirs.* Edited by Harold Rosenthal. London: Remington, 1888; reprinted by Appleton-Century (New York), 1966.

Marchesi, Blanche. *A Singer's Pilgrimage.* Boston: Small, Maynard, 1923.

Marchesi, Mathilde. *Marchesi and Music: Passages from the Life of a Famous Singing Teacher.* New York: Harper, 1898.

Martens, Frederick. *The Art of the Prima Donna.* New York: Appleton, 1923.

Martin, George. *Verdi at the Golden Gate: Opera and San Francisco in the Gold Rush Days.* Berkeley: University of California Press, 1993.

Martin, Sadie E. *The Life and Professional Career of Emma Abbott.* Minneapolis: Kimball, 1891.

Massenet, Jules. *My Recollections.* Translated by H. Villiers Barnett. Boston: Small, Maynard, 1919.

Mathews, W. S. B. *A Hundred Years of Music in America.* Chicago, 1889; reprinted AMS (New York), 1970.

Mattfield, Julius. *A Hundred Years of Opera in New York.* New York: New York Public Library, 1927.

Matz, Mary Jane. *The Many Lives of Otto Kahn.* New York: Macmillan, 1963.

Maude, Mrs. Raymond. *The Life of Jenny Lind.* London: Cassell, 1926.

Mayer, Martin. *The Met: One Hundred Years of Grand Opera.* New York: Simon & Schuster, 1983.

McArthur, Edwin. *Flagstad: A Personal Memoir.* New York: Knopf, 1965.

McGovern, Dennis, and Winer, Deborah Grace. *I Remember Too Much: 89 Opera Stars Speak Candidly of Their Work, Their Lives, and Their Colleagues.* New York: Morrow, 1990.

Melba, Nellie. *Melodies and Memories.* New York: Doran, 1926.

Meneghini, Giovanni Battista. *My Wife Maria Callas.* Translated by Henry Wisneski. New York: Farrar, Straus & Giroux, 1982.

Mercer, Ruby. *The Tenor of His Time: Edward Johnson of the Met.* Toronto/Vancouver: Clarke, Irwin, 1976.

Merrill, Robert (with Sandford Dody). *Once More from the Beginning.* New York: Macmillan, 1965.

Metropolitan Opera Annals. Edited by William Seltsam. New York: Wilson, 1947. *First Supplement: 1947–1957,* 1957; *Second Supplement: 1957–1966,* 1966.

Moore, Edward C. *Forty Years of Opera in Chicago.* New York: Liveright, 1930.

Moore, Grace. *You're Only Human Once.* New York: Garden City Publishing Co., 1944.

The New Grove Dictionary of American Music. Edited by Stanley Sadie and H. Wiley Hitchcock. 4 vols. London: Macmillan, 1986.

The New Grove Dictionary of Opera. Edited by Stanley Sadie. 4 vols. London: Macmillan, 1992.

Noble, Helen. *Life with the Met.* New York: Putnam, 1954.

Notable American Women, 1607–1950: A Biographical Dictionary. 4 vols. Edited by Edward T. James. Cambridge: Belknap Press of Harvard University Press, 1971.

O'Connell, Charles. *The Other Side of the Record.* New York: Knopf, 1947.

O'Connor, Garry. *The Pursuit of Perfection: A Life of Maggie Teyte.* Southampton, England: Camelot, 1979.

Odell, George C. D. *Annals of the New York Stage.* 15 vols. New York: Columbia University Press, 1927–49.

Pahlen, Kurt. *Great Singers from the Seventeenth Century to the Present Day.* Translated by Oliver Coburn. New York: Stein & Day, 1974.

Peerce, Jan (with Alan Levy). *The Bluebird of Happiness: The Memoirs of Jan Peerce.* New York: Harper & Row, 1976.

Perkins, Charles C., and Dwight, John S. *History of the Handel and Haydn Society of Boston, Massachusetts, Vol. 1: From the Foundation of the Society Through Its Seventy-Fifth Season: 1815–1890.* Boston: Mudge, 1883–93; reprinted by Da Capo (New York), 1977.

Pinza, Ezio (with Robert Magidoff). *Ezio Pinza: An Autobiography.* New York: Rinehart, 1958.

Pleasants, Henry. *The Great Singers: From the Dawn of Opera to Our Own Time.* New York: Simon & Schuster, 1966.

Ponselle, Rosa (with James A. Drake). *Ponselle: A Singer's Life.* New York: Doubleday, 1982.

Pougin, Arthur. *Marie Malibran: The Story of a Great Singer.* London: Eveleigh Nash, 1911.

Rasponi, Lanfranco. *The Last Prima Donnas.* New York: Knopf, 1982.

Ritter, Frédéric Louis. *Music in America.* New York, 1890; reprinted by Johnson Reprint (New York), 1970.

Robinson, Harlow. *The Last Impresario: The Life, Times, and Legacy of Sol Hurok.* New York: Viking, 1994.

Ronald, Landon. *Variations on a Personal Theme.* London: Hodder & Stoughton, 1922.

Rorem, Ned. *An Absolute Gift.* New York: Simon & Schuster, 1978.
———. *The Final Diary.* New York: Holt, Rinehart & Winston, 1974.
———. *Knowing When to Stop.* New York: Simon & Schuster, 1994.
———. *Setting the Tone.* New York: Coward-McCann, 1983.
Rosenthal, Harold. *Two Centuries of Opera at Covent Garden.* London: Putnam, 1958.
Rosselli, John. *Singers of Italian Opera: The History of a Profession.* Cambridge, England: Cambridge University Press, 1992.
Sachs, Harvey. *Toscanini.* New York: Lippincott, 1978; reprinted by Da Capo (New York), 1981.
Schoen-René, Anna Eugenie. *America's Musical Inheritance.* New York: Putnam, 1941.
Schwarzkopf, Elisabeth. *On and Off the Record: A Memoir of Walter Legge.* New York: Scribners, 1982.
Scott, Michael. *The Great Caruso.* New York: Knopf, 1988.
———. *Maria Meneghini Callas.* Boston: Northeastern University Press, 1991.
———. *The Record of Singing—Volume 1: To 1914.* London: Duckworth, 1977.
———. *The Record of Singing—Volume 2: 1914 to 1925.* London: Duckworth, 1979.
Shaw, George Bernard. *Shaw's Music: The Complete Musical Criticism in Three Volumes.* London: Bodley Head, 1981.
Sills, Beverly (with Lawrence Linderman). *Beverly: An Autobiography.* New York: Bantam Books, 1987.
Sokol, Martin. *The New York City Opera: An American Adventure.* New York: Macmillan, 1981.
Sonneck, O. G. *Early Concert-Life in America.* Leipzig: Brietkopf & Härtel, 1907; reprinted by Da Capo (New York), 1978.
———. *Early Opera in America.* New York: Schirmer, 1915.
Southern, Eileen. *The Music of Black Americans.* New York: Norton, 1971; 3rd ed., 1997.
———. *Readings in Black American Music.* New York: Norton, 1971.
Steane, J. B. *The Grand Tradition: Seventy Years of Singing on Record.* London: Duckworth, 1974; 2nd ed., Amadeus (Portland, Oreg.), 1993.
Steber, Eleanor (with Macia Sloat). *Eleanor Steber: An Autobiography.* Ridgewood, N.J.: Wordsworth, 1992.
Story, Rosalyn M. *And So I Sing: African-American Divas of Opera and Concert.* New York: Amistad, 1990.
Strang, Lewis C. *Famous Stars of Light Opera.* Boston: Page, 1900.
———. *Prima Donnas and Soubrettes of Light Opera and Musical Comedy in America.* Boston: Page, 1900.
Street, Richard. *The Perils of Pauline.* St. Louis, Mo.: Opera Theatre of Saint Louis Nineteenth Season Program Book, 1994.
Thompson, Oscar. *The American Singer: A Hundred Years of Success in Opera.* New York: Dial, 1937; reprinted by Johnson Reprint (New York), 1969.
Traubel, Helen. *St. Louis Woman.* New York: Duel, Solan & Pearce, 1959.
Truxall, Aida Craig, ed. *All Good Greetings: Letters of Geraldine Farrar to Ilka Marie Stotler, 1946–1958.* Pittsburgh: University of Pittsburgh Press, 1991.

Tuggle, Robert. *The Golden Age of Opera*. New York: Holt, Rinehart & Winston, 1983.

Varnay, Astrid (with Donald Arthur). *50 Years in 5 Acts: Memoirs of an Operatic Career*. Unpublished manuscript, 1995.

Vehanen, Kosti. *Marian Anderson: A Portrait*. Westport, Conn.: Greenwood, 1941.

Wagenknecht, Edward. *Jenny Lind*. Boston: Houghton Mifflin, 1931.

Ware, W. Porter, and Lockard, Thaddeus C., Jr. *P. T. Barnum Presents Jenny Lind: The American Tour of the Swedish Nightingale*. Baton Rouge: Louisiana State University Press, 1980.

Weinstock, Herbert. *Rossini*. New York: Knopf, 1968.

Werner, M. R. *Barnum*. New York: Harcourt, Brace, 1923.

Wood, Henry J. *My Life of Music*. London: Gollancz, 1938; reprinted by Books for Libraries (Freeport, N.Y.), 1971.

Index

Abbott, Emma, 2, 68, 70–76, 125, 198, 262, 342, 488

Abduction from the Seraglio, The. See Entführung aus dem Serail, Die

Adams, Charles R., 104–6, 131, 151

Adams, Suzanne, 191–92, 198

Adriana Lecouvreur, 281

Africaine, L', 100, 133, 273

Africana, L'. See Africaine, L'

Aida, 65, 66, 137, 148, 154, 216, 236, 269, 270, 273, 279, 302, 363, 366, 368, 428, 451, 452, 459, 460, 468, 470, 517, 518, 538

Aiglon, L', 301

Albani, Emma, 68, 82–86, 138, 292, 293

Alceste, 433

Alda, Frances, 176, 197, 199, 220, 221, 298, 303, 310, 311, 312

Almanach de Gotha, 47

Amante Astuto, L', 12

Amara, Lucine, 448, 533–34

Amica, 254

Amore dei Tre Re, L', 236, 269, 347, 364

Ancêtre, L', 254

Ancona, Mario, 128

Anderson, June, 544, 548

Anderson, Marian, 2, 286, 322, 335–40, 394, 454, 459

Andrea Chénier, 273, 303, 315, 408, 434, 492

Aphrodite, 226, 234

Arabella, 408, 463

Arabi nelle Gallie, Gli, 18

Arditi, Luigi, 47, 61

Ariane et Barbe-Bleue, 258

Armide, 169

Arnoult, Émilie, 41, 104

Arroyo, Martina, 448, 535–36

Artaxerxes, 19

Artôt, Désirée, 93

Ascanio, 155

Assedio di Corinto, L', 20, 39, 497

Auber, Daniel-François-Esprit, 40, 88, 90, 92, 253, 254

Augér, Arleen, 563–64

Balfe, Michael, 63, 75

Ballad of Baby Doe, The, 100, 504

Ballester, Vincente, 303

Ballo in Maschera, Un, 44, 57, 209, 310, 314, 340, 420, 423, 434, 504, 530, 534

Bampton, Rose, 368

Barber, Samuel, 400, 408, 411, 517, 536

Barbiere di Siviglia, Il, 8, 9, 10, 12, 14, 49, 104, 122, 173, 184, 320, 437

Barbirolli, John, 292, 376

Barrientos, Maria, 294

Batson, Flora, 329

Battle, Kathleen, 557–59, 575

Beardslee, Bethany, 294, 510

Beecham, Sir Thomas, 194, 342, 372, 392, 535
Belari, Emilio, 131
Belasco, David, 247
Bellezza, Vincenzo, 361
Bellini, Vincenzo, 3, 9, 18, 23, 26, 31, 50, 275, 395
Benedict, Sir Julius, 32, 109
Bentonelli, Joseph, 366
Benzell, Mimi, 398
Berberian, Cathy, 509–10
Bergonzi, Carlo, 424
Berlioz, Hector, 9, 100, 256, 395, 400, 413
Bernstein, Leonard, 19, 430
Bertucca, Appolonia, 131
Bing, Rudolf, 19, 340, 353, 373, 377, 383, 390, 393, 396, 397, 399, 402, 405, 406, 407, 408, 410, 414, 428, 430, 435, 440, 441, 444, 446, 448, 451, 463, 467, 482, 484, 494, 507, 514, 524, 538, 580
Biscaccianti, Eliza, 22–27, 42, 579
Bishop, Anna, 29
Bispham, David, 2, 103–4, 109–17, 145, 171, 192, 308, 313, 316, 573
Bizet, Georges, 65, 93, 95, 240
Bjoerling, Jussi, 429, 507
Blake, Rockwell, 553
Blass, Robert, 157, 192, 201
Bodanya, Natalie, 366
Bodanzky, Artur, 116
Boghetti, Giuseppe, 420
Bohème, La, 242, 244–45, 254, 342, 345, 347, 350, 366, 420, 451, 467, 468
Bohemian Girl, The, 63, 75, 76, 110, 189, 196, 535
Böhm, Karl, 444, 460
Bohnen, Michael, 352
Boito, Arrigo, 243

Bonci, Alessandro, 157, 242
Bonelli, Richard, 320, 366, 406, 439, 446
Bonynge, Richard, 271, 519, 520, 521
Booth, Edwin, 110
Bordogni, Giulio, 46
Bori, Lucrezia, 199, 220, 261, 276, 300, 303, 365, 437
Boris Godunov, 303, 313, 368, 446, 455
Bos, Coenraad, 376
Bouhy, Jacques, 293
Boyce, William, 459
Brandt, Marianne, 106
Braslau, Sophie, 300
Brewer, Christine, 413
Brice, Carol, 459
Briel, Joseph, 272
Brignoli, Pasquale, 130
Bristol, Frederick, 171
Britten, Benjamin, 19, 475, 528, 554
Broadfoot, Eleanor, 214
Broccolini, Giovanni, 107–8
Brooklyn Academy of Music, 66, 77, 91, 320
Brooks, Patricia, 502
Brown, Anne, 456
Browning, Lucielle, 366
Brownlee, John, 318
Bruce, Edwin, 104
Bumbry, Grace, 535, 536–38, 549
Burke, Hilda, 366
Busch, Fritz, 372

Caballé, Montserrat, 479, 494, 496
Caldwell, Sarah, 505
Callas, Maria, 62, 168, 223, 282, 355, 408, 428, 430, 434, 443, 444, 466, 472, 478–86, 487, 494, 496, 514, 548
Calvé, Emma, 128, 141, 148, 152,

161, 189, 190, 212, 215, 250, 268, 348, 384
Campanari, Giuseppe, 157, 161
Campanello, Il, 116
Campanini, Cleofonte, 296, 357
Campanini, Italo, 96
Candidus, William, 106
Cantelli, Guido, 453
Caponsacchi, 313, 318
Carmen, 65, 66, 95, 96, 97, 98, 100, 110, 136, 138, 148, 157, 172, 173, 190, 196, 214, 215, 233, 234, 247, 250, 258, 259, 260, 262, 278, 279, 280, 285, 294, 302, 303, 352, 384, 385, 397, 454, 460, 470, 491
Carré, Albert, 222, 223, 232, 279
Carreras, José, 503, 552, 560
Carte, Richard D'Oyly, 112
Caruso, Enrico, 4, 157, 159, 160, 161, 169, 207, 215, 216, 239–45, 254, 255, 256, 257, 259, 264, 265, 269, 272, 276, 281, 287, 298, 299, 362, 426, 429, 430, 479
Cary, Annie Louise, 64, 65, 208–10
Casa da Vendere, La, 18
Case, Anna, 291–92, 300
Casella, Alfredo, 286
Castle, William, 63, 106–7
Cavalleria Rusticana, 162, 214, 269, 456
Cehanovsky, George, 315
Cenerentola, La, 12, 45, 281
Chadwick, George, 212
Chaliapin, Feodor, 157, 302, 313, 359, 462, 479
Chamlee, Mario, 243, 244
Chapin, Edwin, 71, 77
Chapin, Schuyler, 430
Charpentier, Gustave, 222, 258, 347, 388
Chartreuse de Parme, La, 301

Chorley, Henry, 35, 36, 60
Cigna, Gina, 317
Cimarosa, Domenico, 18
Cinti-Damoreau, Laure, 39, 40
Clément, Edmond, 242, 290, 296, 332
Cleopatra's Night, 243
Cléopâtre, 234
Comer, Thomas, 41
Conley, Eugene, 443
Conly, George, 63
Conner, Nadine, 2, 397, 534
Conried, Heinrich, 159, 160, 174, 194, 215, 255, 256
Contes d'Hoffmann, Les, 176, 178, 197, 268, 288, 298, 303, 356, 463, 494, 501, 521, 533
Cookasian, Lili, 282
Cooper, James Fenimore, 47
Cordon, Norman, 366, 392
Corelli, Franco, 410, 424, 430, 505, 524, 552
Corsaro, Frank, 502
Così Fan Tutte, 393, 408, 410, 446, 453, 517, 540
Cossotto, Fiorenza, 465
Cotogni, Antonio, 66
Creation, The, 28, 104
Crimi, Giulio, 272
Crispino e la Comare, 92
Croft, Dwayne, 553
Crooks, Richard, 2, 366–67
Curtin, Phyllis, 452, 492, 493, 495, 498–500, 542
Curtis-Verna, Mary, 533
Cushman, Charlotte, 20–22, 110
Cyrano de Bergerac, 203, 243

Dalis, Irene, 243–44, 476–77
Damnation de Faust, La, 100
Damrosch, Walter, 115, 142, 203, 292, 301, 375
Daniels, David, 565, 577

Danise, Giuseppe, 312, 396
Da Ponte, Lorenzo, 12, 16, 18
Daughter of the Regiment, The. See Fille du Régiment, La
Davis, Ellabelle, 458–59
Davy, Gloria, 539
Debussy, Claude, 202, 220, 224, 225, 228, 230, 365
DeGaetani, Jan, 294, 511–12, 573
De Gogorza, Emilio, 161, 163, 164
Delibes, Léo, 95, 133, 183, 184, 199, 218
Della Casa, Lisa, 452
Delsarte, François, 131
De Luca, Giuseppe, 298, 312, 348, 359
De Lussan, Zélie, 189–91, 202
De Reszke, Édouard, 128, 155, 156, 190
De Reszke, Jean, 112, 128, 129, 137, 139, 141, 142, 144, 147, 155, 156, 190, 212, 214, 240, 241, 250, 285, 288, 299, 301, 320
Destinn, Emmy, 216, 254, 258, 298
Devriès, David, 201
Devriès, Herman, 201
Devriès, Maurice, 201
De Wilhorst, Cora, 49
Dialogues of the Carmelites, 391, 396
Diamants de la Couroune, Les, 90
Didur, Adamo, 303, 311
Dietz, Howard, 393
Di Giuseppe, Enrico, 504
Dippel, Andreas, 160, 257
Diton, Carl, 329
Dobbs, Mattiwilda, 459–60, 539
Domingo, Plácido, 242, 424, 503, 552, 560
Domino Noir, Le, 253, 254
Don Carlo, 254, 273, 434, 437, 445, 447, 533, 536
Don Giovanni, 12, 39, 47, 87, 92, 93,

107, 132, 183, 278, 370, 408, 445, 519, 542
Donizetti, Gaetano, 3, 9, 39, 46, 57, 61, 104, 108, 116, 119, 208, 243, 339
Don Pasquale, 488
Don Quichotte, 287
Dotti, Marie Louise, 199
Duckworth, Kate, 51
Duesing, Dale, 553
Dufranne, Hector, 227
Duncan, Todd, 456, 457
Dunn, Susan, 544, 546
Duprez, Gilbert-Louis, 40
Dupuy, Joseph, 307

Eames, Emma, 2, 85, 113, 128, 147–64, 169, 185, 212, 221, 257, 548, 549
Easton, Florence, 116, 286–88, 300, 533
Ebers, John, 9
Edoardo e Cristina, 20
Elektra, 287
Elias, Rosalind, 448
Elijah, 29
Elisir d'Amore, L', 240, 333
Elman, Mischa, 293
Emperor Jones, The, 313, 455
Endrèze, Arthur. *See* Krackman, Arthur
Enesco, Georges, 286
Engel, Marie, 199
Engelman, Wilfred, 366
Engen, Keith, 450
Enoch Arden, 114
Entführung aus den Serail, Die, 80, 400, 405
Erkel, Ferenc, 94, 144
Ernani, 23, 273, 400, 434, 517, 530
Errani, Achille, 54, 70, 71, 77, 90
Errolle, Ralph, 300, 301
Esclarmonde, 183, 186

Étoile du Nord, L', 91
Eugene Onegin, 447, 517, 533
Evans, George T., 25
Ewing, Maria, 545–46

Fabri, Ludwig, 390
Falstaff, 157, 297, 303, 304, 318,
   370, 433, 446, 452, 453
Fama, La, 42
Fanciulla del West, La, 258, 287, 298,
   306, 392, 408, 429, 516
Fanti, Clementina, 17, 18
Farini, Antonio, 326
Farrar, Geraldine, 2, 82, 101, 149,
   165, 199, 242, 246–63, 269,
   290, 317, 343, 384, 459, 542,
   544, 545, 580
Farrell, Eileen, 505–7
Fauré, Gabriel, 333
Faust, 57, 59, 62, 63, 80, 93, 94,
   110, 134, 135, 137, 151, 157,
   162, 164, 199, 214, 232, 243,
   247, 250, 252, 258, 287, 299,
   304, 356, 410, 443
Favorita, La, 108, 208, 245, 285, 339
Favorite, Le. See Favorita, La
Fedra, 278
Ferne Klang, Der, 287
Feuermann, Emanuel, 293
Fidelio, 287, 420, 443, 481
Figlia dell'Aria, La, 12
*Figlia del Reggimento, La. See Fille du
   Régiment, La*
Fille de Tabarin, La, 225
Fille du Régiment, La, 57, 62, 72, 189,
   287, 396, 407, 450, 460, 488
Films with American opera singers,
   2, 341, 352
   Farrar, Geraldine, 248, 259, 260
   Garden, Mary, 228
   Kirsten, Dorothy, 383, 391
   London, George, 462
   Melton, James, 442

Merrill, Robert, 440, 441
Merriman, Nan, 453
Moore, Grace, 346
Munsel, Patrice, 393
Namara, Marguerite, 299
Peerce, Jan, 422
Pons, Lily, 353
Ponselle, Rosa, 280
Stevens, Risë, 383, 384
Swarthout, Gladys, 356
Thebom, Blanche, 395
Tibbett, Lawrence, 315, 316, 317,
   341–42
Traubel, Helen, 377
White, Carolina, 298
Fisher, Clara, 21
Fisher, Susanne, 366
Fitziu, Anna, 298
Flagstad, Kirsten, 180, 262, 361,
   368, 369, 375, 376, 378, 379,
   380, 382, 383
Fledermaus, Die, 393, 488
Fleming, Renée, 547–48
Fliegende Holländer, Der, 63, 94, 444
Flotow, Friedrich von, 57, 93
*Flying Dutchman, The. See Fliegende
   Höllander, Der*
Foley, Allan James, 107
Fornia, Rita, 258
Forrester, Maureen, 507–8
Forza del Destino, La, 19, 264, 265,
   269, 272, 281, 402, 429, 434,
   505
Fra Diavolo, 90, 92, 93
Françoise de Rimini, 80
Fremstad, Olive, 2, 138, 157, 165–
   81, 205, 206, 207, 216, 224,
   343, 539, 542
Freni, Mirella, 548

Gadski, Johanna, 115, 157, 176,
   179, 180, 214, 235
Galli-Curci, Amelita, 235, 261, 276,

294, 295, 300, 352, 359, 381, 534

García, Manuel, 8, 9, 10, 13, 14

García, Manuel, II, 42, 44, 45, 96, 149, 201, 210

García, María, 8, 9, 12–13, 14. *See also* Malibran, Maria

Garden, Mary, 4, 149, 177, 186, 189, 220–38, 247, 261, 263, 279, 295, 296, 299, 343, 344, 348, 357, 364, 384, 391, 515, 580

Garrison, Mabel, 116, 294–95

Gatti-Casazza, Giulio, 143, 159, 167, 168, 169, 176, 178, 179, 180, 204, 206, 216, 232, 243, 247, 257, 261, 262, 265, 269, 271, 272, 276, 277, 278, 280, 282, 286, 287, 290, 296, 299, 300, 303, 305, 310, 312, 348, 351, 355, 360, 363, 366, 375, 580

Gazza Ladra, La, 17, 90

Gedda, Nicolai, 424, 430

Gericke, Wilhelm, 151

Gerster, Etelka, 97–98

Ghismonda, 234

Giannini, Dusolina, 366, 368–70

Gianni Schicchi, 287, 288, 521

Gigli, Beniamino, 244, 303, 312, 341, 359, 363, 364, 389

Gilbert, Henry, 116

Gilbert, Sir William, 45, 74, 107

Giles, Edward, 111

Gilfry, Rodney, 553

Gilly, Dinh, 169

Gilmore, Patrick, 77, 131, 132

Gioconda, La, 276, 298, 362, 368, 369, 427, 476, 478

Giulietta e Romeo, 12

Glade, Coe, 298

Gleason, Helen, 366

Gluck, Alma, ·2, 169, 289–91

Godard, Benjamin, 96

Goetz, Hermann, 100

Golden Legend, The, 137

Götterdämmerung, 113, 129, 142, 288, 382, 444

Gottschalk, Louis Moreau, 121, 122

Gounod, Charles, 57, 60, 74, 84, 92, 93, 116, 122, 129, 134, 135, 147, 154, 156, 184, 203, 225, 243, 256

Gramm, Donald, 505

Grau, Maurice, 138, 141, 142, 156, 159, 160, 187, 213, 250, 255

Grau, Robert, 125

Greenfield, Elizabeth, 322–26, 339, 456

Greer, Frances, 398

Grieg, Edvard, 81, 285

Grieg, Nina, 337

Grisélidis, 231

Grisi, Giulia, 35, 579

Grist, Reri, 539

Griswold, Putnam, 192, 202–3

Grobe, Donald, 451

Gruber, Andrea, 546

Gruenberg, Louis, 313

Grüning, Wilhelm, 254

Guard, Billy, 362

Guarrera, Frank, 446

Guercoeur, 301

Guerrabella, Genevra, 51, 52

Gugliemo Tell, 105, 273

Gui, Vittorio, 278

Guiraud, Ernest, 96

Gye, Frederick, 83, 84

Habanera, La, 287

Hackett, Charles, 243, 244, 298

Hackley, Emma Azalia, 329

Haddon, Judith, 551

Hadley, Jerry, 552–53, 570

Hageman, Richard, 313

Hahn, Reynaldo, 301

Hale, Robert, 554
Hampson, Thomas, 570–73, 575, 577
Handel, George Frideric, 28, 29, 85
Handel and Haydn Society (Boston), 28, 29, 44, 104, 109, 208, 211
Hänsel und Gretel, 207
Hanslick, Eduard, 35, 81, 82, 122
Hanson, Howard, 313
Hardy, Emily, 366
Harrell, Mack, 445
Harris, Sir Augustus, 113, 136, 137
Harrison, Benjamin, 328
Harrison, Hazel, 329
Harrold, Orville, 116, 243
Harshaw, Margaret, 2, 397
Hastreiter, Hélène, 210
Hauk, Minnie, 2, 87–101, 136, 138, 183, 313, 316, 384, 580
Haydn, Joseph, 28, 104
Hayes, Roland, 329–35, 340, 343, 457
Hayes, Rutherford B., 326
Heater, Claude, 444
Hedmont, Charles, 107, 197
Hélène, 225
Hempel, Frieda, 199, 261, 294
Henschel, Sir George, 111, 151
Hensler, Elise, 45–48, 579
Heppner, Ben, 552
Hérodiade, 229, 296
Hewitt, James, 23
Hinckley, Allen, 203
Hinckley, Isabella, 49
Hines, Jerome, 446–47
Hinshaw, William, 203–4
Hoffman, Grace, 449
Holland, Charles, 456
Homer, Louise, 2, 166, 169, 205–8, 211–19, 256, 361, 394, 403
Hone, Philip, 16
Horn, Charles Edward, 20

Horne, Marilyn, 479, 495, 518–22, 550
Hotter, Hans, 383, 447, 472
Howard, Kathleen, 288–89
Huehn, Julius, 366
Hughes, Gene, 267, 268
Hugo, John Adams, 287
Huguenots, Les, 133, 137, 143–44, 191, 214, 287, 294, 476
Humperdinck, Engelbert, 207, 258
Hunt, Lorraine, 566–67, 577

Idomeneo, 400

Jagel, Frederick, 363, 366
Jepson, Helen, 299, 356
Jeritza, Maria, 247, 261, 359, 363
Johnson, Edward, 280, 281, 363–71, 372, 376, 379, 380, 394, 395, 397, 407, 414, 416, 421, 427, 440, 443, 448, 481, 580
Jones, Sissieretta, 327–29
Jongleur de Notre-Dame, Le, 229, 230, 231
Journet, Marcel, 214
Juch, Emma, 195–97, 272
Judson, Arthur, 300, 336, 361, 462
Juive, La, 39, 40, 243, 273, 287, 300, 430
Jurinac, Sena, 408, 460

Kahn, Otto, 345, 348, 351
Kalisch, Paul, 171, 172
Karajan, Herbert von, 453, 515
Kaskas, Anna, 366
Kellogg, Clara Louise, 1, 2, 5, 22, 43, 52, 53–68, 70, 71, 90, 91–92, 98, 110, 125, 134, 313, 578, 580
King's Henchman, The, 287, 312, 313
Kirsten, Dorothy, 2, 347, 377, 383, 384, 388–92, 408, 413, 516, 570

Klein, Herman, 84, 96, 97, 101, 112, 114, 119, 143, 183
Klemperer, Otto, 450
Kobbé, Gustav, 111
Koenig, Fidèle, 213
Königskinder, 258
Kostelanetz, André, 354
Koussevitzky, Serge, 457, 459
Krackman, Arthur, 301
Kraus, Alfredo, 424
Krauss, Gabrielle, 152, 154
Kreisler, Fritz, 299
Krips, Josef, 452
Kullman, Charles, 366, 367–68
Kunz, Erich, 460
Kurt, Melanie, 179, 180
Kurz, Selma, 152

Lakes, Gary, 552
L'Allemand, Pauline, 199–200
Lamperti, Francesco, 23, 77, 83, 85, 112, 116, 183
Lanza, Mario, 391, 462
Larmore, Jennifer, 567–68
Lashanska, Hulda, 292–93
Lassalle, Jean, 112
Lauri, Lelia, 199
Lauri-Volpi, Giacomo, 244, 278, 348, 359
Lawrence, Marjorie, 366, 375
Lazzari, Carolina, 298
Lear, Evelyn, 471–73
Leblanc, Georgette, 230
Leech, Richard, 552
Legend, The, 243, 272
Legend of Saint Elizabeth, The, 287
Lehár, Franz, 262, 316, 351
Lehmann, Lilli, 85, 95, 128, 129, 140, 141, 142, 171, 172, 253, 257, 275
Lehmann, Liza, 36
Lehmann, Lotte, 164, 375, 380, 508
Leinsdorf, Erich, 374, 498

Leonard, Myrtle, 362, 366
Leoncavallo, Ruggiero, 240, 247, 254
Lert, Ernst, 306
Leslie-Smith, Kenneth, 457
Levine, James, 547, 575
Lewis, Mary, 350–52, 534
Lied von der Erde, Das, 285
Lind, Jenny, 25, 30–37, 41, 42, 76, 81, 88–89, 119, 123, 244, 579
Linda di Chamounix, 44, 46, 47, 56, 57, 62, 90–91, 356
Litta, Marie, 199
Litvinne, Félia, 128
Lodoletta, 261
Lohengrin, 106, 108, 137, 139, 151, 155, 157, 180, 195, 196, 201, 203, 252, 304, 366, 375, 380, 433, 443
London, George, 460–64, 501, 578
Longone, Paolo, 298
Louise, 202, 222, 223, 224, 225, 226, 229, 232, 233, 247, 258, 261, 347, 400, 458
Love for Three Oranges, The, 235
Lucca, Pauline, 55, 62, 63
Lucia di Lammermoor, 39, 49, 84, 92, 104, 119, 123, 243, 354, 442, 445, 467, 484, 494
Ludwig, Christa, 521, 538
Lynch, Dominick, 7, 8, 9, 12, 16

Macbeth, Florence, 298
McCormack, John, 302
McCormic, Mary, 298–99
McCracken, James, 468–71
McDaniel, Barry, 451
McFerrin, Robert, 459
McKnight, Anne, 451
Maclennan, Francis, 286
MacNeil, Cornell, 529–30
Madama Butterfly, 159, 207, 256, 268,

287, 298, 378, 390, 400, 406, 410, 459, 465, 481, 483
Madeira, Jean, 474–75
Maeder, James, 21
Maeterlinck, Maurice, 230
Mahler, Gustav, 157, 168, 207, 258, 285
Malfitano, Catherine, 544–45
Malibran, Maria, 4, 8, 9, 14, 15, 20, 46, 119, 244, 579. *See also* García, María
Manon, 100, 186, 187, 201, 247, 253, 254, 296, 367, 390, 495, 517, 524
Manon Lescaut, 298, 390, 408
Mansfield-Rudersdorff, Erminia, 78, 79, 81
Mapleson, Henry, 64, 65, 98, 99
Mapleson, James Henry, 59, 61, 62, 72, 73, 79, 83, 93, 96, 97, 98, 100, 107, 108, 123, 124, 135, 136, 163, 193, 201, 208, 326
Mapleson, Lionel, 115
Marafioti, Mario, 344
Marc, Alessandra, 546
Marchesi, Blanche, 185, 188, 191, 192, 194
Marchesi, Mathilde, 93, 147, 149, 153, 154, 162, 185, 191, 192, 193, 194, 197, 210, 221, 251
Maretzek, Max, 43, 62, 90, 91, 92, 105, 118, 131
Mario, Queena, 300, 366, 579
Marsh, Lucie Isabelle, 302
Martha, 57, 75, 131, 151, 185, 209, 240, 302
Martin, Riccardo, 116, 242, 243, 320
Martinelli, Giovanni, 244, 276, 300, 314, 317, 359, 363, 381, 439
Martyr of Antioch, The, 84
Marwick, Dudley, 366
Mascagni, Pietro, 254, 287

Masini, Angelo, 66
Masnadieri, I, 46, 54
Mason, Edith, 2, 295–97, 366
Massé, Victor, 57, 74
Massenet, Jules, 100, 148, 183, 185, 186, 187, 188, 225, 229, 234, 253, 254, 261, 287, 298, 493
Massue, Nicholas, 366
Materna, Amalie, 106
Matilde di Shabran, 17–18
Matrimonio Segreto, Il, 18
Matthews, Edward, 455
Matzenauer, Margarete, 206
Maurel, Victor, 128, 137, 157, 158, 269
Mauro, Ermanno, 504
Maximilien, 301
Maynor, Dorothy, 457, 458, 538
Médicin Malgré Lui, Le, 116
Mefistofele, 214, 455, 501
Mehta, Zubin, 524
Meisle, Kathryn, 361
Meistersinger von Nürnberg, Die, 101, 107, 113, 251, 288, 314, 445, 547
Melba, Nellie, 85, 113–14, 128, 139, 141, 142, 147, 152, 153, 154, 155, 163, 164, 190, 191, 202, 212, 221, 250, 251, 268, 333, 393, 401
Melchior, Lauritz, 5, 243, 286, 349, 355, 359, 376, 383, 426, 444
Melis, Carmen, 296
Melton, James, 2, 392, 420, 442, 443, 553
Mendelssohn, Felix, 28, 29, 35
Menotti, Gian Carlo, 380, 433, 454
Mercer, Ruby, 366
Merrill, Robert, 2, 416, 430, 434, 437–42, 446, 463, 520, 581
Merriman, Nan, 453
Merritt, Chris, 553
Messager, André, 222, 224

Messiah, 111, 196
Metropolitan Opera, 85, 100, 135,
    156, 157, 226, 284, 299–301,
    359–71
  Auditions of the Air, 365, 392,
    396, 405, 431, 433, 439, 440,
    446, 524, 535, 540
  competition at, 2
  See also individual singers
Meyerbeer, Giacomo, 9, 39, 91,
    100, 129, 133, 137, 185
Mignon, 63, 65, 110, 133, 144, 178,
    183, 185, 195, 196, 250, 255,
    287, 356
Mikado, The, 74
Milanov, Zinka, 396
Millard, Harrison, 48
Miller, Mildred, 448
Millet, Émile, 54
Millo, Aprile, 546
Milnes, Sherrill, 282, 442, 530–33,
    553, 581
Mitchell, Leona, 546
Mitropoulos, Dimitri, 394, 400,
    430, 435, 445, 506
Mittelmann, Norman, 451
Moffo, Anna, 465–68, 497
Molese, Michele, 503–4
Montague, Annie, 63
Moore, Douglas, 100
Moore, Grace, 2, 198, 289, 317,
    342–48, 352, 363, 384, 388,
    389, 390, 391
Moore, Isabel, 67
Moore, Mary Elizabeth, 362
Morelli, Carlo, 366
Morgana, Nina, 300
Morris, James, 282, 553, 554
Mozart, Wolfgang Amadeus, 7, 12,
    21, 80, 87, 116, 195, 395, 400,
    407, 450, 452, 515
Muck, Karl, 252, 287
Muette de Portici, La, 40, 47

Mulder-Fabbri, Inez, 104, 105
Müller, Maria, 381
Munch, Charles, 414
Munsel, Patrice, 2, 392–94, 534
Mussorgsky, Modest, 19, 303, 315
Muzio, Claudia, 261, 265, 269, 288,
    295
Muzio, Emanuele, 54, 55, 65

Namara, Marguerite, 299, 491
Nau, Dolorès, 38–41, 48, 87
Naughty Marietta, 243
Navarraise, La, 261
Negri, Giuseppe, 530
Nelli, Herva, 533
Nero, 106, 195
Nevada, Emma, 192–94
Neway, Patricia, 454
New England Conservatory of
    Music, 130, 131, 295, 327,
    403, 406, 413
New York City Opera, 390, 396,
    457, 459, 488, 489, 497, 499,
    500, 504, 520, 532, 533, 540,
    548, 555, 565
Nicolini, Ernest, 79, 84, 123, 125,
    193
Nielsen, Alice, 198–99
Nilsson, Birgit, 397, 505, 514, 524
Nilsson, Christine, 59, 60, 61, 92,
    132, 135, 151, 195, 209
Niska, Maralin, 503
Noces, Les, 286
Noces de Jeannette, Les, 57
Nordica, Lillian, 2, 66, 85, 108,
    128–46, 148, 167, 168, 177,
    215, 250, 251, 348, 414, 546,
    578, 579
Norma, 9, 31, 35, 41, 51, 90, 104,
    138, 249, 275, 276, 278, 279,
    484, 488, 496, 519, 538
Norman, Jessye, 556–57
Notte di Zoraima, La, 278

Nourrit, Adolphe, 40
Novotna, Jarmila, 341, 421, 462
Nozzari, Andrea, 553
Nozze di Figaro, Le, 21, 61, 98, 157, 163, 298, 405, 467
Nuits d'Été, 400

Oberlin, Russell, 564–65
Oberon, 21, 271, 452
Offenbach, Jacques, 176, 197, 300, 393
Olheim, Helen, 366
Orfeo ed Euridice, 207
Ormandy, Eugene, 394, 406, 455, 465
O'Sullivan, John, 298
Oswald, Mark, 553
Otello (Rossini), 12, 13
Otello (Verdi), 138, 155, 157, 318, 453, 468, 469, 470, 531
Othello (Shakespeare), 309
Owen, Catherine Dale, 316

Pacini, Giovanni, 18
Paddon, John, 21
Padilla, Mariano, 93
Paër, Ferdinando, 13
Pagliacci, 240, 252, 296, 304, 315, 433, 436, 457, 533
Parepa-Rosa, Euphrosyne, 70, 130
Parsifal, 139, 140, 171, 173, 180, 243, 300, 302, 364, 443, 463, 528, 529
Pasatieri, Thomas, 283
Pasta, Giuditta, 9, 13, 23, 35, 168
Patti, Adelina, 4, 59, 60, 61, 66, 72, 79, 81, 84, 85, 86, 92, 104, 108, 118–27, 128, 138, 151, 183, 190, 193, 221, 244, 255, 266, 348, 356, 579
Pavarotti, Luciano, 242, 424, 552, 560–61
Pêcheurs de Perles, Les, 240

Peerce, Jan, 2, 406, 416, 417–23, 426, 431, 442, 453, 462, 535
Pelléas et Mélisande, 19, 202, 224, 225, 226, 227, 229, 230, 232, 233, 364, 396
Pelletier, Wilfrid, 405, 433
Perchinsini, Giulio, 108
Périchole, La, 393
Périer, Jean, 227
Perle du Brésil, La, 292
Peter Grimes, 19, 443, 454
Peter Ibbetson, 313
Peters, Roberta, 441, 448, 533, 534–35
Phillipps, Adelaide, 2, 41–45, 48, 52, 55, 65, 104, 579
Phillipps, Mathilde, 44, 45
Pini-Corsi, Antonio, 310
Pinza, Ezio, 5, 19, 314, 359, 381, 554
Pirates of Penzance, The, 107
Plançon, Pol, 112, 113, 128, 157, 202, 203, 215
Pleasants, Henry, 37
Plishka, Paul, 430, 555–56
Polacco, Giorgio, 295
Poleri, David, 454
Pomo d'Oro, Il, 315
Pons, Lily, 4, 189, 352–55, 390, 392, 393, 534
Ponselle, Rosa, 2, 264–83, 305, 306, 320, 321, 348, 365, 368, 384, 491, 544, 546, 578–79
Powers, Marie, 454
Price, Leontyne, 460, 470, 513–18, 519, 535, 546, 578, 579
Price, Stephen, 7, 8, 9
Princesse Osra, La, 225
Prophète, Le, 133, 206, 213, 285
Puccini, Giacomo, 3, 148, 149, 159, 163, 240, 256, 258, 273, 389, 390, 406, 449

Puritani, I, 50, 57, 278, 400, 443, 482, 483, 488, 548

Quartararo, Florence, 398
Quilico, Gino, 553

Radio broadcasts, 2, 19, 162, 244, 277, 280, 281, 313, 314, 318, 341, 347, 355, 357, 369, 378, 385, 412, 419, 427, 428, 431, 506
Raidich, Hubert, 366
Rains, Leon, 203
Raisa, Rosa, 269, 295
Ramey, Samuel, 553, 554–55
Rankin, Nell, 476
Rasely, George, 366
Raskin, Judith, 508
Ravelli, Luigi, 98–99, 136
Rayner, Sydney, 366
Reardon, John, 505
Recordings by American singers, 285, 341
    Anderson, Marian, 338
    Bispham, David, 115
    Blass, Robert, 201
    Caruso, Enrico, 240, 244
    Case, Anna, 291–92
    De Lussan, Zélie, 191
    Eames, Emma, 149, 161
    Easton, Florence, 288
    Farrar, Geraldine, 247, 254, 257
    Fremstad, Olive, 177, 178
    Garden, Mary, 228
    Garrison, Mabel, 295
    Gluck, Alma, 289
    Harrell, Mack, 445
    Haynes, Roland, 334
    Hines, Jerome, 447
    Homer, Louise, 218
    Juch, Emma, 196
    Kirsten, Dorothy, 391
    Kullman, Charles, 367

London, George, 463
McCracken, James, 470
Merriman, Nan, 453
Nielsen, Alice, 199
Nordica, Lillian, 143, 144
Ponselle, Rosa, 268, 273–74, 281, 282
Saville, Frances, 197
Sills, Beverly, 497
Steber, Eleanor, 410, 411, 412
Stevens, Risë, 384–85
Strong, Susan, 198
Swarthout, Gladys, 357–58
Tibbett, Lawrence, 309, 314, 315
Tucker, Richard, 429
Yaw, Ellen Beach, 194–95
Reine Fiammette, La, 225, 261
Reiner, Fritz, 376
Reiss, Albert, 116
Renaud, Maurice, 230
Requiem (Verdi), 269
Resnik, Regina, 2, 395–97
Rethberg, Elisabeth, 314, 359, 375, 439
Rheingold, Das, 179, 207
Ribla, Gertrude, 439
Richter, Hans, 139
Rienzi, 105
Rigoletto, 1, 43, 44, 46, 55, 57, 58, 122, 207, 214, 241, 287, 300, 303, 348, 362, 420, 423, 433, 434, 444, 446, 453, 530
Ring des Nibelungen, Der, 94, 101, 142, 172, 396, 464, 554
Rioton, Marthe, 222, 223
Ritchard, Cyril, 393
Ritter, Frédéric Louis, 17, 18–19
Robert Bruce, 40
Roberti, Margherita, 451
Robert le Diable, 39, 40, 132, 133
Roberto il Diavolo. See Robert le Diable
Robeson, Paul, 454–55
Robinson-Wayne, Beatrice, 455

Rode, Pierre, 46
Roi de Lahore, Le, 254
Roi d'Ys, Le, 213, 273
Roi l'a Dit, Le, 95
Roland von Berlin, Der, 254
Romani, Nino, 270–71, 275, 276, 278, 280
Roméo et Juliette, 74, 92, 162, 199, 254, 287, 356
Rondine, La, 467, 518
Rosa, Carl, 100
Rosenkavalier, Der, 291, 296, 405, 407, 427, 473
Rose of Castile, The, 75
Rose of Persia, The, 194
Ross, Elinor, 533
Rossini, Gioacchino, 3, 7, 8, 10, 12, 13, 17, 20, 26, 29, 39, 40, 46, 51, 57, 90, 105, 494
Rousselière, Charles, 255
Royer, Joseph, 366
Roze, Marie, 64, 65, 66, 98, 108, 208
Rubinstein, Anton, 106, 195, 209
Ruffo, Titta, 281, 312
Ruysdael, Basil, 204, 308, 309, 314, 320

Saint-Saëns, Camille, 155, 187, 225, 240, 254, 281, 433, 527, 538
Salome, 166, 174, 175, 221, 224, 228, 231, 232, 233, 234, 236, 253, 287, 298
Samson et Dalila, 213, 240, 281, 433, 437, 468, 538
Sanderson, Sibyl, 2, 152, 182, 183, 185–89, 222, 253, 296, 493
Sangiovanni, Antonio, 131, 132
Santley, Charles, 60, 61, 110, 197
Saville, Frances, 197
Sbriglia, Giovanni, 185, 202
Scalchi, Sofia, 66, 108, 157
Schippers, Thomas, 507

Schoen-René, Anna, 293, 385, 386
Schuman, Patricia, 542, 543
Schumann, Elisabeth, 296, 450
Schumann-Heink, Ernestine, 128, 144, 206, 267–68
Schwarzkopf, Elisabeth, 274, 452, 473, 543
Scotti, Antonio, 128, 157, 159, 161, 163, 214, 215, 216, 256, 257, 258, 303, 304, 305, 312, 359
Scotto, Renata, 465, 494, 495
Scovelli, Arturo, 108, 132
Seefried, Irmgard, 460
Segreto di Susanna, Il, 258, 298
Seguin, Zelda, 110
Seidl, Anton, 129, 142, 160, 171
Selika, Marie, 326–27
Sembrich, Marcella, 66, 157, 161, 163, 257, 290, 348, 369
Semiramide, 42, 44, 108, 123, 151, 519, 521
Senger-Bettaque, Katherine, 157
Serafin, Tullio, 275, 276, 280, 281, 315, 348, 361, 368, 479, 482
Serkin, Rudolf, 293
Seymour, John, 313
Sheean, Vincent, 220–21, 235, 340, 347
Shicoff, Neil, 551
Shirley, George, 539–40
Sibelius, Jean, 285, 337
Siège de Corinthe, Le. See Assedio di Corinto, L'
Siegfried, 113, 141, 142
Siepi, Cesare, 443, 447, 476, 501
Sills, Beverly, 1, 2, 282, 299, 430, 479, 487–98, 578
Simon Boccanegra, 19, 314, 381, 382, 431, 433, 434, 435, 446, 521
Simoneau, Léopold, 243
Sirène, La, 40
Solti, Georg, 450, 491, 547

Sonnambula, La, 23, 24, 57, 73, 83, 87, 91, 93, 98, 183, 193
Sontag, Henriette, 46
Squires, Henry, 48, 49
Stabat Mater (Rossini), 29, 122, 134
Stahlman, Sylvia, 451
Steber, Eleanor, 2, 243, 377, 398, 399–415, 443, 534, 546, 548, 575
Stellman, Maxine, 366
Sterling, Antoinette, 210–11
Stevens, Risë, 2, 252, 354, 377, 383–88, 390, 391, 392, 394, 395, 397, 413, 570
Stewart, Thomas, 471–73
Stich-Randall, Teresa, 451–52
Stigelli, Giorgio, 55
Still, William Grant, 459
Stillwell, Richard, 553
Stockhausen, Julius, 201
Stokowski, Leopold, 286, 314
Stoska, Polyna, 398, 453, 454
Strakosch, Max, 50, 61, 62, 64, 67, 78, 79, 81, 83, 88, 92, 209
Stratas, Teresa, 448, 464, 522–26, 570
Strauss, Richard, 114, 202, 214, 231, 234, 253, 407, 408, 450
Stravinsky, Igor, 293, 395, 443, 509, 520
Strong, Susan, 197–98
Studer, Cheryl, 500, 542, 544, 546–47
Sullivan, Brian, 443, 453
Sullivan, Sir Arthur, 45, 74, 84, 107, 109, 112, 123, 137, 194, 211
Sumner, Edward, 48
Suor Angelica, 261, 281
Sutherland, Joan, 271, 401, 479, 494, 495, 496, 497, 519, 520, 521, 548

Swarthout, Gladys, 2, 356–58, 384, 491
Sweet, Sharon, 546
Swenson, Ruth Ann, 548–49
Sylvan, Sanford, 565–66, 577
Sylvester, Michael, 552
Symonds, John Addington, 33
Symons, Charlotte, 366
Szell, George, 372, 379

Tagliavini, Ferruccio, 424
Tailleferre, Germaine, 286
Talley, Marion, 348–50, 392, 393, 534
Tamagno, Francesco, 128, 138, 157
Taming of the Shrew, The, 100
Tancredi, 12
Tangeman, Nell, 508
Tannhäuser, 105, 113, 167, 178, 180, 203, 253, 314, 315, 349, 375, 376, 470, 528, 536–37
Tauber, Richard, 341
Taylor, Bayard, 32
Taylor, Deems, 164, 312, 313, 315, 580
Tebaldi, Renata, 62, 408, 466, 472, 484, 514, 546
Television, 2, 367, 388, 401, 406, 407, 442, 465, 470, 515
Telva, Marion, 300
Tentoni, Rosa, 366
Ternina, Milka, 128
Tetrazzini, Luisa, 194, 268
Teyte, Maggie, 116
Thaïs, 187, 202, 213, 221, 224, 225, 226, 227, 228, 229, 232, 234, 261, 296, 299, 467, 497, 515
Thaw, David, 450
Thebom, Blanche, 2, 394–95, 411, 433
Thomas, Ambroise, 80
Thomas, Jess, 473–74

Thomas, John Charles, 2, 299, 320, 321, 366, 367
Thomas, Theodore, 106, 195, 199
Thompson, Oscar, 304
Thomson, Virgil, 356, 358, 392, 452, 455, 458, 459, 463, 508, 514
Thorner, William, 351
Thursby, Emma, 68, 71, 75–82, 250, 425
Tibbett, Lawrence, 303–21, 341, 363, 366, 381, 416, 420, 421, 431, 433, 434, 437, 442, 463, 520, 553, 578, 579, 581
Tietjens, Therese, 60, 61, 84
Tobin, Eugene, 449
Torriani, Ottavia, 65
Tosca, 148, 149, 156, 157, 161, 162, 163, 178, 180, 221, 228, 234, 241, 247, 249, 258, 269, 357, 390, 400, 408, 430, 484, 499, 515
Toscanini, Arturo, 159, 160, 169, 179, 207, 216, 248, 257, 258, 286, 290, 297, 337, 367, 370, 420, 428, 440, 441, 446, 451, 453
Toten Augen, Die, 287
Tourel, Jennie, 370, 562, 563
Tozzi, Giorgio, 475–76
Trabadello, Antonio, 222, 251, 302, 344
Traubel, Helen, 2, 370–71, 373–79, 380, 383, 390
Traubman, Sophie, 199
Traviata, La, 51, 57, 73, 104, 125, 132, 136, 228, 254, 261, 276, 277, 303, 315, 355, 366, 420, 421, 433, 440, 467, 484, 502
Treigle, Norman, 500–2, 555
Tristan und Isolde, 129, 139, 141, 144, 167, 168, 172, 174, 177, 179, 180, 375, 395

Trovatore, Il, 43, 48, 52, 66, 104, 130, 138, 144, 269, 273, 314, 396, 434, 439, 444, 449, 460, 471, 483, 507, 513
Troyanos, Tatiana, 549–60
Troyens, Les, 395, 413
Tucker, Richard, 2, 243, 416, 418, 421, 423–31, 442, 448, 478, 551, 552, 578, 579
Turandot, 451, 505, 524
Turco in Italia, Il, 12

Ugonotti, Gli. See Huguenots, Les
Uhde, Hermann, 447
Uppman, Theodor, 475
Upshaw, Dawn, 294, 500, 542, 543, 544, 573–76, 577

Vaccai, Nicola, 23, 54
Valente, Benita, 508
Valentino, Frank, 445–46
Valleria, Alwina, 96
Vandenburg, Howard, 450
Van Dyck, Ernest, 128, 139
Vaness, Carol, 544, 547
Vanessa, 395, 408, 411
Van Gordon, Cyrena, 298
Vannuccini, Luigi, 403
Van Zandt, Jennie, 63, 183
Van Zandt, Marie, 182–84, 193, 199
Varnay, Astrid, 2, 373, 377, 379–83, 396, 433, 449
Vaucorbeil, Auguste Emmanuel, 134
Vaughan Williams, Ralph, 315, 351
Vehanen, Kosti, 337, 394
Verdi, Giuseppe, 3, 9, 23, 26, 43, 47, 51, 57, 65, 84, 122, 129, 138, 148, 157, 209, 221, 254, 264, 273, 276, 303, 360, 395, 435, 449, 515
Verrett, Shirley, 535, 538–39, 549
Vestale, La, 274, 275, 278

Viardot, Pauline, 9, 45, 46, 209,
210, 299
Vickers, Jon, 424, 526–29
Vinay, Ramon, 424
Vogelhändler, Der, 293
Voice of Firestone, The (television),
367, 388, 401, 406, 442
Voigt, Deborah, 544
Von Stade, Frederica, 568–70
Votipka, Thelma, 366

Wagenknecht, Edward, 37
Wagner, Cosima, 139, 202, 251
Wagner, Richard, 3, 9, 63, 64, 65,
84, 94, 101, 106, 113, 114,
129, 144, 148, 167, 168, 195,
221, 240, 243, 256, 288, 382,
383, 420, 443
Wagner, Siegfried, 139, 203, 251
Wagner, Wieland, 379, 382, 463,
473, 536
Walker, Edyth, 206, 215, 394
Walker, Sarah Jane Layton, 285
Walküre, Die, 142, 144, 176, 214,
285, 308, 314, 366, 380, 420
Walter, Bruno, 285, 367, 372
Walter, Gustav, 285
Ward, Genevieve, 50, 51
Warren, Leonard, 2, 19, 318, 416,
429, 431–37, 442, 448, 463,
520, 581
Watson, Claire, 450, 451, 563
Watson, Henry C., 24
Weathers, Felicia, 539
Weber, Carl Maria von, 21, 196,
271
Webster, David, 396
Weede, Robert, 420, 422, 431, 444,
445, 476
Weigert, Hermann, 379, 380, 382,
383

Werther, 148, 149, 258, 290, 291
Wheatley, Julia, 19–20, 22, 41, 579
Wheeler, Andrew C., 68
White, Carolina, 298
White, Richard Grant, 23, 24
Whitefield, Hugh, 242
Whitehill, Clarence, 2, 201–2, 312
Whiting, Virginia, 51
Whitman, Walt, 37
Whitney, Myron, 109, 116, 212,
403, 554
Whitney, William, 212, 403, 404,
413
Wilhelm Tell. *See Guglielmo Tell*
Williams, Camilla, 459
Williams, Sampson, 326
Wilson, Woodrow, 117
Winters, Lawrence, 459
Witherspoon, Herbert, 116, 203,
204, 363
Wolansky, Raymond, 449, 450
Wood, Henry, 112, 113
Woodward, Sidney, 329
Wozzeck, 390, 408, 445, 472, 506,
521

Yaw, Ellen Beach, 194–95
Yurka, Blanche, 82

Zaïre, 155
Zajick, Dolora, 550
Zampa, 110
Zauberflöte, Die, 186, 405
Zazà, 246, 247, 254, 287
Ziegler, Edward, 348, 365
Zigeunerliebe, 316
Zingarelli, Nicola, 12
Zirato, Bruno, 362